R+

1
4

GENESIS

A COMMENTARY

GENESIS

A COMMENTARY

BRUCE K. WALTKE

WITH CATHI J. FREDRICKS

ZONDERVAN®

ZONDERVAN.com/
AUTHORTRACKER
follow your favorite authors

We want to hear from you. Please send your comments about this book to us in care of zreview@zondervan.com. Thank you.

ZONDERVAN

Genesis: A Commentary
Copyright © 2001 by Bruce K. Waltke

Requests for information should be addressed to:
Zondervan, *Grand Rapids, Michigan 49530*

Library of Congress Cataloging-in-Publication Data

Waltke, Bruce K.
    Genesis: a commentary / Bruce K. Waltke with Cathi J. Fredricks.
      p. cm.
    Includes bibliographical references.
    ISBN 978-0-310-22458-7
    1. Bible. O.T. Genesis — Commentaries. I. Fredricks, Cathi J. II. Title.
BS1235.3 .W34 2001
222'.110770 — dc21   2001017808

Interior design: Melissa Elenbaas

Printed in the United States of America

13 14 15 16 /DCI/ 29 28 27 26 25 24 23 22 21 20 19 18 17 16 15 14 13

Marjorie Elizabeth Mullan Fredricks and
Robert William Fredricks—heroes of the faith
and
The memory of Louise Daab Waltke—
who by faith, though dead, still speaks

Contents

Preface

An extended process of research and collaboration led to the creation of this commentary. The foundation of exegetical notes was laid in the late 1980s when Bruce prepared Genesis notes for the *New Geneva Study Bible*. We are most grateful to the Foundation for Reformation for their permission to use these notes as the starting basis for this commentary. The primary theological reflections and expanded notes focusing on literary analysis were developed when Bruce subsequently taught Genesis at Regent College. In 1997 Bruce and Zondervan realized that the combination of these notes, literary analysis, and theological reflections had the makings of an excellent commentary that would enrich people's understanding of this book of beginnings.

Here Bruce brought Cathi, his teaching assistant at that time, into the project to collaborate with him on the writing, editing, and organizing. Cathi, a former English teacher, seemed a good fit for the project, able to contribute not only to the writing and editing but also to the concerns of literary analysis and of women in biblical studies.

When he wrote his original lecture notes, Bruce analyzed Genesis with a structure of books, acts, and scenes in an effort to capture the literary nature of the text and to help his students grasp the structure and flow of Genesis. As this unusual approach proved effective for helping students study the book, Cathi and Bruce worked together to hone and expand the literary analysis. Cathi provided a skeleton draft of the book. Then, as inevitably happens when one begins a project of this magnitude, Bruce determined that significant additional research was needed to cover the detail of Genesis adequately. He made extensive additions to the literary analysis, exegetical notes, and theological reflections. Cathi edited the whole, making it more readable, probing Bruce with challenging questions, and improving the overall flow by paying special attention to the plot and structure of the narrative. The introduction to the commentary was written by Bruce, including his adaptation of his essay "The Kingdom of God in Biblical Theology."[1] Utilizing Bruce's biblical theology notes, Cathi wrote the section on poetics. The continual process of dialogue and collaboration led to the commentary in its present form.

---

[1]This essay on "The Kingdom of God in Biblical Theology" will appear in a forthcoming book, *Looking into the Future: Evangelical Studies in Eschatology*, ed. David W. Baker (Grand Rapids: Baker, 2001).

It is our hope and belief that the combination of literary analysis, exegetical notes, and theological reflections will be particularly helpful to pastors and lay leaders to teach and preach Genesis. As explained in the introduction, following the design by the author of Genesis, we have outlined Genesis by a prologue and ten books (*tôlᵉḏôt*). At the beginning of each book we have set out the key theme and outline of the book. In an attempt to capture the literary flow of the narrative and for ease of analysis, we have further divided Genesis into acts and scenes. This nomenclature is arbitrary, since the author of Genesis did not work in the structures of a modern play. Nevertheless, we believe our divisions are true to his representation of Israel's history and helpful for demarcating narrative units. The Literary Analysis highlights the major literary features of each act and scene and should provide a helpful starting point for the reader. The analysis is by no means exhaustive nor conclusive. Rather, we have attempted to model a literary approach to Genesis. As readers enter Genesis, it is our hope they will discover its rich literary treasures, uncovering many other possible structures and techniques.

The Exegetical Notes are best read with a Bible in hand. Based on the NIV text unless otherwise noted, they are intended to provide useful summary and explanation. Particular words and phrases that have significance or require historical, social, or geographical clarification are highlighted. The Theological Reflections expand upon the themes of Genesis, drawing connections with the rest of Scripture and making application to the church and the Christian life.

We are indebted to many people for their time, counsel, and assistance in finalizing the detail of this book. We could not have asked for a more talented bibliography crew. Jonathan Bird, Daniel Clark, Matthew Freeman, Otto Guggemous, Poul Guttesen, Bruce Jeffery, Dorothy Kieft, Andrew Lewis, Carol McMahan, Janet Somes, and Kara Wenzel were a pleasure to work with. We would especially like to thank Megan Brown, Peter Chamberlain, and Keith Hyde, who were extraordinary in the giving of their time and talents. We owe a huge debt of gratitude to Bob Buller and Verlyn Verbrugge for their careful and critical editing of the final manuscript. Bruce gladly acknowledges his unending dialectic with the community of readers—writers, teachers, and students—whose ideas he has absorbed and integrated as his own. The footnotes point the reader to some of these sources, but in truth they are too many and too interrelated to credit properly. Cathi would particularly like to thank Kimberly Fredricks, Dorothy Kieft, and Kara Wenzel, along with many other friends for their support during the lengthy process of writing and editing.

Abbreviations

Primary Sources

b. Ned.	Babylonian Talmud, *Nedarim*
b. Taʿan.	Babylonian Talmud, *Taʿanit*
LXX	Septuagint
MT	Masoretic Text
NAB	New American Bible
NASB	New American Standard Bible
NIV	New International Version
NJPS	*Tanakh: The Holy Scriptures: The New JPS Translation according to the Traditional Jewish Text*
NKJV	New King James Version
NRSV	New Revised Standard Bible
REB	Revised English Bible
SP	Samaritan Pentateuch

Secondary Sources

AB	Anchor Bible
ABD	*Anchor Bible Dictionary*. Edited by D. N. Freedman. 6 vols. New York: Doubleday, 1992.
ANEP	*The Ancient Near East in Pictures Relating to the Old Testament*. Edited by J. B. Pritchard. Princeton, N.J.: Princeton Univ. Press, 1969.
ANET	*Ancient Near Eastern Texts Relating to the Old Testament*. Edited by J. B. Pritchard. 3d ed. Princeton, N.J.: Princeton Univ. Press, 1969.
ANF	*Ante-Nicene Fathers*
ASORDS	American Schools of Oriental Research Dissertation Series
AUSS	*Andrews University Seminary Studies*
BA	*Biblical Archaeologist*
BAR	*Biblical Archaeology Review*
BASOR	*Bulletin of the American Schools of Oriental Research*
Bib	*Biblica*
BSac	*Bibliotheca sacra*
BSOAS	*Bulletin of the School of Oriental and African Studies*

BT	*The Bible Translator*
BZAW	Beihefte zur Zeitschrift für die alttestamentliche Wissenschaft
CBQ	*Catholic Biblical Quarterly*
EBD	*The Eerdmans Bible Dictionary*. Edited by Allen C. Myers. Grand Rapids: Eerdmans, 1987.
EvQ	*Evangelical Quarterly*
ExpTim	*Expository Times*
FOTL	Forms of the Old Testament Literature
GKC	*Gesenius' Hebrew Grammar*. Edited by E. Kautzsch. Translated by A. E. Cowley. 2d ed. Oxford: Clarendon, 1910.
HALOT	*The Hebrew and Aramaic Lexicon of the Old Testament*, by L. Koehler and W. Baumgartner; trans. and ed. under supervision of M. E. J. Richardson. 4 vols. Leiden: Brill, 1994–1999.
HTR	*Harvard Theological Review*
IBC	Interpretation: A Bible Commentary for Teaching and Preaching
IBD	*The Illustrated Bible Dictionary*. Edited by J. D. Douglas et al. Wheaton, Ill.: Tyndale, 1980.
IBHS	B. K. Waltke and M. O'Connor. *An Introduction to Biblical Hebrew Syntax*. Winona Lake, Ind.: Eisenbrauns, 1990.
ICC	International Critical Commentary
IDB	*The Interpreter's Dictionary of the Bible*. Edited by G. A. Buttrick. 4 vols. Nashville: Abingdon, 1962.
IDBSup	*Interpreter's Dictionary of the Bible: Supplementary Volume*. Edited by K. Crim. Nashville: Abingdon, 1976.
IEJ	*Israel Exploration Journal*
ILR	*Israel Law Review*
ITC	International Theological Commentary
JAAR	*Journal of the American Academy of Religion*
JAOS	*Journal of the American Oriental Society*
JBL	*Journal of Biblical Literature*
JBR	*Journal of Bible and Religion*
JETS	*Journal of the Evangelical Theological Society*
JJS	*Journal of Jewish Studies*
JNES	*Journal of Near Eastern Studies*
JNSL	*Journal of Northwest Semitic Languages*
JPOS	*Journal of the Palestine Oriental Society*
JQR	*Jewish Quarterly Review*
JSOT	*Journal for the Study of the Old Testament*
JSOTSup	Journal for the Study of the Old Testament Supplement Series
JSS	*Journal of Semitic Studies*

JTS	*Journal of Theological Studies*
NAC	New American Commentary
NBD	*New Bible Dictionary.* Edited by J. D. Douglas and N. Hillyer. 2d ed. Downers Grove, Ill.: InterVarsity, 1982.
NICOT	New International Commentary on the Old Testament
NIDOTTE	*New International Dictionary of Old Testament Theology and Exegesis.* Edited by W. A. VanGemeren. 5 vols. Grand Rapids: Zondervan, 1997.
OBT	Overtures to Biblical Theology
OTL	Old Testament Library
OtSt	*Oudtestamentische Studiën*
RB	*Revue biblique*
ResQ	*Restoration Quarterly*
SBLMS	Society of Biblical Literature Monograph Series
SBT	Studies in Biblical Theology
ScrHier	Scripta hierosolymitana
TDNT	*Theological Dictionary of the New Testament.* Edited by G. Kittel and G. Friedrich. Translated by G. W. Bromiley. 10 vols. Grand Rapids: Eerdmans, 1964–1976.
TDOT	*Theological Dictionary of the Old Testament.* Edited by G. J. Botterweck and H. Ringgren. Translated by J. T. Willis, G. W. Bromiley, and D. E. Green. 11 vols. Grand Rapids: Eerdmans, 1974–.
TLOT	*Theological Lexicon of the Old Testament.* Edited by E. Jenni, with assistance from C. Westermann. Translated by M. E. Biddle. 3 vols. Peabody, Mass.: Hendrickson, 1997.
TNBD	*The New Bible Dictionary.* Leicester, Eng.: Inter-Varsity; Downers Grove, Ill.: InterVarsity, 1996.
TWOT	*Theological Wordbook of the Old Testament.* Edited by R. L. Harris, G. L. Archer Jr., and B. K. Waltke. 2 vols. Chicago: Moody Press, 1980.
TynBul	*Tyndale Bulletin*
UF	*Ugarit-Forschungen*
VT	*Vetus Testamentum*
VTSup	Supplements to Vetus Testamentum
WBC	Word Biblical Commentary
WTJ	*Westminster Theological Journal*
ZAW	*Zeitschrift für die alttestamentliche Wissenschaft*
ZBK	Zürcher Bibelkommentare

Introduction

TITLE AND TEXT

In conformity with the ancient Near Eastern practice of naming a book by its first words, the Hebrew title of the book of Genesis is *berēʾšît* ("in the beginning"). The English title, on the other hand, is a transliteration via the Vulgate (*Liber Genesis*) of the Greek title, probably taken from 2:4, *genesis* ("origin, source, race, creation"). Happily, both titles are appropriate, for this book deals with beginnings *and* origins, broadly of the cosmos (1:1–2:3), of humanity and the nations and their alienation from God and one another (2:4–11:32), and of Israel (12:1–50:26), God's new initiative to save the world.

This commentary is based on the codex of Samuel son of Jacob (ca. A.D. 1000), who "copied, vowel-pointed and Massoretically annotated this codex of the sacred Scripture from the correct manuscript that the teacher, Aaron son of Moses Ben-Asher, redacted . . . and that constitutes an exceedingly accurate exemplar."[1] In a few instances another text or ancient version, such as the Greek Septuagint (LXX), is preferred to this oldest complete manuscript of the Hebrew Bible.[2]

STRUCTURE AND CONTENT

The Basic *tôledôt* Structure[3]

After the prologue representing the creation of the cosmos (1:1–2:3), the author of Genesis introduces ten new divine initiatives in salvation history with a *tôledôt* heading (i.e., "the account of the line of X") and transitions linking these developments:

---

[1]Frontispiece of Leningrad Codex B 19ᵃ. This codex is the diplomatic text of *Biblia Hebraica Stuttgartensia*, ed. K. Elliger and W. Rudolph (Stuttgart: Deutsche Bibelgesellschaft, 1983).

[2]See Waltke, "Reliability," *NIDOTTE*, 1:51–67.

[3]Based on the work of earlier scholars, I. Kikawada and A. Quinn (*Before Abraham Was: The Unity of Genesis 1–11* [Nashville: Abingdon, 1985], 47–48) argue that the Primeval History had the same epic structure as the early second millennium B.C. Mesopotamian epic of Atrahasis (i.e., "The Exceedingly Wise"). That epic consists of a creation narrative, three threats to human existence (plague, famine, and flood), and a resolution, interspersed with references to numerical increase. That structure, they argue, is reflected in Gen. 1–11: creation narrative, three threats (Adam and Eve, Cain and Abel, and the Flood), interspersed with genealogies (2:4; 4:1–2, 25–26; 10:1–32; 11:10–26). Both narratives address the question whether humanity can survive various threats to its existence. In the Atrahasis Epic, population increase is a major problem for the gods; they resolve it by putting threatening checks

Contrary to what one might expect, the accounts are not essentially about the titular ancestor but about his descendants. For instance, the accounts of the lines of Terah, of Isaac, and of Jacob are principally about their offspring: Abraham, Jacob, and the twelve sons of Israel, respectively. In addition, in order that "the account of Noah's line" might pertain to both Noah and his sons, the author intercalates this third account into the second by completing 5:32 in 9:18. Further, the heading of the first account is an ad hoc literary creation. Obviously the inanimate heaven and earth cannot give birth to Adam, but he has no human parentage. Finally, these *tôledôt* headings introduce two types of literature: short genealogies—linear (accounts 2, 5) and segmented (accounts 7, 9[5])—and extended narratives (accounts 1, 3, 6, 8, 10).

---

on it. In the biblical account, human sin threatens humanity's existence. God blesses humanity to multiply but repeatedly intervenes to see it fill the earth according to his intention. Inferentially, God resolves the potential overpopulation problem by scattering people over the breadth of the earth. D. Garrett (*Rethinking Genesis: Sources and Authorship of the First Book of the Pentateuch* [Grand Rapids: Baker, 1991], 111–13) argues that Genesis as a whole has the same thematic pattern, including a prologue (Gen. 1–11), a triadic narrative that describes a threat to the hero (Abraham, Jacob, and Joseph), and a conclusion, with transitional genealogies between these narrative divisions (11:27–32; 25:12–18; 36:22c–40; 46:8–27). But the structural analogues between the Atrahasis Epic and Genesis 1–11 are not totally convincing.

[4]The final details concerning Abraham's children, the settling of Abraham's affairs, and his death (25:1-11) at the conclusion of the preceding book function as a transition to both the accounts of Ishmael and of Isaac.

[5]The segmented and linear genealogy of 36:9–43 is a later addition to Ur-Genesis. See structure in literary analysis of Book 9.

The fourth account, the so-called Table of Nations, is a mixture of these two literary forms.

The Alternating and Concentric Patterns of the Ten *tôlᵉḏôṯ*

Building on the studies of Umberto Cassuto, Michael Fishbane, and J. M. Sasson,[6] Gary Rendsburg notes that the first five *tôlᵉḏôṯ*, which pertain to humanity as a whole, are arranged in a "parallel" (better: "alternating") structure and the last three narrative *tôlᵉḏôṯ* in a concentric structure, divided by two short genealogical *tôlᵉḏôṯ*.[7] He groups the first five under the heading "Primeval History" and gives the others their popular content labels (see below). He backs up this analysis by noting other poetic devices, such as key words, that give coherence to the sections.

Section	Extent	Structure
Primeval History	1:1–11:26	alternating
Abraham cycle	11:27–22:24	concentric
Linking material	23:1–25:18	parallel with 35:23–36:43a
Jacob cycle	25:19–35:22	concentric
Linking material	35:23–36:43a	parallel with 23:1–25:18
Joseph cycle	37:2–50:26	concentric

Below is an adapted summary of Rendsburg's analysis of the main cycles. The first and third narrative *tôlᵉḏôṯ* are modified below in a large measure from David A. Dorsey:[8]

The Primeval History: alternating structure

A Creation story: first beginning; divine blessing 1:1–2:3

    B Sin of Adam: nakedness; seeing/covering nakedness; curse 2:4–3:24

        C No descendants of murdered younger, righteous son Abel 4:1–16

---

[6]U. Cassuto, *A Commentary on the Book of Genesis. Part 2: From Noah to Abraham,* trans. I. Abrahams (Jerusalem: Magnes, 1964), 296; M. Fishbane, "Composition and Structure in the Jacob Cycle Gen 25:19–35:22," *JJS* 26 (1975): 15–38; idem, *Text and Texture* (New York: Schocken, 1979), 50–62; J. M. Sasson, "The 'Tower of Babel' As a Clue to the Redactional Structuring of the Primeval History (Gen. 1–11:9)," in *The Bible World: Essays in Honor of Cyrus H. Gordon,* ed. G. Rendsburg (New York: Ktav, 1980), 211–19.

[7]G. A. Rendsburg, *The Redaction of Genesis* (Winona Lake, Ind.: Eisenbrauns, 1986). This commentary uses the terms *alternating structure* for units of literature arranged in parallel (e.g., ABCA'B'C'), *chiastic* for those structured around a single center or pivot (e.g., ABCB'A', and *concentric* for those arranged around a double center (e.g., ABCC'B'A'). By contrast, Jerome T. Walsh reverses this definition of chiastic and concentric (*1 Kings* [Collegeville, Minn.: Liturgical, 1996], xiv).

[8]D. A. Dorsey. *The Literary Structure of the Old Testament: A Commentary on Genesis-Malachi* (Grand Rapids: Baker, 1999), 55, 60.

D Descendants of sinful son Cain 4:17–26
  E Descendants of chosen son Seth: ten generations from Adam to Noah 5:1–32
    F Downfall: unlawful union 6:1–4
      G Brief introduction to Noah 6:5–8
A′ Flood story: reversal of creation; new beginning; divine blessing 6:9–9:19
  B′ Sin of Noah: nakedness, seeing/covering nakedness; curse 9:20–29
    C′ Descendants of younger, righteous son Japheth 10:1–5
      D′ Descendants of sinful son Ham 10:6–20
        E′ Descendants of chosen son Shem: ten generations from Noah to Terah 10:21–32[9]
          F′ Downfall: rebellious union (Tower of Babel) 11:1–9
            G′ Brief introduction of Abraham, through whom God will bless humanity 11:27–32[10]

The Abraham Cycle: concentric pattern

A Genealogy of Terah 11:27–32
  B Promise of a son and start of Abraham's spiritual odyssey 12:1–9
    C Abraham lies about Sarah; the LORD protects her in foreign palace 12:10–20
      D Lot settles in Sodom 13:1–18
        E Abraham intercedes for Sodom and Lot militarily 14:1–24
          F Covenant with Abraham; annunciation of Ishmael 15:1–16:16
          F′ Covenant with Abraham; annunciation of Isaac 17:1–18:15
        E′ Abraham intercedes for Sodom and Lot in prayer 18:16–33
      D′ Lot flees doomed Sodom and settles in Moab 19:1–38
    C′ Abraham lies about Sarah; God protects her in foreign palace 20:1–18
  B′ Birth of son and climax of Abraham's spiritual odyssey 21:1–22:19
A′ Genealogy of Nahor 22:20–24

---

[9]The alternating structure is violated here to link closely the account of Shem's descendants with the account of Terah's descendants, the lineage that saves the nations from Babel's curse.

[10]The introduction to Book 6 is a janus between books 5 and 6, between the Primeval History (Gen. 1–11) and the Patriarchal History (Gen. 12–50) (see below, Literary Analysis of Book 6).

The Jacob Cycle: concentric pattern

A Oracle sought; struggle in childbirth; Jacob born 25:19–34
  B Interlude: Rebekah in foreign palace; pact with foreigners 26:1–35
    C Jacob fears Esau and flees 27:1–28:9
      D Messengers 28:10–22
        E Arrival in Haran 29:1–30
          F Jacob's wives are fertile 29:31–30:24
          F' Jacob's flocks are fertile 30:25–43
        E' Flight from Haran 31:1–55
      D' Messengers 32:1–32
    C' Jacob returns and fears Esau 33:1–20
  B' Interlude: Dinah in foreign palace; pact with foreigners 34:1–31
A' Oracle fulfilled; struggle in childbirth; Jacob becomes Israel 35:1–22

The Joseph Cycle: concentric pattern

A Introduction: beginning of Joseph story 37:2–11
  B Jacob mourns "death" of Joseph 37:12–36
    C Interlude: Judah signified as leader 38:1–30[11]
      D Joseph's enslavement in Egypt 39:1–23
        E Joseph savior of Egypt through disfavor at Pharaoh's court 40:1–41:57
          F Journeys of brothers to Egypt 42:1–43:34
            G Brothers pass Joseph's test of love for brother 44:1–34
            G' Joseph gives up his power over brothers 45:1–28
          F' Migration of family to Egypt 46:1–27
        E' Joseph savior of family through favor at Pharaoh's court 46:28–47:12
      D' Joseph's enslavement of Egyptians 47:13–31
    C' Interlude: Judah blessed as ruler 48:1–49:28
  B' Joseph mourns death of Jacob 49:29–50:14
A' Conclusion: end of Joseph story 50:15–26

COMPOSITION AND AUTHORSHIP

Who is the literary genius of this artistic masterpiece, which, like a Bach fugue, counterpoints these patterns of structure with plot development? To answer that question one must broaden the discussion to address the authorship and composition of the first five books of the Bible, for the book of Genesis opens up the Pentateuch, which all agree has been edited as a unity. Although a good case can be made that Moses authored the essential shape

---

[11]This analysis is based on J. Goldin, "The Youngest Son or Where Does Genesis 38 Belong," *JBL* 96 (1977): 27–44 (see also the commentary below on Gen. 38).

of Genesis and of the Pentateuch, he clearly did not author the extant text in our hands. To understand the book's composition and authorship it is helpful to consider at least three stages in its development.

Moses and Ur-Genesis

The Pentateuch attributes large portions of its content to Moses. At Sinai the Lord gives him the great legal codes of the Ten Commandments and the Book of the Covenant (Ex. 20:2–23:33; 34:11–26) and the cultic laws and Holiness Code of Leviticus (Lev. 1:1; 27:34). On the journey from Sinai to Moab the Lord gives Moses more instructions, as recorded in Numbers 1:1; 36:13. At Moab Moses expounds the law in his three addresses embedded in Deuteronomy (1:5–4:40; 5:1–26:19; 30:2–20), along with the covenant blessings and curses (Deut. 27–28), his song (31:30–32:43), and his last words (33:1–29).

Jesus and his followers likewise assume this point of view (Matt. 8:4; Luke 16:31; 24:27, 44; John 1:17; Acts 3:22). Jesus says Moses gave the Jews circumcision (John 7:22; cf. Acts 15:1). The regulations of circumcision are given *extensively* in Gen. 17:9–14, not in Lev. 12:3, which suggests that Jesus thought of Moses as the author of Genesis.

Furthermore, Moses is said either explicitly or implicitly to have written some sections of the Pentateuch (e.g., Ex. 24:12; 34:27). The putative Deuteronomist, who during the exile composed the final draft of Deuteronomy–Kings but not Ruth, also cites his law as written down (Deut. 28:58; 29:20–21, 27; 30:10; 31:19, 24; Josh. 1:8; 8:31, 34; 23:6; 1 Kings 2:3), as do the postexilic Chronicler (2 Chron. 23:18; 25:4; 31:3; 35:12) and Nehemiah (8:14; 10:34, 36). The exilic and postexilic writers refer to the Pentateuch as the Law, the Law of Moses, the Book of Moses, and the Book of the Law of Moses (2 Chron. 25:4; 35:12; Ezra 3:2; 7:6; Neh. 8:1). Jesus refers to Exodus as the book of Moses (Mark 12:26).

To many English readers these late titles signify that Moses wrote the extant books of the Pentateuch, but more probably they are conventional ways of referring to the Pentateuch's content and aim to underscore its authority, not the authorship of the book's extant form.

Moses' superb training, exceptional spiritual gifts and divine call uniquely qualified him to compose the essential content and shape of Genesis and of the Pentateuch. Walther Eichrodt, who wrote a classic theology of the Old Testament, contends that Moses is best described as founder of the theocracy to bring in a new world order.[12] As such, Moses of necessity would have given Israel its prior history, meaning, and destiny as well as its laws. Every political and/or religious community must have a memory of its history that defines and distinguishes it. Genesis also reports the origins of

---

[12]W. Eichrodt, *Theology of the Old Testament*, trans. J. A. Baker (Philadelphia: Westminster, 1961), 290–91.

the nations who are destined to come under Israel's rule (e.g., ch. 10). Furthermore, the historical narrative of Genesis repeatedly and emphatically explains that Israel's God, the God of creation and the Lord of history, has called Israel to take possession of Canaan and from that basis to bless the nations (e.g., 12:1–3; 15; 17). Finally, it also foretells the future of the tribes on the basis of their past history (e.g., ch. 49).[13] In sum, the founder of Israel is the most probable person to transpose its national repository of ancient traditions into a coherent history in order to define the nation and its mission. His noble vision stirs the imagination and calls upon its audience to order itself according to that memory.

Having been highly educated in Pharaoh's court as the son of Pharaoh's daughter (Ex. 2:1–10), in the late eighteenth or early nineteenth dynasty (ca. 1400–1300 B.C.), Moses had unique access to the ancient Near Eastern myths that show close connections with Genesis 1–11. For example the Atrahasis Epic and the Sumerian flood story, both dated earlier than 1600 B.C., parallel very closely the thematic content of Genesis 1–11.[14] The Sumerian king list, similar to the pattern in Genesis 5–11, includes a list of antediluvian kings with extravagantly long reigns (cf. Gen. 5), then a mention of the flood (cf. Gen. 6–9), and then postdiluvian kings with much shorter reigns down to ca. 1980 B.C. (cf. Gen. 11:10–27).[15] The creation account in Genesis 1 has parallels with the early second millennium B.C. Babylonian account of creation, the *Enuma Elish*.[16] The closest comparison that can be made with Genesis 2–3 is with the Adapa myth. Adapa was summoned to heaven and offered the bread and water of life. Having been warned by his personal god to reject such an offer, he declined.[17] The Genesis account of the Flood also finds striking parallels in ancient Near Eastern myths (see commentary on Book 3). These myths, against whose worldview Genesis 1–11 is in fact a polemic, were known after Moses' time, so the parallels do not establish Mosaic authorship of Genesis 1–11,[18] but they also existed before his time and Moses had a unique opportunity to know and rebut them.

Moses' training as a budding official in Pharaoh's court also would have given him firsthand education in the ancient Near Eastern law codes. For instance, the Book of the Covenant (Ex. 20:22–23:19) shows too much resemblance to the Code of Hammurabi (ca. 1700 B.C.) to have arisen independently from it; on the other hand, their differences are too great to support a theory

---

[13]J. Sailhamer, *The Pentateuch As Narrative: A Biblical-Theological Commentary* (Grand Rapids: Zondervan, 1992), 34–37.

[14]G. J. Wenham, *Genesis 1-15* (WBC 1; Waco, Tex.: Word, 1987), xxxix–xli.

[15]*ANET*, 265.

[16]A. Heidel, *The Babylonian Genesis: The Story of the Creation*, 2d ed. (Chicago: Univ. of Chicago Press, 1963).

[17]*ANET*, 76–80.

[18]J. Van Seters (*Prologue to History: The Yahwist As Historian in Genesis* [Louisville: Westminster/John Knox, 1992]) thinks that Genesis 1–11 has an affinity with Greek antiquarian writing of the late first millennium as well as with Mesopotamian sources.

of direct dependence upon that code.[19] Furthermore, Mendenhall, using the work of Korošec, shows that the book of Deuteronomy has formal similarities with Hittite suzerainty treaties (1400–1250) at the time of Moses.[20]

Finally, as the greatest of Israel's prophets, Moses would also have had the ability to draw upon God's omniscience and omnipresence in the retelling of Israel's historical traditions (cf. Num. 11:25; Deut. 34:10–11). With his extraordinary gift, confirmed by his spectacular signs and wonders, he was eminently qualified to usher his audience into the heavenly court at the time God created the cosmos (Gen. 1) and to reveal what the Almighty and other humans thought, felt, and intended (6:6, 8; 13:13; 25:34b). In a segue, let it be noted that the real hero of Genesis is the Lord and that, if the stories in Genesis about him are not inspired by heaven, they are fictitious. Thus Sternberg rightly comments: "Were the narrative written or read as fiction, then God would turn from the lord of history into a creature of the imagination, with the most disastrous results."[21]

Sources of Ur-Genesis

As a historian Moses would have used sources. One of them is noted in Genesis 5:1: "the written account [sēper tôlᵉḏôt] of Adam's line."[22] Elsewhere the Pentateuch cites the Book of Wars (Num. 21:14). Similarly, ancient Near Eastern narrators commonly used sources to compose their work.[23]

Literary source critics, however, gainsay the biblical authors' claim to Mosaic authorship of the portions attributed to him, although allowing a kernel of Mosaic material in some of them. Citing the presence of varying divine names (i.e., Yahweh [English versions, "LORD"] and Elohim ["God"]) and other vocabulary in combination with changes in style, doublet accounts of the same event, and differences in theology, they won a broad consensus for about a century (1880–1980) that a redactor in the postexilic period pieced together four formerly continuous documents to compose the present work: J (Yahwist, 950 B.C.), E (Elohist, 850 B.C.), D (Deuteronomist, 620 B.C.), and P (Priestly Code, ca. 500 B.C.). The critics originally dated these

---

[19]S. R. Driver, *The Book of Exodus* (Cambridge Bible for Schools and Colleges; Cambridge: Cambridge Univ. Press, 1911), 418–25.

[20]G. E. Mendenhall, *Law and Covenant in the Ancient Near East* (Pittsburgh: Biblical Colloquium, 1955), 24–50.

[21]M. Sternberg, *The Poetics of Biblical Narrative: Ideological Literature and the Drama of Reading* (Indiana Studies in Biblical Literature; Bloomington: Indiana Univ. Press, 1987), 32.

[22]Evidence exists of varying sources for the genealogies of Genesis. In Gen. 26:34 and 28:9 the wives of Esau are Judith, Basemath, and Mahalath. In 36:2 they are Adah, Oholibamah, and Basemath. The differences probably reflect different sources, and we can only speculate why they differ. In Gen. 11:10 Arphaxad is the only named son of Shem. In 10:22 he is Shem's third son. These are readily harmonized but also may reflect different sources.

[23]J. Tigay, "The Evolution of the Pentateuchal Narratives in the Light of the Evolution of the *Gilgamesh Epic*," in *Empirical Models for Biblical Criticism*, ed. J. Tigay (Philadelphia: Univ. of Pennsylvania Press, 1985), 20–52; idem, "Conflation As Redactional Technique," in *Empirical Models*, 53–94; idem, "The Stylistic Criterion of Source Criticism in the Light of Ancient Near Eastern and Postbiblical Literature," in *Empirical Models*, 149–74.

sources by the assumption of a simplistic evolution of religion and by putting strictures upon the prophetic gifts so that the patriarchs' alleged prophecies were in fact composed at the time of their fulfillment. Accordingly, the prophecies in Gen. 27:40 and 49:1–27 were dated to the early monarchy. New data and approaches, however, have recently seriously disrupted this consensus.

Variations in divine names are now well attested in ancient texts with no prehistory, and their variation in the Pentateuch can be explained as meaningful. For example, Yahweh is used when God's covenantal relationship with Israel is in view, but Elohim is used with reference to his universality over all the nations. Rendsburg notes that the use of Elohim from Gen. 17:3–22:24, in contrast to its absence in 11:27–16:16, occurs appropriately in connection with the name change from Abram ("Exalted Father") to Abraham ("Father of a Multitude of Nations").[24] Nevertheless, it is possible that this meaningful difference already existed in the source material.

There are also doublets in the Pentateuch that represent the same event from different points of view. For example, Genesis 1 views the creation of humanity as male and female under divine blessing, but Genesis 2–3 represents it from a sociological perspective as a husband and wife alienated from God's blessing by their disobedience. Traditional source critics also think that the repetitions such as the "sister-wife" stories (12:10–20; 20:1–18; 26:7–11) represent conflicting variants of a single historical event. But new literary critics, who prefer to consider the text's strategy rather than its strata, explain these repetitions as type-scenes. Ancient audiences loved and looked for repetition and parallels in a unified narrative to emphasize a point.[25] The source critics' parade example of a contradictory doublet is P's claim that Yahweh was not known to the patriarchs (Ex. 6:3), which contradicts J's claim that they knew the name Yahweh as early as Enosh (Gen. 4:26) and gainsays its repeated use in Genesis (e.g., 12:8; 28:13). Eslinger, however, notes that Exodus 6 does not say that the patriarchs did not call upon the name *Yahweh*. He argues that the passive construction "I was not known as Yahweh" is a variant of the active construction, "you will know that I am Yahweh." This "recognition formula" refers to the manifestation of the divine name through miraculous interventions and is common only in Exodus and Ezekiel (more than fifty times).[26] In the former God manifests his miraculous intervention through history; in the latter, through prophecy.[27] Nevertheless, two presentations of the same event in connection with the other

---

[24]Rendsburg, *Redaction*, 106.
[25]R. Alter, *The Art of Biblical Narrative* (New York: Basic Books, 1981), 47–62 ; T. L. Thompson, *The Origin Tradition of Ancient Israel* (JSOTSup 55; Sheffield: JSOT Press, 1987), 59.
[26]R. M. Hals, *Ezekiel* (FOTL 19; Grand Rapids: Eerdmans, 1989), 362.
[27]C. Eslinger, "Knowing Yahweh: Exodus 6:3 in the Context of Genesis 1–Exodus 15," in *Literary Structure and Rhetorical Strategies in the Hebrew Bible*, ed. L. de Regt, J. de Waard, and J. P. Fokkelman (Winona Lake, Ind.: Eisenbrauns, 1996), 188–98.

criteria, such as attested in Genesis 1 and 2, give the appearance of being derived from different sources. Moreover, some repeated situations, such as the different identifications of Esau's wives (26:34; 28:9; cf. 36:2) and the two accounts of Benjamin's birthplace as Bethlehem and Paddan Aram (35:16–19, 22b–26), are hard to harmonize and appear to belong to different traditions. Notably, however, these two glaring examples of apparent contradiction involve genealogies, a literary form that is notorious for establishing family relationships and not historical accuracy.

Variations in vocabulary and style may be due to differing literary genres, which by definition have different styles and call for differing vocabulary. But recognition of these differences, for whatever reason, is important in lexical studies. For instance, *'aḏām* signifies "humanity" as male and female in Genesis 1 but refers to the man/husband in Genesis 2.

In reality, the tools form and tradition critics use to trace the history of a given text or source from its earliest oral stage through to its commitment to writing and finally to its redaction into the present text of Genesis have proved woefully inadequate. After almost a century of research, their practitioners have failed to reach any consensus. After surveying the present state of pentateuchal criticism, Gordon J. Wenham concludes: "Today there is . . . no consensus. 'Every man does what is right in his own eyes.'"[28]

Literary source critics now tend to expand the content of J at the expense of E and to merge them together; in any case, there is still a consensus that J was an originally independent and continuous document. Such scholars tend to think, in contrast to form critics, that the Tetrateuch (Genesis–Numbers) escaped any systematic editing by the Deuteronomist, who clearly edited Deuteronomy through Kings in the Hebrew canon. Cross and others deny P ever existed as an independent narrative document.[29]

Moreover, scholars have dismissed the notion of a simplistic evolution of Israel's religion, thereby undermining the basis of dating the documents, and now recognize that all the alleged documents contain ancient traditions and archaic material. Following Y. Kaufmann, Israeli and American Jewish scholars such as A. Hurvitz, M. Haran, J. Milgrom, and M. Weinfeld argue that P may be contemporary with J and thus precede D.[30] Because the scribes archaized, modernized and smoothed the text, it is extremely difficult to date the sources scientifically. Judgments regarding these literary matters are just that and carry no conviction for the wary.[31] Thus Rendtorff writes, "It must be conceded that we really do not possess reliable criteria for dating

---

[28]G. J. Wenham. "Pondering the Pentateuch: The Search for a New Paradigm," in *The Face of Old Testament Studies: A Survey of Contemporary Approaches*, ed. D. W. Baker and B. T. Arnold (Grand Rapids: Baker, 1999), 116–44.

[29]F. M. Cross, *Canaanite Myth and Hebrew Epic: Essays in the History of the Religion of Israel* (Cambridge: Harvard Univ. Press, 1976), 293–325.

[30]Documented by Wenham, "Pondering," 134 n. 62.

[31]See *IBHS* §1.4.1.

of the pentateuchal literature."[32] In addition, J. G. McConville has offered a serious challenge to the traditional linking of the D document to the Josianic reform (622 B.C.), the anchor point for the traditional dating of the documents. According to him, "Deuteronomy generally legislated for conditions which characterized a considerably earlier period than Josiah," and its "laws are consistently compatible with Deuteronomy's self-presentation as speeches on the verge of the promised land."[33]

In addition, historical and textual evidence supports an earlier date for the so-called Tetrateuch than the Exile. First, those books are written from the viewpoint of Israel's enslavement in Egypt, not from the viewpoint of its exile in Babylon.[34] In Genesis the Lord predicts Israel's enslavement in a "country not their own" (15:12–16), and its author draws his history to conclusion with the entrance of the tribes into Egypt, where Moses single-handedly will forge them into a theocracy. In Genesis and Exodus the author faults the Egyptians for innocent Israel's troubles there, but the Deuteronomist finds Israel guilty of bringing the exile upon itself.

Furthermore, preexilic biblical writers at the least knew the content of the Pentateuch. For instance, in Psalm 8 David (ca. 1000 B.C.) puts the creation account of Genesis 1 into the form of a psalm. Moreover, the prophets are now generally regarded as reformers, not innovators, as traditional source critics once thought.[35] The prophets' austere messages of judgment rest on the lofty ethical laws of the Mosaic Code; their consoling messages of hope, on God's unchanging covenant with the patriarchs. Hosea and Micah, who are among the earliest writing prophets, according to their superscriptions (ca. 750–700 B.C.), mention Abraham, Jacob, and Moses and allude to the contents of both Genesis and the Pentateuch (Hos. 12:12–13; Mic. 6:4; 7:19–20).[36] Cassuto classifies Hosea's allusions to the Pentateuch into six categories: patriarchal narratives, the Exodus story, the Decalogue, the biography of Moses, Deuteronomy 11:13–21, and 33:1–43.[37] Finally, the pre-Samaritan Pentateuch text was probably modernized at the time of Ezra-Nehemiah, which means that the archaic text type of the Pentateuch preserved in the masoretic tradition must be much older.[38]

In sum, one may plausibly and most simply identify Moses as the author of the so-called J and hypothesize that he used fragments of diverse material,

[32]R. Rendtorff, *The Problem of the Process of Transmission in the Pentateuch*, trans. J. J. Scullion (JSOTSup 89; Sheffield: JSOT Press, 1990), 201.
[33]J. G. McConville, *Law and Theology in Deuteronomy* (JSOTSup 33; Sheffield: JSOT Press, 1984), 155.
[34]The reference to Babylon and Assyria in Gen. 10:10–11 is part of the book's intention to explain the origin of the nations surrounding Israel.
[35]J. Van Seters's view that the Torah is modeled on the prophets is rejected by most (*The Life of Moses: The Yahwist As Historian in Exodus-Numbers* [Louisville: Westminster/John Knox, 1994]).
[36]Many critics, however, reckon the verses cited in Micah as later additions to that book.
[37]U. Cassuto, "The Prophet Hosea and the Books of the Pentateuch," in *Biblical and Oriental Studies*, trans. I. Abrahams (Jerusalem: Magnes, 1973), 1:79–100.
[38]B. K. Waltke, "Samaritan Pentateuch," *ABD*, 5:938.

which have been traditionally denominated as P, to construct the skillfully unified Ur-Genesis.[39] It is also possible that Moses himself later interpolated alleged D material into his finished composition (e.g., Gen. 26:5), even as Muhammad secondarily interpolated material into the Koran.[40] In any case, the overall artistry of the whole and its parts, in spite of the few apparent contradictions, show that the author carefully used his sources in an integrated and sustained literary imagination, not as a redactor who crudely patched his material together.

Post-Mosaic Additions:
The Implied Author and Audience

If one assumes the Mosaic authorship of Ur-Genesis, anachronisms such as the mention of Dan (14:14) and the reference to the kings of Israel (36:31)[41] show that the scribes, the official revisers of the text, modernized and supplemented as needed the putative Ur-text of Moses. It is conceivable that they added the second account of Esau's line (36:9–29) and introduced the interlude about Judah (ch. 38) into the so-called Joseph Story during the united monarchy. The historical books as a whole, including Genesis, are probably anonymous in part because they were living texts in the hands of the scribes, who kept the text current for the people of God.[42]

Thus it seems best from a literary point of view to retain the book's own anonymity and to think of its implied author rather than its real author. Although a foundational Mosaic authorship is probable, it is not unquestionable from the text itself. The extent of scribal revisions, though probably minimal, cannot be determined. The identification of Moses as the author of the Law is important from a religious point of view, but his authorship of Genesis and the Pentateuch is not important from a literary viewpoint. More important from this viewpoint is the narrator's evaluative point of view that can be determined from the text itself without considering anything extrinsic to the narrative (see "Poetics and Narrative Theology" below).[43] For these reasons this commentary will refer to the unknown final author as "the narrator" and pay little attention to his uncertain sources.

Similarly, since the specific audience is not named, it is best to think of an implied audience. The book does not name a specific narratee because it was written for the universal people of God who share the narrator's evaluative point of view (2 Tim. 3:16–17). The real hero of Genesis is the Lord, and

[39]Wenham (*Genesis 1–15*, xxxvii–xlv) argues in detail that P is an ancient source used by J as the final editor-author.

[40]G. Widengren, *Literary and Psychological Aspects of the Hebrew Prophets* (Uppsala: Universitets Arsskirff, 1948), 10, 49.

[41]See also a-Mosaica in Gen. 11:31; 12:6; 19:38; 22:14; 32:31–32; 34:7; 47:11, 26; Ex. 11:3; 16:35; Num. 12:3; 21:14–15; 32:34; Deut. 1:1–5; 2:10–12, 20–23; 3:9, 11, 13b–14; 4:41–5:1a; 10:6–7, 9; 27:1a, 9a, 11; 28:68; 29:1a; 31:1, 7a, 9–10a, 14a, 14c–16a, 22–23a, 24–25, 30; 32:44–45, 48; 33:1; 34:1–4a, 5–12.

[42]Waltke, "Reliability," *NIDOTTE*, 1:53–54.

[43]M. A. Powell. *What Is Narrative Criticism?* (Minneapolis: Fortress, 1990), 5.

its stories pertain to the origin and life of the covenant community under the God of Israel. The New Testament often cites the book of Genesis using the present tense and the first-person pronoun "we," not third-person "they," and relates its content to the church.[44] This should leave little doubt about the implied audience of this portion of Scripture.

HISTORICITY AND LITERARY GENRE

The question that must now be raised is whether Israel's memory is historically reliable. Is Israel's faith based on historical fact or on fiction? Is Abraham the creation of faith or the creator of faith?[45] The narrator's inspiration from God, who cannot lie, is sufficient to guarantee its truthfulness without other historical corroboration, but the author of Genesis represents himself as a historian, not as a prophet who receives visions of events. He gives an essentially coherent chronological succession of events, using the Hebrew narrative verb form. He validates his material as much as possible by locating his story in time and space (e.g., 2:10–14), tracing genealogies (e.g., 5:1–32), giving evidence of various sorts that validate his history (e.g., 11:9), and citing sources (5:1). According to Brevard Childs, following W. F. Albright and John Bright, the narrator's reference to "this day"/"today" (19:38; 22:14; 32:32; 47:26) is "a formula of personal testimony added to, and confirming, the received tradition."[46] The narrator's evidence will not satisfy the demands of modern historiography, but it shows that he intended to write real history, not myth or saga or legend. Although historical critics rule out as historically credible his theological interpretation of history, their antisupernatural assumptions do not disprove empirically the prophetic narrator's account of God's hand or interventions in history.

From the viewpoint of modern historiography, internal evidence within the Pentateuch supports the narrator's inferred claim to represent what really happened. The religious practices of the patriarchs both remarkably agree and at the same time considerably disagree with the religious practices Moses commands. For example, on the one hand, Noah without explanation distinguishes between clean and unclean animals (presumably the same as specified in the law) before the law was given (6:19–7:3). On the other hand, the patriarchs worship God under different names, such as El Olam ("the Eternal God," 21:33) and El Shaddai (17:1), that never recur in the Torah, aside from Ex. 6:3. In addition, contrary to the Mosaic law and without the narrator's censure, Jacob erects a stone pillar (maṣṣēḇâ, Gen. 28:18–22),

---

[44]For example, limiting oneself to just the first ten verses of the book of Genesis, compare Gen. 1:1 with Heb. 11:3, Gen. 1:3 with 2 Cor. 4:6, and Gen. 1:6–9 with 2 Pet. 3:3–5.

[45]Cf. J. Goldingay, "The Patriarchs in Scripture and History," in *Essays on the Patriarchal Narratives*, ed. A. R. Millard and D. J. Wiseman (Winona Lake, Ind.: Eisenbrauns, 1983), 30.

[46]B. S. Childs, "A Study of the Formula 'Until This Day,'" *JBL* 82 (1963): 279–92. B. O. Long confirmed Childs's study in his Yale Ph.D. dissertation, later published as *The Problem of Etiological Narrative in the Old Testament* (BZAW 108; Berlin: Töpelmann, 1968).

Abraham marries his half-sister (Gen. 20:12), and Jacob simultaneously marries sisters (Gen. 29:15–30; cf. Deut. 16:21–22; Lev. 18:9, 18, respectively). Moreover, as Sarna notes, "freedom of testation in disregard of natural seniority, as practiced by Isaac and Jacob, is illegal and invalid according to the provisions of Deuteronomy 21:15–17."[47] Were the stories faked, one would expect the author of the Pentateuch to ground his law in the created order or in ancient traditions and, at the least, not cite data that could possibly undermine his teaching. These religious traditions are ancient, having been neither tampered with nor contrived.

Sarna also notes that "the practice of accompanying oath-taking by the gesture of placing a hand 'under the thigh' of the adjurer never recurs." He adds, "of the thirty-eight names by which the patriarchs and their families are called, twenty-seven are never found again in the Bible." Again, "only in Genesis Hebron is called Mamre, and only there is Paddan-aram mentioned."[48] The Kenites and Kenizzites head the list of the ten nations who are to be displaced by Israel at the time of their conquest (15:19). Nevertheless, Israel is never said to have fought against these tribes. Quite the contrary, the Kenites are later represented as befriending Israel (Judg. 1:16; 4:11, 17; 5:24; 1 Sam. 15:6) and the Kenizzites, one of whom is faithful Caleb, are absorbed into Judah (Num. 32:12; Josh. 14:6, 14; 1 Chron. 4:13). Finally the cataloguing of the patriarchs' sins rules out classifying these traditions as hagiography. "The cumulative effect of all this internal evidence," says Sarna, "leads to the decisive conclusion that the patriarchal traditions in the Book of Genesis are of great antiquity"[49] and so implies their historical authenticity.

The internal evidence is supported by texts uncovered at Mari, Nuzi, Alalakh, and Ugarit from the Middle Bronze Age (ca. 1950–1550 B.C.) and slightly later, though no text has yet been found mentioning the patriarchs. The social customs and legal procedures attested in these texts parallel those in the patriarchal traditions. After sifting the data, M. J. Selman cites "thirteen social practices of the patriarchal narratives to be legitimately illustrated and supported from a variety of historical contexts in the ancient Near East."[50] In light of the internal evidence for the early date of these practices, Selman adds, they are better situated in the early second millennium B.C. horizon than in the first millennium. Some data uniquely belongs to the earlier horizon. For instance, Selman notes, "in Genesis 25:23, the Hebrew term for the eldest son is not the usual b^ekor but rab, which is used here only in this sense. The cognate Akkadian word, $rabu$, is also used by itself of eldest son, but so far has turned up only in tablets of the mid-second millennium."[51]

---

[47]N. Sarna, *Genesis* (JPS Torah Commentary 1; Philadelphia: Jewish Publication Society, 1989), xvi.
[48]Ibid.
[49]Ibid., xvii.
[50]M. J. Selman, "Comparative Customs and the Patriarchal Age," in *Essays on the Patriarchal Narratives*, 91–139.
[51]Ibid., 135.

K. A. Kitchen documents several other features in the patriarchal narrative that fit *only* the Middle Bronze horizon. This is true of the price of a slave at twenty shekels of silver (Gen. 37:28), of the form of treaties mentioned in Genesis 14:13; 21; 26; and 31, and of the alliance of Mesopotamian kings in Genesis 14. Prior to and after that time a single power ruled the area.[52] In sum, the cumulative evidence does not prove the historicity of the patriarchal traditions, but it does validate it.

POETICS AND NARRATIVE THEOLOGY

Sternberg argues convincingly that the *inspired* narrator aims to produce a work that is historical, ideological, and aesthetic.[53] The preceding section argues that the narrator's interests are historical. This section demonstrates that his interests are also inseparably didactic and aesthetic. Unlike a geometry textbook that may aim to be only didactic, *Genesis* is literature because it communicates doctrine in an artful way; it is ideological art. The narrator uses words not as a stick but as a web. He teaches by telling stories. This section analyzes how he persuades as he prescribes through his stories his worldview. Poetics deals with the rhetorical techniques that all biblical writers employ to communicate meaning; narrative theology is derived from the application of poetics, along with other methods, to the narratives.

Levels of Signification

In the work of interpreting a text, one must take note of different levels of signification. One may define twelve levels in the biblical text, moving from smallest to largest.[54]

12. book/composition
11. sections/cycles
10. acts or phases
9. scenes or episodes
8. scene parts or incidents
7. frames/speeches
6. sentences
5. clauses
4. phrases
3. words
2. syllables
1. sounds

---

[52]K. A. Kitchen, "The Patriarchal Age: Myth or History?" *BAR* 21 (March/April, 1995): 48–57, 88–95.

[53]Sternberg, *Poetics*, 156.

[54]Adopted and adapted from J. P. Fokkelman, *Narrative Art and Poetry in the Books of Samuel*, vol. 2 (Assen: Van Gorcum, 1986), 4.

Levels 1 and 2 involve sound and sense. For example, Gen. 27:36 reads: *ʾt bkrtî lqḥ whnh ʿth lqḥ brktî* ("My birthright he took, and look, now he has taken my blessing"). The sound play between *bᵉḵōrātî* and *birkātî* in the outer frame of the chiasm effectively links Esau's complaint that Jacob stole "my birthright" and its correlative "my blessing." Likewise, in Gen. 9:6, as McCreesh notes, "The repeated sound patterns in the chiasm *šōpēḵ dam hāʾāḏām bāʾāḏām dāmô yiššāpēḵ* ('whoever sheds the blood of a human being by a human being his blood will be shed') phonically represent the reversal of fortune described."[55]

Levels 3–6 are typically treated in Hebrew grammars and syntaxes.[56] Scenes (level 9), sometimes referred to as episodes, develop the smallest units of plot development that display a significant level of independence from the context. For example, the Abraham cycle contains a number of scenes: the call of Abraham (12:1–9), Abraham's exodus in Egypt (12:10–20), Abraham and Lot separate (13:1–18), and so on. In order to observe the overall dynamic of the story, the scenes can be batched into *acts* (level 10). The scenes in Genesis 12–15 belong to an act that develops the motif of land, the scenes in Genesis 16–22 to an act developing the motif of seed. The thematic analysis of scenes and acts is often validated by other poetic devices such as key words, inclusios, and so forth (see below). For example, the act from Genesis 16–22 begins "Sarai . . . had borne [Abram] no children" (16:1) and draws toward a conclusion by noting, "Sarah . . . bore a son to Abraham" (21:2). A scene plot consists of incidents, and these in turn of dialogues and frames (levels 7–8). The ten *tôlᵉḏôt* sections function as cycles in Genesis, marking the book's major divisions in tracing God's program of bringing the seed of the Serpent under the dominion of the elect seed of the woman. The meaning of the whole book (level 12) is discussed below ("Theme of Genesis and Biblical Theology").

Modern literary criticism has done much to uncover the techniques by which the skillful narrator of Genesis has masterfully woven this story. The writer of Genesis has obviously not related every event and detail of the beginning of history and the beginning of the people of God. Thankfully he did not try to produce such an unreadable and unimaginative report. Hexter explains, "The historical record which is all too exiguous is also paradoxically all too full. In order to make human character stand clear of the clutter of routing action . . . [the historian has to] practice the art of discerning and reporting the telling detail, the illuminating incident, the revelatory remark."[57] The narrator of Genesis has selected the particular stories of Genesis to explain what it means to be the people of God. He has told

---

[55]T. P. McCreesh, *Biblical Sound and Sense: Poetic Patterns in Proverbs 10–29* (JSOTSup 128; Sheffield: Sheffield Academic Press, 1991), 76.

[56]See *IBHS*.

[57]J. H. Hexter, *Doing History* (London: Allen & Unwin, 1971), 167–68.

them in such a masterful way that the heroes of faith emerge as literary icons inspiring the audience to emulate their faithful actions. The readers participate in the story, experiencing with the characters its message, challenge, and exhortation.

The studies of poetics and narrative criticism examine how the narrator has so effectively shaped a story and seek to uncover the layers of meaning within the text. Simplistically, poetics is the grammar of literature, the study of the techniques and devices an author uses to convey meaning in a text; narrative criticism is the application of poetics to narrative. With the tools of these studies the exegete can discern the narrator's evaluative point of view that governs the work as a whole. The reader can enter the narrator's, and thereby God's, world and life views.

Poetics

Adele Berlin defines the study of poetics as "an inductive science that seeks to abstract the general principles of literature from many different manifestations of those principles as they occur in actual literary texts." Its essential aim is not "to elicit meaning of any given text" but rather "to find the building blocks of literature and the rules by which they are assembled." Thus, "poetics is to literature as linguistics is to language." In essence, poetics is the grammar of literature. We must first know *how* a text means before we can know *what* it means.[58]

Just as the rules of grammar change from era to era and language to language, literary methods also change. The narrator's different social and historical setting from that of the contemporary audience creates gaps in the latter's knowledge and understanding of the author's intention, gaps that must be carefully bridged. The task of the Bible student is to discern the "rules" employed in a biblical text as evidenced by that text. This task necessarily involves a heuristic spiral. One approaches the text with ideas about its techniques and principles, which the text then proves or disproves. Thus begins the dialogue with the text that leads the careful listener to learn how the text communicates.

The use of poetics in interpreting the biblical text produces certain implications and expectations. One of the first things noted by literary critics is that biblical authors use words sparingly—each word counts. Therefore, the exegete's attitude should be that every feature in the text is there for a reason and needs to be explained.[59] So, for example, from this vantage the exegete is not primarily concerned with how the change of divine names in Genesis 1 and 2 may reflect different sources but with what function the

---

[58]A. Berlin, *Poetics and Interpretation of Biblical Narrative* (Bible and Literature Series 9; Sheffield: Almond, 1983), 15.

[59]A. Bonchek, *Studying the Torah: A Guide to In-Depth Interpretation* (Northvale N.J.: Jason Aronson, 1996), 15.

change has in the development of the story. As noted, the different names express different aspects of God's character and rule. In Genesis 1 *ʾelōhîm* (God) refers to God's transcendence over the world, while in Genesis 2–3 *yhwh* (LORD) speaks of God's immanence with his elect. When the narrator combines the two names, he makes a bold assertion that the Creator God is the Lord of Israel's history. Just as God ordered creation, he orders history. All is under God's sovereign control, guaranteeing that Israel's history will end in triumph, not in tragedy.

The recognition of the poetic features in the biblical text helps the reader to identify the narrator's interpretive lens. By determining where his emphasis, criticism, and approval lie and where they do not, we are given insight into the narrator's evaluative viewpoint. Identifying that evaluative viewpoint, his world and life view, is the goal of those who want to listen to and apply the text. Below is a sampling of some of the poetic devices frequently employed by the narrator of Genesis.

Key Word (Leitwort)

Martin Buber coined the term *Leitwort,* meaning "lead word" (referred to in this commentary and other literary works as "key word"). He identifies this lead or key word as "a word or word-root that is meaningfully repeated within a text, or a sequence of texts or a complex of texts; those who attend to these repetitions will find a meaning of the text revealed and clarified, or at any rate made more emphatic."[60] Such words provide focus, meaning, or emphasis in a text.[61]

So, for instance, the narrator plays with the word *ṣāyiḏ* "game" in the story of Isaac. Genesis 25:28 literally reads "Isaac loved Esau because of *the game in his mouth.*" This foreshadows Isaac's defining moment of failure in Genesis 27, when he seeks to bless Esau, not elect Jacob, because his moral taste has become so dulled by his sensual appetites. The narrator punctuates the tale of blessing in Genesis 27 with the words "game" (*ṣāyiḏ*), repeated eight times, and "tasty food" (*maṭʿammîm*), repeated six. Isaac is said to "love tasty food" by Rebekah, Isaac himself, and the narrator. The repetition makes the point apparent: Isaac's love for his sensual taste has distorted his spiritual taste (cf. 26:35).

Refrain

A refrain is a repetition of a phrase or sentence. In addition to emphasizing a point, it also helps to divide material. Although this literary technique

---

[60]M. Buber, "Leitwort Style in Pentateuch Narrative," in *Scripture and Translation,* ed. M. Buber and F. Rosenzweig, trans. L. Rosenwald and E. Fox (Bloomington: Indiana Univ. Press, 1994), 114.

[61]Note: These key words may not always be apparent in the English versions. Good English style requires that the translator use different English words to render the same Hebrew word. Other than reading the text in Hebrew, a reader must rely on a more word-for-word translation than the NIV.

is most noticeable in poetry, it also operates in narrative. For example, the refrain "The account of the descendents of . . ." (*tôlᵉḏôt*) divides Genesis into its ten books tracing God's new initiatives in salvation history.

Contrast

Writers use contrast when they associate or juxtapose things that are dissimilar or opposite. Bonchek writes, "It has been said that a sign of the creative individual is his ability to perceive the differences in similar things and the similarities in different things."[62] Biblical writers masterfully contrast similar scenes and events. Alter uses the term "type scene" to refer to a frequently repeated scene. The similarities of such scenes allow the narrator to highlight both the similarities and differences. One notable type scene is "meeting a bride at a well." The contrast between the meeting of Abraham's prayerful servant and Rebekah (Gen. 24) and the meeting of Jacob and Rachel (Gen. 29:1–12) highlights the lack of prayerfulness and spiritual astuteness in Jacob's life. Whereas Abraham's servant begins and ends his meeting with prayer and judges Rebekah on her hospitality, Jacob never prays at the well but instead shows off his brute strength to lift the well stone. His assessment of Rachel is based solely on her beauty.

Comparison

Comparison is an association or juxtaposition of things that are alike or similar. Here again we see the narrator's skillful use of similar scenes and events. The similar stories of the jeopardizing of the matriarch by Abraham and Isaac highlight important comparisons between father and son. On different occasions both father and son act duplicitously and their wives are taken into the harems of foreign kings, only to be protected by God's intervention. Just as Sarah is protected in Abimelech's harem, Rebekah is protected. Just as the Philistine king makes a treaty with Abraham at Beersheba, a Philistine king makes a treaty at Beersheba with Isaac. The comparison demonstrates that Isaac has the same blessing as his father.

Logic and the Law of Reciprocity

The narrator brings order to the text and connects events and scenes through cause and effect. Jacob deceives Isaac through the latter's blindness of sight (Gen. 27:18–24). Laban deceives Jacob through the "blindness" of night (29:25). The story of Joseph's being sold into slavery, where Judah deceives his father by telling him to "recognize" the bloody tunic (37:32–33), is followed by the story of Tamar's deception of Judah and her demand to "recognize" your staff (38:25). A sense of poetic justice often governs the narratives.

---

[62]Bonchek, *Studying*, 59.

Climax/Intensification

Texts commonly reflect escalating action, a sense of movement from the lesser to the greater. This is evident in the first six days of creation in Genesis 1. These days are divided into two triads arranged by intensification. Both vegetation and humanity, symbolizing the fertility of life, were considered pinnacles of creation in the ancient Near East. The first triad ends climactically with the creation of vegetation; the second, the creation of humanity.

Patterns[63]

The narrator uses structural patterns in connection with the elements in all twelve levels of signification. Of the many patterns used by biblical writers, the most common in Genesis are alternating (also called symmetrical), concentric, and chiastic. Examples of the alternating and concentric patterns are seen above in the structure of the *tôledôt* cycles. So, for instance, the elements in the Primeval History are set out in an alternating structure, the Abraham cycle in a concentric pattern. With regard to the symmetrical pattern, Walsh explains, "Parallel patterns tend to invite comparison of the parallel sequences and of the individual parallel elements. Comparison often reveals progression, but not necessarily opposition or contrast, between the parallel components."[64] In the concentric pattern, the first series of elements usually pertain to the plot's rising tension or action, and the second series to its resolution or falling action. The chiastic pattern is similar to the concentric, but unlike the concentric it has a single central element, the turning point or "pivot." Sometimes the respective elements on either side of the pivot contrast. Pratt illustrates the turning-point pattern from Genesis 15:7–21.[65]

A Problem: Abraham's request regarding promised land of Canaanites (15:7–8)
  B Rising action: Covenant ceremony is begun (15:9–11)
    C Pivot: Abraham receives promise in a dream (15:12–16)
  B′ Falling action: covenant ceremony is completed (15:17)
A′ Resolution: God states covenant to give Abraham the land of Canaanites (15:18–21)

In all three patterns there is a delightful sense of balance in the arrangement of the elements and a sense of the Sovereign's order in history.

Janus

Janus, named from the Roman god of doorways with one head and two faces looking in opposite directions, is a term applied to a literary unit that

---

[63]For a more detailed and helpful analysis see R. L. Pratt Jr., *He Gave Us Stories* (Brentwood, Tenn.: Wolgemuth & Hyatt, 1990), 179–230.
[64]Walsh, *1 Kings*, xiv.
[65]Adopted from Pratt, *He Gave*, 201.

looks back and forth to unite the units before and after.[66] The transition passages at the end of each *tôlᵉḏôṯ* (e.g., 4:25–26; 6:1–8; 9:18–29, etc.) are janus sections.

Generalization and Particularization

Generally a narrative moves toward explication that becomes either more specific or more comprehensive. The movement of the first four chapters of Genesis is an example of particularization. Whereas the prologue concerns creation on a cosmic level, Book 1 focuses on the first human beings.

Foreshadowing

Foreshadowing refers to the inclusion of material in one part of the narrative that serves primarily to prepare the reader for what is still to come. As noted before, the mention of Isaac's taste for wild game, at the time a seemingly gratuitous comment, is actually a foreshadowing of Isaac's failure to exercise divine wisdom in blessing his boys.

Summarization

A summarization is a synopsis or abridgment of material that is treated more fully elsewhere. For example, Gen. 2:1, "Thus the heavens and the earth were completed in all their vast array," is a summarization of the entire preceding chapter.

Inclusio

Inclusio refers to a repetition of features at the beginning and the end of a unit. An inclusio may function to frame a unit, to stabilize the enclosed material, to emphasize by repetition, or to establish a nexus with the intervening material for rhetorical effect. In Genesis 16, the narrator uses the terms "Abram," "Hagar," and the verb "to bear" to form an inclusio around the scene, "Hagar and Ishmael Rejected" (Book 6, Act 2, Scene 1).

"Now Sarai, Abram's wife, had borne him no children. But she had an Egyptian maidservant named Hagar" (16:1).

"Abram was eighty-six years old when Hagar bore him Ishmael" (16:16).

This repetition frames the story and emphasizes Sarah's barrenness, particularly in light of her failed attempt to engineer her own solution. As noted above, *Abram/Abraham*, *Sarai/Sarah* and *bore* also form an inclusio around the entire act.

Intercalation

Intercalation is the insertion of one literary unit into the midst of another. For example, as mentioned above, by completing 5:32 in 9:18 the third

---

[66]January, which looks back to the old year and ahead to the new, takes its name from this god.

tôlᵉḏôt, "The account of the line of Noah's line," is intercalated into the second so that the third might pertain to both Noah and his sons.

Irony

Irony, which broadly refers to incongruity, has many forms. Dramatic irony—when the reader and/or certain characters are aware of important elements unknown to other characters—often reduces the ignorant person to a joke. A classic example is blind Isaac blessing Jacob disguised as Esau, thus establishing God's purpose and defeating the patriarch's interest. Lot is an especially hapless figure of irony. Wanting wealth and comfort, he chooses the seemingly glamorous city Sodom and ends up in poverty and incest in a cave.

Narrative Theology

Definition and Hermeneutics

Narrative theology is, among other things, a specific application of "poetics" to narrative. Narrative is a representational form of art. Narrative criticism is an attempt to observe, analyze, and systematically classify how narratives represent their objects, how they tell their stories to communicate meaning. A narrative represents character(s) and event(s), often in distinct settings, whose interaction constitutes plot. Fewell and Gunn note, "Narrative communicates meaning through the imitation of human life, the temporal ordering of human speech and action. It constructs a verbal world that centers on human characters, their relations, desires, and actions in time."[67]

Narrative criticism distinguishes between story (i.e., the brute facts) and discourse (i.e., the artistic representation of the facts). "Story," Powell explains, "refers to the content of the narrative, what the narrative is about."[68] Behind the narrative lie the actual or imagined characters and events that the narrative seeks to portray. According to Powell, "Discourse refers to the rhetoric of the narrative, how the story is told. Stories concerning the same basic events, characters, and settings can be told in ways that produce very different narratives."[69] Discourse is similar to fiction. Both the historian and fiction writer generate a mood stance, such as reflection, exploration, edification, celebration, cathartic cleansing, and/or sheer delight. The biblical historical books are both history and literature.

Through his discourse the narrator leads his audience, God's universal covenant community, to absorb his world and life views. He motivates the audience to surrender its own thought system and life forms in order to enter God's world and to be carried along by the flow of his interpretative report.

---

[67]D. N. Fewell and D. Gunn. "Narrative, Hebrew," *ABD*, 4:1023.
[68]Powell, *Narrative Criticism*, 23.
[69]Ibid.

By inviting the readers to become insiders, the narrator teaches implicitly more than explicitly; he catches readers off guard and exposes them to thoughts and worldviews that might otherwise be met with hostility. Because personhood emerges as life unfolds, the possibility of grasping personal identity arises more readily by seeing another's life whole and clear. The biographies of Genesis are historical "metaphors," often inspiring literary "icons," enabling the reader to compare and construct his or her own life. Moreover, God may be comprehended more readily in his involvement in a person's life than in the nontemporal, abstract theological categories of a systematic theology.

Evaluative Viewpoint

Before analyzing the agencies and means by which the narrator communicates his world and life views, let us remember that his narrative operates on two levels: the historical facts of the story and the narrator's representation of the facts, the discourse. As a result there emerges four evaluative points of view. On the factual level, there is God's viewpoint versus those of the human characters. On the discourse level there are the narrator's viewpoint and that of his audience whom he tries to win over to his point of view. In truth, however, the narrator has the final word. We only know of God's viewpoint and that of the characters within the story to the extent that the narrator records them, and we may assume that he selects and expresses their words in such a way that he communicates his point of view. All contributes to the narrator's intention to win his implied audience over to his inspired viewpoint. Ultimately, however, he is expressing God's viewpoint for he is God's inspired prophet-historian.

Listed below are some of the narrative techniques employed in Genesis to provide insight into the inspired narrator's evaluative viewpoint.

Through Agents and Direct Statement

The narrator communicates a point of view through many agencies and means, the most common of which are delineated below.

God's point of view. When God speaks in the biblical narrative, it is always reliable. At the beginning of Genesis, God communicates mostly in theophany; later to the patriarchs, mostly in visions and dreams; at the end, through providence. Whereas theophany is unambiguous, vision, dreams, and especially providence are less clear. The narrator expresses God's point of view in a variety of ways:

- by direct quote (see Gen. 2:18; 7:1; 22:15–18)
- by the narrator's direct statements about God (see 6:6, 8; 13:13)
- by providence and actions. Although providence is ambiguous, God's providential ordering of the affairs of his people does provide insight into his evaluative viewpoint

Direct statement of narrator's point of view. The narrator's viewpoint is also reliable because he speaks as an inspired spokesperson for God. The audience knows the events and characters of the Bible only as the narrator represents them. It sees and hears only through the narrator's eyes and ears. He is an a priori category constituting the sole means of knowing the story. The covenant community hears and accepts his inspiration; unfortunately, those outside the community sometimes deconstruct his interpretation in order to empower their own world and life views in place of his. The narrator is usually hidden in the story but occasionally steps outside of it to address the audience directly. Thus, in Gen. 16:6 the narrator judges Sarah's actions against Hagar in the direct statement, "Sarah mistreated Hagar." Regarding Esau's sale of his birthright, the narrator says, "Esau despised his birthright" (25:34b). Sometimes he uses retrospects: "So when God destroyed the cities of the plain, he remembered Abraham, and he brought Lot out of the catastrophe that overthrew the cities where Lot had lived" (19:29). Other times he uses prospects: "For this reason a man will leave his father and mother and be united to his wife" (2:24).

Indirect statement of narrator's point of view. Sometimes the characters within the story, the actual participants in the narrative, express the narrative's evaluative viewpoint.

- Hero's words: The main character may declare a truth about God. So Jacob, who prior to this point rarely spoke of God, declares, "the God of my father has been with me" (31:5).
- Agent's words: Even one who is not the hero of the narrative may confirm a viewpoint expressed by the narrator. For example, Abimelech says to Abraham, "God is with you in everything you do" (21:22).

Without confirmation by other means, it is sometimes difficult to determine if the participant is reflecting the narrator's viewpoint, for even the great heroes of faith are flawed.

Through Poetics and Other Techniques

The narrator also communicates an evaluation of the events, characters, and settings that constitute his discourse in several other ways besides the poetic techniques analyzed above.

Hints of style. The narrator's choice of vocabulary is often a subtle but important clue to his viewpoint. The subtle but crucial difference between Abel's sacrificial gift of "fat portions from some of the *first*born" and Cain's gift of "*some* of the fruits of the soil" indicts Cain's tokenism and explains why his gift was unacceptable (Gen. 4:3–5).

Gaps. A *gap* is an intentional omission, whereas a *blank* is an inconsequential omission. The gap of the expected book entitled the *tôlᵉḏôt* of Abraham (i.e., Isaac's narrative) is glaring (compare the *tôlᵉḏôt* of Terah [Abraham's narrative], the *tôle̠dôt* of Isaac [Jacob's narrative], and the *tôle̠dôt* of Jacob [Joseph and Judah's narrative]). This obviously intentional gap stands as an implicit judgment against the miracle child who in his later years gives himself over to sensual pleasures at the expense of spiritual discernment.

Anachrony. With this textual feature the narrator tells the story out of order or withholds information, revealing it later for dramatic effect. By this method the narrator reveals the meaning of place and temple in the story of Jacob's Bethel dream (Gen. 28:10–22). At the story's beginning the narrator reports that Jacob arrived at "a certain place," essentially calling it a "no-place." But this no-place becomes the axis of heaven and earth, God's presence transforming it into a place of meaning. At the end of the story (28:19), the narrator anachronistically identifies this place as Luz, a thriving Canaanite city. By this anachrony the narrator suggests that Luz has to be emptied of its Canaanite grandeur and be reduced to a no-place before it can be seen as God's house.[70]

Through Characterization

The narrator employs a variety of techniques to help the reader evaluate a character, whether that character is God, a supernatural being, or a human being.

Outer description. Biblical narrative rarely describes someone's appearance. Consequently, when it does it has a purpose, usually serving the plot. Esau is described as "hairy," Jacob as smooth. These descriptions explain the goatskin in Jacob's ruse to steal the blessing.

Direct characterization. In rare occasions the narrator breaks the frame to make his evaluation of a character unambiguous. Thus in a direct statement he says, "The serpent was more crafty," "Noah was a righteous man," and so forth.

Revelation of a character's thoughts. The narrator's disclosure of Esau's thoughts (27:41) reveals the extent of his hatred for Jacob and the covenant family (see also Gen. 8:21; 18:17; 37:34). The Lord gave Leah children because he "saw" that she was not loved (29:31), and years later "God remembered Rachel . . . and opened her womb" (30:22).

Direct speech. Usually the narrator relies on the human character's direct speech for portrayal. For example, Adam's only words prior to the Fall are words about his wife: she is my equal. His speech indicates the robust solidarity he feels toward his wife before sin hinders their relationship (see also Gen. 17:17; 30:2; 31:31). Jacob confesses to the Lord, "I am unworthy" (32:10), and "I am afraid" (32:11).

Action. Noah's tender care of the dove returning to the ark (Gen. 8:9) reveals him to be a gentle conservationist, living out God's love for creation.

---

[70]J. P. Fokkelman, *Narrative Art in Genesis: Specimens of Stylistic and Structural Analysis,* 2d ed. (Sheffield: JSOT Press, 1991), 69.

Speech and actions. Upon his return from the field, famished Esau pleads, "Red stuff, red stuff!" (lit., 25:30). Then the narrator encapsulates his actions, "He ate and drank, and then got up and left" (25:34). In other words, Esau is man of immediacy and reaction rather than reflection and wisdom.

Contrast. In some cases character is revealed by contrasting one person with another. For example, Jacob is contrasted with Esau. Despite all his flaws, Jacob values the birthright. Esau does not.

Naming. Often the name or descriptive phrase used for a character either identifies the narrator's perspective on the person or reveals something about the speaker. Thus the weak "Jacob" is later renamed "Israel" to reveal his new strength. Bonchek points out the shifting names for Dinah in Gen. 34:1–4. In 34:1, when she goes out to visit the women of the land, she is called "the daughter [of] Leah." In 34:2, when she is treated as an object and raped, she is referred to simply as "her," "her," "her." In 34:3, when Shechem wants to marry Dinah, she is called "the daughter of Jacob"; when he wants to woo her, "a young woman" (lit.). In 34:4 when Shechem speaks to his father about her, he refers to her as "child" (lit.).

Through Plot

The plot structure typically consists of an exposition or introduction, a rising tension, a climax or peaking of the tension, and a resolution and denouement. Biblical narratives often begin with exposition, preparing the narrative. Bar-Efrat explains: "The situation at the beginning of the action is presented in what is usually called the exposition. This serves as an introduction to the action described in the narrative, supplying the background information, introducing the characters, informing us of their names, traits, physical appearance, state in life, and the relations obtaining among them, and providing the other details needed for understanding the story."[71] It may also set forth the problem or tension. The story of Abraham's sacrifice of Isaac (Gen. 22) opens with two sentences of exposition, which not only establish the setting but also explain that this unusual scene is directed by God's desire to test Abraham.

The plot tension is often structured by a pattern such as the ones highlighted in poetic techniques above and/or by summarization and particularization. The protagonist, the leading character (whether good or bad), is displayed and developed in the plot's rising tension usually in conflict with the antagonist, the leading character arrayed against him or her. Often God's sublime character is displayed in the denouement: he keeps his promises, rewards the faithful, punishes the evildoer, graciously overlooks the foibles of his people, and so. The evaluative viewpoint is often seen in how the story turns out.

---

[71]S. Bar-Efrat, *Narrative Art in the Bible* (Bible and Literature Series 17; JSOTSup 70; Sheffield: Almond/JSOT Press, 1989), 111.

Through Scenic Depiction

Sometimes the description of the scene correlates with a character's situation and provides a clue to the narrator's perspective. For example, the setting sun marks the beginning of Jacob's flight to Laban as he enters a dark period of testing (Gen. 28:10–11). At the end of those twenty long years, Jacob limps toward home as the sun rises above (32:31).

Through Symbols

The narrator may use symbols and imagery to depict a character's state. In the life of Jacob, stones, such as the pillow-cum-pillar of Bethel (Gen. 28), mark significant moments. The story of Jacob features stones, that of Joseph features robes. Such palpable objects symbolize something of a character's social and/or spiritual situation.

Law of Parsimony

As the careful exegete approaches the text, one principle will guide him or her well: the law of parsimony, which states that the simple, yet most comprehensive, interpretation is preferred over the complex and circumscribed. Bonchek remarks, "An interpretation that resolves several difficulties in the text in one fell swoop is not only more elegant, it has the ring of truth." For instance, Rashi and Ibn Ezra both suggest explanations for why Joseph imprisons Simeon in Gen. 42:24. Citing Genesis 34, where Simeon and Levi massacre Hamor, Shechem, and their city, Rashi argues that they have a violent nature and thus "it was Joseph's intention to separate him from Levi, lest the two of them conspire to kill him." However, based on Reuben's speech in 42:22–23, Ibn Ezra reasons that Joseph has probably just learned that Reuben was not responsible for his enslavement and that now Joseph assumes that the next eldest Simeon must be responsible. In contrast to Rashi's explanation, which requires leaps and unstated allusions to much earlier material, Ibn Ezra's explanation fulfills the law of parsimony for its simplicity, rationality, and its ability to make sense of the connection in verses 22–24.[72]

THEME OF GENESIS AND BIBLICAL THEOLOGY[73] ──────

Introduction: The Kingdom of God

The theme of Genesis and its subordinate motifs are best understood in light of the whole Bible. So, one must ask, what is the entirety of the Bible all about?

---

[72]Bonchek, *Studying*, 16.

[73]This section of the introduction has been adapted from the essay by B. K. Waltke in "The Kingdom of God in Biblical Theology," *Looking into the Future: Evangelical Studies in Eschatology*, ed. D. W. Baker. (Grand Rapids: Baker, forthcoming).

The kingdom of God is a central tenet in the teachings of the Lord Jesus and plays an important role in Paul's teaching. Although the expression "kingdom of God" never occurs in the Old Testament and its equivalents are relatively rare and late,[74] the concept informs the whole. The Primary History, which traces Israel's history from the creation of the world (Gen. 1) to the fall of Israel (2 Kings 25), is all about what the New Testament calls "the kingdom of God."

Though composed of many earlier blocks of writings, the Primary History in its final form consists of two great collections. The Pentateuch (Genesis–Deuteronomy) traces the history of Israel from the creation of the cosmos to Israel's being perched on the threshold of entering the Promised Land. The so-called Deuteronomistic History (Deuteronomy–Kings)[75] continues that history from Israel's entrance into the land to its exile from it. The lynch pin of the Primary History, binding together these two great histories, is the book of Deuteronomy. Paradoxically, Deuteronomy is both the capstone of the Pentateuch and the foundation stone of the Deuteronomistic History. This is so because the core of the original book of Deuteronomy is Moses' three addresses to Israel, his song about Israel's future course of history, and his blessings on the tribes of Israel. To these the Deuteronomist during the Exile added fifty-six verses in order to incorporate the core within the narrative of his so-called Deuteronomistic History. Through this double authorship it becomes the janus or transition book that binds together the two great documents of the Primary History.

This history is the backbone of the Old Testament. The superscriptions of the prophetic books, of the Psalms, and of Proverbs are set within the context of this history. Just as in the case of other heuristic theological schemes, such as the Trinity, it may be possible to identify a theme in the Old Testament, such as the kingdom of God, even though the term itself is not used.

Paul Drake draws two conclusions about Jesus' use of the phrase. First, it has a historical dimension: "The kingdom comes at the end of time as the culmination of everything that has happened from the creation until now."[76] Second, this eschatological reality has a legal dimension. God exercises the authority of a sovereign in a realm where his subjects obey his commands. Citing the Lord's Prayer, Drake defends the conclusion "that the synoptic tradition understands the kingdom of God as the establishment of God's sovereignty over the human race."[77] The Matthean version reads, "your king-

---

[74]Psalms 22:29 [Eng. 28]; 103:19; 145:11–13 [4x]; Obad. 21; Dan. 2:44; 3:33 [Eng. 4:3]; 4:31 [Eng. 34]; 6:27 [Eng. 26]; 7:14, 18, 27; 1 Chron. 17:14; 28:5; 29:11; 2 Chron. 13:8.

[75]Joshua 1 is a pastiche of Deuteronomy; Judg. 2:6 repeats Josh. 24:28, but in a chiastic structure bringing closure; 1 Samuel 8 brings closure to the period of the judges; and 1 Kings 1–2 brings the so-called "succession narrative" begun in 2 Samuel 9 to closure. We need here only to observe this unity, not debate how it came to be.

[76]P. Drake, "The Kingdom of God in the Old Testament," in *The Kingdom of God in 20th Century Interpretation*, ed. W. Willis (Peabody, Mass.: Hendrickson, 1987), 67–79.

[77]Drake, "Kingdom," 71.

dom come, your will be done on earth as it is in heaven. Give us this day our daily bread" (Matt. 6:10–11). The Lukan version, however, reads, "your kingdom come. Give us each day our daily bread" (Luke 11:2), lacking the petition, "your will be done on earth as it is in heaven." Matthew probably added "your will be done" to explicate the petition for the coming of the kingdom.[78] Drake, however, fails to differentiate adequately between God's universal kingdom and the particular kingdom in view in the Lord's Prayer. By the former, theologians mean God's activity in exercising his sovereignty over all things, even giving the nations their pagan deities (Deut. 4:19). By the latter, Jesus Christ meant God's activity in establishing a realm in which his subjects obey *ex animo* his law.

In the Primary History, God's kingdom mostly takes the shape of national Israel, a political state with geospatial boundaries in contradistinction to other nations. The principal concern of the Primary History is the irruption (i.e., the breaking in from without), not eruption (i.e., the breaking out from within), of God's righteous kingdom through the political state of Israel.

The Call of Abraham (12:1 – 3): The Key to the Primary History

D. J. A. Clines demonstrates that the episode recounting God's call of Abraham (Gen. 12:1–3) expresses tersely and succinctly the theme of the Pentateuch.[79] In truth, it also presents the scheme for understanding the Primary History. God's seven promises to Abraham pertain to three expanding horizons, from God's call to Abraham to disassociate himself from his family (12:1), to God's making him into a nation of blessing (12:2), to God's blessing the whole earth through him (12:3). On the part of Abraham and his nation, they bless the earth only to the extent that they submit themselves to God's moral law. Elsewhere God says, "For I have chosen [Abraham], so that he will direct his children and his household after him to keep the way of the LORD by doing what is right and just, so that the LORD will bring about for Abraham what he has promised him" (Gen. 18:19). The nations, on their part, qualify themselves for this blessing by recognizing that Abraham and his obedient nation are possessed of God's power to mediate abundant and effective living and then by praying for God's blessing upon Abraham and his nation.

In order to unpack this idea that God is establishing his moral rule over the earth through national Israel, it is helpful to analyze it into its four constituent motifs. A nation consists of a common people, normally sharing a common land, submissive to a common law, and led by a common ruler. The book of Genesis is concerned principally in identifying both the people who submit to God's commands and the land that sustains them. The rest of the

---

[78]R. Hamerton-Kelly, *God the Father* (Philadelphia: Fortress, 1979), 73–74.
[79]D. J. A. Clines, *The Theme of the Pentateuch* (JSOTSup 10; Sheffield: JSOT Press, 1978).

Pentateuch focuses mainly on God's law, while the Deuteronomistic history (especially, Joshua–Kings) develops the theme of the nation's ruler.

First Motif: The Seed

Genesis sometimes uses the metaphor of "seed" for human offspring. Fundamental to that metaphor is the notion of reproduction "after its kind." To oversimplify the matter, just as the seed of plants and trees produce according to their kind (Gen. 1:11–12), so human seed grows according to the type of person that produces the seed. In the beginning God creates humanity in his image, that is, as his regents to represent his rule on earth. In the temple-garden of Eden his first word to humanity is a command. They must not eat of the tree of the knowledge of good and evil. That famous tree symbolizes the ability to discern good (i.e., what advances life) and evil (i.e., what hinders life). Such knowledge belongs to God alone because, as Agur inferentially argues in Prov. 30:1–6, one must know comprehensively in order to speak absolutely about what is good and bad.

However, finite humanity in Adam and Eve refuses to accept this limitation and transgresses the established boundary. Tempted by Satan to doubt God's goodness and the truth of his word, with an illicit reach of unbelief and defiance against God's rule they eat the forbidden fruit, making themselves their own lawmakers apart from God. As God has threatened, they become alienated from God and from one another. In response to their rebellion in setting up a rival kingdom, the gracious Sovereign intervenes by changing Eve's religious affections so that she will love God and submit to his rule and hate Satan who defies it. Addressing Satan, God says, "*I will* put enmity between you and the woman, and between your offspring [seed] and hers" (Gen. 3:15). From then on humanity is divided broadly into two spiritual races, though both physically reproduce Adam and Eve. The seed of the woman as seen in Abel reproduces her love for God, and the seed of the Serpent as seen in Cain reproduces his spiritual enmity against God.

The book of Genesis is all about this seed of the woman. It is structured by means of linear genealogies to trace this holy seed from Adam and Eve to the twelve tribes of Israel (see "Excursus: Genesis Genealogies"). A decisive development in this theme occurs in God's call of Abraham. God elects Abraham and his offspring who reproduce his faith to represent God's moral rule and to mediate God's blessing to all the tribes and nations of the earth. In a binding covenant God obligates himself to make Abraham and his circumcised seed the unique representatives of his blessed rule. His promise to make them as numerous as the stars of heaven is fulfilled at the time of Israel's conquest of the Holy Land (Gen. 15:5; Deut. 1:10). God's covenant with faithful Abraham in Genesis 17 explicates in a fresh way the Lord's promise in Gen. 12:3 to bless all nations through Abraham's offspring. Now

God declares, "I am going to make you a father of many nations . . . and kings will come from you" (lit., Gen. 17:5–6).

God's promise to make Abraham a father of many nations should be understood, on the one hand, in a purely biological sense. Through Hagar, Abraham physically "begets" the Ishmaelites (see 17:20; 21:13; 25:12–18); through Keturah, the Midianites, among others (25:1–4); and through Isaac and Rebekah, the Edomites (see 25:23; 36:1–43). This interpretation is validated by the genealogies of Keturah (25:1–4), Ishmael (Book 7, Gen. 25:12–18), and Edom (Book 9, Gen. 36). On the other hand, the promise should also be understood as a reference to the nations that reproduce his faith; this cannot be said of the Ishmaelites, the Edomites, or the descendants of Keturah. Significantly, whereas God says that kings will come from Abraham's loins, God does not say that of the nations Abraham will father. The psalmist supports this interpretation. He anticipates the nations becoming part of the people of God by rebirth: "I will record Rahab and Babylon among those who acknowledge me—Philistia too, and Tyre, along with Cush—and will say, 'This one was born in Zion.' . . . The LORD will write in the register of the peoples: 'This one was born in Zion'" (Ps. 87:4–6).

Turning to the New Testament, Jesus essentially severs the link between the people of God and Abraham's physical offspring. At the end of Matthew our Lord asserts his authority over all nations and commissions his disciples, not old Israel, to make disciples of the nations, teaching them to obey everything he had commanded them (Matt. 28:18–20). Similarly, Mark records a scene where Jesus' physical mother and brothers symbolically stand outside the house where he is teaching. To those seated in the circle around him he asks, "Who are my mother and my brothers?" Looking at this same group of people he declares, "Here are my mother and brothers! Whoever does God's will is my brother and sister and mother" (Mark 3:33–35). In Luke, Jesus forecasts through the parable of the tenants that God will take the vineyard (i.e., the right to be the people chosen to mediate his moral rule) away from Israel and give it to the Gentiles (Luke 20:9–19). In John Jesus speaks of having other sheep (i.e., the Gentiles) who "are not of this sheep pen" (i.e., physical Israel, [John 10:16]).

Paul and Barnabas fulfill what Jesus predicts. Abraham's physical offspring had the first opportunity to represent God's rule and mediate the blessing (Acts 3:25), but when the Jews, for the most part, reject the gospel, Paul turns away from them to the Gentiles (Acts 13:46; 18:6). By the second century the church was composed almost entirely of Gentiles. In Galatians, Paul refers to the seed God covenanted to give Abraham as finding fulfillment both uniquely in Jesus Christ and collectively in all, Jew and Gentile alike, baptized into Jesus Christ (Gal. 3:15–29). In Romans, Paul interprets God's promise to make Abraham a father of many nations in the sense that they reproduce his faith. The church at Rome undoubtedly had representatives from many nations at that center of the Roman Empire. To them the apostle writes, "the promise ... [is] guaranteed to all Abraham's offspring—not only to those who are of the law but also to those who are of the faith of Abraham. He is the father of us all. As it is written: 'I have made you a father of many nations'" (Rom. 4:16–17). In Rom. 16:20 the apostle probably identifies the promised seed of the woman with the church at Rome, which represents the nations subject to his rule: "The God of peace will soon crush Satan under your feet." However, in that letter Paul also teaches that God is not yet finished with Abraham's physical progeny. God always retains a remnant among them who also reproduce Abraham's faith. Indeed, the apostle implies that they may again become the dominant group among the people of God (Rom. 11). Finally, using language reminiscent of Gen. 15:6, Rev. 7:9 envisions "a great multitude that no one could count, from every nation, tribe, and people and language, standing before the throne and in front of the Lamb," praising God.

In sum, under the old covenant Abraham's spiritual seed is mostly, but not exclusively, reproduced in Abraham's physical offspring. Under the new covenant his spiritual seed is reproduced mostly, but not exclusively, among the Gentiles.

Second Motif: The Land

When God creates the world, he gathers the primeval waters to let dry land appear, and in it he causes all kinds of vegetation to grow. In this way he provides both space for the representatives of his rule to live and food to sustain them. More particularly, he places his earthly rulers in a garden, that is, in an enclosed, protected area where the flora flourishes. This garden represents unique territorial space in the created order where God intends human beings to enjoy bliss and harmony with him, one another, the animals, and the land. God is uniquely present in this temple-garden, but humanity loses this temple when it sets up its rival kingdom. Later, when God calls Abraham to become a great nation, he promises to give Abraham's offspring the land of the defiled Canaanites.

Just as God's covenant with Abraham in Genesis 17 explicates the promise in Gen. 12:3 to make Abraham and his seed a blessing to the nations, so his covenant with Abraham to give him the land of Canaan (Gen. 15) explicates his promise in 12:2 to make him into a great nation. God reckons Abraham's faith in the Lord's promise to give him innumerable offspring as qualifying Abraham to become the recipient of an irrevocable land grant, idealized as extending from the river of Egypt to the Euphrates (Gen. 15:6–19). In this land flowing with milk and honey, his people will be protected and sustained. This land promise is fulfilled progressively several times but never consummated. God initially fulfills the promise through Joshua (Josh. 21:43–45), but not completely (Josh. 13:1–7); through David and Solomon (1 Kings 4:20–25; Neh. 9:8), but still not completely (see Ps. 95:11; Heb. 4:6–8; 11:39–40).

In the New Testament the land theme undergoes a paradigm shift similar to that of the seed theme. As the physical aspect of the seed was mostly dropped in favor of the spiritual, so also the physical aspect of land is downplayed in favor of its spiritual significance. The paradigm shift can be inferred from the fact that the term *land,* the fourth most frequent word in the Old Testament, is never used in the New Testament with reference to Canaan. Indeed, the Old Testament's use of the term *land* with reference to Canaan is resignified to encompass the whole earth in Matt. 5:5 and Rom. 4:13.[80] Neither Christ nor his apostles ever teach that dispersed ethnic Israel will again return to Canaan.[81] Rather, for them *Canaan* seems to function as a type of the Christian's life in Christ, both from a historical or chronological perspective and from a conceptual perspective. As Wright explains, "According to Hebrews [13:14], the only thing which we do not have is an earthly, territorial city."[82]

Regarding the historical aspect, one notes a number of important parallels between Israel and the church and their relationship to the "land." (1) Israel is saved from slavery and death in Egypt under the tyranny of Pharaoh; the church is saved out of the slavery of sin and death in the world under Satan. (2) Israel is delivered by the blood of the Passover lamb and by the wind at the Red Sea; the church is delivered by Christ the Passover Lamb and by the Spirit (Acts 2; 2 Cor. 5:17). (3) Israel is baptized with Moses in the sea and feeds on manna on its pilgrimage to the land; the church is baptized in Christ through water and feeds upon Christ the true manna from heaven (John 6; 1 Cor. 10:1–4). (4) Israel is tested in the wilderness before inheriting the land; the church suffers in its wilderness on the way to the celestial city where Christ is the light. (5) Israel finally enters the land, but they will not enter its antitype without the church (Heb. 11:39–40).

Significant parallels between the two "lands" also exist on the conceptual level: (1) both are a divine gift (Gen. 15:7, 18; Deut. 1:8; Rom. 6:23); (2) both are entered by faith alone (Num. 14:26–45; Josh. 7; John 3:16); (3) both are an inheritance (Deut. 4:20; Acts 20:32; Eph. 1:14);[83] (4) both uniquely offer blessed rest and security (Ex. 23:20–31; Deut. 11:12; 12:9–10; 28:1–14; Matt. 11:28; John 1:51; 14:9; Heb. 4:2–3); (5) both offer God's unique presence; (6) both demand persevering faith (Deut. 28:15–19; Heb. 6; 10); (6) both have an already-but-not-yet quality (see Heb. 11:39–40; Rev 21:1–22:6).

---

[80]In the latter case, Paul changes the ʾereṣ (LXX: gē) of Gen. 12:1 to *kosmos,* meaning "whole world."

[81]See W. M. Blanchard, "Changing Hermeneutical Perspectives on 'The Land,'" Ph.D. dissertation Southern Baptist Theological Seminary (Ann Arbor, Mich.: University Microfilms International, 1986), 38.

[82]C. J. H. Wright, "A Christian Approach to OT Prophecy concerning Israel," in *Jerusalem Past and Present in the Purpose of God,* ed. P. W. L. Walker (Grand Rapids: Baker, 1994), 18–19.

[83]See the discussion on fellowship in C. J. H. Wright, *An Eye for an Eye: The Place of the Old Testament Ethics Today Ethics Today* (Downers Grove, Ill.: InterVarsity, 1983).

Garrett eloquently develops "alienation" as a primary theme of Genesis.[84] Sinful Adam is expelled from the garden, and the depraved human race becomes scattered and dispersed into warring nations. Abraham must separate himself from his family, and he and his descendants live as sojourners in Canaan. Jacob is an alien wherever he goes, alienated as he is from his brother in Edom and from his Aramean uncle. Later, because of the violence of his sons, he becomes a stench in the land (Gen. 34:30). Joseph is ever an alien. His story begins with his brothers hating him and selling him as a slave into Egypt, where he is a man without rights. Says Garrett, "When Joseph dies, his body lies strangely out of place in a coffin in Egypt."[85]

Garrett thinks that the promises of God only mitigate this theme of estrangement and homelessness. In fact, however, God's promise to establish his kingdom through his grace that overcomes human sin is the governing theme of Genesis. God promises a seed that will destroy the Serpent, entailing that through it humanity will regain the Paradise it lost. Abraham is sent to bless the alienated nations. The narrator develops the cycles of Abraham, Jacob, and his sons in a concentric pattern to teach that true Israel strives and prevails (see "Structure and Content" above). The seed is born and raised from the dead, and Sarah is buried in the land as an anchor that holds Israel's future. Prayerless Jacob is in exile in Paddan Aram, but he returns as a prayerful saint with his sons, all twelve, the biblical number denoting government. The book ends with Israel in Egypt but with the promise that Joseph's bones will be carried back to the Promised Land. Thus, although alienation lurks on every page, God's resolve to establish his kingdom victoriously marches through the book.

Third Motif: God's Rule

If Genesis presents God as making an irrevocable covenant with the patriarchs to make of them a nation to be a light to the Gentiles, Exodus–Deuteronomy represent Israel as accepting God's covenant or laws to become that light to the nations. In connection with transforming the twelve tribes of Israel into a nation, God gives the people a covenant setting forth in detail their religious and ethical obligations. Not surprisingly, in that context Israel for the first time calls God "King" (Deut. 33:3–5; cf. Ex. 15:18; Num. 23:21) and God refers to Israel as "a kingdom of priests" (Ex. 19:6). All Israel is a priesthood (i.e., separated as holy to mediate between God and the nations) by virtue of its obedience to God's covenant.

Although the motif of God's rule is not as dominant in Genesis as in Exodus–Deuteronomy, Genesis does make important contributions to it. First,

---

[84]Garrett, *Rethinking Genesis*, 233–35.
[85]Ibid., 234.

prior to God's mediation of his laws to Israel through Moses, God makes known his laws through the general revelation of conscience (and occasionally through special revelations such as theophanies and visions), showing that through it God rules all people (see Gen. 4:7; 6:9; Rom. 2:1–12). Second, Genesis also teaches that, apart from God's grace, humanity on its own, even in the ideal environment, cannot and will not submit itself to God's law (Gen. 3:6; 8:21). Third, Abraham by faith keeps even the Mosaic law (Gen. 15:6; 18:19; 26:5), since his faith is a gift of God that entails regeneration (3:15; Eph. 2:8–9). In short, Abraham participates in the provisions of the new covenant before God administers his kingdom through that means of grace. Apart from that gracious enabling, natural Israel cannot and will not keep the law (Deut. 31:29; Josh. 24:19–27).

The old Mosaic covenant threatens the nation with exile, should they break their covenant obligations. Eventually the longsuffering God sends disobedient Israel into exile, but in that connection he promises to make a new covenant with them. The new covenant does not replace the eternal substance of the Mosaic law as expressed in the Ten Commandments and summarized by Jesus in terms of love for God and for one's neighbor. Rather, it replaces its mode of administration. Among many differences between the two styles of administration, suffice it to note here that the old covenant was effected through the blood of animals, the new through the cleansing blood of Jesus Christ. The old covenant was written on rock and copied in ink, while the new is written on the heart by the Spirit (Jer. 31:33–34; 2 Cor. 3:3). Finally, Israel obligated itself to keep the old covenant, but God obligates himself to keep the new (Heb. 8:6).

In sum, God now reckons the church, because it is baptized into Jesus Christ, who is the true Judah and Israel, as the recipients of the new covenant (cf. Heb. 8). Thus Peter says to a church composed of Jews and Gentiles, "But you are a chosen people, a royal priesthood, a holy nation, a people belonging to God, that you may declare the praises of him who called you out of darkness into his wonderful light. Once you were not a people, but now you are the people of God; once you had not received mercy, but now you have received mercy" (1 Peter 2:9–10). In a similar vein, Paul calls the church "the Israel of God" (Gal. 6:16). With respect to the third motif, one must conclude that Christ administers this "nation" (i.e., the church) by means of the new covenant.

Fourth Motif: The Ruler

Prior to the establishment of the monarchy as recorded in Samuel, the Primary History regards God as the sole ruler of his kingdom. When the people ask for a king, the Lord regards it as a rejection of his rule over them as their king (1 Sam. 8:6–8). Nevertheless, with the institution of kingship in the days of Saul, the Lord hands over the rule of Israel to a human king, which by definition entails dynastic succession.[86] The Chronicler even speaks of the king as sitting on "the throne of the kingdom of the LORD" (1 Chron. 28:5), though God still maintains his ultimate rule by choosing the king through prophetic designation (Deut. 17:15) and by retaining the right to transfer the kingship from one house to another if a king fails to adhere to God's moral standards as expressed in the Mosaic law. Selman comments, "If God has a kingdom to give, then he too must have a kingship of his own, and one that is of a higher order than that which is . . . entrusted to Saul, David, or Abijah. . . . God was directly involved with this one, specific, earthly kingdom, and through it he, as well as the human king, worked out his royal purposes."[87] Thus, after the rejection of the Benjaminite Saul, the Lord anoints David from the tribe of Judah as king and fulfills Jacob's prophecy that Judah will rule his brothers and subdue the nations (Gen. 49:8–12). Moreover, God's covenant with David promising that his house will rule God's kingdom forever lays the foundation for the future course of history (2 Sam. 7; 1 Chron. 17; Ps. 89). It also fulfills, confirms, and supplements the Abrahamic covenant, which was first introduced in Genesis.

In fulfilling the Davidic covenant's promise to give the nation rest from its oppressors, the Lord inferentially fulfills his promises to Abraham. For example, when Solomon assumes his father's throne, Abraham's seed has become as numerous as "the dust of the earth" (2 Chron. 1:9), "the sand on the seashore" (1 Kings 4:20), and "the stars in the sky" (1 Chron. 27:23), the standards of comparison for the multitude of Abraham's promised offspring (Gen. 13:16; 15:5; 22:17).[88] David's military victories, also promised in the Davidic covenant, expand the kingdom that Solomon inherits from the river of Egypt to the Euphrates (1 Kings 4:21), the dimensions promised in the Abrahamic covenant (Gen. 15:18).

In addition to being linked in terms of promise and fulfillment, the Abrahamic and Davidic covenants are remarkably similar in style and content. Both are the Lord's grants as rewards to faithful servants, yet their eternal dimensions far exceed their investments in a single lifetime. Both occur in a nocturnal vision, see into the remotest future, and reshape the course of history. Moreover, both pertain to the beneficiaries' seed and land. The center of attention in both is the son from the body. God's covenant with Abraham promises him an eternal posterity, his covenant with David an eternal dynasty. In addition, David's dynasty mediates the kings whom the Lord promises to give from Abraham's and Sarah's own bodies.[89] Fokkelman argues that the choice of "from your own loins" (*mimmēʿêkā*) in 2 Sam. 7:12

---

[86]T. Ishida, *The Royal Dynasties in Ancient Israel* (New York and Berlin: Walter de Gruyter, 1977), 7–25.

[87]M. J. Selman, "The Kingdom of God in the Old Testament," *TynBul* 40 (1989): 161–83.

[88]O. T. Allis, *Prophecy and the Church*, 2d ed. (Grand Rapids: Baker, 1978), 58.

[89]B. Mazar, "The Historical Background of the Book of Genesis," *JNES* 28 (1969): 75.

links the two covenants, for it is the sole occurrence of the term since Gen. 15:4. Thus Mendenhall rightly comments, "In David, the promise to the patriarchs is fulfilled and renewed."[90]

Although both covenants are unconditional with reference to their enduring seed as an institution, the enjoyment of their provisions by their sons as individuals is conditioned on their obedience to the Mosaic covenant. Their descendants experience the benefits of the covenants only to the extent that they are loyal to the Lord and obey his law.

The grant that David's house will rule God's kingdom forever lays the foundation for the messianic hope. J. J. M. Roberts explains, "The . . . claim that God had chosen David and his dynasty as God's permanent agent for the exercise of the divine rule on earth was the fundamental starting point for the later development of the messianic hope."[91] Thus Israel's kings are always regarded in a general way as God's *messiah* (literally, "anointed"). Their prophetic anointing publicly designates them as God's chosen, consecrates them as God's property, bestows authority on them, and equips them for the task.

But the term takes on a narrower meaning in connection with the Exile. This development can be seen in the use of the Psalter. The Psalms augment in an idealistic way the royal ideology associated with the historical king. The Psalter envisions God's son, as the king was called, as endowed with justice and righteousness, and as such his rule extended from sea to sea and from the River to the ends of the earth (Ps. 2, 72). For the psalmist, the king stands in God's stead: "Your throne, O God, will last for ever and ever" (Ps. 45:6 [Eng. 7]). These songs celebrating the king are like royal robes with which Israel drapes each successive son of David at his coronation, but none has shoulders broad enough to wear them. Shakespeare says of Macbeth, when he is exposed as Duncan's traitor, "How does he feel his title hang loose about him, like a giant's robe upon a dwarfish thief."[92] The Psalter's giant robes hang loosely on David's dwarfish successors, though some, like Hezekiah and Josiah, have broader shoulders than others. After Jehoiakim, the psalmists' hope for an ideal king slips off the stooped shoulders of David's successors, leaving Israel with a wardrobe of magnificent purple robes waiting for an Anointed One from David's house worthy to wear them. Thus during the Exile the royal Psalms—and most of the Psalter—were referred to a coming, hoped-for son of David. At this point the term *Messiah* acquires its specifically eschatological and strict sense vis-à-vis the expected king and deliverer of Israel. That hope for this ideal king is also

---

[90]G. E. Mendenhall, "Covenant," *IDB*, 1:718.

[91]J. J. M. Roberts, "In Defense of the Monarchy: The Contribution of Israelite Kingship to Biblical Theology," in *Ancient Israelite Religions: Essays in Honor of Frank Moore Cross*, ed. P. D. Miller Jr., P. D. Hanson, and S. D. McBride (Philadelphia: Fortress, 1987), 378.

[92]*Macbeth*, 5.2.20–22.

augmented in the prophetic literature and heightened in the apocalyptic literature and in the intertestamental Jewish literature (200 B.C.–A.D 100).[93]

In the fullness of time God sent his Son incarnate in Jesus of Nazareth. Here was a son of David with shoulders broad enough to wear the Psalter's magnificent robes. At his birth an angel of the Lord proclaimed, "Today in the town of David a Savior has been born to you; he is Christ [Messiah] the Lord" (Luke 2:11). John the Baptist identifies Jesus as the Messiah (John 1:19–34), and the disciples confess him to be the Messiah (Mark 8:29; Luke 9:20; John 11:27). Furthermore, John writes his Gospel that his audience might believe that Jesus is the Christ. The words of Jesus and his works bear witness to his deity and are all done in truth, righteousness, and justice. He is the one who will reign forever and ever, the only one worthy to rule over all humanity.

Conclusion

Jesus Christ's offer of the kingdom of God in the Synoptic Gospels brings the expectation of the Primary History that God will establish his moral kingdom over the nations through national Israel to its fulfillment. On the other hand, in the New Testament God's kingdom now transcends the geospatial boundaries of national Israel. The people of the kingdom are now no longer primarily Abraham's physical progeny but the nations themselves. The theme of land has been "Christified." His law is no longer written on rock tablets housed in Jerusalem but inscribed by the Holy Spirit on the hearts of all the subjects of this kingdom. Finally, the king's throne is no longer in earthly Jerusalem but in heavenly Mount Zion, from which the King of kings and Lord of lords administers his kingdom through the Holy Spirit. May God use us to hasten the day when at the name of Jesus Christ every knee will bow and confess that he is Lord and so submit to his rule.

---

[93]See M. de Jonge, "Messiah," *ABD*, 4:785–86.

PROLOGUE (1:1 – 2:3)

The prologue announces that the God of the covenant community is the same as the Creator of the cosmos. God is the implicit king of this cosmos, making provision, establishing order, and commissioning regents. The life-support systems of air, water, and land provide creation's abundance of all sorts of living species with sustenance and space to live. It is the stage on which the drama of history under God will be played.

God steps creatively into the primordial abyss and darkness to transform it into a magnificent, ordered, and balanced universe. Those who submit themselves to the Creator's rule are assured that their history will not end in tragic darkness and chaos but will continue in triumphant light and order.

As God unfolds the drama of creation in successive days, building to a climax, so God develops the drama of history through successive epochs, which reach a dramatic climax when all volitional creatures bow to Christ.

The order of this creation will undergird God's later revelations regarding humanity's social order. His law (the teachings of Scripture) is in harmony with the created order. Thus, to flout his revealed moral order is to contradict creation, his created reality.

OUTLINE OF THE PROLOGUE ——————————————————

LITERARY ANALYSIS OF THE PROLOGUE ───────────

The Pattern of Creation: Process and Progress

Process of Creation

The creation account is a highly sophisticated presentation, designed to emphasize the sublimity (power, majesty, and wisdom) of the Creator God and to lay the foundations for the worldview of the covenant community.

Creation is divided into six days or "panels," each following a basic process of creation. The key words—"said," "separated," "called," "saw," "good"—as actions and thoughts of God, emphasize his omnipotent and omniscient presence in creation. The process of creation typically follows a pattern of *announcement, commandment, separation, report, naming, evaluation,* and *chronological framework.*

Each day begins with an *announcement*: "And God said." Much of the detail of the account is framed in narration, but it is the direct speech of God, however brief, that drives and forms the account. Thus Hamilton rightly concludes, "God is the soloist; the narrator is the accompanist."[1] The hero of creation is God. Each event occurs according to God's expressed will and through the agency of his word. Speech signifies that God is intimately bonded to his creation.

Announcement is followed by *commandment*: "Let there be" (or its equivalent). God's word in conjunction with his Spirit is irresistible and creative; consequently, it overcomes chaos and emptiness (cf. 2 Cor. 4:6).

Third, God's powerful words bring *separation*, dividing day and night, waters and land, fish and fowl. Boundaries are important in both the created and social orders. When everything keeps to its allotted place and does not transgress its limits, there is order, not chaos.

The narrator's subsequent *report*, "And so God made" (or its equivalent), affirms that everything exists by God's expressed will, purposes, and word.[2] God also displays his sovereignty on the first three days by *naming* the elements ("And he called. . ."). Naming, an indication of dominion,[3] reveals God as the supreme ruler. Even the negative elements of the precreated state, darkness and chaotic waters, are under his dominion and brought within his protective restraints.

Then, of each piece of handiwork, God offers his *evaluation* ("God saw that

---

[1]V. P. Hamilton, *The Book of Genesis: Chapters 1–17* (NICOT; Grand Rapids: Eerdmans, 1990), 119.

[2]This stands in marked contrast to ancient Near Eastern accounts of creation, in which creation erupts from the battles among the gods. God fights with no one to create this ordered universe. He speaks. His words take form. For examples of the ancient Near Eastern myths, see Heidel, *Babylonian Genesis.*

[3]Cf. Num. 32:38; 2 Kings 23:34; 24:17. See also G. von Rad's discussion of God's dominion through creation by word in Gen. 1:3–5 and of naming as appropriation in Gen. 2:18–25 (*Genesis*, trans. J. H. Marks [OTL; Philadelphia: Westminster, 1972], 49–51, 80–83.

it was good").[4] Everything, including the bounded darkness and sea, satisfies God's purpose. Because God is completely benevolent, as well as all-powerful, humanity has nothing to fear from creation. Accompanying the *evaluation* of living creatures is God's "blessing" (i.e., potency for life). Beginning with the fish and fowl, God blesses each creature with procreativity.

Finally, all of the acts of creation follow a *chronological framework*. God does not create in time, but with time. The week becomes the basic unit of time: six days of work and one of rest.[5] The careful use of numbers throughout the account attests to God's logical and timely shaping of creation.[6]

Progress of Creation

Utilizing the structure of the creative process, the narrator constructs the story with billowing detail and movement. With crescendo the narrator devotes more time and space to each day until the climactic apex of creation, when motion ceases and God rests.

The creation account is divided into two triads, which contrast with the unformed (*tōhû*) and unfilled (*bōhû*) state of the earth when the story begins.

Form/"The Resource" (versus *tōhû*)		Fill/"The Utilizer" (versus *bōhû*)[7]	
Day			Day
1	Light (1:3–5)	Lights (1:14–19)	4
2	Firmament (1:6–8)	Inhabitants (1:20–23)	5
	sky	birds	
	seas	fish	
3	Dry land (1:9–10)	Land animals (1:24–25)	6
	Vegetation (1:11–13)	Human beings (1:26–31)	

The movement and development of each triad reveals a progression within creation. The first triad separates the formless chaos into three static spheres. In the second triad, the spheres that house and shelter life are filled with the moving forms of sun, moon, and living creatures. The inhabitants of the second triad rule over the corresponding spheres: the sun and the moon rule the darkness,[8] while humanity (head over everything) rules the earth.[9]

---

[4]This pattern of evaluation is altered slightly on the second and third days. See Exegetical Notes below.

[5]See Theological Reflections below on the significance of time in this account with regard to the imitation of the Creator.

[6]The structured use and repetition of numbers is readily apparent. The key numbers are three (i.e., three namings, three uses of "created" [*bārāʾ*]), seven (i.e., seven reports, seven evaluations, seven uses of "made" [*ʿāśâ*] in the suffix or prefix conjugations), and ten (i.e., ten "And God said" announcements, ten "according to their kind," and ten occurrences of *ʿāśâ* in all their forms).

[7]The terms "Resource" and "Utilizer" are suggested by Sarna, *Genesis*, 4.

[8]The rule of sun and moon is poetic (Ps. 136:7–9), determining the amounts of light and darkness. They evoke feelings of grandeur and awe among those who experience their rays.

[9]Although not expressly stated, there is a certain poetic sense in which the fish have dominion over the sea and the birds have dominion over the air.

Each triad progresses from heaven to earth (land) and ends with the earth bringing forth. In the first triad, the land brings forth vegetation; in the second, the land brings forth animals. The number of creative acts also increases within each triad: from a single creative act (days 1 and 4) to one creative act with two aspects (days 2 and 5) to two separate creative acts (days 3 and 6).

Action in the creation account also escalates.[10] Within the first triad, there is simple movement from light to dark, from firmament and seas to growing vegetation. Within the second triad, there is an eruption of kinetic energy. Sun and moon arch across the sky; birds and fish swarm the air and sea; land animals rove across the ground. The pattern of movement in the second triad occurs progressively. The lights follow a predictable and structured pattern. The animals travel with limited levels of freedom, bounded by their instinctual patterns of migration and habitation. Human beings have the greatest freedom, limited only by the earth itself.

The entire account is unified by a basic week time structure. Structure affirms the consonance and symmetry, the harmony and balance in God's world.

EXEGETICAL NOTES TO THE PROLOGUE ─────────

Summary Statement (1:1)[11]

1. In the beginning. The daring claim of verse 1, which encapsulates the entire narrative, invites the reader into the story. Its claim and invitation is that in the beginning God completed perfectly this entire cosmos. "Beginning" refers to the entire created event, the six days of creation, not something before the six days[12] nor a part of the first day. Although some have argued that 1:1 functions as merely the first event of creation, rather than a summary of the whole account, the grammar makes that interpretation improbable.[13]

God [*ʾĕlōhîm*]. The form is plural in Hebrew to denote God's majesty.[14] This name of God represents his transcendent relationship to creation. He is the quintessential expression of a heavenly being. God, unlike human beings, is without beginning, begetting, opposition, or limitations of power.

created [*bārāʾ*]. This telic verb refers to the completed act of creation.[15] Although many verbs denote God's activity of bringing creation into

---

[10]L. Strauss, "On the Interpretation of Genesis," *L'Homme* 21.1 (1981): 11–13.

[11]For a detailed exegesis of Gen. 1:1–3, see B. K. Waltke, "The Creation Account in Genesis 1:1–3," *BSac* 132 (1975): 25–36, 136–44, 216–28; 133 (1976): 28–41.

[12]This is a relative beginning. As verse 2 seems to indicate, there is a pre-Genesis time and space.

[13]Those who hold to that view believe that 1:2 clarifies 1:1, that is, God creates the earth as an unformed mass. Martin Luther, arguing for this view, said, "heaven and earth are the crude and formless masses ... up to that time" (*Luther's Works*, Vol. 1, *Lectures on Genesis Chapters 1-5*, ed. J. Pelikan [Saint Louis: Concordia, 1958], 6). John Calvin also took this position (*A Commentary on Genesis*, ed. and trans. J. King [London: Banner of Truth, 1965], 69–70).

[14]Considered an honorific plural (*IBHS* §7.4.3b).

[15]A telic verb (i.e., die or sell) only finds meaning at the end of a process. The Hebrew term *bārāʾ*, meaning "to create," only refers to a completed act of creation (cf. Deut. 4:32; Ps. 89:12; Isa. 40:26; Amos 4:13), so it cannot mean that, in the beginning, God *began* the process of creating the cosmos.

existence,[16] *bārā* distinguishes itself by being used exclusively of God. His creation reveals his immeasurable power and might, his bewildering imagination and wisdom, his immortality and transcendence, ultimately leaving the finite mortal in mystery. The earth endures in part because it is brought into existence through God's wisdom, which entails his righteousness. His creation embodies both physical and sociocultural aspects of reality (see Prov. 3:19–20; 8:22–31).[17] Because of God's largess, the apple tree does not produce one apple but thousands, and the grain of wheat multiplies itself a hundredfold.

the heavens and the earth. This merism represents the cosmos,[18] meaning the organized universe in which humankind lives. In all its uses in the Old Testament (cf. Gen. 2:1, 4; Deut. 3:24; Isa. 65:17; Jer. 23:24),[19] this phrase functions as a compound referring to the organized universe.[20]

Negative State of Earth before Creation (1:2)

2. Now the earth.[21] The starting point of the story may be somewhat surprising. There is no word of God creating the planet earth or darkness or the watery chaos.[22] The narrator begins the story with the planet already present, although undifferentiated and unformed. In God's creative power he will transform the darkness into an ordered universe.

earth. This term is used in three ways in the Prologue: to signify the cosmos, when part of a compound phrase with "heaven" (see 1:1); to signify dry land (see 1:10); and, as it is used here, to signify what we would call the planet.

formless and empty [*tōhû wābōhû*]. This phrase is an antonym to the "heavens and the earth," signifying something uncreated or disordered (Jer. 4:23–27). According to David Tsumura, this syntagm "refers to the earth as an empty place, i.e. 'an unproductive and uninhabited place.'" Tsumura

---

[16]See, for example,*ʿśh* "make, do" (Isa. 45:18); *pʿl* "make, work" (Ex. 15:17); *yṣr* "form, shape" (Isa. 45:18); *kwn* "to establish, make firm" (Prov. 8:27).

[17]See R. Van Leeuwen, "*brʾ*," *NIDOTTE*, 1:731.

[18]A merism is a statement of opposites to indicate totality. For instance, "day and night" means "all the time." In such usage the words cannot be understood separately but must be taken as a unity. Just as the English expression "part and parcel" cannot be understood by studying *part* and *parcel* as independent terms, so the merism of the Hebrew words *heavens* (*šāmayim*) and *earth* (*ʾereṣ*) cannot be understood by studying the words separately but only by studying the unit. As a unit this refers to the organized universe.

[19]In the Apocrypha, Wisdom of Solomon 1:14 refers to the heavens and earth of Gen. 1:1 as *ho kosmos* ("the world").

[20]In his otherwise superb commentary, Wenham invests this compound with the unique meaning "totality" in contradistinction to "ordered cosmos," but his unsubstantiated meaning violates accredited philology (Wenham, *Genesis 1–15*, 15).

[21]One novel suggestion resolves the seeming contradiction of verses 1 and 2 by limiting "the earth" to the land of Israel (see J. Sailhamer, *Genesis Unbound* [Sisters, Ore.: Multnomah, 1996], 47–59). This suggestion does not make sense of the inclusio formed by 1:1 and 2:1. Since 1:1 refers to the cosmos, so also must 2:1 and, consequently, the entire narrative. The argument also fails in its analysis of day four, since grammatically *rʾh* does not mean in the Qal stem "to appear," as he suggests.

[22]Genesis 1:2 tells us nothing about an old earth or a young earth.

convincingly argues that the concern of the narrative is for life: birds, animals, and vegetation. The negative state of the earth reflects a situation in which the earth is not producing life.[23] Chronologically, this must describe the state of the earth prior to verse 1, as it would be a contradiction to represent the creation as formed cosmos and the earth as unformed.

darkness was over the surface of the deep. The earth is a dark abyss, inhospitable to life. "Darkness" and "deep," as opposites of "light" and "land," connote surd evil (Ex. 15:8; Prov. 2:13). They too become part of God's creation, doing his will (see Gen. 45:5–7).

Spirit of God [*rûaḥ ʾelōhîm*]. Since the word rendered "Spirit" (*rûaḥ*) can also mean "wind,"[24] some argue that this should be translated "wind of God" or "mighty wind." A good case can be made for either "Spirit" or "wind." In the re-creation after the Flood, God again sends a *rûaḥ*—there clearly a wind—over the waters (8:1). Here, however, the *rûaḥ* is modified by *ʾelōhîm*, which in the rest of this chapter always means "God," not "mighty." Thus, Spirit better fits the context.[25] Hovering eaglelike over the primordial abyss, the almighty Spirit prepares the earth for human habitation. John Sailhamer connects the role of the Spirit in building God's cosmic temple (cf. Ps. 104:1–3, 30) with the Spirit's filling of Bezalel to build his tabernacle on earth (Ex. 31:1–5).[26]

Creation by Word (1:3–31)

Day One (1:3–5)

3. And God said. See *announcement* in Literary Analysis above. Into the negative state enters the word of God that puts light in the midst of darkness, land in the midst of sea, air in the midst of water and that overcomes the uninhabitable world that marked the setting of creation. Gerhard von Rad observes, "The idea of creation by the word preserves first of all the most radical essential distinction between Creator and creature. Creation cannot be even remotely considered an emanation from God ... but is rather a product of his personal will."[27] Subtly but implicitly, the Genesis creation account serves as a polemic against the ancient Near Eastern myths.[28] Whereas the forces of nature are often deities in the ancient Near Eastern creation myths, here all derive from and are subject to God's word (see also "light" and "two great lights" below). Though creation is not part of God's being, all creation is utterly dependent on God for its subsistence and sustenance (cf. Neh. 9:6; Acts 17:25, 28).

[23]D. T. Tsumura, *The Earth and the Waters in Genesis 1 and 2: A Linguistic Investigation* (JSOT-Sup 83; Sheffield: JSOT Press, 1989), 42–43.
[24]An absolute superlative (*IBHS* §14.5b).
[25]For a helpful summary of the arguments for "Spirit," see Hamilton, *Genesis 1–17*, 111–14.
[26]Sailhamer, *Pentateuch*, 32.
[27]von Rad, *Genesis*, 49–50.
[28]See U. Cassuto, *A Commentary on the Book of Genesis. Part 1: From Adam to Noah*, trans. I. Abrahams (Jerusalem: Magnes, 1961), 7–8.

Let there be. See *commandment* in Literary Analysis above. God's word has the power to bring into existence what was not (Heb. 11:3). God's will is irresistible, carried out by divine imperative.

light. Light symbolizes life and blessings of various sorts (cf. Ps. 19:1–6; 27:1; 49:20 [Eng. 19]; 97:11). Since the sun is only later introduced as the immediate cause of light, the chronology of the text emphasizes that God is the *ultimate* source of light. The dischronologization probably functions as a polemic against pagan religions, which worship the creation or creatures, not the Creator upon whom the creation depends.

4. saw. This is a metaphor for God's spiritual perception.

good [*ṭôḇ*]. Although the eggshells of the precreated state, darkness and seas of abyss, are still present, they can now be called "good" (i.e., beneficial and desirable) because they are bounded by light and land, respectively, and serve useful tasks (Ps. 104:19–26). Creation is imbued with God's goodness and *joie de vivre* (Prov. 8:30–31).

separated [*bāḏal*]. See *separation* in Literary Analysis above. This term denotes the separation of what does not belong together as well as the separation of the components of a particular task. Light and darkness—like waters above and below the firmament—do not belong together and have distinct tasks.

5. called. See *naming* in Literary Analysis above. In biblical thought a name is equated with existence. By naming the positive life-support systems (light, atmosphere, and land) as well as their counterparts (darkness and chaotic water), God shows his sovereignty over even the negative elements of the precreated state (see Theological Reflections below).

day [*yôm*]. Several interpretations have been proposed for the "days" of the creation account, including literal twenty-four-hour periods, extended ages or epochs, and structures of a literary framework designed to illustrate the orderly nature of God's creation and to enable the covenant people to mime the Creator. The first two interpretations pose scientific and textual difficulties.[29] The third interpretation is consistent with the text's emphasis on theological, rather than scientific, issues. The presentation of creation through "days" reveals God's sovereign ordering of creation and God's care to accommodate himself to humanity in finite and understandable terms. God's decision to create the cosmos through successive days, not instantaneous fiat, serves as a paradigm for his development of humanity through successive eras of history.

evening, and there was morning—the first day. One might translate this, "Evening came, and then morning. . . ." The idea, as expressed by the

---

[29]In the case of the first suggestion, most scientists reject a literal twenty-four-hour period. In the case of the second, the pattern in the text of morning-evening seems inconsistent with the epoch theory. For further discussion of the days, see "Excursus: The Literary Genre of the Creation of the Cosmos," below.

Hebrew, is that the first day ends when the darkness of the evening is dispelled by the morning light.

Day Two (1:6 – 8)

6. expanse [*rāqîaʿ*]. This seems to be the atmosphere or sky, which in 1:8 is called *šāmayim*, "heavens" or "skies." The expanse separating the waters is part of the sky. Elsewhere it is said to be hard as a mirror (Job 37:18) and like a canopy (Isa. 40:22).

water from water. The expanse separates the source of rain from the waters on earth.

8. the second day. The Hebrew literally reads, "a second day." The lack of the definite article on each of the first five days suggests they may be dischronologized.[30] On the second day, when God creates the firmament, he does not offer an evaluation.[31] The three life-supportive systems are not yet in place, and rain is of no use without the land to fructify.

Day Three (1:9 – 13)

10. land. The earth produces and sustains all life, provides wealth of life and the necessary space for land creatures and people (see 1:9–13, 24; 2:7, 12). The word *land* connotes that which is benevolently ordered by God's sovereignty in the interests of human life and security (Ps. 24:1–2; cf. Prov. 2:21–22).

11. Let the land produce. The earth is the agent through which God mediates his generative power. So-called "nature" is God's mediated power and life. There is no excuse for deifying it as "Mother Nature."

according to their various kinds. All created species follow God's master design and appointed purposes. The vegetation serves as food for higher life forms (1:29–30).

12. good. With the life-support systems now in place, God evaluates creation and twice declares it good (1:10, 12).

Day Four (1:14 – 19)

14. in the expanse of the sky. Some translations read "in the heavens," but the description is phenomenological (i.e., as things appear to the eye).

signs to mark seasons. The Hebrew literally reads, "for signs and for seasons." The lights mark out a comprehensive divine order for Israel's sacred seasons, not the zodiac or astrology.

16. two great lights. This expression serves as a polemic against the principal deities of a pagan pantheon (see Jer. 10:2). Whereas in the ancient Near

---

[30]M. Throntveit. "Are the Events in the Genesis Account Set Forth in Chronological Order? No," in *The Genesis Debate*, ed. R. F. Youngblood (Nashville: Thomas Nelson, 1986), 53; and D. A. Sterchi, "Does Genesis 1 Provide a Chronological Sequence?" *JETS* 39 (1996): 529–36.

[31]Even God did not say that Mondays are good!

Eastern myths, the sun and the moon are principal deities, here they are nameless objects designed by the one Creator God to serve humanity.[32]

govern. As noted in the Literary Analysis above, the elements of the second triad rule over their respective spheres in the first triad.

the stars. The slight, almost passing mention of the stars may have a polemical function, since ancient Near Eastern people often believed stars directed people's destinies.

Day Five (1:20–23)

20. Let the water teem. Water does not have the power for spontaneous generation. It produces life only through God's efficacious word.

creatures [*nepeš*].[33] The Hebrew word *nepeš*, used for all the living creatures, is sometimes translated "soul."[34] It refers to the passionate appetites and desires of all living things (Isa. 5:14; cf. Deut. 23:24; Ps. 78:18; Jer. 2:21). These appetites and desires include the drives for food and sex. The craving for God distinguishes human *nepeš* from animal *nepeš* (Ps. 42:2–3 [Eng. 1–2]; 63:2 [Eng. 1]; 84:3 [Eng. 2]; 119:20, 81).

21. great creatures of the sea. Old Testament poetry alludes to the dreaded sea dragons of pagan mythology, who rival the creating gods (cf. Leviathan [coiled one], Rahab [arrogant one], and Tannin [Dragon]; Job 3:8; Ps. 74:13–17; 89:9–10; Isa. 27:1; 51:9–10; Jer. 51:34). Hebrew poets adopt pagan imagery, but not pagan theology. The primeval monsters, which symbolize rebellion in ancient Near Eastern myths,[35] are here depicted as merely a few of God's many creatures, depending upon and ultimately serving God.[36]

22. blessed. This word means to be filled with the potency of life, overcoming defeat and death. God blesses the creatures to be procreative, in spite of death.

23. Be fruitful and increase in number. This entails the notion of multiplication so as to rule (cf. 1:28). The birds and fish rule their realms through multiplication.

living creatures [*nepeš*]. The Hebrew *nepeš* is traditionally rendered "soul" with reference to humanity (see "Soul" in Theological Reflections below).

---

[32]See G. Hasel, "The Polemic Nature of the Genesis Cosmology," *EvQ* 46 (1974): 81–102; idem, "The Significance of the Cosmology in Genesis 1 in Relation to Ancient Near Eastern Parallels," *AUSS* 10 (1972): 1–20.

[33]See also B. K. Waltke, "*nāpash*," *TWOT*, 2:587–91.

[34]In the OT a human being *is* a soul; in the NT a human being *has* a soul (Matt. 16:26; 1 Thess. 5:23).

[35]See the discussion of Leviathan in Waltke, "Creation . . . Part 1: Introduction to Biblical Cosmogony," *BSac* 132 (1975): 32–36; M. K. Wakeman, *God's Battle with the Monster: A Study in Biblical Imagery* (Leiden: Brill, 1973); and C. H. Gordon, "Leviathan: Symbol of Evil," in *Biblical Motifs: Origins and Transformations*, ed. A. Altmann (Cambridge: Harvard Univ. Press, 1966), 1–9.

[36]Psalm 104: 26 reduces the Leviathan to a duck in God's bathtub.

Day Six (1:24–31)

24. livestock . . . wild animals. The contrast between domesticated and wild animals distinguishes cattle from carnivores. The Hebrew phrase for "wild animals" is the same as that in Job 5:22; Ps. 79:2; Ezek. 29:5; 32:4; and 34:28.

25. God . . . good. The absence of the blessing on the land animals is striking. They are not to have dominion over humanity, who is blessed to rule them. The fish and birds, however, receive blessing since they inhabit different spheres and pose no threat to people.

26. Let us. The impersonal "let there be" (or its equivalents) of the seven preceding creative acts is replaced by the personal "let us." Only in the creation of humanity is the divine intent announced beforehand. The formula "and so it was" is replaced by a threefold blessing. In these ways, the narrator places humankind closer to God than the rest of creation.[37]

us. See also 3:22; 11:7. Various referents have been suggested for the "us."[38] The traditional Christian interpretation, that it represents a plurality within deity, has some textual support and satisfies the Christian theology of the Trinity (John 1:3; Eph. 3:9; Col. 1:16; Heb. 1:2). That God is a plurality is supported by the mention of the Spirit of God in 1:2 and the fact that the image itself is a plurality. This interpretation would also explain the shifts in the text between the singular and plural. The primary difficulty with this view is that the other four uses of the plural pronoun with reference to God (3:22; 11:7; Isa. 6:8) do not seem to refer to the Trinity. The explanation that better satisfies all such uses of the pronoun is that God is addressing the angels or heavenly court (cf. 1 Kings 22:19–22; Job 1:6; 2:1; 38:7; Ps. 29:1–3; 89:5–6; Isa. 6:8; 40:1–6; Dan. 10:12–13; Luke 2:8–14). It seems that in the four occurrences of the pronoun "us" for God, God refers to "us" when human beings are impinging on the heavenly realm and he is deciding their fate. In Gen. 3:22, God sees that human beings have grasped

---

[37]Sarna, *Genesis*, 11.

[38]Suggestions include an unassimilated fragment of myth, an address to creation, a plural of majesty or intensification, or a plural of self-deliberation. See P. D. Miller Jr., *Genesis 1–11: Studies in Structure and Theme* (Sheffield: Department of Biblical Studies, Univ. of Sheffield, 1978), 9–26. The idea that the "us" is an unassimilated fragment of myth is theologically objectionable. The Torah, especially Gen. 1, polemicizes against mythic thinking. That the "us" is an address to creation is textually objectionable. The text denies that creation has volition, and Genesis 1 aims to distinguish God and humans from the rest of creation.

A plural of majesty or intensification does occur in Hebrew with nouns (the word for God, *ᵓelōhîm*, is plural for that reason), not however with pronouns. Pronouns are always countable plurals. For this reason, grammatically the "us" cannot be a plural of majesty or intensification (P. P. Joüon, *Grammaire de l'Hébreu biblique* [Rome: Pontifical Biblical Institute, 1947], 309; 11 n. 1).

Some have suggested a plural of self-deliberation (W. H. Schmidt, *Die Schöpfungsgeschichte der Priesterschrift* [WMANT 17; Neukirchen-Vluyn: Neukirchener Verlage, 1964], 130). GKC finds grammatical support for this interpretation (§124g n. 2), which would also explain the "us" in 11:7. However, Cassuto debates the grammatical merit of such a plural. Also, this meaning does not explain the other uses of "us" in 3:22 and Isa. 6:8 (Cassuto, *From Adam*, 55–56).

the knowledge of good and evil and have become like divine beings. In Genesis 11 the heavenly court comes down to see what the earth-bound are building to attain the heavenly space. In Isa. 6:8, God is clearly addressing the heavenly court, which the prophet in his vision has entered. It is not surprising that God would address the heavenly court, since angels play a prominent role in Scripture (e.g., Gen. passim; Job 38:7; 1 Tim. 3:16),[39] and there is much commerce in Genesis between the angelic realm and human beings.[40]

image [*selem*].[41] Fundamental to Genesis and the entirety of Scripture is the creation of humanity in the image of God.[42] The expression "image of God" is used uniquely with reference to human beings and so sets them apart from the other creatures. Whereas the other creatures are created "according to their kinds" (Gen. 1:21, 24, 25), humanity is made "in the image of God." Being made in God's image establishes humanity's role on earth and facilitates communication with the divine. D. J. A. Clines details a number of characteristics of being made in the image of God.[43] First, the term *image* refers to a statue in the round, suggesting that a human being is a psychosomatic unity. Second, an image functions to express, not to depict; thus, humanity is a faithful and adequate representation, though not a facsimile.[44] It is often said that the Bible represents God anthropomorphically (i.e., as a human being). More accurately, a human being is theomorphic, made like God so that God can communicate himself to people. He gave people ears to show that he hears the cry of the afflicted and eyes to show that he sees the plight of the pitiful (Ps. 94:9). Third, an image possesses the life of the one being represented.[45] Fourth, an image represents the presence

---

[39]Psalm 8 is, as Franz Delitzsch rightly asserts, a "lyric echo" of Gen. 1:26–28 (*Biblical Commentary on the Psalms*, vol. 1 [London: Hodder & Stoughton, n.d.], 177). In David's reflection upon our text he speaks of *ʾādām* as being "a little lower than the heavenly beings [*ʾelōhîm*]." Since the rest of the psalm depends on Gen. 1:26–28, David more probably derived his thought from the text than created it ad hoc. However, some prefer to invest *ʾelōhîm* with its most common meaning, God. First, against this interpretation, the Greek translation, the oldest interpretation of the psalm, understood this as a reference to angels. Second, the inspired writer of Hebrews assumes this meaning (cf. Heb. 2:7). Third, the psalmist consistently addresses God in the second person. Had he meant "God," he would have said, "You made him a little lower than yourself" (see also P. Humert, *Études sur le récit du paradis et de la chute dans la Genèse* [Neuchatel: Universite, 1940], 170).

[40]The main argument against this interpretation is that angels are not involved in creation (see Cassuto, *From Adam*, 55). However, God's address of the heavenly court does not mean that they participate in the act of creation. For instance, in Isa. 6:8 when God says, "Whom shall I send? And who will go for us?" God is the primary actor, but he is acting in concert with a heavenly dimension.

[41]The word *selem* occurs seventeen times in sixteen verses in the OT: five passages pertain to humanity being in God's image; the other eleven refer to a physical image (such as a statue or representation). The Aramaic form of the word also occurs seventeen times in Dan. 2–3.

[42]A most readable summary and treatment of "image" is given by A. A. Hoekema, *Created in God's Image* (Grand Rapids: Eerdmans, 1986). See also B. K. Waltke, "Relating Human Personhood to the Health Sciences: An Old Testament Perspective," *Crux* 25 (September 1989): 2–10.

[43]D. J. A. Clines, "The Image of God in Man," *TynBul* 19 (1968): 53–103.

[44]Moreover, some discontinuities exist between the divine and human. For instance, God is asexual but we are sexual.

[45]Pagans sought to achieve this through magic.

of the one represented. Fifth, inseparable from the notion of serving as a representative, the image functions as ruler in the place of the deity. Hart explains,

> In the Ancient Near East it was widely believed that a god's spirit lived in any statue or image of that god, with the result that the image could function as a kind of representative of or substitute for the god wherever it was placed. It was also customary in the ANE to think of a king as a representative of a god; obviously the king ruled, and the god was the ultimate ruler, so the king must be ruling on the god's behalf. It is therefore not surprising that these two separate ideas became connected and a king came to be described as an image of a god.[46]

The Hebrew perspective bears a distinct difference. In ancient Near Eastern texts only the king is in the image of God.[47] But in the Hebrew perspective this is democratized to all humanity. "The text is saying that exercising royal dominion over the earth as God's representative is the basic purpose for which God created man,"[48] explains Hart. He adds, "man is appointed king over creation, responsible to God the ultimate king, and as such expected to manage and develop and care for creation, this task to include actual physical work."[49] Finally, in the context of Genesis, the image refers to the plurality of male and female within the unity of humanity. This concept is also distinct from the ancient Near Eastern perspective.[50]

likeness. The important addition of "likeness" underscores that humanity is only a facsimile of God and hence distinct from him. Whereas the image of the deity is equated with the deity itself in the ancient Near East, the word *likeness* serves to clearly distinguish God from humans in the biblical worldview.[51]

---

[46]I. Hart, "Genesis 1:1–2:3 As a Prologue to the Books of Genesis," *TynBul* 46 (1995): 318. This functional understanding of "image" in Genesis has become the dominant interpretation, supplanting the interpretation of image as "spiritual qualities."

[47]A correspondent to a seventh-century Assyrian king, Esarhaddon, writes, "A (free) man is as the shadow of god, the slave is as the shadow of a (free) man; but the king, he is like unto the (very) image of God" (R. H. Pfeiffer, *State Letters of Assyria* [New Haven, Conn.: American Oriental Society, 1935], 234 (no. 345), quoted in Clines, "Image," 84.

[48]Hart, "Genesis 1:1–2:3," 322. Here Hart notes especially the close syntactical and grammatical connection to the following phrase to rule over the creatures.

[49]Ibid., 324. This connects well with the theme of six days of work.

[50]Karl Barth (*The Work of Creation*, vol. 3.1 of *Church Dogmatics*, trans. and ed. G. W. Bromiley and T. F. Torrance [Edinburgh: T. & T. Clark, 1960], 182–206) rightly recognizes relationships as a part of the image, but he goes too far when he makes this entailment the definition itself and rules out that it refers to humanity's structure and qualities. Genesis 5:1–3 and 9:6 show clearly that "the image of God" pertains to the individual himself or herself, not to relationship. Genesis 9:6 reads, "Whoever sheds the blood of ʾāḏām [generic person], by ʾāḏām shall his blood be shed; for in the image of God has God made ʾāḏām." Here ʾāḏām refers to every human being, male or female, not a duality of male or female. Clearly the image of God refers to the structure of the individual, and his or her capacity for companionship with a female or male respectively is an entailment. The "image" is found in the psychosomatic wholeness of each individual, who cannot come into being apart from the male-female relationship, and who is intended to live in relationship as man and woman.

[51]Recent scholarship, in contrast with medieval theology, argues that the Hebrew terms *image* and *likeness* are synonymous. Both are incorrect. The medieval distinction of "image" referring to natural

27. So God created. . . . This verse is the first poem in the Bible. The shift to poetry highlights God's creation of humanity as God's image bearers. The truth expressed here undergirds all of Genesis. The unique repetition of the word "create" (*bārā'*) intensifies this significant act. Humanity is uniquely shaped by the hand of God.

28. blessed. Three times God blesses[52] humanity, and it is this blessing that enables humanity to achieve its twofold destiny: to procreate in spite of death and to rule in spite of enemies.

and said to them. The blessing is uniquely given to God's image in the form of direct address.

Be fruitful and increase in number; fill the earth and subdue it. Humanity is given a twofold cultural mandate: to fill the earth and to rule the creation as benevolent kings (Gen. 9:2; Ps. 8:5–8; Heb. 2:5–9).[53]

30. I give. The creatures are totally dependent on God's grace.

31. very good. This is a divine evaluation of the total creation prior to the Fall.

the sixth day. The definite article is used only with the sixth and seventh days, perhaps to signify the climax of the narrative on these two important days.

Summary Statement (2:1)

1. the heavens and the earth were completed. The concluding summary statement underscores that the creator has perfectly executed his will with regard to the first triad.

their vast array. This refers to the second triad.[54]

Epilogue: Sabbath Rest (2:2 – 3)

2. the seventh day. Unlike the previous days, the number of this day is marked three times, indicating its significance above all other days.

God had finished. This is the climactic moment that stands apart from creation, not following the structure of the previous six days. In the first six days space is subdued; on the seventh, time is sanctified. This day is blessed to refresh the earth. It summons humanity to imitate the pattern of labor and rest of the King and so to confess God's lordship and their consecration to him.[55] On this day they cease to subdue the earth.

---

reason and "likeness" referring to original righteousness lost in the Fall cannot be supported from the text. The narrator's careful selection of words throughout also makes the synonymity of the terms unlikely. The word *likeness* serves to ensure the distinctness of humanity from God.

[52]The word *blessing* denotes all that fosters humanity's fertility and assists them to achieve dominion.

[53]The natural human can rule the animal (Gen. 1:28) and plant (1:29) kingdoms, but he or she cannot rule the heavenly powers, especially Satan (ch. 3; Eph. 6:10–12) (see Theological Reflections below).

[54]In 1:1 the merism "heaven and earth" functions as a synecdoche for all the vast array as well.

[55]This sign of a covenant with God (Ex. 31:13, 17) and type of Christ (Col. 2:16–17) gives promise of divine rest both now and forever (Matt. 11:28).

he rested. No mention is made of "evening and morning," perhaps because the Sabbath ordinance continues and humans are exhorted to participate in it (Ex. 31:17) and to look forward to the eternal, redemptive Sabbath rest (Heb. 4:3–11).

3. blessed the seventh day. It is infused with procreative power. The blessing and sanctity of the seventh day is unique to the biblical account of creation. "In fact, the concept of a seven day week is unique to Israel."[56]

made it holy. The seventh day is the first thing in the Torah to which God imparts his holiness and so sets apart to himself (Ex. 20:11). Other creator gods built temples as a sign of their victory over the wild forces of chaos, but God institutes the Sabbath rest instead. This will be the temporal shrine in which the people of Israel can rest from their labors each week with their God.

THEOLOGICAL REFLECTIONS ON THE PROLOGUE ———

Theology Proper

God's existence is not explained but is axiomatic and self-evident (cf. Rom. 1:19–20). His character emerges through his intimate activity with creation. God's transcendence is echoed by the repeated phrase, "and so God made." The entire account is structured to convey God's omnipotence and transcendence.

Surd Evil

The narrator chooses not to explain the origins of what we call the planet earth and of its states hostile to life (darkness and depth), that is, evil.[57] Where do surd evil (physical conditions hostile to physical life) and moral evil (volitional beings hostile to the social order) come from? The narrator does not answer these questions. However, one should not infer an eternal dualism from this silence. Other Scriptures clearly state that only God is eternal—he made everything (e.g., Neh. 9:6; Job 41:11; Ps. 102:25; Heb. 11:3; Rev. 1:8). Here the narrator is only concerned with the relative beginning of creation. He wishes to establish the creative power of God and his relationship to humanity as well as the covenant community. Although the narrator does not explain the existence of the darkness or the abyss that becomes the sea, he is clear that God bounds and controls it.

The precreated state of the earth with darkness and chaos suggests that everything hostile to life is not a result of sin.[58] This is Job's discovery (Job 38–41). Job is mystified by his whole experience of suffering. God's response is to make clear that everything negative in creation from the human perspective is not a result of human sin. The chaotic forces—sea, darkness, and the like—

---

[56]Sarna, *Genesis,* 14.

[57]As we shall see in Gen. 3, Satan is the expression of moral evil. Where or how this evil originates, the narrator also does not explain.

[58]However, human sin does have an impact on ecology. For example, see Gen. 3:17 and the Noah account.

are a mystery to human beings. Although these forces seem, for the moment, hostile to life, human beings can still trust the benevolence of the Creator because the malevolent forces of creation operate only within his constraints. The sea is always bounded by the land and the darkness of night by the light of the morning. To be sure, there are local floods and fires, but they are confined within the good earth that sustains life. All is bounded by God's control.

Creation by Word

Since everything exists by the word of God, we must not think of creation independently of God. The word of God is the creative and binding force of life. Just as God calls the world into being, he also calls Abraham and the church into existence (Rom. 4:17; Heb. 11:3; 2 Peter 3:5). Through God's word creation is bound to God and the products of creation to one another. Christ as the Logos of God powerfully illustrates this (Col. 1:15–17). Through Christ, the Father binds people to the triune God.

Separation

Just as God commands the light and dark as well as the land and sea to separate, God calls the Israelites to separate from the pagan nations. Separation is a fundamental concept both to creation and to Israel's existence (Gen. 3:15; 12:1; Lev. 20:24–25; Num. 8:14). However, while the nonvolitional elements of the cosmos retain their place and preserve the creation, the volitional, by disobedience, collapse the social order.

Blessing

Because of God's blessing, the natural world is teeming with life. Blessing is God's gift of potency and power. Thus Armstrong says, "People experience this divine blessing as an enabling power that [helps them] to transcend [their] fears and discover a new source of strength in the depths of [their] being."[59] Blessing enables God's creatures to fulfill their natures and to live in their element.

Image of God

Understanding that we are made in the image of God is essential for understanding our destiny and relationship to God (see further the exegetical note and "image" at 1:26). Without revelation humans become confused or depreciate themselves. Emil Brunner says, "The most powerful of all spiritual forces is man's view of himself, the way in which he understands his nature and his destiny, indeed it is the one force which determines all the others which influence human life."[60] Our being and function[61] come from

---

[59]K. Armstrong, *In the Beginning: A New Interpretation of Genesis* (New York: Ballantine, 1996), 16.
[60]E. Brunner, "The Christian Understanding of Man," in *The Christian Understanding of Man*, ed. T. E. Jessop (London: Allen & Unwin, 1938), 146.
[61]Hoekema, *Created*, 69.

God's image. As representatives mirroring God and breathing God's life, we may live in relationship with God and exercise our dominion over all the earth. This can take many forms; for example, the cultural mandate gives dignity and meaning to the arts and sciences.

Furthermore, we are theomorphic. At the very least this entails that human beings, like God, are persons. As such, we are not only creatures dependent upon God but also persons with volition free to make decisions. Hoekema says, "To be creatures means that God is the potter and we are the clay (Rom. 9:21 [Isa. 45:9]); to be persons means that we are the ones who fashion our lives by our own decisions (Gal. 6:7–8 [cf. Josh. 24:15])."[62] Accordingly, humanity has the potential to sin *and* to accept God's grace.

The Christian understanding of the image of God must be separated from New Age thinking. We are made in God's image, but we are only a likeness (1:26). We are not God. This concept, set out in Genesis, is further developed throughout the Old and New Testaments. The image is not erased after the Fall but continues seminally to every individual (Gen. 5:1; 9:6). However, after the Fall the first Adam (and all of humanity) can only partially fulfill the cultural mandate: procreating and subduing in sorrowful toil.[63] Only Christ, the Second Adam (cf. Ps. 8 and Heb. 2), can completely fulfill the regent function of the image.[64] The One who is uniquely the express image of God's person, the heavenly Son of Man and Rider of the Clouds, is the true Image[65] and so God's true King on earth. He brings salvation to fallen humanity. He completes perfectly humanity's twofold function. He makes the church his bride (Eph. 5:23–32) and fills the earth with spiritual children (Isa. 53:10–11; Matt. 12:46–50; John 1:11–13; Gal. 3:29).[66] He blesses his disciples and fills them with the Spirit of life (cf. *emphysaō* in LXX of Gen. 1:7 and John 20:22). He brings everything under his dominion (Luke 10:18–19; Eph. 1:22; Col. 1:18–20), including Satan and evil (Gen. 3:15; Matt. 4:1–11; Col. 3:10), and enters into the rest of God (Heb. 1:3).

Soul

The Old Testament understanding of "soul" (*nepeš*) differs from the New Testament's notion of "soul" (*psychē*). In the Old Testament a human being

---

[62]Ibid., 6.

[63]Adam exercises dominion by naming parts of creation (Gen. 2:19), but he subjects himself to Satan. He procreates and subdues the earth, but there is painful labor in childbearing and in toiling the soil (3:16–19). Civilization exhibits creative gifts of God (4:21–22) but also honors violence and worships human creation (4:17, 23–24). All is subject to the futility of death (Eccl. 2:22–23; 9:3).

[64]The Lord Jesus completes the spiritual dimension of the cultural mandate when he blesses his disciples to multiply spiritually (Matt. 28:18–20; Luke 24:50–51).

[65]Christ is a heavenly being, the Image of God in his deity (Rom. 8:29; 1 Cor. 15:49; 2 Cor. 3:18, 4:4; Col. 1:15–20).

[66]The Great Commission is a redemptive correlative to the command to be fruitful (Matt. 28:19–20). Christ raises seed from children of death, imparting an everlasting name to those cut off without seed (Isa. 56:4–8). He also heads a race of righteous people (Rom. 5:19).

is a *nepeš*, while in the New one has a *psychē*. Essentially *nepeš* means "passionate vitality." Along with the rest of the creatures, human beings have drives and appetites for food and sex. What distinguishes humanity from animals is the *imago Dei* and a passionate appetite for God (cf. Ps. 42:1). Our distinctive *nepeš* distinguishes us from the rest of creation, but more important, it is the *imago Dei* that sets us apart for God. We are to be distinguished by our godlike compassion in connection with our ruling. Like God, we are to be merciful kings.[67]

Sabbath

Seven-day periods were well known in the ancient Near East, and other cultures distinguish between days for work and days for rest. Moreover, ancient Near Eastern literature provides numerous examples of the use of the seventh day as the climax of a cataclysmic or cosmic event.[68] Israel, however, uniquely sanctifies the seventh day for rest.

The fourth of the Ten Commandments in Exodus 20 is grounded in God's creative action of working six days and resting on the seventh, as recorded in Gen. 1:1–2:3 (cf. Ex. 16). The order of creation stands behind Sabbath observance. God's work in one week becomes stamped upon his people as a repeating design for their sanctification. The Sabbath, says Jesus, is meant for humanity (Mark 2:27). Moreover, this fourth commandment is a janus linking the first three commandments pertaining to God with the last six pertaining to humanity. By ceasing from work and economic commerce on the Sabbath (cf. Ex. 31:12–17; 34:21; Num. 15:32–36; Neh. 10:31; 13:15–22; Jer. 17:22), Israel keeps the day holy to the Lord, but this practice aims to give rest to all animals and all people, slave and free. Nevertheless, the priests offer sacrifices (Num. 28:9; Matt. 12:5) and circumcise infants on the Sabbath (John 7:22), and Israel's army marches on this holy day (Josh. 6:3–4). Although observing the Sabbath is not connected with religious practices in the Old Testament, by the time of the New Testament the Scriptures are also read and argued on the Sabbath (Mark 1:21; Luke 4:16–20; Acts 13:13–45; 15:21; 17:2).

Observing the design of creation weekly sanctifies Israel in several ways. First, it reminds Israel again and again that God completes his work. As he consummates his work in creation, he will bring to perfection his work in history through his elect people. He who calls Israel to bring salvation will not fail (cf. Isa. 45; Phil. 1:6; Heb. 12:2).

Second, by observing the Sabbath Israel confesses regularly that their God is Lord of all. He made the Sabbath holy to celebrate his rest "from all

---

[67]Waltke, "*nāpash*"; see also A. R. Johnson, *The Vitality of the Individual in the Thought of Ancient Israel* (Cardiff: Univ. of Wales, 1949).

[68]Cf. *ANET*, 904. The number seven signifies "completeness" (see also "Literary Analysis of Book 2: Genealogical Structure").

the work of creating that he had done" (Gen. 2:3). Kline summarizes, "Observance of the Sabbath by man is thus a confession that Yahweh is Lord and Lord of all lords. Sabbath-keeping expresses man's commitment to the service of the Lord."[69] In the creation God ordains hierarchies of government in assigning the luminaries to govern day and night (1:18) and human beings to rule the earth (1:28). The Sabbath reminds God's image that they are his regents to serve him.

Third, God blesses the Sabbath and makes it holy in the best interest of all people and all animals (Ex. 20:8–11). The rabbis, however, multiply its rules and regulations and make it a heavy burden on the people. But Jesus as the Lord over the Sabbath releases the people from this heavy burden, teaching that the Sabbath is meant for people, not people for the Sabbath. It is a time to heal and do good (Matt. 12:1–14; Mark 2:23–28; John 5:9–15). As apostle of the Lord of the Sabbath, Paul abrogates the law and regulations of Sabbath observance as binding upon the church (Col. 2:16). Observance or nonobservance of days is a matter of an individual's conscience, service to the Lord, and faith (Rom. 14:5–23).

Fourth, the Sabbath is the sign that the Creator has set Israel apart for a special covenant relationship with him (Ex. 31:17). In the rabbinic literature circumcision, dietary practices, and Sabbath observance become the distinctive marks of Judaism. In the New Testament, believers gather together on the first day of the week, the Lord's Day (Rev. 1:10), to break bread and to read, teach, and study Scriptures (John 20:1, 19–23; Acts 20:7; 1 Cor. 16:2). A person who feels inclined to work seven days a week should examine what god he or she worships. God is that "to which your heart clings and entrusts itself."[70] Those who find their security and significance in Mammon or professionalism find community worship on the first day of the week a burden.

Fifth, Sabbath observance reminds Israel that they were slaves in Egypt but that the mighty Lord has redeemed them from servitude into rest (Deut. 5:15). Today its typical significance has been fulfilled in Christ (Col. 2:16–17).

Sixth, in the book of Hebrews the Sabbath rest gives concrete expression to the church's realized eschatology (Heb. 4:1–11). The Sabbath rest assures saints that, just as God entered his rest after the working for six days, so also they live in the hope that when they cease from their labors after their fleeting days they too shall enter an eternal rest. In Christ, New Testament saints already by faith enter that rest. Thus Wilson says, "When we keep Sabbath by resting from our labors, we acknowledge that our life . . . is sustained by God. We rest from our labors because we know that our hope is in the Lord,

---

[69]M. G. Kline, *Kingdom Prologue* (Hamilton, Mass.: Meredith Kline, 1993), 25.

[70]M. Luther, *Large Catechism*, in *The Book of Concord*, trans. T. Tappert (Philadelphia: Fortress, 1959), 365.

not in our labors. Sabbath rest also reflects our larger hope in the Lord for the sustenance of creation and for the completion of redemption."[71]

Seventh, it can be inferred from the creation narrative that the Sabbath is a day to recognize and celebrate the significance of time. We are not just creatures of space but also creatures of time. As Heschel observes, "Technical civilization is man's conquest of space. It is a triumph frequently achieved by sacrificing an essential ingredient of existence, namely, time. In technical civilization, we expend time to gain space. To enhance our power in the world of space is our main objective. Yet to have more does not mean to be more. The power we attain in the world of space terminates abruptly at the borderline of time. But time is the heart of existence."[72] Participating in God's rest gives us significance as we reflect on what we have done and allows us to participate in something eternal (transcendent time). Heschel argues,

> The higher goal of spiritual living is not to amass a wealth of information, but to face sacred moments. In a religious experience, for example, it is not a thing that imposes itself on man but a spiritual presence. What is retained in the soul is the moment of insight rather than the place where the act came to pass. A moment of insight is a fortune, transporting us beyond the confines of measured time. Spiritual life begins to decay when we fail to sense the grandeur of what is eternal in time.[73]

In the imitation of God's rest, we find our sustenance in God and the true meaning of our labor and God's good creation.[74] Again Heschel comments, "To disparage space and the blessing of things of space, is to disparage the works of creation, the works which God beheld and saw 'it was good'.... Time and space are interrelated.... What we plead against is man's unconditional surrender to space, his enslavement to things. We must not forget that it is not a thing that lends significance to a moment; it is the moment that lends significance to things."[75]

EXCURSUS: THE LITERARY GENRE OF THE CREATION ACCOUNT

"The Spirit of God who spoke through them did not choose to teach about the heavens to men, as it was of no use for salvation."
AUGUSTINE

"The Bible tells us how to go to Heaven, not how the heavens go."
GALILEO GALILEI

---

[71]J. R. Wilson, *Gospel Virtues: Practicing Faith, Hope and Love in Uncertain Times* (Downers Grove, Ill.: InterVarsity, 1998), 129.
[72]A. J. Heschel, *The Sabbath: Its Meaning for Modern Man* (New York: Farrar, Straus & Giroux, 1986), 3.
[73]Ibid., 6.
[74]See ibid., 28.
[75]Ibid., 6.

"The function of setting up goals and passing statements of value transcends the domain of science."

ALBERT EINSTEIN

The historicity and scientific accuracy of the Genesis creation account has been the subject of much controversy and debate. Questions concerning the relationship of the Genesis creation account and science can only be addressed intelligently by determining the literary genre of Gen. 1:1–2:3. Generally, the creation account is slotted into one of four categories: myth, science, history, or theology. The determination of the genre of any passage must always be founded on the text, and careful textual analysis of Genesis 1 reveals that it is problematic to assign this passage to any one of these categories.[76]

Creation and Myth

Is Genesis myth? That question is complicated by the many definitions of the word *myth*.[77] If by the word *myth* one means a story that explains phenomena and experience, an ideology that explains the cosmos, then the Genesis account of creation is myth. In this sense, myth addresses those metaphysical concerns that cannot be known by scientific discovery.

However, most commonly the word *myth* is understood to represent things fanciful or untrue. In this case, the word *myth* misrepresents the Genesis account and does an injustice to the integrity of the narrator and undermines sound theology.

Creation and Science

Is Genesis scientific? As an account that describes life-support systems, heavenly bodies, species of flora and fauna, and other natural elements of earth, the creation account has a scientific dimension. But the Genesis creation account has distinct differences from a scientific document.

First, Genesis and science discuss essentially different matters. The subject of the Genesis creation account is God, not the forces of nature. The transcendent God is a subject that science cannot discuss.

Second, the language of Genesis and science is entirely different. The creation account is formed in everyday speech, nontheoretical terminology, rather than mathematics and technical terminology.[78] More

---

[76]For a more detailed examination of these questions, see B. K. Waltke, "The Literary Genre of Genesis 1," *Crux* 27 (December 1991): 2–10.

[77]For twelve definitions of *myth*, see J. W. Rogerson, "Slippery Words: V. Myth," *ExpTim* 90 (1978): 10–14; and G. J. Brooke, "Creation in the Biblical Tradition," *Zygon* 22 (1987): 233.

[78]Its style is not in contrast to scientific language. The Hebrew language is nonscientific, not prescientific (which might imply that science is the only accurate standard). The perspective of the creation narrator is entirely different from a scientist.

important, Genesis 1 is concerned with ultimate cause, not proximation.[79] The intent of the creation account is not to specify the geological and genetic methods of creation but to definitively establish that creation is a result of God's creative acts. When the psalmist says "You knit me together in my mother's womb" (Ps. 139:13), he is not intending to comment on genetics or immediate cause. To suggest otherwise is to distort the text. This is a clear example of why scientific and theological accounts should not be pitted against one another. In Genesis, the narrator only tells us that God commands the earth to bring forth life. He does not explain how that bringing forth occurs.

Third, the purposes of Genesis and science also differ. Genesis is prescriptive, answering the questions of who and why and what ought to be, whereas the purpose of science is to be descriptive, answering the questions of what and how. The narrator of the creation account is not particularly concerned with the questions a scientist asks; rather, he wants to provide answers to the questions science cannot answer— who has created this world and for what purpose?

Fourth, since they are addressed to different types of communities, Genesis and science require distinct means for validation. Science, speaking to the academic scientific community, requires empirical testing for validation. Genesis, addressed to the covenant community of God, requires the validation of the witness of the Spirit to the heart (Rom. 8:16). For these reasons, the Genesis creation account cannot be delineated as a scientific text.[80]

Creation and History

If not science, is Genesis history? It certainly has historical elements. It is factual in the sense that God created the cosmos and all that is in it, and the genealogies that trace the history of Israel back to Adam and Eve speak to the narrator's concern with historicity. However, Genesis bears little resemblance to modern conceptions of history (see "Historicity and Literary Genre" in the introduction). In short, it is not straightforward or positivistic history.

---

[79]That is, Genesis 1 is not concerned with Aristotle's efficient cause but with his formal (plan) and final clause (purpose). Langdon Gilkey complains about those who mix these categories: "They ignore the (scholastic) distinction between *primary* causality of a First Cause, with which philosophy or theology might deal, and *second* causality, which is causality confined to the finite factors" ("Creationism: The Roots of the Conflict," in *Is God a Creationist? The Religious Case against Creation-Science,* ed. R. Mushat Frye (New York: Scribner, 1983), 60.

[80]This should not be understood as an argument for or against evolution. If the creation account is not meant as science, then it should not be pitted against scientific theories. Rather, scientific theories should be critiqued by scientific method. This is not the Bible's concern. (We must also distinguish between science and scientism, between evolution and evolutionism.) For an argument against evolution see P. Johnson, *Darwin on Trial* (Washington, D.C.: Regnery Gateway, 1991); M. Pitman, *Adam and Evolution: A Scientific Critique of Neo-Darwinism* (Grand Rapids: Baker, 1984); and M. M. Denton, *Evolution: A Theory in Crisis* (Bethesda, Md.: Adler & Adler, 1986).

The creation account is unlike any other history. History is generally humanity recounting its experiences. The Genesis creation account is not a record of human history, since no humans are present for these acts.

Even in modern history, there is a tension between the historical referent and authorial creativity in the writing of history. The Bible gives great scope to creativity in interpreting and presenting the data. The biblical narrator even feels license to dischronologize the events.[81] Certain "difficulties" in the order of the days seem clearly to represent a dischronologization. On the first day (1:5) God creates the evening and morning, but he does not create the luminaries to divide them until the fourth day (1:14).[82] If this is a straightforward historical account, God created evening, morning, and days without luminaries and then created luminaries in order to effect them.[83] Are we really to conclude that the division occurs without the dividers? It seems reasonable to assume that the narrator has offered a dischronologized presentation of the events in order to emphasize a theological point. God is not dependent on the luminaries. The narrator also subtly suggests a dischronologization by speaking of each of the first five days as "a day," not "the day."[84] The narrator's concern is not scientific or historical but theological and indirectly polemical against pagan mythologies. The narrator wishes clearly to establish that it is God who has created all and has dominion over all, including the seas, sun, and moon.[85]

Other aspects of the Genesis creation account likewise suggest that it is not concerned with presenting a strict historical account. The sym-

---

[81]As early as the eleventh century, the great Jewish commentator Rashi pointed out that Genesis 1 does not describe a literal sequence of events. Other biblical writers rearrange events for theological purposes (e.g., Gen. 10/11; Ex. 4–11/Ps. 105:28–36; the Synoptic Gospels). In each of these examples, the events are recast to emphasize a theological point.

[82]There are other difficulties of chronology. Differences seem to exist between the order of events in the first and second accounts (i.e., Gen. 1:1–2:3; 2:4–25). In the second account there is the chronological difficulty of the trees. Assuming that God planted the garden on the third day of creation, when he formed the vegetation, the trees grew and bore fruit before the creation of the woman on the sixth day. To be sure, creation may assume apparent age, but the text says unambiguously that "the LORD God made all kinds of trees grow" (2:9). That cannot have happened within the three days according to a normal reading of the text, and the narrator does not represent the growth of the trees as an instantaneous act. It is also difficult to imagine that Adam named all the animals (both domestic and wild), underwent an operation, woke up, and composed a poem all within the daylight hours of the sixth day. It seems clear that the two chapters were not written to be read sequentially and according to strict chronology.

[83]The suggestion that he caused them only to appear on the fourth day (having already been created on the first day) is unconvincing.

[84]Throntveit, "Are the Events," 53; and Sterchi, "Does Genesis," 529–36. Sterchi's article provides a good summary of this particular issue and offers some helpful illustrations.

[85]J. L. McKenzie writes, "The Hebrew author enumerates all the natural forces in which deity was thought to reside, and of all of them he says simply that God made them. Consequently, he eliminates all elements of struggle on the cosmic level; the visible universe is not an uneasy balance of forces, but is moderated by one supreme will, which imposes itself with effortless supremacy upon all that it has made"(*The Two-Edged Sword* [New York: Image, 1966], 101).

metrical nature of the account (see Literary Analysis above) and the similarities of patterns with ancient Near Eastern material, including the use of the widely attested seven-day typology of the ancient world, may suggest that the narrator is using a stereotypical formula to speak of divine activity and rest.[86] Youngblood adds, "I would point out that the omission of the definite article ("the") from all but the sixth day allows for the possibility of random or literary order."[87]

The days of creation may also pose difficulties for a strict historical account. Contemporary scientists almost unanimously discount the possibility of creation in one week, and we cannot summarily discount the evidence of the earth sciences. General revelation in creation, as well as the special revelation of Scripture, is also the voice of God. We live in a "universe," and all truth speaks with one voice.

One of the key ways in which the text distances itself from a bare-facts retelling of the events of creation is its metaphorical language.[88] As soon as we talk about God in heaven, we are in a realm that can only be represented by earthly figures. The narrator must use metaphor and anthropomorphic language[89] so that the reader can comprehend. When the text says that God said, commanded, called, and saw, are we to understand that God has vocal cords, lips, and eyes?[90] Obviously this language is anthropomorphic, representational of the truth that God creates. If the narrator's descriptions of God are anthropomorphic, might not the days and other aspects also be anthropomorphic? The anthropomorphic allows us to enter into and identify with the creation account. The time of creation is presented in the anthropomorphic language of days so that humankind might mime the Creator. Since we cannot participate in vast stretches of time, how else could we imitate the creator, except with finite terms such as a week?

In sum, the narrator has an agenda very different from the modern historian. He has a theological agenda: to tell us that God created the earth and that it is all very orderly.

---

[86]Within ancient Near Eastern material, the pattern of six as incompleteness and seven as resolution is quite common.

[87]R. Youngblood, *The Book of Genesis: An Introductory Commentary* (Grand Rapids: Baker, 1992), 26 n. 29.

[88]The metaphorical language is carefully chosen best to represent God in understandable ways. We cannot, however, change the metaphors by which God chose to reveal himself without changing our understanding of God. To reimage God is idolatry.

[89]H. N. Ridderbos explains, "Is . . . the author not under the necessity of employing such a method, because this is the only way to speak about something that is really beyond all human thoughts and words?" ("The Meaning of Genesis I," *Free University Quarterly* 4 (1955–1957): 222.

[90]Young, although he does not admit to an anthropomorphic understanding of the days, clearly recognizes the anthropomorphic language here: "It is certainly true that God did not speak with physical organs of speech nor did he utter words in the Hebrew language" (E. Young, *Studies in Genesis 1* (Philadelphia: Presbyterian & Reformed, 1973), 55–56.

Creation and Theology

If the narrator has so clearly crafted the Genesis creation account around theological concerns, can we call the account theology? Once again the answer is yes and no. Genesis is theological in that it is concerned with divine matters and with teaching the covenant community important truths about God and his relationship with his world, but it is not theology as we usually understand it. The narrator does not systematically present abstract truths about the divine; rather, he tells us a story about the Creator and his creation.

What, then, is the genre of the Genesis creation account? Following Henri Blocher,[91] we can describe the creation account as an artistic, literary representation of creation intended to fortify God's covenant with creation. It represents truths about origins in anthropomorphic language so that the covenant community may have a proper worldview and be wise unto salvation. It represents the world as coming into being through God's proclamation so that the world depends on his will, purpose, and presence.

---

[91]H. Blocher, *In the Beginning: The Opening Chapter of Genesis* (Downers Grove, Ill.: InterVarsity, 1984), 50–59.

THE ACCOUNT OF THE HEAVENS AND THE EARTH (2:4 – 4:26)

THEME OF BOOK I

The perspective now shifts from God as sole actor to humanity as reactor. The subtle change from "the heavens and the earth" (1:1) to "the earth and the heavens" (2:4b) may point to the shift in perspective.[1]

The account of the heavens and the earth records the drastic change from the pristine "very good" creation to the harsh realities now experienced outside the temple-garden. Through the Fall, sin and death enter the human race and the earth becomes cursed. Both humanity and the earth are in need of redemption.

In the historical event of the Fall, Adam and Eve function as archetypes for humanity's disobedience. The priestly guardians of the sanctuary are tested for their fidelity to their King. Obedience entitles them to life with God (cf. Deut. 30:15–20). Failure points to their need for justification and sanctification through the covenant of redemption established with and through Jesus Christ.

OUTLINE OF BOOK I

---

[1]Sarna, *Genesis*, 16–17.

LITERARY ANALYSIS OF BOOK I ————————————

Genre

Like the creation account, the account of the heavens and the earth has historical solidity. The story is based on events in time and space, a real Adam and Eve.[2] But it is not merely a historical account. The style is artistic and figurative rather than scientific and literalistic.[3] The scenes of creation are painted as an artist might envision them: God, as a potter, forming the man; as a gardener, designing a garden of beauty and abundance; and as a temple builder, raising the woman from the rib of the man.

The suprahistorical dimension is also essential for the theology of this account. On this register, Adam and Eve represent every man and woman (Gen. 3:16–19; cf. 2:24; Matt. 19:4–6; Rom. 5:12).[4] They represent our own rebellion, fallenness, and need for God's graceful redemption. This is as important as the historical dimension. Therefore, both the historical and the suprahistorical should be held in proper tension.

Structure and Plot

In contrast to the static and balanced report of creation in the prologue, the account of the heavens and the earth unfolds like a drama with all the elements of scenic depiction, contrast, conflict, and climax. This is a drama of three acts opening with paradise, falling to despair, and resolving with a seed of hope.

Each act opens with a setting and concludes with a poem (which captures the theme of the act), followed by an epilogue (cf. 2:23 with 24–25; 3:14–19 with 20–24; 4:23–24 with 25–26). The first act begins with Adam in a par-

---

[2]We should assume Adam and Eve to be historical, since the narrator makes no distinction between the narratives of Adam and Eve and the patriarchs. Adam is connected to Abraham by a royal genealogy that extends to David in the book of Ruth and to Jesus in the New Testament. The Chronicler (1 Chron. 1) and the NT (Matt. 19:4–5; Luke 3:23–38; Rom. 5:12–19; 1 Cor. 15:21–22; 1 Tim. 2:13–14) assume the historicity of Adam and Eve.

[3]If read literally, a number of problems would ensue. For instance, on a literal level how can 2:9 be harmonized with 1:11–13, 26–30?

[4]Most of us already read it this way intuitively. We assume the judgments given to Adam and Eve apply to us. We do not think the curse of pain in childbearing or the struggle with the soil apply only to Eve and Adam.

adisiacal garden separated from the rest of creation. The garden is a temple, and its priest is the man with the woman to help him. Scene 1 features vegetation, which has a prominent role in the probation. Scene 2 presents the animals, which are important to the "gift of the bride." The poem concluding this act celebrates God's gift of a wife.

The second act begins with the crafty serpent. Against the backdrop of the same lush and holy garden, humanity forfeits its priestly role. Plants and animals together have important roles in this moment of decision for the protagonists. The act concludes with a poem of judgment and salvation.

The third act begins outside the garden with the woman giving birth. The setting outside of the paradisiacal garden conveys humanity's failure, but Eve's childbirth conveys God's grace and the hope that remains. The concluding poem of this act, Lamech's song of revenge, forcefully depicts humanity's escalating sin and violence.

The first two acts are closely related by a chiasm:

A Creation of man: his happy relationship with the earth and his home in the garden, where he has freely growing food and access to the tree of life (2:4–17)
  B Creation of woman: her happy relationship with man (2:18–25)
    C Conversation of serpent with woman: his tempting of her (3:1–5)
      X The sin and God's uncovering of it (3:6–13)
    C' Punishment of serpent: its spoiled relationship with woman (3:14–15)
  B' Punishment of woman: her spoiled relationship with man (3:16)
A' Punishment of man: his spoiled relationship with the earth and expulsion from his home in the garden; he now has to toil to secure food and will no longer have access to the tree of life (3:17–24).[5]

This analysis exposes the crucial moment as Adam and Eve's choice to eat the forbidden fruit. The chiasm may justify combining acts 1 and 2 into one act: "the expulsion of man from the Garden."[6]

Escalation

The acts display humanity's worsening situation. The serpent tempts Adam and Eve to sin, but Cain sins after God encourages him to do what is right. Adam and Eve eat the forbidden fruit, but Cain murders his brother, fears being killed and his offspring repeatedly kill in unbridled revenge and debase God's ideal for marriage by polygamy. Not surprisingly, Cain's punishment is more severe than Adam's. According to Dorsey, "Adam is . . .

[5]So Dorsey, *Literary Structure*, 50.
[6]So Wenham, *Genesis 1–15*, 49–51.

- driven from the garden, to settle in a new home east of Eden
- forced to till the soil to get food
- separated from the source of perpetual life (the tree of life), while Cain is...
- driven out, doomed to wander forever with no permanent home
- not even able to till the soil for his food
- hounded by death (would-be killers) wherever he goes."[7]

Characters

Three characters deserve special mention: Adam as God's image and dust, woman as helper and hinderer, and the serpent as subtle and lovely. The latter trait in each case is emphasized in connection with sin. Adam and Eve, as main characters, develop and change. Adam, who begins as the hero, is banished along with his wife when they embrace the seductive words of the serpent and rebel against God. But Adam and Eve return to God's care and participate in redemption as they build a family and produce a line of godly descendants. Each character of this book participates in the great themes and conflicts of life's drama: love, revenge, judgment, salvation.

Conflict

The conflicts of these acts set the stage for the conflicts that will trouble characters throughout Genesis: the battle of seed, strife in marriage, the fight to master sin, and rivalry among siblings. Adam and Eve's conflict with God extends to conflicts with one another, leading first to blaming, then to power struggle, and eventually to violence.

Irony

The events of Adam and Eve's lives are tragically filled with irony. They use speech, which is meant to bind them together, to alienate one another. Moreover, they use speech, which enables them to rule, in a way that forfeits that rule. The ground from which the man came and that is intended to serve him becomes his enemy. The helper becomes a hindrance. The brother becomes a murderer. The narrator uses word plays throughout the account to highlight these ironies. For instance, when God comes to investigate in the garden, Adam hides because he says that he "heard" God. It is precisely his lack of "hearing" that leads to that painful situation. With poetic justice, however, the serpent receives due punishment. The animal more crafty (ʿārûm) than any other becomes most cursed (ʾārûr).

---

[7]Dorsey, *Literary Structure*, 50.

Innertextuality[8]

Sailhamer argues plausibly that the alternating structure of narrative, followed by a poem and an epilogue in this account suggests the compositional strategy for Genesis 1–11, Genesis as a whole and even the Pentateuch. The creation of Adam and Eve in Genesis 2 is drawn to conclusion with Adam's poem about his wife (2:23) followed by an epilogue (2:24). The account of the Fall concludes with a poem (3:14–19) and an epilogue (3:20–24). The story about Cain concludes with Lamech's poem (4:23–24) and an epilogue (4:25–26). The third account, essentially the story of the flood (6:9–9:23), is drawn to conclusion with Noah's prophetic poem (9:24–27) also followed by an epilogue (9:25). Possibly Lamech's words in 5:29 after the genealogy of the second account function in the same way. Sailhamer also notes that the four major poems in the Pentateuch (Gen. 49; Ex. 15; Num. 23–24; and Deut. 32–33) follow the same compositional pattern. Finally, he notes that these poems are linked in their content, including their royal focus for the last days.[9] One might say that they point indirectly to the Messiah. The Lord's poem points to the saving seed of the woman (3:15), Lamech's to the one who will bring comfort from the curse on the earth (5:29), Noah's to the blessed line of Shem (9:26), Jacob's to Judah (49:8–12), Balaam's to Israel's future king (Num. 24:7), and Moses' to the tribe of Judah who will come to his people and defeat his enemies (Deut. 33:7).

EXEGETICAL NOTES TO BOOK I ――――――――――

Superscription (2:4a)

4a. This is the account [*tôlᵉḏōṯ*]. This word is the signal marker for the beginning of each of the ten books of Genesis (see "Structure and Content" in the introduction). *Tôlᵉḏōṯ*, from the root *yld*, meaning "to bear children," here signifies "what is produced or brought into being by someone." It is the nominal form of the root, meaning "descendants."[10] The account pertains to what the cosmos has generated, not the generation of the cosmos.

the heavens and the earth (see 1:1 and "Structure and Content" in the introduction).

---

[8]In this commentary, the term "innertextuality" refers to textual relationships within Genesis as opposed to "intertextuality," which refers to relationships between Genesis and other books of the Bible.

[9]J. Sailhamer, "A Wisdom Composition of the Pentateuch," in *The Way of Wisdom: Essays in Honor of Bruce K. Waltke*, ed. J. I. Packer and S. K. Soderlund (Grand Rapids: Zonderan, 2000), 15–35.

[10]Many of the older English translations render the word as "descendants" or "generations," since "what is produced" are the descendants. Either because "beget" is understood as a metaphor for successive events or because these descendants have stories associated with them, the NIV committee decided to translate the word as "account" here and as "account of X and his descendants" in the subsequent passages.

Act I: Humanity on Probation (2:4b – 25)

Scene I: Man on Probation: Humans Retain Paradise by Obeying God (2:4b – 17)

Setting (2:4b – 6)

4b. the earth and the heavens. The change in order from 1:1 and 2:4a is possibly a subtle signal to the change in perspective (see "Theme of Book 1," above).

LORD God [*yhwh ʾelōhîm*]. Here the narrator introduces an additional name for God: *yhwh* (see "Exegetical Notes to the Prologue," above). The term *God* (*ʾelōhîm*) represents him as sovereign Creator, while LORD (*yhwh*) designates him as the one who initiates a unique covenant commitment with Abraham and his seed and who oversees its fulfillment in history (see also Ex. 3:14–15). The combination of names shows that the Creator of the cosmos rules history through chosen humanity.

5. no shrub of the field . . . no plant of the field. This describes part of the negative state of the earth before the Fall. The Hebrew terms here refer to inedible vegetation (cf. 3:18) and cultivated (cf. 3:17, 23) grains won from a cursed ground.[11] As in the preceding account and ancient Near Eastern creation myths, the story begins with a negative state (cf. Prov. 8:24–30).[12] Because of the crucial role of the garden, trees, and the cursed ground in the Fall, the introduction focuses on plants, not animals. The animals, however, are featured in the gift of the bride story.

ground. *ʾadāmâ* is a technical term for arable land.[13] Hiebert comments, "The role of human beings is to serve the land, turning it into that which can support life, and God's role, to provide the rain." These two roles of humanity and of God, argues Hiebert, are "the most fundamental facts of existence, the absence of which signify the state of the world before creation."[14]

6. streams came up. Prior to the Fall, vegetation is not dependent on rain but relies on subterranean waters that rise, like the Nile, and irrigate the earth.

---

[11]The shrub of the field (*śiaḥ*) represents wild growth, thorns, and thistles (cf. the definition in *HALOT*, 1321). The term *plants* (*ʿēśeb*) represents wheat, barley, and other grains, since humans had not yet been assigned to cultivate grains (see Gen. 3:18, 23; Cassuto, *From Adam*, 101–3). David Tsumura argues that the terms refer to any uncultivated plants, regardless of their edibility (*Earth*, 87–88). But Cassuto's argument stands, based on his evidence that "plants of the field" in 3:18 clearly means cultivated grains and subsequently "shrubs" seems to refer to "thorns and thistles." He also argues that these should be distinguished from the vegetation of 2:5. Cassuto's interpretation also satisfies the exegetical expectations drawn from other "creation" accounts that the negative state at the beginning of the narrative will be transformed by the end of the story.

[12]The present state of a cursed earth and painful toil is the result of the Fall and will be lifted in the new creation.

[13]T. Hiebert, *The Yahwist's Landscape: Nature and Religion in Early Israel* (New York: Oxford Univ. Press, 1996), 61, 97.

[14]Ibid., 72.

Creation of Man (2:7)

7. LORD God. He continues to be the chief actor (cf. Gen. 1:3).

formed. The image is of a potter and clay: God as the Artist is bonded to his work. The image signifies a deliberate, not accidental creation.[15] The same metaphor is used for the creation of every human being (Job 10:8–9).

man . . . ground [ʾā**ḏ**ām . . . ʾa**ḏ**āmâ]. The word play shows the man's close connection with the ground, his cradle, his home, his grave (see 2:5, 15; 3:19). The first Adam is fashioned in a natural body for an earthly existence.[16]

breath of life. Animals also have breath, but it is the narrator's intention to stress that human beings have the very breath of God sustaining them.[17] Michelangelo powerfully depicts this scene with God's mighty finger reaching to touch the man's flaccid and lifeless hand. Humans have been given God's life.

living being [nepeš]. This is traditionally translated "soul" (see "Theological Reflections on the Prologue: Soul," above).

The Paradisiacal Setting of Probation (2:8 – 14)

8. garden [gan]. From the Hebrew root gnn, meaning "to be enclosed, fenced off, protected," "garden" probably denotes an enclosed, protected area where the flora flourishes. It represents territorial space in the created order where God invites human beings to enjoy bliss and harmony between themselves and God, one another, animals, and the land. God is uniquely present here. The Garden of Eden is a temple-garden, represented later in the tabernacle.[18] Cherubim protect its sanctity (Gen. 3:24; Ex. 26:1; 2 Chron. 3:7) so that sin and death are excluded (Gen. 3:23; Rev. 21:8). Active faith is a prerequisite for this home. Doubt of God's word or character cannot reside in the garden.

east. Where the sun rises represents light and life, versus the west, which represents death.[19] But movement to the east in Genesis is usually negative, in the context of judgment (3:24; 4:16), vainglory and greed (11:2; 13:11), and alienation (25:6).

Eden. The likely etymology of the word is a Hebrew term meaning pleasure, delight, or lush fecundity.[20] The topography, foliage, and heavenly river

---

[15]The depiction is widespread in the ancient world; however, the biblical account "omits all mythological details" (Sarna, Genesis, 17–18).

[16]The heavenly Son of Man (cf. Dan. 7:13) shared in this earthly state in order to secure for fallen humanity a spiritual body of imperishable glory in the resurrection (1 Cor. 15:42–49; see Theological Reflections below).

[17]Here is an example of narrative depiction versus scientific analysis.

[18]The Holy of Holies will have all the trees of the garden and life. The eschatological temple is compared with Paradise (Rev. 20–21).

[19]An illustration of this ancient Near Eastern thinking can be seen on the Nile, where all the gods of life are on the east bank and all the pyramids and gods of death are on the west.

[20]It may also derive from an Akkadian term meaning "plain" or "prairie."

all depict a scene of paradise[21] in the Garden of Eden. It is the archetypal sanctuary. By inference from the text, Eden, a place larger than the garden residing within it, is a mountain representing heaven (Gen. 2:10).[22] The water flows through the garden and then divides into four headwaters to fructify the earth.

put the man. God's placement of the man in the garden suggests that humanity is meant for fellowship in the garden, with God, its Creator and Gardener. Adam and Eve's expulsion will make them feel as castaways in a strange land.

9. all kinds of trees. This orchard is both aesthetically pleasing and practical. Life in the garden is represented as a banqueting table—good for food and delightful to the eye. Humanity has no need to eat the forbidden fruit.

tree of life. God gives the humans the potential for life in its highest potency, representing life that transcends the natural. In Proverbs "tree of life" is used to refer to anything that heals, enhances, and celebrates life: righteousness (11:30), longing fulfilled (13:12), and a tongue that brings healing (15:4).[23] The "tree of life" is mentioned first, but Adam and Eve focus on the second tree. The primary quest of humanity is power, not life.

tree of the knowledge of good and evil. This knowledge creates ethical awareness, as Adam and Eve later experience when they discover their nakedness, a symbol of their vulnerability and ability to use or abuse sex. "Good and evil" is a merism for all moral knowledge: the capacity to create a system of ethics and make moral judgments. The knowledge of good and evil represents wisdom and discernment to decide and effect "good" (i.e., what advances life) and "evil" (i.e., what hinders it).[24] Unless we know everything, we only know relatively; unless we know comprehensively, we cannot know absolutely. Therefore, only God in heaven, who transcends time and space, has the prerogative to know truly what is good and bad for life. Thus, the tree represents knowledge and power appropriate only to God (Gen. 3:5, 22).[25] Human beings, by contrast, must depend upon a revelation from the only one who truly knows good and evil (Prov. 30:1–6), but humanity's temptation is to seize this prerogative independently from God (see 3:7).

10–14. A river. . . . The description of the rivers of Eden functions as a pause in the narrative.

10. river. The heavenly river, in contradistinction to the streams coming up from the earth outside the garden (cf. 2:6), represents the dissemination

---

[21]The term *paradise* is derived from the LXX's rendering of *Eden* by *paradeisos* from Old Persian *pairi-daêza*, which meant "an enclosed park and pleasure ground." The term *paradise* later came to designate the place where the righteous are rewarded after death (Luke 23:43).

[22]Ezekiel depicts Satan's rebellion as taking place on a heavenly mountain (Ezek. 28:13–14; Rev. 21:10; 22:1–2).

[23]See R. Marcus, "The Tree of Life in Proverbs," *JBL* 62 (1943): 117–20.

[24]See "wisdom" in Gen. 3:6; cf. Ezek. 28:6, 15–17.

[25]In his grace, God shares this ability with his king whom he anoints to judge the holy nation (2 Sam. 14:17).

of heavenly life. Its abundant supply flows from Eden through the temple-garden and then branches out to the four corners of the earth. It provides food and healing and is symbolic of the springs of living water, the life that issues from the throne of the living God (Ps. 36:8–9; 46:4; Jer. 17:7–8; Ezek. 47:1–12; Rev. 22:1).[26]

11–13. Pishon . . . Gihon. Their identity is problematic.[27] Havilah is in Arabia, so Pishon should be identified with Arabia, possibly the Persian Gulf. According to Gen. 10:8, Cush should be in western Iran. Is Gihon one of the rivers or canals of Mesopotamia?

11. Havilah. The geographic depictions express the historical basis of the account.

12. gold. God provides for humanity's enrichment outside the garden as well. Later the riches outside of the Israelite temple will be brought into it and dedicated to God.

The Probation (2:15 – 17)

15. work it and take care of it. Work is a gift of God, not a punishment for sin. Even before the Fall humanity has duties to perform. Elsewhere in the Pentateuch this expression describes activity only of priests. The latter term entails guarding the garden against Satan's encroachment (see 3:1–5). As priest and guardians of the garden, Adam and Eve should have driven out the serpent; instead it drives them out.

16. commanded. These first words of God to man assume man's freedom to choose and thus his formed moral capacity. In this covenant arrangement, God graciously offers human beings life, but he demands an active faith-obedience to keep his commands.

17. not eat from. . . . This unique prohibition (cf. 1:29) confronts humans with the Creator's rule. The tree is good, but it belongs exclusively to God. Sin consists of an illicit reach of unbelief, an assertion of human autonomy to know morality apart from God. The creature must live by faith in God's word, not by a professed self-sufficiency of knowledge (Deut. 8:3; Ps. 19:7–9; Ezek. 28:6, 15–17).

Surely die. The verdict for disobedience is the death penalty (see 20:7; Ex. 31:14; Lev. 24:16).[28] Although the statement may refer to physical death, primarily in view is spiritual death, which entails loss of relationship with God and with one another. When the man and woman eat from the tree, they immediately damage their relationship with God and with one another (see

---

[26]Its antitypes are the word of God flowing from the temple (see Mic. 4:1–4) and the Spirit of God from temple-believers (John 7:37–39).

[27]For bibliography, see *HALOT*, 926.

[28]Although one must admit the possibility that the Hebrew means "may die" or "is liable to death" in the legal literature, the context of the narrative makes it clear this is not the meaning here. For its possible meaning in legal literature, see B. Gemser, "The Importance of the Motive Clause in Old Testament Law," VTSup 1 (1953): 50–66.

3:7–13). Physical death, an additional judgment, is an indirect blessing, ending life's pain and opening the prospect for life apart from sin and death.

Scene 2: Gift of the Bride (2:18–23)[29]

Setting (2:18)

18. not good [$lō$ʾ $tôḇ$]. The phrase $lō$ʾ $tôḇ$ is highly emphatic.[30] Essentially, it is bad for Adam to be alone.[31] God intends marriage, which entails intimacy and sexual relationship.[32] Relationship is modeled after God who does not exist in isolation but is a triunity, surrounded by a heavenly court.

helper [ʿ$ēzer$]. God creates the woman to help Adam, that is, to honor his vocation, to share his enjoyment, and to respect the prohibition. The word *help* suggests that the man has governmental priority, but both sexes are mutually dependent on each other. The man is created first, with the woman to help the man, not vice versa (see also 1 Tim. 2:13); however, this does not mean ontological superiority or inferiority. The word *helper,* used for God sixteen of the nineteen times it appears in the Old Testament, signifies the woman's essential contribution, not inadequacy.[33]

suitable [$negḏô$]. The Hebrew means "equal and adequate." Men and women differ in sexuality but are equals as bearers of God's image and in their standing before God.[34]

Preparation of Man for the Gift (2:19–20)

19. L<small>ORD</small> God had formed . . . all the beasts. The creation of the animals is mentioned now because of their importance to the gift of the bride story.

called. The narrator blanks the origin of language, but he later explains its diversity.[35]

---

[29]The ancient Near Eastern texts have no account of the formation of woman. The biblical account, by contrast, devotes one verse to the creation of man and six to woman! Her appearance brings the creation to completion (Sarna, *Genesis*, 21).

[30]The usual way of expressing a less than ideal situation is ʾ$ên$ $tôḇ$, "it is lacking in goodness."

[31]That it is not good for man to be alone must be qualified by the NT teaching. Marriage is good, but it is even better to be married to Christ (1 Cor. 7:29–40).

[32]In the OT, even those set apart for holy duties marry (high priest, Lev. 21:13; Nazirite rules do not include celibacy, Num. 6:1–4).

[33]The OT and NT affirm this structured, dependent relationship of men and women: (1) In the OT a woman may serve as a prophetess but not priestess; (2) The relationship of the Godhead is Father, Son, Spirit (not Parent, Child, Spirit); (3) In the NT the apostles were all men; (4) As presented in 1 Cor. 11:3–16, the wife is to the husband as the husband is to Christ and as Christ is to God; (4) 1 Peter 3:6 reminds women that Sarah called Abraham "master" in her self-talk (Gen. 18:12).

[34]This complete equality before God is seen throughout Scripture. Women pray directly to God (Gen. 30:1–2; 1 Sam. 1:9–14; 2:1–10), participate in sacrifice and ministry (Lev. 12:6; Luke 8:1–3), are Nazirites (Num. 6:2; 1 Cor. 7:32–35), parent with equal standing before the children (Lev. 19:3; Prov. 1:8; 31:26), receive and communicate divine revelation (Gen. 25:22–23; Ex. 15:20; Judg. 4:4–7; 2 Kings 22:13–20; Isa. 8:3), and serve and minister in the church (Phoebe, Priscilla, Junia, Euodia, Syntyche— *diakonos, synergos, apostolos,* Acts 21:9; Rom. 16:1–3, 7; Phil. 4:2–3).

[35]From the empirical evidence, language is devolving, not evolving.

20. gave names. See also 1:5. Adam assumes the lead in naming (prior to the creation of the woman).[36] Following the cultural mandate (1:26), Adam imitates God and brings the world under his dominion. In the order of creation, humans are lower than the heavenly beings and higher than the animals (Ps. 8:5).

no suitable helper was found. Why does God determine that it is not good for Adam to be alone and then give him animals? Should he not have given the woman first? In fact, Adam must realize that it is not good to be alone. Rather than squandering his most precious gift on one who is unappreciative, God waits until Adam is prepared to appreciate the gift of woman.

Creation of the Woman (2:21 – 22a)

21. one of the man's ribs. The intimacy and harmony that should support the marriage relationship is captured perfectly with this image (see also Eph. 5:28). In the famous words of Matthew Henry, the woman is "not made out of his head to top him, not out of his feet to be trampled upon by him, but out of his side to be equal with him, under his arm to be protected, and near his heart to be beloved."[37] So also says Cassuto: "Just as the rib is found at the side of the man and is attached to him, even so the good wife, the *rib* of her husband, stands at his side to be his helper-counterpart, and her soul is bound up with his."[38]

Gift of the Bride (2:22b – 23)

22b. he brought her. This first marriage, set in the sacred temple-garden and designed by God, signifies the holy and ideal state of marriage. God plays the role of attendant to the bride. He gives the man his wife.

23. This is now . . . man. Here we read Adam's only recorded words before the Fall. With poetry, he celebrates the bond[39] and equality of man and woman. In naming her "woman" (*ʾiššâ*) he also names himself "man" (*ʾîš*). The narrator names him by his relation to the ground, but Adam names himself in relation to his wife.[40] A man and woman are never more like God than on their wedding day when they commit themselves unconditionally to one another.[41]

called. The man's twofold naming of his wife entails his authority in the home (3:20; cf. Num. 30:6–8). In ancient times the authority to name implied authority to govern (Gen. 1:5; 2:19).

---

[36]B. K. Waltke, "The Role of Women in the Bible," *Crux* 31 (September 1995): 29–40.
[37]M. Henry, *A Commentary on the Holy Bible* (London: Marshall Brother, n.d.), 1:12.
[38]Cassuto, *From Adam*, 134.
[39]The image of shared flesh illustrates the complete bond of marriage. All that affects one, affects the other. To hurt one is to hurt the other (Eph. 5:28–29).
[40]Sarna, *Genesis*, 23.
[41]Christ, the model, will go even further and die for the other. In marriage we imitate the gospel, giving up our rights and even our life for the other.

Epilogue (2:24–25)

24. For this reason. This aside by the narrator indicates the archetypal intent of the story. Every marriage is divinely ordained. The inspired explanation aims to correct cultures that give priority to the parental bonds over the marital bonds.

leave. Because husband and wife are one flesh, the bond of marriage has priority over the bond of procreation. The husband's obligations to his wife take precedence over other priorities.

united. This is the language of covenant commitment. Marriage depicts God's relationship to his people (Hos. 2:14–23; Eph. 5:22–32).

one flesh. God's intention that marriage be monogamous is implied by the complete unity and profound solidarity of the relationship.

25. no shame. In this ideal state, man and woman view their person and sexuality with wholeness and thus feel no shame in their nakedness. Here their nakedness is an image of openness and trust. With the loss of innocence in the Fall, they will feel shame and temptation and so need to protect their vulnerability by the barrier of clothing (3:7).

Act 2: The Fall and Its Consequences (3:1–24)

Scene I: The Temptation and Fall (3:1–7)

The Shape of the Tempter (3:1a)

1. serpent. In the ancient Near East, in varying contexts, serpents are symbols of protection (Egyptian uraeus), of evil (deadly poison [Egyptian apopis]), of fecundity (Canaanite fertility goddess), or of continuing life (renewal of skin)[42] (cf. Job 26:12–13; Isa. 27:1). Here the serpent is a symbol of antigod. Although not named here, he is the adversary of God and humanity, called the Satan (Hebrew *śāṭān* ["adversary, persecutor, or accuser"]) in the Old Testament and the devil (*diabolos*, the Greek equivalent) in the New Testament. He originates in heaven, standing outside earth's natural order.[43] He is malevolent and wiser than humans, bringing them under his rule. He knows divine matters (3:5)[44] and uses speech to introduce confusion.[45]

crafty [*ʿārûm*]. The word play of "nude" and "shrewd" (*ʿārûm* in 2:25 and 3:1) links the two scenes and draws attention to Adam and Eve's painful vulnerability. Satan's craftiness is seen in his cunning distortion of God's words. With subtle guise, the adversary speaks as a winsome angelic theologian.

---

[42]Cf. A. Heidel, *The Gilgamesh Epic and Old Testament Parallels* (Chicago: Univ. of Chicago Press, 1949), 212 n. 92.

[43]Seemingly (a mystery) he does not belong to this creation, which is good.

[44]This inference becomes explicit in later revelations (Job 1:6–12; Zech. 3:1–2).

[45]Cf. John 8:44; 2 Cor. 11:14; Rev. 12:9. Despite his power, he will be destroyed by Christ and his seed (Gen. 3:15; Luke 10:18–19; Rom. 16:20).

had made. The snake is not a mythological figure but a part of real history.

he said.[46] God gives humanity language to subdue the earth, to bring everything under dominion. The serpent perverts language, using it to bring confusion and to draw Adam and Eve under his control.

The Shape of the Temptation (3:1b – 5)

1b. Did God really say. . . . Satan smoothly maneuvers Eve into what may appear as a sincere theological discussion, but he subverts obedience and distorts perspective by emphasizing God's prohibition, not his provision, reducing God's command to a question, doubting his sincerity, defaming his motives, and denying the truthfulness of his threat.

not [to] eat from any tree. The serpent's subtle changes to God's words entirely distort the truth. He wants God's word to appear harsh and restrictive.

2–3. We may . . . or you will die. Eve gradually yields to the serpent's denials and half-truths by disparaging her privileges, adding to the prohibition, and minimizing the threat.[47]

4. You will not surely die. Trying to remove her fears, the serpent contradicts God's word (2:17).

5. like God, knowing. The Hebrew word for "knowing" is *yōdēʿa,* a masculine plural participle. The meaning is ambiguous. On the one hand, the plural can be used as an honorific form for God, in which the given translation is legitimate.[48] On the other hand, it can be a countable plural, in which case the translation should be "you will be like divine beings, knowers of good and evil." The latter meaning is more probable, since, after they eat of the forbidden fruit, the text says unambiguously, "They have become like one of us, knowers of good and evil" (lit., Gen. 3:22). In any case, the serpent makes God appear to be restricting them from full humanity.

The Shape of Sin (3:6)

6. fruit . . . wisdom. Eve's decision gives priority to pragmatic values, aesthetic appearance, and sensual desires over God's word. Armstrong states, "What Adam and Eve sought from the tree of knowledge was not philosophical or scientific knowledge desired by the Greeks, but practical knowledge that would give them blessing and fulfillment."[49] They are not seeking

---

[46]Although the serpent was a real, historical figure, it is possible that the narrator, in recording the serpent's speech, is verbalizing the psychological dynamics of temptation. Would anyone else have heard the dialogue between the serpent and Eve? Similarly, the witch sees Samuel but does not hear him; Saul hears him but does not see him, and probably his servants hear and see nothing (1 Sam. 28:3–25; Acts 22:9). Probably Adam, who is with Eve, also hears and sees nothing; he is not deceived.

[47]Walter Brueggemann notes, "The serpent engages in a bit of sociology of law in order to relativize even the rule of God. Theological-ethical talk here is not to serve but to avoid the claims of God" (*Genesis: A Bible Commentary for Teaching and Preaching* [IBC; Atlanta: John Knox, 1982], 47–48).

[48]*IBHS* §7.4.3.

[49]Armstrong, *Beginning,* 27.

more information but hunger for power that comes from knowledge—knowledge that has the potential for evil ends as well as for good.

good. In light of chapter 1, this statement is surely ironic. Good is no longer rooted in what God says enhances life but in what people think is desirable to elevate life. They distort what is good into what is evil.

wisdom [*haśkîl*]. This is better understood as "prudence" or "competence" (i.e., to give attention to a threatening situation, to have insight into its solution, to act decisively, and thereby effect success and life and prevent failure and death).

he ate. The man chooses to obey his wife, not God (see 3:17).

The Shape of Sin's Consequences (3:7)

7. the eyes of both of them were opened. Ironically, their opened eyes bring them shame. This knowledge of good and evil is not a neutral state, desired maturity, or an advancement of humanity, as is commonly argued. God desires to save humans from their inclination for ethical autonomy. Because Adam and Eve have attained this sinful state, they must not eat of the tree of life and are consigned forever to the forbidden state of being inclined to choose their own code of ethics (Gen. 3:22). By contrast, in God's kingdom one chooses to know God and live upon his word (Deut. 8:3).

naked [*ʿārûm*]. In the Bible, *ʿārûm* usually describes someone stripped of protective clothing and "naked" in the sense of being defenseless, weak, or humiliated (Deut. 28:48; Job 1:21; Isa. 58:7). With an awareness of guilt and a loss of innocence, the couple now feels shame in their naked state.[50] Their spiritual death is revealed by their alienation from one another, symbolized by sewing fig leaves together for barriers, and by their separation from God, symbolized by hiding among the trees.

7. fig leaves. These are leaves strong and broad enough for clothing.

Scene 2: The Shape of Judgment (3:8–19)

8. Lord God as he was walking in the garden. The Gardener has not abandoned his garden. The proof of love is the unwillingness to abandon the object of love even when love fails to achieve its desired end.

cool of the day. This is literally the "wind" or "spirit" of the day. The wind/spirit is the symbol of God's presence (see 1:2).

hid. Their actions are an implicit admission of guilt.

9–13. Where? ... Who? ... What? God models justice. The just King will not pass sentence without careful investigation (cf. 4:9–10; 18:21). Although omniscient, God questions them, inducing them to confess their guilt.[51]

---

[50]One image of God's redemption is his covering for human sin (3:21; cf. Ex. 25:17).

[51]However, God pronounces judgment without investigation to Satan, who has already rejected redemption.

10. heard [*šm^c*]. Ironically, the Hebrew word may also mean "obey," which is precisely what Adam did not do.

afraid. Actions motivated by fear are not motivated by faith and so cannot please God.

12–13. The woman you put here . . . the serpent . . . I ate. The couple shows their allegiance to Satan by distorting the truth and accusing one another and ultimately God (see James 1:13). They are preoccupied with "I."

14. to the serpent. Satan, who has instigated this evil, is not questioned or given opportunity to explain. The judgment refers to both the serpent and Satan.

cursed [*ʾārûr*]. Consigned to impotence, the serpent's seed does not have the productivity of God upon it. It cannot overcome final death to live forever.

dust. This symbolizes abject humiliation (Ps. 44:25; 72:9) and total defeat (Isa. 25:12; Mic. 7:17) in the Bible.

all the days. The serpent's final defeat under Messiah's heel (3:15) is delayed to effect God's program of redemption through the promised offspring. In the interim, God leaves Satan to test the fidelity of each succeeding generation of the covenant people (Judg. 2:22) and to teach them to "fight" against untruth (Judg. 3:2).

15. I will put enmity. In sovereign grace God converts the depraved woman's affections for Satan to righteous desire for himself.

your offspring and hers. "Offspring" renders *zera^c* "seed," which is used commonly as a figure for descendants. Like the English word, *zera^c* can refer to an immediate descendant (Gen. 4:25; 15:3), a distant offspring, or a large group of descendants. Here and throughout Scripture, all three senses are developed and merged.[52] In this Genesis text we can infer both the single and collective senses. Since the woman's seed struggles against the serpent's seed, we infer that it has a collective sense. But since only the head of the serpent is represented as crushed, we expect an individual to deliver the fatal blow and to be struck uniquely on his heel.

The seed of the serpent is not literal, as in little snakes, for it has already been established that the serpent is only a masquerade for a heavenly spirit. Neither is the seed demons, for such an interpretation does not fit the context and Satan does not father demons. Rather, the seed of the serpent refers to natural humanity whom he has led into rebellion against God. Humanity is now divided into two communities: the elect, who love God, and the reprobate, who love self (John 8:31–32, 44; 1 John 3:8). Each of the characters of Genesis will be either of the seed of the woman that reproduces her

---

[52]The immediate seed is Abel, then Seth. The collective seed is the holy offspring of the patriarchs (Gen. 15:5; 22:17). After Genesis we do not hear again of the promised seed until God promises David a seed (2 Sam. 7:12), which should also be understood in all three ways. The unique fulfillment of this seed promise, Jesus Christ, comes into the world through the seed of the woman: the patriarchs and David. Paul refers to the seed of Abraham as the individual Jesus Christ (Gal. 3:16) but then also includes the church in Christ as Abraham's seed (Rom. 16:20; Gal. 3:29).

spiritual propensity, or of the seed of the Serpent that reproduces his unbelief.[53] The unspoken question to the reader is, "Whose seed are you?"

he . . . you. God announces a battle of champions, and there will be a seed that conquers Satan. Because natural Adam has failed, ultimately the woman's offspring must be a heavenly Adam and his community (See Dan. 7:13–14; Rom. 5:12–19; 1 Cor. 15:45–59; Heb. 2:14; Rev. 12).

crush . . . strike [*šup*]. Both English words translate the same Hebrew root. The parallelism suggests that both individuals are grievously wounded. There must be struggle, affliction, and suffering to win this battle over the Serpent (see Isa. 53:12; Luke 24:26, 46–47; Rom. 16:20; 2 Cor. 1:5–7; Col. 1:24; 1 Peter 1:11). God's judgment reveals that suffering plays a part in those who identify with God's overcoming of the Serpent. As a result, morality will not be confused by pleasure and reward. Adam and Eve must serve God out of a desire for righteousness, not from a desire for self-gratification, which originally led to this place of judgment (see Theological Reflections).

16. To the woman. The woman is frustrated within her natural relationships in the home: painful labor in bearing children and insubordination toward her husband. Control has replaced freedom; coercion has replaced persuasion; division has replaced multiplication.

pains. The context indicates that physical pain is meant here. Just as the man's toil over the resistant ground will now be very difficult and painful, the woman's toil in childbearing may involve great pain (cf. this concept of painful toil in Ps. 127:2 and Prov. 5:10).

childbearing. Immortality is replaced by progeny, opening the door to redemptive history. The privilege of bearing and raising covenant children saves women from their loss of leadership (1 Tim. 2:15).

desire. The chiastic structure of the phrase pairs the terms "desire" and "rule over," suggesting that her desire will be to dominate. This interpretation of an ambiguous passage is validated by the same pairing in the unambiguous context of 4:7.

rule over. Ironically, man will dominate her. Their alienation from one another is profoundly illustrated by God's description of the power struggles, rather than love and cherishing, that is to come.[54] Male leadership, not male dominance, had been assumed in the ideal, pre-Fall situation (see 2:18–25; Theological Reflections).

17. to Adam. As with the others, God's punishment fits the crime. In response to Adam's sin of eating, God's speech to Adam mentions "eating" no less than five times (3:17–19).[55] Adam also will suffer pain and frustration in natural relationships.

---

[53]This division will emerge almost immediately in the hostility between Cain and Abel (see Gen. 4).
[54]The restoration of a love relationship is found in a new life in Christ (see Matt. 20:25–28).
[55]Hamilton, *Genesis 1-17*, 202.

ground. The man's natural relationship to the ground—to rule over it—is reversed; instead of submitting to him, it resists and eventually swallows him (see Gen. 2:7; Rom. 8:20–22). The ecology of the earth is partly dependent on human morality (Gen. 4:12; 6:7; Lev. 26; Deut. 11:13–17; 28; Joel 1–2).

painful toil. The narrator uses the same term as for the woman's anguish. Work itself is a blessing of the working God, not a curse (see 2:15), but now it is cursed by the estrangement of humanity from the life-giving soil. No longer will humanity always gain reward for harsh labor.

18. thorns and thistles. The inedible growth robs the earth of plant life that people need for their subsistence. The hostile creation that must be overcome by work serves as a parable for spiritual hostility that must be overcome by heavenly wisdom (see Prov. 24:30–34).

19. dust you will return. Ironically, transgressing the divinely ordered boundaries does not bring the man and the woman the elevated lives they had hoped for but instead brings them chaos and death. Physical death is both bane and boon. It renders all activity vain but delivers mortals from eternal consignment to the curse and opens the way to eternal salvation that outlasts the grave.

Epilogue: Salvation beyond the Fall (3:20 – 24)

20. named. To the woman's generic designation, Adam adds a personal name that defines her destiny.

mother of all the living. Adam's naming of Eve is the beginning of hope. Adam shows his restoration to God by believing the promise that the faithful woman will bear offspring that will defeat Satan. While this story is filled with death—judgment on the serpent, painful labor, conflict of wills—a ray of hope remains in the promise that the seed of the woman who feels enmity toward the serpent will defeat the incarnation of evil.

21. garments. Adam and Eve's "coverings" of 3:7 were only loincloths, inadequate to cover their shame. Now with the "sacrifice" of an animal,[56] God crafts for them tunics that reach down to the knees or ankles. Brueggemann explains, "With the sentence given, God does (3:21) for the couple what they cannot do for themselves (3:7). They cannot deal with their shame. But God can, will, and does."[57]

clothed. This depicts an image of God's tender care for the couple. Through his sacrifice, he restores the alienated couple to fellowship with him and one another.

22. us. See the note on 1:26. The best explanation of the first-person plural is that God is referring to the heavenly court. Concerning the knowledge of good and evil, Adam and Eve are now like other heavenly beings. It seems improbable that God is referring only to himself (2 Sam. 14:17).

---

[56]The killing of an animal necessary to make garments of skin may suggest/imply the image of a sacrifice for sin.
[57]Brueggemann, *Genesis*, 50.

live forever. In their fallenness, humans must not participate in immortality. Death is both a judgment and a release.

23. banished. Thus God cleanses his temple-garden (cf. John 2:12–17; Rev. 21:27).

24. cherubim. Like the angelic cherub in Ezek. 28:14 whose task possibly is to block one's ascent to the summit throne (cf. Isa. 14:13), these flaming beings have the monitory role to prevent sinners from grasping at immortality. Winged sphinxlike throne bearers are attested throughout the ancient Near East.[58]

Act 3: Escalation of Sin in the Line of Cain (4:1–24)

Scene 1: Cain and Abel (4:1–16)

Setting (4:1–2)

1. lay with. The Hebrew literally means "knew." In the Bible, "knowing" someone involves a personal and intimate involvement, not an impersonal knowing of information. Here "knowing" is used of the most intimate, hallowed relationship between a husband and a wife. "Knowing" is never used of animals, for which coitus only fulfills an instinctual appetite.

Cain. His name may mean to "acquire, get, possess." If so, it is a foreshadowing of his primary proclivities.

With the help of the Lord I have brought forth. The woman is the first to use the covenantal name (see "Composition and Authorship" in the introduction). However, although acknowledging the Lord's role in procreation here, the naming betrays a synergism (God does his part; I do mine).[59] Essentially Eve says, "I have done this."[60] The reader is signaled to expect problems in the life and line of Cain.

a man. The Hebrew term refers to a mature male, not to a baby. The unexpected term may have been chosen as an echo of 2:23. Woman (ʾiššâ) originally came from the man (ʾîš); now man originates from the woman. The sexes are mutually dependent on one another, and both are dependent on God (see 1 Cor. 11:8–12).

2. Later. This literally reads, "she again." The prophesied battle between the seed of the serpent and the seed of the woman is already apparent in their offspring. Even though Adam and Eve have been restored to God, they have two distinct seeds even within the covenant home. The principle of primogeniture, favoritism of the first, is rejected. This begins an important theme of this book.

---

[58]*ANEP*, 159–60, plates 456, 458.

[59]The Hebrew here is somewhat difficult. Most likely the preposition is "*with* the Lord."

[60]Contrast this with the birth hymns of Hannah (1 Sam. 2:1–10): "My heart rejoices in the Lord.... Do not keep talking so proudly or let your mouth speak such arrogance.... The Lord brings death and makes alive"; and Mary (Luke 1:46–55): "My soul glorifies the Lord and my spirit rejoices in God my Savior, for he has been mindful of the humble state of his servant. From now on all generations will call me blessed, for the Mighty One has done great things for me...."

Abel. Eve's lack of comment (cf. Cain) is fitting in light of his name, which means "vapor, breath," and is used metaphorically for what is insubstantial and fleeting. Here also in the name is an ominous foreshadowing of his life.

flocks . . . soil. In spite of the Fall, humans still carry out the cultural mandate to manage the earth's resources (1:26, 28).

Cain's Offering: Tokenism (4:3 – 5a)

3. Cain brought. Cain first fails at the altar, and because he fails at the altar, he fails in the field. Because he fails in his theology, he will fail in his ethics.

offering [*minḥâ*]. This is the common Hebrew word for "tribute," normally in the Mosaic law the cereal offering, the firstfruits. With this offering, the giver acknowledges the superiority or rule of the receiver (Lev. 2:14; 1 Sam. 10:27; 1 Kings 10:25). Both Cain and Abel bring an offering. They both come as priests, worship the same God, and desire God's acceptance, but only Abel brings acceptable tribute (see below).

4. Abel and his offering. The worshipper and his offering are inseparable.

5. did not look with favor. Why does God reject one sacrifice and not the other? Two common interpretations suggest Cain's lack of faith or his sacrifice's lack of blood.[61] Drawing from Heb. 11:4, Calvin argues that only Abel's sacrifice is offered in faith.[62] This is only half correct, for it does not directly engage the Genesis text. Gerhard von Rad points out that Cain's offering is bloodless and suggests that "the sacrifice of blood was more pleasing to Yahweh."[63] The problem with this view is that, in the Pentateuch, the tribute (*minḥâ*) is a bloodless sacrifice (see above). In actuality, the key to Cain's failure is found in the narrator's careful descriptions of Cain and Abel's tribute. Cain brings "some of the fruits." There is no indication these are the first or the best. Abel brings the best, fat from "the firstborn." Cain's sin is tokenism. He looks religious, but in his heart he is not totally dependent on God, childlike, or grateful.

Cain's Bad Feelings, Unbelief, and Impenitence (4:5b – 7)

5b. Cain was very angry.[64] Cain's failure in worship and subsequent anger are basic to his unethical behavior. The elect and nonelect are differentiated by their basic attitudes toward God. Ironically, Cain tries to hide his internal thoughts from the omniscient God who knows his anger.

---

[61]Wenham (*Genesis 1–15*, 104) actually outlines five interpretations, including Gunkel's suggestion that God prefers shepherds to gardeners and Westermann's view that God is inscrutable. Gunkel's suggestion is contrary to the text. Since God himself creates the Garden of Eden (2:8) and appoints Adam and Eve to be its gardeners (2:15), it seems improbable that he would not like gardeners. Westermann's suggestion that God is inscrutable is essentially a claim that God is capricious. This is theologically objectionable and does not match with God's concern to explain the failure to Cain (4:7).

[62]Calvin, *Genesis*, 193–96.

[63]von Rad, *Genesis*, 104.

[64]For the meaning of *ḥrh* without *ʾap* meaning "to be angry," see *HALOT*, 351.

6. Why? As before, God begins his admonition with a question designed to allow the listener to confess his failure (cf. 3:9).

7. If you do what is right. This narrative illustrates original sin. Cain has a God-consciousness of right from wrong but rebels against it.

will you not be accepted? The question demands an answer. It takes faith to believe that God always does what is right. Cain, however, by leaving the question unanswered, shows he lacks the kind of faith that pleases God.

crouching at your door. The depiction of sin as a demon or a vicious animal lying in wait to devour is possibly an allusion to the serpent waiting to strike the heel (3:15; cf. 1 Peter 5:8).

it desires to have you, but you must master it. "Freud may have first named it 'id.' But he did not first discern it. This story-teller already knows about the power of sin that drives, even to death."[65]

Fratricide (4:8–9)

8. Now Cain said. Cain's answer to God's questioning is not recorded in his words to God but in his words and actions toward his brother.

to his brother. The key word *brother* occurs seven times in Gen. 4:2–11. This is the emergence of sibling rivalry, a problem that will plague each of the godly families of Genesis. In hatred, Cain begins the first religious war. Because he renounces God, he renounces his image.

attacked . . . killed. Cain's bad feelings against God spill over into irrational behavior and an unjustifiable jealous rage against his brother. The sundering of the familial bond, begun in chapter 3, here escalates to fratricide in one mere generation.

9. Am I my brother's keeper? His question is absurd. Having dispatched his brother, he now denies any responsibility. His play at innocence reprises his father's attempt at concealment.

God's Investigation, Cain's Alienation (4:10–12)

10. What have you done? Again, God investigates. God's outrage is apparent.

11. curse. God now links Cain with the serpent in the cursed state (3:14).

11–12. driven from the ground . . . will be a restless wanderer. Cain alienated himself from his brother and God, so God will alienate Cain from the arable soil. He will be a nomad without home or security.

12. no longer yield. Once again earth's ecology is impacted by human morality (see 3:17).

Cain's Response (4:13–14)

13. more than I can bear. Cain responds with self-pity instead of repentance. He fears physical and social exposure but not the invisible God who has made him.

---

[65]Brueggemann, *Genesis*, 58.

14. hidden from your presence. The rebel irrationally fails to believe that God, who made him and sees his heart, can see his situation and prevent the world from dissolving into anarchy.

whoever finds me. The narrator blanks the time between the expulsion and procreation. For instance, whom does Cain have to fear, or where does Cain get his wives? Obviously, this information may be inferred from the reference to his siblings and their descendants (4:17, 25–26; 5:4). However, the narrator's focus is on the human condition, not history per se.

kill me. Ironically, none will be "his keeper." The murderer fears death (cf. Num. 35:19).

God's Protective Grace (4:15 – 16)

15. seven times over. Seven denotes a complete cycle, and so here perfect justice.

mark. This is apparently a protective tattoo, allowing him to live out his natural life span.

land of Nod. This symbolic name means "wandering." The person alienated from God is a person without an abiding place.

Scene 2: Cain's Progeny: Lamech (4:17 – 24)

From the First Connected with a City (4:17 – 18)

17. Cain. What follow are the genealogy of Cain and the accomplishments of his descendants. The genealogy is linear: seven generations, counting Cain, are segmented at the end into four children of Lamech. His lineage gives us the first metallurgy, the first poetry, and the first cities. His lineage is symbolic of human culture with great civilizations and no God. At the same time, the narrator silently polemicizes against the pagan myths that attribute the advances of the cultural mandate to divine and semidivine figures.[66]

lay[67] with his wife . . . gave birth to Enoch. In God's common grace, family life is enjoyed by unbelievers as well as by believers. No law as yet forbids marrying a sister (see 5:4).[68]

city [ʿîr]. The city refers to some form of fortification. Hulst explains, "Any settlement, more-or-less permanently inhabited, protected by the erection of a 'fortress' or simple wall, can be called ʿîr."[69] The earthly city provides both civilization and protection but culminates in 11:4 in the building of a city that challenges God's supremacy.[70] The city functions as an anodyne to

---

[66]For example, the Ugaritic texts attribute the discovery of using iron to the god Koshar, the divine artisan and smith. The Cypriot god Cinyras was credited with the invention of the lyre, the Greek god Pan with the flute.

[67]Literally, "knew" (see 4:1).

[68]For many other differences between accepted religious and social practices before and after the Mosaic law, see "Historicity and Literary Genre" in the introduction.

[69]A. R. Hulst, "ʿîr," *TLOT*, 2:881.

[70]The faithful, by contrast, look for a heavenly city (Phil. 3:20; Col. 3:1–4; Heb. 11:10, 16; 12:22; 13:14).

wandering and alienation and as a protection against human irrationality and retaliation. The ambiguity of godless human culture is portrayed by paralleling advances in civilization and violence.

named it. Instead of honoring God, the unbeliever honors humanity. This perverse reversal will give rise to a self-idolizing, Machiavellian state.

17–18. Cain . . . Enoch . . . Irad . . . Mehujael . . . Methushael . . . Lamech. The names are similar to those in Genesis 5, not to represent variations of the same source, but to parallel and contrast the two offspring of Adam. The seventh from Adam through Cain and through Seth, respectively the ungodly Lamech (4:19–24) and the godly Enoch (5:24), stand in sharp contrast to one another. The former inflicts death; the latter does not die.

Tyrannical Lamech (4:19–24)

19. Lamech. Lamech represents both a progressive hardening in sin—polygamy (cf. 2:24; Matt. 19:5–6) and grossly unjust vendetta—and the extension of the cultural mandate from animal husbandry (Gen. 4:20) to the arts (4:21) and sciences (4:22).

two women. The escalation of sin is now extended to the marital relationship. Polygamy is a rejection of God's marital plan (2:24).

21–22. Jubal . . . Tubal-Cain . . . Naamah. The name *Jubal* is connected with being productive; *Naamah,* pleasant. This family line is a tragic image of sin's distortion and destruction. The arts and sciences, appropriate extensions of the divine cultural mandate, are here expressed in a depraved culture as means of self-assertion and violence, which climaxes with Lamech's song of tyranny.

21. harp and flute. Although invented by the godless, they are used by the godly to praise the Lord (1 Sam. 16:23).

23. hear my words. The section ends with a poem: Lamech's song of revenge.[71] Cain's descendants embrace greater violence and vindictiveness. Whereas Cain feared God's authority, Lamech fearlessly takes authority for his personal gain.

24. seventy-seven times. This formulaic number represents unlimited violence. Cain flagrantly and abusively bolsters reputation with retaliation; hence, Cain's identity, which was *marred* by violence, engenders his progeny's identity, which is *marked* by violence (see also 6:1–6).

Epilogue: A Godly Remnant (Transition to Book 2) (4:25–26)

25. Adam lay[72] with his wife again. Clearly this story has been dischronologized. The line of Cain through tyrannical Lamech is presented to illustrate the consequences of the sin of revenge. Now the story flashes back

---

[71]Contrast Lamech's revenge of seventy-seven-fold and Christ's forgiveness of seventy-seven times (Matt. 18:22), Lamech's unending revenge versus God's unending forgiveness.
[72]Literally, "knew" (see 4:1).

to the birth of Seth to reveal hope in the progress of the godly seed. Despite the vicissitudes of history, God is keeping his promise to provide a seed to destroy the serpent (3:15).

Seth. His name, derived from the Hebrew verb translated "granted" and meaning "to set, place," expresses Eve's faith in God to continue the covenant family in spite of death.

God has granted. In contrast to the earlier naming of Cain, Eve now properly credits God alone for giving her a child.

26. Enosh. His name means "weakness," and in his weakness he turns to God with his petition and praises (see Ps. 149:6). Sarna notes, "It is the consciousness of human frailty, symbolized by the name Enosh, that heightens man's awareness of utter dependence upon God, a situation that intuitively evokes prayer"[73] (see Theological Reflections below).

call on the name of the LORD. This is an image of prayer: "to enter into an intensive relationship as someone who calls."[74] The covenant family, making its petition and praise in the name of the Lord, glorifies God, not humans (cf. 4:23–24).

THEOLOGICAL REFLECTIONS ON BOOK I

Temple[75]

The garden is a temple from which the heavenly waters flow to the rest of the earth. This is a foreshadowing of the life of Christ and his church as temple. The living water of the Spirit now pours out from the temple of believers (cf. John 2:19–22; 7:37–39; 1 Cor. 3:16; 6:19; 2 Cor. 6:16; Eph. 2:21–22; Heb. 3:6).

Depravity

This garden is Paradise: if humanity fails in this ideal setting, then there is no hope for humanity to keep faith anywhere else. The failure of Adam and Eve in the Garden of Eden has profound theological significance. Since Adam was the only human being who could have resisted temptation, his failure implies that humanity cannot keep covenant with God. If Adam before the Fall proved unfaithful in Paradise, how much more will Israel fail in the land when surrounded by the depraved Canaanites (cf. Deut. 31:20; Josh. 24:19)? People cannot keep the law. Their only hope is to call out to God to save them. In contrast to much sociological thinking, namely, that the way to improve humans is to improve their environment, humanity at its best rebels in the perfect environment. Sodom and Gomorrah, where humanity sunk to the lowest levels of violence and sex, was at the

---

[73]Sarna, *Genesis*, 40.
[74]*HALOT*, 1130, 9c. *HALOT* defines this expression as such in its uses in Genesis.
[75]See the Exegetical Notes on 2:18–23 and the Theological Reflections on Book 8, Act 2, Scene 1.

time like the "garden of the LORD" (Gen. 13:10). Our modern world is no better.

Adam and Eve's original sin leads to a corruption of their nature, as shown by their fear after they have disobeyed God. This corruption involves a transfer from an original integrity to the corruption of human nature at its source. Adam and Eve pass on the pollution of their sin and its guilt to their descendants. Sin pollutes Cain and his descendants (Gen. 4), and death, sin's consequence, has the final word among righteous Seth's descendants as well (Gen. 5). Even after the Flood, humanity is not purged. God says that "every inclination of [the human] heart is evil from childhood" (Gen. 8:21; see also 1 Kings 8:46; Ps. 58:3; 130:3; 143:2; Prov. 20:9; Eccl. 7:20; Jer. 17:9; John 3:3; Rom. 3:23; 8:7; Eph. 2:3; 4:17–19; Titus 1:15–16; James 3:2).

Orthodox theologians speak of "original sin," which reflects the truth that sin has originated with Adam and has its source at the conception of every descendant of Adam. The narrator and his audience understand that Adam acts as his descendants' representative head. Paul in the New Testament also presents Adam as the representative head of everyone in his choice to disobey God (Rom. 5:12–21; 1 Cor. 15:21–22). By contrast, Jesus Christ is the representative head of all who believe in him, in his active obedience to God, and in his resurrection from the dead. Nevertheless, depraved humanity continues ambiguously to fulfill its cultural mandate as seen in the accomplishments of Cain's descendants (see Exegetical Notes on 4:17–18).

Satan and Angels

The shape of the tempter is given in Gen. 3:1a (see Exegetical Notes and footnotes) so that we will not be deceived by him (2 Cor. 11:3; 1 Peter 5:8). The frequency of angels is extraordinary in Genesis in comparison to the rest of the Primary History. These unnamed divine beings accompany God (see Exegetical Notes on 1:26); know good and evil, as he does (3:22); and are his ministering spirits (cf. 16:7–9; 18; 19:1, 15; 21:17; 22:11, 15; 24:7, 40; 28:12; 31:11; 32:1–2; 48:16). Cherubs symbolize God's transcendent presence on his throne (Ex. 25:18–20; 37:7–9; 1 Sam. 4:4; 1 Kings 6:23–28) and protect it. They come in various shapes: flaming (Gen. 3:24), winged (Ex. 25:18–20), and multidimensional (Ezek. 1:5–28).

Temptation

The shape of Satan's temptation is given in 3:1b–5 (see Exegetical Notes). Adam and Eve are surrounded by wonderful trees and provisions in the garden, including the tree of life, but all Eve can see is the one tree of which they cannot partake. Once Satan can get our eyes on what we cannot do, we are sure to do it. The focus of the Christian should be on all the good that God offers, not on the few restrictions that have goodness of which we may be unaware.

Sin

Sin is essentially a breach of trust, an illicit reach of unbelief, an assertion of autonomy. The spiritual death of Adam and Eve is shown by their alienation from one another, symbolized by sewing fig leaves together for barriers, and their separation from God, symbolized by hiding among the trees. Sin is transgressing divine boundaries, which results in alienation, deteriorating ecology, and physical death. "Freedom which does not discern the boundaries of human life leaves us anxious," says Brueggemann.[76] The attempts to resolve anxiety in our culture are largely psychological, economic, cosmetic. They are bound to fail because they do not approach anxiety's causes. Our public life is largely premised on an exploitation of our common anxiety. The advertising of our consumerism and the drives of the acquisitive society, like the serpent, seduce us into believing that there are securities apart from the reality of God.

Like Adam and Eve, we hide ourselves among "trees." The theologians and ministers hide themselves among the marble columns of the church; the activist, among the picket signs of causes. We are busy but not resonating with the Spirit of God.

In God's words to Cain about mastering sin (4:7), we can hear the voice of Moses instructing Israel. Sin is like a lion crouching at the door—lethal. It wants to devour. Sin is larger than Cain, and he cannot rule it (cf. Rom. 7:17). Only Christ can do that. Unless it is checked immediately by faith, sin spreads like wild fire (see above "Literary Analysis: Escalation"; 4:1–24; 6:1–8; Rom. 1:28–31; 1 Cor. 5:6–7; James 1:14–15; 3:5–6).

Clothing

Adam and Eve's nakedness (2:25) does not idealize nudity but shows why human beings must wear clothes. With the Fall came a tragic loss of innocence (together with resulting shame). When people's minds are enlightened by the gospel, they understand their moral frailty and practice customs of dress that shield them against sexual temptation.

Seed and Second Adam

The seed that will rule the earth is now differentiated into those with the woman's restored religious affections of animosity toward Satan and those who share Satan's religious affections of disparaging the goodness of God's character and the truthfulness of his word (see "Theme of Genesis and Biblical Theology" in the introduction). Early in the history of Christian doctrine the church recognized in Jesus Christ the quintessential expression of that seed.[77]

---

[76]Brueggemann, *Genesis*, 54.
[77]H. P. Ruger, "On Some Versions of Genesis 3.15, Ancient and Modern," *BT* 27 (1976): 106.

Humanity must return to the garden without sin and without death. That will require the second Adam, who by clothing us in his righteousness will take us into the garden. The first Adam, representing all people, fails and brings death upon all. The active obedience of the last Adam satisfies God's demands and gives the faithful eternal life (Rom. 5:12–19; 1 Cor. 15:45–49). The story of paradise regained is true only through Christ. The coming heavenly Adam, who bears the curse of toil, sweat, thorns, conflict, death on a tree, and descent into dust, will regain the garden, tearing apart the veil of the temple on which the cherubim were sewn (Ex. 26:1; Matt. 27:51; Heb. 6:19; 9:3; Rev. 22:1–3, 14). This suggests a consummation distinct from the present world through the promised offspring who projects a new spiritual race into this fallen world.

Faith

Adam and Eve fail in their confrontation with Satan because they fail to trust the goodness of God's character and the truthfulness of his word. The second Adam, faced with similar temptations, routs Satan by faith combined with the Word of God (Luke 4:1–13). Saints receive the benefits of the second Adam's active obedience by faith in him (see Theological Reflections on Faith in Book 6, Act 1, Scene 5). Eden contains the tree of life—life in its highest potency, transcending the natural realm. Adam and Eve's sin cuts them off from this tree, but it is available to those who reenter the garden through the second Adam (see Gen. 3:22; Rev. 2:7; 22:14; cf. John 6:53). It must be eaten by faith. As God by his sovereign grace puts enmity against the Serpent in Eve's heart, by his mercy and grace he puts the pure virtue of faith into the heart of his seed elected out of depraved humanity (Eph. 2:8–9; James 1:17).

Sacrificial Suffering

God's judgment reveals that victory comes with sacrifice. Were the rewards of faith given apart from sacrifice, we would be tempted to serve God for self-gratification. But by winning the victory through sacrifice, grace is imparted (see Rom. 5:3–5). The suffering Christ is victorious. He has already won the victory at the cross by providing an atonement for the redeemed (Col. 2:13–15), and he will consummate it at his second Advent (2 Thess. 1:5–10).

Husbands and Wives

The story about the gift of the bride (see Exegetical Notes at 2:18–23) represents marriage ideally before the Fall, providing a basis for the laws against adultery (Ex. 20:14; Heb. 13:4), a model for marriage in the church (Matt. 19:3–12), the basis for government in the home and church (1 Cor. 11:3–12; 1 Tim. 2:9–10), and a type of Christ's relationship to his Church (Eph. 5:22–

32). This latter represents their relationship by the metaphor of the gospel. As Christ dies for his church, the husband dies for his wife; as the church obeys her Lord in everything, the wife obeys her husband. After the Fall the man and the woman become divided and struggle in their relationship (Gen. 3:16), but God works in the faithful to restore them to their "gospel" relationship.

The Cain in Us

In Jude 11 we are warned against false teachers, and in 1 John 3:12 we are warned not to be like Cain. Jude uses Cain as an exemplar of false teachers, who advocate libertarianism. In 1 John 3:12, *all* Christians are warned not to be like Cain. True Christians recognize their propensity to be irresponsible and their hate toward brothers and sisters, but, unlike Cain, they repent because they know God does what is right.

Weakness

Abel, signifying insignificance, by faith offers an acceptable sacrifice; Enosh, signifying weakness, by faith offers an acceptable prayer. These two together are the expression of true religion. Ironically, when we are weak in ourselves we find the potential to be strong in the Lord.

EXCURSUS: GENESIS GENEALOGIES

Genealogies in this book of genealogies (see 2:4) serve several purposes, depending in part on the nature of the genealogy.[78] *Broad* genealogies present only the first generation of descendants (e.g., "The sons of Leah ... the sons of Rachel..." in Gen. 35:23–26; cf. 6:9–10; 25:13–15). *Deep* genealogies list sequential descendants, in this book usually numbering from two to ten.[79] *Linear* genealogies display only depth (e.g., "Cain ... gave birth to Enoch. To Enoch was born Irad..." 4:17–18; cf. 5:1–31; 11:10–26; 36:31–39, 40). *Segmented* genealogies display both depth and breadth (e.g., "This is the account of Shem, Ham and Japheth.... The sons of Japheth: Gomer ... The sons of Gomer..." 10:1–29; cf. 11:27–29; 19:36–38; 25:19–26; 36:1–5, 10–30; 46:8–25).[80] The distinctions of broad, deep, linear, and segmented genealogies help explain the various functions of genealogies. Of the nine purposes for biblical genealogies presented by M. D. Johnson, five are particularly important to Genesis.[81]

[78]See D. Howard, *An Introduction to the Old Testament Historical Books* (Chicago: Moody Press, 1993), 249–50.

[79]There are ten generations from Adam through Seth to Noah. In the eleventh generation the genealogy becomes segmented.

[80]Apart from the genealogy of the "kings of Edom" (36:31–43), the linear genealogies become segmented with the last generation (cf. 4:19–22; 5:32; 11:26).

[81]M. D. Johnson, *The Purpose of the Biblical Genealogies* (Cambridge: Cambridge Univ. Press, 1969), 77–82.

First, broad and segmented genealogies display the existing relations between kinship groups by tracing their lineage back to a common ancestor. Tribal societies use genealogies to express social relationships with their rights and privileges, rather than to describe strict biological kinship. The Table of Nations (Gen. 10) expresses the kinship and distinctions between Israel and the nations. She emerges from the nations and is destined to bless them (Gen. 12:3). The segmented lists of tribes in Gen. 46:8–25 display both the unity of all Israel and the distinctness of its tribes.

Second, the linear genealogies in Gen. 4:17–18, 5:1–31; 11:10–26 establish continuity over stretches of time without narrative. Because the genealogies are concerned to propel the story and establish relational links, they cannot be used to compute absolute chronology, as evidenced by the following data: (1) Although the antediluvian genealogy of Gen. 5:1–31 and postdiluvian genealogy of 11:10–26 record the ages when descendants father a son and die and compute the years of their life spans, they do not give the complete sum of time, a surprising omission if the narrator's aim was to establish an absolute chronology. (2) Comparison of longer and shorter genealogies elsewhere in the Bible, covering the same time periods, suggests that the shorter ones contain gaps. For example, Ex. 6:14–25 presents four generations from Levi to Moses, but 1 Chron. 7:23–27 presents a more realistic ten generations for the same period, and Ezra 7:1–5 omits six names that are given in 1 Chron. 6:3–14. (3) The division of humanity between Adam and Abraham into two equal divisions of ten generations (5:1–32 and 10:10–26) seems artistic, like the division of history into three periods of fourteen generations in Matthew 1 (see v. 17), which is known to be creative. (4) "Son" (Hebrew *ben*) may bear the sense of "grandson," as in Gen. 31:28, 55, or "descendant," as in the "sons of Israel."[82] By analogy, the verbal equivalent "beget" also may be flexible.

Third, Johnson explains, linear "genealogies were also used to demonstrate the legitimacy of an individual in his office or to provide an individual of rank with connections to a worthy family or individual of the past."[83] This purpose was unaffected by the omission of names. The genealogy of Book 2 establishes Noah as the legitimate descendant of Adam through Seth. By beginning Noah's ancestry with Adam, whom God created in his image, this genealogy represents Noah and his ancestry as the worthy bearers of the divine image mandated to

---

[82]The ancient Near Eastern king lists "may omit several generations (up to seventy among the Sumerians) between one king and his ancestor. Yet even when separated by numerous generations, the latter may still refer to himself as a 'son'" ("Genealogy," *EBD*, 407). Turning to Egypt, "King Tirhakah (c. 670 B.C.) honors his 'father' Sesostris III (c. 1870 B.C.)" (Mitchell, "Genealogy," *TNBD*, 400).

[83]Johnson, *Purpose*, 79.

rule the earth. As Wilson states, "The entire linear genealogy thus deals with the transmission of the divine image and the blessing through a series of firstborn sons."[84] Moreover, Seth connects Noah with the seed of the woman destined to destroy the Serpent.

Fourth, by terminating the ten-descendant linear genealogies of both the antediluvians and the postdiluvians with a segmented eleventh generation, the narrator prepares the way for further delineation of the elect seed. Thus, from Noah's three sons (5:32), Shem will be chosen (11:10–25); from Terah's three sons (11:26), Abraham.

Fifth, the author of Genesis brings together these probably once-isolated genealogies to create a coherent and inclusive genealogical system (see "Introduction: Composition and Authorship").[85] By linking the genealogies by *tôledōt* and connecting the twelve tribes of Israel to Noah's son, Shem, the narrator demonstrates the legitimacy of the twelve tribes of Israel as the image bearers, destined to subdue the earth, and as the worthy seed of the woman that will vanquish the Serpent. From those tribes Judah emerges as leader at the end of Genesis. His eternal son will rule forever over the nations (Gen. 49:8–12). The chart on the following page shows the connection of these genealogies.[86]

---

[84]The mention of Arphaxad as third in one genealogy and the legitimate heir in another suggests Wilson is overreading the text when he specifies "firstborn" (R. R. Wilson, *Genealogy and History in the Biblical World* [New Haven, Conn.: Yale Univ. Press, 1977], 164).

[85]Evidence exists of varying sources for these genealogies. In Gen. 26:34; 28:9 the wives of Esau are Judith, Basemath, and Mahalath. In 36:2 they are Adah, Oholibamah, and Basemath. The differences probably reflect different sources, and we can only speculate why they differ. Are they other wives or different names for the same women? In Gen. 11:10 Arphaxad is the only named son of Shem. In 10:22 he is Shem's third son. These are readily harmonized, but they may reflect different sources.

[86]See Alexander, *From Paradise*, 10; and Johnson, *Purpose*, 23.

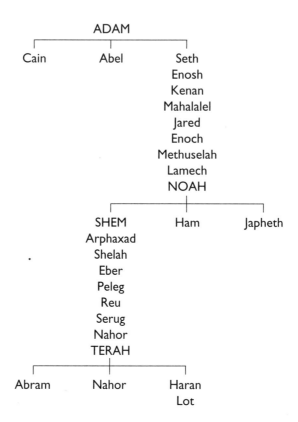

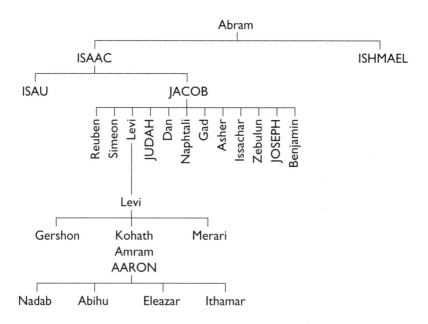

THE ACCOUNT OF ADAM'S DESCENDANTS (5:1 – 6:8)

THEME OF BOOK 2

Genesis begins the process of identifying the seed that will rule the earth (Gen. 1:26–28) and crush the Serpent (3:15). Book 2 traces that lineage from Adam to Noah, even as the matching ten-generation genealogy of Book 5 traces it from Shem to Abraham. Book 2 concludes with the progressive and rapid hardening of sin and the inability of the godly seed of the woman on its own to reverse it. Sin, like the Serpent, is too strong for them.[1] Clearly, both God's judgment and deliverance are needed.

OUTLINE OF BOOK 2

Superscription	5:1a
Act 1: Covenant line of Seth	5:1b–32
Act 2: Transition: Escalation of sin before the Flood	6:1–8
Scene 1: Tyranny by the sons of God and God's resolve, 6:1–4	
Scene 2: Universality of sin and God's resolve, 6:5–8	

LITERARY ANALYSIS OF BOOK 2

Book Structure

The two acts of this account are linked by the reference to Noah in their final verses (5:32; 6:8). Act 1 traces the generations from Adam to Noah, demonstrating that Noah is the legitimate seed to build the culture pleasing to God. This act consists of an introduction giving the setting of this genealogy

---

[1]God's gift of the Spirit at Pentecost will reverse this. His church goes into all the world (Acts 1:8), and the gates of Hades cannot overcome it (Matt. 16:18).

as the creation of *ʾādām* in God's image (5:1b–2), a tenfold linear genealogy from Adam to Noah (5:3–31) and a segmented eleventh generation (5:32). Both the setting and the unique citations of Enoch and Lamech link this lineage with God.

The second act corroborates Noah's right by contrasting him with his own generation. The whole world has become so utterly corrupt that God determines to wipe out the human race; however, Noah finds favor with God (6:8). The second act also forms a transition to Book 3, the account of Noah (6:9–9:29).

The second act falls into two scenes. The first scene specifies a particularly heinous crime among the rulers of the earth; the second, as noted by Vos, shows "*firstly:* the intensity and extent of evil ('great in the earth'); *secondly:* its inwardness ('every imagination of the thoughts of his heart'); *thirdly:* the absoluteness of the sway of evil excluding everything good ('only evil'); *fourthly:* the habitual, continuous working of evil ('all the day')."[2] God escalates his resolve from withdrawing life to wiping out the whole creation to assuage his great pain. The scenes are linked by the characters "LORD" and "man" (6:1, 5) and by God's expressed resolve (6:3, 7).

Genealogical Structure

After a prologue, 5:1–2, this chapter contains ten identically crafted paragraphs, one for each generation in Adam's line from Adam to Seth to Noah. Each paragraph is patterned accordingly: (1) name; (2) age; (3) additional years after birth of son; (4) acknowledgement of other children; (5) total life span; and (6) the refrain "then he died" (See "Excursus: Genesis Genealogies," above).

After underscoring that God created *ʾādām,* male and female, in his likeness, repeating Gen. 1:26–28, the narrator states that Adam "had a son in his own likeness, in his own image" (5:3), not simply that "he became the father of," as in the rest of the narrative. This unique variation reveals humanity participating in the creative act of God by the seminal transference of the image of God to each successive generation. Moreover, by linking the creation of the image with Seth, and not with Cain, the narrator implies that God's purpose for his image will be realized through Seth and his named descendants. Still, the refrain "then he died" is a bittersweet echo of humanity's original sin and God's grace. To each generation, humanity bequeaths life and death.

Deviation from the structured pattern highlights important persons and truths. Instead of simply saying that Lamech "became the father of Noah," the narrator adds, "He named him Noah" with the etymological explanation that this son will bring comfort. The narrator introduces Noah not with the

---

[2]G. Vos, *Biblical Theology: Old and New Testaments* (Grand Rapids: Eerdmans, 1948), 51.

customary "when Noah had lived 500 years," but with the unique "after Noah was 500 years old, he became the father . . . ." In another significant deviation, the records of the godly Enoch and Noah do not end with the refrain of death. Enoch's unusual ending is a testimony to the hope of righteousness in the line of Seth. Noah's unfinished record leaves an opening for the story of the Flood.

The narrator also highlights great moments in history and important personages by creatively schematizing his genealogies.[3] By presenting ten generations both before and after the Flood, the narrator sets the Flood as the great divide between Adam and Abraham. Noah is the savior at the end of the antediluvian history, and Abraham is the savior at the close of the postdiluvian history. With Noah, the Creator makes a covenant to save his creation; with Abraham, the Lord of history makes a covenant to save the nations. The number ten indicates simple completeness and a convenient round number.[4] Seven is the most important symbolic number in the Bible and often signifies divine completeness.[5] In this genealogy, Enoch is featured as the seventh from Adam (see Jude 14) and thereby featured as a favorite of God because of his righteousness.

The Use of Numbers

The expansive and incredible ages of the antediluvians have led some to explore the symbolic and poetic functions of numbers in the genealogy. In light of the narrator's schematized use of ten and seven, it should come as no surprise if the other numbers in this genealogy also have symbolic value.

M. Barnouin[6] has proposed connections between the ages of the antediluvians and the astronomical periods known to the Babylonians. For instance, Enoch's 365 years (5:23) equal the days of the year, Lamech's 777 years (5:31) equal the synodic periods[7] of Jupiter + Saturn, and Yared's 962 years (5:20) equal the synodic periods of Venus + Saturn. Also, if the sum of the years at the time of fathering and of the total life spans from Adam to Lamech are each divided by sixty—based on the Babylonian sexagesimal

---

[3]Ezra schematizes his own priestly genealogy around the pivot of Azariah, the first priest in Solomon's temple. He presents seven priests between himself and Azariah and seven between Aaron and Azariah. In this way he legitimates himself as the right one to reconstitute the Mosaic system as first practiced under Aaron(Ezra 7:1–5).

[4]Cf. the ten plagues (Ex. 7:8–11:10), the Ten Commandments (20:2–17), the tithe (Deut. 26:12), and a quorum of ten men (Gen. 18:32).

[5]Cf. creation in six days and divine rest on the seventh (Gen. 2:3; Ex. 20:8–11); the sabbatical year; after seven sabbatical years, a Year of Jubilee (Lev. 25); the seven-day Feast of Tabernacles (23:34) and Feast of Unleavened Bread (Ex. 34:18); the seven branches of the lampstand (25:31–39); the seven days' march with the seven priests around Jericho climaxing on the seventh day with a march seven times around (Josh. 6:3–4); and the seven river dippings of the proud, leprous Naaman in order to restore his skin (2 Kings 5:14). Seven may also signify simple completeness, such as Cain's sevenfold revenge and Lamech's boast to avenge himself seventy-seven times (Gen. 4:24; cf. Prov. 6:31; 24:16).

[6]M. Barnouin, "Recherches numèriques sur la gènéalogie de Gen. V," *RB* 77 (1970): 347–65.

[7]A synodic period is the time it takes a planet to return to the same place in the sky.

system—the sum of the remainders is 365, again perhaps representing the perfect life span.[8] The cycles of a man's years may match the cycles of the heavenly spheres to show that their lives follow a meaningful pattern and end with a completed cycle. The symbolism is significant!

However, it would be mischievous to pit this possibly symbolic use of numbers against their historical use. In Book 1 the narrator showed himself competent to present a story as both historical and symbolic. We have no reason to think that his artistic use of numbers is not restrained by real history. Its historicity is enhanced by its comparison and contrast with the list of Sumerian kings. The total number of years of the eight kings detailed in the Sumerian King List is 241,000. By contrast the total in Genesis 5 is a modest 1,656. The Sumerian King List then details twenty-three kings, who ruled 24,510 years, 3 months, and 3 1/2 days, which parallels the shorter generations of Gen. 11:10–26.[9]

Innertextual Links

The genealogy of Book 2 forms an intricate web of relations with the surrounding accounts. The repetitions between Gen. 5:1–3 and 1:26–28 establish beyond question the link between the line of Seth and the original creation of humanity in the image of God.

Another significant connection is that between Book 2 and the genealogy of Cain. The two genealogies (4:17–24; 5:1–32) compare in structure, AB/A'B'. Both begin as linear and conclude by segmenting the line into three sons (see 4:20–22; 5:32).[10] However, they contrast sharply in theme. The God-loving Seth, replacing Abel, is juxtaposed to the self-loving Cain. Whereas the genealogy of Cain presents the curse-laden line that ends with a murderer fathering a murderer (see 4:17–24), the genealogy of Seth presents the progression of the seed of promise, linking the founder of humanity, Adam, with its refounder, Noah (see notes on 4:25, 26). Although both genealogies share several names (Enoch, 4:17; 5:21–24; and Lamech, 4:18; 5:25), the characters are radically different. The righteousness and hope exhibited by the Enoch and Lamech of Seth's line sharply contrast with the violence and despair in the line of Cain. Enoch, the seventh in Seth's line, walks with God (5:24), in contrast to the seventh in Cain's line, Lamech, the bigamist and vengeful murderer who boldly sings of his violent deeds. The

---

[8]R. K. Harrison records a similar symbolic use of numbers in the parallel Antediluvian Sumerian King List. The Sumerian King List can be understood by dividing the regnal years of the king by 602, the "ideal" constant: "Perhaps, after all, base-60 squared was intended to serve as a symbol of relative power and importance, which the compilers of the ancient Sumerian King List associated with those men whose reigns they recorded" ("Reinvestigating the Antediluvian Sumerian King List," *JETS* 36 (1993): 7. He also mentions that the ancient Sumero-Babylonian sexagesimal system included the unit 602. The word identifying this unit had an antecedent meaning "universe." See also O. Neugebauer, *The Exact Sciences in Antiquity*, 2d ed. (New York: Harper, 1957), 141.

[9]See T. Jacobsen, "The Sumerian King List" in *ANET*, 265.

[10]The same is true in 11:10–26.

Lamech in Seth's line looks for deliverance from the Lord's curse on the ground (5:29). Whereas Cain's son, Enoch, has a city named after him (4:17), Seth's son, Enosh, calls upon the name of the Lord (4:26). The line of Cain begins with a city builder and terminates with three sons who carry the divine image as culture makers of various aspects of nomadic and urban civilization: sheep-breeders, musicians, smiths,[11] and poets (4:20–24). However, unlike the line of Seth, they are not characterized by complete and full life spans, and they and their culture become too wicked to survive the Flood. By contrast, the bearers of Adam's image, as culture makers pleasing to God, are noted for their long and full lives, not for their arts and sciences, and Noah is worthy to survive the Flood. Cain's line leads to judgment, Seth's line to salvation.

Finally, by only completing Noah's genealogy in 9:29, the narrator skillfully intercalates Book 3 into Book 2. In this way, he features Noah, not his three sons, as the hero of the Flood story.

EXEGETICAL NOTES TO BOOK 2

Superscription (5:1a)

1. written (see 2:4). The mention of a written account suggests that the author used sources (see 11:10–26). Possibly this source contained a written form of an earlier oral tradition.

account of Adam's line (*tôlᵉḏōt*). The author is not concerned with Adam as much as with his sons and the covenant line (see *tôlᵉḏōt* in "Exegetical Notes to Book 1"), which means that this is actually "the account of Adam's descendants."

Act I: Covenant Line of Seth (5:1b – 32)

Introduction (5:1b – 2)

likeness. This reference to the prologue of Genesis establishes a firm connection between Adam's line and God's intentions for creation. The godly line of Seth, in contradistinction to that of Cain (4:1–24), is linked with the original creation.

2. male and female. Adam and Eve's names have personal and generic meaning. Their creation also represents God's creation of all humanity. God is explicitly the Father of the covenant seed (see Luke 3:38) and implicitly of all humanity (see Gen. 10:1).

likeness . . . image. The disobedience of the Fall did not destroy God's image. The verbal linkage with 1:26–28 presents human procreation as the continuation of God's creative act. The image of God continues seminally

---

[11]Johnson (*Purpose*, 12 n. 4) credits the first three terms to S. Mowinckel, "The Two Sources of the Predeuteronomic History (JE) in Gen. 1–11" (1937), 11, 21.

within each line (cf. Eccl. 12:7). Although the breath/spirit of God is passed on seminally (see Gen. 5:1–3), God gives his breath/spirit to all who breathe and so creates each one (Ps. 104:29–30).

called. This exercise of God's dominion is not mentioned in the prologue, but implied in 1:26. It is made explicit here to show that each generation is a continuation of humanity's original creation.

Genealogy (5:3 – 32)

3. had a son . . . named. The pattern of "birth" and "naming" furthers humanity's connection to divine activity. The connection between God and the first parents and the first parents and their children is established by the similarity between 5:1–2 and 1:26–28, the naming of the "offspring" (5:2), and the repetition of "likeness . . . image" (5:3).

Seth. This also links the passage with the previous account (4:25–26).

4. 800 years. The nondiminishing longevity in the line of the antediluvians contrasts sharply with the essentially logarithmic decline in the postdiluvians.[12] Presumably, the postdiluvian world is more hostile to life than the antediluvian (see also above "Literary Analysis: The Use of Numbers").

5. 930 years. The numbers are radically different in the different recensions of the text. The three principal texts of the Pentateuch—the traditional Masoretic (MT), the Greek (LXX), and the Samaritan (SP)—differ on the ages of the antediluvians: in MT the Flood comes in the year 1656 B.C. after the creation of Adam, in SP in 1307 B.C., and in LXX in 2242 B.C. In MT, Methuselah dies in the year of the Flood; in SP, Yared, Methuselah, and Lamech died in that year; and in LXX, Methuselah lives fourteen years beyond it! The MT is given credibility by its overall textual superiority to the other two text types[13] and by its symbolic use of numbers, which can hardly have been a coincidence[14] (see also above "Literary Analysis: The Use of Numbers").

he died. Through Adam's transgression death has come upon all (see also Rom. 5:12–14). On the other hand, God's blessing assures the stability of the created order. In spite of judgment and death, God's grace preserves the messianic line (Gen. 3:15) even while sin abounds in the earth (4:17–24).

18. Enoch. The description of Enoch deviates from the genealogy pattern, highlighting his righteousness. In this line, he is listed seventh, a position often favored in biblical genealogies (see note on 5:1–32; Heb 11:5; Jude 14). Enoch is a symbol of the covenant strength within this line.

22. walked with God. This rare expression (only 5:22, 24; 6:9; Mal. 2:6), denotes to enjoy supernatural, intimate fellowship with God, not merely to

---

[12]See D. Patten, *The Biblical Flood and the Ice Epoch* (Seattle, Wash.: Pacific Meridian, 1996), 215.

[13]See B. K. Waltke, "The Samaritan Pentateuch and the Text of the Old Testament," in *New Perspectives on the Old Testament*, ed. J. B. Payne (Waco, Tex.: Word, 1970), 212–39.

[14]Barnouin, "Recherches." Regrettably, this work is overlooked in R. W. Klein, "Archaic Chronologies and the Textual History of the Old Testament," *HTR* 67 (1974): 255–63.

live a pious life.[15] Enoch's life affirms that those who "walk with God" (5:22, 24) in this fallen world will experience life, not death, as the last word (see Deut. 30:15–16; 2 Kings 2:1, 5, 9–10; Ps. 49:15; 73:24; Heb. 11:5).

23. 365 years. Perhaps a symbolic number corresponding to the days of the solar year and signifying a life of special privilege (see above "Literary Analysis: The Use of Numbers"). Although longevity is often a sign of divine favor (Ps. 91:16), the blessed Enoch's relatively short life span, especially compared to his son Methuselah, shows that being in God's presence is an even greater privilege.[16]

24. was no more, because God took him away. This describes a sudden and mysterious disappearance. Of all recorded Old Testament saints, only Enoch and Elijah are represented as not experiencing physical death (2 Kings 2:1–12; Heb. 11:5). The expression "took him" (*lāqaḥ*) differs radically from "to take the life of someone," referring to an untimely death (cf. Jonah 4:3) or "to take from" (*lqh min*), referring to depriving someone of life (cf. Ezek. 24:16). Schmidt rightly renders "took him" in Gen. 5:24 and 2 Kings 2:3, 5 as "to rapture."[17]

29. He will comfort us. Whereas the Cainite Lamech sought to redress wrong through revenge (see 4:24), the Sethite Lamech looks for deliverance from the curse. Noah fulfills the prophecy by beginning viticulture and viniculture (see 9:20).

32. After Noah was 500 years old. The precise age of Noah at the birth of these sons is uncertain. Later time-frame data suggests the order of sons listed does not represent the birth order (see 10:21 and 11:10).

Shem, Ham, and Japheth. See 9:18 where their story is resumed.

Act 2: Transition: Escalation of Sin before the Flood (6:1 – 8)

Scene 1: Tyranny by the Sons of God and God's Resolve (6:1 – 4)

1. When men. . . . This section forms a connection between Books 1, 2, and 3, recalling the ominous situation at the end of the Cainite lineage (see 4:17–24) and forming a transition from the godly line of Seth to the Flood story (6:9–9:17).

2. sons of God. This problematic expression has been defined as Sethites, angels, or a dynasty of tyrants who succeed Lamech.[18] All three interpretations

---

[15]Piety is commonly expressed by "to walk in connection with the LORD" (see 17:1; 24:20). So BDB, 236b.2 and *IBHS* §26.1.2b. The Hithpael stem of the verb here signifies a durative-iterative notion. D. J. Wiseman thinks it denotes here God's active presence among his people, but he does not carefully differentiate the uses of the Hithpael *hlk* with different prepositions ("Abraham Reassessed," in *Essays on the Patriarchal Narratives*, ed. A. R. Millard and D. J. Wiseman [Downers Grove, Ill.: InterVarsity, 1980] 155 n. 31).

[16]See also John 17:24. The same language is used of resurrection (Ps. 49:15; Ps 73:24).

[17]Schmidt, "*lqh*," *TLOT*, 2:651. He also notes that the rapture of Utnapishtim in the Gilgamesh Epic is reported with the analogous Akkadian verb *legu*.

[18]Although many academics regard this story as myth or "demythologized" myth, I discount that view because the inspired narrator regarded it as history.

can be defended from the Hebrew grammar.[19] The traditional Christian interpretation since the third century, supported by Luther and Calvin, understood the sons of God and the daughters of men to be the sons of Seth and the daughters of Cain, and the sin the mingling of the two seeds, defiling the line.[20] Superficially this best fits the immediate context contrasting the cursed-laden line of Cain with the godly line of Seth, but it must be rejected for philological reasons. Genesis 6:1 reads "when men [$hā^{\prime}ādām$] began to increase ... and daughters [$bānôt$] were born to them." $hā^{\prime}ādām$ is generic for humanity and $bānôt$ refers to all their female offspring. It is arbitrary (i.e., the burden of proof rests upon the exegete to prove a change of meaning) in the next verse to limit $^{\prime}ādām$ to the Sethites and $bānôt$ to the Cainites. If anything, "daughters" in this context refers to Seth's, for in his lineage the begetting of daughters is repeated nine times (5:4, 7, passim), and the narrator never mentions daughters in Cain's lineage. The view that angels had sexual relations with mortals is extremely ancient. This interpretation was held in the early apocalyptic literature, in rabbinic Judaism, and by the early church fathers.[21] This interpretation probably informs 1 Peter 3:19–20 and Jude 6–7.[22] This interpretation, however, does not fit the context of the Flood, since the flood judgment is against humanity (Gen. 6:3–5) and not the heavenly realm. God specifically labels the offenders in 6:3 as "flesh" ($bāśār$ "mortal" in NIV). This interpretation also contradicts Jesus' statement that angels do not marry (Matt. 22:30; Mark 12:25). It is one thing for angels to eat and drink (see Gen. 19:1–3), but quite another to marry and reproduce.

The interpretation that sees this designation as referring to royal tyrannical successors of Lamech finds historical support in an ancient Jewish interpretation that the "sons of God" were nobles, aristocrats, and princes who married girls outside their social status and took great numbers of them into their harems.[23] M. Kline broke fresh ground when he modified "sons of God" to mean "divine" kings.[24] In his view, these tyrants, a continuation of the cursed line of Cain, were supposed to administer justice, but instead they claimed for themselves deity, violated the divine order by forming royal harems, and perverted their mandate to rule the earth under God. Their off-

---

[19]Human beings are called "sons of God" in Hos. 1:10, angels/heavenly beings in Job 1:6, and divine kings in 2 Sam. 7:14; Ps. 2:7; 82:6. Angels are called "sons of God" because they belong to the world of $^{\prime}el\bar{o}h\hat{i}m$, although not in a mythological, physical, or genealogical sense.

[20]Calvin, *Genesis*, 10.

[21]Cf. *1 Enoch* 6:1–7; *Testament of Reuben* 5:6; *Jubilees*; Zadokite Fragment; probably 2 Peter 2:4; Jude 6–7 ("the angels who did not keep their positions of authority" shows strong influence by the apocryphal literature).

[22]W. A. VanGemeren, "The Sons of God in Genesis 6:1-4," *WTJ* 43 (1981): 345–46. Jude compares the fallen angels characterized by hubris to the sexual immorality and perversions of Sodom and Gomorrah.

[23]U. Cassuto, "The Episode of the Sons of God and the Daughters of Man," in *Biblical and Oriental Studies*, vol. 1, trans. I. Abrahams (Jerusalem: Magnes, 1973), 18.

[24]M. G. Kline, "Divine Kingship and Sons of God in Genesis 6:1-4," *WTJ* 24 (1962): 187–204.

spring, he further notes, were the Nephilim-heroes (*nᵉpîlîm, gibbōrîm*, 6:4), "evidently characterized by physical might and military-political dominance" (see Gen. 10:8–10).[25] This interpretation best explains "any of them they chose" (6:2). For example, Pharaoh took to bed whom he would (12:10-20), and so did David (1 Sam. 11). It also fits the immediate context of the Flood, the theme of Genesis, and connects the reference to the Nephilim and heroes in 6:4 to 6:1–3. However, the meaning "divine rulers" is somewhat questionable, whereas "angels" is well established. In addition, Kline's interpretation is recent and seems to undercut the interpretation of 1 Peter 3:19 and Jude 6–7. The best solution is to combine the "angelic" interpretation with the "divine king" view. The tyrants were demon possessed. Gispen avers: "The text presents us with men who are controlled by fallen angels."[26] Their perverted psyches allowed this entrance of the demonic. Eichrodt asserts, "God's power operates . . . within the evil which has been begun by the perversion of the creature's will."[27]

saw . . . beautiful . . . any of them they chose. The Hebrew reads literally: "saw . . . good . . . took." Their sin repeats the pattern ("saw . . . good . . . took") of the original sin in 3:6. They are driven by lust, not spiritual discernment.

married. Literally, "they took wives to themselves," which refers to permanent intermarriage, not fornication.

3. My Spirit. The Spirit of God is the source of natural life (Ps. 104:29–30).

contend [*yāḏôn*]. The meaning of the unique Hebrew word is uncertain. Although the Greek translator only guessed at the meaning "contend," the most recent authoritative lexicon prefers this meaning.[28] Speiser argues for the meaning "to shield/to protect" on the basis of an Akkadian cognate.[29] Brueggemann explains the sense, "The judgment is that God will not endlessly and forever permit his life-giving spirit to enliven those who disorder his world. The breath of life (Gen. 2:7; Ps. 104:29–30) remains his to give and to recall."[30]

a hundred and twenty years. This is probably the span of time between this proclamation and the Flood (see 5:32; 7:6), rather than the years of an individual's life span.[31] God's judgment is seasoned by grace (cf. 1 Peter 3:20). The 120-year delay allows time for people to repent and provides testimony of the coming judgment through Noah and his huge ark.

---

[25]Kline, *Kingdom*, 115.

[26]W. H. Gispen, *Genesis I: Kommentaar op het Oude Testament* (Kampen: J. H. Kok), 221, cited favorably by VanGemeren, "The Sons," 348. My independent investigations lead me to the same conclusion.

[27]Eichrodt, *Theology*, 2:179.

[28]*HALOT*, 217.

[29]E. A. Speiser, "YDWN. Gen 6:3," *JBL* 75 (1956): 128.

[30]Brueggemann, *Genesis*, 72.

[31]It may refer to an individual's life span, but that seems contradicted by the age of the postdiluvians who at first lived much longer (see Gen. 11) and then much less (see Ps. 90:10).

4. Nephilim. Also called "heroes," these are the offspring of the demonic tyrants filling the earth with violence (see 6:11; Num. 13:33). The Hebrew root (*nāpal*) means "to fall" and may suggest their fate (see Ezek. 32:20–28). God will not allow any tyrant to oppress and terrorize the land forever.

and also afterward. This parenthetical remark reminds the book's audience that the same kind of horrible people exist after the Flood (see Num. 13:32–33).

heroes [*gibbōrîm*]. The Hebrew here is also used for Nimrod and his bestial kingdom (10:8–11).

men of renown. These heroes may provide the historical base behind the accounts of semidivine heroes, such as Gilgamesh, of mythology. Instead of the Bible representing myth as history, as is commonly alleged, perhaps the ancients transformed history into myth.

Scene 2: Universality of Sin and God's Resolve (6:5–8)

5. The LORD saw . . . wickedness. Contrast this statement with Genesis 1 (passim). Before, what the Lord saw was good. Now humanity's "creation" has corrupted the earth. This act of looking upon the earth also signifies that God does not bring judgment without full awareness of the situation (cf. 3:8–14; 19:21).

every inclination. This is a vivid portrayal of the depth and comprehensiveness of human depravity (see 8:21). The situation portends the end of history at the second coming of Christ (Luke 17:26–27; 18:8; 2 Tim. 3:1–5; Rev. 20:7–10, and Jewish apocalyptic literature).

heart. Moderns have no equivalent term for the Hebrew, which refers to the locus of thought, feeling, volition, and morality.[32]

6. grieved . . . pain. Note the word play with "comfort" and "painful toil" in 5:29. God and humans are pained by sin.[33] Noah brings comfort to both.

was grieved. The Hebrew here is also translated "changed his mind," a reference to a change of attitudes and actions. The unchanging God is always pained by sin. Moreover, because he is immutable, he will *always* change his plans to do good if people persist in their sin: "If it [a nation] does evil in my sight and does not obey me, then I will reconsider the good I had intended to do for it" (Jer. 18:10; see also Ex. 32:12, 14; 1 Sam. 15:11; 2 Sam. 24:16; Jer. 18:11; Amos 7:3, 6).[34] God's change of mind about the human race at the

---

[32]O. R. Brandon, "Heart," in *Evangelical Dictionary*, ed. W. Elwell (Grand Rapids: Baker, 1984), 498–99.

[33]God allows himself to be pained. To say God is impassable is not to suggest that God does not have emotions but that emotions do not rule Him. See J. I. Packer, "Theism for Our Time," in *God Who Is Rich in Mercy: Essays Presented to Dr. D. B. Knos*, ed. P. T. O'Brien and D. G. Peterson (Grand Rapids: Baker, 1986), 7–8; and D. A. Carson, *The Gagging of God: Christianity Confronts Pluralism* (Grand Rapids: Zondervan, 1996), 236–37.

[34]R. Pratt ("Historical Contingencies and Biblical Predictions," in *The Way of Wisdom: Essays in Honor of Bruce K. Waltke*, ed. By J. I. Packer and S. K. Soderlund [Grand Rapids: Zondervan, 2000], 180–203) convincingly analyzes prophetic prediction into three categories: (1) predictions qualified by conditions; (2) predictions qualified by assurances; and (3) predictions without qualification.

time of the Flood is entirely consistent with his unchanging character. God is not fickle; he does not change his mind (Num. 23:19; 1 Sam. 15:29), including his mind to reconsider. People can count on God always to reconsider his original intention to do good or evil according to the human response.

pain. The Hebrew here means "indignant rage." Christ's sacrifice will pacify God's bitter indignation against sin (see 8:21).

7. I will wipe . . . from the face of the earth. God's judgment upon the first cosmos, lasting from creation to the Flood, is a prophetic paradigm of the coming second judgment on the current second cosmos, lasting from the Flood to destruction by fire (see 2 Peter 3:5–7).

animals . . . air. As the ground must endure the consequences of its ruler's sin, so also must the animals (see 3:17).

8. found favor. This statement appears climactically at the end of the account of Adam's descendants. Noah represents a new beginning, an inversion that was anticipated in 5:29. Noah finds God's grace not in spite of sin but because of his righteousness (see 6:9). The narrator leaves it to the audience to realize that Noah's righteousness is not his own but a gift of God's grace, just as much as it was the gift of sovereign grace that put enmity against the Serpent in Eve's heart. God works in Noah as in all the saints both to will and to do according to his good pleasure (Phil. 2:13).

THEOLOGICAL REFLECTIONS ON BOOK 2 ————

God's Mercy, Justice, and Sovereignty

Saints and sinners were found among all of Adam's children, as well as in the messianic lineage. God raised up prophets, such as Enoch (see Jude 14–15) and Noah (see 2 Peter 2:5), who communed with God and preached to their generations. The world may understand God's forbearance as a lack of will, but in truth it is God's long-suffering grace. God's judgment and delay of 120 years (Gen. 6:3) demonstrates that while God gives people time to repent, still he will not clear the guilty (2 Peter 3:9). Ultimately, judgment will come. Yet the ten generations from Seth to the climactic figure Noah, matching the ten generations from Shem to Abraham (11:10–26), represent history not as a succession of meaningless generations but as human activity under the hand of God leading to climactic salvation in the fullness of time.

Image of God

The image of God subsists, independent of the Fall and the Flood (Gen. 5:2–4). Although sin will be ever present, each life is still valuable, made in the image of God. Saints and sinners, however, will express that image differently. The Cainites, ruling the earth in self-love, corrupted it. The Sethites, walking in love for God, preserved it. Nevertheless, both have value in God's sight as his image bearers and, when not guilty of taking innocent life, both must be protected (9:6).

Faith

The righteous life of Noah in the midst of a world terrorized by evil people (6:18) is a model of pious persistence and commitment. The truly righteous are willing to risk themselves in faith during great peril. In spite of crime, they reach out to the needy. In spite of giants, they do good and accept weakness as their posture. Of course, the righteous in themselves are unable to stop the rapid and progressive pervasiveness and hardening of sin, as in the line of Cain and in the human situation at the time of the Flood. Saints need the empowering of the Holy Spirit to reverse the tide.

Hope

As seen in the life of Enoch, "Where communion with God has been restored, there deliverance from death is bound to follow."[35]

---

[35]Vos, *Biblical Theology*, 47.

THE ACCOUNT OF NOAH AND HIS FAMILY (6:9 – 9:29)

THEME OF BOOK 3 ————————————————————

    Noah, who comes exactly midway in the genealogies between Adam and Abraham, is a pivotal figure in Genesis 1–11, and the account of Noah and his family, which comes in the middle of the books between the creation of Adam and the call of Abraham, records a pivotal event in that history. Whereas the narrator races through the millennia between Adam and Noah, and between Noah and Abraham, he slows the action to a standstill and devotes a full book to the six-hundredth year of Noah's life.

    In that year through a cataclysmic flood, God wipes out the seed of the Serpent, which had become utterly corrupt. By means of a divinely specified ark God spares the righteous seed of the woman via Noah and his family, and with them his creation in miniature. Noah and his family, having survived the punishing and purging Flood, emerge from the ark to a renewed earth that will last to the end of time as we know it. Tragically, however, Noah and his family again give birth to the seed of the Serpent, though they also perpetuate as the seed of the woman (see 8:21).

OUTLINE OF BOOK 3 ————————————————————

---

[1] A term borrowed from cinematography. Here it represents partial scenes.

LITERARY ANALYSIS OF BOOK 3 ——————————————

Plot

Frame 1 (6:9b–12) introduces the audience to the characters of Act 1, namely, the righteous Noah and his family (6:9b–10) versus the corrupt people of the corrupt earth in which he lives (6:11–12). This contrast sets up the two tensions of the act, presented in Frame 2 (6:13–22). The Lord resolves to destroy the corrupt people and earth by means of the Flood and to preserve in the ark the righteous and the creation they were created to rule. To do so the Lord must control the Flood, first unleashing it and then restraining it on schedule. The tension, between the Lord and the corrupt earth, peaks in Frame 5 (7:17–24). In this frame the Flood "triumphs" over even the highest mountains and wipes out all life. The pivot, Frame 6 (8:1a), forms the transition from one tension to the other. The second tension begins to subside in the denouement in Frame 9 (8:15–19). In this frame, Noah and the survivors disembark from the ark to the renewed earth. In the final denouement of the tenth frame (8:20–22), the Lord, who is pacified by

Noah's atoning sacrifice, resolves never again to destroy the earth and all its people, for humanity is incurably stained with original sin. Frames 11 (9:1–7) and 12 (9:8–17) elaborate upon that resolve.

More profoundly, however, there is a delicious tension between the covenant partners, the Lord and Noah. The issue is whether or not they can count on each other in the crisis. The very important theological word *covenant* (Hebrew *bᵉrît*) occurs for the first time in the Bible in 6:18. It signifies that the maker of a covenant obligates himself to keep self-imposed commitments either on condition of the favored recipient's continued faithfulness or as repayment (Josh. 9:11, 15–16).[2] The former arrangement is in view here in frames 1–9; the latter, in frames 10–12.

According to 6:18 God elects Noah for a covenant relationship before his six-hundredth year, the year of the Flood. The Lord obligates himself to preserve Noah throughout the imminent Flood. Noah, on his part, must build an ark to preserve life and enter it according to the Lord's directions.

Can God count on Noah? To be sure, God authors the covenant, but it cannot be effected without Noah's fidelity (see 7:1). If Noah does not build the ark and enter it, not only Noah and all life will perish, but so will God's purpose to rule the earth through Adam and his promise to crush the Serpent through the woman's seed. The future of salvation history rides on Noah's faithfulness.

On the other hand, can Noah count on God? God calls upon Noah to trust him to keep his threat to wipe out the earth and his promise to preserve him, his family, and the life of all that breathes. If the Lord does not send the threatened Flood, Noah will have wasted years of his life and of his three sons building the ark, and "Noah's folly" will become the laughingstock of history. And if God does not keep his promise to preserve Noah and his family through the Flood, their faithful service is in vain. The plot develops as the divine and human covenant partners commit themselves to one another.

It should now be clear that the character of the covenant partners drives the plot. The narrator feels no need to explicitly characterize God as just, merciful, and faithful to his word. God's actions speak for themselves as he both unleashes the Flood on time and spares Noah in time. It comes as no surprise that God remembers Noah at the pivot. The character of the human partner, however, is more up in the air as the story begins. Thus, the narrator explicitly and forcefully characterizes Noah in the very first words of the act, escalating his godly virtues from "righteous" to "blameless" to his highest accolade, "he walked with God" (6:9b). Then the narrator quotes the Lord himself: "I have found you righteous" (7:1). These terms do not refer to Noah's good works as such; they characterize the way true faith expresses

---

[2]E. Kutsch, "*bᵉrît*," *TLOT*, 1:259.

itself. The narrator reinforces his characterization by the refrain, "Noah did everything just as God/the LORD commanded him." These refrains occur in connection with the two critical actions of building the ark (6:22) and entering it (7:5). Noah also displays his faith-righteousness by his concern for the animals. He not only lives for a full year in his zoo-boat in the most hostile environment imaginable, but at the end he still tenderly retrieves the anxious dove that finds no resting place for its foot (8:9). Even after he sees the earth has dried out, he waits patiently almost another two months until the divine word that it is safe to disembark.

Structure

Act 1 features Noah as the righteous hero who saves humanity and the land animals; Act 2, as the drunken sinner who precipitates the threefold division of humanity into the curse-laden line of Canaan and the blessed line of Seth with Japheth finding salvation in Seth.

Act 1 can be analyzed broadly into two scenes. The first (6:9b–8:22) features God's covenant with Noah to preserve him as the bridge between the antediluvian and the postdiluvian worlds. The second features God's covenant with humanity never again to destroy the earth while the earth endures. The poem at the end of Scene 1 (8:22; cf. 1:26–28; 2:22b–23; 3:14–19; 4:23–24; 9:24–27), which celebrates God's preservation of a fruitful earth, is a janus between the two scenes, just as the poem at the end of Act 2 (9:24–27) is a janus to Book 4. Scene 1 of Act 1 can be analyzed according to its ten frames, and Scene 2 according to its two frames (See Exegetical Notes for specific literary analysis of frames).

The genealogical notice in 9:18–19, paralleling 6:10, functions as an introduction to Act 2 of this book.[3] Building upon the last three frames of Act 1 (8:20–22; 9:1–7, 8–17), Act 2 foreshadows and predicts the future course of history. After an editorial preface (9:18–19), the act unfolds in two scenes. Scene 1, in prose, represents intoxicated Noah, stripped naked in his tent and the response of his sons to it. Scene 2, in poetry, presents Noah's prophecy about their future based on how they had responded. Act 2 constitutes the transition to Book 4 (10:1–11:9); it lays the theological foundation for the classification of Noah's three sons in the following Table of Nations (ch. 10).

Intercalation

The genealogy of the antediluvian patriarchs, presented in 5:1–32, does not conclude until 9:28–29. The narrator inserts the account of Noah and his family (6:9–9:27) as a parenthesis within Book 2, and in this way he transforms Book 3 into an account principally about Noah, not his sons.

---

[3]K. A. Mathews, *Genesis 1–11:26* (NAC; Broadman & Holman, 1996), 349–50.

Patterns of Structure

Source critics hold up the account of Noah and his family as a model of the value of source criticism.[4] By noting the changes of the divine name (e.g., "God" [6:9–22] and "Lord" [7:1–5]) and the presence of doublets sometimes combined with alleged inconsistencies (e.g., a 40-day flood [7:17] versus a 150-day flood [8:3]), these critics divide the account into at least two sources. Since narrators in the ancient Near East commonly used sources to compose their work, perhaps some variations are due to the author's sources.[5] However, this approach to the text is wrongheaded: the alleged sources cannot exist independently; repetitions can be explained as due to Hebrew epic style; the alleged inconsistencies can be explained; and the narrator has total control over his sources not vice versa. The finished composition, a complete account, exhibits a masterful structure (see "Composition and Authorship" in the introduction), illustrated in at least four specific ways. First, Act 1 and the transitional introduction to Act 2 exhibits a chiastic (i.e., mirror image) pattern[6]:

A Transitional introduction: superscription 6:9a

    B Noah and his world at the time of the Flood 6:9b–12

        C Provision for the Flood with a divine monologue establishing God's covenant to preserve Noah, preceded by reflections on Noah and human behavior 6:13–22

            D Embarkation 7:1–5

                E Beginning of Flood: Noah and animals are main actors 7:6–16

                    F The triumphant Flood: 7:17–24

                        X God remembers Noah 8:1a

                    F' The waning Flood 8:1b–5

                E' Ending of Flood: Noah and birds are main actors 8:6–14

            D' Disembarkation 8:15–19

        C' Provision for the post-Flood world with a divine monologue to preserve the earth, with reflections on human behavior (8:20–22)

    B' Noah and the world conditions after the Flood 9:1–17

A' Transitional introduction 9:18–19

The chiastic arrangement helps form the bridge between the antediluvian and postdiluvian worlds. A and A' frame the act. B and B' show that human

---

[4]J. Skinner writes, "The resolution of the compound narrative into its constituent elements in this case is justly reckoned amongst the most brilliant achievements of purely literary criticism, and affords a particularly instructive lesson in the art of documentary analysis" (*A Critical and Exegetical Commentary on Genesis*, rev. ed. [ICC; Edinburgh: T. & T. Clark, 1930], 147).

[5]Tigay, "Evolution," 20–52; idem, "Conflation," 53–94; idem, "Stylistic Criterion," 149–74.

[6]The suggestion is based on B. W. Anderson, "From Analysis to Synthesis: The Interpretation of Genesis 1–11," *JBL* 97 (1978): 23–29; R. E. Longacre, "The Discourse Structure of the Flood Narrative," *JAAR* 47 Sup (1976): 89–133; and Wenham, *Genesis 1–15*, 157–58.

depravity continues after the Flood. However, whereas God terminates the corrupt antediluvian world, he covenants with all humanity never again to treat the earth with contempt as long as it endures. To achieve this end he institutes ordinances, especially capital punishment, "to make possible and safeguard this [new] programme of forbearance."[7] C and C' both contain a divine monologue to Noah, reflecting on the depravity of the human race (6:13; 8:21), making provisions to preserve Noah and his family in spite of original sin. However, C and C' contain differences. The situation in 6:13 (cf. 6:5, 11–12) refers to the historical culmination of humanity's progressive degradation that called for God's judgment, while 8:21 describes the natural state of the human heart apart from a historical hardening.[8] Moreover, whereas Noah's obedience in building the ark provided humanity's salvation through the Flood (6:22), his soothing sacrifice provides salvation after it (8:20–21). D and D' contain divine commands to Noah, first to enter the ark (7:1–4) and then to leave it (8:15–17). Both frames feature Noah's obedience (7:5; 8:18–19), revealing that Noah's faithfulness preserves life through the Flood. E and E', unlike the preceding pairs, are purely narration and feature Noah as a conservationist. In E the animals come to Noah and enter the ark to be spared. In E' he sends forth the birds to see if it is safe for the ark's inhabitants to disembark. Even after he knows the waters have receded, he waits another seven days to be sure. Wenham also notes, "This pair of scenes contains the long date formulae specifying the date of the flood's onset (7:6, 11) and its termination (8:13, 14) by reference to Noah's life."[9] They feature the number seven (7:4, 10; 8:10, 12). F and F' feature the Flood and the ark as the plot's agents. The Flood effects the devastation of God's creation and the ark its preservation. The Flood drama peaks in F, when the triumphant Flood covers the entire earth and snuffs out the breath of life except for the flickering flames within the ark; the preservation of life climaxes in F', when the inhabitants of the ark step out on to dry, arable ground. Literary critics refer to the pivot (X) as the "peripateia," the sudden reverse of circumstances in the drama. When God remembers Noah, the frames of Act 1 begin to mirror one another.

Second, not only does Act 1 as a whole exhibit a chiastic pattern; the number of days in Scene 1 betray a concentric pattern (Wenham):[10]

> 7 days of waiting for the Flood (7:4)
>> 7 days of waiting for the Flood (7:10)[11]
>>> 40 days of flooding (7:17a)
>>>> 150 days of water triumphing (7:24)

---

[7]Vos, *Biblical Theology*, 52.
[8]Ibid.
[9]Wenham, *Genesis 1–15*, 158.
[10]Ibid., 157.
[11]The first mention of the seven days of waiting for the Flood refers to the divine word; the second, to its fulfillment.

150 days of water waning (8:3)[12]
40 days of waiting (8:6)
7 days of waiting (8:10)
7 days of waiting (8:12)

Third, the janus framing of Scene 1 (8:20–22) and Scene 2 (9:1–17) is chiastic:

A God's resolve never again to destroy the earth or humanity 8:20–22[13]
  B Command to be fruitful 9:1
    C Legislation with regard to blood 9:2–6
  B' Command to be fruitful 9:7
A' God's covenant and sign never again to destroy all flesh 9:8–17

Finally, Acts 1 and 2 reveal an alternating pattern:

A Genealogical introduction 6:9–10
  B Setting 6:11
    C Narrative 6:12–8:21
      D Poem 8:22
        E Epilogue 9:1–17
A Genealogical introduction 9:18–19
  B Setting 9:20
    C Narrative 9:20–24
      D Poem 9:25–27
        E Epilogue 9:28–29

Comparison and Contrast

The narrator underscores his theme of the Flood as re-creation by selecting remarkable parallels between Adam and Noah, between God's creative and re-creative acts, and perhaps between time markers for the days.

Parallels between Adam and the Original Creation and Noah and the Re-creation[14]

The Flood defaces the original creation headed by Adam and cleanses the earth for its re-creation headed by Noah. Warren Gage[15] notes striking parallels between the prediluvian and postdiluvian worlds, making Adam the father of all humanity and Noah its father in the postdiluvian world. (1) Both "worlds" are created out of a watery chaos in closely parallel acts (see phases

---

[12]The 150 days from the beginning of the Flood to the grounding of the ark are viewed from two perspectives.
[13]This janus section can be reckoned a part of Scene 1 or of Scene 2.
[14]See "Structure and Content" in the introduction.
[15]W. Gage, *The Gospel of Genesis: Studies in Protology and Eschatology* (Winona Lake, Ind.: Carpenter, 1984), 9–15, here modified slightly and supplemented with the insights of Mathews, *Genesis 1–11:26*, 351.

of re-creation below). (2) Both Adam and Noah are uniquely associated with the "image of God,"[16] "in the Adam narrative as the basis of man's identity and in the Noah narrative as the basis of man's protection"[17] (Gen. 1:27; 5:1–3). (3) Both "walk with God" (3:8; 6:9). (4) Both rule the animals: Adam by naming (2:19), Noah by preserving (7:15). (5) God repeats almost verbatim his commission to be fruitful, to multiply, and to rule the earth (1:28–30; 9:1–7).[18] (6) Both work the "ground" (cf. 3:17–19; 9:20). (7) Both follow a similar pattern of sinning, the former by eating and the latter by drinking (3:6; 9:21). (8) The immediate result of their sin is shameful nakedness (3:7; 9:21), connected with "knowing"[19] (3:5; 9:24) and being clothed by another (3:21; 9:23). (9) Both have three named sons (4:1–2, 25; 6:10). (10) As a remote result from Adam's sin, judgment falls on all; from Noah's, a curse on Canaan. (11) Among their three sons is judgment and hope, division into elect and nonelect. The conflict between the seed of the Serpent (i.e., the curse-laden Cainites) and the seed of the woman (i.e., the Yahweh-worshiping Sethites), is now carried on between the cursed seed of Canaan and the seed of Shem, whose God is the LORD.[20] In addition, in both halves of the Prehistory (books 1–3 and 4–6), human disobedience impinges on the heavenly sphere and God responds using the first-person plural ("like one of us"; "let us"; 3:22; 11:7), and alienation is part of his judicial sentence (from the Garden of Eden and from Shinar; 3:24; 11:9; cf. 4:12).

Seven Progressive Phases of Creation and Re-creation

Seven progressive phases of renewing creation parallel the progression of creation during the first week.[21]

Phase 1: precreation. Just as God's Spirit hovered over the abyss (1:2), God sends a wind over the engulfing waters to renew the earth.

1:2	"earth," "deep," "Spirit" (*rûaḥ*), "waters"
8:1b–2	"wind" (*rûaḥ*), "earth," "waters," "deep"[22]

Phase 2: second day. Just as God initially divided the waters (1:6–7), God regathers the waters, reestablishing the boundaries between sky and earth.

1:6–8	"waters," "sky"
8:2b	"sky"

---

[16]The precise expression is found in only Gen. 1:26–28; 5:3; and 9:6.

[17]Gage, *Gospel*, 11.

[18]The narrator subtly links the two by uniquely referring to Noah as a man of the "soil" (lit. "ground" *ᵃdāmâ*, 9:20) , a deliberate echo of 2:7: "the LORD God formed the man from . . . the ground [*ᵃdāmâ*]."

[19]"Found out" (NIV) renders the Hebrew verb "to know."

[20]Subsequently, just as the Cainites from Adam sought their security in cities, the Canaanites from Ham son of Noah will seek theirs in a tower. The elect from Seth called on "the name of the LORD" (4:25), as will Abraham (12:8; Heb. 11).

[21]Mathews outlines the word comparisons of this chart (*Genesis 1–11:26*, 383).

[22]There is no need for re-creation of light after the Flood (cf. the creation of the first day, 1:3–6).

Phase 3: third day. Just as God separated the dry, arable ground from the water to sustain vegetation, so again, the dry ground emerges in successive stages.

| 1:9[23] | "water," "dry ground," "appear" |
| 8:3–5 | "water," "tops of the mountains," "appear"[24] |

Phase 4: fifth day. The sky once again houses the winged creatures, as God first proclaimed it so to be.

| 1:20–23[25] | "birds," "above [*al*] the ground [NIV, 'earth']" |
| 8:6–12 | "raven," "dove," "from [*mēʿal*] . . . the ground" |

Phase 5: sixth day. The living creatures of sky and land are called out from the ark, as in their first creative calling from the voice of God.

| 1:24–25 | "creatures," "livestock," "creatures that move along the ground," "wild animals" |
| 8:17–19 | "creature," "birds," "animals," "creatures that move along the ground" |

Phase 6. The reappearance of the nuclear family, all of whom bear God's image, as the heads and sole representatives of the human race functions as a reprise of the creation of *ʾāḏām,* male and female in God's image.

1:26–28	"man," "image of God," "male and female"
8:16, 18	Noah and his wife
9:6	"man," "image of God"

Phase 7. The heavenly King graciously grants his blessing on humanity, feeds them with the fruit of the restored earth, and, renewing the cultural mandate, restores them as lords over the creation.

| 1:28 | "blessed," "be fruitful," "increase in number," "fill the earth," "rule . . . every living creature" |
| 9:1–2[26] | "blessed," "be fruitful," "increase in number," "fill the earth," "fear . . . of you . . . upon every creature" |

Markers of Days in Creation Account and in Flood Account

Using Jaubert's hypothesis that this account's unusually precise chronology is informed by the 364-day calendar used in *Jubilees,* Wenham dates

---

[23]There is no need to renew vegetation (1:11–13), as seen by "freshly plucked olive leaf" (8:11).

[24]NIV, "became visible." Also, there is no need after the Flood to re-create the luminaries, which were originally created on the fourth day (1:14–19). Kline (*Kingdom Prologue,* 139) suggests as a possibility that the removal of the ark's canopy resulting in the uncovering of the canopy of the heavens corresponds to the creation of the luminaries. He regards the ark as a symbolic representation of the cosmos in miniature.

[25]There is no need for renewing fish.

[26]See also 8:17.

the ten events as follows (asterisks indicate the date is not given but computed):[27]

1.	Announcement of the Flood	(7:4) *10.2.600	Sunday
2.	Flood begins	(7:11) 17.2.600	Sunday
3.	Flood lasts forty days and ends	(7:12) *27.3.600	Friday
4.	Waters triumph	(8:4) 17.7.600	Friday
5.	Mountain tops appear	(8:5) 1.10.600	Wednesday
6.	Raven sent out	(8:6–7) *10.11.600	Sunday
7.	Dove's second flight	(8:10) *24.11.600	Sunday
8.	Dove's third flight	(8:12) *1.12.600	Sunday
9.	Waters dry up	(8:13) 1.1.601	Wednesday
10.	Noah leaves ark	(8:14–18) 27.2.601	Wednesday

Remarkably, the Flood begins to "corrupt" the creation on a Sunday, the day creation began, and ends its work triumphantly on Friday, the day creation was finished. However, just as striking from this hypothesis, the acts of re-creation occur on Sunday and Wednesday, the days that began the two triads in the first week of creation.

Parallels between Noah and Lot

The New Testament links the destruction of the wicked city of Sodom with the judgment of the Flood (Luke 17:26–30; 2 Peter 2:5–8). In that connection, Noah's deliverance from the Flood foreshadows Lot's deliverance from Sodom.[28] Whereas the parallels with the first creation underscore that Noah is the reprise of Adam in the postdiluvian world, the following parallels with Lot and Sodom uncover the fingerprint of God in judging sinners and saving his saints: (1) the judgment is due in part to sexual impropriety (6:1–4; 19:1–11); (2) God remembers the elect (8:1; 19:29); (3) divine warnings precede the judgment (6:13–22; 19:15–22); (4) the Lord brings the elect to a place of safety and shuts the door (7:16; 19:10); (5) the Lord "rains" (*māṭar*) down judgment (7:4; 19:24); (6) the wicked are destroyed (*šāḥat*) (6:17; 19:13); (7) Lot, like Noah, finds grace in God's eyes (6:8; 19:19); (8) one family alone escapes (7:21–23; 19:15, 25–29); (9) the survivor becomes drunk, which results in family sin (9:22–23; 19:30–38).

Key Words and Refrain

Key words and phrases in this account include "water" and "floodwater" (*mabbûl*, cf. 7:6, 17; 9:11, 15), "ark" (*tēbâ*, see 6:14), "life/to keep alive" (*ḥāyâ*, 6:17, 19, 20; 7:3, 11, 14, 15, 22; 8:21; 9:3, 5, 10, 12, 15, 16), "you and

---

[27]Wenham, *Genesis 1–15*, 100.
[28]W. M. Clark, "The Flood and the Structure of the Pre-patriarchal History," *ZAW* 83 (1971): 184–211, esp. 194–95; I. M. Kikawada, "Noah and the Ark," *ABD* 4:1129–30.

your sons and your wife and your sons' wives with you" (6:18; 8:16, 18; cf. 7:1, 13), and the Hebrew root *nwḥ* (*nōaḥ*, Noah [6:9 passim]; *nûaḥ*, "to rest" [8:4]; *mānôaḥ*, "resting place" [8:9]; *nîḥōaḥ*, "soothing/pleasing" [8:21]). A key refrain is, "and Noah did all that the LORD commanded him" and its equivalent, "just as God commanded him" (6:22; 7:5; cf. 7:9, 16; see Exegetical Notes and Theological Reflections).

Inclusio

The inclusio of Act 1, "I will/now establish my covenant with you" (6:18: *waháqīmōṯî ʾet-bᵉrîṯî ʾittāk;* 9:9: *waʾᵃnî hinnî mēqîm ʾet-bᵉrîṯî ʾittᵉkem*), theologically undergirds the first act and marks the advance in salvation history. The shift from a singular "you" (*ʾittāk*) in 6:18 to a plural "you" (*ʾittᵉkem*) in 9:9 marks the significant advance from God's covenant with Noah to preserve him through the Flood to his covenant with humanity to preserve the earth.

Blanks and Gaps

The narrator blanks as unessential to his narrative descriptions of the shape of the ark and of how Noah and his family managed to bring a year-long food supply for so many animals or disposed of the manure as they rode out the heaving storm.[29] He also blanks how God spoke to Noah (6:13) and how Noah distinguished between clean and unclean animals (7:8).

The narrator, however, intentionally and meaningfully gaps the preservation of antediluvian arts and sciences on the ark. The narrator implies that Noah carried on the ark either in artifacts or in memory the skills of the ancient culture because he says that Cain's descendants *are* the "fathers" (i.e., founders of professions) of all those who are sheep-breeders, musicians, and smiths (4:22). This gap contrasts sharply with the parallel Babylonian account. That flood hero reports: "What I had of silver I laded upon her; whatever I had of gold I laded upon her. . . . All my family and kin I made go aboard the ship. The beasts of the field, the wild creatures of the field, *all the craftsmen I made go aboard.*"[30] The biblical narrator probably gapped this information because, although ideally the arts and sciences are rooted in the cultural mandate (see 1:26), in fact they were developed out of human hubris and associated with those opposed to salvation history. However, God redemptively works out his cultural mandate in the progress of holy history through such people as Noah, who built the saving ark, and as Bezalel (Ex. 36:1) and Huram (1 Kings 7:14), who built the tabernacle and the temple, respectively, to God's glory.

---

[29]Morris and Whitcomb suggest the animals went into hibernation (H. M. Morris and J. C. Whitcomb, *The Genesis Flood: The Biblical Record and Its Scientific Implications* [Philadelphia: Presbyterian & Reformed, 1961], 70).

[30]*ANET,* 94, lines 81–86, italics mine.

Historicity

Eliade notes,

> As has been well known since the compilations made by R. Andree, H. Usener, and J. G. Frazer, the deluge myth is almost universally disseminated; it is documented in all the continents (though very rarely in Africa) and on various cultural levels. A certain number of variants seem to be the result of dissemination from Mesopotamia and then from India. It is equally possible that one or several diluvial catastrophes gave rise to fabulous narratives. But it would be risky to explain so widespread a myth by phenomena of which no geological traces have been found. The majority of the Flood myths seem in some sense to form part of the cosmic rhythm: the old world, peopled by a fallen humanity, is submerged under the waters, and some time later a new world emerges from the aquatic "chaos." In a large number of variants, the Flood is the result of the sins (or ritual faults) of human beings; sometimes it results simply from the wish of a divine being to put an end to mankind.[31]

To be sure, stories of a great flood are found all over the world. For example, Deucalion, son of Prometheus, and the only survivor of the flood brought on by Zeus, offers him a sacrifice like the one at Medone, and it is accepted. In that account the gods are also present, and they feed on the sacrifices[32] or on the smoke that rises from the burning fat.[33]

However, no deluge accounts are so strikingly similar to the Noah account as those of ancient Mesopotamia. The three parallels most striking are: (1) the Sumerian account with the hero Ziusdra, (2) the Old Akkadian account with the hero Atrahasis, and (3) the Old Babylonian account contained in the Gilgamesh Epic, Tablet 11, with the hero Utnapishtim. Although these accounts share many similarities with the biblical account, the biblical account stands apart in significant ways. In the Mesopotamian stories the petty gods bring the flood to control overpopulation and/or to get rid of the annoying noise of people. Once the flood comes, they are frightened by it, and afterward they hungrily gather around the sacrifice. In contrast, God sovereignly brings the Flood because of human wickedness, and in response to Noah's sacrifices, he pledges never again to destroy the earth. Whereas in the Atrahasis Epic the problem redressed by the flood is overpopulation, in Genesis life is an unqualified good (for other specific comparisons, see Exegetical Notes below).[34]

---

[31]M. Eliade, *A History of Religious Ideas*, trans. W. R. Trask (Chicago: Univ. of Chicago Press, 1985), 62.

[32]*Iliad* 1.423–24; 8.548–52.

[33]*Iliad* 1.66–67.

[34]For detailed arguments pro and con with respect to the universality of the flood, see S. A. Austin and D. C. Boardman, *The Genesis Debate*, ed. R. Youngblood (Grand Rapids: Baker, 1991), 210–29. Youngblood and many other evangelicals favor a local flood (Youngblood, *Genesis*, 105–15), but the

EXEGETICAL NOTES TO BOOK 3 ─────────────────

Superscription (6:9a)

9. the account [*tôledōt*] **of Noah.** The Hebrew literally reads, "the descendants of Noah." This account is about Noah in Act 1 and his children in Act 2 (see "Literary Analysis: Intercalation," above).

Act 1: Noah and the Flood:
The Preservation of Life (6:9b – 9:17)

Scene 1: The Flood (6:9b – 8:22)

Frame 1: Noah and His World at the Time of the Flood (6:9b – 12)

In this diptych of two verses each, the narrator paints Noah as pure white (6:9b–10) and his world as pitch black (6:11–12). Noah serves the community as a model of piety in a hostile world. The contrast hearkens back to the seed of the woman versus the seed of the Serpent.

9b. righteous. This is the first time *righteous* and *blameless* are used in the Bible. Righteousness combines piety and ethics. Olley explains, "There is dynamic concern to bring about right and harmony for all [in physical and spiritual realms]. . . . It finds its basis in God's (or the gods') rule of the world."[35] To serve the interest of the creation (see Gen. 8:9; 12:10), their neighbors (cf. Ezek. 18:5–9), and their King, the righteous are willing to disadvantage themselves to advantage others. The standards for what is right are revealed in natural moral law (i.e., conscience [Gen. 3:10]) and in special revelation.

blameless. This literally means "whole, complete," signifying wholehearted commitment and wholeness of relationship.[36] The pairing of "blameless" and "righteous" suggests that Noah is wholly committed to righteousness (cf. Deut. 32:4; Ps. 18:30; 19:7–8), "giving his contemporaries no excuse to criticize his conduct."[37] *Blameless* denotes to abstain from sin, not to be without sin. David, though an adulterer and a murder, can still claim "I have been blameless before him" (2 Sam. 22:24).

walked with God. This phrase links Noah with Enoch in the godly line of Seth (5:24). Enoch is saved from death, Noah from the Flood.

─────────────────────────────

narrator, even allowing for oriental hyperbole, seems to have in mind a universal flood. The geological arguments favoring a local flood assume that the history of the earth's geology is uniform, but the text represents a geological cataclysm and the re-creation of the earth. I am not competent to judge whether the scientific data favors or disallows a universal flood (see Morris and Whitcomb, *Genesis Flood*; F. A. Filby, *The Flood Reconsidered: A Review of the Evidences of Geology, Archaeology, Ancient Literature and the Bible* [London: Pickering, 1970]; versus D. A. Young. *Creation and the Flood: An Alternative to Creation and Theistic Evolution* [Grand Rapids: Baker, 1977]). The evidence of "arkeology" (the sightings of the ark on Mount Ararat) is not compelling.

[35]J. W. Olley, "'Righteous' and Wealthy? The Description of the *Ṣaddiq* in Wisdom Literature," *Australian and New Zealand Theological Review: Colloquium* 22 (May 1990): 38.

[36]von Rad, *Genesis*, 193.

[37]Youngblood, *Genesis*, 89.

10. Noah had three sons. The genealogical notice serves several functions: (1) to introduce Acts 1 and 2 (see 9:18–19), (2) to link Noah with Adam and his three sons, (3) to present Noah as head of the nuclear family, and (4) to foreshadow the destiny of Noah and his three sons as the common ancestors of humanity.

11. was corrupt [*šāḥat*]. This could be translated, "had become corrupt." The expression, which occurs seven times in the narrative, signifies "to spoil or disfigure." Generally it describes a wide number of matters: spring (Prov. 25:26), belt (Jer. 13:7), city (Gen. 18:28), nation (Jer. 4:7), and earth. Here the parallel "violence" shows that moral behavior and its consequences are in view.

violence [*ḥāmās*]. Haag defines *ḥāmās* as "the cold-blooded and unscrupulous infringement of the personal right of others, motivated by greed and hate and often making use of physical violence and brutality."[38] He adds, "a favorite instrument of [*ḥāmās*] is false accusation and unjust judgment."[39] Mathews comments, "Whereas God has blessed the human family with the power of procreation to fill the earth (1:28; 9:1), these culprits have 'filled the earth' by procreating 'violence' (cf. v. 13; Ezek. 8:17; 28:16)."[40]

12. God saw. This statement implies investigation of the facts and readiness to action (see 6:5).

all the people. Elsewhere in the narrative the phrase (lit., "all flesh") consistently refers to the animals as well as people (6:19; 7:16; 8:17; 9:11, 15–17), making the NIV's unique use unlikely. Animals too, like the goring bull, transgress the hierarchy of being (God-humanity-animals-plants), and whoever does so, intentionally or unintentionally, is liable to capital punishment (Gen. 9:6; Ex. 21:28).[41] The narrator links human morality with the state of the animal and natural worlds (see Gen. 3:17–19; Rom. 8:20–21). The connection can be suggested by concrete illustrations: matadors enrage bulls, cruel children infuriate dogs, and wicked people excite cock-fights. However, something more profound than these illustrative analogies is in view. Both people and animals have transgressed the parameters of their order and the hierarchy ordained by God.[42] As Dumbrell states, "This is a picture of the total rupture of created relationships on the part of the creature."[43] "Flesh" underscores their mortality. The new divine provision for the postdiluvian world to put the fear of people in animals (9:2) and to give them over as food (9:3) implies that here animals have also transgressed their boundaries.

---

[38]Haag, "*ḥāmās*," *TDOT*, 4:482.
[39]Ibid., 483.
[40]Mathews, *Genesis 1–11:26*, 359.
[41]See D. Patrick, "Studying Biblical Law as Humanities," *Semeia* 45 (1989): 27–47.
[42]D. J. A. Clines, "Noah's Flood: I: The Theology of the Flood Narrative," *Faith and Thought* 100 (1972–1973): 133–34.
[43]W. J. Dumbrell, *Covenant and Creation* (Exeter: Paternoster, 1984), 14.

Frame 2: Provision for the Flood with a Divine Monologue Affirming God's Covenant with Noah, Preceded by Reflections on Noah and Human Behavior (6:13 – 22)

13. God said. In contrast to the gods of the Babylonian flood account, who keep their decisions secret from any person so that all will be killed,[44] God takes Noah into his confidence (Gen. 18:17; 2 Chron. 20:7; Ps. 25:14; Isa. 41:8; Amos 3:7; John 15:15; James 2:23). The text blanks how this communication occurs. Is it in a theophany? Whatever it might be, Noah's experience is not unlike that of Christians who hear the word of God unmistakably in Scripture and are willing to risk their lives on it. God is always present in word and rarely in sight. The people of God are the people of the ear, not of the eye.

destroy [šāḥat]. This is the same word translated "corrupt" in 6:12. With poetic justice, just as the people have corrupted the earth, so God will disfigure the earth so it can no longer feed them. Sarna notes, "The idea is that humankind cannot undermine the moral basis of society without endangering the very existence of its civilization. In fact, through its corruption, society sets in motion the process of inevitable self-destruction."[45]

14. make yourself. The Lord specifies the construction of the ark, just as he specified the construction of his tabernacle. He does not entrust the means of salvation to human imagination.

ark. This key word is used seven times in the instructions to build the ark and seven times in the report of the subsiding of the waters (8:1–14), and only once again in Scripture: in the salvation of baby Moses (Ex. 2:3–5).[46] The narrator does not mention a rudder or navigational aids, suggesting that the fate of the ark depends solely on the will of God. By contrast, the hero of a Mesopotamian parallel employs a boatsman to navigate.[47]

cypress wood [gōper]. The Hebrew word is an unknown species of a tree. The NIV opts for "cypress" because of the similar consonants with the Hebrew (c/g-p-r) and because the ancients used it in their shipbuilding due to its resistance to rot.

rooms. The Hebrew literally means "nests."

15. 450 feet long, 75 feet wide and 45 feet high [135 m long, 22 m broad, and 13 m deep]. The narrator blanks its exact shape, but its length (half again as long as a football field) and its dimensions, like those of modern ships, give it the necessary capacity for its cargo and make it seaworthy. The massive size of this handmade wooden craft staggers the imagination, and its

---

[44]*ANET*, 95, lines 170–87.

[45]Sarna, *Genesis*, 51.

[46]"If Moses was indeed the author of Genesis and Exodus, these striking similarities between the story of his own deliverance and that of Noah must have impressed him deeply" (Youngblood, *Genesis*, 89).

[47]*ANET*, 94, line 944.

seaworthy proportions incite admiration. The ship in the parallel Babylonian epic was an unstable 180-foot cube and about four times larger in tonnage than Noah's ark.[48]

17. floodwaters [*mabbûl*]. The Hebrew is a technical term for the "celestial sea" associated with the Deluge[49] and "indicates the unparalleled cataclysmic nature of the event."[50] The Flood both punishes and purges the world. In the Babylonian tradition, the flood got out of control and the frightened gods "cowered like dogs."[51] God, however, sovereignly rules over it (Ps. 29:10).

all life under the heavens. A worldwide flood may be indicated (see 7:19–23; 8:21; 9:11, 15; 2 Peter 3:5–7); however, such comprehensive language can be used for limited situations (see Gen. 41:56–57; Deut. 2:25; 1 Kings 4:34; 10:24; 2 Chron. 36:23; Dan. 2:38; 4:22; 5:19; Luke 2:1).

breath [*rûaḥ*]. This is the same Hebrew word as that for Spirit in 6:3 (see 1:2, note).

18. establish. The term "he established/confirmed" (*qûm*), rather than "made" (*kārat*), signifies the confirmation of preexisting terms, whether a promise (Num. 23:19), vow (Num. 30:14), oath (Gen. 26:3), covenant (Gen. 17:7, 19, 21; 2 Kings 23:3), or the like. A covenant solemnizes and confirms a social relationship already in existence. The audience knows from 6:8 that Noah enjoys God's favor prior to this confirming covenant. In all likelihood, God chose Noah to be his covenant partner at his birth when Noah's father probably in faith and hope named him as the one to bring comfort to humanity's hard labor (5:29).[52] We can infer that the Lord obliged himself to bless and prosper his favored and chosen servant. However, in Noah's six-hundredth year, God more specifically obligates himself to preserve him through the imminent Flood.

my. This personal pronoun underscores that God is the author of the covenant. He sets the grant and provides its sanctions.

covenant [*bᵉrît*]. The important theological word *covenant* occurs for the first time in the Bible in 6:18 (see "Literary Analysis: Plot," above).

with you. God's covenant is with Noah. His grant is worked out through Noah's building of the ark (6:14–16) and his provisioning and entering it (6:19–21).

your sons and your wife and your sons' wives with you. This key expression (7:7, 13; 8:16, 18; cf. 7:1) emphasizes that God preserves humanity in its basic family structure. His salvation extends to the children. The

---

[48]*ANET*, 93, lines 57, 58.
[49]*HALOT*, 541.
[50]Sarna, *Genesis*, 53.
[51]*ANET*, 94, lines 105–23, esp. 115.
[52]The pseudepigraphal book of *1 Enoch* says that at birth Noah "opened his eyes and made the whole house bright" and "opened his mouth and blessed the LORD of Heaven" (*1 En.* 106:2,11; cited by Mathews, *Genesis 1–11:26*, 356 n. 12).

Babylonian parallel adds to the passenger list other relatives, artisans, and the boatsman.[53]

20. of every kind. This is an unmistakable echo of Gen. 1:20–23. The language of 6:19–21 indicates the continuity of all kinds of animals through the Flood.

will come to you. God's power can be discerned in the instinctual coming of the animals to Noah (see 7:8–9).

21. food. The vegetable kingdom continues to serve its lords within the ark (cf. 1:26, 29–30). In spite of the Flood, the "freshly plucked olive leaf" from the renewed earth before Noah disembarks shows that vegetation survives outside the ark (see 8:11).

22. Noah did. These few words underscore that Noah lived by faith (Heb. 11:7) but blank the tremendous effort and investment involved. It must have taken Noah years of work to cut down the multitude of needed trees, convey them to his building site, and fit and join the huge planks. Moreover, he must have spent a fortune to build a boat of such a prodigious size and to provision it with a sufficient and varied food supply for so many animals.[54] The Mesopotamian stories focus on the flood hero's actions;[55] Genesis, on God's activity and Noah's obedience.

Frame 3: Embarkation (7:1 – 5)

1. you righteous. The "you" is singular, but it cannot be inferred that the seven other family members are not righteous. According to Ezekiel (14:20; 18:20), Noah's righteousness cannot save his family. Rather, God holds each family member responsible. To be sure, Ham will act vilely after the Flood, but Noah also sins. God saves Ham through the Flood and then blesses him. Noah's curse is on his grandson, Canaan, son of Ham.

I have found. The Hebrew literally reads, "I have seen," forming a striking contrast with 6:5, 12.

righteous. The narrator's characterization of Noah (6:9) is affirmed by the Lord. Noah's righteousness is not a work to gain merit with God but the outcome of his faith in God, as seen in his building and provisioning the ark in the preceding frames.

generation. Noah's righteousness in his generation saves his righteous family and the living creatures; his sacrifice after the Flood provides salvation to future generations (see 8:21).

2. Take with you. . . . These directives clarify, not contradict, those of 6:19–20.

seven. In typical Semitic style, the summary injunction to take pairs of animals into the ark is now developed by the more specific injunction to

---

[53]*ANET*, 94, lines 84–85, 94.
[54]See Calvin, *Genesis*, 260–61.
[55]*ANET*, 93–94, lines 53–86, 131–37.

take seven pairs of clean animals. To make the capacity of the ark more capable of saving every kind of land animal and bird, Whitcomb and Morris argue that the Hebrew means seven of each clean species, not fourteen, and that the supernumerary animal is the one Noah offers after the flood.[56] However, the next phrase "male and its female" (see also 7:3) calls their interpretation into question.

clean [*ṭāhôr*]. The Hebrew means "pure" (i.e., "pure-formed"). This is the first occurrence of the root (see Lev. 11 and Deut. 14:3–12). The earth's future depends on these typical, sacrificial animals. Noah may have known of the distinction between pure and impure through his walks with God. The fundamental institutions of the "ceremonial law," Sabbath (see 2:1–3) and sacrifice (3:21; 4:3–5), reach back to the original creation, unlike some other patriarchal religious and social practices (see "Historicity and Literary Genre" in the introduction).

3. male and female. This specification anticipates the command to be fruitful and to increase in number and so replenish the earth (8:17; 9:1).

bird. The Samaritan Pentateuch and Septuagint add "clean bird," but the raven is unclean (see 8:7, 20; Lev. 11:15).

4. seven days. Seven days are needed for the animal occupants to board the ark and to be accommodated.[57] Noah and his family, however, enter the ark the day the Flood begins (7:13).

forty days and forty nights. Forty is a conventional number for a long time and represents the introduction of a new age.[58]

5. commanded. This word identifies a key refrain (see 6:22).

Frame 4: Beginning of Flood: Noah and Animals Are Main Actors (7:6 – 16)

The increasing detail of this frame signifies the escalating tension. The narrator first represents the essential facts of the frame (7:6–10): the date of Noah's six-hundredth year, the broad classification of the ark's occupants, and the seven-day time span prior to the Flood. The frame of this historic moment continues with greater detail and flourish (7:11–16). The precise date is the seventeenth day of the second month of Noah's six-hundredth year (7:11), the rain begins and lasts forty days (7:12), and on the very day that the Flood begins, Noah and his wife as grand marshals, followed by

---

[56]Morris and Whitcomb, *Genesis Flood*, 65. In part they base their argument on Koenig's *Syntax*, 85, 316b and Gesenius' *Grammatik*, rev. by Kautzsch, 134g).

[57]A hundred and twenty years were needed to build the ark and one week to fill it. The Gilgamesh Epic seems to imagine seven days to build a ship much bigger than Noah's and a flood lasting seven days (*ANET*, 94, lines 127–31).

[58]Isaac and Esau marry their wives at forty years of age (25:20; 26:34); Moses is on the mountain forty days (Ex. 24:18); Israel's spies are in the land forty days, and upon their unbelief God sentences them to forty years of wilderness experience before bringing Israel into the land; Elijah takes forty days and nights to return to Mount Sinai (1 Kings 19:8); and the resurrected Christ appears to his disciples for forty days before his ascension (Acts 1:3).

their sons and their wives, enter the ark. As the animals parade two by two into the ark—which, in fact, happens during the preceding week—the narrator calls off with greater specificity the names of the embarkees. He draws this frame to the climactic conclusion: "Then the LORD shut him in" (7:16b).

8. animals . . . came to Noah. Reminiscent of when God brings the animals to Adam to name them (2:19), God now brings them to Noah to preserve them.

11. seventeenth day of the second month.[59] Precise dates, which are unique in Genesis and elsewhere usually reserved for kings, invest the story with importance and historical credibility (see above, "Markers of Days in Creation Account and in Flood Account").

springs . . . floodgates.[60] The narrator offers a poetic expression for the unrestrained release of water (see Ps. 78; Isa. 24:18; Mal. 3:10). The earth is being returned to its precreation chaos by the release of the previously bounded waters above and by the upsurge of the subterranean waters (see 1:2, 6–9; 8:2). Mathews notes, "The prophets also appeal to the imagery of creation's reversal to depict the day of the Lord's judgment (e.g., Isa. 24:18b; Jer. 4:23–26; Am. 7:4)."[61] The brief and powerful description contrasts with the elaborate details given in the Babylonian parallel. God is proving himself trustworthy to the one who trusts his word.

12. forty days and forty nights. This defines the period that the deluge fell, whereas 150 days (see 7:24) defines the period that the deluge is on the earth. One hundred and ten days after the rain stops falling from the celestial sea, the earth is completely dry.

13. On that very day. This phrase connotes a memorable occasion (see 17:23, 26; Ex. 12:41, 51; Deut. 32:48).

15. breath [*rûaḥ*]. This is also translated "spirit" (see 6:17 and note).

16. the LORD shut. God's action marks the climactic conclusion of this frame. In the Mesopotamian parallels, the heroes shut the hatch themselves. Noah's salvation is due to divine grace. God's act signals the divine protection that keeps the raging flood from capsizing the vessel. God's works of grace are both sovereign and particular.

Frame 5: The Triumphant Flood (7:17–24)

Both the historical Flood itself and its narrative representation peak in this frame. The summary statement of 7:23—the hostile Flood prevails, leaving only Noah and those with him in the ark—states the theme of this melancholy frame. The key words "rose" (*gāḇar*) and "all/every" (*kol*) capture the

---

[59]Israel had two calendars: one began in the fall, the other in the spring. It is uncertain which one is being used for this account.

[60]The NIV renders freely Hebrew *ʾarubbâ*, "hole." It is used of a hole in a wall, once for a chimney (Hos. 13:3), and once for where doves fly (Isa. 60:8). Here it refers to the holes in the heavens through which rain pours down.

[61]Mathews, *Genesis 1–11:26*, 376.

total devastation inflicted by the Flood. The narrative covering the forty awe-some days comes to a complete standstill to depict the eerie, now silent dev-astation, with only the tiny ark riding its waves. Everything God has threatened and promised in Frame 2 is now fulfilled.

18. rose [gāḇar]. This key word expresses "triumph [in battle]" (in NIV "rose" [7:18, 19, 20] and "flooded" [7:24]). The terrible, chaotic waters, which originally covered the earth, are implicitly likened to hostile warriors attacking and undoing God's creation. The rhythmic repetition of this term with the crescendo of the waters and the repetition of "every living thing" mimics the rising of the waters and the pitching of the ark.

19. all/every [kol]. This key word, translated "all, entire, every, and everything" (7:19 [2x], 21 [3x], 22 [2x], 23) denotes the all-encompassing devastation and death inflicted by the Flood.

20. twenty feet. The gloss is approximate. The ark's draft is half its height (i.e., 15 cubits or 22.5 ft.) The mountains are submerged to a depth of fif-teen cubits, a depth sufficient to keep the ark from grounding.

21. birds . . . mankind. Creatures are listed in the order of their creation.

23. Only . . . him. The water is death and judgment for the evil world but also divine cleansing and preservation for the elect remnant.

Frame 6: God Remembers Noah (8:1a)

The narrator's terse theological evaluation, "But God remembered Noah," forms the hinge of the larger diptych that constitutes Scene 1 (6:13–8:22). Frames 1–5 paint in ever darker tones the Flood and its devastation (6:13–7:24), but frames 7–9 paint in ever brighter hue the renewal of the earth (8:1b–19). The narrative tension relaxes as the waters retreat. In those three frames the narrator chronicles the progress of creation through seven phases that closely correspond to the first week of creation (see "Seven Progressive Phases of Creation and Re-creation," above).

1a. remembered [zkr]. Unlike English "remembered," which refers merely to mental recall and entails having forgotten, the Hebrew term, espe-cially with reference to God, signifies to act upon a previous commitment to a covenant partner (see 9:14–15; 19:29; 30:22; Ex. 2:24; 6:5; 32:13; 1 Sam. 1:19; Judg. 16:28; Job 14:13; Ps. 8:4; 9:12; 74:1–3; 98:3; 105:8; 106:45; 111:5; Jer. 15:15). By acting on his earlier promise to Noah (see 6:18), God shows himself to be a trustworthy covenant partner. This crucial expression shows that the subsiding waters of the Flood are subject to God's undisputed will. By contrast, in the Babylonian accounts "the gods were terror-struck at the forces they themselves had unleashed. They were appalled at the conse-quences of their own actions over which they no longer had control."[62] It is only the remembering of God that gives hope and makes new life possible.

---

[62]Sarna, *Genesis*, 56–57.

Frame 7: The Waning Flood (8:1b – 5)

1b. wind [*rûaḥ*]. The Hebrew is rendered "Spirit" in a similar context in 1:2.

4. mountains of Ararat. The ark rested in the area of ancient Urartu (2 Kings 19:37), now part of eastern Turkey, southern Russia, and northwestern Iran. The reference is too imprecise to specify the mountains, suggesting that the narrator himself is uncertain.

Frame 8: Ending of Flood: Noah and Birds Are Main Actors (8:6 – 14)

7–8. raven . . . dove. Noah's release of the birds into the air is the first sign of renewed life. In the Babylonian account, the hero sends out a dove, a swallow, and then a raven.[63] The difference in the sequence profiles again the superiority of the biblical account. The raven braves the storm, can feed on carrion, and as the stronger bird can remain in flight much longer. It makes sense, as in the biblical account, to send out the stronger raven before the gentle, timid, and low-flying dove, but none to reverse the sequence, as in the Babylonian epic.

9. reached out . . . took the dove . . . brought it back to himself. The narrative speed, which has been racing through weeks in one verse, slows dramatically to focus on this one brief event. This series of verbs provides a cameo of Noah. He has the heart of a conservationist (see Prov. 12:10), modeling God's concern to preserve the creation. Skinner says, "The description of the return and admission of the dove is unsurpassed . . . for tenderness and beauty of imagination."[64]

11. freshly plucked. Trees and plants are growing again.

13–14. ground was dry . . . dry. The verbs of 8:13 and 14 rendered "dry" in NIV differ. Even after Noah sees the earth has dried out (Heb. *ḥārēb* [8:13]), he waits patiently almost another two months until it is completely dry (Heb. *yābēš* [8:14]), waiting for the divine word that it is safe to disembark.

Frame 9: Disembarkation (8:15 – 19)

17. multiply. The bright hope of fertility and life in the renewed earth differs from the Babylonian parallel. In that dark epic, when its hero looks out on the world after the flood, he sees "all of mankind had turned to clay."[65]

15, 18. God said . . . Noah came out. The almost word for word pattern of 8:16–17 and 18–19 illustrates Noah's consistent obedience. Calvin remarked, "How great must have been the fortitude of the man, who, after

---

[63]*ANET*, 94–95, lines 145–54.
[64]Skinner, *Genesis*, 156.
[65]*ANET*, 94, line 133.

the incredible weariness of a whole year, when the deluge has ceased, and new life has shone forth, does not yet move a foot out of his sepulchre, without the command of God."[66]

Frame 10: Provision for the Post-Flood World with a Divine Monologue to Preserve the Earth, with Reflections on Human Behavior (8:20–22)

20. Noah built an altar. Significantly, Noah's first act after emerging from the ark is to worship God. Whereas God spares the earth on the basis of Noah's righteousness (cf. 6:9, 18), now on the basis of Noah's sacrifice he resolves never again to destroy it in spite of humanity's sin.

burnt offerings. The offering animal, apart from the hide, is wholly burnt up on the altar and offered to the Lord. It is a way of calling upon the Lord and carries an atoning effect for the worshiper (Lev. 1:4; Job 1:5).

21. smelled. The figure derives from the Canaanite roots of the Hebrew language. It is a technical term, no longer mythological, and expresses God's favor and pleasure toward the sacrifice and worshiper (cf. Ex. 29:18; Lev. 1:9; 3:16; Num. 15:3).

pleasing. It is the burning of the offering that makes it a pleasing aroma. The play on words with the root of this word (it is the same as in Noah's name) signifies the pleasure God takes in the obedience and worship of his people. This sweet savor offering pacifies God's indignation against sin (see 6:6). This reveals a sharp contrast to other Flood accounts in which the Mesopotamian gods gather "like flies" around the sacrifice.[67]

in his heart. The Septuagint paraphrase, "having considered," explains clearly the intended connection between the sacrifice and God's resolve. God's heart at the time of the Flood is full of pain because of people's sin (6:6). Human sin inflicts pain upon God's heart only because he graciously humbles himself to become fully involved with humanity. Now that pain and indignation is assuaged by the atoning sacrifice.

Never again . . . curse the ground. God is not lifting the curse of 3:17 but promising not to destroy the earth again (see 6:13; Isa. 54:9). In 3:17 "curse" renders the Hebrew ʾārar and signifies "to inflict an anti-blessing, disastrous misfortune (i.e., privation, not fertility, and subservience, not dominion)." Here it renders the Hebrew qālal and signifies "to treat with contempt."[68]

even though. The gracious character of this so-called Noahic covenant is underscored by the divine promise, despite the continuing presence of human sin deserving judgment.[69]

---

[66]Calvin, *Genesis*, 280.
[67]*ANET*, 95, lines 158–61.
[68]Cf. H. N. Wallace, "The Toledot of Adam," in *Studies in the Pentateuch*, ed. J. A Emerton (VTSup 41; New York: Brill, 1990), 26–27.
[69]God's amazing grace also underlies his preservation of Israel (see Ex. 33:3; 34:9).

every inclination of his heart is evil. The Flood effects no fundamental change in humanity, but Noah's sacrifice effects a change in God by pacifying his righteous indignation against sin.

from childhood. Adam's original sin continues to be passed on seminally to everyone after the Flood. Before the Flood, the degradation of sin had culminated in history (6:5). This statement pertains to the natural state of sin, not its historical progression. Sarna thinks the term implies "that the tendency to evil may be curbed and redirected through the discipline of laws. Hence, the next section deals with the imposition of laws upon postdiluvian humanity."[70]

22. As long as the earth endures. This expression qualifies "never again" in 8:21. God will providentially preserve the earth and its ecology until the final judgment (1 Peter 3:20–21; 2 Peter 2:5–12).

seedtime and harvest. In this allusion to 1:11–12, God guarantees the continuation of humanity until the end of history by guaranteeing its sustaining food supply.

day and night. This is an allusion to 1:14.

As long . . . never cease. Act 1 concludes with a poem. So also Act 2 (9:24–27; cf. Book 1, Act 1 [2:23], Act 2 [3:14–19], and Act 3 [4:23–24]).

Scene 2: Noah and the World Conditions after the Flood (9:1–17)

Scene 2 (9:1–17) elaborates upon Frame 10, God's provision for the post-Flood world. It consists of two frames: God institutes ordinances to safeguard his forbearing program of blessing sinful humanity (9:1–7), and God grants a sign to guarantee his promise of forbearance (9:8–17).

Frame 11: God's Ordinance to Safeguard His Program of Forbearance (9:1–7)

G. Vos summarizes the three ordinances of this frame: (1) the propagation of life (9:1, 7), (2) the protection of life, from both animals and humans (9:2a, 4–6), and (3) the sustenance of life (9:2b–3).[71] The commands "be fruitful and increase in number" form the outer frame (9:1, 7) and underscore the theme of divine blessing on human life. The inner core presents necessary legislation to sustain life and to protect both animal and human life. To protect human life and to curb violence, God prescribes capital punishment both of guilty animals and human beings (9:5), succinctly summarized in a memorable poem with a rationale (9:6). The legislation is necessary to preserve life in the face of human depravity. Before the Flood the lack of capital punishment led to blood vendettas (see Gen. 4), and without instinctive

---

[70]Sarna, *Genesis*, 59.
[71]Vos, *Biblical Theology*, 52.

fear, the animals corrupted their behavior. Thus Sarna says, "The destruction of the old world calls for the repopulation of the earth and the remedying of the ills that brought on the Flood. Society must henceforth rest on more secure moral foundations."[72]

1. blessed. The statement summarizes God's seventh and climactic act to reestablish the creation (see Literary Analysis). This is the third time God blesses human beings (see 1:28; 5:2) and commands them to be fruitful (see 1:28; 8:17). "Responsible parenting and societal protection" celebrate God's blessing.[73]

Be fruitful. Unlike the Mesopotamian parallel, Genesis 1–11 presents human life as an unqualified good. In the Atrahasis Epic, the older Mesopotamian account of the Flood, overpopulation precipitates the Flood. To ensure that the problem will not reoccur, the gods reach a compromise by inflicting women with sterility, a high infant mortality, and artificial barrenness by cult practices.[74]

2. fear . . . of you. This military term seems to be stronger than to "rule" in 1:28 and implies that the interaction between humans and animals will not be peaceful, just as 9:6 suggests the same of human beings. It was God's intention that human beings voluntarily submit to him and animals to them (see Isa. 11:6–8). But both humans and animals in hubris transgressed their assigned roles. Apparently before the Flood, when all flesh corrupted its behavior (see 6:12), animals got out of control, having no fear of human beings. Despite human sin, God now confirms and enhances human dominion over animals.

given into your hands. God adds animals to the human diet to protect human life. Humanity has the power of life and death over the animal kingdom.

3. Everything . . . everything. For the human diet, God at this time makes no distinction between clean and unclean.

that lives. Presumably animals that die of themselves are forbidden. Subsequently, only the covenant people are prohibited from eating an animal found dead (see Lev. 11:40; Deut. 14:21).

4. not eat . . . lifeblood. Blood is equated with life in the Old Testament (Lev. 17:11). Here blood is equated with the animal's "soul" (i.e., its passionate vitality).[75] By forbidding the eating of blood, this regulation instills a respect for the sacredness of life and protects against wanton abuse (see Lev. 3:17; 7:2–27; 19:26; Deut. 12:1–24; 1 Sam. 14:32–34).[76] Adding meat to the human diet is "not a license for savagery."[77] Noah's descendants are predators on the top of the food chain. However, as animals are not to eat

---

[72]Sarna, *Genesis*, 60.
[73]Mathews, *Genesis 1–11:26*, 399.
[74]Kikawada and Quinn, *Before Abraham*, 47.
[75]See B. K. Waltke, "*Nāpash*," *TWOT*, 2:587–91; cf. also Johnson, *Vitality*, 1949.
[76]Vos, *Biblical Theology*, 53.
[77]Sarna, *Genesis*, 60.

human beings after a carnivorous fashion, so human beings must show a proper respect for life as a sacred thing (see 9:10).[78]

5. I will surely demand an accounting. "Accounting" signifies an exacting compensation, as 9:6 clarifies. The law protects human life from human assault. If animal life is sacred, how much more human life that bears God's image? No sanction against the offender is stated for violating animal life. But with respect to the taking of human life, the threefold repetition of this phrase brings emphatic attention to the value God bestows on it. The principle is first stated generally, then specified to human beings and finally to animals. Animal blood may be shed for food, but human blood may not be shed at all, except to compensate for homicide (see 9:6). In 9:6 the matter of making compensation is given over to humankind, but ultimately God will exact from each individual without exception. In the case of homicide God will vindicate the life of the murdered (see Theological Reflections).

from every animal. So valuable is human life that a compensation of life for life will even be exacted from animals (see "all the people," i.e., "all flesh" in 6:12; cf. Ex. 21:28–29).

fellow man. The Hebrew word here is translated "brother" in 4:8–11, suggesting a connection between this command and the way God avenges Abel's blood. Where there he does not exact blood for blood, from now on he will.

6. Whoever sheds the blood . . . shall his blood be shed. The chiastic style matches the concept of poetic justice: life for life (see "Capital Punishment" in Theological Reflections below). Unlike other law codes in the ancient world, money cannot ransom a murderer (Num. 35:31).

by[79] man. Human beings are God's agents for exacting compensation by capital punishment. They stand in God's stead as rulers (see 1:26). The legislation lays the foundation for government by the state. As Mathews states, "Exacting retribution is not a personal matter but a societal obligation"[80] (cf. Rom. 12:19; 13:1–5; 1 Peter 2:13–14).

image. God's determination to spare the creation is inextricably linked with the value he places on his image. The image of God continues in depraved humanity (see 8:21) and explains why homicidal blood, in contrast to animal blood, must be compensated.

Frame 12: God's Covenant Sign Never Again to Destroy the Earth (9:8–17)

Framed by an inclusio (9:8–11 and 17) is God's covenant sign of a rainbow (9:12–16).

---

[78]G. M. Tucker, "Rain on a Land Where No One Lives: The Hebrew Bible on the Environment," *JBL* 116 (1997): 11 and n. 22.

[79]The preposition could be read "in exchange for." Most English versions rightly understand the preposition to indicate agency. This is its normal meaning with Niphal (*IBHS* §23.2.2f); it avoids a tautology with 9:5 and lays a solid foundation for capital punishment as exacted later in the Mosaic law (cf. Ex. 21:12–14; Num. 35:16–32; Deut. 17:6–7; 19:15).

[80]Mathews, *Genesis 1-11:26*, 405.

9. I [myself] establish . . . my covenant [*ᵃnî . . . mēqîm ʾet-bᵉrîtî*]. This verse repeats key vocabulary from 6:17 and so forms an inclusio around Act 1. This covenant is God's unconditional promise given as repayment for Noah's offering (see "Literary Analysis: Plot" above). God unilaterally takes full responsibility to preserve the earth and its complete ecology forever in order to sustain his image bearer (8:20–22). The covenant confirms God's preexisting relationship with all creatures when he blessed them at the time of their creation.[81]

10. every living creature. The repetition of this phrase (9:10a, 10b, 12b) and its equivalents, "all life" (9:11b, 15b, 17b) and "all living creatures of every kind" (9:15a, 16b)—a total of eight times in this scene—affirms God's passionate concern for and certain commitment to the preservation and care of all living species on the earth (see Theological Reflections).

11. never . . . be cut off. The phrase "cut off" refers to God handing over someone to the realm of death, which lies outside of God's providential care (cf. 17:14; Lev. 7:20; 17:4; and "destroy" [literally "cut off"] in Micah 5:10–13 [Heb. 9–12]).

12. sign. God certifies his covenants by signs: for the covenant with Abraham, circumcision (Gen. 17:11); with Israel at Sinai, Sabbaths (Ex. 31:13, 17); with Christ and new Israel, the cup (Luke 22:20).[82]

13. rainbow. The Hebrew reads simply "bow," a battle weapon and a hunting instrument. In ancient Near Eastern mythologies, stars in the shape of a bow were associated with the hostility of the gods.[83] Here the warrior's bow is hung up, pointed away from the earth.[84] Kline states, "The symbol of divine bellicosity and hostility has been transformed into a token of reconciliation between God and man."[85] The relaxed bow stretches from earth to heaven and extends from horizon to horizon, reminding God of his universal commitment. Delitzsch's comment is helpful: "Stretched between heaven and earth, it is a bond of peace between both, and, spanning the horizon, it points to the all-embracing universality of the Divine mercy."[86] The [rain]bow and the signs of other biblical covenants consecrate already common events and invest them with new and sacred significance.

15. remember. See 8:1 and the note there. God in his transcendence is omniscient, but in his immanence he involves himself with the affairs of earth. This latter perspective of God is in view here.

---

[81]God likewise follows up his promises to Abraham in Gen. 12:1–3 with his covenants and their signs in Gen. 15 and 17. The pattern is promise, covenant confirmation, and covenant sign.

[82]No sign was needed with David, for the promise included the birth of a son.

[83]See Sarna, *Genesis*, 63.

[84]Kline writes, "The war-bow is mentioned in God's arsenal of wrath. . . (cf., e.g., Deut. 32:42; Ps. 7:12[13]; 18:14[15]; 64:7[8]). However, in the sign of the rainbow, the bow is not raised vertically and drawn taut in the face of the foe but is suspended in the relaxed horizontal position" (Kline, *Kingdom*, 152).

[85]Ibid.

[86]F. Delitzsch, *A New Commentary on Genesis*, trans. S. Taylor (Edinburgh: T. & T. Clark, 1899), 2:290.

16. see. This stands in contrast to the evil God "saw" in 6:12. The transcendent God, who humbles himself to involve himself with people, deliberately chooses to reflect on this colorful vision rather than humanity's evil.

everlasting. The important eschatological and covenantal term *ʿôlām* may be relativized by the context (Gen. 17:13); here, by "as long as the earth endures" (8:22).

Act 2: Prophecies about Noah's Sons (9:18–27)

Editorial Preface (9:18–19)

18. The sons of Noah. These two verses shift the focus from Noah to his sons and future generations. The genealogical notes of 9:18–19 (cf. 6:9) and 9:28–29 frame this act. The following story illustrates the piety and virtue of the Shemites and of the Japhethites and the moral degradation of the Hamites, who include the Egyptians, Babylonians, and Canaanites.[87] Noah's sons carry on both the seed of the Serpent and the seed of the woman.

father of Canaan. The narrator prepares the audience for the important topic of the Canaanites. The immoral action of their father foreshadows their spiritual degradation and arms Israel against its contagion.

19. the three sons . . . scattered over the earth. "Scattering" entails that God blesses them and makes them fruitful. The mentioning of the scattering of the three sons functions as a transition between the account of Noah and his family (6:9–9:29) and the account of the descendants of Shem, Ham, and Japheth (10:1–11:9). In the former they emerge out of the ark into the renewed earth armed with God's covenant (8:16, 18; 9:8–17); in the latter they are scattered (10:18; 11:4, 8–9).

Scene 1: Noah's Nakedness (9:20–23)

20. Noah. The scene unfolds with Noah being the chief actor and then his sons.

soil (*hāʾǎḏāmâ*). The narrator adds the unnecessary expansion to connect Noah with Adam, who was formed from *hāʾǎḏāmâ* (2:7; see "Literary Analysis: Parallels between Adam and the Original Creation and Noah and the Recreation") and with Lamech's prophecy. Lamech named his son Noah *nōaḥ*, "rest," because he would bring *nḥm*, "comfort" (i.e., relief), from the Lord's curse on *hāʾǎḏāmâ* (5:29). Before Noah develops viniculture, the land produces through painful human toil the food for sustenance, but little else. Now he subdues the land to produce wine, which uniquely cheers, comforts, and gladdens the heart (Judg. 9:13; Ps. 104:15).[88]

---

[87]Leviticus 18:3 lumps the Egyptians and Canaanites together in their abominable sexual perversion (see also Gen. 12:10–20; 19:5–8; 20; 26:7–11; 34; 38–39).

[88]The making of wine had such an important place in ancient epic traditions that they attributed the origin of wine-making to some god or demigod. The biblical story emphasizes that viniculture is a human invention (Cassuto, *From Noah*, 160).

proceeded. The verb, which literally means "he began,"[89] implies a new, not a renewed, activity.[90] The text implies that Noah develops viticulture (the science of growing grapes) and viniculture (the science of making wine). As in 4:17–22, human advance in technology is distorted by human depravity.

plant. The implied time lapse between the two acts is further underscored by the fact that presumably Noah now has a grown-up grandson.

vineyard. The vine comes from Armenia, where the ark grounded (see 8:4).

21. became drunk. Walter Brown argues convincingly that *skr* "to become drunk" does not necessarily have negative connotations in the Old Testament (cf. Gen. 43:34; Song 5:1; Hag. 1:6). He is less convincing, however, when he argues that it should be rendered here "he became fully content" or "he was satiated to sleep" in a laudable sense. The verb may have a negative sense (Lam. 4:21; Isa. 29:9; 49:26; Jer. 25:27; Nah. 3:11). Brown dismisses the four prophetic passages as irrelevant because "the depiction of drunkenness in these texts is obviously symbolic." However, drunkenness in these texts pictures the LORD's judgment, not blessing, on people. Moreover, though David fails, he tries to get Uriah drunk in order to remove Uriah's religious scruples against untimely and improper sex (2 Sam. 11:13). Lot's daughters make him drunk to commit incest (Gen. 19:31–35). To sustain his argument that Noah's drinking to satiation is positive and laudable, not negative and despicable, Brown excuses Noah's uncovering himself as a private, not public, matter.[91] Nevertheless, at the least his exposing himself occasioned his younger son's sin, and his older sons felt it necessary to cover their father's nakedness, a precaution Noah did not take. Although the precise working in Hab. 2:15 and Lam. 4:21 differs somewhat from Gen. 9:21, the prophets nevertheless censor nakedness in connection with being satiated with wine, suggesting the narrator also condemns, not commends, Noah's drinking and uncovering himself. Wine can bring joy, when drunk in moderation (see "soil" above), moral laxity and sorrow, when drunk in excess.

lay uncovered. This is better understood as, "he exposed himself."[92] Habakkuk thunders, "Woe to him who gives drink to his neighbors, pouring it from the wineskin till they are drunk, so that he can gaze on their naked bodies" (Hab. 2:15). Habakkuk connects exposing one's nakedness through intoxication with "prurient voyeurism,"[93] an act that deprives another of his or her dignity and desire for propriety (cf. Lam. 4:14). Naked-

---

[89]NIV translates *hll* by forms of "to begin" in 4:26; 11:6; 41:54; and by "first" (1 Sam. 14:35; cf. "grew" in Gen. 10:8).

[90]Compare with Mathews, *Genesis 1–11:26*, 416.

[91]W. Brown, "Noah: Sot or Saint?" in *The Way of Wisdom: Essays in Honor of Bruce K. Waltke*, ed. J. I. Packer and S. K. Soderlund (Grand Rapids: Zondervan, 2000), 36–60.

[92]*HALOT*, 192. The Hithpael can be passive, "he was exposed" (*IBHS* §26.3a), but more probably has its normal reflexive sense here (*IBHS* §26.2).

[93]H. C. Leupold, *Exposition of Genesis* (Grand Rapids: Baker, 1942), 1:346.

ness is associated with shame (Gen. 3:7, 21), is publicly demeaning (2 Sam. 6:16, 20), and is incompatible with living in God's presence (Ex. 20:26; cf. Deut. 23:12–14). When human beings fell into sin, they became aware through their nakedness of the potential for doing good and evil. The regulations against nakedness aim to protect people from sin. Noah's nakedness occasions Ham's sin.

inside his tent. Although Noah sins in exposing himself through drink, he exposes himself in private, not in public. This makes Ham's invasion of his privacy more contemptible and his guilt more culpable.

22. saw his father's nakedness. The Hebrew *rā'â* here means "to look at (searchingly)" (Song 1:6; 6:11b), not a harmless or accidental seeing. Rabbinical sources think either that he castrated his father or that he committed sodomy.[94] However, they are guilty of adding to the text. Some are guilty of special pleading as they argue that the text has been purged of earlier sordid details. Probably just Ham's "prurient voyeurism" is meant (see Hab. 2:15). His voyeurism, however, is of the worse sort. Voyeurism in general violates another's dignity and robs that one of his or her instinctive desire for privacy and for propriety. It is a form of domination. Ham's, however, is perverse, for his is homosexual voyeurism. Worse yet, he dishonors his father, whom he should have revered in any case (Ex. 21:15–17; Deut. 21:18–21; Mark 7:10), and then increases the dishonor by proclaiming it to others. Ham's brothers thought it sin merely to look at their father's nakedness and took every effort not to do so. In a Canaanite epic reflecting the ideals of that world, Baal prays that El his father will bless a certain Daniel with a son "who takes him by the hand when he's drunk, carries him when he's sated with wine."[95] Noah's leaven of exposing himself spreads to Ham's homosexual, parent-dishonoring voyeurism and will sour fully into Canaan's rampant sexual perversions so that the land will vomit them out (see Lev. 18:24–30; Deut. 12:29–32).

23. took a garment . . . would not see their father's nakedness. The narrator highlights the honorable character of Shem and Japheth with the elaborate description of their actions. "The shameless sensuality of Ham, the modesty of Japheth and Shem, marked a difference in common morality."[96]

Scene 2: Noah's Prophetic Invocations (9:24–27)

24. found out. Did Shem and Japheth tell him?

25. he said. These are the only words Noah utters in the whole account. Although in the form of prayerful requests, they function as prophecies (see Gen. 49:1; Deut. 33:1). "They are in effect his last will and testament."[97] God's words (9:1–17) pertain to human history in general; Noah's to redemptive

[94]Sarna, *Genesis*, 66.
[95]*ANET*, 150, lines 32–33.
[96]Vos, *Biblical Theology*, 56.
[97]Mathews, *Genesis 1–11:26*, 415.

history. His prophecies repeat the antediluvian history: As Adam's three children were divided into the ungodly Cainites and the godly Abel, replaced by Seth and his descendants (see 4:17–5:32), so Noah's descendants are divided into the reprobate Canaanites and the godly Shemites, who will be succeeded by the Japhethites.

cursed [*ʾārar;* cf. 8:21]. The Canaanites succeed the Cainites as the curse-laden descendants of the Serpent (3:14–15; 4:11). This curse on Canaan is essentially repeated in connection with each prayer of blessing (9:26, 27).

Canaan. Why Canaan rather than Ham? Since the curses and blessings on the three sons have their descendants in view, it is not strange that the curse falls on Ham's son rather than on Ham himself (9:18–22), especially since God has already blessed this righteous survivor of the Flood (9:1). As the youngest son wrongs his father, so the curse will fall on his youngest son, who presumably inherits his moral decadence (see Lev. 18:3; Deut. 9:3). In addition to the Canaanites, Ham's descendants include some of Israel's most bitter enemies: Egypt, Philistia, Assyria, Babylon (see 10:6–13). Behind Noah's prophecy is the concept of corporate solidarity. The ancestors reproduce their own kind (see "Theme of Genesis and Biblical Theology" in the introduction). Noah's righteousness is reproduced in Shem and Japheth, his immorality in Ham. The hubris of Ham against his father will be worked out in his descendants, and the modesty of Shem and Japheth in theirs.

The lowest of slaves. Cassuto explains, "The Canaanites were to suffer the curse and the bondage not because of the sins of Ham, but because they themselves acted like Ham, because of their own transgressions"[98] Canaan's slavery is spiritual, not just political. The curse placed upon Canaan links him with the curse on the Serpent (3:14) and on Cain (4:11). However, the general curse is not without exception. As the first scene clarifies, the difference between the future prospects of the ancestral brothers pertains to their morality, not to their ethnicity as such. The family of the Canaanite prostitute Rahab will become part of the covenant people (Josh. 2:14; 6:17, 22–25; Matt. 1:5; Heb. 11:31), and the family of the Judean Achan will be cut off (Josh. 7). When Israel behaves like the Canaanites, the land also vomits them out (2 Kings 17:20).

26. He also said. The double "he said" introduction (9:25, 26) distinguishes the curse on Canaan to abject slavery (9:25) from the blessings on Shem and Japheth (9:26, 27).

blessed. Through this doxological benediction, Noah asks that the covenant-keeping God be recognized and hallowed as the author of Shem's life and victories.

God of Shem. Shem is identified by his relationship with God, and "the LORD" is identified by his being the God of Shem. The blessed Creator of all

---

[98]Cassuto, *From Noah,* 155.

life and Lord of all history commits himself to Shem. This is the first indication that God elects the line of Shem to rule the earth (Gen. 1:26–28) and
crush the Serpent (Gen. 3:15; 4:26). Sovereign grace always opens a blessed
future, as when God chooses as Shem's successors, Abraham, not Nahor;
Isaac, not Ishmael; Jacob, not Esau; Judah, not Joseph.

slave of Shem. The Hebrew reads "their slave"[99] (see next verse).

27. God. Noah uses God's personal name, "LORD," for his covenant relationship with Shem, but he uses "God" for his transcendence over the
Japhethites.

Japheth. Note a word play with "may he enlarge" (*yapt*). The Japhethites
spread out principally in Anatolia and Greece (see Gen. 10:2–5).

live in tents. "Live" renders Hebrew *škn*, "to dwell." The figure implies
displacement. This interpretation finds support in Job 18:14–15: "He is torn
from the security of his tent. . . . Fire resides (*škn*) in his tent."

his slave. This is best translated "their slaves." In all three petitions, Noah
asks that Canaan be subjugated to slavery by his brothers. He regards Shem
and Japheth ruling over Canaan together. The plural "their" probably refers
to the descendants of Shem and Japheth.

Epilogue: Noah's Epitaph (9:28 – 29)

he died. The genealogical record begun in 5:32 is now completed according to the pattern of chapter 5. Book 3 is a parenthesis within Book 2.

THEOLOGICAL REFLECTIONS ON BOOK 3

God's Judgments

Ronald Youngblood suggests that the Flood narrative illustrates five truths
about God's judgments: they are not arbitrary, are announced beforehand,
allow time for repentance but are otherwise carried out, result in death, and
are due to his justice.[100]

A Foreshadow of the End of the Earth and
the Resurrection of Saints

The theme of this *tôledôt*, the annihilation of the seed of the Serpent's
kingdom and the earth they have corrupted and the preservation of the seed
of the woman through it to a renewed earth (see Theme of Book 3), foreshadows the future destruction of this present, evil world by fire and the
preservation of the faithful by the specified salvation in Christ to inherit a
regenerated earth that will never pass away (Matt. 24:30–31, 37–39; Luke

---

[99]Hebrew *lāmô* (9:26b, 27b) is best taken as a third masculine plural pronoun "to them" (GKC
§103f, k), not third masculine singular (GKC §103g, n. 3; *IBHS* §11.1.2d), because it is parallel to "his
brothers" in 9:25.
[100]Youngblood, *Genesis*, 99–100.

17:26–32; 2 Thess. 1:5–9; 2 Peter 3:6–7). The elect covenant family going through a sea of death and coming forth from their burial chamber (Isa 26:19–21) is a pledge that the redeemed will be brought through the cataclysm of the final judgment.

The seed of the Serpent (i.e., Noah's evil generation) are like Satan, their head, pretenders to the throne, whereas the seed of the woman (i.e., Noah and his family) are its legitimate heirs (cf. Matt. 4:8; 2 Thess. 2:1–12; 1 Peter 1:4; 2 Peter 3:13; Rev. 11:15; 12:10).[101] The account of the Flood guarantees that the pretenders finally will be deposed and the legitimate heirs will be victors.

A Foreshadow of Israel's History

Later stories of the Old Testament will bear echoes of Noah's righteousness and God's faithfulness. The unique word for "ark" and the mention of "pitch" (see Gen. 6:14) will be used in Ex. 2:3 for the ark (of bulrushes) that protects Moses, which God also uses to bring forth a new humanity from a world under judgment.

Moreover, just as the Lord uniquely specifies the design for the building of the ark (Gen. 6:14), he will specify the wilderness tabernacle and Solomon's temple. The ark preserves Noah's covenant family through chaotic water, and these later structures will preserve the covenant people among the chaotic nations.

The ark door in particular functions as a type of their history. When God slams shut the door of the ark, he radically distinguishes between the righteous and the wicked (see 7:16). Elsewhere in Scripture, doors provide safety for God's people in times of judgment. Lot (19:10), Israel (Ex. 12:23), and Rahab (Josh. 2:19) find safety behind closed doors while God rains judgment on the wicked. Jesus uses this symbol of separation in describing the safety of the righteous in the day of the Lord's coming (Matt. 25:10–13).

Christian Baptism

As in Christian baptism, the covenant family emerges out of the waters that symbolize the death of an old world to emerge into a new life (1 Peter 3:20–21).

The Future Course of History

Noah's prophecies to his sons, which foreshadow the future of God's covenant people and the future course of history, find fulfillment in the New Testament. Apart from Canaan and his descendants, Noah blanks the future of Ham's other sons and their descendants. However, the narrator makes clear that they include the Egyptians (Ps. 78:51; 105:23), who enslave Abraham's

---

[101]For this language and viewpoint that the wicked people of Noah's day represent an anti-Christ kingdom, I am indebted to M. Kline, *Kingdom*, 132–33.

children at the beginning of Israel's history, and the Babylonians, who enslave them at its end. Politically, Noah's prayer for Shem's subjugation of Canaan to abject slavery is realized with respect to the Canaanites (Gen. 15:18–21; 50:24–25; Ex. 3:8; Deut. 7:1–2; Josh. 12; Judg. 1; 1 Chron. 13:5). However, the biblical Shemites politically never subjugate Egypt and Babylon. God's victory through Shem over degraded moral practices is ultimately spiritual and fulfilled in the messianic age, which is inaugurated by the greatest of the Shemites, Jesus Christ.[102] In that age, both Egypt and Babylon find new birth in Jerusalem and are numbered with the people of God (Ps. 87; Isa. 19:19–25; 66:19–20). Moreover, in the messianic kingdom, the Japhethites are enlarged and displace the Shemites as the victors over evil.

Politically, the Japhethites displace the Shemites (i.e., Israel) by the conquests of Persia, Macedonia, and Rome after the Old Testament period. However, their political victory over the Shemites can scarcely be in view, because God has committed himself to bless Shem. Theologically, after the victorious death, resurrection, ascension, and glorification of Jesus Christ and the pouring out of his Spirit upon the elect of Israel, Japhethites displace Israel when Paul turns from unbelieving Israel to the Gentiles, most of whom live in Anatolia and Greece (Acts 13:44–52; 14:27; 18:6). Spiritual displacement to inherit God's blessing is in view, as the church fathers recognized. Thus, today the seed of the woman and the heirs of Abraham's covenants are mostly Gentiles, who originally inhabited Anatolia, Greece, and Rome (see Rom. 16:20). Using Paul's metaphor of Rom. 11:16–24, the natural branches (i.e., ethnic Israel) of the olive tree (the historical covenant community) have been mostly broken off, while the wild shoot (i.e., Gentiles) has been grafted in to be nourished by the sap of the tree (i.e., God's spiritual life that flows from a covenantal relationship with him; Gal. 3:26–29; Eph. 2:11–22; 1 Peter 2:9–10). Delitzsch says, "We are all Japhethites dwelling in the tents of Shem."[103]

Apart from the preservation of an elect remnant within ethnic Israel, these ethnic divisions no longer exist in God's administration. Today his church includes the Ethiopian eunuch (Ham), Peter and Paul (Shem), and Cornelius (Japheth). God is no respecter of a person's ethnic origin but only of his or her spiritual condition. In God's household, none is unclean (Acts 10), and in Christ there is neither Jew nor Greek, for all are Abraham's seed (Gal. 3:26–29).

---

[102]Some scholars find the fulfillment of Japheth's expansion when the Sea Peoples from Anatolia and Greece entered Canaan in 1225 B.C. and again at 1175 B.C. Many of these scholars also date Israel's settlement in the land to this same time. However, this cannot be the narrator's meaning. He identifies the Philistines as Hamitic (see 10:14), and he would have not have wished for the expansion of the Sea Peoples. Furthermore, to judge from what we know of the Philistines (see Judg. 14–16), he would not have credited them with virtue.

[103]C. F. Keil and F. Delitzsch, *The Pentateuch*, trans. J. Martin (Grand Rapids: Eerdmans, n.d.), 1:160.

God's Covenant

The elect beneficiaries live by faith in God, trusting him to fulfill his covenant promises. Noah, on his part, "did all that the LORD commanded him" (7:5). He builds the ark (6:22) and provisions it (7:5). The Lord, on his part, proves himself a covenant-keeping God. He himself shuts Noah in the ark (7:16) and remembers him when the Flood triumphs (8:1). Calvin's hymn, "I Greet Who My Sure Redeemer Art" captures the faith of Noah well:

> Our hope is in no other save in Thee;
> Our faith is built upon thy promise free;
> Lord, give us peace, and make us calm and sure,
> That is Thy strength we evermore endure.

The Lord's covenant with all humanity never again to destroy the earth as long as it endures is a unilateral covenant (8:20–22; 9:8–17), given as a repayment for past faithful service. In this case it is the reward for Noah's pacifying offering (8:21). God's covenants with Abraham, David, and the church are likewise unilateral, given as repayment for faithful service. However, his "repayment" is a hundred times more than the investment; it is enriched with a large measure of grace. All saints are dependent upon the active obedience of Jesus Christ, who alone satisfies for them God's righteous standards.

Noah the Paragon of Righteousness

Noah is distinguished from his vile age by his being the only person left in the ancient world who is totally committed to righteous living (see 6:9).[104] Along with Job and a certain Daniel of antiquity, he is legendary for being a righteousness man outside of Israel (Ezek. 14:14, 20). The writer of Hebrews holds him up as an example of a righteousness that comes by faith: "By faith Noah, when warned about things not yet seen, in holy fear built an ark to save his family. By his faith he condemned the world" (Heb. 11:7). Peter bestows on him the unique appellation "a preacher of righteousness" (2 Peter 2:5).[105] Here is a covenant partner who counts upon God to keep his word and upon whom God can count to live by his word. An unregenerate person, shackled in sin, cannot generate that kind of virtue. Such faith is

---

[104]Jewish literature celebrated his righteousness (e.g., Sirach 44:17; *Jubilees* 5:19; Wisdom of Solomon 10:4; *1 Enoch* 67:1).

[105]This depiction of Noah is unique in Scripture, but not in Jewish literature. Jewish and Christian traditions also taught that Noah was persecuted. Mathews summarizes, "Noah is depicted as the stalwart preacher forewarning doom, but the people 'sneered at him, each one, calling him demented, a man gone mad' (*Sib. Or.* 1.171–73). Josephus' account envisions that the patriarch felt threatened for his life and fled the country with his family (*Ant.* 1.3.1). Luther supposed, 'More than one miracle was necessary to prevent the ungodly from surrounding and killing him'" (*Genesis 1–11:26*, 357). However, the notion that he was persecuted overreads the biblical texts. According to the New Testament, his preaching and lifestyle condemned sinners. We need not detain ourselves here to exegete the disputed "[Christ] preached to the spirits in prison . . . in the days of Noah" (1 Peter 3:19–20).

God's gift to those whom he chooses as covenant partners. God knew the one to whom he extended such grace.

Instructively, the first three heroes of faith listed in Hebrews are from Genesis 4–6: Abel, Enoch, and Noah. All believed God, but their destinies were significantly different. Abel believed God and died. Enoch believed God and did not die. Noah believed God, and everyone else died in the Flood; eventually he died a natural death at the good old age of 950 years. We cannot dictate where faith will lead. The human tendency is to see only Enoch as the example of faith, but Abel is also given as our example.[106] What all three have in common is that they walked by faith and pleased God. That faith is an example to us.

Yet Noah was not perfect. The striking parallel and contrast between the saintly Noah before and during the Flood (6:8–9) and the drunken sinner, who exposes his nakedness after the Flood (9:21), directs the audience to look to God, not humans, for salvation.

Ecology

Book 3 has much to say about the modern Christian's relationship to ecological concerns. First, life on the ark represents the social hierarchy God intends. Within this miniature cosmos, which is designed by the Creator (see 6:15), human beings under God tend to the creation (6:18), animals submissively stay within their space (6:20), and vegetation sustains its lords (6:20). The text implies that when humans overstep their boundaries and usurp the place of God, animals likewise transgress (see 6:12). To keep animals in their place, God has had to instill them with fear and dread, setting up hostility between human beings and animals.

People, however, have a responsibility to care for and to preserve animals. Humans have the power of life and death over the animal kingdom (9:2). The intentional repetition of the phrase "every living creature" (and "all life"), eight times in Frame 12 alone (see 9:10), affirms God's desire to preserve every species. The human annihilation of species is a matter of grave concern to the Creator. If he will not extinguish the species, how much more must the creature honor that commitment. This desire and concern should call Christians to speak against and to take appropriate action to stop the modern destruction of species. Christians should not leave it to non-Christians to take the lead here. The species must be preserved to glorify and please God. Righteous Noah models the ideal (8:9).

With regard to the earth and the care of its vegetation, we need to remind ourselves that God wiped out the first earth because greedy people defaced

---

[106]It is often overlooked that at the same time that God performed spectacular miracles through Elijah, the faithful Obadiah hung a question mark over God's ways. While Elijah was calling fire down from heaven, Jezebel was killing prophets, one hundred of whom Obadiah hid in two caves (1 Kings 18). The writer of Hebrews holds up martyrs as well as victors as examples of faith (Heb. 11:35–38).

it (6:13). Christians should take a stand against raping the earth. Again, if God acts to ensure that life on the earth can reproduce to sustain itself (see 8:22), then Christians have the same obligation to preserve the earth and the reproduction of all forms of life for future generations. This is not a call to stop cutting down trees—Noah must have cut down a small forest to build the ark (see 6:22)—but it is a call for responsible management.

Family Salvation

Although Noah's righteousness by faith did not save his generation, his family was saved with him. Had any of Noah's peers repented of their violence and by faith entered the ark with Noah and his family while they were building the ark, they would have been saved just as surely as Rahab in her generation (Josh. 2). Is this not implied in Noah's preaching to them? By contrast, the refrain "you, your sons, your wife and your sons' wives" (see key words above) gives evidence that the Lord saves by families. This does not mean that God reckoned Noah's righteousness to each family member (see Ezek. 14:14, 20) but rather that each one embraced his faith. By faith his grown sons and daughters-in-law freely chose against their peers to enter the ark (see 7:1). Belonging to a holy family has distinct advantages, but each member is individually accountable to God (see Gen. 19:26; Josh. 24:15; Acts 16:31; 1 Cor. 7:14; 1 Peter 3:1–2).

The doctrine of corporate solidarity must be held in tension with individual accountability. The ancestor's seed reproduces him or her. Thus, the descendants of Shem and Japheth differ from those of Ham (see 9:24–27), just as the descendants of Lot differ from those of Abraham.

Overpopulation

The Old Testament's valuation of human life and bearing children starkly contrasts with other ancient Near Eastern views. Pagans hoped for sterility and high infant mortality and employed artificial contraception (see 9:1 in Exegetical Notes). Poignantly, the capricious gods of other flood accounts wipe out the earth because of overcrowding. The biblical account presents an entirely different picture. God, with great pain, only destroys humanity because it is destroying itself and the earth, and he chooses a remnant to restore hope to humanity. After the Flood, God repeats his earlier command to humanity to "be fruitful and increase in number and fill the earth" (9:1, 7). God desires as many people as possible to eat at his banqueting table of life. Any Christian discussions regarding modern concerns of overpopulation must take into account this divine command and the value that God places on all human life. We should take seriously Carl Sandburg's definition of a baby as "God's opinion that the world should go on."[107]

---

[107]Cited by Youngblood, *Genesis*, 57.

An Elect Remnant

The eight people on the ark give evidence that the sovereign, merciful Lord preserves a righteous remnant of covenant people during the darkest crises of their history (Isa. 54:9–10). Although the whole corrupt world perishes in the Flood, God preserves for himself one family (1 Peter 3:20). Likewise, although the whole nation apostatizes in the time of Elijah, God keeps seven thousand who do not bow their knees to Baal (1 Kings 19:18). He preserves a remnant through the Assyrian invasions (Isa. 1:9; 10:20) and the Babylonian exile (Micah 4:7; 5:3, 7; 7:18) and brings back a remnant under Zerubbabel, Ezra, and Nehemiah (Ezra 9:8). Today he preserves a remnant of ethnic Israel as part of his church (Rom. 11:5).

Capital Punishment

The instruction about capital punishment (Gen. 9:5–6) is set within the frame of the Lord's promise (8:20–22) and covenant (9:8–17), which is given to all humanity, to preserve all human life. In that context, the legislation to execute capital punishment pertains to all people (9:5–6). Capital punishment is founded upon the truth that all human beings bear the image of God, setting them apart from the rest of the living creatures.[108] "No one can be injurious to his brother without wounding God himself."[109] "The offense itself is not against the murdered, nor his family, nor society at large (obviously it impacts them as well)," but against God.[110] So valuable is human life as the bearers of God's image that God will exact compensation for shedding its life blood not only from the murderer but even from animals. Obviously, the murderer does not come under the protection of the sixth commandment, which prohibits the taking of innocent life (cf. Num. 35).

The principle of *lex talionis* (i.e., life for life) is clarified in the Lord's commands to his covenant people regarding the murderer (Num. 35:16–21) and in Paul's teaching about the Christian and the state. In the case of manslaughter, the guilty are consigned to cities of refuge, not penitentiaries, until the death of the high priest (Num. 35:22–28). In the case of murder, however, capital punishment is exacted.

In the New Testament Christians must not avenge themselves for any wrongdoing but leave room for God's wrath to avenge it (Rom. 12:19). God, in turn, appoints the civil government as his minister, an avenger to execute wrath on the one who practices evil (Rom. 13:4). The supreme Lord and King arms the civil authority with the sword, the instrument of death, for the

---

[108]Humanity loses its dignity without reckoning itself as God's image.

[109]Calvin, *Genesis,* 295–96. The interpretation that the assault on the image of God in human beings furnishes the reasons for this extreme penalty is better than the interpretation that God invests human beings with the authority to take human life because they are in his image. The poem in 9:6 seems to elaborate upon 9:5, where God takes measures to protect human life.

[110]Mathews, *Genesis 1–11:26,* 403.

punishment of evildoers. The legislation, "whoever sheds the blood of man by man shall his blood be shed," gives evidence that the civil authority as God's minister now has the responsibility to execute capital punishment for a capital offense.

This is an obligation, not an option. Three times God says, "I will demand an accounting" (9:5). Blood shed through homicide must be dealt with. It invests the guilty with its pollution (Num. 35:33; Ps. 106:38) and secures its expiation by the death of the murderer (see Gen. 9:6; 1 Kings 2:32) or through atonement (see Deut. 21:7–9). The high priest must die before the one guilty of manslaughter goes free. If the blood is not compensated by capital punishment or atoned for, it brings the Lord's judgment on the land (Deut. 19:13; 2 Sam. 21; 1 Kings 2:9, 31–33).

The law carefully protects the innocent. There must be at least two or three witnesses to convict a person of a crime (Deut. 19:15). Moreover, if a witness commits perjury, then the judges hearing the case will do to the perjurer as he or she intended to do to the accused, including life for life (Deut. 19:16–21). Finally, the witnesses themselves must be involved in the execution (Deut. 17:2, 7).

However, the murderer who truly repents of the crime should find mercy (Prov. 28:13). Although David took away the purity of Bathsheba and murdered her husband, he found forgiveness on the basis of God's sublime attributes of grace, unfailing love, and mercy (2 Sam. 12:13–14; Ps. 51). Indeed, the blood of Christ atones for all the sins of all his elect forever (Heb. 7:23–28).

Diet

In this same context, God gives three directions regarding eating animals. First, every animal may be eaten (Gen. 9:2). Noah distinguishes between clean (i.e., pure-formed) and unclean (i.e., mixed) animals in the ark, but when God adds meat to the human diet he does not make that distinction (Gen. 9:2–3). That distinction is unique to the Old Testament administration (Lev. 11; Deut. 14:3–21). It aims, like the Israelite laws not to mix linen and wool in clothing or to sow fields with different kinds of seed, to separate Israel from their pagan environment. In the church, which embraces all ethnic groups, that distinction is abolished (Mark 7:19; Acts 10:9–16; 1 Tim. 4:3), though the principal of spiritual separation remains (2 Cor. 6:14–18).

While every kind of animal is given for food, it has to be moving, that is, it must be killed for the purpose of eating it (Gen. 9:3). Subsequently, however, that law for all humanity is modified. Israel could give to an alien or sell to a foreigner an animal that died of itself (Deut. 14:21; cf. Lev. 17:15–16). The law aims to consecrate Israel to God.

Finally, eating the blood of animals is proscribed to teach people the value of blood, which can make atonement, and to prevent human beings from reducing themselves to savagery (see 9:4). This law is repeated for Israel (Lev. 17:10–14; 19:26).

All three laws are essentially abolished in the New Testament. In short, the Christian is no longer bound by dietary laws. Their observation tends to reduce religion to outward acts and to inculcate pride and false notions of religion. Moreover, they are unable to change the heart and the lusts of sinful people (Col. 2:20–23). What is needed is the regeneration of the human heart (Mark 7:19–23). However, so as not to offend Jews whose consciences forbid the eating of blood and strangled food, Christians in their company abstain from these (Acts 15:19–21).

Wine

Noah fulfills his father's dream that his son would bring comfort from the painful toil of the earth by beginning the science of growing grapes and of making wine, which uniquely gives people joy (see 9:18–20). The same text, however, illustrates its grave dangers. The rest of Scripture likewise both looks favorably on wine (Num. 15:5–10; Deut. 14:26; Ps. 104:15; John 2:1–11) and soberly warns of its dangers (Prov. 21:17; 23:20–21, 29–35; Isa. 5:22; 28:7), especially moral laxity as displayed in self-exposure (Lam. 4:21; Hab. 2:15). The holy Nazirite (Num. 6:3–4), the officiating priests (Lev. 10:9), and rulers making decisions (Prov. 31:4–5) abstain from it. John abstains from it; Jesus does not (Matt. 11:17–19).

Sacrifice

Noah, the priest, and his burnt offering are prototypes of Israel's priests and their sacrifices (cf. Job 1:5; 42:8) and prefigure Jesus Christ, the High Priest, and his sacrifice. Mathews astutely observes, "The manifestation of Christ has taken away these ancient shadows."[111] The value God places upon the sacrifice of Christ can be inferred from his reaction to Noah's offering. His atoning sacrifice so assuages God's heart in spite of humanity's original sin that God resolves never again to destroy the earth (8:21). For the covenant people of God, Christ's sacrifice secures their cleansing from all sin and secures for them eternal life with God (Heb. 10:11–24).

---

[111]Ibid., 281.

THE ACCOUNT OF SHEM, HAM, JAPHETH AND THEIR DESCENDANTS (10:1 – 11:9)

THEMES OF BOOK 4

Setting the stage for Book 5, the descendants of Noah's son Shem, Book 4 represents the descendants of Noah's sons multiplying under God's blessing and being scattered with many languages under God's wrath.

Act 1, "The Table of Nations," represents the nations as of one blood, multiplying under God's blessing as distinct tribes and nations. The Table represents God's broad concern for all peoples, not just the Israelites, which is understood by the omission of Israel from this Table. The narrator presents a symbolic seventy nations based on ethnic, geographic, linguistic, and political factors.

Act 2, "The Tower of Babel," reveals the formerly unified people building a tower in a collective, titanic rebellion against God. The strength of their unity is their common language and the symbol of their unity, the tower.

Their pride-filled sin is threefold. They disobey the divine command to fill the earth by their aim "that we may ... not be scattered" (11:4). They also scheme "that we may make a name for ourselves," thereby seeking their significance independently from God. Finally, in their hubris, they transgress the boundaries of heaven and earth, as established in Gen. 1:6–7. As God explains, "Nothing they plan to do will be impossible for them" (11:6). To restrain their titanic, societal rebellion to usurp God's rule, the Lord confounds their speech.

Chronologically, Act 2 is a flashback that explains the Table of Act 1. By anachrony, the narrator represents the nations first and foremost as of one blood, multiplying under God's blessing (see 9:1), not under

Babel's curse.[1] The judgment on the nations in Act 2 will form the proper background for God's call of Abraham to be a light to them and to provide a way of salvation for them.

OUTLINE OF BOOK 4

Superscription	10:1
Act 1: Table of Nations	10:2–32
Act 2: Tower of Babel	11:1–9

BOOK 4, ACT 1: TABLE OF NATIONS (10:1–32)

LITERARY ANALYSIS OF BOOK 4, ACT 1

Although here the two acts are analyzed separately for clarity, they must be read together, for they hold in tension the unity of the tribes and nations as of one blood under God's blessing and their diversity into many languages under God's wrath.

Structure

The Table presents a segmented genealogy of Noah's three sons with two biographical notes about Nimrod and Peleg, both of which foreshadow the Tower of Babel narrative. The Table does not aim to give an exhaustive list of all peoples (see 10:5). Rather, its intentions are theological (see below).

According to traditional source criticism, the Table is an amalgam of fragments. To be sure, there are discernible stylistic peculiarities, yet the narrator is not subject to his alleged sources but employs them to create a clearly unified document. Its broad structure, marked off by refrains, is clearly set forth by Mathews:[2]

Introduction: "This is the account of [*tôlᵉḏōṯ*] . . . Noah's sons . . . after the flood" (10:1).

- "The sons of Japheth. . ." (10:2)
  "territories," "clans," "nations," "language" (10:5)
- "The sons of Ham. . ." (10:6)
  "clans," "languages," "territories," "nations" (10:20)
- "Sons were also born to Shem. . ." (10:21)
  "clans," "languages," "territories," "nations" (10:31)

Conclusion: "These are the clans of Noah's sons, according to their lines of descent [*tôlᵉḏōṯ*] . . . after the flood" (10:32).

The introductory and concluding refrains in connection with each of the three sons clearly mark off the tripartite arrangement, thereby linking the tribes and nations with Noah's prophetic invocations (see 9:24–27). The

---

[1]So Clines, *Pentateuch*, 74.
[2]Mathews, *Genesis 1–11:26*, 433–34.

Chronicler (1 Chron. 1:5–23) presents a convenient summary of the Table, following the same order.

Inclusio

The narrator frames the Table of Nations by a similar introduction and conclusion (10:1 and 32; see structure above). This frame underscores that all the nations spring from "Noah's sons . . . after the flood." The focus is on the unity of all people. The segmented genealogies between the inclusio show the relationship of peoples to one another (see ch. 5).[3]

Keywords and Foreshadowing

Although Acts 1 and 2 radically differ in their structure and themes, the superscription and connecting key words nevertheless show that they were intended to be read as one book. Two key words in their refrains tightly bind them together: "territories/earth" (ʾereṣ, 10:5, 20, 31–32; 11:1, 8–9) and "language" (lāšôn [lit., "tongue"], 10:5, 20, 31 and its equivalent śāp̄â [lit., "lip"] 11:1, 6–7, 9).

More subtly, the narrator foreshadows the Tower of Babel narrative by key words in the biographical note about Nimrod (10:8–12). Both Nimrod and the tower builders "build," bānâ, "cities," ʿîr (10:11–12; 11:4–5), in "Babylon" and "Shinar" (10:10; 11:2, 9). Moreover, in both of these narratives the narrator inserts the only two references to "the Lord" in the book. Both pertain to God's sovereignty over the godless humans and their cities. Nimrod's deeds were "before the Lord" (10:9), and the "Lord came down to see the city [Babylon]" (11:5; cf. vv. 6, 8–9).[4] The narrator reserves the key word for judgment, "scattered" (pûṣ), for the curse-laden Canaanites (10:18; 11:4, 8–9). He also foreshadows the Tower of Babel incident by mentioning that the earth is divided in the days of Peleg, whetting the reader's appetite for clarification.

Paronomasia

The name Peleg (10:25) constitutes a significant word play, a *nomen est omen*, in Act 1. Peleg ("Division") is so named "because in his time the earth was divided [pālaḡ]." The resulting division of Peleg son of Eber from his brother Joktan is crucial to salvation history. Peleg's descendants through Abraham, not Joktan's descendants, will be the legitimate bearers of God's image to rule the earth and of the woman's conquering seed.

Climax

The Table of Nations moves from the Japhethites, who are most removed from Israel, to the Hamitic peoples, Israel's closest and most bitter neighbors,

---

[3]By contrast, the linear genealogy of Book 5 aims to show that Israel is the legitimate heir of Shem's God, "the Lord."

[4]Mathews, *Genesis 1–11:26*, 428.

and finally to the Shemites from whom Israel springs.[5] The narrator's arrangement, a reversal of his otherwise consistent presentation of Shem, Ham, and Japheth in that order (5:32; 6:10; 9:18), seems intentional, just as in 9:24–27 the narrator deliberately changed the arrangement emphatically to put Canaan under the curse.

However, even though Shem's descendants are placed last, this lineage is not the climax before the call of Abraham. The line of Shem itself must be divided into the nonelect (i.e., Joktan to Jobab, 10:26–30) and the elect (i.e., Peleg to Abraham, 11:18–26). By linking the rejected descendants of Shem through Joktan with the tower narrative and by isolating the chosen line of line of Shem through Peleg in a separate book, the narrator identifies the former as under the Tower of Babel's judgment and in need of the salvation that will come from the latter through its famous descendant, Abraham.

Generalization and Particularization

In Noah's prophetic invocation, he both emphasizes the curse of Canaan and intentionally gaps any reference to Ham participating in Shem's blessing. In the Table of Nations, the narrator singles out Nimrod, a descendant of Cush son of Ham, for special mention. Surprisingly, however, he is a mighty conqueror, not a slave. In this way, the narrator pushes the fulfillment of Noah's blessing of Shem and Japheth into the future, after the call of Abraham.

Comparison and Contrast

This segmented and linear genealogy is a highly stylized account of Israel's known world. Seventy nations are given: fourteen from Japheth, thirty from Ham, and twenty-six from Shem. Seventy, a multiple of seven and ten (both connoting completeness), represents a large (see Judg. 8:30; 2 Kings 10:1) and complete number (see below).[6] This number compares with the number of Abraham's seed at the end of the book. By the time of their descent into Egypt they, too, have reached the symbolic, complete, and full number.[7] Thus, the sovereign God has laid a firm foundation for making this microcosm of the nations into a nation able to bless the earth (cf. Gen. 46:27; Ex. 1:5).

In addition to the intentional sum of "seventy," the narrator shows a preference for "seven" and its multiples. Japheth has seven sons and seven grandsons. Ham has seven descendants of Cush (10:6–7) and seven of

---

[5]Amos likewise moves in a circle from Israel's remote neighbors, to nearer neighbors, and finally to Israel itself (see Amos 1–2).

[6]For example, U. Cassuto notes, "according to the concepts of the Canaanites concerning the origin and genealogy of the deities in their pantheon, the family of the gods—the sons of El and the sons of Asherah—comprised seventy souls" (*From Noah*, 175).

[7]The narrator again uses the number seventy to show completeness in connection with Jacob's children that descend into Egypt (Gen. 46:27; Ex. 1:5; Deut. 10:22; cf. Judg. 8:30; 9:2, 5; 2 Kings 10:1, 6, 7).

Mizraim (excluding the Philistines) (10:13). Counting Cainan (see below), fourteen distinct names are given in the lineage from Shem to Eber. The last of the elect ancestors before the line of Shem is divided between Eber's sons, Peleg and Joktan. This number is contrived by throwing in the name of Japheth (10:21–24). The number of Shem's named sons to Eber's two sons is also fourteen, again counting Cainan. The narrator gives fourteen names in the "cul-de-sac" line of Shem, Joktan, and Jobab (10:26–29). "Sons of" (*bᵉnê*) occurs fourteen times, seven times in 10:1–7, before Nimrod, and seven times in 10:20–32 (i.e., after the Hamitic lineage).[8] Cassuto also notes, "if we add to these the other terms that are characteristic of a genealogy, *ʾăbhî* ['the father of'] . . . *bānîm* ['sons'], *tōlᵉḏōṯ* ['generations of,' 'history of'] and the forms of the verb *yālaḏ* ['to bear'] we obtain twenty-eight—four times *seven*."[9] By contrast, there are uniquely no sevens in the structuring of the Canaanite genealogy. The representation of the Canaanites in the Table of Nations stands apart by its asymmetry to match their chaos.

EXEGETICAL NOTES TO BOOK 4, ACT I ──────────────

Superscription (10:1)

1. This is the account [*tōlᵉḏōṯ*] of Shem, Ham and Japheth. See the discussion of *tōlᵉḏōṯ* at 2:4.

themselves had sons. The Hebrew reads literally "sons were born to them," making them the recipients, not the actors. The word *sons* and its synonyms have broad meaning. The refrains mention "clans," "territories," "language," and "nations," showing that the descendants of Noah's three sons are being divided by their ethnicity, geography, language, and politics. Of the names in this genealogy, some are persons (e.g., Japheth, Nimrod), others are people groups (e.g., Ludites . . . Caphtorites), and others are place names (e.g., Egypt [Mizraim], Sidon, Sheba). Matching those concerns, the terms *sons of* or *fathered* might refer to political, geographical, social, and/or linguistic relationships (see also 4:20, 22; 10:31).[10] For example, the "sons of Javan" are, in the first place, Elishah and Tarshish (i.e., place names),[11] and in the second place, nations (Kittites, etc.). Some (e.g., Havilah and Sheba) occur twice in the chapter.[12]

---

[8]Cassuto, *From Noah*, 179.

[9]Cassuto finds twelve sons of Canaan but he has to count Canaan (ibid.).

[10]A. P. Ross, "Studies in the Book of Genesis, pt. 2: The Table of Nations in Genesis 10—Its Structure," *BSac* 137 (1980): 343–44.

[11]Similarly, the Chronicler says that Shobal was the father of Kiriath Jearim (1 Chron. 2:52) and that Salma was the father of Bethlehem (1 Chron. 2:51).

[12]Cassuto explains: "Although one man can have only one father, a tribe may be composed of different elements, and in such instances the Bible apparently intends to indicate that these tribes comprised some ethnic elements pertaining to Cush and others belonging to Joktan, like the Manahathites mentioned in Chronicles, half of whom were assigned to Shobal (i Chron. ii 52; compare Gen. xxxvi 23) and half to Salma (i Chron. ii 54)" (Cassuto, *From Noah*, 182).

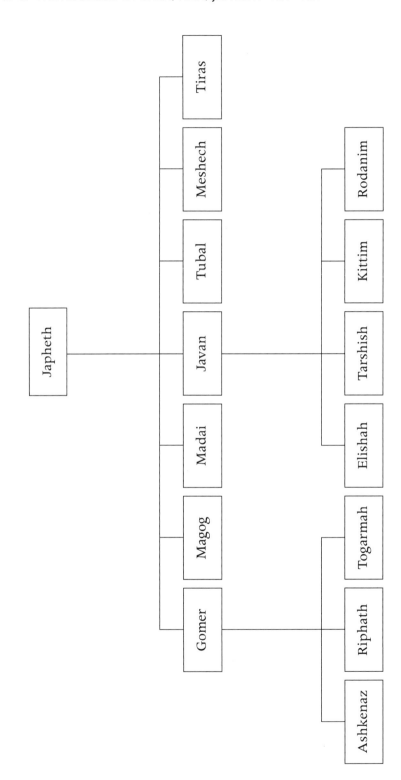

Table 1: Sons of Japheth (10:2 – 5)

Seven Sons of Japheth (10:2)

2. sons of Japheth. All are locatable to some degree in the area of Anatolia. Ezekiel associates "Gog, of the land of Magog" with Meshech and Tubal (Ezek. 38, passim), with Gomer and Beth Togarmah (38:6), and with the coastlands (39:6).

Japheth. See 9:27 and the notes there.

Gomer. This refers to the later Cimmerians, a nomadic people to the north of the Black Sea, who later overran much of the region of Anatolia in the seventh century B.C.

Magog. Lydia.[13]

Madai. These are the later Medes, who inhabited modern Northwest Iran (see 2 Kings 17:6; Jer. 51:11; Dan. 5:28).

Javan. Ionian Greeks.[14]

Tubal. The prophets often mention Tubal with Meshech (Ezek. 27:13; 38:2).[15]

Meshech. Phrygia.

Tiras. Identification of Tiras is somewhat uncertain, but this probably refers to Turcsha, one of the Sea Peoples, from the region of the Aegean Sea. Some relate them to Thrace; others, assuming a metathesis, to the Etruscans, who eventually settled in Italy.

Seven Grandsons by Gomer and Javan (10:3 – 4)

3. Ashkenaz. Scythians.

Riphath. The identification is uncertain. This term is Diphath in the MT of 1 Chron. 1:6, but many Hebrew MSS, LXX, and Vulgate of 1 Chron. 1:6 support the reading here. The alteration of *r* and *d* in Hebrew is a common scribal error (see Rodanim in 10:4).

Togarmah. This lies somewhere in the region of Uraratu (Armenia).

4. Elishah. The identification is disputed, but it is probably Cyprus.

Tarshish. Its identification with the region of the Mediterranean Sea is uncertain. Proposals range from Carthage to Tartessus in southwest Spain.

Kittim. This refers to people from southern Cyprus.

Rodanim. These are people from the island of Rhodes. The Hebrew reads Dodanim, but the reading "Rodanim" has support from 1 Chron. 1:7, SP, and LXX (see Riphath in 10:3).

---

[13]See A. Millard, "Gog and Magog," *NIDOTTE*, 4:685–87.

[14]J. Brinkman, "The Akkadian Words of 'Ionia' and 'Ionian,'" *Daidalikon* (1989): 53–71.

[15]The Greek text inserts Elishah between them, but according to 10:4 Elishah properly belongs as a son of Javan.

Inhabitants of the Mediterranean, Settling Its Coastal Regions and Islands (10:5)

5. from these. The pronoun refers to the whole Japhethite stock (see 10:32). The generalization shows that the Table is selective, not exhaustive.

maritime [*'iy*]. The Hebrew term means "islands."

spread out . . . own language. This actually occurs after the Tower of Babel (11:1–9).

Table 2: Sons of Ham (10:6–20)

Four Sons (10:6)

6. sons of Ham. The Egyptians, Babylonians, Assyrians, and Canaanites, Israel's most bitter and influential neighbors, are mentioned in this list. Although only Canaan is cursed, no distinctive blessing of the Lord is placed upon this genealogy.

Cush. Possible identifications are Nubia and Northern Sudan; the country bordering the southern Red Sea; the land of the Kassu, along the Araxes; or the vast area in the south, reaching far to the east.

Mizraim. This is Egypt (see Ps. 78:51), first Israel's host and then the infamous house of Israel's slavery (see 10:13–14).

Put. This is Libya. The narrator does not include his children, if any (cf. Cush, Mizraim, and Canaan).

Canaan. This refers to the southern Levant from southern Syria, so including Phoenicia and the whole of Palestine west of Jordan.

Five Sons of Cush and Two Sons of Raamah (10:7)

7. sons of Cush. Most settled in South Arabia.

Seba. This is in northern Africa (see Isa. 43:3; cf. 45:14). Based on Josephus, Seba is generally located at Meroe, the ancient capital of Ethiopia.

Havilah. Southwest Arabia.

Sabtah. South Arabia, possibly Shabwat, capital of Hadramaut.

Raamah. South Arabia in the region of Najran.

Sabteca. Unknown area of South Arabia.

Sheba. This is a region of South Arabia that probably had commercial colonies in North Arabia.

Dedan. North Arabia.

The Biography of Nimrod Fathered by Cush (10:8–12)

8. Cush was the father. The following biographical notation foreshadows the Tower of Babel and explains the racial, political, and spiritual origin of Babylonia and Assyria, the two great Mesopotamian powers that conquered Israel and held them as exiles. Nimrod founds his empire on naked aggression (10:8). His might is so great that it becomes proverbial in

Israel (10:9). His empire included all of Mesopotamia, both Babylonia in the south (10:10) and Assyria in the north (10:10–12). As the chief centers of his empire, he founds the great city of Babylonia, most notably Babylon (10:10), and subsequently, having moved into Assyria, greater Nineveh (10:11). His identity with known historical kings is disputed. The most likely candidate is King Sargon of Akkad (2350–2295 B.C.).

Nimrod. His name means, "We shall rebel" (see 11:1–9).

grew. The Hebrew "began to be" (see 4:26; 6:1; 9:20; 11:6) denotes an important innovation and development in history. Nimrod achieves his ascendancy by aggression; he is not characterized by spreading out.

warrior in the earth [*gibbōr bāʾāreṣ*]. The Hebrew means "tyrant," linking Nimrod with the infamous tyrants of 6:4.

9. mighty hunter. Ancient Near Eastern kings prided themselves on their hunting prowess. They were not shepherd kings.

before the LORD. The polyvalent *before* here means "in the estimation of" (i.e., even in God's estimation Nimrod is a mighty warrior and tyrant).[16] The phrase functions as a superlative, signifying Nimrod as a hunter to be greatly feared.

10. first centers. The Hebrew may be read as "first centers" and/or "chief centers," to show their political prominence as well as their chronological priority.

Babylon. Located on the Euphrates, south of where the Euphrates and the Tigris Rivers approach, Babylon was in Israel's world what Rome was to the Middle Ages. It represented the spiritual and political antithesis to Jerusalem. It eventually terminated Judah as an autonomous nation.[17]

Erech. This is modern Warka, the site in southern Iraq where archaeologists situate the birth of civilization. Inhabitants of this area are later deported to Samaria by the Assyrians (Ezra 4:9–10).

Akkad. The home of the famous Sargon I (2350–2295 B.C.), its location is unknown.

Calneh. Unidentified and unknown from Akkadian sources, this is not the Calno of Syria (Isa. 10:9; Amos 6:2). Some emend the vowel points of the Masoretic text from *kalnēh* to *kullānâ* ("all of them"). In that case the text would read "Erech and Akkad—all of them in. . . ."

Shinar. This refers to the whole of Mesopotamia.[18]

11. Assyria. Micah (ca. 700 B.C.) labels Assyria, in the northern part of Mesopotamia, as the land of Nimrod (5:6). Assyrians are one of the cruelest, if not the cruelest, conquerors known in ancient history, the infamous destroyers of Israel's northern kingdom.

---

[16]So also BDB, 817, 4.a(g); *HALOT*, 942, 4e; Jenni, *TLOT*, 2:1003.
[17]The victory of Jerusalem over Babylon must wait for the advent of Jesus Christ and his ascension to the heavenly Jerusalem.
[18]*HALOT*, 1485. Daniel 1:2, where it means Babylonia, is an exception.

built. Nimrod built cities, not altars to the Lord.

Nineveh. This great city lies on the east bank of the Tigris, opposite Mosul, in Northern Iraq.

Rehoboth Ir. The term, meaning "plazas of the city," designates either a suburb of Nineveh or a place situated nearly.[19]

Calah. Modern Tell Nimrud, approximately 20 miles south of Nineveh.

12. Resen. Probably modern Selamiyeh, about 2.5 miles northwest of Nimrud.

great city. This could refer to Calah or Nineveh (see Jonah 1:2; 3:2–3; 4:11).

Seven Sons of Egypt (10:13 – 14)

13. Ludites. These are probably the Lydians of North Africa and not the Lydians of Asia Minor (cf. 10:22).[20]

Anamites. The identification is uncertain; they are possibly Egyptian people.

Lehabites. Unidentified.

Naphtuhites. Inhabitants of Middle or Lower (i.e., northern) Egypt.

14. Pathrusites. These are people of Pathros in Upper (i.e., southern) Egypt.

Casluhites. Unidentified.

Philistines. They are probably not to be counted as one of the nations but mentioned parenthetically to identify Israel's bitter foe at the end of the period of judges and the beginning of the monarchy. The Egyptian and Cretan cultures are connected. The Philistines may have migrated to Caphtor (Crete) and from there settled in southwest Canaan around 1200 B.C. Amos 9:7 says that the Lord brought the Philistines out of Crete in the same way that he brought the Israelites out of Egypt, suggesting that Crete may not have been the Philistines' ultimate place of origin. The references to the Philistines in Genesis 21 and 26 may be anachronisms due to the scribal tendency to modernize the text (see "Composition and Authorship" in the introduction) or, more probably, a reference to smaller settlements of Sea Peoples who arrived already in the patriarchal period and lived there intermittently.[21] In any case, they differ from the later Philistines. The early Philistines are ruled by a king; the later ones by five lords. The early Philistines are peaceful and reasonable; the latter, highly aggressive warriors.

Caphtorites. Cretans.

---

[19]*HALOT*, 1213.
[20]*HALOT*, 522.
[21]K. A. Kitchen, *Ancient Orient and Old Testament* (Downers Grove, Ill.: InterVarsity, 1966), 80–81; T. C. Mitchell, "Philistines, Philistia," *IBD*, 3:1222; N. Bierling, *Giving Goliath His Due: New Archaeological Light on the Philistines* (Grand Rapids: Baker, 1992), 24.

The Eleven Descendants of Canaan and Their Land
(10:15 – 20)

15. Sidon. This is Canaan's firstborn, located in Sidon.

Hittites. The Hebrew literally reads Heth, probably the ancestor of the biblical Hittites, one of the progenitors of Jerusalem (Ezek. 16:3). In the patriarchal period the Hittites live in Judah's territory, especially around Hebron (see Gen. 23). Their immorality repulses Isaac and Rebekah, but Esau intermarries with them (Gen. 26:34–35; 27:46).

16. Jebusites. These are the pre-Israelite inhabitants of Jerusalem (Judg. 19:10–11; 2 Sam. 5:6–9).

Amorites. According to Ezek. 16:3, the Amorites were the other progenitors of Jerusalem. They were scattered throughout Israel's hill country on either side of the Jordan (Num. 13:29). At the time of Jacob, they are found in Shechem (Gen. 48:22) ; at the time of Moses, in Transjordan from the Arnon to Mount Hermon (Deut. 3:8) and from the wilderness to the Jordan (Judg. 11:22); at the time of Joshua, in five towns of Judah (Josh. 10:5); and in the next generation, in three towns (Judg. 1:35). In the period of the judges, they also reside in Gilead (Judg. 10:8).

Girgashites. This is a little-known Canaanite tribe (see Gen. 15:21; Deut. 7:1; Josh. 3:10).

17. Hivites. Part of the Canaanite population and uncircumcised (Gen. 34:13–24), they were at Shechem (Gen. 34), Gibeon (Josh. 9:1, 7), Lebanon (Judg. 3:3), and near Mount Hermon (Josh. 11:3; 2 Sam. 24:7).

Arkites. Identified with Tell 'Arqa, northwest of Tripoli.

Sinites. Inhabitants of a city-state south of Ugarit (modern Ras Shamra) in Phoenicia.

18. Arvadites. Inhabitants of Ruad, a North Phoenician island town.

Zemarites. They are located approximately 12 miles south of Arwad.

Hamathites. These are inhabitants of modern Hama, the ancient Syrian city on the Orontes River. It marked the northernmost boundary of the land of Canaan (Num. 34:8; Josh. 13:5; 2 Sam. 8:9–10; 1 Kings 8:65; 2 Kings 14:25–28).

scattered. This key word foreshadows the punitive judgment on the tower builders in Act 2.

19. borders of Canaan. The territory lies on the Via Maris, the north-south seacoast highway, connecting Egypt with Mesopotamia. The border extends from Sidon in the north to Gaza in the south. From there it extends to Sodom and Gomorrah east or southeast of the Dead Sea. The narrator paces off the Canaanite border because it is this land that the Lord will dispossess for Israel (for a more detailed description, see Num. 34:2–12; cf. Gen. 15:18; Ezek. 47:15–20; 48:1–28).

Gerar. This is modern Tell Abu Hureira, 11 miles southeast of Gaza, or Tell esh-Sheri'a, west of Beersheba.

Gaza. Modern Gaza.

Sodom, Gomorrah, Admah and Zeboiim. Sodom and Gomorrah are east or southeast of the Dead Sea. They occur fifteen times together, in connection with Adamah and Zeboiim here and in Gen. 14:2, 8; Deut. 29:23. Admah and Zeboiim also occur together in Hosea 11:8. All four are overthrown when God rains down fire and brimstone upon them (Gen. 19).

Lasha. This is in the region of the Dead Sea, perhaps its northern end.[22]

Table 3: Sons of Shem (10:21–31)

Introduction (10:21)

21. Sons were also born. The segmented genealogy of 10:21–24 traces Shem's lineage to Eber. Of Shem's five sons, the narrator blanks the lineages of Elam, Asshur, and Lud. Aram's genealogy is broad, presenting only the first generation of four descendants. The blessed line runs through Arphaxad to Eber. With Eber's two sons, Peleg and Joktan, a major division takes place. The nonelect line of Joktan is traced in 10:26–29 and connected with the rebellion against God at the Tower of Babel. The elect line of Peleg will constitute Book 5 and trace the linear lineage down to Abraham, making him the legitimate heir of Shem's blessing.

Shem. The elect line is presented last (see Literary Analysis above).

whose older brother was Japheth. The ambiguous Hebrew could also indicate Shem as the older brother. However, in light of the time frame indicated in Shem's genealogy (see 11:10 in Book 5), Japheth is likely the older brother.

ancestor. The Hebrew word is translated "father" elsewhere. Actually, Shem is at the least Eber's great-great-grandfather (see 10:24; 11:13–14).

all the sons of. The narrator highlights the importance of Eber's sons.

Eber. This genealogy accents Eber by mentioning him out of order (see 10:21, 24), by repeating his name as son of Shelah and as father of Peleg and Joktan, and by mentioning at the outset that Shem is the father of all his sons. The narrator does this because Eber is the last ancestor in the in-depth lineage from Shem to Abraham before the division between his sons into the nonelect through Joktan and the elect through Peleg.

Twelve Sons and Fourteen Names of Shem to Eber (10:22–24)

22. Elam. Modern southwestern Iran (see 14:1, 9; Ezra 4:9; Isa. 11:11).

Asshur. This son may have given his name to the land of Assyria (see 2:14; 10:11). According to archaeological evidence, the earliest inhabitants of Assyria were Sumerians (Hamitic), and they were supplanted by the Semitic culture that spread throughout Mesopotamia.

Arphaxad. The territory is uncertain. The linear lineage of Arphaxad is expanded in 11:12–17.

---

[22]*HALOT,* 537.

Lud. Related to Lydians in Asia Minor (cf. Gen. 10:13).

Aram. As a place name, it refers to the whole kingdom of the Aramean tribes or to diverse sites in Syria and Mesopotamia. Amos 9:7 traces the Arameans to Kir, perhaps in southern Babylonia in the vicinity of Elam (see Isa. 22:6), though their movement to this southern location may have been as secondary as Israel's in Egypt and the Philistines in Crete.

23. sons of Aram. Little is known about them, but the patriarchs have close relations with them (see 25:20; 31:20; Deut. 26:5).

Uz. This is the head of the Aramean tribe. As a place name, Uz is the homeland of Job, but the site is unknown. Suggestions from the Old Testament include a southern land to the east of the Jordan (Edom) or a northern land to the east of the Jordan in Aramean territory.

Hul, Gether. Unidentified.

Meshech. The Greek version and 1 Chron. 1:5 read Meshech (see 10:2). If so, both Japheth and Shem have sons named Meshech. The Hebrew reads "Mash"; if correct, it could be connected with Mount Masius of northern Mesopotamia or the mountains of Lebanon and Antilebanon.

24. [father of Cainan]. The LXX adds this here and in 11:12–17. The addition provides the anticipated ten names between Shem and Abraham. It is easier to explain the omission as due to haplography than to explain the addition. Cainan's name is part of the lineage of Jesus Christ (Luke 3:35–36).

Shelah. Of uncertain identity (cf. Gen. 38:5, 11), it probably means "sprout, branch, descendant." The full name may be Methushelah.

Eber. The adjectival form "Hebrew" may come from this name.[23] This last descendant of God's blessing before the narrator divides Shem's lineage probably gives his name to the patriarchs and to Israel (e.g., 14:13; 39:14; 40:15; 41:12; Ex. 2:11; 3:18).

Eber's Two Sons (10:25)

25. Peleg. His name, which means "division," probably prophesies the dispersal of the nations at Babel (see Lamech's prophecy in 5:29). It may also signify the separation of the elect line of Shem from the nonelect line.

earth was divided. This is probably a reference to the division of the peoples into nations in Act 2. In Ps. 55:9, the same Hebrew verb is used in the phrase "confound their speech [tongue]." The brothers are divided by the Tower of Babel both in history and in the narrative of books 4 and 5.

Joktan. Bearing an Aramaic name meaning "watchful," Joktan is the forefather of tribes of south Arabia.[24] In contrast to his brother's line, which leads to Abraham (see 11:16–26), Joktan's nonelect branch will reach a cul-de-sac.

---

[23]Some derive "Hebrew" from its etymology, "across" (i.e., the one who is from beyond the other side). Others attribute it to Akkadian *abiru/apiru,* which designates social outcasts of different ethnicity who served as mercenaries.

[24]The descendants of Ishmael (25:13–16) inhabited north Arabia (F. V. Winnett, "Studies in Ancient North Arabian Genealogies," *JAOS* 107[1987]: 239–44).

Shem's Sons by Eber through Joktan:
Fourteen Names (10:26–30)

26. Almodad.[25] Ancestor, region, or tribe in Yemen.

Sheleph. A Yemenite tribe.

Hazarmaveth. The south Arabian region Hadramaut.

Jerah. Location unknown.

27. Hadoram. Arabian tribe.

Uzal. Traditionally the pre-Islamic name of Ṣana'a, capital of Yemen.

Diklah. South Arabian oasis meaning "palm-land."

28. Obal. Between Ḥodeida and Ṣana'a in southwest Arabia.

Abimael. Unidentified.

Sheba. This is probably the same location as Seba of 10:7.

29. Ophir. Situated between Sheba and Havilah in southwest Arabia and with gold in its wadis (Job 22:24), it possibly included the coast of Africa opposite, the land of Punt in Egyptian sources.

Havilah. This is probably the same location as the Havilah of 10:7.

Jobab. Located in southern Arabia; more precise locations are disputed.

30. region where they lived. The reference to the region of Joktan's sons shows the importance of the Shemites to the narrator.

from Mesha. Territory in North Arabia, far south of Hadramaut.

toward Sephar. This is traditionally identified with Iṣfar in the south of Hadramaut or Ẓafar harbor city in Oman or in Yemen.

Conclusion to Act 1, Transition to Act 2 (10:32)

32. Noah's sons. This phrase forms an inclusio with 10:1, framing Act 1.

these the nations. LXX and SP read "these islands of the nations."

spread out. The shift from "had sons" (10:1) to "spread out" (10:32) prepares the way for Act 2 in chapter 11.

THEOLOGICAL REFLECTIONS ON ACT 1 ———————————

God's Sovereignty over All the Nations

The numbers seven and seventy in the Table of Nations represent the nations as dependent upon their Creator and under his sovereignty, whether they acknowledge him as such or not. It is not without interest that such a table of the nations is unique to Old Testament literature. Neither the hieroglyphic nor the cuneiform worlds produced a parallel document. "The theological value of the Table is that it affirms Israel as part of one world governed by one God."[26] The Table also underscores that God is the God of the Gentiles by omitting Israel.[27] Gowan comments, "Without referring to

---

[25]The following identifications are taken from *HALOT*.

[26]Hamilton, *Genesis 1-17*, 346.

[27]The Table also uses *gôy*, "nation," not *ʿam*, "people."

chp. 11 one would not have a clue where Israel will belong in the Table of Nations. Here we have expressed an interest in all people, in their own right."[28] Mathews adds, "There was a world of peoples before the call of Abraham, and it is that map of peoples that concerns the God of Abraham ultimately. Out of concern for the salvation of the nations, God calls Abraham and his posterity."[29]

Although the Table does not mention it, the nations receive their time and place as the outworking of God's sovereignty. According to Moses and the Deuteronomist (i.e., the final author of Deuteronomy–2 Kings, not including Ruth), God assigns the nations their territories: "The Most High gave the nations their inheritance, when he divided all mankind" (Deut. 32:8; cf. also Amos 9:7). Paul comments, "[God] determined the times set for them and the exact places where they should live" (Acts 17:26). It is important to keep in mind that the godless cities Nimrod builds, Babylon and Nineveh, are the cities that eventually bring the northern and southern kingdoms of Israel to their knees. What a comfort for the godly exiles from these kingdoms to know that their covenant-keeping God is sovereign over Nimrod's cities (see also "Theological Reflections on Act 2").

City of Man versus City of God

By establishing the borders of the curse-laden Canaanites (Gen. 10:19), the narrator sets the stage for what God will take away from them because of their iniquity and give to his chosen people to sanctify. The seventy nations also stand over against the seventy sons of Israel. Israel is in microcosm similar in form to the macrocosm. God has set the microcosm apart to bless the macrocosm.

BOOK 4, ACT 2: ESCALATION OF SIN IN BABYLON (11:1–9)

LITERARY ANALYSIS OF BOOK 4, ACT 2[30] ———————

Anachrony

Act 2 is a flashback that explains why the three sons of Noah became divided at the time of Peleg son of Shem (10:25; see above).

Structure and Plot

The Tower of Babel narrative can be divided into four scenes: the initial setting on the plains of Shinar (11:1–2); the human word to construct a city

---

[28]D. E. Gowan, *Genesis 1–11: From Eden to Babel* (ITC; Grand Rapids: Eerdmans, 1988), 114.

[29]Mathews, *Genesis 1–11:26*, 430.

[30]The Babel story is not dated, but similar elements are found in early Akkadian literature in the second millennium B.C. (cf. the confusion of language [Enmerkar] and the refusal of humanity to worship the gods [Atrahasis]).

and tower (11:3–4); the divine word to deconstruct by confounding speech (11:5–7); and the final setting, the nations scattered (11:8–10). The story is equally divided between humanity and God. The first setting and dialogue feature humanity. The second dialogue and final setting feature God.

The structure of this terse short story can be analyzed as alternating or chiastic:

Alternating structure:

Words of the people 11:1–4
A One language and a common speech
  B "Come" + 2 cohortatives
    C "Let us build ourselves a city, with a tower"
      D Let us "make a name"
        E Lest we be scattered over the face of earth
Words of the Lord 11:5–9
A′ One people and one language
  B′ "Come" + cohortative
    C′ Ceased to build
      D′ Its "name" [Heb.] was Babel
        E′ The Lord scattered them over the whole earth

This structure exposes the tension of the act: the struggle of human endeavor against God, matched by God's punitive response. The plot pits the word of humanity against the word of God. It peaks when God confuses humanity's speech. Its denouement occurs in the scattering of the people.

Chiastic structure:[31]

A All the earth (*kol-hāʾāreṣ*) one language
B People settle together there (*šām*)
  C Said to each other (*rēʿēhû*)
    D Come now, let us make bricks (*hāḇâ nilbᵉnâ*)
      E A city and a tower
        X And the Lord came down
      E′ The city and the tower
    D′ Come now . . . let us confuse (*hāḇâ . . . nāḇᵉlâ*[32])
  C′ [Not understand] each other (*rēʿēhû*)
B′ People disperse from there (*šam*)
A′ Language of the whole earth (*kol-hāʾāreṣ*)

This chiastic structure exposes the theme of reversal around the pivot, "The LORD came down." The plot moves from humanity's construction of a

---

[31]I. M. Kikawada, "The Shape of Genesis 11:1-9," in *Rhetorical Criticism: Essays in Honor of James Muilenburg*, ed. J. J. Jackson and M. Kessler (Pittsburgh: Pickwick, 1974), 18–32.
[32]MT omits *meteḡ*.

city and a tower to God's deconstruction of them. A/A′ set forth the contrasting settings. The act begins with the whole world speaking a common language and ends with the whole world confused, speaking different languages. B/B′ contrast the centripetal energy of the people to remain consolidated at Shinar and the divine centrifugal energy that scatters them. C/C′ contrast the strength of their unification in opposition to God with their divided communication and resulting segregation. D/D′ contrast the people's resolve to build in hubris against God versus the resolve of God and his court to confound. The reversal is nicely accented by the reversal of the broken sequence of their resolves: *nlbnh* ("let us make bricks") versus *nblh* ("let us confound"). E/E′ contrast the human and divine viewpoints toward the city and tower. For the rebels, the city and tower symbolize the ability of collective humanity to defy the rule of heaven. From the viewpoint of the divine council, they symbolize the human societal threat to divine dominion. X is the focal point on which the narrative turns. The turn entails the dramatic irony that the heavenly court has to descend to see the puny tower and city.

Inclusio

The inclusio of Act 2 focuses on the earth and language, commencing with one unified language (11:1) and concluding with a cacophony of confused languages dividing people from one another (11:9).

Key Words and Paronomasia

The key expression of this act, "all the world/earth" (*kol-hāʾāreṣ*, 11:1, 4, 8, 9 [2x]) represents the whole earth as tainted with human sin. "Language" also occurs five times and gives the act its focus. The setting presents humanity as unified both in language (11:1) and in habitation (11:2). Their unity is underscored by *kōl* ("whole") earth and *ʾeḥāṯ* ("one"/"common") language/speech.

Comparisons

The Babelites and their hubris compare significantly with those who precede them. Humanity's building of a tower with its lofty head in the clouds represents the final and climactic expression of human hubris. As Adam and Eve transgressed the limits of human wisdom and sought, by eating the forbidden fruit, to be like God (Gen. 3:22) and as the sons of God transgressed the boundaries of marriage (6:1–2, 4), the tower builders seek meaning and fame by transgressing into the dwelling place of God. They infringe upon the divine sphere and God himself draws the conclusion that "nothing they plan to do will be impossible for them."

The postdiluvian tower builders are the spiritual heirs of the line of Cain, not of Seth, as these comparisons show: both migrate eastward (4:16; 11:2); both build a city to establish a secure place and a meaningful existence without God (4:17; 11:4); both are proud manufacturers (4:19–24; 11:3–4); both

are judged by being forced to migrate (4:12–13; 11:8); both continue to prop-
agate under the Lord's blessing (4:17–24; ch. 10).

Irony

In the ancient Near East, Babel claimed to be the center of the world in the
same way as Rome was widely regarded as the religious center of the Holy
Roman Empire in the Middle Ages. The Tower of Babel story lampoons this
boast. To its founders "Babel" meant "gate/residence of the gods," but the
narrator parodies that significance by a Hebrew by-form *bll,* meaning "confused" (cf. English, "a babel of voices"). Its builders think their temple tower
reaches into heaven; it is so low that the Lord has to descend from heaven
just to see it!

EXEGETICAL NOTES TO BOOK 4, ACT 2 ───────────

Scene 1: The Initial Setting: On the Plains of Shinar (11:1–2)

1. whole world. "Whole" may be a relative term (cf. 13:9, 15; Deut.
11:25; 19:8; 34:1), but nothing in the context suggests a restricted use (cf.
Gen. 19:31; Ex. 19:5; Num. 14:21). This image of the whole world underscores the people's unity.

one language. The Hebrew is literally "one lip" (so also 11:7; Ps. 81:5;
Isa. 19:18).[33]

a common speech. The text literally reads "one words." They are
entirely unified by language and vocabulary.

2. moved. The image is that of people "pulling up stakes" for travelling.
The survivors of the Flood are represented initially as anxious nomads.

eastward. As Mathews notes, "[Eastward] marks events of *separation* in
Genesis. By this spatial term the narrative also conveys a metaphorical
sphere, meaning the Babelites are outside God's blessing"[34] (cf. Gen. 3:24;
4:16; 13:10–12; 25:6; 29:1).

Shinar. See comments on 10:10.

settled there. This represents the theological opposite of God's command
to fill the earth (9:1) and the lexical opposite of "scattered from there" (11:8).

Scene 2: The Human Word: To Construct
a City and Tower (11:3–4)

3. They said. By quoting them, the narrator allows the people to condemn themselves.

let's make bricks [*nilbᵉnâ lᵉbēnîm*] **and bake them thoroughly** [*niśrᵉpâ
liśrēpâ*] . . . **tar for mortar** [*ḥēmār . . . lāhem laḥōmer*]. The similar sounds

---

[33]The Sumerian epic entitled Enmerkar and the Lord of Aratta also speaks of a time when "the
whole universe in unison spoke to Enlil in one tongue." It then reports that speech was confounded as
a result of jealousy and strife between two gods. Here it is a divine judgment against human hubris.

[34]Mathews, *Genesis 1–11:26,* 478.

match their similar speech (note the sequence of *l, b, n* in the first phrase; *s, r, p* in the second; and *ḥ, m, r* in the third; with *l* uniting all three). The importance of their determination to manufacture their own building materials can be inferred by the detail presented of its manufacture.[35]

They used . . . mortar. The narrator has to explain to his Israelite audience, who used readily available stone, the Mesopotamian building practice.[36]

4. Come, let us build. They continue to use the mood of willful resolve, underlined by the rare exclamation, *hāḇâ*, "come [now]."

city. A defensive wall is the hallmark of a city (see 4:17). Cities in the ancient Near East were not designed to be lived in but were intended for religious and public purposes.

tower [*migdāl*]. The Hebrew from the root *gdl*, "to be great," has a wide range of meanings. Here with reference to Mesopotamia, which did not have the defensive stone watch towers of Canaan, it designates the Mesopotamian ziggurat.[37] The ziggurat was a massive and lofty, solid-brick, staircase structure. It was an inseparable part of the city, and sometimes the temple complex was the entire city.

that reaches to the heavens. Like Jacob's staircase (see Gen. 28:12), the ziggurat mountain, with its roots in the earth and its lofty top in the clouds, served in mythopoeic thought as a gate to heaven. This humanly created mountain gave humanity access to heaven (28:17) and served as a convenient stairway for the gods to come down into their temple and into the city. For example, the ziggurat at Larsa was named "The House of the Link Between Heaven and Earth" and the most famous ziggurat of all, at Babylon, "The House of the Foundation of Heaven and Earth." The ziggurat culminated in a small shrine at the top, often painted with blue enamel to make it blend with the celestial home of the gods. Here the addition "to the heavens" shows they are vying with God himself. The Lord, not humankind, dwells in the heavens (Gen. 19:24; 21:17; 22:11, 15; Deut. 26:15; Ps. 115:16).

that we make a name for ourselves. "Name" (*šem*), occurring twice in this act, constitutes a sound play with "there" (*šam*), which occurs five times. Since *name* connotes fame and progeny, these city builders are futilely attempting to find significance and immortality in their own achievements (see 6:4). The Babelites earn for themselves the ignominious name "Confusion." It is not the construction of cities but the human pride and security that people attach to the cities (Gen. 4:12–14, 17) that displeases the Lord.[38]

---

[35]Sarna writes, "Akkadian building inscriptions, which hail the achievements of the great kings, repeatedly emphasize the making of bricks. Indeed, the modeling of the first brick was regarded as an important rite and was accompanied by elaborate ceremonies" (*Genesis*, 82).

[36]Instructively, he employs the accredited grammatico-historical method of interpretation.

[37]From Akkadian, *zaqāru* "to build high."

[38]In contrast, Israel celebrates the holy city of Jerusalem.

and not [*pen*]. The meaning is, "otherwise we will be." Their sin is similar to Adam's and Eve's. They transgress boundaries and the divine prohibition in order to satisfy material and spiritual aspirations independently from God.

be scattered. This skyscraper is a symbol of their united titanic societal self-assertion against God, who commands them to "fill the earth" (9:1). These proud sinners, like Cain, fear both a loss of place (i.e., existential meaning) in their isolation from God and perhaps from one another (see 4:14). Like him, they find their solution for meaning in an abiding city rivaling God.

Scene 3: The Divine Word: To Deconstruct by Confounding Speech (11:5 – 7)

5. came down. As seen throughout Genesis, God thoroughly investigates a situation before giving a judicial sentence (3:8–13; 4:9–10; 18:21). The ziggurat builders imagine themselves ascending to the heavens and their gods descending down their staircase. They do not expect the true God to descend.

to see. Ironically, the tower is so puny that God has to come down to see it (see 1:4; Isa. 40:22). Sarna explains, "This figurative usage implies no limitation on God's omnipotence, for the divine 'descent' presupposes prior knowledge of human affairs from on high, and God's subsequent counter-action unqualifiedly exhibits His absolute sovereignty."[39]

men. The Hebrew literally reads "sons of humankind." This emphasizes that the builders are nothing more than frail, mortal earthlings.

were building. The project is incomplete, as 11:8 indicates. Nevertheless, as much as they have built is represented as complete through the literal Hebrew here: "they built."

6. one people. This phrase emphasizes their kinship.

speaking the same language. Their common language is the source of their strength and unity, symbolized by the tower.

have begun to do. The endeavor to find fame, existential significance, and unity through technology is a new innovation of boundary crossing in postdiluvian history. Describing this building project as just having begun also has polemical significance. This counters the Babylonian creation myth that presents Babylon as founded at the time of the original creation.[40]

nothing . . . will be impossible. Literally, "all they plan to do will not be withheld from them." God clearly exposes that humanity's sin in building the tower is its refusal to live within God-given boundaries.

7. Come, let us. The rallying cry of heaven matches the mortals'. The "us" refers to the divine council (see 1:26).

---

[39]Sarna, *Genesis*, 83.
[40]According to Berossus, it was created at the beginning and rebuilt after the Flood (cf. Josephus, *Contra Apionem* 1.19).

confuse. The confounding of their language is matched by the confounding of the consonantal sequence from *nilbᵉnâ* ("let us make bricks," 11:4) to *nābᵉlâ*[41] ("let us confound," 11:7).

not understand. The absence of a common language leads to the lack of a common understanding, which terminates the project.

Scene 4: The Final Setting: The Nations Scattered (11:8 – 10)

8. the LORD scattered them from there. He reverses "and [they] settled there" (11:2).

over all the earth. In spite of their rebellion, the Sovereign fulfills his design that people fill the earth.

9. Babel. The narrator parodies Akkadian *bāb-ilu,* meaning "gate of god," with its Hebrew phonological equivalent *bābel,* meaning "confusion." Babel likely refers to the city of Babylon (cf. 10:10, with the same Hebrew word). The mention of Shinar (10:10; 11:2) and Babel/Babylon connects this city and its tower with Nimrod's antigod kingdom. Nimrod built cities that replicated the original Babel and its ziggurat.

confused the language. This reverses "one language and a common speech" (11:1).

THEOLOGICAL REFLECTIONS ON BOOK 4, ACT 2 ———————

God's Sovereignty

Act 2 points to the Lord's sovereignty over all nations. The narrator draws its final scene to conclusion with the inclusio: "The LORD scattered them . . . over [the face of] all the earth" (11:8a, 9b). He sandwiches in between: "the LORD confused the language of the whole world" (11:9a). Before assigning the nations their territories, God first confounds their speech and scatters them.

Unity and Diversity of the Nations

On the one hand, the segmented genealogies of the Table present the interconnectedness of all people. They are all descendants of Adam and Noah, are under God's fertility blessing, and have dignity as bearers of God's image to subdue the earth. That emphasis restrains the negative affects of tribalism. Mathews says, "Genesis 10–11 shows that a disproportionate consideration on 'races,' as in our modern world, forfeits our inherent unity and may lead to a primitive tribalism that fosters war."[42] The nations' original unity portends their ultimate unity when nation shall not lift up sword against nation, neither shall they learn war any more (Isaiah 2:4 and Micah 4:3).

---

[41]Note that MT omits *meṯeḡ.*
[42]Mathews, *Genesis 1–11:26,* 429.

On the other hand, the Tower of Babel narrative shows the need for division. Depraved humanity are united in their spiritual endeavor to find, through technology, existential meaning apart from God and the means to transgress its boundaries. Unless God intervenes and divides them by confounding their speech, nothing can stop human beings in their overweening pride and their desire for autonomy. They will drive over the boundaries the Creator has established. Like Adam, they seek to usurp the rule of the divine council itself. Fokkelman says: "Implicitly they want, perhaps as yet unconsciously, to make impossible the salvation-history, which according to the biblical message is essentially the thrilling dialogue between God and man. Implicitly they want to penetrate the strictly divine and become divine themselves. What drives them is hubris."[43]

Fokkelman goes on to note that this hubris has both a positive and a negative aspect: "We see how, in a nutshell, the narrator conveys in language the idea that hubris has not only a 'positive' component, megalomania, wanting-to-be-like-God, but also a negative one, fear, the fear of being scattered abroad, of having to live without safety and existential security, of being lonely and vulnerable."[44] Is the United Nations building in New York a long shadow of the Tower of Babel?

The result of being divided into nations, however, has been catastrophic. Their hubris against God on the vertical axis also finds expression in their refusal to recognize boundaries on the horizontal axis of human relationships. Individuals, unwilling to submit to the Creator's boundaries as expressed in conscience and the Ten Commandments, transgress each other's boundaries in order to kill, rob, plunder, and destroy one another. The characterization of Nimrod as a rebel against God and a tyrannical ruler over people shows the connection between transgressing heavenly and earthly boundaries. His cities replicate the Tower of Babel city in its rebellion against God, but they also represent tyranny on the horizontal axis. The human spirit to idolize itself led in the twentieth century to titanic world wars. In World War II, fifty million people were killed.

Thus, society apart from God is totally unstable. On the one hand, people earnestly seek existential meaning and security in their collective unity. On the other hand, they have an insatiable appetite to consume what others possess. Because of this tension, the United Nations is doomed to frustration and failure in its quest for peace without the Prince of Peace.

City of Man Versus City of God

The cities that Nimrod built replicate Babel and its tower. They represent the human spirit to achieve significance and security through their collec-

---

[43]Fokkelman, *Genesis*, 17.
[44]Ibid.

tive technology, independently from God. At the heart of the city of man is love for self and hatred of God. The city reveals that the human spirit will not stop at anything short of usurping God's throne in heaven. Today, self-idolizing humanity is storming outer space, hoping to subdue even the heavenly bodies, and through genetic engineering has the potential to clone and shape humanity according to its own imagination. What had historically been the prerogative of God alone has now come under the dominion of depraved humanity. The prospect is frightening.

In and of itself, the construction of cities does not cause the Lord's displeasure; for example, Israel celebrates holy Jerusalem. Rather God censures the human pride and security that people attach to their cities (Gen. 4:12–14, 17). By contrast, Abraham was content to be a wandering Aramean with God (Deut. 26:5), looking for a city with foundations, "whose architect and builder is God" (Heb 11:10). As a reward, God gave him and all who, like him, honor God's name, an enduring name. The Babelites, in their longing for a humanly constructed, human-glorifying city, earn for themselves the ignominious name "Confusion."

Technology

Technology, which enables human beings to subdue the earth and in part sets them above animals, is God's good gift to people. However, people pervert it. Since the word *name* connotes fame and progeny, the city builders were futilely attempting to find significance and immortality in their technology and their achievements. However, technology cannot give divine blessing. Only God can give an everlasting name (see Gen. 12:2), and he gives it to those who magnify his name and not their own achievements (see 4:26; 2 Sam. 7:8–9; 8:13; Isa. 63:12, 14). Today the city and its civilization are signs of humanity's separation from God. It cannot renew the divine intimacy of the lost paradise.

The failure of secular technology is symbolized by the incompleteness of their project. Whereas God establishes a complete number of nations, the tower builders, under divine wrath, cannot complete their project. Fox says, "By portraying an unfinished tower, by dispersing the builders, and by in essence making fun of the mighty name of Babylon, the text functions effectively to repudiate the culture from which the people Israel sprang."[45]

Language

As human beings abuse God's good gift of technology for dominion, they also abuse language. God gives them language to bring the world under dominion by naming, but they use it to rival God. God judges humanity by

---

[45]E. Fox, *In the Beginning: A New English Rendition of the Book of Genesis* (New York: Schocken, 1983), 43.

confounding their languages and forcing them to separate from one another. As noted, the result has been catastrophic destruction, not dominion, as unbridled nations go to war against one another. That damaging confusion and devastating destruction is reversed at Pentecost (Acts 2:5–18). The Spirit does not remove diverse languages but allows the regenerate people to hear and understand one another. The Spirit alters the effects of their languages from deconstructing the community to reconstructing the new community of the church. With the Holy Spirit, we hear and understand; without him, we misunderstand through our fear, distrust, and self-ambition. Unity cannot be engineered; it is matter of the Spirit.[46] Filled with the Holy Spirit, we hear, understand, and sacrifice in love for one another.

---

[46]See E. F. Roop, *Genesis* (Scottdale, Pa./Kitchener, Ont.: Herald, 1987), 84–85.

THE ACCOUNT OF
SHEM'S DESCENDANTS (11:10–26)

THEME OF BOOK 5 ————————————————————

The ten-name, linear genealogy of Book 5 forms the transition from the Flood to Abraham. By tracing the lineage from the God-blessed Shem to his legitimate heir, Abraham, who will become God's means of blessing all tribes and nations, the genealogy inferentially presents God's gracious presence in the midst of prideful humanity. In the context of God's scattering rebellious humanity over the face of the earth (11:1–9), the Lord preserves the seed to whom he has committed himself to be their God. Dorsey explains, "The cadenced, highly structured format again communicates a sense of restored order, in contrast to the structurally (and thematically) fractured preceding unit. This sense of well being is confirmed by the unit's positive conclusion: the birth of Abraham, Israel's revered ancestor."[1] These bearers of the image of God are the legitimate rulers of God's creation and the seed that will destroy the Serpent. This is the lineage of Jesus Christ and his church (Luke 3:34–35; Gal. 3:29). Although before the Flood tyrants transgressed the marriage ordinance and after the Flood humanity collectively breached the boundary separating earth and heaven, God's program to save humanity cannot be stopped.

OUTLINE OF BOOK 5 ————————————————————

---

[1]Dorsey, *Literary*, 53.

LITERARY ANALYSIS OF BOOK 5 ───────────────

Structure and Plot

The account consists of the typical superscription (11:10a), the initial chronological setting, "two years after the flood" (11:10b), the linear genealogy (11:10b–25), and the segmented genealogy of Terah (11:26). The tension of this act pertains to God's promise to be the God of Shem. Each generation waits expectantly to see if God will fulfill his elective purpose. He does not fail. The genealogy concludes with the birth of Abraham, the man of faith par excellence, who stands against an unbelieving world.

Janus

Book 5 is a janus book between books 3–4 and 6. It looks back to Book 3 by mentioning the Flood (11:10) and Shem (cf. 9:27) and by uniquely featuring the genealogy of Shem, to whom the Lord committed himself (9:27). It also looks back to Book 4 by repeating the genealogy of Shem to Peleg (cf. 10:22–25; 11:10–16).

Book 5 also looks ahead by concluding with Terah and his family (11:26), the subject of Book 6 (11:27–25:11). Moreover, the death of Terah is not noted until the end of the introduction to Book 6 (11:32), thereby dovetailing these two books together.

Comparisons and Contrasts

This genealogy is similar to the genealogy of Book 2 (Gen. 5), which presents the transition from Adam to the Flood.[2] Both quickly sketch extended periods of time. Both are linear, aiming to show the legitimate descendant of God's election. Both, using the same vocabulary and literary pattern, announce the age of the patriarch at the birth of his firstborn son, his number of years after that birth, and his fathering of sons and daughters. Both segment into three sons at the conclusion, naming the elect descendant first (i.e., Noah and Abraham). Both are open, not closed, schematizing the extended time spans involved by restricting themselves to ten (a number of completion) names (see below).

Finally, the seventh generation figures prominently in both genealogies. Enoch as the one who walked with God is in the special seventh slot in the Adam-to-Noah genealogy, and Eber as the father of the "Hebrews" (cf. 10:21, 24–25) is seventh from the end in the Shem-to-Abraham genealogy. Moreover, in the combined genealogies, Eber is listed in the fourteenth (seven times two) generation from creation, and Abraham, according to the LXX, is in the twenty-first (seven times three) (see note on 11:12).[3]

───────────────

[2]The parallel Sumerian King List likewise interrupts the genealogies of the notable kings by the Flood story and shows a dwindling in the longevity of the kings after the Flood, though the figures are still relatively enormous (see *ANET*, 265).

[3]In MT Abraham is reckoned as seventh from Eber; see J. M. Sasson, "Generation, Seventh," *IDB-Sup*, 354–56.

However, the Sethite genealogy, unlike Shem's, adds together the patriarch's age before and after the birth of the elect descendant[4] to give the sum of years and the announcement "and he died."[5] Those additions underscore that the antediluvian patriarchs live complete and full lives with no reduction of their longevity.[6] In comparison, the ages of the postdiluvian patriarchs at the birth of the firstborn son and the number of remaining years reveals a logarithmic[7] reduction of the longevity of the postdiluvians.[8] Shem lives only about two-thirds of Noah's life span (600 years versus 950; cf. 11:10–11 and 9:29), and Arphaxad, only two-thirds of Shem's (438; 11:12–13).

The two omissions in the Shemite genealogy also cause the audience to "speed read" to Abraham. The omission of the "and he died" refrain gives a more optimistic color to the Shemite genealogy, by focusing on birth and future hope, not on inevitable death.

This linear genealogy of Shem overlaps with Shem's segmented genealogy in 10:22–25. The two genealogies of Shem part company at the point of Eber's sons Peleg and Joktan. Genesis 10:26–29 ends in a cul-de-sac with the rejected line of Jobab, but 11:10–26 ends open to the future of salvation history by not mentioning the death of Terah. Here is a diagram of the two genealogies of Shem:

Shem

10:22–24 (cf. 11:14–15)

Eber

Peleg	*at the time*	Joktan
(11:16–26)	*of Babel*	(10:25–31)
Abraham	*(11:1–9)*	Jobab
no children		

Shem's genealogy through Joktan in Book 4 was followed by humanity's sin at the Tower of Babel and God's judgment. Shem's genealogy in Book 5 ends with the promise of Abraham's birth. Shem in Hebrew means "name." Ironically, the tower builders were seeking to "make a name" but have no names, and the city they built receives the shameful name "Confusion." God gives the elect of Shem an everlasting name in this genealogy, and above all, he will exalt the name of the faithful descendant Abraham (see 12:2).

EXEGETICAL NOTES TO BOOK 5

Superscription (10:10a)

10a. account of [*tôlᵉdōt*]. See comments on 2:4 in Book 1.

---

[4]The SP also presents the sum of the two figures in Book 5.
[5]R. S. Hess, "The Genealogies of Genesis 1–11 and Comparative Literature," *BSac* 70 (1989): 243–44.
[6]For example, Adam lived 930 years, and Methuselah (eighth generation) lived 967 years.
[7]See Patten, *Biblical Flood*, 214–16.
[8]Shem lived 500 years, and Nahor (ninth generation) lived 110 years.

Shem. The Hebrew means "name," which is a key word linking with 11:4 and 12:2 (see above).

The Linear Genealogy from Shem to Terah (10:10b–25)

The narrator intentionally schematizes this transitional genealogy to just ten names. He does not name every descendant in order to establish an absolute chronology. If one regarded the Masoretic text as closed (i.e., without chronological gaps), the events of Genesis 9–11 would cover less than three centuries[9] and all of Abraham's ancestors would have been living when he was born. Shem would have outlived Abraham by thirty-five years, and Shem and Eber would have been contemporaries with Jacob![10] By schematizing the genealogies of Genesis 5 and 10:10–26, the narrator effectively unifies the Proto-History from Adam to Abraham, who constitutes the turning point in salvation history and of this book.

10b. Two years after the flood. This setting announcement links Book 5 with Book 3, but the given time frame, along with the announcement, "when Shem was 100 years old, he became the father of...," creates a chronological problem. According to Gen. 5:32; 7:6, Noah was 500 years old when he fathered his three sons and 600 at the time of the Flood. If Shem were the firstborn, his son Arphaxad would have been born the year of the Flood, not two years later. The simplest solution is to read the ambiguous Hebrew of Gen. 10:21 as announcing Japheth as the older brother. Then the precise age of Noah at the time of Shem's birth is unknown. The NIV achieves this interpretation by adding "After Noah was 500 years old" in 5:32.[11]

From Shem to Peleg (10b–17)

10–16. Shem . . . Peleg. The first five names of this linear genealogy overlap with the segmented genealogy of 10:21–25.

10b. father. The Hebrew term here may mean "ancestor."

Arphaxad. In 10:22 Arphaxad is mentioned as the third of Shem's four sons. Here he occurs alone, suggesting that priority in lineage is not based on being the firstborn but on God's election.

11. other sons and daughters. The mention of other children shows both God's progeny blessing and the selective nature of the linear genealogy.

---

[9]The textual recensions of the SP and of the LXX add one hundred years to the ages of the patriarchs from Arphaxad to Serug at the first son's birth. Perhaps they did so to distance Abraham from Shem and to assure that only Abraham's near ancestors were still alive when he was born. As a whole, the Masoretic text shows itself as more reliable than the other two smoothed recensions, but its omission of Cainan between Arphaxad and Shelah is probably secondary. See Waltke, "Samaritan Pentateuch," 212–39; and G. Larsson, "The Chronology of the Pentateuch: A Comparison of the MT and LXX," *JBL* 102 (1983): 401–9.

[10]Cf. D. V. Etz, "The Numbers of Genesis V 3–31: A Suggested Conversion and Its Implication," *VT* 43 (1993): 171–89, esp. 188–89.

[11]It is unlikely that either 500 in 10:32 and/or 100 in 11:10 are round numbers because the other numbers in both genealogies are precise.

12. When Arphaxad had lived 35 years, he became the father of Shelah. This should read, "When Arphaxad had lived 35 years, he became father of Cainan. And after he became the father of Cainan, Arphaxad lived 430 years and had others sons and daughters. When Cainan had lived 34 years he became the father of Shelah. And after he became the father of Shelah, Cainan lived 330 years and had other sons and daughters." This reading is based on the Greek text and Luke 3:35–36 (see Gen. 10:24). From a text-critical point of view, it is much simpler to explain an accidental deletion of a name than an addition. This deletion is explained easily by the similarity of the two entries,[12] a common scribal error. In all likelihood, the Masoretic text then was corrected as necessary to accommodate the omission. This seems more likely than a scribe adding a name to a fixed genealogy. Some, supporting the Masoretic text, argue that Abraham is the tenth generation, but the parallel is imprecise, for they include the segmented genealogy as part of the linear, unlike the ten linear names in Genesis 5.

From Peleg to Terah (11:18–25)

18. Peleg. With Peleg, the lines of Shem through Eber divide between the nonelect and the elect.

19. 209 years. Beginning with Peleg, the life span is even further drastically reduced (see above, "Literary Analysis: Comparisons and Contrasts"). From Arphaxad to Eber the patriarchs live about 450 years. From Peleg to Serug they live a little less than 250 years, and Nahor lives to be only 148.

20. Reu. Aside from the biblical genealogies, the name is unattested. Since Peleg's descendants settled in Upper Mesopotamia, the same may be suspected of Reu.

22. Serug. This is an Akkadian place name approximately 45 miles (60 km) west of Haran in Upper Mesopotamia.

24. Nahor. This is also attested as a place name in Upper Mesopotamia (see 22:23 and 24:10).

The Segmented Genealogy of Terah (11:26)

Terah. The concluding segmented genealogy forms a natural transition to the account of Terah's descendants. Terah is also a place name on the Balikh River near Haran. Terah and his sons first migrate to Ur in southern Mesopotamia (11:28) and then to Canaan (11:31).

70 years. Whereas his ancestors from Arphaxad to Nahor father their firstborn in their early thirties, Terah has to wait another forty years. The delay foreshadows the fate of his son Abraham, who is one hundred, and of

---

[12]LXX reads 130 years, but the additional 100 years is presumably the typical later correction of that recension (see n. 9 above).

his grandson Isaac, who is sixty, when they father children. Moreover, seventy represents a complete number, disclosing the fingerprint of God.[13]

father of. Just as the genealogy of Noah's three sons was segmented to show the relationship of the elect Shem to his brothers, so Terah's lineage is segmented to single out the elect Abraham from his family.

Abram. Based on the recension represented in part by the Samaritan Pentateuch, Abram is Terah's firstborn. Abram, whose name is later changed to Abraham (see 17:5), means "exalted father" or "the father is exalted," suggesting his noble lineage. Abram stands apart from his brothers by being mentioned first, like Shem (5:32), but also by his faith. His family was steeped in pagan idolatry (Josh. 24:2). This is clearly the case with Terah's great-grandson Laban by Nahor (see 22:22; 25:20; 29:5; 31:19). Mathews notes that Abram chastises his father for his idolatry in *Jubilees*.[14]

Nahor. Abram's brother was named after their grandfather (see 11:22–24). In the genealogies of Genesis 5, 10, and 11, this is the only instance of naming after an ancestor, possibly suggesting that the family is closely knit. If so, it will be all the more difficult for Abraham to leave. Nahor and Haran will be important for their descendants, Rebekah and Lot.

THEOLOGICAL REFLECTIONS ON BOOK 5

Sin and Grace

Scholars have noted in the Proto-History of Genesis the pattern of increasing sin matched by God's saving grace. The chart on the following page diagrams that alternating pattern.

In each story God's rule is expressed either through his direct commands (i.e., not to eat of the tree) or through his gift of common grace that allows each person to discern right and wrong. On that basis the narrator may evaluate Noah as righteous, in contrast to his wicked generation. When God speaks to Cain before Cain's crime of fratricide, he warns, "If you do what is right, will you not be accepted? But if you do not do what is right, sin is crouching at your door; it desires to have you, but you must master it" (4:7). Consciousness of right and wrong is assumed.

Nevertheless, humanity, in its hubris, batters against the boundaries God has established. With each story the rebellion grows, symbolized by the disintegrating ethics and the escalating violence. In an illicit reach for autonomy, Adam and Eve decide for themselves what should be right. This rootless self-determination begins the spiraling decline of their descendants who will assert their own right to choose, even at the cost of murdering their

---

[13]See the comment on the seventy nations and the seventy sons of Jacob. Seventy is a multiple of the two numbers symbolizing fullness and completion, seven and ten (see "Comparison and Contrast" in Literary Analysis of Book 4, Act 1).

[14]Mathews, *Genesis 1–11:26*, 499 n. 32.

	Adam	Cain	Noah	Babel
Rule	Eat of all the trees except the tree of good and evil	Common grace: right and wrong assumed in conscience (4:7)	Common grace: right and wrong assumed in conscience	To spread out and fill the earth
Rebellion	Choosing to eat of the forbidden tree; an illicit reach for autonomy	Tokenism and fratricide	Every imagination of the heart only evil continually	Refusal to obey; relying on their unity and self-determination for security (symbolized in the tower)
Judgment	Spiritual death: loss of relationship with God and one another; cast from the garden	Cast off the land to become a nomad and a wanderer	Flood; earth destroyed	Confusion of language; beginning of tyrannical nations
Mitigation	The promise of a seed that will bring salvation and conquer the Serpent	A mark upon Cain that protects him and allows him to live out his years	Noah and creation in the ark as the hope of God and humanity	The call of Abraham— one nation that will bring salvation to all the families

brothers. Eventually every imagination will be evil, and humanity will determine to reach the heavens and tower against God's command to fill the earth.

Their evil brings God's just judgment upon them. Their alienation from God leads to their alienation from each other until eventually they are scattered into separate nations with divided languages. Brother against brother becomes nation against nation, a turbulence that still continues (the last World War of nations led to fifty million deaths).

God's grace, however, will not let his people entirely destroy themselves. While humanity was still in the Garden of Eden, he planted a seed of hope.

From the woman, one will come who will defeat evil. Out of the nations God will call one nation to be his special people to bring salvation to all of the nations. Book 5 is God's gracious response to humanity's failure at the Tower of Babel. Shem's seed preserves the line of blessing that will lead to Abraham. Abraham initiates the new innovation in history: one nation that will bless the nations.

Grace and Historical Guilt

Although God initiates in each case a new means of grace, the historical consequences of sin are painfully apparent. God forgives David for murdering Uriah and committing adultery with Bathsheba, but the murdered husband cannot be revived, and the wife's purity cannot be restored. The genealogy of Book 5 presents God's grace in preserving a blessed descendant of Shem, but the dwindling longevity of the patriarchs shows the devastating consequences of the Flood upon humanity. Noah, the last of the antediluvians, lived 950 years, but Nahor, the last of the postdiluvians whose age is cited in this genealogy, lived only 148 years (11:24–25).

THE ACCOUNT OF TERAH'S DESCENDANTS (11:27–25:11)

THEME OF BOOK 6

God's division of the world into nations (see Book 4) provides the backdrop for God's innovation to elect one particular nation from Shem's lineage (Book 5) to bring universal salvation. The extensive but unified narrative of Book 6 presents God's grant to Abraham of a covenant.

On God's part, the Lord elects this descendant of Shem for this unique covenant relationship. With the call of Abraham, God commences the story of creating Israel, both old and new (i.e., the church), as his covenant people. God's original blessing on all humanity (1:28) now finds its fulfillment through Abraham and the nation that springs from him. In this call of Abraham and his people, the Lord reveals his freedom in being merciful to Israel, his holiness in judging them for infidelity, his faithfulness in restoring them, and his absolute sovereignty over all history.

Abraham, on his part, must live by faith that God will keep his promises. The narrator characterizes Abraham's faith to show the kind of person with whom God grants his covenant.

First, Abraham is not without flaws. As with each of the heroes of faith, his flaws will be as instructive as his virtues. The faithful patriarchs wander in and out of the Promised Land, the place of blessing and light, but with each step God's guiding hand will be evident, since even "if we are faithless, he will remain faithful, for he cannot disown himself" (2 Tim. 2:13).

As Abraham's faith matures, God increasingly commits himself to Abraham. He begins by promising to bless Abraham and to make him into a nation (Gen. 12:2) and through him to bless the earth

(12:2–3). God then puts the promise to make Abraham into a nation into the form of an immutable covenant (ch. 15) and still later confirms his promise to bless the nations through Abraham by confirming the covenant (ch. 17). Finally, the Lord swears to it (ch. 22).

Abraham is *the* biblical hero of faith. The writer of Hebrews in the role call of the heroes of faith normally devotes one verse to each; to Moses he devotes six. However, to Abraham the author gives a full twelve verses (Heb. 11:8–19). Abraham and the other heroes of faith in Genesis—Isaac, Jacob, Joseph, and Judah—are the holy root from which the Lord Jesus Christ sprouts and of the tree into which the Gentiles have been grafted (Rom. 11:17–21). Abraham is the father of all who believe (Rom. 4:16–17).

Abraham's story begins with God's call to venture from the "city of man" and family security to find the city of God. It is a call that every saint hears and that guides God's people on their pilgrimage to the celestial city. Readers perceive themselves as recipients or addressees of these direct acts of commitment or of promise. They are members of this community.

OUTLINE OF BOOK 6

Scene 3: Gift of Rebekah to Isaac, 24:1–67
Scene 4: Isaac the sole heir, 25:1–6
Scene 5: Death of Abraham, 25:7–11

LITERARY ANALYSIS OF BOOK 6 ————————————

Book 6, as a cohesive narrative, is unified by several broad literary features (for a detailed analysis of the literary aspects of the acts and scenes, see the discussion of each act and scene).

Structure and Plot

Book 6, though consisting of a number of clear scenes, is a single, tightly woven narrative, from the birth of Abraham (11:27) and the introduction of his barren wife, Sarah (11:29–30), to the death of Sarah and of Abraham (23:1–20; 25:7–11).

After the typical superscription that separates the ten books of Genesis (11:27a), Book 6 consists of three clearly defined sections: an introduction (11:27b–32), the main body (12:1–22:19), and the transition to the next book and generation (22:20–25:11). The introduction presents the book's characters. The main body develops the plot's tension through the testing of Abraham's faith. The concluding transition sandwiches the scene of securing a bride for Isaac between scenes of Sarah's and Abraham's deaths (23:1–20; 25:1–11). This provides the necessary background for the account of Isaac (that is, of Isaac's and Rebekah's descendants; 25:19–35:29).

The plot is driven by Abraham's struggle to trust God in the face of a series of conflicts testing his faith. His faith develops as he trusts God in spite of a childless wife, famine in the Promised Land, exile in a hostile land, the kidnapping of his wife in pagan kings' harems, an ungrateful nephew who seizes land for himself, war against mighty kings, family strife between rival wives and their children, his withering body, and death itself with the promise unfulfilled. In addition, Abraham's God is mysterious, asking Abraham to sacrifice the child in whom his offspring will be reckoned.

Gary Rendsburg argues convincingly that the narrator unifies the Abraham cycle by a concentric pattern (see "Structure and Content" in the introduction).[1] This pattern, as in a Bach fugue, functions as counterpoint to the plot structure.

Inclusios

The main body (see B to B,' "Structure and Content" in the introduction), the heart of the narrative, begins and ends with God's radical challenge to Abraham and God's promise to bless all nations through Abraham and his offspring:

---

[1]Rendsburg, *Redaction,* 28–29.

- "Go from (*lek-lᵉkā,* NIV 'Leave') . . . your father's household . . . to the land I will show you" (12:1).
- "All peoples on earth will be blessed through you" (12:3).

- "Go (*lek-lᵉkā*) . . . on one of the mountains I will tell you about" (22:2).[2]
- "Through your offspring all nations on earth will be blessed" (22:18).

At the beginning and end of this narrative (B and B') Abraham must leave all that is familiar to set out for a place he does not know. In Genesis 12 Abraham is called to leave his past out of simple trust in God's promises, and in Genesis 22 Abraham is called to abandon his future out of simple trust in God. Each call for radical obedience is followed by God's abundant promises.

The main body, 12:1–22:19, consists of two acts, marked off by inclusios pertaining to their distinctive themes and the two aspects of Abraham's becoming a nation. The first act pertains to the land (chs. 12–15). It begins with the command "Go to the land I will show you" (12:1) and ends with God's covenant guaranteeing his promise: "To your descendants I give this land" (15:18).

The second act pertains to the seed. It begins: "Now Sarai . . . had borne him no children" (16:1). It comes to a partial resolution with the announcement, "Sarah became pregnant and bore a son" (21:2). It culminates with the climactic conclusion, "I will surely bless you and make your descendants as numerous as the stars in the sky" (22:17).

Climax

The tension comes to a magnificent climax in Genesis 22. Abraham demonstrates that his faith has fully matured by offering Isaac as a sacrifice and, as it were, receives him back from the dead. God swears to keep the promise he originally made to Abraham: "I swear by myself, declares the LORD, that because you have done this and have not withheld your son, your only son, I will surely bless you and make your descendants as numerous as the stars in the sky. . . . Your descendants will take possession of the cities of their enemies, and through your offspring all nations on earth will be blessed, because you have obeyed me" (22:16–18; see also Heb. 6:13–20).

Characterization: Development and Contrast

The narrative is a study of Abraham in the school of faith. With great candor, the narrative presents Abraham's development through failures and successes as an obedient servant of God. Abraham begins in "elementary school" (12:1–3). Here he lives in a divine imagination (i.e., seeing things

---

[2]The phrase *lek-lᵉkā,* which does not occur anywhere else in the OT in precisely this form, links the two passages.

that are not, as though they were), informed by the word of God, especially his promises. The writer of Hebrews says Abraham "saw" God's promised seed and land and "welcomed them from a distance" (Heb. 11:13b).

As a "college student," however, Abraham must learn that God's covenant partners must live in this imagination when the heavenly vision seems impossible in light of harsh and contrary realities (see Gen. 15). Called at seventy-five years of age to this venture of faith, he must watch his own body petrify like a dead tree that has lost its sap and Sarah's womb wither like a dead flower. At one point he exclaims, "What can you give me since I remain childless" (15:2). To assist his imagination God takes him outside at night and, pointing to the starry heavens with its "Milky Way," promises, "so shall your offspring [lit., 'seed'] be" (15:5). Abraham, however, does not always rely steadily on these incredible promises. Repeatedly he fails to trust God for protection (12:10–13; 20:11–13), and before finally receiving the promised seed, he and Sarah try to engineer their own fulfillment with devastating consequences (16:1–4).

In "graduate school," Abraham learns that living in the imagination informed by the word of God entails a radical obedience (Gen. 22). The narrator focuses the faith of Abraham and Sarah upon Isaac. At the climax of their lives, God commands Abraham to sacrifice him, thereby negating the hope that has reversed their years of disappointment. Abraham's actions signify a decided maturation in his faithful reliance on God. Contrary to all reason and convention, Abraham obeys, confident that God will somehow provide the sacrifice (22:1–19). The author of Hebrews writes, "Abraham reasoned that God could raise the dead, and figuratively speaking, he did receive Isaac back from death" (Heb. 11:19).

This matured faith of Abraham remains steadfast, even when at the end of his life he still has not seen the fulfillment of God's promise of land. Abraham's only portion in the land is the cemetery plot that he purchased at a very high price in order to bury his wife (Gen. 23). His extravagant purchase, however, signifies his faith that this land has been given to him and his descendants.

The narrative records the development of Sarah's character and faith as well. Sarah emerges—albeit with faltering steps—from simply a barren wife to a beautiful woman to a scheming and jealous wife and then to a miraculous mother who honors God and protects her son and whose council is validated by God (21:12).

Many other minor characters contribute to this narrative. Their qualities serve to complement and contrast with Abraham and Sarah. For instance, Lot's folly serves a foil to Abraham's faith, and Hagar and her natural child, Ishmael, offers a foil to Sarah and her supernatural offspring, Isaac.

The presence of the primary character often goes unnoticed. Abraham appears as the main character, but the development of each character, including Abraham, occurs from encounters with the prime director of the narrative, God. In this narrative in particular (cf. Gen. 37–50), God's intimate presence is readily perceivable throughout. He communicates his will, good pleasure, and judgment in varied forms throughout the narrative: through the spoken word, physical appearances, visions, dreams, and messengers of the Lord. Even the significant absences of God's speech, particularly to Abraham (e.g., 12:10–20), convey God's intentions.

Key Words

Pertaining to God's promises to Abraham are these key words: "see,"[3] "land," and "seed."

Foreshadowing

With the statement, "Now Sarai was barren," and the emphatic phrase, "she had no children" (11:30), the introduction foreshadows the tension of barrenness that drives the Abraham narrative. In addition, Terah's migration with his family (11:31) foreshadows Abraham's pilgrimage to the land of promise.

Typology

God's promises and covenants with Abraham typify the gospel of Jesus Christ; Garrett calls them "The Gospel of Abraham."[4] The hope of Abraham and of the nations for salvation depends on God fulfilling his promises to give a son (Gen. 15:1–6; Luke 2:28–32). To that end, the births of both Isaac and Jesus are miraculous (Gen. 17:15–18; 18:12–14; Matt. 1:18–25). Paradoxically, however, both sons have to die and be raised from the dead before they can fulfill their missions: Isaac typically, Jesus Christ literally (Heb. 11:19). Furthermore, God enacts his covenant with Abraham in connection with a sacrifice (Gen. 15:18) and initiates the new covenant with the church through the sacrificial act of the crucifixion of Jesus (Luke 22:20). In addition, circumcision is the sign of Abraham's covenant (Gen. 17); the communion cup is the sign of the new covenant (Luke 22:20). Moreover, Abraham has to leave his home to establish his community as a group of aliens and sojourners (Gen. 12:1), and the church today confesses itself to have its citizenship in heaven and not of this world (John 15:19; Phil. 3:20). Finally, both Abraham and the church are founded on the eschatological hope of a new heaven and earth (Heb. 11:39–40).

---

[3]Martin Buber noted "see" as a key word of the narrative ("Abraham the Seer," in *On the Bible*, ed. N. N. Glanzer (New York: Schocken, 1982), 42.
[4]See Garrett, *Rethinking*, 164–68.

BOOK 6, INTRODUCTION (11:27–32)

LITERARY ANALYSIS OF BOOK 6, INTRODUCTION ———

Structure

The introduction consists of the prefatory superscription (11:27a), Terah's segmented genealogy (11:27b–30), his migration (11:31), and obituary (11:32). Dorsey notes its concentric pattern: [5]

A Introduction: Terah and his offspring (11:27)
  B The family lives in *Ur of the Chaldeans;* Haran dies (11:28)
    C Abraham *takes* (*lāqaḥ*) *Sarai* as his *wife;* Nahor marries Milcah, *whose father is Haran* (11:29)
      X Sarai is barren; she has no children (11:30)
    C' Terah takes (*lāqaḥ*) Abraham, along with Abraham's *wife Sarai* and Lot, *whose father is Haran* (11:31a)
  B' The family leaves *Ur of the Chaldeans* and settles in Haran (11:31b)
A' Conclusion: summary of Terah's life; his death (11:32)

Janus

The introduction forms a transition between Books 5 and 6 by repeating almost verbatim in its first verse the last verse of Book 5 (see 11:26, 27). Moreover, the introduction completes the genealogical pattern of Book 5 in a varied form. Instead of a summary statement such as "Terah had other sons and daughters" (cf. 11:12–25), it names the children (11:27–30), adds a biographical note (11:31), and uniquely concludes, "And he died in Haran." That obituary tightly closes the door to the Proto-History. Genesis 12:1–3 will open a new door in salvation history.

EXEGETICAL NOTES TO BOOK 6, INTRODUCTION ———

Superscription (11:27a)

27. account of Terah's descendants. See the comments on *tôlᵉdôt* at 2:4.
  Terah. See 11:26. The father of the principal hero (Abraham) gives his name to the family whose history is recorded here. He will not be mentioned again, for he does not share Abraham's faith. The introduction infers that Terah's family worships the moon god Sin. He settles in Ur and Haran (see 11:31), both of which were important centers of the moon-god cult. The daughters Sarai and Milcah are probably named after the name and title of Sin's consort and daughter respectively (see 11:29). His own name Terah may be related to the Hebrew *yeraḥ,* meaning "moon." This comports well with Josh. 24:14.

---

[5]Dorsey, *Literary,* 54.

Segmented Genealogy (11:27b–30)

Terah became the father. The repetition of 11:26 explicitly links Book 6 to the previous book. The segmented genealogy introduces Terah's children and their relationships. Abraham, Sarah, and Lot are full and developing characters; the others are agents.

28. Haran died. His premature death may have influenced Abraham's migration from there (see 12:4–5). It explains the fate of Haran's children in this closely knit family (see 24:3; 27:46; 31:50). Nahor marries Haran's daughter, Milcah (11:29), who will bear him eight sons, one of whom is Bethuel, father of Laban and Rebekah. Terah and Abraham care for orphaned Lot (11:31; 12:4).

Ur of the Chaldeans. This is modern Tell el-Miqayyar in Lower Mesopotamia. The name "Chaldean" is probably a modernization reflecting the later editing of the book of Genesis (see "Composition and Authorship" in the introduction). The Chaldeans entered southern Mesopotamia in the first millennium B.C. and became the ruling caste there in the seventh to sixth centuries B.C. Some think Ur refers to Urfa (Edessa) in northern Mesopotamia or some other Ur near Haran, but these interpretations contradict Acts 7:2.

the land of his birth. The same Hebrew words are rendered "land" in 11:28 and "country" in 12:1, establishing Ur of the Chaldeans (rather than Haran) as the place where Abraham receives his call (cf. 15:7; Neh. 9:7; Acts 7:2).

29. Sarai. If based on Hebrew, her name means "princess"; if based on Akkadian *sharratu*, it means "queen." Sharratu was the female consort of the moon god Sin, the principal deity of Ur. Sarai was the daughter of Terah by a different mother than Abraham's (20:12). The law against this kind of incest was unknown in patriarchal times (see "Historicity and Literary Genre" in the introduction).[6]

Nahor's wife. The law did not prohibit marrying one's niece.

Milcah. Her name, a variant form of Hebrew *malkâ,* means "queen." Akkadian *malkatu* is a title of the goddess Ishtar, daughter of the moon god Sin.

Iscah. She plays no role in the Abraham narrative.

30. barren. Brueggemann declares this to be "an effective metaphor for hopelessness . . . no human power to invent a future."[7] Sarah's infertility tests Abraham's faith and drives the whole story. The theme of God's purposes overcoming symbolic barrenness (see Isa. 54:1) recurs with Rebekah (Gen.

---

[6]See Lev. 18:9; 20:17; Deut. 27:22. Later this will be forbidden. The law probably aimed to protect a woman from the uncaring passion of a half-brother. A full brother was more likely to be protective of his full sister; he would guard her virginity, but a half-brother would not naturally have this same concern. The difference is well-illustrated by the rape of Tamar by her half-brother Amnon and her protection by her full brother, Absalom (2 Sam. 13).

[7]Brueggemann, *Genesis,* 116.

25:21), Rachel (29:31), and Hannah (1 Sam. 1:2), and it foreshadows the virgin birth (Luke 1:26–38). All these women actively commit themselves to God's grace.

Migration from Ur to Haran (11:31)

31. Terah took. The migration to Canaan does not begin as a pilgrimage following a vision but as a family decision. Genesis 12:1 suggests that Abraham is told to leave by himself for Canaan, but he does not separate himself until his father dies. This introduction represents Abraham as slow to believe.

Haran. Not to be confused with the personal name, Haran the place is located on the bank of the Balikh River, 550 miles (885 km) northwest of Ur and close to the present-day Syrian-Turkish border. Like Ur, it was an important center of moon worship.

settled there. Instead of pressing on to Canaan, Terah and his family settle down at another center of moon worship.

Death of Terah (11:32)

32. 205 years. The original text probably read "145 years." This reading is attested in the Samaritan Pentateuch, which preserves an early text type and informs Acts 7:2–4. If the Masoretic text is original, Terah was 130 when Abraham was born (see 11:26; 12:4). This seems unlikely for three reasons: (1) it accords badly with the rest of the genealogy from Shem to Terah, who have their firstborn in their early thirties; (2) there would be nothing exceptional in Abraham fathering Isaac at 100 years of age; (3) Stephen could not have known that Abraham left Haran after his father's death, for Abraham could have left Haran before his father's death (see Acts 7:2–4).[8]

THEOLOGICAL REFLECTIONS ON BOOK 6, INTRODUCTION

Sovereign Grace

This dark introduction profiles God's grace that will follow in the rest of Book 6. Terah is steeped in pagan idolatry. One of his sons dies, leaving two orphans; another is married to an infertile wife, and Terah himself will die, having settled for a land short of Abraham's heavenly vision. Against this hopelessness, God's sovereign call of Abraham offers bright hope. Indeed, Sarah's sterility (see 15:2–3; 17:17) emphasizes the fact that God's grace is beyond human imagination. She will bear children not by natural generation but by supernatural life that faith engenders. Through this childless couple, God will bring into being a new humanity that is born not of the will of a husband but by the will of God.

---

[8]See Waltke, "Samaritan Pentateuch," 212–39.

BOOK 6, ACT 1: ABRAHAM AND THE PROMISED LAND (12:1–15:21)

LITERARY ANALYSIS OF BOOK 6, ACT 1 ─────────

The five scenes of this act all pertain to the Promised Land: Abraham's faithful embrace of the land and the conflicts in the land that test Abraham's faith. Abraham sets out for this land (12:1–3), and when he arrives he sets up altars at Shechem and Ai, thereby claiming it for God (12:4–9). In fear of famine he migrates from the Negev into treacherous Egypt, where Sarah is kidnapped (12:10–20). Upon his return to the Negev, strife between Lot's and Abraham's herdsmen motivates Lot's separation from his blessed uncle (13:1–18). That scene closes with Abraham building an altar at Hebron. Then foreign kings invade the Dead Sea area and kidnap Lot. After Abraham valiantly rescues him, he is greeted by kings of Sodom and Salem near to Jerusalem (14:1–24). The act closes climactically with God making a covenant to give Abraham all the land of the Canaanites, counting them off one by one (15:1–21). As noted, the key word "land" forms a frame around the act.

BOOK 6, ACT 1, SCENE 1: THE CALL OF ABRAHAM AND ABRAHAM'S MIGRATION TO THE PROMISED LAND (12:1–9)

LITERARY ANALYSIS OF BOOK 6, ACT 1, SCENE 1 ───────

Plot and Themes

The gracious God's broad new strokes to bless the earth come suddenly and brilliantly upon the canvas of sacred history. The Lord has not spoken to his saints since his covenant with Noah, in which he resolved to bless the earth and never again to treat it with contempt (8:20–9:17). Now suddenly his creative word to bless the tribes and nations—which he has scattered—redirects the course of history. This word of benediction counterbalances his words of malediction against the tower builders.

Reciprocally, Abraham, with astounding suddenness, charges out in obedience and faith. The description of Abraham's pilgrimage is structured according to a very selective itinerary: (1) the journey from Haran to Canaan (12:4–5), featuring Abraham's obedience; and (2) his journey through the land from north to south, from Shechem to the Negev (12:6–9), featuring his worship. The latter involves a series of movements: his journey (a) to the religious center of Shechem, where he builds an altar (12:6–7), (b) to Ai where he builds another altar (12:8), and (c) to the Negev (12:9).

Innertextuality

God's call to Abraham echoes earlier books. God's call to Abraham to bless the world in redemptive grace parallels God's appointment of Noah to do the same for creation in common grace (see 8:1 and comments there). The pattern of God's call to Abraham recalls God's pattern of creation—announcement, command (12:1), and report (12:4–9) (see "Literary Analysis of the Prologue")—with an addition of God's promise (12:2–3) in order to encourage Abraham's faithful obedience.

The repetition of "blessing" human beings (five times in 12:1–3 compared to five times in chs. 1–11, see 1:22, 28; 2:3; 5:2; 9:1[9]) and "cursing" is also an allusion to the creation account. These links confirm that Abraham is of the seed of the woman.

God's call of Abraham, attended as it is with blessings and curses, also anticipates the blessings and curses attending the Mosaic covenant (cf. Lev. 26; Deut. 28). Moreover, in sovereign grace God calls a particular individual or a people, which entails not selecting others, to mediate his blessing. This pattern will be repeated in his election of Isaac rather than Ishmael, of Jacob rather than Esau, and of Judah rather than his brothers to be king.

Key Words

The fivefold repetition of the key word *blessing* points to the theme of this scene. It is narrowed by another key word, *you,* which is repeated at least a dozen times. One individual will bring universal blessing and salvation.

Symbolism

God's call contains seven (i.e., the symbolic number of completeness) elements: (1) "I will make you into a great nation"; (2) "I will bless you"; (3) "I will make your name great"; (4) "you will be a blessing"; (5) "I will bless those who bless you"; (6) "whoever curses you I will curse"; and (7) climactically, in the favored seventh position, "all peoples on earth will be blessed through you."

Climax

These seven promises pertain to three expanding horizons. The scene begins within the narrow confines of the call of Abraham to disassociate himself from his family (12:1). This call expands to the Lord's promise to make Abraham into a nation of blessing, and it is within that context that he will experience the first four blessings (12:2). Finally, the last three elements of Abraham's call expand the horizon of Abraham's blessings to the whole earth for all time (12:3).

Contrast

There is a striking contrast between Abraham's first migration directed by his father and pagan family (11:31) and this one, which takes place in solitary response to the Lord's command.

---

[9]In Gen. 9:26 people bless God.

Blanks and Gaps

Apart from Abraham's family ties (11:27–32), the narrator blanks the first seventy-five years of Abraham's life and draws a veil over Abraham's slowness to believe. Instead, the narrator focuses on God's call to Abraham to be his means of blessing and Abraham's obedient step of faith, which will change forever the course of history and open up a door of hope that will never close.

The narrator also blanks why Terah pulls up stakes to go to Haran and the great religious and economic centers Abraham undoubtedly passes through on his journey, for this migration and these centers would only distract from the narrator's purpose. He does not explain why Abraham limits his journey to the hill country, though his statement that "the Canaanites were in the land" (12:6) suggests that Abraham avoids infringing upon their territory. The description of Abraham's journey selectively highlights only religious sites and locations that give insight into Abraham's faith and religion.

Foreshadowing

God's call (12:1–3) explains all that follows in this narrative: Abraham's migration to and sojourn in the Promised Land and his anticipation of descendants (see also Theological Reflections below).

EXEGETICAL NOTES TO BOOK 6, ACT I, SCENE I ————

God's command to Abraham (12:1)

1. had said.[10] The past perfect tense is used because God calls Abraham in Ur before his father dies, not in Haran (see 11:28, 31; 15:7; Acts 7:4). Or does God call Abraham a second time, as he does with Jeremiah (1:4–19; 15:19–21)? The same word that summoned the cosmos into existence now summons Abraham to bring a nation into existence. The narrator chooses not to explain how God speaks to Abraham,[11] but it is probably not a theophany, which uses the formula "And the Lord appeared and said" (see 12:7). Abraham does not know where he is going (Heb. 11:8; see Theological Reflections below).

to Abram. God's particular election can only be explained by God's sovereignty and divine wisdom. Abraham does prove to be a faithful covenant partner, but there were other righteous people at the time, certainly Melchizedek (Gen. 14:18–20) and probably Job and a certain Daniel (Ezek. 14:14).

---

[10]For the use of *wayyqtl* to designate the pluperfect tense, see *IBHS* §33.2.3.

[11]Cf. G. Martin, *Reading Scripture As the Word of God: Practical Approaches and Attitude*, 2d ed. (Ann Arbor, Mich.: Servant, 1982), 3–4, 96–97.

leave [*lek-lᵉkā*]. The Hebrew expression is that of "determinedly dissociating oneself,"[12] literally "leave by yourself."[13] Calvin's paraphrase captures the essence of this faith-demanding command: "I command thee to go forth with closed eyes, . . . until, having renounced thy country, thou shalt have given thyself wholly to me."[14]

land. This is the key word of this act (see 12:7).

show. This is a form of the key word "to see" (see 12:7).

God's Promises regarding the Nation (12:2)

2. I will make. The Hebrew literally reads, "so that I might make you . . . bless you . . . make your name great."[15] The covenant structure is apparent. God obligates himself to Abraham while assigning him a task. God's commands are fulfilled in Abraham's obedient faith (see note on "left" in 12:4; cf. 6:9–22; 17:1–2). In truth, the promise engenders the capacity to embrace it by faith.

great. The reference is both to numbers and to significance. The magnitude of the promise to a husband with a barren wife tests Abraham's faith to the limit. By not surrendering to unbelief, Abraham serves as an exemplar to the covenant people (Isa. 51:2).

nation. See "Theme of Genesis and Biblical Theology" in the introduction.

bless. "Bless," which occurred five times in Genesis 1–11, now occurs five times in 12:1–3, perhaps linking these texts (see "Innertextuality" in Literary Analysis, above). The three nuances of bless—prosperity (13:2, 5; 14:22–23; 24:35; 26:12–13; 30:43; 32:3–21), potency/fertility (1:28; 13:16; 15:5; 22:17; 26:4; 28:3, 14; 35:11), and victory (cf. 1:22)—are spelled out in 22:17.[16] Horst says, "Blessing brings the power for life, the enhancement of life, and the increase of life."[17]

make your name great. In the ancient Near East, a name was not merely a label but a revelation of character. Thus a great name entails not only fame but high social esteem "as a man of superior character."[18]

blessing. God blesses Abraham to be his blessing bearer. The procreative intentions of divine blessing are always within the context of loyalty to the spiritual transformation of future generations.

---

[12]T. Muraoka, "On the So-Called *Dativus Ethicus* in Hebrew," *JTS* 29 (1978): 495, cited in *IBHS* §11.2.10d.

[13]God's call is repeated in Jesus' call, "Follow me" (see Luke 9:57–62).

[14]Calvin, *Genesis*, 344.

[15]Since ᵃgaddᵉlâ is unambiguously cohortative, we may assume the same for the ambiguous verbal forms. For *waw* + cohortative after a volitional form to denote a final clause, see *IBHS* §34.6a.

[16]For NT connections, see Acts 3:25–26 (Christ is sent first to Israel to bless); Gal. 3:14 (to Gentiles); cf. Matt. 5:3–12; Luke 1:42–45; 6:20–26.

[17]F. Horst, *Gottes Recht: Gesammelte Studien zum Recht im Alten Testament* (Munich: Chr. Kaiser Verlag, 1961), 194, cited by Roop, *Genesis*, 98.

[18]Sarna, *Genesis*, 89.

God's Promise regarding
the Universal Blessing (12:3)

3. I will bless . . . I will curse. This constructive "I" speech of God contrasts with the destructive "I" speech of humans (Gen. 3:10–13; 11:3–4). The extent of God's gracious desire to bless rather than curse is indicated by the grammatical differences of the two phrases in Gen. 12:3. First, the statement is in a form indicating resolve ("I will bless"), intentioned toward plural recipients ("those who bless"). Second, it shifts to a simple statement of fact ("I shall curse") and a singular recipient ("whoever curses"; see also 27:29; Num. 24:9).

those who bless you. This refers to those who through prayer seek to mediate God's blessing on this agent of blessing, Abraham, and his faithful descendants.[19] Until Christ comes, Abraham and his descendants play a representative messianic role and prefigure Christ. The promise does not pertain today to unbelieving, ethnic "Israel" (see Rom. 9:6–8; Gal. 6:15) but to Jesus Christ and his church (see 12:7; 13:16 and notes; Gal. 3:16, 26–29; 6:16).

will be blessed. The ambiguous Hebrew form could be reflexive: "will bless themselves by you." The alternative rendering could mean that people will take Abraham's blessing as the desired standard for their own blessing. It is sometimes argued that the verbal form in the parallel text of 22:18 must be reflexive, but it too can be passive or reflexive.[20] The reflexive, however, could also mean that the nations bless themselves by mediating blessing through their prayers for Abraham. In that sense the meaning is not much different from the passive. In either case, God mediates his blessing to the nations through Abraham (see also Theological Reflections on Book 10, Act 4, Scene 2, "Blessing and Reciprocity").[21]

The Journey from Haran to Canaan (12:4–5)

4. left. The first word describing Abraham's response, *hālak*, "to go, walk," matches the first verb of God's command (12:1).

as the LORD had told him. His "walk" is transformed from a migration to faith's pilgrimage, looking for the heavenly city.

---

[19]Divine "blessing" may be mediated through a sacred person such as a patriarch (Gen. 27:7), a priest (cf. Lev. 9:23), a king (2 Sam. 6:18), a dying man (Job 29:13), and the sacred congregation. Probably the "blessings" are the words of blessing that prayerful people utter on the heads of the righteous. In the book of Ruth the Lord's blessings are mediated by the prayer of the faithful: the workers for Boaz (Ruth 2:4), Naomi for Boaz (2:19–20), Boaz for Ruth (3:10), and the congregation for Boaz and Ruth (cf. 4:11). When blessings are mediated through others, benedictory words and power become mingled notions. A person who dispenses blessings is a *nepeš berākâ* (Prov. 11:25), but "the Northwest Semites always understood the deity as a true giver of blessing even when they do not explicitly mention him" (Sharbert, "*brk*," *TDOT*, 2:283).

[20]*IBHS* §26.3a. The change to Hithpael in 22:8 may reflect a later stage of editing, for passive Hithpael tends to oust the passive Niphal.

[21]This more likely passive sense is supported by the ancient versions (*Targum Onqelos*, LXX, and Vulgate).

Lot went with him.[22] Unlike when Terah took Abraham and Lot with him, Lot agrees on his own to go with his uncle in his venture of faith. Abraham is not violating the command to go it alone.

Seventy-five. Ten years beyond modern retirement, Abraham begins his new venture. The text blanks the reason for the decreasing life span after the Flood, declining from Arphaxad (438 years, 11:13) to Abraham (175 years, 25:7) to Jacob (147 years, 47:28) to Joseph (110 years, 50:22). By the time of Moses seventy or eighty years is normal (Ps. 90:10).

5. He took. The change of verb indicates that Abraham takes responsibility for this entourage. They do not go against their will.

they set out . . . they arrived. The Hebrew verbs *yṣ'*, "to go forth," and *bô'*, "to come, enter," repeat 11:31. The first migration to Canaan under Terah failed. This one under God succeeds.

Journey through the Land (12:6 – 9)

6. through the land. The royal nomad keeps to the hill country, where he will not infringe on the rights of others.

site [*māqôm*]. The Hebrew means "sacred site."[23] The mention of Shechem suggests it was an ancient sanctuary.

great tree. This is probably an oak tree whose greater height makes it a preferred place of worship (see 13:18; 14:13; 18:1; 21:33). Pagans worshiped fertility deities under such trees. With its lofty top in the heavens, it could be considered an axis between heaven and earth and a place for revelation. Abraham's altar at this location may indicate his hope in God's promise of offspring and his hope that God will again speak to him. Although Abraham still worships according to the religious customs of his time, the content of his worship differs significantly. Abraham's faithful worship, longing for a heavenly city (Heb. 11:10), is dedicated to the one true God and will yet endure through long years of infertility. The seed he hopes for will be holy. He will instruct his seed in righteousness (Gen. 18; 19), and his seed will bring salvation to the nations.

Moreh. The name means "teacher," and it probably is a pagan site for oracles. The Lord sanctifies it by appearing to Abraham (12:7).

Shechem. This ancient city is regarded as lying in the heart of Canaan (see Josh. 20:7).

At that time. This is an "a-Mosaica." Again, the hand of the later editor shows itself. Such a comment would have been unnecessary for Moses, since the Canaanites were still in the land during his time (see "Composition and Authorship" in the Introduction).

---

[22]Hamilton suggests that the double reference to Lot (12:4–5) may hint at the dispute and difficulties to come involving Lot (*Genesis 1-17*, 376).

[23]See *HALOT*, 627, entry 6.

Canaanites. This is a generic term for the pre-Israelite inhabitants. Two obstacles stand in the way of God's promises: Sarah's barrenness (11:30) and the Canaanites in the land who prevent Abraham from settling.

7. appeared. Again a key word is used at a crucial moment (see 12:1). God said that he would show Abraham the land, and now he appears, perhaps in a theophany, to confirm that he has arrived in the Promised Land.[24] God appears three times to Abraham (17:1; 18:1), twice to Isaac (26:2, 24), and once to Jacob (35:9).

give. The holy land is a sacred gift. It is now legally Abraham's, but actual ownership must await the divinely appointed time.

offspring. Although Abraham does not yet understand, this will be no natural offspring but a supernatural one, raised from Abraham and Sarah's withered and virtually dead bodies (see Rom. 4:18–21).[25]

land. The crucial key word looks back to the implicit promise in 12:1.

built an altar. Abraham does not use a Canaanite altar. His altar is an expression of gratitude (see 8:20) and consecration of the Promised Land to God (see also 12:8; 13:18; 22:9; 26:25; 35:7; Ex. 20:24; Josh. 22:19).[26] Here also Abraham sanctifies a religious custom of his day. In pagan religions, land and deity are inseparable. Abraham acknowledges God to be the Lord of this land, which Abraham has chosen to own (Lev. 25:23).

8. Bethel. This city was formerly called Luz (see 28:19). It is identified with modern Beitin, approximately 10 miles (17 km) north of Jerusalem. Only Jerusalem is mentioned more often in the Old Testament than this site, which will become one of the two capitals and cult centers of the northern kingdom.

Ai. It is usually identified as et-Tell, a large city east of Bethel. But Joshua speaks of it as a small city (Josh. 7:2–8:28), calling the traditional identification into question. The narrator gives no reason why Abraham builds an altar between Bethel and Ai.

THEOLOGICAL REFLECTIONS ON BOOK 6, ACT I, SCENE I

The Progress of Redemption

This scene is the thematic center of the Pentateuch. The call of Abraham to the Promised Land, with its attendant promise to give him that land, explains the geographical movement at the end of each of the five books of the Pentateuch. Genesis ends with Joseph having his brothers swear to take

---

[24]The root $r^ʾh$, like $ḥzh$, "to see," belongs to the vocabulary of prophecy and may denote "auditions" (see 1 Sam. 3:15; Isa. 1:1; Amos 1:1).

[25]Grammatically "O/offspring" is a collective singular: it pertains uniquely to Jesus Christ (Gal. 3:16) and to all those who share Abraham's faith in God who raises the dead (Rom. 4:16; Gal. 3:26–29). The OT saints looked forward to the coming Christ (see 15:6; John 8:56; Gal. 3:6–9), and the NT ones reflect upon him (John 3:11–21).

[26]The patriarchs never build an altar outside the Promised Land.

his bones with them when they leave Egypt to fulfill God's promise to Abraham, Isaac, and Jacob (Gen. 50:22–26). Exodus ends with the expectation that God's glory cloud will lead them from Sinai to the Promised Land (Ex. 40:34–38). Leviticus draws to a conclusion with the summary statement: "These are the commands the LORD gave Moses on Mount Sinai" (27:34). That statement is repeated in Num. 36:13, with the substitution "plains of Moab" for Sinai. Deuteronomy also ends on the plains of Moab, but Joshua has been appointed the leader to fulfill the promise (Deut. 34).

The call of God to Abraham is the sneak preview for the rest of the Bible. It is a story of God bringing salvation to all tribes and nations through this holy nation, administered at first by the Mosaic covenant and then by the Lord Jesus Christ through the new covenant. The elements of Abraham's call are reaffirmed to Abraham (12:7; 15:5–21; 17:4–8; 18:18–19; 22:17–18), to Isaac (26:24), to Jacob (28:13–15; 35:11–12; 46:3), to Judah (49:8–12), to Moses (Ex. 3:6–8; Deut. 34:4), and to the ten tribes of Israel (Deut. 33). They are reaffirmed by Joseph (Gen. 50:24), by Peter to the Jews (Acts 3:25), and by Paul to the Gentiles (Gal. 3:8).

The expansion of the promise of 12:1–3 from individual to national to universal salvation is the essential movement of Scripture. The Bible is a missionary guide: concerned with bringing salvation to all the families of the earth. Abraham as a blessing bearer of salvation is an anticipation of the blessing-bearing Christ. When Christ ascends into heaven, he extends his pierced hands, hands that blessed infants and gave sight to the blind, to bless his church (Luke 24:50–53).

Faith and Pilgrimage

The life of faith entails prompt obedience to God's word in a pilgrimage based on a revealed and perceived vision (Deut. 26:5; Ps. 105:12–15). Faith demands a ruthless abandonment of the past. Abraham has to leave the consolation of familiarity and tradition far behind. He has to jettison his family, his homeland, and the old ways of worship.[27] But this abandonment leads to his fulfillment. Brueggemann asserts that "departure from securities is the only way out of barrenness."[28] The pilgrim's citizenship is in heaven, and he or she looks for a city whose architect and builder is God (Phil. 3:20; Heb. 11:9–10, 13–16).

Revelation and Illumination

The modern Christian's experience is not unlike Abraham's. Abraham hears God speak a call and promise. The believer today opens Scripture and hears God's word. Christians are people of the ear, not of the eye. God does not appear to be seen but speaks to be heard. God is always present in words that bind. The community of faith is built around these speech acts.

---

[27]Cf. Armstrong, *Beginning*, 55.
[28]Brueggemann, *Genesis*, 118.

Offspring

The promise of offspring finds singular and collective fulfillment. The singular Offspring through whom the world is blessed is Jesus Christ (Gal. 3:16). The collective offspring finds partial fulfillment in old Israel (see Num. 23:10; 1 Kings 4:20; 2 Chron. 1:9; Acts 3:25) and consummation in the New Israel, composed of Jews and Gentiles (see Gen. 12:3 and note; Rom. 4:16–18; Gal. 3:29; Rev. 7:9). The one people of God consists of two choirs: Old Testament saints sang in anticipation of Christ's sufferings and glory (Luke 24:45–46; John 5:46; 8:56; 1 Cor. 15:4; 1 Peter 1:10–12; 2 Peter 1:21), and New Testament saints sing in remembrance of his life, death, resurrection, and ascension, and in celebration of his anticipated second coming in glory. This promise regarding the covenant people of God must not be confused with Abraham's offspring outside of faith in Jesus Christ (see Gen. 16:10).

Land

The land promises also are fulfilled several times but never consummated.[29] God fulfills the promise through Joshua (Josh. 21:43–45), but not completely (Josh. 13:1–7); through David and Solomon (1 Kings 4:20–25; Neh. 9:8), but still not completely (see Ps. 95:11; Heb. 4:6–8; 11:39–40).

BOOK 6, ACT 1, SCENE 2: DELIVERANCE FROM EGYPT (12:10–13:2)

LITERARY ANALYSIS OF BOOK 6, ACT 1, SCENE 2 ———

Structure

The form and content of this scene match those of the other two scenes in which the matriarch finds herself in a pagan king's harem (20:1–18; 26:1, 7–17). Garrett helpfully notes the parallels:[30]

Scene A (12:10–20)

Section	Verses	Content
Migration	10	Abraham goes to Egypt because of a famine.
Deception	11–13	He sees Sarah is beautiful, so tells her to say she is his sister.
Abduction	14–16	Pharaoh takes Sarah and rewards Abraham.
Deliverance	17	The Lord afflicts Pharaoh.
Confrontation	18–19	Pharaoh rebukes Abraham.
Conclusion	20	Abraham leaves with wealth.[31]

---

[29]See "Second Motif: The Land" in the introduction.
[30]Cf. Garrett, *Rethinking*, 132.
[31]In our analysis 13:1 is a janus between Scenes 2 and 3, functions as an inclusio in Scene 2, and is the setting for Scene 3.

Scene B (20:1–18)

Section	Verses	Content
Migration	1	Abraham goes to Gerar.
Deception	2a	He tells Abimelech that Sarah is his sister.
Abduction	2b	Abimelech takes Sarah.
Deliverance	3–8	The Lord rebukes Abimelech in dream.
Confrontation	9–13	Abimelech rebukes Abraham.
Conclusion	14–18	Abimelech rewards Abraham, and Abraham prays for Abimelech.

Scene C (26:1, 7–17)

Section	Verses	Content
Migration	1	Isaac goes to Gerar because of a famine.
Deception	7	He says that Rebekah is his sister when men of Gerar ask about her.
Abduction		No abduction.
Deliverance	8	Abimelech sees Isaac caressing Rebekah.
Confrontation	9–16	Abimelech rebukes Isaac, but God protects him; the Lord blesses Isaac.
Conclusion	17	Isaac separates from Abimelech when rivalry develops.

Garrett also notes that the three scenes are remarkably bound by a pattern in which a narrative element section is consistently present in two out of the three scenes. A and C begin with a famine, but not B. In A and B, the patriarchal couple is Abraham and Sarah, but in C, it is Isaac and Rebekah. In A, the location is Egypt, but in B and C the location is Gerar. A and C mention the beauty of the wife, but not B. In A and C, the host's servants first notice the beautiful woman, but not in B. In A and B, the wife is taken into the harem, but not in C. In A and B, deliverance comes by direct intervention of God, but in C deliverance comes by a providential accident. The host rewards the patriarch in A and B, but God blesses the patriarch in C. God is called "the LORD" in A and C, but in B he is Elohim. In A and C, the patriarch explicitly departs, but in B his departure is implicit.[32] This pattern tends to debunk the view that these are doublets of the same event.[33]

Plot and Theme

The three scenes, which transcend the acts of Genesis, are also linked thematically. Viewed as a unity they represent a triple threat to the holy seed.[34] However, since they are isolated from one another, within each act they

[32]Garrett, *Rethinking*, 133.
[33]See, e.g., H. H. Rowley, *The Growth of the Old Testament* (New York: Harper & Row, 1986), 17–18.
[34]Garrett speculates that in an earlier stage in the development of the Genesis material they existed as a literary unity.

function differently. In this act, Scene 2 is the first of three scenes of conflict related to the issue of land: Abraham versus famine and Pharaoh (12:10–20), Lot (13:1–18), and the eastern kings (14:1–24). After receiving the promise of land, Abraham must now, despite hardship and conflict, trust God to provide for him inside the land and protect him outside of it. In his first challenge to believe in God's fruitfulness when the land is barren, Abraham will fail to act rightly.

The plot's tension thickens from danger with a famine (12:10) to Abraham's fear for his life (12:11–12) to his foolish scheme (12:13) to Sarah's desperate plight in the Pharaoh's harem (12:14–16). The profane scheming of the elect couple almost shipwrecks their faith pilgrimage. The Lord's gracious intervention, however, provides the plot's resolution and saves them (12:17–20). Lesson learned, they return to the Promised Land and God's intimate fellowship (13:1–2).

Inclusio and Scenic Depiction

The geographical frame of this scene symbolizes Abraham's failure to progress. The scene is framed by the movement to and from Egypt: "went down to Egypt" (12:10) "went up from Egypt" (13:1). Though the verbs "went down" and "went up" are normal vocabulary for this movement,[35] they also symbolically depict his spiritual and physical pilgrimage out of God's blessing and back into it. Although in the previous scene Abraham has received great promises from God of land and offspring, here Abraham's circular excursion has led him nowhere.

Gap and Contrast

The narrator intentionally gaps any mention of altars or God's presence by word and promise. The lack of God's direct interaction with Abraham signifies his disapproval. Whereas God had specially favored Abraham with his voice, Abraham must now receive his rebuke from a pagan king.

EXEGETICAL NOTES TO BOOK 6, ACT I, SCENE 2————

Migration: Abraham Goes to Egypt Because of a Famine (12:10)

10. Now there was. The rapidity of the narration between Abraham's journeying in 12:9 and his leaving in 12:10 gives the impression that he walked right through and out of the Promised Land.

famine in the land. Famine can result from a plague of locusts (Deut. 28:38; Joel 1–2), from enemy sieges (Deut. 28:49–52; 2 Kings 6:25; 25:3), and from drought (Deut. 28:22–24; 1 Kings 17:1–18:3).

---

[35]Sarna (*Genesis*, 358 n.1) notes that a term similar to "went up" is found in the journal of an Egyptian frontier official (ca. 1225 B.C.) to designate a journey from Egypt to Asia (*ANET*, 258, no. 1).

went down to Egypt.[36] Egypt would be appealing to Abraham, since he has no means for long-term food storage and Egypt has a dependable water supply in the Nile. However, Abraham's movement to Egypt is paralleled by his return in 13:1. Since he receives no revelation to sojourn in Egypt (cf. 12:1; 26:2–6; 46:2–3),[37] he is stepping out of the stones in God's will to find bread.

to live [*gûr*]. The verb is similar to *yšb* "to dwell," rendered "settled there" in 11:31 (see 20:1; Jer. 49:18, 33; 50:40). *Gûr* is also rendered "linger" or "abide" in Judg. 5:17. Konkel asserts, "It lends itself as a metaphor for the pilgrimage of life."[38] The narrator represents Abraham as going to Egypt to live, but not as a native citizen.

the famine was severe. The addition suggests that Abraham leaves only under great duress.

Deception: Abraham Tells Sarah to Say She Is His Sister (12:11 – 13)

11. he said. Abraham speaks out of fear of humans, which is incompatible with faith in God.

a beautiful woman. Although sixty-five years old (see 12:4), Sarah retains her beauty.

12. When the Egyptians see you. Abraham may not have anticipated precisely what Pharaoh's officials do (12:14–15). He is not necessarily selling Sarah's honor to save his own skin but perhaps deceitfully stalling for time to exploit suitors without actually giving her away (see Laban with Rebekah [24:55] and the Israelite brothers with Dinah [34:13–17]).

kill me. The situation resembles the days of Noah: harems and violence (see 6:1–8). However, Abraham's fear demonstrates a lack of trust in God's recent promises. Although God has promised to make Abraham's seed abundant (a promise still to be fulfilled) and to curse those who curse Abraham, Abraham fears for his life.

13. say. This is better translated, "Please say," a request, not an order. Sarah pragmatically consents. Their philosophy is "Better defiled than dead." This is not a philosophy that establishes God's kingdom in a pagan world.

sister. Abraham suggests an equivocating half-truth. She is actually his sister, and it was also a Hurrian practice to adopt a wife as a sister to elevate her social standing.[39] However, he is willing to risk his honor and his wife's purity to advantage himself on this technicality.

---

[36]An Egyptian frontier official from the age of Ramesses II (ca. 1300–1250 B.C.) sent this message to his superior: "We have finished letting the Bedouin tribes of Edom pass the fortress . . . to keep them alive and to keep their cattle alive" (*ANET*, 259).

[37]The Israelites will also find that, out of the land of blessing, they are under a curse (cf. 26:1; 47:4; Ruth 1:1).

[38]A. H. Konkel, "*gûr*," *NIDOTTE*, 1:837.

[39]E. A. Speiser, *Genesis* (AB; New York: Doubleday, 1964), 91–93.

Abduction: Pharaoh Takes Sarah and Rewards Abraham (12:14–16)

14. woman. This impersonal identification signifies Sarah's treatment as an object.

15. Pharaoh. This is actually a title meaning "Great House," not a personal name; it is a metonymy, like "Crown" for the British monarch.

Pharaoh's officials . . . praised her to Pharaoh. This is probably more than Abraham has bargained for. Only divine intervention can correct this situation.

was taken. Although ambiguous, the Hebrew here does not necessarily entail sexual intercourse (see 20:2, 6); to signify intercourse the text might have included "and violated her" (see 34:2) or "and lay with her" (see 38:2).

16. he treated Abram well. Each of the wife-sister episodes has the motif of the patriarch's enrichment in connection with his deception (20:14–16; 26:12–14). However, in this first story the Pharaoh enriches Abraham after the matriarch's abduction; in the case of Abimelech and Sarah, the Philistine rewards Sarah to compensate for his wrong (20:14–16); in the case of Abimelech and Rebekah, the Lord blesses Isaac (26:12–14). In spite of the patriarchs' failure of faith, God extends them grace and plunders the real criminal, who we may presume would have killed Abraham to gratify his lust (see 12:12–13 and notes on 12:17 below).

sheep. The Hebrew word can also include goats.

cattle. The Hebrew denotes domesticated bovines.

male . . . maidservants. Hebrew reads "male donkeys, menservants, maidservants, and female donkeys." The narrator depicts Abraham's caravan precisely according to the order in which it moves. The donkey wranglers separated male donkeys, with their strong sexual drives sparked by the scent of the female donkeys, by placing them in the front and the human servants between to keep order.

donkeys. The donkey was an important animal for riding and plowing. Sarna comments, "Its [the male-donkey's] importance may be gauged from the fact that it is the only unclean animal whose firstling requires redemption [cf. Ex. 13:13]."[40]

menservants and maidservants. The Hebrew word also denotes "slaves." People who failed financially for one reason or another became indentured slaves. A person of modest means had at least several slaves (cf. Judg. 6:15 with 6:27). Even a "nobody" had at least one (Prov. 12:9). On the other hand, in the law, the kidnapping of a person to sell him or her into slavery was a capital offense (Ex. 21:16), and an Israelite slave was set free with a generous hand after six years (Deut. 15:12–15).

camels. The Hebrew word does not distinguish between the one-humped dromedary of Arabia and the two-humped beast of Iran. The reference to

---

[40]Sarna, *Genesis*, 96.

camels in the patriarchal narratives has raised questions about their historicity. Some contend from archaeological evidence that the effective domestication of the camel did not occur before the twelfth century B.C. Speiser, however, suggests that "the camel may have come into limited use at an early period (as did also the horse), but required centuries before it ceased to be a luxury."[41] K. A. Kitchen also cites counter archaeological evidence for a limited domestication of the animal as early as 3000 B.C.[42] Sarna cites evidence proving knowledge of the dromedary in Old Babylonian times (ca. 2000–1700 B.C.).[43] Possession of the rare animal signaled wealth and status (Gen. 24). At the rear of the caravan, the wealthy and dignified members of the family rode high upon their camels looking gratefully over all their blessings that stretched out in front of them.

Deliverance, Confrontation, and Resolution: The Lord Afflicts Pharaoh; Pharaoh Rebukes Abraham; and Abraham Leaves with Wealth (12:17–20)

17. The LORD inflicted. Through the plagues, Pharaoh recognizes the providential blessing and protection on Sarah. In contrast with his later dealings with Abimelech (20:6), however, God does not acquit Pharaoh as innocent. In all likelihood, Pharaoh's general behavior has been the reason for Abraham's fear.

serious diseases. Though the nature of the diseases is unexplained, it probably pertains to sex so as to suggest to Pharaoh that Sarah is their cause. Instead of bringing blessing and life, Abraham brings death upon Egypt (see 12:3).

18–19. What? . . . Why? . . . go! The silence of Abraham expresses his guilt.

18. Why didn't you tell me. The narrator blanks the fact that Sarah must have told the suspicious Pharaoh.

Return to the Land (13:1–2)

1. went up from Egypt to the Negev. See Literary Analysis above.

Lot went with him. This is a necessary comment to set the stage for the next scene. Sarna notes, "By placing him [Lot] last in the list, after Abraham's possessions, the text hints at a degree of estrangement."[44]

2. wealthy. Hebrew *kābēḏ* is translated "severe" in 12:10, inviting a contrast of Abraham's situation before and after he goes to Egypt. This also sets the stage for the strife between his herdsmen and Lot's in the following scene.

---

[41]Speiser, *Genesis*, 90.
[42]K. A. Kitchen, "Camel," *NBD*, 162.
[43]Sarna, *Genesis*, 96.
[44]Ibid., 97.

in livestock and in silver and gold. Only the livestock can be attributed to the gifts of Pharaoh. By the mention of silver and gold, the narrator inferentially points to the Lord as the ultimate Blesser, though the immediate cause may have been various sorts of commercial transactions. Precious metals afford a measure of security and protection in times of famine.

THEOLOGICAL REFLECTIONS ON BOOK 6, ACT 1, SCENE 2

Suffering and the Test of Faith

God's promises to his pilgrim-covenant partners are not intended to bring quiet and repose. Suffering is a necessary part of the pilgrim's perfection. Were God's blessings given without suffering, the saint would confound morality with pleasure. Saints would serve God for what they could get out of it, a system of ethics known as eudaemonism. By interrupting acts of faith from their rewards with hardships, God saves his people from selfishness and develops such virtues as faith, hope, patience, and upright character (see Rom. 5).

This scene tests the saint with choosing famine and stones in God's will or bread outside of it. Abraham fails the test, but not our Lord (Luke 4:1–4). God leads Jesus into the wilderness, where he endures hunger for forty days. Though he has the power to change stones in God's will into bread out of it, he resists the temptation. At the end of the temptation, the angels of God feed him. We, who would live the life of faith, will also encounter such temptation. Will we abide with the stones in God's will or go out of God's will to find bread? Out of God's will we may find food, but we will be living in Satan's rude world and will become spiritually famished.

Ethics

The pilgrim frequently faces difficult moral choices. Abraham fears he can only escape death by tarnishing his honor through lies and by jeopardizing the honor and purity of his wife. Is being defiled better than death? If we act out of fear, we are not acting out of faith. Without faith we cannot please God (Heb. 11:6), and whatever is not of faith is sin (Rom. 14:23). Furthermore, the coward denies God the opportunity to glorify himself. Jesus said that unless we take up his cross, the symbol of death, we are not worthy to be his disciples (Matt. 16:24–27). Jesus forewarns Peter that Satan will tempt him to disown his Lord to save himself (Luke 22:31–34). Afterward Peter repents of his cowardice (Luke 22:54–62).

God's Grace

Though Abraham fails the tests of faith and ethics, God proves faithful. Though we are unfaithful, he is faithful (2 Tim. 2:13) and takes pity upon his children (Ps. 103:13). He supernaturally intervenes to protect his own, though this is not always so (1 Kings 18:13; Heb. 11:35b–38), and he even enriches Abraham materially. Nevertheless, Abraham pays a price. He loses God's voice, builds no altars, and brings no blessing on others. Instead of blessing, he brings a rebuke upon himself.

Canonical Foreshadowing

The first mention of Egypt in the Bible "prefigures the ambiguity of future relationships—on the one hand as a place of shelter and succor in time of distress, on the other hand as a place of mortal danger."[45] Abraham's exodus from Egypt typifies the nation's later Exodus: God sends a famine (Gen. 12:10; 47:4); the Egyptians afflict them (12:12–15; Ex. 1:11–14); God plagues the Egyptians (Gen. 12:17; Ex. 7:14–12:30); the Egyptians let them go with great wealth (Gen. 12:16, 20; Ex. 12:33–36); they return to the land by stages through the wilderness (Gen. 13:3; Ex. 17:1); and finally arrive back in the land where they worship the Lord (Gen. 13:3–4; Ex. 15:17; see also Ps. 105:14–15; 1 Cor. 10:1–4).[46]

As noted above, this is also the first of three typical scenes in which the matriarch finds herself trapped in a pagan king's harem (Gen. 20:1–18; 26:1, 7–11).[47] The repetition typifies the situation and projects it into the future. Esther will also find herself in a pagan king's harem. Saints find themselves plundered by tyrants in all sorts of ways, but few are so richly provided for in this lifetime as Abraham is.

Grace to the Gentiles

Remarkably, as Sarna notes, "there is no hatred of Egypt in the Bible. To the contrary, Israel is enjoined: 'You shall not abhor an Egyptian, for you were a stranger in his land' (Deut. 23:7). Notwithstanding repeated prophetic denunciations of Egypt for its duplicity and fickleness in international relations, Isaiah can envisage a future partnership of Israel and Egypt, and so God says: 'Blessed be Egypt my people' (Isa. 19:25)."[48]

---

[45]Ibid., 93.

[46]For other striking parallels, see Sailhamer, *Pentateuch*, 142.

[47]The repeated experience is not surprising nor probably due to varying contradictory sources narrating the same event. Abraham anticipated such treatment when he set out on his pilgrimage in the first place and made provision for it. As he explains to Abimelech, who also kidnapped Sarah, "When God had me wander from my father's household, I said to her [Sarah], 'This is how you can show your love to me: Everywhere we go, say of me, "He is my brother."'" Moreover, Biblical narrators delight in repetition to emphasize a point. Finally, Ugaritic and Greek epics provide parallels to the motif of the abduction of the hero's beautiful wife (see Sarna, *Genesis*, 94).

[48]Sarna, *Genesis*, 93.

BOOK 6, ACT I, SCENE 3:
SEPARATION OF LOT FROM THE
LAND OF PROMISE (13:3 – 18)

LITERARY ANALYSIS OF BOOK 6, ACT I, SCENE 3 ————

Structure

The events of this scene can be arranged chiastically:

A Abraham at his Bethel altar with contentious Lot (13:3–7)
   B Abraham's speech: his offer of the land (13:8–9)
      X Lot's choice of Sodom (13:10–13)
   B' God's speech: his offer of the land (13:14–17)
A' Abraham at his Hebron altar alone (13:18)

A/A' set the physical and spiritual tone of scene. Geographically the scene moves from Bethel/Ai in the north to Hebron in the south. Spiritually, Abraham is back at his altar in the heart of the Promised Land. Lot's spiritual situation is blanked, although one might guess it, since Lot makes such a poor choice.

In B/B', with an amazing generosity Abraham gives up his rights and offers Lot the pick of the land. The Lord affirms Abraham's peacemaking by reaffirming his promise in the legal language of the time.

In X, Lot's wicked decision not to defer to his esteemed uncle marks their decisive separation: one to cursed prosperity (cf. Acts 8:20), the other to eternal life and true prosperity.

Garrett notes the parallel structure of the three Lot scenes in this book:

Scene A (Gen. 13:1–18)

Section	Verses	Content
A	13:1–4	Initial setting: Abraham wealthy and pious at Bethel/Ai
B	13:5–7	Threat to Lot: strife of Abraham's and Lot's herdsmen
C	13:8–13	Abraham saves Lot; Sodom very wicked
D	13:14–18	The Lord blesses Abraham

Scene B (Gen. 14:1–24)

Section	Verses	Content
A'	14:1–11	Initial setting: War
B'	14:12	Threat to Lot: taken as prisoner of war
C'	14:13–16	Abraham saves Lot
D'	14:17–24	Melchizedek blesses Abraham; Sodom very wicked

Scene C (Gen. 18:1–19:38)

Section	Verses	Content
A″	18:1–15	Initial setting: Annunciation of Isaac's birth an ironic contrast to births of Moab and Ammon
B″	18:16–21	Threat to Lot: the Lord threatens Sodom
C″	18:22–19:29	Abraham/the Lord saves Lot; Sodom very wicked
D″	19:30–38	Lot's tragic end[49]

Plot and Character Development

Paradoxically, whereas in the previous scene the plot's tension arose out of the severity of famine, the plot tension of this scene arises out the prosperity of Abraham and his nephew Lot. On a deeper level, the plot's tension involves a test of character for both men. Will Lot defer to his esteemed uncle and benefactor or assert his own self-interest? Will Abraham give up his right to choose in order to retain peace with his kinsman and trust God to give him the Promised Land? Abraham, not Lot, proves the worthy covenant partner.

Inclusios

The scene begins and ends with Abraham at an altar, the symbol of worship and fellowship. As in the previous scene, this scene is framed by movement, but with the important addition of altars built in the north (13:3) and south (13:18) of the Promised Land.

Altar Motif

The building of altars in this scene is the key to Abraham's spiritual triumph. In Egypt, when Abraham feared for his life and doubted God's promises, there were no altars. In this scene, the altars signify Abraham's return to faith and his proclamation of claiming the land in the name of God. The narrator underscores Abraham's return to the place of faith and worship by the repetitive phrase "as far as the site where his tent had been earlier, to the site where he had first built an altar" (lit., 13:3–4).[50]

Contrast

Three contrasts underscore Abraham's faith in this scene. First is the contrast between Abraham in Pharaoh's palace out of the land of blessing (12:15) and Abraham in a nomad's tent in the land of blessing.

Second, Abraham's faith in the land is contrasted with his own cowardice in Egypt. Abraham had journeyed away from the land and his altar and failed to trust God. The silencing of God's voice to Abraham and the absence of the symbolic altars in that scene alluded to Abraham's lack of faith. By

---

[49]Cf. Garrett, *Rethinking*, 138.
[50]The NIV diminishes the impact of the apposition by adding "and" to join the clauses.

contrast, in this scene Abraham's faith in God is so secure that he can extend land to Lot to make peace. In faith and worship, he builds altars to the Lord, and God rewards him with his voice of promise to give him the land.

Third, Abraham's faith is contrasted with Lot's foolishness. Both Lot and Abraham look around (13:10, 14), are offered all the land (13:9, 15–17), and travel to their allotted portions (13:11–12, 18)—but Lot chooses by sight (see 27:18–27) and will later only barely escape destruction (see 14:12, 16; 19:1–29). Lot serves as a foil to Abraham, who chooses by faith and receives God's affirmation, with promises of eternal enrichment.

Foreshadowing

The narrator underscores the folly of Lot's choice by framing his decision (13:10–13) with two parenthetical remarks foreshadowing Sodom and Gomorrah's destruction. The first remark anticipates God's destruction of the cities of the plain that Lot chooses (13:10), while the second notes their wickedness that causes the destruction and that Lot in unbelief chooses to ignore (13:13).

EXEGETICAL NOTES TO BOOK 6, ACT I, SCENE 3 ————

Abraham at His Bethel Altar with Contentious Lot (13:3 – 7)

3. From the Negev. This reference forms a smooth, almost seamless, transition from the conclusion of the previous scene. Scene 3 will transpire between Ai and Bethel in the north (13:3) and Hebron in the south (13:18).

he went. Socially, Abraham is a wealthy nomad and an alien resident among the Canaanites. Spiritually, he is a pilgrim in quest of the heavenly vision of a holy land and city.

from place to place. Hebrew *lᵉmassāʿāyw*, not *māqôm*, denotes "to move by stages" (i.e., from one watering hole to the next).

the place [*māqôm*]. This is better translated "the sacred site" (see 12:6).

tent. This is a nomad-pilgrim's residence (see 13:12).

3–4. earlier . . . first. The repetition of synonyms underscores Abraham's physical and spiritual return to his initial step of faith.

4. altar. This has significance on both the story and discourse levels. The physical symbol is a reminder to Abraham of God's promises and Abraham's earlier faith. The narrator's comment on this image suggests to the reader that Abraham has returned to a position of faith, the place where the reader should also dwell.

and where. The Hebrew literally reads, "unto the site" (*māqôm*, see 12:6).

5. Lot . . . also had. Abraham mediates blessing to those with him.

6. the land could not support them. Ironically, the problem is the "severity" of blessing that causes strife among family.

7. Canaanites and Perizzites. The Perizzites are not listed as descendants of Canaan (10:15–18). Rather than an ethnic term, it probably denotes a social class of Canaan's descendants, "a section of the population driven out of a town and living in the open country" (see Deut. 3:5; 1 Sam. 6:18; Est. 9:19).[51] If so, the Canaanites may represent the citizens connected with the walled cities.[52] Together, they composed the indigenous population that restricts the pasturage and watering holes, making it impossible for the kinsmen to sustain the fertility of their flocks and herds grazing together (see 21:25; 26:13–22).

Abraham's Speech: His Offer of the Land (13:8–9)

8. we are brothers. Abraham treats his orphaned nephew as an equal. He puts the peace between family before individual prosperity.

9. the whole land before you. Some commentators find fault with Abraham for offering the land to Lot. However, the narrator's criticism of Lot and God's affirmation of his promises to Abraham (cf. Pharaoh's criticism of Abraham in the previous scene, 12:18–19) are evidence of the narrator's approval of Abraham's choice.

Let's part company. Sometimes brothers must separate for the sake of peace (see Acts 15:39; 1 Cor. 7:10–16).

If . . . left. The magnanimity of the patriarch of the clan and the uncle of the orphan is truly remarkable. The social superior humbles himself before the inferior to preserve peace, thereby proving himself the spiritual superior. Abraham's faith gives him the freedom to be generous (see 14:20).

Lot's Wicked Choice (13:10–13)

10. Lot looked up and saw. He is probably standing on an elevation close to Bethel (2,886 ft. [880 m] above sea level) and has a magnificent view of the Jordan Valley to the southeast.

plain of the Jordan. It is not entirely clear whether it is part of the Promised Land, the edge of the Promised Land, or possibly just beyond it (see 10:19; Num. 34:2–12). It is contrasted with Canaan in 13:12.

well watered. Like Egypt, which has the Nile, the area is fed by streams, brooks, springs, and oases from the base of the Jordanian Rift. By contrast, the central ridge where Bethel and Hebron are located depend upon the Lord to send rain (see Deut. 11:10–12).

like the garden of the Lord. See 2:10 and "Regeneration" in Theological Reflections below.

like the land of Egypt. After Abraham's disastrous choice to go to Egypt, similarity with Egypt should be a warning (see Literary Analysis).

before the Lord destroyed Sodom and Gomorrah. The narrator ensures that his audience understands Lot's poor choice by identifying this land with the cities that are so evil that they incur God's fiery judgment.

---

[51]*HALOT*, 965.

[52]In addition to its being a collective proper name, *Canaanite* can denote "tradesmen."

Zoar. This is probably on the southern end of the Dead Sea.

11. So Lot chose for himself. Lot selfishly intends to advantage himself by disadvantaging his uncle.

east. With the banishment of Adam and Eve from Eden, as Armstrong notes, "the easterly direction had come to symbolize distance and exile from the divine presence [see 11:2], and without the sacred there could be no blessing."[53]

set out. This is the same root rendered "from place to place" in 13:3. Lot is a nomad headed for the city of destruction.

12. Abram . . . Canaan/Lot . . . Sodom. The narrator stops the action to contrast the two choices.

pitched his tents. This is the verbal form of "tent" in 13:3. Abraham's tent is at the Bethel altar; Lot's camp points toward the evil Sodom (see 14:12 and note).

Sodom. The story anticipates the episodes of Genesis 14, 18, and 19.

The Lord's Reaffirmed Promise in Legal Language (13:14–17)

14. The LORD said. In the legal language of the ancient Near East, God conveys the Promised Land to Abraham (see below).

after Lot had parted. This comment marks a new innovation in salvation history. The partner, unfit for covenant, separates himself from the people of God.

place. The Hebrew is *māqôm* (see 12:6; 13:3–4).

Lift up your eyes . . . and look. The narrator invites comparison to Lot's survey of the land in 13:10. "Look" (i.e., "to see") is a key word in this book.

look north and south, east and west. This may reflect a legal practice of transferring property rights by "sight and intention."[54] The Lord invites Moses to a similar panoramic overview of the land (Deut. 34:1–4). In each case, the invitation is given to confirm the promise to one who himself will not participate in the dispossessing of the Canaanites.

15. land . . . forever. See 12:1, 7.

offspring. See 12:7.

16. like the dust. See 32:12 and Neh. 9:23.

17. Go, walk. Abraham's walking about the land symbolizes his legal acquisition of it. Kings asserted their right to rule their territory by symbolically tracing out its boundaries.[55] In Egypt (from ca. 3000 B.C.), on the day of his enthronement, the new pharaoh circumambulated the fortified wall in

---

[53]Armstrong, *Beginning*, 59.

[54]D. Daube, *Studies in Biblical Law* (Cambridge: Cambridge Univ. Press, 1947), 28–36. This is a concrete way of bringing Israel into legal possession of the land (cf. Deut. 3:27; Isa. 39:1–4; Luke 4:5; Mark 11:11).

[55]T. H. Gaster, *Myth, Legend, and Custom in the Old Testament* (New York: Harper & Row, 1969), 2:411–12.

a festal procession known as the "circuit of the wall." The Hittite king (ca. 1300 B.C.) toured his realm at the annual winter festival of Nun-ta-ri-ya-shas. In a poem of Ugarit (on the coast of Syria about 1400 B.C.), Baal made the rounds of "seventy-seven towns, eighty-eight cities" in order to assert his new kingship over gods and humans. Similarly, the priests within Joshua's army carried the Lord's throne around the walls of Jericho for seven days presumably to stake out their claim (Josh. 6). Sarna notes, "Early Jewish exegesis (Targ. Jon.) understood this traversing of the length and breadth of the land to be a symbolic act constituting a mode of legal acquisition termed *hazakah* in rabbinic Hebrew"[56] (see 12:7b and note; Josh. 1:3; 18:4; 24:3).

Abraham Settles at Hebron (13:18)

18. moved his tents. Presumably Abraham did this after having toured his claim.

great trees. The Masoretic text also offers a plural form of the same Hebrew word in 14:13 and 18:1, but a singular form in 12:6. In the Greek, Syriac, and Vulgate, the word is consistently singular.

Mamre. Here the word is a proper name of a location. The person Mamre, whose name is associated with the site, is an Amorite who seeks security in an alliance with Abraham. He will be blessed through Abraham (see 14:13, 24).

Hebron. The Hebrew means "confederacy" and may reflect that a number of clans are united in some kind of alliance.[57] As the highest town in Palestine (ca. 3,050 ft. [927 m]), Hebron is strategically located midway on the "Ridge Route" between Jerusalem and Beersheba. There is evidence of a settlement on the site from the third millennium B.C. Its foundation as an Egyptian fortified administrative center was laid in 1737 B.C. (cf. Num. 13:22). The resident population in Abraham's day are the Hittites (see Gen. 23). At the time of the conquest, it is populated by the descendants of Anak (Num. 13:22, 28, 33). Abraham and Sarah, Isaac and Rebekah, and Jacob and Leah are buried here (Gen. 49:31; 50:13).

built an altar. Abraham offers a proper response to God's renewed promises (cf. 12:7–9) and an appropriate conclusion to this scene (see 13:3–4).

THEOLOGICAL REFLECTIONS ON BOOK 6, ACT I, SCENE 3 ——————————

Biblical Economics

Paradoxically, God's largess, not famine, provokes the problem of scarcity of land, and Abraham's generous relinquishment brings peace and God's further blessing. These days, an economy of scarcity and an assumed consumerism lie behind both capitalism and communism, but true Christianity

---

[56]Sarna, *Genesis*, 100.
[57]Its older name was Kiriath Arba, "city of the four" (Josh. 14:15; Judg. 1:10).

renounces consumerism. Instead, Christians are to relinquish their rights in order to enrich others, trusting God's promises to provide. Abraham, secure in God, can give up his land. When we are secure in Christ, we do not have to grasp greedily for possessions.

Faith versus Sight

Lot, who chooses by sight and separates himself from the carrier of blessing, is a foil to Abraham. Calvin explains, "[Lot] fancied he was dwelling in paradise, [but he] was nearly plunged into the depths of hell."[58] Abraham, giving up his rights and implicitly risking the Promised Land to the reprobate Moabites and Ammonites (19:37–38; Deut. 23:3–6; Ezra 9:1), by faith inherits forever "all the land" and "an offspring like the dust" (see Gen. 13:15–16). He prefigures Christ, who humbles himself to the cross and then is so highly exalted that every rational being in heaven and earth will bow the knee at his name.

Peacemaking

Abraham's generosity, coupled with his willingness to forego his rights, reconciles the conflict with Lot (see 13:9). A major theological concern of this story is the priority of peace between brothers. Christians are to give up their rights and prosperity to restore relationship between people. Generosity and peacemaking kiss one another (Prov. 25:21–22). As Wenham explains, "The generosity and peaceableness displayed by Abraham on this occasion is applauded from one end of Scripture to the other (e.g., Lev. 19:17–18; Ps. 122; 133; Prov. 3:17, 29–34; Heb. 12:14; James 3:17–18). Indeed, peacemaking and reconciliation are so central to God's character as revealed in Christ (cf. Matt. 5:22–26, 43–48) that Paul often calls God 'the God of peace' (e.g., Rom. 15:33; 2 Cor. 13:11; Phil. 4:9; 1 Thess. 5:23; cf. Eph. 2:14–17)."[59]

Pentateuchal Foreshadowing

Abraham's generosity to Lot typifies that of Israel to Moab and Ammon, Lot's descendants (see Deut. 2:8–19). In the description of the Jordan Plain as "like the land of Egypt," Lot's choice and its disastrous consequences foreshadow the desire of the Israelite rebels to return to Egypt (see Ex. 16:3; Num. 11:5; 14:2–3).

Regeneration

Peace is not secured by creating the ideal environment. In the ideal environment of Eden, sin originated, and in this scene in a land that is "like the garden of the LORD" (13:10), conflict abounds. Only surrendering the heart and will to God creates peace.

---

[58]Calvin, *Genesis*, 373.
[59]Wenham, *Genesis 1-15*, 300.

BOOK 6, ACT 1, SCENE 4:
VICTORY OVER EASTERN KINGS (14:1–24)

LITERARY ANALYSIS OF BOOK 6, ACT 1, SCENE 4 ————

Plot

The plot's tension begins when four eastern tyrants suppress a revolt by five kings in the Dead Sea area. The tension mounts as they raid and conquer all of the Transjordan and the south of Palestine on their way to punish the rebels. It escalates further when they thoroughly rout the rebels and now bring Abraham onto the scene by kidnapping wealthy Lot with his possessions as part of the plunder. Abraham, with his allies, musters an armed force from his own household and leads a military campaign. In most literature, one might expect the climax to be Abraham's successful attack and routing of the enemies. But the story actually builds to the climactic recognition of God, unmentioned previously in this scene, as the battle's true victor and the subsequent blessing and affirmation of Abraham by the priest-king Melchizedek. In an anticlimax to this tremendous scene of worship, the pagan king of Sodom, speaking disrespectfully to Abraham, tries to assert his nonexistent authority and tempt Abraham with the plunder. But the faithful Abraham cannot be dissuaded from glorifying God.

Abraham continues to face conflicts and temptations that test his faith in God's promises for the land. Abraham's leadership in this scene signifies a much different Abraham from the cowardly man who endangered his wife just two scenes previously. His loyal defense of his foolish nephew reveals the depth of his honorable brotherly love. His refusal to accept the plunder from the king of Sodom also demonstrates his continuing reliance on God— and not the spoils of war—to provide the blessing.

Structure[60]

The battles develop in an alternating pattern:

A Dead Sea kings rebel against eastern kings		1–4
B Eastern allies conquer Transjordan and South		5–7
A′ Dead Sea kings plundered by eastern kings		8–12
B.′ Abraham and allies conquer eastern allies		13–16

Abraham's encounter with the king of Sodom and the priest-king Melchizedek is structured with both an alternating and chiastic pattern. It alternates the kings' greetings to Abraham (14:17–18) with their speeches and Abraham's responses (14:19–24). However, whereas the narrator begins the greetings with the king of Sodom, he opens the speeches with Melchizedek. As a result Abraham's relationship with the king of Sodom forms the outer frame, and his relationship with Melchizedek the inner core.

---

[60]See also Garrett's parallel structure between the Lot scenes cited above in Scene 3.

A King of Sodom and Melchizedek meet Abraham   14:17–18
    King of Sodom mute and empty-handed, 14:17
    Melchizedek's banquet, 14:18
A′ Melchizedek blesses and king of Sodom demands   14:19–24
    Melchizedek's blessing and Abraham's tithe, 14:19–20
    King of Sodom's demand and Abraham's oath, 14:21–24

The mention of the king of Sodom in 14:21–24 also forms a stylistic inclusio with the king's first mention in 14:2, thus unifying the entire chapter.

Key Word

The word *king* appears in this chapter twenty-eight times. A host of royal players make up this scene: five kings of Canaan, four kings of Mesopotamia, Abraham, Melchizedek the priest-king, and implicitly the Lord. Israel's God, Yahweh, however, stands above all as King of kings (see gaps). The Lord is sovereign over Philistia (Gen. 20; 26); Egypt (Ex. 1–15); Sihon and Og (Numbers); Canaan (Deuteronomy). By repeating *king*, precisely naming the kings and their countries from all over the Fertile Crescent and beyond, and by spreading the battles of this war all over Transjordan and south Palestine, the narrator magnifies the greatness of his hero, Abraham. On earth, God's faithful warrior, though lacking the title *king*, is in fact a greater king.

Comparisons and Contrasts

Abraham came up out of Egypt at the end of Scene 2 (13:1–2) a very wealthy man. At the end of Scene 3 (13:14–18), the Lord conveys into his hand the land of the Canaanites. At the end of this scene he holds in his hand the plundered wealth of the six nations who live in Transjordan and the south as far as Paran and of the pentapolis around the Dead Sea. This wealth even includes Lot's.

The decisive and courageous warrior at Mamre has done a complete about face from the duplicitous and cowardly husband in Egypt. The man of faith is not shackled by his past failures but saved from them. The man of peace, with reference to his relative, becomes a man of war, with reference to those who plunder him.

By contrasting two campaigns of the war, the scene contrasts the strength of the four eastern kings (14:5–7), the weakness of the five Dead Sea kings (14:8–12), and the superiority of Abraham to both (14:13–16). The battle lines of the kings of the pentapolis contrast with Abraham's surprise attack. The plundering kings have to be defeated in an unconventional way.

The scene also contrasts Abraham's covenant loyalty to his nephew with his nephew's disloyalty in the preceding scene. Even now Lot has not changed, as is indicated by his settling directly in wicked Sodom (14:12). In back-to-back verses, the narrator contrasts the dwellings of the man of vision and the man of sight. In this scenic depiction, Lot lives (*yšb*) in the city of Sodom (14:12), Abraham "tents" (*škn*) near the great trees of Mamre, "where he built an altar"(13:18; 14:13).

The attitudes of Melchizedek and Abraham toward the plunder contrast radically with that of the king of Sodom. The king of Sodom "came out" (14:17), but Melchizedek "brought out" (14:18). Melchizedek's first words were "Blessed be Abram," and the king of Sodom's were "Give me."

Blanks and Gaps

The narrator blanks details about the nature of the relationship of the Dead Sea vassals to their overlords. He also blanks details about the war. What interests many commentators and the ancient chroniclers of Near Eastern wars are of no interest to him.

However, the narrator's curious omission of any mention of the Lord in these battles, giving it a secular feeling, must be intentional. This omission cannot be an unintentional blank occasioned by his source.[61] The narrators of sacred Scriptures exercise control over their sources and aim to celebrate Israel's God. Here, however, the narrator cloaks God's presence in a straightforward war story. He colors his narrative as precise history by giving precise dates and ancient names, adding in parenthesis their modern names for his audience. However, the cloak is an opaque veil, to be lifted at Melchizedek's climactic blessing of Abraham in which he honors God's sovereignty over the enemies. Abraham's deeds confirm this truth. First, Abraham goes forth to battle from his sacred site at Mamre (14:13–14). Second, and most significantly, Abraham gives a tithe of the plunder to Melchizedek, the priest-king of the Most High God at Jerusalem (14:18–20). By giving God the firstfruits of the plunder, he signals that the Lord is the victor. The ambiguity of providence explains why Abraham declines the plunder that is rightfully his as victor. Abraham declines his rightful prize because the pretentious king of Sodom would irrationally think that he, not the Lord, has made him rich (14:23).

The narrator blanks the fate of the king of Sodom between his flight from the battle (14:10) and his meeting with Abraham as unimportant for salvation history. Presumably, Abraham's military campaign deep into northern Syria takes several weeks. In the interim, the king of Sodom has regained control over his plundered city (see 14:10).

However, the narrator's silence about Melchizedek can scarcely be intentional. Here is a king-priest of the Most High God who is able to mediate God's blessing to Abraham, God's mediator of blessing to the nations (12:3). Accordingly, Melchizedek is greater than any earthly king. Yet he emerges suddenly on the narrator's canvas without comment on his birth or ancestry. Just as quickly he disappears without mention of his fate or death. The

---

[61]An unusual spectrum of literary features, including a consistent modernization of place names, suggests that the narrator is updating an ancient record.

final editor of Genesis was likely aware of Psalm 110. In that psalm David anticipates a future king-priest after the order of Melchizedek who will rule and judge the nations. Presumably, the narrator did not intentionally gap the expected information but lacked it and stood in awe of this mysterious heavenly figure whom David calls "my Lord" (Ps. 110:1).

EXEGETICAL NOTES TO BOOK 6, ACT I, SCENE 4 ─────

Dead Sea Kings Rebel against Eastern Kings (14:1–4)

1–2. At this time . . . went to war. This is better translated, "At the time when Amraphel . . . went to war."[62] The Hebrew grammar of 14:1 (i.e., *wayyĕhî* + adverbial phrase and no narrative verb forms) shows that the section presents background information. We may presume that the story occurs about the same time as Scene 3 because in both scenes Abraham is at Mamre (cf. 13:18; 14:13). However, the narrator does not establish a chronology.

1. Amraphel . . . Tidal. The four eastern kings are listed in alphabetical order, though Kedorlaomer is their leader.[63] None of these kings has been definitely identified in extrabiblical sources. Attempts have been made, but none convincingly. Their names suggest a very wide area from the Black Sea to the Persian Gulf, the whole Mesopotamian Valley, all of what later is Babylon and Asher. One explicitly comes from Elam (part of modern Iran) and another from Shinar (modern Iraq). The other two are probably from Turkey. This historical situation of several powers, rather than one, only fits the Middle Bronze Age, Abraham's horizon (see "Historicity and Literary Genre" in the introduction).

Amraphel. He was formerly thought to be Hammurab/pi of Babylon.

Shinar. See 10:10; 11:2.

Arioch. This is also the name of a son of King Zimrilim of Mari (ca. 1750 B.C.).

Ellasar. *Genesis Apocryphon* identifies this ancient Babylonian city with Cappadocia (Turkey); Symmachus and Jerome, with Pontus on the Black Sea.

Kedorlaomer. The first element, from *kudur,* appears as a component of several Elamite names, and the second element sounds like the goddess Lagamar. If so, it means "servant of Lagamar."

Elam. See 10:22.

Tidal. This is a Hittite royal name.

Goiim. The Hebrew literally means "Gentile nations." These are perhaps the Umman Manda, barbarian hordes to the north of Mesopotamia (see Josh. 12:23). Tidal may have led this horde.

2. war. For the first time in the Bible, tribes and nations[64] now war against each other in the intensification of sin and the confusion from Babel.

---

[62]NIV, which locates it at the same time ("at this time"), over-reads the Hebrew.

[63]Sarna, *Genesis,* 102.

[64]In Canaan, rather than ruling tribes and nations, the kings ruled over city-states, as in this Canaanite confederacy.

Bera . . . Birsha . . . Shinab . . . Shemeber. Note the alliterative pairs.[65] Sodom and Gomorrah also commonly occur together. Current archaeological evidence points to five sites at Bab edh-Dra (on the tongue of land that juts into the Dead Sea on its eastern side) and nearby as the most likely locations for these five cities.

Bera. This name may mean "to triumph."

Sodom . . . Zeboiim. See 10:19.

Bela (that is, Zoar). The need to modernize the name suggests that the account is based on a precise historical source.

Zoar. See 13:10.

3. joined forces. This act of allying for war will only intensify in the many centuries to follow.

Valley of Siddim. This geographical note foreshadows 14:8. This former valley on the south end of the Dead Sea is now about 20 feet below the surface. Its northern end is approximately 1,300 feet (400 m) deep.

Salt Sea. The Dead Sea is called the Salt Sea because its average 32 percent saline content is about ten times more than the 3 percent average of the oceans.

4–5. twelve years . . . thirteenth year . . . fourteenth year. These details are another indication of a precise historical source.

4. subject to. The Hebrew means "served." They had been required to pay him tribute, to give him whatever he demanded.

rebelled. They probably refused to pay the annual tribute.

Eastern Kings Conquer Transjordan and South Canaan (14:5 – 7)

5. went out. The Hebrew reads "came." The narrator presents the war from a westerner's, not easterner's, viewpoint. As the eastern kings campaign towards the Valley of Siddim, they conquer four peoples in Transjordan. They probably transverse the length of the "King's Highway" (Num. 21:22) that runs through the hill country of Transjordan.

fourteenth year. See above.

Kedorlaomer. This king heads the eastern confederacy.

the Rephaites. The Hebrew lacks the article (cf. 15:20). The meaning of the Hebrew is uncertain, though LXX renders the term "giants." They inhabited Bashan, the northernmost part of Transjordan (Deut. 3:13). The Ammonites called them Zamzummites (Deut. 2:20).

Ashteroth Karnaim. Ashteroth near Karnaim was capital of Bashan, but its precise location is unknown.

Zuzites. These people are not otherwise mentioned. *Genesis Apocryphon* identifies them with Zamzummim, who may have been an offshoot of the Rephaites.

---

[65]Sarna, *Genesis*, 102.

Ham. Tell Ham is approximately 19 miles (30 km) east of Beth Shean.

Emites. The original inhabitants of Moab, they were strong, numerous, and giants (Deut. 2:10–11). Their name means "terrors."

Shaveh Kiriathaim. This is probably the plain of Kiriathaim, the well-known city in the Moabite tableland, 6 miles (10 km) due west of Medeba.

6. Horites. Their identity is uncertain. Perhaps the Horites, the aboriginal inhabitants of Mount Seir, are the Hurrians, known from ancient Near Eastern documents of the second millennium B.C. (see Deut. 2:12, 22). Or, if the name derives from a Hebrew root meaning "cave," they may have been cave dwellers.

Seir. This is the hill country southeast of the Dead Sea along the Arabah.

El Paran. This is possibly the same as Elath, the harbor at the northern end of the eastern bay of the Red Sea. Paran is a general name for the wilderness of the eastern Sinai Peninsula.

7. went. The Hebrew reads "came" (see 14:5).

En Mishpat (that is, Kadesh). Kadesh is also known as Kadesh Barnea, a group of springs 46 miles (75 km) south of Beersheba.

Amalekites. A seminomadic tribe living primarily in the Negev (Num. 13:29), they were so despicable that eventually blotting them out was the only appropriate response toward this warlike people, who provoked unwarranted attacks against God's people and took advantage of the weak (Deut. 25:17–18; 1 Sam. 27:8–11; 30:1–20). The term may come to refer sometimes to any group of people who resist God's purposes (cf. Ex. 17).

Amorites. See 10:16.

Dead Sea Kings Plundered by Eastern Kings (14:8–12)

8. marched out. The verb is the opposite of "came" that introduced the two Transjordan battles. Thus, this is the first mention of resistance. The verb is singular, suggesting that the king of Sodom heads the Dead Sea coalition.

drew up their battle lines. The narrator describes a traditional battle matching strength against strength, five kings on the home ground against four kings far removed from their homeland. The contrast underscores the might of the eastern kings.

10. tar [ḥēmār]. This refers to a dark, bituminous substance that in ancient times was used as cement and mortar (see 11:3). Today, in addition to being found in natural beds, it is obtained as a residue in petroleum refining.

fled. The point seems to be that they escape from the battle (see 14:17).

some of the men fell into them. The Hebrew, "they fell into them," is ambiguous. It could mean that "[the kings] threw themselves into" the pits. "To fall" is also often a term in battle, but verses often cited to support "threw themselves into" include an additional preposition that clarifies the meaning. Probably this verse refers to the troops, not the kings, since the "rest" (of the troops) is juxtaposed with "they." The meaning then is that during their flight, the troops fall into the pits. The forces of nature under the invisible hand of Providence also conspire against the wicked men of Sodom to bring them down in defeat.

rest fled. Does this include the king of Sodom (14:17)?

12. Abram's nephew Lot. The narrator identifies the occasion for Abraham's involvement (see 14:14).

living in Sodom. Lot is still a fool. Note the progressive identification of Lot with Sodom: choosing it (13:11), camping near it (13:12), living in it (14:12), and a respected citizen in it (19:1, 6; see Ps. 1:1). He compounds his folly later by three more steps downward, for a total of seven: he flees to Zoar (19:18–23), settles in a cave (19:30), and in a drunken stupor incestuously begets Moab and Ammon (19:31–38).

Abraham and Allies Conquer Eastern Kings (14:13–16)

13. One who had escaped. Again, this shows the invisible hand of Providence.

the Hebrew [ʿibrî; cf. 10:21]. There is uncertainty about the meaning of this word during this time period. Some think it is a geographic term, deriving from the Hebrew root ʿbr, "to pass over," and thus meaning "one from beyond" (cf. Josh. 24:2). Others think it is a social term, designating a landless people of many ethnic backgrounds known in West Semitic as the ʿapiru, who hired themselves out as slaves or mercenaries and could be a socially disruptive force in society. Though a reputable leader and head of the allies,[66] Abraham is landless (see Gen. 23). Others think it is an ethnic term, connected with Eber, the last ancestor in the line of Shem before the earth is divided (10:21–25). The latter is the preferred meaning based on the following: (1) The form (ʿibrî) consists of ʿēber + a gentilic î, like Israeli or Israelite from Israel; (2) this form is appropriate with the proper name Eber, not with ʿapiru; (3) the term always occurs in opposition to other ethnic groups, especially the Egyptians and Philistines; (4) though landless, the other characteristics of Abraham do not fit the ʿapiru. The Bible ascribes the term only to Abraham and his descendants to show that they are the legitimate descendants of Shem through Eber.

dwell [škn]. Hebrew škn denotes a more temporary dwelling than yšb (see 14:12).

great trees of Mamre. See 12:6; 18:1. The narrator links this scene with the preceding one by noting that Abraham still resides "near the great trees of Mamre" (13:18; 14:13) and Lot has moved into Sodom. Indeed, both scenes pertain to Abraham's relationship with his nephew Lot.

Amorite. See 10:16. Sometimes this is a blanket term for the earlier inhabitants of Palestine (see 48:22; Deut. 1:44; Josh. 2:10).

---

[66]Wiseman, "Abraham Reassessed," 144–49.

Mamre . . . Eshkol . . . Aner. The three brothers were probably the heads of aristocratic families in Hebron. Since their own kinsmen are attacked, they too have reason to uphold their treaty with Abraham.

allied. The Hebrew literally refers to "those bound by a treaty." Centuries later, the law forbids Israel to make treaties with the Amorites, for they would steal away the covenant children from Israel's faith. Nothing in this text suggests that Abraham plays the fool by making a treaty with them here. Rather, they seem to have recognized Abraham as a mediator of blessing. They accompany him in battle (see 14:24) and find blessing (see 14:19–20; cf. 12:3).

14. relative. The Hebrew here is usually rendered "brother," as in 13:8. The term explains Abraham's action: the godly display "loving-loyalty" toward their kin.

called out. One should read *wayyādek* with the Samaritan Pentateuch and translate this "muster." The Masoretic text reads "empty out" (*wayyā-req*). The difference reflects the common scribal confusion of *d* and *r* (see Gen. 10:3 and 10:4).

318. Since this is a sizeable army in Abraham's time (cf. Gideon, Judg. 7), it is a clear indication of Abraham's great wealth even before he recovers the plunder. There is some evidence from Egyptian sources and from the *Iliad* that the number is symbolic.[67]

trained. The meaning of the unique Hebrew term is derived from an Egyptian cognate meaning "retainer."

born in his household. These would be Abraham's most reliable slaves.

Dan. The name is modernized from Laish after the time of Moses (see Judg. 18:29; also "Composition and Authorship" in the introduction). Tell Dan lies at the southern foot of Mount Hermon. It represents the northern extremity of Palestine (Judg. 20:1; 1 Sam. 3:20).

15. During the night. Abraham attacks when least expected.

divided. The Hebrew reads, "divided against them," perhaps a technical military term.

men. Literally, they are his "servants" or "slaves."

routed them. As Roop says, "No foreign king can exercise power against the blessing of God, as Pharaoh discovered by accident."[68]

King of Sodom Meets Abraham (14:17)

17. came out [*yṣ', Qal*] to meet. In the Hebrew text this expression introduces the scene. Its meaning is ambiguous. It can mean "to greet" (1 Sam. 18:6) or "to confront" (Num. 20:20 ["against them" NIV]). Since the king of Sodom meets the victors mute and empty-handed, unlike Melchizedek, the former meaning is not viable. His unnatural lack of gratitude and preoccupation with the spoils of war provides an index of Sodom's wickedness.

---

[67]Wenham, *Genesis 1–15*, 314.
[68]Roop, *Genesis*, 107.

After . . . Kedorlaomer and the kings allied with him. The narrator adds this chronological note to emphasize the greatness of Abraham and the wickedness of the king of Sodom's ingratitude and pretentious demand.

Shaveh. Apart from the narrator's explanation, the meaning would be uncertain. The King's Valley is probably close to Jerusalem (2 Sam. 18:18).[69] Some identify it as the fairly flat area north of Jerusalem, but most refer to the valley west of the City of David in Jerusalem.[70]

Melchizedek's Banquet (14:18)

18. Then. The Hebrew simply has "and," suggesting that Melchizedek comes out at the same time as the king of Sodom.

Melchizedek. The name means "king of righteousness" or "my king is righteous" (see Heb. 7:2),[71] just as the name Adoni-Zedek means "righteous lord" or "my lord is righteous" (Josh. 10:1).[72]

Salem. This is probably Jerusalem (Ps. 76:2),[73] but the identification is uncertain. The name may have been shortened to suggest a connection with shalom, "peace."

brought out [ys', Hiphil]. The Hebrew pun with 14:17 underlines the contrast.

priest. This is the first reference to priests in the Bible. The Hebrew has no definite article ("a priest" rather than "the priest"), suggesting the existence of other priests of God. Though the fusion of the offices of priest and king is attested in Assyria and among the Hittites, it is not attested in Ugarit (i.e., Syria ca. 1400 B.C.).

bread and wine. "Bread" probably means "food." The combination is a merism for a full dinner, a royal banquet (see 2 Sam. 17:27–29; Prov. 9:5).[74]

God Most High [ʾēl ʿelyôn]. The Hebrew word ʾēl is essentially a common appellative for "divinity" and therefore may be accompanied by a specifying term. For instance, Jacob calls his Shechem altar El Elohe Israel (33:20). The background for ʾēl may be a Canaanite name for the head of their pantheon; therefore, some argue that Melchizedek's God is ʾēl the head Canaanite deity.[75] The word ʾēl occurs in compounds in Canaanite and in the Old Testament,[76] but never as ʾēl ʿelyôn.[77] Corresponding names, which in fact

---

[69]Josephus, *Antiquities* 7.10.13.

[70]L. Jonker, "šwh," *NIDOTTE*, 4:60.

[71]This meaning is more probable than "Malki is righteous" or "my king is Zedek" or "legitimate king" (see *IBHS* §8.2c).

[72]*HALOT*, 16.

[73]*Jeru + salem* means "city of salem."

[74]A Ugaritic text affords an interesting parallel: "Eat of the food, ho! Yea drink of the ferment of the wine, ho!" (J. Gray, *The Legacy of Canaan: The Ras Shamra Texts and Their Relevance to the Old Testament* [Leiden: Brill, 1965], 94).

[75]F. M. Cross "ʾēl," *TDOT*, 1:256.

[76]Cf. El Roi (El Who Sees Me, 16:13); El Olam (El Eternal, 21:33).

[77]El and Elyon appear as separate deities in Northwest Semitic inscriptions, but it is plausible that "Most High" was one of El's titles, like Baal Elyon, which is attested.

do not entirely occur here, do not constitute identity. To be sure, Abraham's specification of the personal name *Yahweh* (14:22) is probably a latter addition to the text, but it accurately reflects the narrator's intention and understanding of the events. Moberly argues that the narrator of Genesis, though aware that the Lord first reveals his name Yahweh to Moses (Ex. 6:2–3), uses Yahweh to insist that God, who is worshiped by the patriarchs as El, El Shaddai, and the like, is indeed Yahweh.[78] Though his thesis is unlikely (see "Composition and Authorship" in the introduction), he is certainly right that the God of the patriarchs is Yahweh, not El of the Canaanite pantheon. The Canaanite *ʾēl*, to judge from texts at about 1400 B.C., was as depraved as the Canaanites themselves. The narrator certainly does not think a pagan priest of such a depraved god can confer a divine blessing upon Abraham; nor would Abraham, who is consecrating the land to the Lord (see 12:7; 13:3), honor such a blessing and give tithe to such a priest. It is mischievous to reconstruct a historically different religion of Israel distinct from the narrator's intention. It impugns his moral integrity and needlessly calls into question his historical credibility. Unquestionably, he identified *ʾēl ʿelyôn* with "the Lord," though *yhwh* may not have been in the original text.[79]

Melchizedek's Blessing and Abraham's Tithe (14:19–20)

19. blessed Abram. As a priest-king, Melchizedek mediates God's potency, power, and protection by placing God's name on Abraham (see 1:22; Num. 6:22–27; 1 Chron. 16:2). One may infer from this that Melchizedek is greater than Abraham (Heb. 7:7).

Blessed be. Noah's doxological benediction on Shem (see 9:26) is now specified to Abraham: the Japhethites will find salvation in him and the Canaanites will become his slaves.

Creator[80] of heaven and earth. Habel argues convincingly that the title is a metonymy for God as the source of life, buoyancy, and joy in the trials of the day, not just as the source of origins.[81] A similar expression occurs in Ps. 115:15; 121:2; 124:8; 134:3; and 146:6, which speak not just

---

[78]R. W. L. Moberly, *The Old Testament of the Old Testament: Patriarchal Narratives and Mosaic Yahwism* (OBT; Minneapolis: Fortress, 1992), 177.

[79]The book of Daniel commonly uses the title "God Most High" (3:26; 4:17, 24–25, 32, 34; 5:18, 21; 7:18, 22, 25, 27), not with reference to the Canaanite El but with reference to Israel's God. "[*ʾēl ʿelyôn*] is used in contexts in which the sweep of faith goes beyond the history of Israel to make universal claims for this God" (Brueggemann, *Genesis*, 136). In the NT, the title the "Most High God" is linked to Jesus (Mark 5:7; Luke 8:28).

[80]NIV offers the option "Possessor," the usual meaning of *qnh*. However, *qnh* mean "to bring forth" (Gen. 4:1; Deut. 32:6 [cf. Deut. 32:18; Isa. 64:8; Mal. 2:10]; Ps. 139:13; Prov. 8:22 [cf. 8:24]) and was translated on occasion by the Greek word *ktizō*, "to create." This is probably its meaning in Northwest Semitic inscriptions where it is used as a title of El. Here, too, the biblical authors adopt a liturgical tradition of the ancient Near Eastern religions and adapt it to the monotheistic religion of Israel.

[81]N. Habel, "Yahweh, Maker of Heaven and Earth: A Study in Tradition Criticism," *JBL* 91 (1972): 321–37.

of God as the originator of creation but also of God being intimately involved in this present reality. In Ps. 121:2; 124:8; 146:6, it is associated with ʿāzar, "to help."

20. And blessed be. This is better translated, "And praise be to" (see also 1 Sam. 25:32–33).

delivered. The Hebrew here is the same root as "shield" in 15:1, providing a key word linking the two scenes.

tenth. This is a one-time tithe of the booty (cf. Num. 31:25–41), not an annual tithe to the priest (cf. Lev. 27:30–33; Num. 18:21). Tithing is an old and ancient practice in the biblical world (see 7:2). Kedorlaomer's tribute is paid as a tithe to the Lord! With the institution of monarchy, a greedy king demands the annual tithe along with the priest (1 Sam. 8:15, 17).[82] The text does not suggest that Melchizedek has come to collect his tithe, though some foist that suggestion upon it. Melchizedek celebrates Abraham as God's warrior and blesses him. Abraham recognizes Melchizedek as the legitimate priest and king of his God.

everything. This refers to the booty.

King of Sodom's Demand and Abraham's Oath (14:21 – 24)

21. Give. The king of Sodom addresses Abraham with a command[83] rather than honor and praise. It reflects an ungrateful heart.

People [nepeš] . . . goods [rᵉḵuš]. Though nepeš can refer to animals as well as people (see 1:24, 30; "Image of God" in Theological Reflections on the Prologue), that meaning is screened out by rᵉḵuš. Rᵉḵuš sometimes specifically denotes domestic animals, the economic backbone of Abraham's agricultural context. Here it more broadly denotes all moveable property, including the livestock.

keep. His proposal is fair and probably generous. The victor is due his share for risking his life and fortune. If it is wrong to keep stolen property (cf. Ex. 22:9), it is also wrong to keep plundered booty. In the case of plunder, however, there is some moral ambiguity, since the victor risks life and fortune to recover it. What is wrong with the king of Sodom's proposal is his audacity and attitude. The victor, not a defeated king, has the right to stipulate the disposition of the spoils of war. Moreover, the king's attitude is deceitful and begrudging. He does not greet Abraham with joy and gladness. Abraham anticipates that, were he to accept the offer, the king of Sodom would claim that he disadvantaged himself in order for Abraham to be advantaged.

22. I have raised my hand. One could translate this, "I raise my hand."[84]

---

[82]A royal tithe is attested at Ugarit.
[83]He does not add the particle of entreaty, "Please" (cf. 12:13).
[84]*IBHS* §30.5.1d.

Lord. God's name is omitted by the original Greek, Syriac, and a Dead Sea scroll; the Samaritan Pentateuch reads "God." In all probability, "Lord" is a secondary addition in the Masoretic text.

23. nothing belonging to you. Abraham will not be stained with the moral ambiguity of keeping a victim's plunder.

a thread or the thong. Reference to a narrow and a wide strap is a merism and synecdoche for all the plunder.

I made Abram rich. Abraham wants a clear, unambiguous moral claim to all his possessions.

24. to the men who went with me. The spoil is their rightful share (cf. 1 Sam. 30:16–25). This distribution of the goods emphasizes Abraham's fairness and generosity.

THEOLOGICAL REFLECTIONS ON BOOK 6, ACT 1, SCENE 4 ————————

Faith and Brotherly Love

Abraham escalates his commitment to his kinsman Lot from humility and generosity in order to preserve peace, to risking his life and fortune to rescue him. Lot's foolish choice of Sodom has put him in this danger. Now kidnapped, he loses his possessions and faces slavery. Abraham's attitude to his nephew is not, "He made his own bed, let him lie in it." In spite of grave danger, Abraham, the faithful uncle, sets out to rescue Lot. Such brotherly love is affirmed throughout Scripture. Judah is crowned with kingship partly because, in loyalty to his family, he offers himself as a slave in the place of his brother, though Benjamin appears to have stolen Joseph's goblet (Gen. 44:33). Christ dies for his spiritual brothers and sisters while they are still sinners (Rom. 5:8). He commands his disciples to love one another as he has loved them (John 15:12–13).

Faith and Just War

The patriarchs do not go to war on behalf of the promised seed and land. They depend entirely on God's providential intervention to preserve the matriarch and the holy seed in the harem of pagan kings (Gen. 12:10–20; 20:1–18; 26:1–11). Jacob even censures Simeon and Levi for using their swords to cut down the Shechemites (Gen. 34) and bypasses them from kingship for being rash hotheads (Gen. 49:5–7). However, the patriarchs are not pacifists. When Lot is unjustly kidnapped, Abraham commences an all-out military campaign to rescue him.

Faith and Insuperable Odds

Abraham does not cower before the four victorious kings. Incredibly, he risks himself and wins against an alliance that has ravaged six tribes and defeated five kings. This is an encouragement to the people of God, even in the Exile. Even powerful nations can be defeated by the faithful and righteous.

Faith and Means

Faith is sometimes passive, depending entirely upon God apart from human means, as when Abraham offers Lot the choice of land. Here, however, Abraham's faith is active, using the normal means of warfare to win. He has already entered into an alliance with the aristocrats at Hebron and has trained his slaves to fight. He takes advantage of the darkness of night and divides his fresh troops to take advantage of the battle-weary and depleted eastern armies. He presses the attack until he has fully routed them and recovered all the plunder (14:14–16). The saint must be sensitive to God's plan. Sometimes it requires more faith to take action than to remain passive.

Faith and Providence

See "Blanks and Gaps" in the Literary Analysis above.

Faith and Alliances

After the conquest of the land, the law forbids intermarriage and treaties with the Canaanites because they would subvert Israel's holiness (Deut. 7:1–6). Abraham, though he does not allow his son to intermarry with them (Gen. 24:3), does not fear that an alliance with them will subvert his faith, represented by his altar in their midst at Mamre (13:18; 14:13). In fact, through their alliance with him, he mediates blessing to them.

Unbelief and Progressive Hardening in Sin

Lot chooses by sight, spiritually blind to the wickedness of the Sodomites. He progressively becomes hardened toward their sin, settling at first *near* Sodom, then *in* it, finally becoming an active citizen (see 14:12; 19:1) and calling them "my brothers" (lit., 19:7). He should have learned from this misadventure to leave it. Tragically, he does not and eventually loses even his family. Nevertheless, in spite of his progressive assimilation to the Sodomites, they never consider him one of them because he retains a fundamental righteousness (19:9; 2 Peter 2:6–8).

Faith and Property

As the conquering hero, Abraham has the right to a share of the property plundered from the king of Sodom, but he wants no share of what the pagan king offers him with a grudge. Abraham wants to be above any reproach in the eyes of his pagan neighbors, and he will not allow the name of his God to be tarnished by moral ambiguity. Because of love for others, Christians must be ready to surrender their rights. Thus Paul refuses his right to payment for his ministry in order not to hinder the ministry (1 Cor. 9:7–19; 2 Cor. 2:17; 11:7–12; cf. 2 Kings 5:15–27).

Unbelief and Property

The king of Sodom, seed of Satan (see 3:15), insinuates that he has the right to stipulate the disposition of the spoils of battle. Abraham rejects the false claim as decisively as his greater Seed (see Luke 4:1–12; 22:25). Unbelievers arrogantly think they own property on this earth and can dictate its disposition. God alone owns the cattle on a thousand hills. We simply make use of them for about a century by his grace. He alone has the right to dictate its use and distribution.

Incarnation Theology

God meets Abraham at his level of understanding. Abraham's religion looks outwardly similar to pagan modes of worship. They worship under fertility trees, set up altars to commemorate sacred experiences, and use the titles for God from the pagan mythologies. Nevertheless, Israel's ethical monotheism, though expressed in this external guise, has no umbilical cord to the religions of the ancient Near East. God incarnates himself in the language and culture of the time. The Hebrew language is Canaanite, but despite this earthly skin, its wine is heavenly. Jesus Christ appears just like any other man and speaks the languages of his culture, but people who hear him say no one ever spoke like this. The religious forms of the Bible are like those of their culture, but their religious substance differs radically.

Canonical Foreshadowing

The presentation of Melchizedek foreshadows the New Testament interpretation in Hebrews 7.[85] The writer of Hebrews argues from the text itself that Jesus Christ belongs to the order of this priest-king.[86]

BOOK 6, ACT 1, SCENE 5:
GOD'S COVENANT WITH ABRAHAM (15:1–21)
LITERARY ANALYSIS OF BOOK 6, ACT 1, SCENE 5————

Structure

Scene 5 consists of two divine encounters (15:1–6 and 7–21) involving dialogue between the Lord and Abraham and powerful images symbolizing God's presence and promises. The first occurs at night (15:5) as a vision (15:1) and pertains to the promised seed. The second occurs at sundown (15:12), partially in a deep sleep (15:12), and pertains to the promised land.

These separate encounters are united by the narrator through a parallel ABC/A'B'C' structure:

---

[85]Carson, *Gagging*, 249.
[86]The sectarians at Qumran identify Melchizedek as an eschatological savior figure independently from the biblical text (V. Woude, "Melchisedek als Himmlische Erlösergestalt in den Neugefundenen Eschatologischen Midraschim aus Qumran Höhle XI," *OtSt* 14 (1965): 354–73.

A The Lord makes a promise to Abraham, using the formula "I am" (15:1).

  B Abraham apprehensively questions the Lord, addressing him with the rare title "Sovereign LORD" (15:2–3).

    C The Lord reassures Abraham by symbolic acts: the display of stars with reference to the seed (15:4–6).

A′ The Lord makes a promise to Abraham, using the formula "I am" (15:7).

  B′ Abraham apprehensively questions the Lord, addressing him with the rare title "Sovereign LORD" (15:8).

    C′ The Lord reassures Abraham by symbolic acts: the burning torch and the smoking kiln through the carcasses with reference to the land (15:9–21).

Janus

The narrator's theological evaluation (15:6) provides a janus between the two encounters. The human partner counts on God to give him offspring, and the divine partner credits that faith as righteousness. On that basis, the Lord grants Abraham his immutable covenant (15:7–21). Scene 5 (15:1–21) also serves as a janus between the first two acts of the Abraham narrative, linking the two key themes: seed (15:1–6; chs. 16–22) and land (15:7–21; chs. 12–14).

Escalation and Innertextual Links

This scene brings the act pertaining to the land to its climactic conclusion. Until now God's promise of the land of Canaan has been conditional on Abraham's obedience, and the Lord has found Abraham's heart to be faithful. Abraham acted, believing God's promises to give him offspring and the land of Canaan (ch. 12). He withstood the challenges to his faith (chs. 13–14) and fully expressed his faith in God's reward (14:22–23). Now, in this scene, to reassure Abraham, the Lord unconditionally obligates himself in an immutable covenant. Abraham's posterity will receive the land of the ten nations who occupy Canaan (see Neh. 9:7–8).

The covenant that God declares in the Abraham narrative is unfolded in two stages conforming to the earlier promises to make Abraham into a nation (12:2) and to make him a blessing to the nations (12:3). Act 1, Scene 5 reveals the phase of the covenant pertaining to the nation, its seed and land; the next phase of the covenant pertaining to the nations will be revealed in Act 2 (17:1–27).

Key Words

Several key words unite and illuminate the last two scenes of Act 1. The Lord's claim for himself, "I am your shield" (*māḡēn,* 15:1), responds to

Melchizedek's description of God as the one "who delivered" (*miggēn*, 14:20) Abraham's enemies into his hand. The Lord's covenant (*bᵉrît*, 15:18) takes the place of the Amorite allies (*baᶜᵃlê bᵉrît*, lit. "owners of a covenant," 14:13). "Possessions" in 15:14 (*rᵉkuš*) is the same word rendered "goods" and "possessions" in 14:11, 12, 16, 21. Abraham's faithfulness is rewarded, not with tainted booty, but with God's countless riches.

EXEGETICAL NOTES TO BOOK 6, ACT 1, SCENE 5 ——————

First Divine Encounter:
Covenant Regarding the Seed (15:1–5)

God's Promise of Reward (15:1)

1. **After this. . . .** Although "after this" may refer to all the scenes of Genesis 12–14, it is most closely connected to chapter 14. M. Kline comments appropriately, "Coming on the heels of the battle, the Lord's word to Abraham (Gen. 15:1) has the character of a royal grant to an officer for faithful military service."[87] He adds, "The 'reward' [*śākār*] is used for the compensation due to those who have conducted a military campaign."[88] God's reward takes the place of the spurned booty (14:22–24). Moreover, God's command, "Do not be afraid," suggests that Abraham expects reprisal from the kings he defeated in combat.

word of the Lord came. This phrase elsewhere in the Old Testament introduces a revelation to a prophet, but it is unique in Genesis. The inference that Abraham is a prophet is made explicit in Gen. 20:7 and Ps. 105:15.

vision. The rare term derives from a root that is connected with revelation to a prophet (cf. Num. 24:4, 16; Ezek. 13:7).

Do not be afraid. This is the way a prophet speaks to a king as assurance of victory before a battle.[89] According to von Rad, "It is as good as certain that the concept of faith—in other words, that confident trusting in the action of Yahweh—had its actual origin in the holy war and that from there it took its own peculiar dynamic character."[90] Although von Rad's statement is rash and reckless, it nevertheless underscores the importance of faith in connection with warfare. In that context Israel is often exhorted not to fear (Ex. 14:13–14; Deut. 20:3; Josh. 8:1; 10:8, 25; 11:6; Judg. 7:3; 1 Sam. 23:16–17; 30:6). If trust means victory, fear means defeat.

shield [*māgēn*]. The metaphor depicts God as one who protects his warrior. The pun with "delivered" (*miggēn*) (see 14:20 and note) suggests that the

---

[87]Kline, *Kingdom*, 216.

[88]Ibid., 216.

[89]J. Van Seters, *Abraham in History and Tradition* (New Haven, Conn.: Yale Univ. Press, 1975), 254. See also "Oracles Concerning Esarhaddon," *ANET*, 449–50.

[90]G. von Rad, *Holy War in Ancient Israel*, trans. and ed. M. J. Dawn (Grand Rapids: Eerdmans, 1981), 71.

Lord is confirming Melchizedek's benediction. Abraham may not have the reward, but he has the God of the reward.

reward [*śākār*]. This is probably a term for a mercenary's pay (see Isa. 40:10; 62:11; Ezek. 29:19). Abraham's reward for faithful service is much greater than the tarnished booty the king of Sodom offered. Only God can reward Abraham with innumerable offspring and land that others possess. Abraham's greatest treasure, however, is having the Lord himself as his God (Gen. 17:8; Deut. 10:21).

Abraham's Complaint (15:2 – 3)

2. Sovereign LORD. This is a rare title of God used when pleading with him (cf. Deut. 3:24; 9:26). "Sovereign" means "master, lord." In his complaint, Abraham does not compromise his role of being the Lord's slave. The narrator's theological comment in 15:6 assures his audience that Abraham complains out of his faith, not his unbelief. It takes spiritual energy of faith to complain in contrast to despairing in silence.

remain. The Hebrew here means "walking, going" and depicts life as a journey; the same verb is used in 12:1, 4, 5, 9; 13:3. Faith is living in imagination in God's word when the situation by sight seems impossible.

childless. To be childless may be a sign of God's judgment (e.g., for incest [Lev. 20:20–21] or wickedness [Jer. 22:30]) or an opportunity for God to do signs and wonders (Judg. 13:2; 1 Sam. 1:1–2:10; Isa. 54:1–5).

the one who will inherit my estate [*ben-mešeq*]. The Hebrew expression is unexplained, though it has been traditionally rendered "the one in charge of my house" (so Targums, the Vulgate, Saadiah, Ibn Janaḥ, and Rashi).

Damascus. The meaning of the word, in the Hebrew, *dammeśeq,* and its location is disputed.[91]

3. servant in my household will be my heir. This helps interpret the unexplained *ben-mešeq.* The Nuzi tablets (mid-second millennium B.C.) give some evidence that in Abraham's culture a childless man could adopt someone to be the guardian and heir of his estate as compensation for the person's performing the duties of a son. If a son was subsequently born, the adopted man could not disinherit the natural son. The adoption of one's own slave, however, is found in only one Old Babylonian letter.[92]

Assurances: The Lord's Promise and Sign (15:4 – 5)

4. Then the word of the LORD came. The English "then" does not capture the Hebrew emphatic particle *hinnēh* ("look"), which aims to involve the audience in the narrative.[93]

---

[91]For discussion see Sarna, *Genesis*, 382–83.

[92]See E. A. Speiser, "Notes to Recently Published Nuzi Texts," *JAOS* 55 (1935): 435–36; C. H. Gordon, "Biblical Customs and Nuzu Tablets," *BA* 3 (1940): 2–3; for an evaluation of the arguments see Wenham, *Genesis 1–15*, 328–29.

[93]See S. Kogut, "On the Meaning-Syntactical Status of *hinneh* in Biblical Hebrew," in *Studies in Bible*, ed. S. Japhet (ScrHier 31; Jerusalem: Magnes, 1986), 133–54.

5. Look up at the heavens and count the stars. See 22:17; 26:4; cf. 13:16; 22:17; 28:14; 32:12. The representation of offspring like the uncountable stars is not just an amazing promise but an assurance of God's creative and sovereign power.

offspring. See 12:7; 13:16.

Janus Verse: Abraham's Faith (15:6)

6. believed [ʾāman]. The Hebrew is better translated "trusted." Abraham considers God true, reliable, and trustworthy. Abraham is the father of all who believe (see Rom. 4:11; Gal. 3:7).

he credited it. The verb denotes "the evaluative categorization of persons."[94] The subject is God and the object of reference is Abraham's faith in the promised offspring. The expression means that God reckons Abraham's faith in the promise as righteousness.

righteousness. The word refers to behavior that serves the community according to God's norms (see 6:9; 7:1). Gerhard von Rad plausibly proposes a cultic background to this theological evaluation.[95] When worshipers wish to enter the sanctuary, the priest interrogates them concerning their manner of life. One of the requirements for admittance is that a worshiper serve the community, not self (Ps. 15). The qualified are admitted into the life and blessing of God's presence. God also makes judgments about whether a person behaves faithfully and establishes the well-being of the community. He reckons Phinehas's bloody intervention to stop the destruction of the community by the wicked as equivalent to "righteousness for endless generations to come" (Ps. 106:31). God reckons Abraham's faith in his promise as righteousness, and in this context, the divine reckoning qualifies Abraham to become the recipient of a land grant to be transmitted to his descendants.

Second Divine Encounter: Covenant Regarding the Land (15:7–21)

God's Promise Concerning the Land (15:7)

7. I am the LORD. The introductory formula, "I am...," which is attested in other ancient Near Eastern royal proclamations and grants, connotes the unimpeachable authority of the declaration that follows.

who brought you out. The ancient royal covenants included a historical prologue. The historical prologue in this covenant together with "I am the LORD" foreshadows the Exodus and the Ten Commandments that follow (Ex. 20). Abraham's exodus from his homeland and Israel's Exodus from Egypt are the two pivotal events in the formation of national Israel.

land. See 12:1–2, 7; 13:15.

---

[94]Schottroff, "bšh," TLOT, 2:480.
[95]G. von Rad, *Problem of the Hexateuch and Other Essays*, trans. E. W. Trueman Dicken (London: SCM, 1984), 125–30.

take possession of [*yāraš*]. The Hebrew word here, the same one translated "heir" in 15:4, connotes a sense of possession by dispossession.

Abraham's Request for Guarantee (15:8)

8. how can I know. The question could be interpreted as unbelief, but
that understanding would not fit the narrator's evaluation that Abraham
trusts God (15:6). More likely, Abraham's request for a sign is motivated by
faith (see 15:6; cf. Isa. 7:10–14). Complaint and faith are not antithetical;
complaint is based on taking God seriously.

Preliminaries of Covenant-Making Ritual (15:9)

9. heifer. . . pigeon. Although a sacrifice is probably not in view, these
are all the species that could be offered on the Lord's altar.

three years old. The animals are all of the prime age, since full-grown
and broken for service (cf. 1 Sam. 1:24).

Abraham's Provision (15:10 – 11)

10. cut them in two [*btr*]. The narrator blanks how Abraham knew that
he should cut them. Possibly the list of animals suggested to Abraham that
the Lord was about to make [Hebrew "to cut"] a covenant with him.

birds, however, he did not cut in half. Were they too small (cf. Lev.
1:17)?

11. birds of prey. The verbal root may mean to fall upon with shouting
(1 Sam. 15:19). The noun, denoting a powerful and swift bird of prey that
swoops upon carrion, is used as a metaphor for a conqueror in Isa. 46:11.
Here the noun may be singular or collective (see Isa. 18:6; Jer. 12:9) and
accordingly represents either Pharaoh[96] or the Egyptians who will threaten
the emergence of the nation.

drove them away. Abraham is symbolically defending his promised
inheritance against foreign attackers (see also his actions in Gen. 14).

Prophecy of Sojourn and Affliction in Egypt (15:12 – 16)

12. As the sun was setting. This marks the beginning of the second
encounter. The eerie scene of intensifying darkness matches Israel's dark-
ening and declining fortunes in Egypt. Stephen summarizes this vision in
Acts 7:6–7.

a deep sleep. This divinely induced and abnormally heavy sleep (see
2:21) connected with a divine revelation (Dan. 8:18; 10:9) may also symbolize death.

a thick and dreadful darkness. This is a symbol of Israel's enslavement
and mistreatment in Egypt.

---

[96]In Egypt, the falcon symbolized the god Horus with whom the Pharaoh identified himself.

13. strangers. See "to live" at 12:10.

four hundred years. This is a round number for the more precise figure of 430 years (see Ex. 12:40–41; Acts 7:6; 13:20). Compare the 120-year delay before the Flood (see Gen. 6:3). God's people must learn to live with delay (2 Peter 3:8–10).

14. the nation. Clearly, the nation is Egypt (Ex. 6:6; 7:4; 12:12).

punish . . . come out with great possessions. The promise of "great possessions" offers justice for enslavement and mistreatment (15:13).

great possessions. See Ex. 12:35–39.

15. good old age. "Old age" is literally "gray-headed." Since sorrow and sadness can just as likely come to the old (Gen. 42:38; 44:29, 31; 1 Kings 2:6, 9), "good" is added to denote a prosperous life (Judg. 8:32; 1 Chron. 29:28). God keeps his promises (Gen. 25:7–8), giving assurance to the patriarchs that he will keep his promises to their descendants.

16. In the fourth generation. *Generation* (*dôr*) denotes a "cycle of time, a life span," which is here calculated to be one hundred years (cf. Ps. 90:10; Isa. 65:20). In Egypt at the time of the patriarchs, 110 was the ideal life span (see Gen. 50:22).

the sin of the Amorites has not yet reached its full measure. *Amorites* (see 10:16; 14:13) here functions as a synecdoche for the ten nations listed in 15:19–21. God will dispossess them in favor of his elect in full agreement with his moral governance of the world. Indeed, it is not until the nations become totally saturated with iniquity that God dispossesses them (Lev. 18:24–28; 20:23). So also he does not send the Flood until the earth is fully corrupt (Gen. 6:5, 12), and he does not destroy Sodom and Gomorrah until he has satisfied himself that not even a quorum of righteous are left in the city. Israel's conquest and settlement of Canaan is based on God's absolute justice, not on naked aggression. Later, when Israel's iniquities have become full, God will drive even his elect nation from the land (Deut. 28:36–37; 2 Kings 24:14; 25:7). The Ugaritic texts (ca. 1400 B.C.) discovered on the Syrian coast in 1929 document the iniquities of the Amorites. The gods they worshiped degraded themselves in violent atrocities and in sexual promiscuity.[97]

The Lord Makes a Covenant (15:17–21)

17. smoking firepot with a blazing torch. These are both symbols of God's awesome presence. Perhaps the cloud of smoke rising from the pot-like, earthenware oven and the soaring tongue of flame from the torch foreshadow the cloud and fire that symbolize God's presence at the Exodus (cf. Ex. 19:18; 20:5; 24:17; 34:5–7; Deut. 4:11, 24, 33).

passed between the pieces. Since only God walks between the pieces, the covenant is based on Abraham's past faithfulness (see 6:18). To judge

---

[97]W. F. Albright, *Archaeology and the Religion of Israel*, 4th ed. (Baltimore: Johns Hopkins Univ. Press, 1956), 71–84.

from ancient Near Eastern texts and Jer. 34:18, God is invoking a curse upon himself if he does not keep his covenant. An eighth-century Assyrian text from North Syria includes the following clause: "This head is not the head of a lamb, it is the head of Mati'lu [his sons, officials and people]. If Mati'lu sins against this treaty, so may, just as the head of this spring lamb is torn off, . . . the head of Mati'lu be torn off, and his sons."[98] Once the animal was killed, the one making the covenant could expect the same fate as the animal if he broke covenant. The sacrifice is thus an enactment of the oath.

18. made [*ktr*]. The Hebrew literally means "cut."

covenant. God's covenant with Abraham has parallels with ancient Near Eastern royal land grants bestowed by kings to loyal servants and their descendants in perpetuity.[99]

this land. The land is delineated in geographic (15:18) and ethnographic terms (15:19–21). However, the geographic dimensions given here are far greater than the ethnographic.

river of Egypt. Since the text uses "river" (*nāhār*), not "wadi" (*naḥal*),[100] the Wadi el-'Arish that divides Canaan from the Sinai is not in view (contra Num. 34:3–5; Josh. 15:2–4). On the other hand, neither is the Nile (*yeʾōr*) in view. Probably the text refers to the Nile's most easterly branch that emptied into Lake Sironbis, not far from Port Said. It is unlikely, however, that even in Solomon's day, Israel's border extended to this boundary.[101]

Euphrates.[102] The geographic boundaries represent an ideal that cannot be matched with Israel's history. At its height, the Davidic Empire exercised political and economic control to the Euphrates (2 Sam. 8:1; 1 Chron. 18), but Israel did not attempt to dispossess the people beyond the geographic boundaries of Canaan (Gen. 10:19). Since the geographic description is much larger than the ethnographic and the ethnographic matches Israel's history but the geographic does not, the geographic is best regarded as an idealization. The narrator aims to place Israel with the great nations of the ancient Near East[103] and to convey the spiritual significance of the land. Similarly, although Mount Zion is not the highest in its environment, in its significance as the mountain of God it is said to be the "highest" mountain in the world (cf. Ps. 48:2–3; Isa. 57:15–16; Mic. 4:1 [= Isa. 2:2]); so too the physical reality of the Jordan is much smaller than its metaphysical reality in Judaism and Christianity.

---

[98]"Treaty Between Ashurnirari V of Assyria and Mati'ilu of Arpad," *ANET*, 532.

[99]See M. Weinfeld, "*bᵉrit*," *TDOT*, 2:270–72.

[100]Some emend the text to *naḥal*. A wadi is a temporary river that flows with great force in the rainy season and that is otherwise a dry riverbed.

[101]A. Malamat, "Aspects of the Foreign Policies of David and Solomon," *JNES* 22 (1963): 1–17.

[102]W. C. Kaiser Jr. thinks that the Great River is modern Nahr el-Kebir [= "Great River"], which flows through the valley that forms the modern border between Lebanon and Syria. However, a modern name cannot override the biblical evidence that specifies the great river as the Euphrates ("The Promised Land: A Biblical-Historical View," *BSac* 138 [1981]: 304).

[103]M. Gorg, "Egpyt, River Of," *ABD*, 2:378.

19. the land of. . . The list of ten nations inhabiting Canaan is longer than the seven nations listed in Deut. 7:1. Both numbers aim to represent completeness rather than an exhaustive catalogue. Canaan's varied topography occasioned the isolation of diverse ethnic groups that migrated through this land bridge connecting Africa with Asia.

Kenites. This is a tribe or people whose name suggests that they were metalworkers. They are parallel with Amalekites in Num. 24:20–22 (cf. 1 Sam. 15:5–6, 32). They were located on the border of Judah with Edom, southeast of Arad.[104]

Kenizzites. They were a nomadic clan around Hebron and Debir.[105]

Kadmonites. The Hebrew literally means "Easterners."[106] This is the only reference to them. Based on their placement in this list, Ishida suggests that the first three names in the list "represent the foreign elements in the south whose absorption into the tribe of Judah was complete by the time of David."[107]

20. Hittites. See 10:15; 23:3.

THEOLOGICAL REFLECTIONS ON BOOK 6, ACT 1, SCENE 5 ────────

Abrahamic Covenant

God reveals his covenant with Abraham and his descendants in progressive stages. Genesis 12:1–3 foretells of God's extensive covenant relationship with Abraham. Just as promised, God is now committing himself to make Abraham into a great nation. God's further covenant commitment to make Abraham and his descendants a light to the Gentiles will be concretized in chapter 17. The psalmist's recounting of the successive covenant promises and renewals with Abraham, Isaac, and Jacob (cf. Gen. 26:3–4; 28:13–15; 35:11–12) praises God for a unified covenant act (Ps. 105:8–15; cf. Mic. 7:20). The progressive promises and renewals constitute a complete covenant commitment of grace.

Justification by Faith

Genesis 15:6 is foundational to the doctrine of justification by faith, not by works (see Gal. 3:6–14). Abraham is not sinless, but he believes the promise of the birth of an heir from the dead (see Rom. 4:17–21; Heb. 11:11–12), and God counts that equivalent to meeting the moral demands later stipulated in the Mosaic covenant (see Ps. 15). According to Nehemiah (Neh. 9:8), God makes a covenant with Abraham because he finds Abraham's heart

---

[104]B. Halpern, "Kenites," *ABD*, 4:18–19.
[105]*HALOT*, 1114.
[106]Ibid., 1002.
[107]T. Ishida, "The Structure and Historical Implications of the Lists of Pre-Israelite Nations," *Bib* 60 (1979): 461–90.

faithful. Abraham is the model for our faith in the resurrection of Jesus Christ, faith that God will credit to us as righteousness (Rom. 4:22–25).

Faith

Abraham's life reveals truths of faith for the Christian. Abraham requests assurance that he will possess the land, for he understands that possessing the land will require dispossessing the pagans. Bolstering Abraham's faith, God concretizes his covenant. The land belongs to God. For Christians to possess life in Christ, the old "kings" and "gods" must be dispossessed. To this order God has promised his Spirit as a guarantee of our inheritance (see Eph. 1:11–14).

God will remain faithful to his covenants, despite the weaknesses of his human partners. As the next scene (Gen. 16) of Abraham's story will show, Abraham and Sarah's faith is "defective." Likewise, Noah, Israel, David, and Peter fail after God covenants with them. Nevertheless, God's covenant stands. He remains faithful.

Prophecy

To Abraham, God specifically predicts four hundred years of oppression in Egypt, Israel's deliverance with great riches, and the possession of Canaan. Abraham functions as a prophet of God, entrusted with knowledge of the future tribulations and exaltations of his descendants. In this prophetic trust, God humbles himself to obligate his life to his people. In passing through the carcasses, he commits to death if his word is untrue. The reason the God of Israel lives in the petitions and praises of his people is that he keeps his prophetic promises. God's prophecy also reveals his sovereign control over history. To be sure, other religions have seers and prophets, but none has prophets who give such a comprehensive view of history and such specific detail as Israel's prophets. No other god of the ancient Near East survives; all passed away, for none could reveal history or speak truth like the God of Israel (cf. Isa. 41:21–29).

BOOK 6, ACT 2: ABRAHAM AND THE PROMISED SEED (16:1–22:19)

LITERARY ANALYSIS OF BOOK 6, ACT 2 ——————

Theme and Conflict

Whereas Act 1 was concerned with land, Act 2 is dominated by the promise of seed, scarcely mentioning land. The plot of Act 2 winds through conflicts caused by the excruciating delay of the fulfillment of God's promise. The act opens, "Now Sarai, Abram's wife, had borne him no children" (16:1), and not until 21:2, "Sarah . . . bore a son," does the conflict begin to resolve. Even then, the tension of seed does not completely subside until the final climactic scene of Act 2, when Abraham confronts the challenge to sacrifice this promised son. Throughout the act, the narrator underscores the delay by the circuitous route of his story and by the marking of time (16:16; 17:1, 17, 24; 18:12; 21:5).

Characters and Conflict

As in Act 1, the characters clash with each other and themselves, trying to engineer their own fulfillment of the promises and struggling to maintain faith. These problems and their significance are epitomized by the conflict between Sarah and Hagar. Both mothers and their boys are characterized by tension that reaches into future generations. Hagar and her son, representing the natural seed of human engineering, are a foil to Sarah and her son, representing the promised seed of election and the interventions of God that must be embraced by faith. The external conflict between Hagar and Sarah symbolizes the internal conflict of both Sarah and Abraham to believe the promise and maintain faith despite delay.

Act 2 also marks significant development in the characters of Abraham and Sarah. The first scenes depict Abraham's tentative faith. His hope and belief are troubled by questions, doubt, human scheming, and passivity towards conflicts in his home. Out of the struggles emerges a righteous man of faith who models hospitality, speaks boldly for justice before God, and then with incredible faith unquestioningly faces God's greatest demand. Sarah's faith and strength also increases. Her early responses to the delayed promises are scheming, anger, and incredulity. However, by the end of the act, she is a faith-filled, decisive woman, whose council is validated by God.

BOOK 6, ACT 2, SCENE 1:
HAGAR AND ISHMAEL REJECTED (16:1–16)

LITERARY ANALYSIS OF BOOK 6, ACT 2, SCENE 1 ————

Structure

The opening scene of Act 2 is a forceful assertion that the covenanted Abraham and Sarah must act only out of radical faith in obedience to divine direction. The frame of the scene, marked by the words "Abram," "Hagar," and the verb "to bear," portrays the consequences of their faithless engineering:

- "Now Sarai, Abram's wife, had borne him no children. But she had an Egyptian maidservant named Hagar" (16:1).
- "Abram was eighty-six years old when Hagar bore him Ishmael" (16:16).

The scene consists of two incidents involving first Sarah and Hagar and then the angel of the Lord and Hagar. The first (16:2–6) follows an alternating structure:

A Sarah proposes (16:1–2a)
B Abraham agrees (16:2b)
    C Sarah's action (16:3)
        D Hagar's reaction (16:4)
A´ Sarah proposes (16:5)
B´ Abraham agrees (16:6a)
    C´ Sarah's action (16:6b)
        D´ Hagar's reaction (16:6c)

The second (16:7–14) follows a concentric construction:[108]

A Angel finds Hagar by spring (16:7)
B Dialogue between Angel and Hagar (16:8–9)
    C Angel's first prophecy (16:10)
    C´ Angel's second prophecy (16:11–12)
B´ Hagar's worshiping response (16:13)
A´ Hagar names well (16:14)

The two incidents are linked by the verb "fled"/"running away" (*bāraḥ*, 16:6, 8) and the titles "mistress" and "maidservant" (for other possible structures see "Comparison and Contrast" below).

Naming

The descriptions used for Sarah and Hagar in this scene identify the divine intentions for their relationship. With reference to Abraham, Sarah is named "wife of Abraham" (16:1, 3), and "mistress" with reference to Hagar (16:4, 8, 9), while Hagar is called "maidservant" (16:1, 2, 3, 5, 6, 8). Sarah's title "wife" suggests that the Lord's promise to make Abraham into a great nation from an offspring out of his own loins, not from an adopted son, also applies to Sarah with whom he is reckoned as one flesh (2:24). Prior to this scene, Sarah and Abraham apparently assumed this to be the case, and the narrator confirms this assumption in Genesis 17.

The title "mistress" for Sarah and "maidservant" for Hagar, in the mouths of all the characters, including God, also confirms that Hagar is in the wrong when she tries to transgress social boundaries by elevating herself above Sarah.

Blanks and Gaps

From the timeline, Sarah's age can be determined to be about seventy-five years. Later, the narrator states clearly that at ninety years of age Sarah was well past the age of childbearing (see 18:11). It is reasonable to suppose menopause had at least begun by her age in this scene, which might explain

---

[108]A modification of Wenham's palistrophic structure (G. J. Wenham, *Genesis 16–50* [WBC 2; Waco, Tex.: Word, 1994], 4).

her remark, "the LORD has kept me from having children" (16:2). Radical faith, however, is so crucial to the narrator that he draws no attention or sympathy to Sarah's age.

Comparison and Contrast

Garrett notes a striking similarity in structures between the two Hagar scenes (16:1–16; 21:1–21).

Genesis 16:1–16

Section	Verses	Format Content
A	1	Sarai's infertility
B	2–3	Sarai's response: "Sleep with my maidservant"
C	4	Hagar pregnant, abuses Sarai
D	5–6	Sarai complains and drives out Hagar
E	7–9	Angel of the Lord speaks, sends Hagar back
F	10	Promise: "I will . . . increase your descendants"
G	11–14	Second word from angel: "Ishmael will be lone wanderer in the desert"
H	15	Ishmael born to Abraham
I	16	Ishmael born of Hagar

Genesis 21:1–21

Section	Verses	Format Content
A′	1–5	Sarah's fertility
B′	6–8	Sarah's response: praise and laughter
C′	9	Ishmael older, abuses Isaac
D′	10	Sarah complains: "Drive out Hagar"
E′	11–12	God speaks: "Send Hagar out"
F′	13	Promise: "I will make the son of your maid a nation"
G′	14–18	Hagar and Ishmael alone in the desert; second word from God
H′	19–20	Ishmael saved
I′	21	Hagar gets Ishmael a wife[109]

In both scenes Hagar emerges as a heroic figure who receives mercy from God in the face of great adversity, presumably because of her connection with Abraham and Sarah in spite of her own unrighteousness.

A number of striking comparisons can also be seen between the characters in Genesis 16 and other characters in the Genesis narrative. For example, Sarah's scheme, contrived without seeking the Lord, contrasts with Abraham, who earlier asks God about the option of adopting a son. Had

---

[109]Garrett, *Rethinking*, 144.

Sarah also sought God's counsel, we can be sure he would have ruled out surrogate motherhood for her as he had ruled out adoption for Abraham (Gen. 15:1–4; cf. 17:19; 18:9–15).

In addition, both Act 1, after Abraham has gone to Canaan, and Act 2 begin with the patriarch taking his own initiative to fulfill the promise. When a famine strikes the Promised Land, Abraham leaves it without divine authorization; when God delays giving him the promised seed, Abraham listens to Sarah's scheme, again without divine consultation. No good comes of either initiative.

Abraham and Sarah also bear similarity to Adam and Eve. Both Adam and Abraham act upon suggestions from their wives that are not prompted by faith (3:17; 16:2). Consequently, they bring conflict into their homes.

EXEGETICAL NOTES TO BOOK 6, ACT 2, SCENE 1 ————

Setting: Barren Sarah Has a Maidservant, Hagar (16:1)

1. Sarai . . . had borne him no children. The narrator foreshadowed the problems of Sarah's barrenness in his introduction to the account in 11:30. The problem has now reached a crisis. The complication of seed resembles the complication of land in 12:10. This dilemma will not be resolved until 21:2, near the end of the act.

Abram's wife. This designation of Sarah emphasizes her rightful standing. The promised son should come from her.

Egyptian. Hagar was possibly among the maidservants Abraham acquired under Pharaoh's patronage (12:16).

maidservant. A maidservant is a personal servant owned by a rich woman, not a slave girl answerable to the master. Hagar's relationship to Sarah resembles Eliezer's to Abraham (see 15:2); she is answerable to Sarah. The angel of the Lord will reassert this identification (16:8).[110]

Incident 1: Sarah and Hagar (16:2–6)

Unbelief: Sarah's Scheme and Abraham's Consent (16:2)

2. The Lord has kept me . . . perhaps I. Sarah was about sixty-five years old when Abraham left his father and homeland. Still childless a decade later, and perhaps already in menopause, Sarah draws the conclusion that the offspring the Lord has promised Abraham will not come from her body. She recognizes the Lord as Creator of life; however, she does not interpret her infertility in terms of God's promise.[111] Her complaint condemns her for seizing the initiative from his hands. Without a word from God to authorize her scheme, she is guilty of synergism. Her plan to deal with the problem compares with Abraham's in 12:11–13 (cf. also Eve's synergism 4:1).

---

[110]A. Jespen, "Amah und Schiphchah," *VT* 8 (1958): 293–97.
[111]Roop, *Genesis*, 118.

Go, sleep. The text literally reads "go into," a Hebraism for coitus.

I can build a family. Literally "I can be built," this phrase is a Hebraism for "obtain a son" (see 30:3).

through her. The practice of surrogate motherhood for an infertile wife through her maidservant seemed to be an acceptable social practice, as can be judged from Gen. 30:3–12, the Code of Hammurabi (ca. 1700 B.C.),[112] a Nuzi text (ca. 1500 B.C.), an Old Assyrian marriage contract (nineteenth century B.C.), and a Neo-Assyrian text.[113] According to the Old Assyrian marriage contract, after the chief wife procured an infant for her husband, she could sell the surrogate mother whenever she pleased. According to the Code of Hammurabi, however, she could not sell her (see "whatever you think" below).

agreed to what Sarai said. The Hebrew here occurs only in Gen. 3:17. Like Adam, Abraham agrees to his wife's faithless suggestion. Abraham's careless passivity sharply contrasts with his valiant actions on behalf of Lot (Gen. 14; 19).

Sarah and Hagar: Conflict in the Home (16:3–4)

3. ten years. See 12:4; 16:16.

Sarai . . . took [lqḥ] . . . gave [ntn] . . . to her husband. This is the same progression of verbs at the Fall in 3:6. Hagar is treated as property with no personal rights.

his wife. The repetition of this designation (16:1) punctuates the foolishness of Sarah's scheme.

4. despise [qll]. The Hebrew here is translated "curses" in 12:3. Already the plan has deconstructed. This attitude is also a crucial mistake for Hagar. She arrogantly turns on the one who has requested her help.[114] Laws of Ur-Nammu 22–23 and the Law of Hammurabi protected the first wife against this natural response.[115] Because Hagar treats Sarah with disdain, she is alienated from the family of blessing, as is Lot (See Prov. 30:21–23).

Sarah and Abraham: Sarah Complains to Abraham and Drives Out Hagar (16:5–6)

5. You are responsible. Like Eve, Sarah now shifts the blame, and like Adam, Abraham shrugs off responsibility. Abraham alone has the judicial authority to effect a change and up to now has not acted to protect their marriage.

wrong [ḥāmās]. The Hebrew suggests a "flagrant violation of law" (see 6:11).

---

[112]"The Code of Hammurabi," *ANET*, 172, par. 146.

[113]All are cited in Hamilton, *Genesis 1-17*, 444.

[114]Cf. ibid., 447.

[115]The Code of Hammurabi reads, "If later that female slave has claimed equality with her mistress because she bore children, her mistress may not sell her; she may mark her with the slave-mark and count her among the slaves" (*ANET*, 172, par. 146).

I am suffering. Although the NIV is a paraphrase of the Hebrew expression meaning "the wrong against me," it captures the right sense. Sarah takes her complaint to Abraham as to a judge to right the injustice. Agur's proverb affirms her implied meaning: "Under three things the earth trembles, under four it cannot bear up: . . . a maidservant [šipḥâ] who displaces her mistress [geḇirtāh]" (Prov. 30:21–23).

despises. In this incident the narrator's sympathy lies with Sarah; in the next, with Hagar. This is evident because in 16:4 he confirms Sarah's evaluation of the situation by using the same vocabulary as Sarah. Sternberg says, "The reader infers from the equivalence in language an equivalence in vision where the character's involvement might otherwise cast doubt on her objectivity."[116]

may the LORD judge between you and me. Sarah appeals to a still higher court (see 31:53; Ex. 5:21; 1 Sam. 24:12, 15)[117] and confesses her faith in God. If Abraham will not offer the legal protection to which she is entitled, Sarah hopes confidently that the Lord will.

6. whatever you think. According to the Code of Hammurabi, the despised mistress in this situation could not sell her maidservant, but she could mark her with the slave mark and count her among the slaves. The Law of Ur-Nammu prescribed that an insolent concubine have "her mouth scoured with one quart of salt."[118]

mistreated [ʿānâ]. This is the same Hebrew verb as in 15:13 for the Egyptian mistreatment of the Israelites (cf. Ex. 1:12). Sarah's reaction is too severe. Victimized by barrenness and Hagar, Sarah now becomes the victimizer. Neither Sarah nor Hagar acquit themselves well here: the mistress is harsh and overbearing; the maidservant is unrepentant and insubordinate.[119]

fled. Like Israel, Hagar flees her mistreatment (Ex. 14:5). The narrator's sympathies now are on the side of the oppressed maidservant.[120] Nevertheless, Hagar's deliverance does not lie in returning to Egypt, her native land, but in submitting to the mother of Israel and not despising her.

Incident 2: Hagar's Encounter with the Angel of the Lord (16:7–14)

Setting: Angel Finds Hagar in the Wilderness (16:7)

7. angel of the LORD. Like all angels, he is a heavenly being sent from the heavenly court to earth as God's personal agent. In the ancient Near East the

---

116Sternberg, *Poetics*, 402.

117See C. Mabee, "Jacob and Laban: The Structure of Judicial Proceedings (Genesis xxxi 25-42)," *VT* 30 (1980): 206.

118"The Laws of Ur-Nammu," *ANET*, 525, par. 22.

119See A. Brenner, "Female Social Behaviour: Two Descriptive Patterns within the 'Birth of the Hero' Paradigm," *VT* 36 (1986): 257–73, esp. 261.

120The Mosaic law assumes that a runaway slave has been mistreated. This is evidenced by the stipulation in Deut. 23:15: "If a slave has taken refuge with you, do not hand him over to his master."

royal messenger was treated as a surrogate of the king (Judg. 11:13; 2 Sam. 3:12–13; 1 Kings 20:2–4). So also the Lord's messenger is treated as God and yet as distinct from God, as God's angel (cf. Gen. 21:17; 22:11; 31:11; Ex. 3:2; 14:19; 23:20; 32:34). For instance, Manoah and his wife, like Hagar, think the man they have seen is God (13:21–22; cf. 6:22–23; cf. Ex. 33:20). This angel's name is beyond knowing (Judg. 13:18), and he is associated with worship (13:15). Some equate him with the second person of the Trinity, yet the New Testament never makes this identification. If we may equate him with the *angelos kyriou* of the New Testament, he announces the birth of John the Baptist (Luke 1:11) and of Jesus (Matt. 1:20, 24; Luke 2:9) and identifies himself as Gabriel (Luke 1:19).

found Hagar. Divine intervention is purposeful and deliberate, not a fortuitous accident (cf. Gen. 12:17).

spring. This sign of life in the desert is a symbol of hope, despite suffering.

Shur. The name means "wall," probably a reference to the Egyptian border forts along the line of the Isthmus of Suez in order to protect Egypt from the incursion of Asiatics (see 25:18; 1 Sam. 15:7). Hagar was fleeing toward her home in Egypt.

Angel's Speech and Hagar's Response (16:8–14)

Initial Exchange (16:8–9)

8. Hagar. This is the only known instance in ancient Near Eastern literature where the deity addresses a woman by name. The greeting makes a trustful response possible.

servant of Sarai. The same Hebrew word is translated "maidservant" in 16:2. This designation of Hagar by the angel confirms Hagar's appointed place.

where. This rhetorical question elicits her participation (see 3:9).

my mistress. Hagar offers an honest and humble response.

9. Go back. The child she carries belongs to Abraham.

submit. This is the same root as "afflict" (*ʿānâ*). The woman who wanted esteem and freedom must submit herself. A servant advances not by discarding social boundaries but by honoring them (Prov. 17:2; 27:18).

Angel's Announcement (16:10–12)

10. The angel added. This is the first of several birth announcements by this heavenly messenger (cf. 17:19; Judg. 13:3, 5, 7; Luke 1:11–20, 26–38). The announcements predict the birth and destiny of those who play a significant role in salvation history.

increase your descendants. God's command to Hagar to submit is graciously accompanied by a promise. The promise is reaffirmed in Gen. 17:20 and fulfilled in 25:13–16. Abraham will father many descendants (13:16), both elect and nonelect. The nonelect will also be protected by God and made into a great nation (17:20).

11. heard of your misery [*ʿonyeḵ*]. The Hebrew word translated "misery" is a nominal form of the same root as "mistreated" (16:6) and "submit" (16:9).[121] God's commitment to Abraham does not void his commitments to the nonelect who also have a future within God's plans. The Lord looks after the oppressed (29:32; Ex. 3:7; 4:31; Deut. 26:7; 1 Sam. 1:11), redeems human error, and protects the wronged.

Ishmael. The name, which means "God hears," is explained more fully by "The LORD has heard of your misery."

12. wild donkey. The fearless and fleet-footed Syrian onager is a metaphor for an individualistic lifestyle untrammeled by social convention (Job 24:5–8; 39:5–8; Jer. 2:24; Hos. 8:9). Ishmael is not a child in whose seed the nations will be blessed; his blessing will be away from the land of promise, living by his own resources.

hostility. His passion for freedom will lead him into conflict with everyone. The fierce aggression of the Ishmaelites is contrasted with the nomadic lifestyle of the patriarchs.

all his brothers. By the end of the Abrahamic narrative, Ishmael and Isaac live in separation (Gen. 25:18).

Hagar's Worship and Etiology (16:13–14)

13. She gave this name to the LORD. This is the only instance in the Bible where a human being is represented as conferring a name on God. Hagar gives God a name that expresses his special significance to her. She responds to the person, not to the promise. She no longer gloats that she is pregnant but marvels at the Lord's care for her.

You are the God who sees me. This sentence name is "You are El-Roi" (lit., "God of my seeing"). The name is a pun, meaning either "the God who sees me" (so NIV), which fits the context, and/or "the God I see," which fits her explanation. The former speaks of his care for her; the latter, of her experiences of God's manifestation.

I have now seen the One who sees me. The Hebrew is difficult and literally reads, "Have I also/even here looked at the back of[122]/after[123] my seeing one?" Her question, which demands an emphatic affirmative, probably entails both that she has looked at God and he has seen her.

14. well [*beʾēr*]. This is a watering place of underground water, but in 16:7 it is called "a spring" (*ʿayin*). Perhaps a well had been dug close to the spring for convenience.

Lahai Roi. The Hebrew means "belonging to the living one, my seeing one," thus referring to the same pun (cf. Gen. 24:62; 25:11).

still there. Today the site is uncertain.

Kadesh. See note on 14:7.

---

[121]*HALOT*, 856.
[122]BDB, 907, 6a.
[123]*HALOT*, 35, B.1.

In Abraham's Tents (16:15–16)

15. So Hagar bore Abram a son. Contrast this with 16:1, which notes that Sarah has borne Abraham no children. The cost of Sarah's human engineering is to watch Hagar give birth to and raise a child for Abraham. The tension for the promised son is only heightened.

Ishmael. The genealogy is given in 25:12–18.

THEOLOGICAL REFLECTIONS ON
BOOK 6, ACT 2, SCENE 1 ───────────────────────

Synergism

This scene illustrates the contrast between sovereign grace and freedom and human effort and slavery (see Gal. 4:21–31). The covenant people are dependent on God's sovereign works and purposes. To attempt to independently help God accomplish his purpose is what theologians call synergism. Synergism only leads to disaster. Hagar and Ishmael function as a foil to living by faith in God's promises. Through her own initiative and impatience, Sarah tries to fulfill the divine promise through her maidservant Hagar. The immediate result is strife in the home, and its long-term consequence is the mixed blessing of numerous progeny that will inherit Hagar's defiant spirit. Through synergism, the entire household loses: Sarah loses respect, Hagar loses a home, and Abraham experiences heartache for a lost wife and a rejected son. This natural generation brings hostility to future generations, not peace. Nevertheless, God takes compassion on the proud who humble themselves. He intervenes to relieve the oppressed Hagar. Abraham and Sarah must find promise through dependence, and Hagar must find freedom through submission.

Grace

God seeks out the sinful and rejected. God's concern for and revelation to the defiant Egyptian woman Hagar anticipates the way Jesus deals with the sinful Samaritan woman (John 4). Both are sinful women, not of Abraham's family. Nevertheless, the Lord reaches out to both with great compassion. Hagar is the only woman in the ancient Near Eastern literature called by name by a deity, and she is the only person in the Old Testament who confers a name upon God. That name, "The One Who Sees Me" and "The One I See," epitomizes their special relationship.

Foreshadow of Exodus

The annunciation and career of Hagar also foreshadows Israel's Exodus (Deut. 26:6–7), flight to the wilderness (Ex. 14:3, 5), and an encounter there with the angel of the Lord (Ex. 14:19; 32:34). If the compassionate God answered Hagar's cry, how much more Israel's.

Birth Announcement

The angel's announcement to Hagar bears striking similarities to his announcement to Mary (Luke 1:28–33, 46–56): the greeting of the messenger (Gen. 16:8; Luke 1:28), the announcement of conception (Gen. 16:11; Luke 1:31), God's favor (Gen. 16:11; Luke 1:30b), the name of the child with etymology (Gen. 16:11; Luke 1:31), and the child's future achievements (Gen. 16:12; Luke 1:32–33), followed by thankful response (Gen. 16:13; Luke 1:48). In that light the contrast between these two offspring is more remarkable.

BOOK 6, ACT 2, SCENE 2: GOD'S COVENANT TO BLESS NATIONS THROUGH ABRAHAM'S AND SARAH'S SEED (17:1 – 27)

LITERARY ANALYSIS OF BOOK 6, ACT 2, SCENE 2 —————

Structure and Plot

In this scene of covenant dialogue between God and Abraham, God renews his promises. God, the primary actor of the Abrahamic narrative and the one who must supply the supernatural promises, carries most of the dialogue.

Sarna helpfully notes an alternating AB/A'B' structure of this scene.[124]

A Abraham the progenitor of numerous nations and of kings; his name is changed (17:1–8)
  B Law of circumcision set forth (17:9–14)
A' Sarah the progenitrix of numerous nations and of kings; her name is changed (17:15–22)
  B' Law of circumcision carried out (17:23–27)

The expansion of God's covenant promises requires Abraham to be completely committed and obedient. The implicit question of this scene—"Will Abraham respond with righteousness and covenant fidelity?"—forms the underlying tension. On this basis, the scene can also be divided by the Lord's granting of the covenant (17:1–22) and Abraham's acceptance (17:23–27). The Lord's grant is marked by the introduction, "the LORD appeared to him" (17:1), and by the conclusion, "God went up from him" (17:22). Three parts, indicated by the repeated formula "As for. . . ," make up this covenant grant. At Abraham's swift acceptance (17:23) the scene peaks. The details of his obedient response (17:24–27) form the denouement.

Key Words

Two words characterize the divine presence and provision in this dialogue of covenant: the word *covenant* (*berît*), which occurs more than a dozen

---

[124]Sarna, *Genesis*, 122.

times, nine times as "my covenant"; and the Hebrew verb *ntn,* "to give," rendered "confirm" (17:2), "made/make" (17:5, 6, 20) and "give" (17:8, 16).

Naming

Naming is an important device of this scene, revealing characteristics or developments in each person. The narrator begins the scene by referring to God as "the LORD," his covenant-keeping name especially with reference to Israel (17:1). He then identifies him by the name "God Almighty" probably to confirm God's power to produce supernatural offspring. After that, and for the first time in Book 6, the narrator refers to God as *ʾelôhîm,* signifying God's transcendence over the nations. This reference to God occurs appropriately in connection with God's renaming of Abraham, "father of a multitude [of nations]" (see "Sources of Ur-Genesis" in the introduction). God's renaming of the patriarch and matriarch signals God's dominion (see 1:5; 2:19), acknowledges their faithfulness, and reveals their new destiny and mission. The name *Isaac,* which means laughter, reminds Abraham and the reader of the incredibleness and joy of God's miraculous blessings.

Blank, Janus, and Inclusio

Scenes 1 and 2 of Act 2 are hinged by successive references to Abraham's age. Scene 1 closed by marking Abraham's age at eighty-six years (16:16). Scene 2 opens counting Abraham's age now at ninety-nine years. The importance of those gapped thirteen years seems to be their delay of the promised seed. In Scene 2, the marking of Abraham's age as "ninety-nine years old" also forms an inclusio around the scene (17:1, 24).

EXEGETICAL NOTES TO ACT 2, SCENE 2 ————————

Abraham the Progenitor of Numerous Nations and of Kings; His Name Is Changed (17:1–8)

1. ninety-nine. See above, "Literary Analysis: Blank, Janus, and Inclusio." Ishmael, age twelve or thirteen, is entering manhood (cf. 16:16). God must make clear to Abraham that Ishmael is not the blessing carrier.

I am God Almighty [*ʾēl šadday*]. El Shaddai, God's principal name in the pre-Mosaic period (cf. Ex. 6:2–3), may signify his universal dominion. Shaddai is attested primarily in Genesis and Job, as a theophoric element in three personal names of tribal representatives at the time of the Exodus (Num. 1–2), and in an Egyptian servant's name, probably Semitic, of the late fourteenth century B.C. Because of its antiquity, its meaning was lost by the time of the translators. The LXX, among many other ways, rendered it by "your God." Jerome based his translations (*deus omnipotens*) "God Almighty" and its equivalents on another rendering in the LXX, *kyrios pantokratōr* (Job 15:25). The Targum often transliterated the term. Like the ancient translators, modern scholarship has reached no consensus on the basis of philology. The most probable suppositions are (1) "The Powerful, Strong One" from the root *šdd;* and (2) "The One Who Suffices" from *še* and *day*.[125] Whatever its exact meaning, the contextual uses suggest, as Wenham states, that "Shaddai evokes the idea that God is able to make the barren fertile and to fulfill his promises."[126]

walk before me and be blameless. See 6:9. Total obedience is the necessary condition to experience the covenant promises. To walk before God means to orient one's entire life to his presence, promises, and demands. Westermann states, "God orders Abraham (now representing Israel) to live his life before God in such a way that every single step is made with reference to God and every day experiences him close at hand."[127] This significant command is later repeated to Israelite kings (Solomon, 1 Kings 9:4–5; Hezekiah, 2 Kings 20:3).[128] Such a high standard is appropriate for Abraham, who will become the father of kings (cf. Gen. 24:40; 48:15).

blameless. The Hebrew word signifies wholeness of relationship[129] and integrity rather than no sin (see 6:9).

2. I will confirm. This is better translated "that I might give." Although Abraham is responsible to walk in companionship with God and to abstain from sin, the covenant is still entirely a gift from God.

my covenant. The three divisions of this covenant—"As for me. . ." (17:4–8), "As for you. . ." (17:9–14), and "As for Sarai. . ." (17:15–16)—recognize the obligations of all the partners. God promises commitment to Abraham and his offspring (17:4–8, 15–16); they follow his commands (17:9–14). This unequal partnership always depends on the divine presence and provisions.

3. Abram fell facedown. This is a typical act of worship (Lev. 9:24; Josh. 5:14; Ezek. 1:28).

4. As for me. This formula marks the first division of the covenant obligations: God's responsibilities.

5. Abram . . . Abraham. See 11:26. His former name spoke of his noble God, of his noble ancestry, or of his own eminence; his new name speaks of his many offspring. This is the name God will make great (12:2). Abram, composed of *ʾāb* ("father") and *rām* ("to be high"), means "Exalted Father," a reference either to God, Terah, or himself.[130] His new name Abraham, by a word play of *ʾāb* ("father") plus *hām* (*hāmôn*, "crowd"), sounds like "father

[125]See M. Weippert, "*šaddat*," *TLOT*, 3:1306.
[126]Wenham, *Genesis 16–50*, 20.
[127]C. Westermann, *Genesis 12–36: A Commentary*, trans. J. J. Scullion (Minneapolis: Augsburg, 1985), 311.
[128]Because of these occurrences, some argue the command is "royal" language; however, it would be an overstatement to consider this an exclusively royal obligation.
[129]von Rad, *Genesis*, 193.
[130]D. Wiseman argues that the biblical narratives present Abraham as a person of authority and standing in his community. Abraham's wealth and behavior and people's responses to him suggest he was already a leader, maybe a local governor ("Abraham Reassessed").

of a multitude." Although this etymology is disputed, this is how the text explains his name: "[because I will make you] the father of many nations [ʾāḇ-hᵃmôn]" (17:4 and 5).

have made you. The Hebrew is better translated, "I will make you."[131]

father of many nations. See 15:5; 28:3. In "Theme of Genesis and Biblical Theology" (see introduction), I argue that God's promise to make Abraham a father of many nations should be understood in both a biological sense and in a spiritual sense. The biological interpretation is validated by the genealogies of Keturah (25:1–4), Ishmael (Book 7, Gen. 25:12–18), and Edom (Book 9, Gen. 36). The interpretation that he fathers the nations that reproduce his faith finds support both within the immediate text and within the canon. In contrast to the promise that kings will come out of his loins, it is not said the nations he fathers are thus begotten. Moreover, circumcision, the sign of the covenant, is extended to every male in Abraham's household, "whether born in your household or bought with your money" (17:12–13; see also Theological Reflections below). The psalmist (Ps. 87:4–6) and the apostle Paul (Rom. 4:16–17; cf. Gal. 3:15–19) both interpret the text with reference to the Gentiles becoming Abraham's offspring. According to this spiritual interpretation, "father" designates a spiritual relationship; it is so used to describe the relationship of Joseph to Pharaoh (Gen. 45:8) and a Levite to Micah (Judg. 17:10).[132]

kings. In primary view are Israel's kings (see 35:11; 49:10; 2 Sam. 7:8–16) but also the messianic king (see Theological Reflections below).

will come from you. This is a reference to physical offspring.

7. everlasting covenant. See 12:3; 15:5. God's covenant endures forever because he is faithful and does not change (see Theological Reflections below).

between me and you and your descendants. This legal formulation guarantees that at the death of the owner the land will be passed on to the next generation in perpetuity.

to be your God. This is the heart of the covenant, guaranteeing that God will protect his people and provide them with life and prosperity (cf. 17:8; Jer. 24:7; 31:33; Ezek. 34:30–31; Hos. 2:1; Zech. 8:8).

8. land . . . everlasting possession. See 13:15. Later "this gift of an unending covenant" (God, seed, land) will become "a critical affirmation for Israel in the time of the exile in Babylon,"[133] enabling them to hope for the future.

Canaan. See 12:1, 7; 13:15; and 15:18 regarding the Promised Land.

---

[131]For this use of the suffix conjugation, see *IBHS* §30.5.1d.

[132]Sarna (*Genesis,* 124) also thinks it has a universal significance in light of the history of world religions: "['Father of many nations'] has a more universal application in that a larger segment of humanity looks upon Abraham as its spiritual father."

[133]Roop, *Genesis,* 122.

Law of Circumcision Set Forth (17:9 – 14)

9. As for you. This marks the second division of the covenant obligations: Abraham's responsibilities.

keep my covenant. Wenham explains, "Whereas inaugurating the covenant was entirely the result of divine initiative, confirming it involves a human response, summed up in v 1 by 'walk in my presence and be blameless' and spelled out in the demand to circumcise every male."[134]

10. circumcised.[135] This ritual marks something as set apart. Here the organ of procreation is consecrated to God (cf. Deut. 30:6; Jer. 4:4). Roop argues that circumcision is also a sign of solidarity. The circumcised become members of the community with whom God has an unending relationship[136] (see Theological Reflections below).

12. eight days old. Some cultures circumcise their children at puberty as a rite of passage from childhood to adulthood in the community. God employed the sign for infants to show that the children, coming under the authority of the parent who confesses faith, are "holy" (i.e., they are separated from the profane world and belong to the covenant community; see Rom. 11:16; 1 Cor. 7:14). Fox argues that circumcision in infancy is a "daring re-interpretation, at once defusing the act of exclusively sexual content while at the same time suggesting that the covenant is a lifelong commitment. The males of the tribe are not simply made holy for marriage. They bear the mark upon their bodies as a sacred reminder of their mission."[137] By the eighth day the baby has completed the cycle of time corresponding to the course of creation (cf. Ex. 22:30; Lev. 22:27).[138]

born . . . bought . . . not your offspring. The covenant promises are extended to all the circumcised, who are reckoned as members of the faithful family (cf. 14:14).

13. covenant in your flesh . . . everlasting. The finite physical mark symbolizes a spiritual reality as indicated by Abraham's spiritual fatherhood and the promise of an everlasting covenant. The Hebrew ʿôlām, translated "everlasting," means "the most distant time," a relative concept according to a text's horizon (cf. Ex. 12:14; 27:21; Lev. 3:17; Num. 10:8; Deut. 15:17). As long as God administered his nation by their physical lineage from Abraham, Isaac, and Jacob, the sign of physical circumcision endured.

14. will be cut off. God will sever the disloyal descendant from the covenant community and from its benefits of blessing and life. The disloyal is doomed to extinction and is liable to premature death.

---

[134]Wenham, *Genesis 16–50*, 20.

[135]Assumedly this circumcision followed the Western Semitic practice, which involved complete removal of the foreskin, in contrast to an Egyptian practice of slitting the foreskin (see also B. K. Waltke, "Circumcision," in *The Complete Book of Everyday Christianity*, ed. R. Banks and R. P. Stevens [Downers Grove, Ill.: InterVarsity, 1997], 143–44).

[136]Roop, *Genesis*, 121–23.

[137]Fox, *Beginning*, 70.

[138]Sarna, *Genesis*, 125.

he has broken. This expresses the opposite of keeping God's covenant (17:9).

Sarah the Progenitrix of Numerous Nations and of Kings; Her Name Is Changed (17:15–22)

15. As for Sarai. This marks the third division of the covenant obligations: the responsibilities of Sarah and Abraham's seed.

Sarai . . . Sarah. Sarah's importance to salvation history is borne out by the fact that she is the only woman in the Bible whose name is changed and whose age at death is detailed (23:1).[139] The exact meaning of her name change is unclear. Though the LXX associates the new name *Sarah* with a Hebrew word meaning "strife," both *Sarai* and *Sarah* are probably dialectical variants meaning "princess." The promise that she will bear kings supports this interpretation. *Sarai,* her birth-name, probably looks back on her noble descent, whereas *Sarah,* her covenantal name, looks ahead to her noble descendants (see "father of many nations," 17:5).

16. bless her . . . give you a son. See 1:22; 12:2.

nations . . . kings . . . from her. Primarily her spiritual motherhood is in view (see "father of many nations," 17:5).

17. fell facedown. Is his humble posture (see 17:3) a cover-up for his inner skepticism?

laughed. Abraham again stumbles in incredulity after the covenant has been given (cf. 12:10–20). Isaac means "he laughs." The name is punned upon in 18:12–15; 21:6.

18. If only Ishmael. As Roop describes, "Abraham reacts . . . not with joy and celebration, but with consternation: it is a complication in his life."[140]

19. you will call him Isaac. Isaac's name means "he laughs." It is as if God, responding to Abraham's doubtful laughter, says, "You laugh, but I will bring about my promises with joy." Both Abraham and Sarah first laugh in disbelief (see 18:12), but at Isaac's birth Sarah will laugh with joy at the supernatural work of grace (21:1–7; Rom. 4:19–21).

20. as for Ishmael . . . twelve rulers . . . great nation. God pastorally reassures Abraham that Ishmael will not be excluded from a blessing. Indeed he too will father a great nation, with twelve tribes corresponding to the twelve tribes of Israel (cf. 25:12–16).

21. with Isaac. Isaac represents the living God's triumph over barrenness. By his own sovereign counsel the Lord elects Isaac, not Ishmael. The Lord's chosen race will not come by natural generation but by supernatural grace at the ordained time (see Rom. 9:6–13).

---

[139]Fox, *Beginning*, 73.
[140]Roop, *Genesis*, 124.

Law of Circumcision Carried Out (17:23 – 27)

23. On that very day. This expression marks a significant moment (see also 7:13): the scene's climax when Abraham shows himself a faithful covenant partner by immediately fulfilling his obligations.

26. Ishmael. Both the elect and nonelect children receive the sign of the covenant.

THEOLOGICAL REFLECTIONS ON
BOOK 6, ACT 2, SCENE 2

Theology of Covenant

Here the Lord expands his covenant with Abraham in several ways. God's covenant with Abraham as recorded in Genesis 15 pertained to the promise to make Abraham into a nation (12:2), specifically to give his descendants the land of Canaan. The supplement of Genesis 17 escalates the motif of land (17:8) and descendants (17:7, 16, 19–20). The Lord commits himself forever to be the God of Abraham and his descendants (17:7) and, as their God, to grant them the land of Canaan forever (17:8). The promise to be their God entails that the descendants in view participate in the new covenant (Jer. 24:7; 31:31–34; Ezek. 34:25–31; Hos. 2:23; Zech. 8:8). But unlike in Genesis 15, the promises made in Genesis 17 are made in connection with the promise to make Abraham and his descendants a blessing to the nations (12:3). God will make Abraham the father of a multitude of nations through numerous physical and spiritual progeny (17:4–6). Kings from his own body will rule the nations (cf. Deut. 17:14–20). Nehemiah treats the covenants of chapters 15 and 17 as two aspects of the Abrahamic covenant, connecting the land grant of chapter 15 with the change of Abraham's names in chapter 17, and regards the Abrahamic covenant as having been fulfilled (Neh. 9:7–8).

Although in chapter 15 Abraham was a passive partner to whom God unconditionally committed himself, this supplement calls Abraham into active partnership. Just as Noah lived righteously and was rewarded with the Noahic covenant by the Lord, Abraham must "walk before" the Lord (living in fellowship with him and being taught by him) and be blameless (living with integrity) in order to enjoy the covenant blessings. In fact, only after Abraham shows his total commitment to the Lord by his willingness to offer up Isaac as sacrifice does God take an oath to fulfill this covenant (22:15–18). From henceforth the covenant supplement is unconditional. Nevertheless, the formulation suggests that for Abraham's descendants to increase and be a blessing they too must walk before God and be blameless. The suggestion becomes explicit in the formulas of blessings and curses in the Mosaic covenant (Lev. 26; Deut. 28).

Faith

The God who alone can satisfy the benevolent provisions of this covenant is faithful and will keep his grant to Abraham, but only those who trust in this Covenant Keeper will enjoy its provisions. Like Abraham, all participants in this covenant must believe God's promise regarding a supernatural Seed, one raised from the dead, as it were. Nevertheless, Abraham's faith sometimes wavered with skepticism. God's grace is greater than our doubts.

Circumcision and Baptism

Circumcision was the crucial symbol of the Abrahamic covenant (cf. Gen. 21:4; Luke 1:59; Phil. 3:5). It was performed on the organ of procreation because the covenant pertained to descendants set apart to God. However, circumcision in the flesh was of no spiritual value unless accompanied by a circumcised heart—the reality that it symbolized. Throughout salvation history, God made it patently clear that only the circumcised heart satisfies the conditions of the covenant relationship (Deut. 10:16; 30:6; Jer. 4:4; Ezek. 44:7–9).[141]

Today God defines his people not by their physical descent from Abraham but by their relationship with Jesus Christ, the only descendant of Abraham who kept God's covenant without transgression. Moreover, God administers them by a new covenant. In this new covenant he grants his people his Holy Spirit and writes the law on their hearts, guaranteeing their circumcision (Jer. 31:31–34; esp. 33; Rom. 2:28–29; 2 Cor. 3:2–6; Gal. 6:15). Circumcision, the old sign of initiation into the covenant community, is replaced by a new sign, baptism. This rite symbolizes that the saint is "circumcised, in the putting off of the sinful nature, not with a circumcision done by the hands of men but with the circumcision done by Christ" (Col. 2:11). It also symbolizes that they live not naturally but supernaturally by faith, "having been buried with him in baptism and raised with him through [their] faith in the power of God, who raised him from the dead" (Col. 2:12). Baptism is the symbol of inclusion in Christ's church, the new expression of God's covenant people, and the symbol of the cleansing of sin (Rom. 6:1–14; 11:16; 1 Cor. 7:14; Col. 2:11–12; 1 Peter 3:20).

In the baptism ritual God continues to use the family institution (see Gen. 7:1; Acts 16:31). Because in Christ's body there is neither male nor female, all may come, male, female, parent, and child (Luke 18:15–17; Gal. 3:26–29; Col. 2:11–12; cf. Luke 1:59; 2:21; Phil. 3:5). However, once again the community must guard against the danger of participating in an initiation rite without living the life of God's new covenant.[142]

Blessing to the Nations through New Birth

Psalm 87:4–6 speaks of converted Rahab (i.e., Egypt) and Babylon, the two notorious enemies of Israel, as being "born" in Jerusalem: "I will record Rahab and Babylon among those who acknowledge me . . . and will say, 'This

---

[141]See Waltke, "Circumcision," 143–44.
[142]Roop, *Genesis*, 123.

one was born in Zion.' Indeed, of Zion it will be said, 'This one and that one were born in her.'" This prophecy, correlating to the provision of the Abrahamic covenant to be a blessing to the nations, is wholly fulfilled in Jesus Christ and those who are baptized into him (cf. John 1:13; Rom. 4:16–17; 15:8–12; Gal. 3:29; Rev. 7:9; 21:24). The Gentiles do not become Abraham's children through circumcision, but through faith, just as Abraham was also justified by faith prior to circumcision (see Rom. 4:11, 16–17).

Messiah

God's promise that kings will come from Abraham foreshadows the one true king, the Messiah Jesus Christ who will reign in heavenly Mount Zion (Heb. 12:22–24) and be worshiped by all other kings (Isa. 52:15; see also "Fourth Motif: The Ruler" in the introduction).

BOOK 6, ACT 2, SCENE 3: THE VISITATION OF THE LORD AND HIS ANGELS: ABRAHAM AS PROPHET (18:1–33)

LITERARY ANALYSIS OF BOOK 6, ACT 2, SCENE 3 ———————

Repetition and Key Word

Several literary devices link Scene 3 to Scene 2. A key word of the Abraham cycle, "to see," appears again in 18:2, 21 and in the passive form "to be seen" ("appeared") in 18:1 (see also 17:1). Scenes 2 and 3 are also connected by God's address to Abraham (17:5; 18:5) and Sarah (17:15; 18:10–15) and God's announcement of their son (17:15–16; 18:10–11).

Structure and Plot

The incredible relationship between Abraham and God, highlighted by the visions and covenant confirmation in Scene 2, intensifies in Scene 3 as Abraham stands as a prophet before God. The contrast between Abraham and the characters of Scene 4 will only affirm this characterization of Abraham.

The two incidents of Scene 3 relay the pronouncements of God: his blessing and judgment. In the first, at the tents of Hebron, three men, later identified as "the LORD" and two angels, announce the birth of Isaac to Abraham and Sarah (18:1–15). In the second incident, while walking to the heights overlooking Sodom, God and Abraham debate the destruction of Sodom and Gomorrah (18:16–33).

The first incident consists of the appearance of divine visitors (18:1–2), the hospitality of Abraham (18:3–8), and the annunciation of Isaac's birth (18:9–15). Not long before, the Lord had appeared to Abraham, promising covenant and requiring Abraham to walk blamelessly. The opening of this scene, "The LORD appeared...," carries an implicit question, "Why has the Lord returned? What will come of his promises?" The crucial moment answers those questions with the unmistakable announcement of Isaac's birth. Abraham's actions in this scene also demonstrate that he is indeed walking blamelessly before God. Abraham's extravagant hospitality illustrates his noble character and reveals him worthy of the prophetic revelation his divine visitors unveil (see 17:1).

The second incident consists of two parts: divine reflection on Abraham and Sodom (18:17–21) and Abraham's intercession with God for Sodom (18:23–32). Journey notes (18:16, 33) enclose these speeches. Abraham has shown his noble character through his generous hospitality; now he must prove himself worthy of "fathering" the great nation that will bless the earth (18:18). Through his actions of this incident, Abraham teaches his offspring to keep the way of the Lord by doing what is right and just (18:19).

Characterization

Abraham is portrayed as a model of hospitality. His gracious hosting is epitomized by his speedy exertion—"hurried," "quick," "ran"—to serve his guests and by the lavish meal he offers. This characterization is only heightened by the later contrast with Lot and Sodom as failed hosts (see Literary Analysis of Book 6, Act 5, Scene 4). In affirmation of Abraham's character, God reveals his plans of blessing and judgment to Abraham.

EXEGETICAL NOTES TO BOOK 6, ACT 2, SCENE 3 ————

Incident One: Announcement of Isaac's Birth (18:1–15)

Appearance of Divine Visitors (18:1–2)

1. **appeared.** To "appear" and "see" is a key of this scene (18:1, 2 [2x], 21; see also 19:1, 28).

The LORD appeared. With the Lord's return appearance (see 17:1), he confirms his revelation of 17:19 and declares certain and swift fulfillment. This appearance also clearly identifies Abraham as a prophet who is given foreknowledge of God's plans and judgments.

great trees of Mamre. See 13:18; 14:13.

entrance to his tent. Contrast this with 19:1. Abraham sits in the shade of a sojourner's tent, a welcoming place to travelers; Lot will sit at the gate of an evil city, hazardous to strangers who enter.

heat of the day. Abraham lives by his subjective experience of the day's downy light, noon-day heat, and cool evening breeze, not by hours and minutes. During the heat of the day travelers seek shade and rest. Abraham does not appear inconvenienced by the interruption of his siesta or by the labor he must do in the day's heat.

2. **three men.** This is actually the Lord and two angels (see 18:1, 10; 19:1). The later identifications of the "men" (18:10, 13, 16–17, 33; 19:1) confirm their manifest difference. One man is none other than the Lord, as 18:2–3

and especially 10, 13–15 make explicit. However, the Lord and his heavenly assembly in their incarnation appear in human form (see 16:7).

standing nearby. The narrator describes the oriental equivalent of knocking at the door.

When he saw them, he hurried. Abraham's rush to welcome his guests is immediate.

bowed low to the ground. Abraham's address, "my LORD" (see below) and his reference to himself as "your servant" are accompanied with an appropriate gesture of awe and humility (18:3).

Abraham's Hospitality (18:3 – 8)

3. found favor. This is always spoken to one of higher rank.

my lord. This is better translated "my LORD." The translation "my lord" is misleading, since the Hebrew text refers to a title for God.[143] NIV translates the same Hebrew in 18:27 as "the Lord" (see 18:1, 13, 17), although it should be written in upper case. Abraham addresses "the LORD" (singular) in 18:3 and all three men (plural) in 18:4–5.

your servant. The consummate host offers himself humbly.

4–5. wash your feet . . . rest . . . eat . . . refreshed. Abraham attends to all his guests' unspoken needs.

6–7. hurried . . . Quick . . . ran . . . hurried. The narrator creates an intimate picture of Abraham, the consummate host, rushing to prepare a great feast for his guests. Throughout the story Abraham is completely at their service.

6. seahs. A seah is two gallons (eight liters) of a grain.

fine flour. Given the rapid preparation of Abraham's meal, it is likely that he also offered bread without yeast, but the narrator blanks this fact to feature Abraham's bread made of fine flour in contrast with Lot's bread made without yeast (see 19:3).

7–8. choice, tender calf . . . curds and milk. Abraham's offering of "something to eat" turns out to be a royal banquet. In the ancient Near East, goat's milk was especially prized because of its energy and easy digestibility.

8. While they ate. The narrator slows the story from action to dialogue. The initiative passes to the strangers, specifically to "the LORD" as the prime speaker.

Annunciation of Isaac's Birth (18:9 – 15)

9. Where. This is a rhetorical question, since the Lord knew what Sarah was doing behind him (see 18:13–15). The question conveys the Lord's concern and secures Sarah's attention for the announcement.

10. I will surely return. This is a clear indication that the speaker is the Lord, since he alone can faithfully promise life out of barrenness and decay.

---

[143]The Hebrew reads ᵃdōnāy ("LORD") not ᵃdōnî ("lord" or "sir") (cf. HALOT, 13, B.2).

about this time next year. The promise (15:4) and covenant (17:16–21) is now escalated to a precise time.

Sarah . . . son. God makes a promise demanding faith (see below, "God's Promise and Faith" in the Theological Reflections).

11. past the age of childbearing. The Hebrew literally reads, "Sarah no longer experienced the cycle of women." Her body is procreatively dead (see Rom. 4:19; Heb. 11:11–12; see also "God's Promise and Faith" below).

12. Sarah laughed. Both Abraham and Sarah first laugh unbelievingly at God's promises (see 17:17).

my master. See 1 Peter 3:6. Sarah understands her social identity and significance in her relationship to Abraham.

pleasure. This is a unique Hebrew term, of uncertain meaning, translated "conception" by an ancient Aramaic translation, "lust" by *HALOT*,[144] and "delight" by J. D. Price.[145] Abraham and Sarah have accepted barrenness as normal.

13–14. Why did Sarah laugh . . . is anything too hard. As assurance of his miraculous power, the Lord verbalizes Sarah's secret thoughts. His rhetorical question declares that, since he is God, everything is possible (see 15:4–6; Heb. 11:11; cf. Jer. 32:17; Mark 10:27; Luke 1:37).

15. lied. The Bible does not gloss over the sins of its hero and heroine of faith (cf. 12:13).

you did laugh. This is both a restorative rebuke (Prov. 28:13) and an assuring sign: the one who reads her thoughts can open her womb.

Incident Two: Abraham Pleads for Sodom (18:16–33)

Journey Note Overlooking Sodom (Janus Verse for Incidents One and Two) (18:16)

16. they looked down toward Sodom. The strangers effect beginnings and endings as the messengers of hope and life to Abraham and Sarah and of judgment and death to the people of Sodom and Gomorrah (Deut. 32:39; 1 Sam. 2:6; Ps. 76:7; Isa. 45:7).

Divine Reflections on Abraham and Sodom (18:17–21)

17. the LORD said [or "thought"]. The narrator records God's internal dialogue for the reader, in order to explain the true nature of the discussion that follows. This dialogue between the Lord and Abraham is for Abraham's benefit, to challenge him to act wisely and nobly for justice. The narrator is a prophet in his own right (see "Moses and Ur-Genesis" in the introduction).

Shall I hide. God so esteems his servants, the prophets, that he "does nothing without revealing his plan" to them (see Gen. 20:7; Jer. 23:16–22; Amos 3:7; John 15:15).

144*HALOT*, 793.
145J. D. Price, "ᶜdn," *NIDOTTE*, 3:329.

18. a great and powerful nation. See 12:2–3. Such a nation has to learn justice beginning with its father, Abraham (18:17–19). The Lord models justice to Abraham in his treatment of the Sodomites (18:20–33) and through this remarkable dialogue he educes Abraham's integrity.

19. I have chosen him. The text literally reads, "I have known him" (i.e., "I have an intimate relationship with him"; see 4:1).

direct. The same term, which means "to command, to charge," is used in connection with the law of Moses. Pedagogy in ancient Israel was strict and urgent.

his children and his household. Israel's inspired spiritual and ethical heritage was passed down through generations within the home (see, e.g., Deut. 6:6; Prov. 1:8). That heritage originated in the revealed will of God through gifted individuals such as Moses and Solomon, who in turn handed their law and wisdom to the parents to teach the next generation. There is no record of a school in Israel before the late intertestamental period; families were the source of all education, including trades.[146]

the way of the LORD. The phrase is a technical metaphor for right behavior that leads to a right destiny due to one's relationship with the Lord. Eugene H. Merrill explains, "The way (*derek*) is . . . the whole course of life lived in conformity to covenant obligation."[147]

right and just [*ṣᵉdāqâ ûmišpāṭ*]. Righteousness portrays a way of living in community that promotes the life of all its members, a life promoting social order in recognition of God's rule (see 6:9). A righteous person rightly orders community, and a just one restores broken community, especially by punishing the oppressor and delivering the oppressed.

so that. The conditional aspect of the Abrahamic covenant is explicit here (see 17:2; 22:15–18; 26:4–5).

20. outcry [*zᵉʿāqâ*]. In 18:21 and 19:13 the term *ṣᵉʿāqâ* is used; here its synonym occurs. As the Judge of the earth, the Lord receives all cries of wrongdoing (see 18:25; 4:10). The Hebrew word play with the "right" (*ṣᵉdāqâ*) actions of Abraham highlights the moral failure of Sodom.

their sin. The narrator spoke earlier of Sodom's wickedness (13:13; see also ch. 19, esp. vv. 4–5 and note; Ezek. 16:49–50).

21. go down and see. This is the narrator's figurative way of saying that God always thoroughly investigates the crime before passing sentence (see 3:11–13; 4:9–12; 11:5).

Abraham Intercedes for Sodom (18:22–33)

22. The men. This is presumably the two angels/messengers (18:1; 19:1). Appropriately, two go to confirm the crime, as later in Mosaic law two witnesses are needed for capital punishment.

---

[146]See B. K. Waltke and D. Diewert, "Wisdom Literature." in *The Face of Old Testament Studies: A Survey of Contemporary Approaches,* ed. D. Baker and B. T. Arnold (Grand Rapids: Baker, 1999), 308–9.
[147]E. H. Merrill, "*drk,*" *NIDOTTE*, 1:989.

Abraham remained standing before the LORD. Although the scribes attempted to keep the text "correct" (*b. Ned.* 37b–38a), they sometimes changed it.[148] According to their own notes, the original text read, "The LORD remained standing before Abraham." This expression of God's condescension was so great it seemed blasphemous to the scribes. If their note on the original is the correct reading, it suggests that the Lord is challenging Abraham to play the role of a righteous judge.

23. Abraham approached him. Abraham the great host is also Abraham the compassionate prophet who intercedes and upholds justice. He stands as a "preserver" in the line of Enoch and Noah. Fox argues, "Without this story Abraham would be a man of faith but not a man of compassion and moral outrage, a model consistent with Moses and the Prophets of Israel."[149]

Will you sweep away the righteous with the wicked? Abraham's arguments for sparing Sodom are founded on a concern for justice, not merely the presence of his nephew Lot in the city. Roop states, "Acting as the one chosen to promote life, Abraham . . . [proposes] that the future of everyone be determined not by the wicked ones in the midst of the community, but by the righteous ones."[150] God agrees. God spares the righteous when he judges a nation, as in the cases of Rahab (Josh. 2), Assyria (Jonah 3–4), and Israel (see Ezek. 14:12–20). The situation differs considerably, however, in cases of natural disaster that are not judicial judgments (see Job 9:22; 12:4, 16; Luke 13:4).

24. fifty. This is about half of a small city (Amos 5:3).[151]

25–32. Far be it from you! . . . I am nothing but dust and ashes. . . . This is an expression of profound deference and humility. Abraham evidences his leadership qualities in his boldness, moral wisdom, and skillful speeches to God.

25. kill. The language carries overtones of a judicial sentence (Lev. 20:4; Num. 35:19, 21).

Will not the Judge of all the earth do right? The Hebrew literally means "to do justice" (i.e., to restore a community's right order under God's rule by punishing those who destroy it with oppression of the weak and by delivering the oppressed). The question could be read as a challenge to God,[152] but sound theology demands it be read as a deliberative prayer asserting faith in God's just character and as a "conduit for the divine fulfillment."[153]

---

[148]B.K. Waltke, "Textual Criticism of the Old Testament and its Relations to Exegesis and Theology," *NIDOTTE*, 1:58–59.

[149]Fox, *Beginning*, 67.

[150]Roop, *Genesis*, 130.

[151]One hundred is a common number for small ancient Near Eastern cities.

[152]So C. S. Rodd. "Shall Not the Judge of All the Earth Do What Is Just?" *ExpTim* 83 (1971–1972): 137–39.

[153]S. E. Balentine, "Prayers for Justice in the Old Testament: Theodicy and Theology," *CBQ* 51 (1989): 597–616.

26. If I find fifty righteous people in the city of Sodom. Like the people of Noah's age, the Sodomites had opportunity to repent and change their wicked ways. As with everyone, their time of grace to repent comes to an end.

I will spare. The Hebrew literally means "lift up." It is unclear whether this means to "lift up [face]," meaning to show grace, or to "lift up [sin]," meaning to forgive.

32. ten. Ten is still a community; fewer than ten can be saved individually, as happens in Genesis 19.

33. he left. It is now established that the judgment on Sodom and Gomorrah, the paradigm for God's future judgments, is just. The Lord investigates the accusations thoroughly (18:22), ensures two objective witnesses, involves the faithful in his judgment, displays active compassion for the suffering, and prioritizes divine mercy over indignant wrath (i.e., not to be destroyed if even ten are righteous). The Lord himself will not appear again in this act; in the next scene he will rain down the judgment from heaven (see 19:24).

THEOLOGICAL REFLECTIONS ON BOOK 6, ACT 2, SCENE 3

Abraham As Prophet

This scene presents Abraham as a noble prophet. Amos declares, "Surely the Sovereign LORD does nothing without revealing his plan to his servants the prophets" (3:7). To Abraham God announces the birth of Isaac through Sarah a year hence. He reveals the imminent destruction of Sodom and Gomorrah, just as God warned Noah in advance of the Flood. Abraham's compassion and sense of righteousness and justice prove him a worthy prophet. He pleads, like the weeping prophet Jeremiah, for the deliverance of the righteous in Sodom and Gomorrah.

Hospitality[154]

Abraham's receptive hospitality is a model for welcoming God's presence. Abraham requests that the three visitors remain with him, saying, "Do not pass your servant by" (18:3). So should the church respond when Christ knocks to be invited in for fellowship (see Matt. 25:31–46; John 6:53–58; Rev. 3:20; 19:7).

God's Promise and Faith

God's promise of a son is so miraculous that Sarah responds not with joy but with doubt (Gen. 18:11–15). But nothing exceeds God's power (18:14), not even virgin birth and resurrection. The word of promise characteristically falls outside of reason. Sarah's body is procreatively dead (see Rom.

---

[154]See also Theological Reflections on Book 10, Act 3, Scene 4.

4:19; Heb. 11:11–12). It is not reasonable to believe in resurrection. But faith transcends reason. Israel's existence is supernatural, not natural (see John 1:13). God's promises, embraced by faith, open the door of hope and future (see Gen. 11:30; 15:2–4; 16:11; 17:15–16). Abraham's recognition of God's power is the kind of faith that believes God raised our Lord Jesus from the dead, a faith that justifies (Rom. 4:22–25; cf. Judg. 13:18–25; Luke 1:37–38, 45). We are not locked into lives of barrenness.

Such faith, exercised according to God's promise and purpose, not according to individual wants, bridges the impossible (Mark 14:36). Lot's daughters will lack such faith (see Book 6, Act 2, Scene 4 below). Cut off from God's promises by their father's decision to leave Abraham, they think of their procreation solely in terms of "the way of all the earth," presumably including the animals. Bondaged to their desire for social immortality, they rely on independent schemes that lead to incest with their drunken father and nations with a troubled future.

Birth Announcement

The joyful announcement of Isaac's supernatural birth prefigures the divine announcement of Jesus Christ's birth (see Isa. 9:6; Luke 2:10–11). The announcement, made by angels (Gen. 18:1–15) and seemingly impossible to fulfill, will come to fruition and accomplish God's plans.

BOOK 6, ACT 2, SCENE 4: JUDGMENT ON SODOM AND GOMORRAH (19:1–38)

LITERARY ANALYSIS OF BOOK 6, ACT 2, SCENE 4 ———

Structure and Plot

The close links between Scenes 3 and 4 are immediately apparent.[155] As Scene 4 opens, less than forty-eight hours have elapsed since the incidents of the Scene 3. This scene of judgment also consists of two incidents. In the first, at Lot's home, the two messengers pronounce God's judgment on Sodom and Gomorrah (19:1–29). The second incident functions as a coda or epilogue, reporting the incestuous intercourse between Lot and his daughters in a cave near Zoar and the birth of Lot's grandsons, Moab and Ammon (19:30–38).

Sarna analyzes with alliteration the three movements of the first incident: "the demonstration by the Sodomites of their irredeemable evil [19:1–11]; the deliverance of Lot [19:12–22]; the devastation of the region [19:23–26]."[156]

---

[155]These scenes are closely woven together. Genesis 18:16 functions as a janus between the first and second incidents in Scene 3, and the second incident of Scene 3 functions as a janus between Scenes 3 and 4. The narrator unites the second incident of Scene 3 and the first incident of Scene 4 by an inclusio mentioning the Lord and Abraham and their looking down from the heights of Hebron upon Sodom (18:16; 19:28) and by his summary statement, "when God destroyed the cities of the plain, he remembered Abraham, and he brought Lot out of the catastrophe" (19:29).

[156]Sarna, *Genesis*, 134.

The scene peaks when the Lord carries out his threat of judgment by raining burning sulfur on Sodom and Gomorrah (19:24–25). In the denouement, Lot's wife suffers the consequences of looking back and the narrator summarizes the destruction. The narrator draws the incident to a conclusion by circling back to the perspective of Abraham as he witnesses Sodom's just destruction (19:27–29).

Incident two functions as a coda that brings the account up to date by explaining the questionable origins of Israel's neighbors, Moab and Ammon. The etiology also aims to establish the scene's historicity (see also "Historicity and Literary Genre" in the introduction).

Comparison and Contrast

Once again Lot is compared and contrasted with Abraham. In Scene 3 the angels arrived in the heat of the day, and Abraham the pilgrim was at his tent's entrance. In Scene 4 they arrive at Sodom in the evening, and Lot, possibly one of the city's leading citizens, is at the city gate. Abraham is "complete" in his devotion to God (cf. "blameless" in 17:1), while Lot has become "complete" in his urbanity.

Both scenes begin with the arrival of the messengers, the greeting by the host, the welcome into the home, and the serving of a meal. In this one parallel the hospitality of both men differs from the rest of Sodom. This is indicative of the righteousness that saves Lot. However, whereas Abraham was the model host, Lot is the sincere but fumbling failure. Abraham's exemplary hosting is epitomized by his speedy exertion—"hurried," "quick," "ran"—to serve his guests and by the lavish meal he offers. In contrast, Lot "rises" to greet his guests, "hurries" them away from the rape gang at his door, and can only offer bread without yeast (cf. 18:6 and note). After Abraham's meal, the angels ask where Sarah is; after Lot's meal, the angels ask if he has any additional relatives besides those in the house. Sarah laughs when she hears that she is to bear a child, but Lot's sons-in-law, when told that the Lord is about to destroy the city, think he is joking. Sarah repents of her laughter of unbelief and receives only a rebuke. Lot's sons-in-law do not repent and lose their lives. In contrast to them, Lot's immediate family is saved. Scene 3 concluded with Sarah humbled but promised a son; Scene 4 ends with Lot's wife turned to salt.[157] Abraham's leadership and oratory skill in Scene 3, even to debate with God, markedly contrast with Lot's excruciating hesitancy and inability to convince even his own family to leave the doomed city. Abraham pleaded for the righteous of Sodom and Gomorrah on the basis of justice; Lot pleads for Zoar on the basis of his self-interest (19:18–20, 30). Lot plays a counter role with respect both to land and seed. He chose by sight and now ends with a cave and descendants by incest.

---

[157]For these contrasts between Scenes 3 and 4, see Garrett, *Rethinking Genesis*, 142.

Sodom and Gomorrah also contrast with the perfect host Abraham. The word play between Abraham's righteousness and justice ($s^ed\bar{a}q\hat{a}/mi\check{s}p\bar{a}t$) and the outcry ($s^{ec}\bar{a}q\hat{a}$) of violence and injustice in Sodom that reaches God illustrates the clear differences. Whereas Abraham extended himself to serve his guests, the Sodomites try to consume their guests in service to themselves. Sodom perverts goodness: "know" refers to illicit and coerced sex; "door" should be the point of contact but is the point of confrontation.[158]

Lot's wife, who is nameless, also invites comparison to Sarah. Both women fail to believe the word of God. Sarah's unbelief was one incident in the life of a woman who showed her faith and godliness by calling her husband "my lord" (see 1 Peter 3:1–6). The Lord's verbal rebuke of her was remedial. She later names Isaac "Laughter," not in unbelief, but in the joy of faith. By contrast, the unbelief of Lot's Sodomite wife, expressed in turning back towards Sodom, is probably exemplary of a life lacking faith. The Lord's palpable rebuke of her is penal; she becomes a pillar of salt.

Scenic Depiction

The scenic depictions not only mark time but also serve as images of the moral conditions in Sodom and of God's judgment. The angels enter the city of Sodom in the evening as the sun is setting, matching the moral darkness of its citizens. They leave the city as the sun is rising. At this time of justice, the Lord rains down on the city burning sulfur, a foreshadow of hell.

Irony

Lot tries to be a blessing but instead appears as a bungler and buffoon.[159] He fails as a host, as a citizen, as a husband, as a father. He wants to protect his guests but needs to be protected by them; he tries to save his family, and they think he is joking; afraid to journey to the mountains, he pleads for a little town, but afraid of the town, he flees to the mountains. His salvation depends on God's mercy (19:16) and Abraham's blessing (19:29).

EXEGETICAL NOTES TO BOOK 6, ACT 2, SCENE 4 ———

Incident One: The Destruction of Sodom and Gomorrah (19:1 – 29)

Demonstration by the Sodomites of Their Irredeemable Evil (19:1 – 11)

1. two angels. The narrator blanks the correspondence between "the men" of the previous scene (18:2, 16, 22) and the two angels. Similarly, he blanked the connection between the men and "the LORD," who was one of

---

[158]Cf. Fox, *Beginning*, 73.

[159]G. Coats, "Lot: A Foil in the Abraham Saga," in *Understanding the Word: Essays in Honour of Bernhard W. Anderson*, ed. James T. Butler et al. (JSOTSup 37; Sheffield: JSOT Press, 1985), 128.

them (cf. 18:10–15, 17–21, 22–33). He obviously intends his audience to make connection between the phenomenological and the theological. As narrator-historian he describes them from the earthly viewpoint: they appear to be "men" (see 18:2, 8; 19:16); as narrator-prophet he describes them from the heavenly perspective: they are divine messengers. The writer of Hebrews reflects on both points of view: "Do not forget to entertain strangers, for by so doing some people have entertained angels without knowing it" (Heb. 13:2).

in the evening. Considering the distance between Abraham's camp and Sodom (20 miles), it may not be the same day. Etymologically, the Hebrew term for "evening" means "black." The physical darkness of the city, with the setting of the sun, matches the moral blackness of the events that follow.

sitting in the gateway. A city gate was usually made of monumental edifices shading the narrow passageway and side chambers of the city entrance. Here the elders and officials sat on stone benches to adjudicate legal matters and discuss local affairs. The gate was the physical symbol of collective authority and power. Lot's presence here suggests that politically he has become one with the Sodomites, if not a leader among them. Curiously, Lot is alone at the focal point of communal life, suggesting that he alone is concerned about the community's interests and well-being. The events that follow substantiate this. Though politically one with them, theologically Lot remains distinct.

bowed down. Although Lot blunders and bungles the situation, his hospitality to strangers throughout the story demonstrates his desire to do righteousness (see 18:2; 2 Peter 2:6–8). Hospitality is a law that has almost a sacral character.[160] Spiritually, Lot has been cut from a different cloth than his neighbors.

2. My lords. . . . Compare Lot's speech with Abraham's. The dialogue is similar but lacks the attentiveness of Abraham's conscientious hosting.

house. Lot has exchanged his tent, formerly pitched *near* the city, for a house in Sodom (see 13:12).

3. insisted so strongly. Is Lot only showing conventional hospitality, or does he anticipate the treachery of his neighbors? The latter interpretation is confirmed by the events that follow, by his instruction that they be on their way early in the morning—presumably so that they can slip in and out of the city unnoticed—and by the parallel incident of the Benjaminites at Gibeah. There too the host, an old man, cautions his guest about the peril of spending the night in the city square of the evil place (Judg. 19:18–20).

meal [*mišteh*]. The Hebrew denotes a banquet, a sumptuous entertainment of guests with food and drink (see Gen. 21:8; 26:30; 29:22).[161] Like

---

[160]B. Vawter, *On Genesis: A New Reading* (Garden City, N.Y.: Doubleday, 1977), 235.
[161]R. H. O'Connell, "*šth*," NIDOTTE, 4:260–62.

Abraham, Lot extends gracious hospitality to his visitors; however, in the narrator's descriptions of the two events, Lot's feast and acts of hospitality cannot measure up to Abraham's lavish meal and generous service.

bread without yeast. This could be prepared quickly for the unexpected guests.

4. all the men from every part . . . young and old. These details are necessary to show that everyone destroyed is wicked (see 18:16–33; also 6:5; 8:21; Rom. 1:26–32). Nevertheless, the language cannot be forced to include Lot's sons-in-law in the mob (Gen. 19:14). The angels reckon them as part of Lot's family (19:12), not of Sodom.

Sodom. The city is guilty here of two crimes: violation of guests and unnatural lust. The men of the city cry not just for homosexuality but for rape. Elsewhere the other noted sins of Sodom and Gomorrah are social oppression (Isa. 1:10, 17); adultery, lying, and abetting the criminal (Jer. 23:14); and arrogance, complacency, and showing no pity on the needy (Ezek. 16:49).

5. that we can have sex with them. The Hebrew is literally "that we may know them" (see 4:1; cf. 18:19). These men have degraded the intimacy of marriage to the lowest level of sexual intercourse; they know nothing of true intimate commitment. They rape the mind, emotions, and body, trivialize the sacred, and legitimatize the vulgar. Homosexuality is a capital offense in the Old Testament (Lev. 18:22; 20:13). The sin of Sodom's act is presumably the worst sort of sexual offense: homosexual gang rape (cf. Judg. 19; Jude 7). Their defiant immorality is the antithesis of Abraham's passion for justice and hospitality (see "Homosexuality" in Theological Reflections below).

6. shut the door behind him. This is probably an act of courage to risk himself and protect his guests, not a deception to conceal from them his morally questionable offer.

7. friends. The Hebrew word is literally "brothers." Lot appeals to them as equals to win their good will (see 29:4).

this wicked thing. His appeal assumes his righteousness (see 2 Peter 2:6–7). Lot knew right from wrong because of conscience and through Abraham. Sarna explains, "Tacitly, though unequivocally, the narrative declares that all socially approved actions and all societal values must be subordinated to the higher obligations of the divinely ordained moral order."[162]

8. I have two daughters. Lot himself is now confronted with the tragic consequence of choosing to identify with Sodom rather than with his God-blessed uncle (see ch. 13). He faces woeful immoral choices—whatever he does will be wrong. On the one hand, he has the obligation to protect his home, including the sanctity of his daughters who are presumably pledged

---

[162]Sarna, *Genesis*, 135.

to be married (19:14). In Mosaic law, the violator of a betrothed woman's sanctity was subject to death by stoning (Deut. 22:23–27). Most important, as bearers of God's image, their persons are sacrosanct. Possibly Lot's suggestion is meant to stress to the men the seriousness and fatal consequences of their evil plan. Nevertheless, by handing his daughters over to be violated, Lot would implicate himself in the crime. On the other hand, Lot has the obligation to protect his guests, who have come under the protection of his home. They too are God's image-bearers. (Lot seemingly does not know at this point that he is entertaining angels.) If he hands himself over, his family and guests are left without a protector. Since the holy angels could have intervened before this, they force him to make the choice. Presumably, had Lot handed the angels over, his family would not have been spared in the judgment on Sodom. He is saved, but only by the skin of his teeth (see "Consequences" in Theological Reflections below).

9. This fellow. The Hebrew literally reads "the one." By replacing his name with a contemptuous, indefinite "one," they aim to strip him of identity and significance. Did the ungrateful mob forget that approximately fifteen years before they had been rescued because of Lot's connection with Abraham (see Gen. 14:14–16)? They allow him to live in the city and even to sit at the gate. Men of the community are also engaged to his daughters, yet they reject his righteousness. To Lot's credit he stands apart morally and spiritually (Luke 6:26).

now . . . judge. Translated literally, this reads, "Now he even plays the judge."[163] An abusive Israelite accused Moses of the same "wrong" (Ex. 2:14; Acts 7:27).

10. Reached out . . . door. See Theological Reflections below, "Justice and mercy."

11. blindness [*sanwērîm*]. The normal Hebrew term for blindness is *ʿiwwēr*. The Hebrew term here occurs elsewhere only in the similar context of 2 Kings 6:18. To judge from Jewish Aramaic and these two texts, it means "to dazzle" and/or "to deceive," suggesting they were blinded temporally by a blazing light.

Deliverance of Lot (19:12 – 22)

12. sons-in-law, sons or daughters. God is concerned with the salvation of the whole family (see 7:1). The narrator uniquely mentions the sons-in-law before sons probably to accent God's grace. Even his sons-in-law are reckoned part of the family that can be saved.

13. we are going to destroy . . . outcry. The outcry has now been confirmed by two credible witnesses (see 18:22, 33).

---

[163]It is so translated because of the climatic, post-positive use of the infinitive absolute (see *IBHS*, §35.3.1f).

destroy. The use of the same Hebrew term as in 6:13 echoes the judgment at the time of the Flood.

14. sons-in-law. They were probably not part of the blinded mob (see 19:4).

pledged to marry. The Hebrew may also mean "who had married." If so, these daughters were left behind with sons-in-law over whom Lot had no authority. More probably, however, the daughters are those of whom he said, "they have never slept with a man." That language is used in ancient Near Eastern texts of a woman pledged to be married.

joking. Lot had no moral persuasion, a marked contrast from Abraham, who reasoned with God (See 2 Peter 3:3–4).

15. your wife . . . two daughters. The family is saved as a unit.

16. hesitated. Lot felt more secure inside an evil city than outside of it with God (see 19:18–21).

merciful. The narrator makes plain that Lot's salvation does not depend upon his own righteousness but on God's mercy. That is true of all humanity (Titus 3:5).

17. flee [*mlṭ*]. This is a word play on Lot's name, *lṭ*. The command to flee is a standard warning to someone to escape the general destruction of war (1 Sam. 19:11; Jer. 48:6; 51:6, 45).

18. But Lot said. His rescue is characterized by exasperation. Here his long speech wastes precious time.

19. found favor. Contrast this with Abraham's speech in 18:3.

this disaster will overtake me. Lot's fear illustrates the irrationality of unbelief. God has sent his servants to rescue Lot, and Lot still fears he will not be protected. Other motives also lurk behind his expressed concern. As his next petition reveals, he cannot face life apart from living in a city.

20. it is very small, isn't it? Lot is pleading that God spare Bela (see 14:2), one of the cities of the plain otherwise under God's judgment (19:25). He argues that, since the walled village is small, its quantity of sin is less and/or it is not worth bothering with. His argument betrays a lack of faith, a jaded spiritual evaluation of justice, and an effete taste for depraved urbanity (see note on 19:18). His selfish plea that God spare Zoar as a place for him to live without regard to righteousness functions as a foil to Abraham's plea for Sodom on the basis of God's compassion and righteousness.

21. I will not overthrow. God's grace to very imperfect people is amazing and accommodating (see 16:9).

Devastation of the Region (19:23–26)

23. Zoar. The town was known to the narrator and his audience, but archaeologists have not yet identified the site.

the sun had risen. In the ancient Near East, court was held symbolically at the rising of the sun (cf. Job 38:12–15; Ps. 5). Shamash, an Akkadian sun deity, was the god of justice.

24. The LORD rained down burning sulfur. Scientifically, the fire and cataclysmic destruction of Sodom and Gomorrah may be explained by an earthquake. Heat, gases, sulfur, and bitumen would have been spewed into air through the fissures formed during a violent earthquake (see 14:10). The lightning that frequently accompanies an earthquake would have ignited the gases and the bitumen.

LORD. The narrator frames the immediate cause, "burning sulfur," with the ultimate cause, the Lord. It is theologically mischievous to dismiss either the scientific causes of historical events because of theological explanation or vice versa.

25. entire plain . . . also the vegetation in the land. In reference to the plain, see 13:10. Like the total destruction of the Flood (see 7:21–23).

26. Lot's wife. The narrator does not explain the origin of Lot's wife. Possibly she was a resident of Sodom, along with Lot's sons-in-law.

looked back. Lot's wife vacillates, probably longing for what she left behind, and experiences the fate of city with which she identifies (Luke 17:32).

salt. In the biblical world, a site was strewn with salt to condemn it to perpetual barrenness and desolation (e.g., Deut. 29:23; Judg. 9:45; Ps. 107:34; Jer. 17:6).[164]

Conclusion: Abraham Looks toward Sodom (19:27–29)

27. returned to the place. The narrator unites Scenes 3 and 4 by an inclusio referring to the discussion between the Lord and Abraham overlooking Sodom (18:16; 19:27–28).

29. remembered. Just as God remembered Noah and his righteousness, God remembers Abraham and saves Lot for his sake. Abraham is the blesser, and his blessing is efficacious even to Lot. Twice Abraham has saved Lot (14:1–16; 19:1–29).

Incident Two: The Birth of Moab and Ammon (19:30–38)

30. afraid. The narrator blanks why Lot is afraid to stay in Zoar. Perhaps he discerns a lifestyle like Sodom and anticipates its future overthrow.

cave. This is converse to Lot's prosperity and prospects in 13:1–13.

31. the older daughter. The narrator indirectly censures the women by not naming them, even as he does Naomi's nearest relative in the story of Ruth (cf. Ruth 4:1).

said. The daughters are an illustration of people doing what is right in their own eyes.

Our father. The narrator offers a contrast of Abraham and Lot. Whereas Abraham will teach his children righteousness and justice (18:18–19), Lot's

---

[164]See F. C. Fensham, "Salt As Curse in the Old Testament and the Ancient Near East," *BA* 25 (1962): 48–50.

children have gleaned little from him. His sons-in-law mock him, and his daughters think of bearing of children "as is the custom all over the earth" (19:31).

old. She presumably means that Lot is too old to remarry and have sons by whom they could have children (cf. Ruth 1:12–13).

no man. Marriages were arranged. She may mean that the family has no social connections for such an arrangement after the destruction of their social life.

as is the custom all over the earth. Her evaluative standard is society at large, not the covenant community under God dependent on his blessing of life.

32. Let's get our father. Lot has taken no initiative to handle the situation. His daughters act out the immorality of Sodom, and their daughters continue in sexual immorality, seducing Israel's men (see Num. 25).

to drink wine. See 9:21. They know their father would not agree to their plan. The older daughter conspires to replace her father's authority.

preserve our family line through our father. The Hebrew literally reads, "to preserve from our father's seed." Her commendable loyalty to her father and her concern for his social immortality is tarnished by her immoral scheme, borne out of fear, not faith. She makes no mention of the Lord who opens the womb (contrast 16:2). Her immoral and self-determined choice contrasts with Abraham and Sarah's faith in the Lord's promise to bring life from their dead bodies.

33. not aware. This is repeated in 19:35. Lot has become totally passive. Lot, who would offer his daughters to be "known" by gang rapists, now does not know his daughters even as he impregnates them.

37–38. Moabites . . . Ammonites. This typical genealogical conclusion begins the story of the bitter animosity of Moab and Ammon against Israel (see Num. 23–25; 2 Kings 3). The Moabites and Ammonites were rejected by God, however, not because of their questionable lineage but because of their mistreatment of Israel (see Deut. 23:3–6). Yet from this lineage will come Ruth, and so Jesus Christ (see Ruth 4:18–22; Matt. 1:5). Because of Ruth's faith, she will be reckoned among the tribe of Judah.

THEOLOGICAL REFLECTIONS ON
BOOK 6, ACT 2, SCENE 4 ───────────────

Hospitality[165]

Abraham solicitously entertains the Lord with a lavish nomad's banquet (18:1–7), and the Lord rewards his hospitality with a gift, the announcement of Sarah's imminent childbirth (18:9–10). Lot likewise retains the nomad's value of hospitality within the city, and the Lord rewards him by

─────────────────

[165]See Theological Reflections on Book 6, Act 2, Scene 3 and Book 10, Act 3, Scene 4.

rescuing both him and his daughters. It is a high virtue to entertain pilgrims and strangers, and Abraham becomes the model of hospitality. The New Testament admonition to show hospitality (see Heb. 13:2) finds motivation in incidents such as these (see also Judg. 6; 13).

Homosexuality

The apostle Paul traces the spiritual source of this sexual perversion to people's failure to gratefully acknowledge God: "Although they knew God, they neither glorified him as God nor gave thanks to him. . . . Therefore God gave them over in the sinful desires of their hearts to sexual impurity for the degrading of their bodies with one another. . . . God gave them over to shameful lusts. . . . The men also abandoned natural relations with women and were inflamed with lust for one another" (Rom. 1:21–27). Jude writes his epistle to encourage the church to contend against false teachers "who change the grace of our God into a license for immorality" (Jude 4). He reminds them, "Sodom and Gomorrah and the surrounding towns gave themselves up to sexual immorality and perversion. They serve as an example of those who suffer the punishment of eternal fire" (Jude 7).

Justice and Mercy

Scene 3 established that God does not punish the righteous along with the wicked. Quite the contrary, he spares the wicked for the sake of the righteous. Scene 4 establishes that God does not bring judgment without careful investigation (18:20–21; 19:13), that he most certainly avenges the oppressed by punishing all oppressors (19:4, 24), that the prayers of the faithful are the conduit of judgment, and that before judging sinners he gives them opportunity to repent (19:7–8). God's judgment on saints is remedial (see Prov. 3:11–12), but when his final judgment falls on the unrepentant, like those in the Flood and Sodom, it is penal.

The following chart schematizes God's justice:

	Sodom	Lot
The Assessment	guilty (19:13)	hospitable/righteous (19:2–3)
The Judgment	destruction (19:24–28)	rescue (19:15–29)

At the same time, God is sovereign in granting mercy. He extends mercy to Lot's family (19:16; see also Theological Reflections on Book 3, "Family Salvation"),[166] including Lot's sons-in-law (19:14). He even accommodates Lot's urbanity by granting him to live in a little city close by, but he judges Lot's wife for clinging to Sodom. She becomes a sobering lesson against vacillating when God's judgment is at hand (see Luke 17:28–37; 2 Peter 2:6).

---

[166]Whereas we tend to think of the salvation of individuals, Scripture thinks in terms of the salvation of families (though cf. Ezek. 18).

God's destruction of the wicked and the deliverance of the righteous in the case of Sodom and Gomorrah versus Lot finds striking parallels with the story of Noah—two cataclysmic acts of divine "destruction" on outrageously sinful communities with only the righteous and their family spared because God "remembers" the saint. In both narratives the Lord "rains" down his judgment from heaven. He or his angels shut a door to separate the righteous from the wicked (7:16; 19:10), and in both a hand is stretched out to provide protection (see 8:9; 19:10). Both narratives draw to a conclusion with drunkenness and sexual immorality. These parallels emphasize that, when God judges the wicked, he mercifully spares the righteous. They become a paradigm for God's judgment on sin (see 2 Peter 2:5).

Consequences

Lot ends up a joke because of his earlier foolish decision to choose by sight, not by faith. Enticed by the lush valley land, he leaves the bearer of blessing and eventually sets up home in a vile and unjust city. He tries to be a host and father but fails to offer his guests real safety or his family decisive leadership. The story of Lot's offer of his daughters seems to reveal Lot as sincerely desiring to do right, but failing miserably. So corrupted by the city he had embraced, he offers an equally immoral act to stop an atrocity.

The desperate scheme by Lot's daughters to preserve seed from their drunken father brings to a conclusion the tragic account of Lot, which began with his separation from Abraham. In spite of Lot's affiliation with Sodom and the unbelief of his family, the Lord mercifully protects his lineage and land (see Deut. 2:16–19) because of Lot's condemnation of the wickedness of the men of Sodom (2 Peter 2:7–8), his hospitality to strangers, and his relationship to Abraham.

BOOK 6, ACT 2, SCENE 5:
MATRIARCH AND PATRIARCH DELIVERED
FROM PHILISTIA (20:1 – 18)

LITERARY ANALYSIS OF BOOK 6, ACT 2, SCENE 5 ———

Structure and Plot

After God's promise-filled pronouncement and Abraham's prophetic leadership, one might expect an immediate birth narrative. Instead, tension escalates as Abraham once again jeopardizes Sarah, the matriarch. More than a mere plot twist, however, Scene 5 serves an important thematic function of testing the nature of the covenant between the Lord and his elect human partner (see "Characterization" below). Once again, though the human partner is unfaithful, God is faithful. He does not cast aside his flawed saint but restores him in order to work his elective purposes through him.

The scene can be divided by the following chiastic structure:

A Abimelech takes Sarah into his harem (20:1–2).
  B God sues against Abimelech (20:3–7).
    X Abimelech and officials become afraid (20:8).
  B′ Abimelech sues against Abraham (20:9–13).
A′ Abimelech compensates Abraham and Sarah, and Abraham prays
  for Abimelech (20:14–18).

Comparison and Contrast

At the beginning of Abraham's pilgrimage and now toward its climactic end, the Lord blesses Abraham for leaving his home to follow him and overlooks his fear (Gen. 12:1–20). In this scene Abraham implicitly confesses that he lacked the faith to believe that God would and/or could protect him from rapacious kings whom he would encounter in his venture to the Promised Land. In fear, he and Sarah engineered a deceptive solution (20:12–13). Remarkably, in spite of their sinful, unbelieving deception, God rescues the kidnapped ancestress from the pagan harems, blames the kings for their covetousness, and overlooks the failure of his flawed saints.

In the second scene of Act 1 the Lord blessed Abraham in Egypt in spite of the deception (12:10–20); now in Act 2 God again enriches Abraham in spite of the same lie in Gerar. In fact, God escalates the protection and blessing of his elect. There is an ambiguity as to whether or not Pharaoh committed adultery with Sarah (12:15–16). Abimelech, however, clearly has no sex with her (20:6). The Pharaoh enriched Abraham with servants and livestock while in Egypt, but when he learned the truth that Sarah was Abraham's wife, he expelled them from Egypt's rich pastureland. By contrast, when Abimelech learns the truth, in addition to giving both Abraham and Sarah servants and livestock, he adds a fantastic amount of money (20:14, 16) and offers Abraham the pick of pasturelands. Moreover, whereas Abraham and Sarah remained childless after the deliverance from Egypt, in the next scene God blesses them with Isaac (21:1–7). Instead of punishing the flawed pilgrim, God punishes the kings who threatened them (Ps. 105:12–15). Though his saints are unfaithful, he remains faithful (2 Tim. 2:13). However, God does not inflict Abimelech with diseases, as he had Pharaoh, because Abimelech takes Sarah innocently. Unlike Pharaoh, this God-fearing king would not have killed Abraham had he known of their marriage, because to him adultery is a great sin (Gen. 20:9). Abraham, we may presume, accurately judged Pharaoh's impiety and violence (12:12), but he misjudges Abimelech's piety and ethics.

However, even though Abraham misjudges Abimelech's religion and moral behavior, he remains the Lord's covenant partner through whom God mediates his blessing to the nations (Gen. 12:2–3). As such, he must intercede to preserve Abimelech's life, for the king has taken a married woman into his harem (20:7).

Characterization

The presentation of Abraham's weaknesses is significant to the picture of Abraham's character. The biblical heroes, God's covenant partners, are never superhuman; their great acts of faith are often bounded by failings and fears. Abraham clearly struggles with his own flawed patterns. The fears he confesses here actually distinguish his obedience and faith. At Abraham's great moments of faith and leadership, the narrator does not reveal his inner thoughts. But the man presented in this scene must have overcome his fears as he left his homeland at God's command, as he risked war for brotherly commitment and justice, or as he dared to approach God to protect the righteous. Abraham has just demonstrated tremendous leadership (Act 2, Scene 3), and he will soon faithfully obey God's most challenging command (Act 2, Scene 7). By revealing Abraham's weaknesses in the midst of these significant events, the narrator captures the magnitude of Abraham's obedience and also inspires the readers' own faith struggles. The disclosure of Abraham's failures also confirms God's sovereignty and power. He is gracious in election and capable of working out his good purposes through his human servants.

Inclusio and Key Words

The stories about the jeopardy of the ancestress in pagan kings' harems form an inner frame around the Abraham cycle before the transition to the next cycle in 22:20–25:11. After Abraham's initial call to the Promised Land to become a great nation, he immediately jeopardizes Sarah in Pharaoh's harem. Now, immediately before the birth of the promised seed, he jeopardizes the matriarch in Abimelech's harem.

Within Scene 5, the key word "his wife Sarah"/"Abraham's wife Sarah" forms an inclusio (20:2, 18). Semantic equivalents occur throughout the chapter (20:3, "the woman"; 20:7, "the man's wife"; 20:11, 12, "my wife"; 20:14, "his wife"), emphasizing the vital relationship of the couple that they jeopardize with their scheme.

Escalation

One notes in this scene a developing bond between the Lord and Sarah. In Act 1, Scene 2, Sarah is implicitly the child-bearer, but she is scarcely mentioned. Even in Pharaoh's harem, though protected, she plays a minor role. In Act 2, she is explicitly included in the Abrahamic covenant (17:15–16), included in the birth announcement (18:13–15), and now receives a fabulous sum of money to restore her violated honor (20:16; see comment below).

Act 2, Scene 5 opens with Abraham settled by an oasis in the extreme south of Canaan, which has an annual rainfall of less than four inches per year. He then makes a visit to the royal city of Gerar (20:1). The scene ends with Abraham settled in the royal pasturelands around Gerar.

EXEGETICAL NOTES TO BOOK 6, ACT 2, SCENE 5 ————

Abimelech Takes Sarah into His Harem (20:1 – 2)

1. from there. Abraham has been near Mamre (18:1).

into the region of the Negev and lived. The narrator provides the same ominous beginning as with Abraham's encounter with the Pharaoh: "set out . . . toward the Negev" (12:9), "to Egypt to live" (12:10).

Kadesh and Shur. The area between the oasis at Kadesh and the Egyptian defense wall at Shur (see 14:7; 16:7). Although Abraham settles in Kadesh and Shur, a grazing area, he stays for a while near the Philistine royal city of Gerar, a town located about halfway between Beersheba and Gaza.

2. my sister. Abraham's reason for his half-truth, fear for his life, is given in 20:11 and 12:11–13. However, he is without excuse for acting out of fear rather than faith. God has pledged that the promised seed will be through Sarah, a bond now even more firm than when they had traveled to Egypt (17:18; 18:9–15).

Abimelech. This is attested as a personal name for Gideon's son (Judg. 8:31), for a Philistine king at the time of David (heading to Ps. 34), for an Israelite priest (1 Chron. 18:16), and for the king of Tyre in the El-Amarna Letters. This common West Semitic name means "My father is king." Probably this Abimelech is a father or grandfather of the Abimelech Isaac will encounter (see 26:1).

sent for Sarah. Sarah's youthful beauty has been rejuvenated (see 12:11; 18:11, 13). The king brings to his harem a woman in her nineties (see 12:4; 17:17; 18:12; 21:6–7).

took. See 6:2; 12:15.[167] On the brink of Isaac's conception (see 18:10–14; 21:1–2), the program of redemption is placed in jeopardy. There is no doubt that salvation depends on the faithful Lord, not on unfaithful humans.

God Sues against Abimelech (20:3 – 7)

3. God. The narrator uses "God" in relation to people in general, rather than "LORD," God's name to the covenant people (see 2:4 and "Naming" in Literary Analysis of Book 6, Act 2, Scene 2).

in a dream. Dreams were a mode of revelation, even to those outside of the covenant (see 28:12; 31:24; 37:5–9; 40:5; 41:1; Num. 22:9, 20). In Genesis 1–11 and in the early years of the patriarchs, God communicates through theophany and dreams and visions; by the end of Genesis, only by providence. This development resembles the Hebrew canon. In the Torah God simply speaks to Moses; to the prophets he gives visions and dreams; and in the Writings he works mostly through providence.

You are as good as dead. Because of general revelation, people recognize the sacred character of marriage (cf. Lev. 20:22; Deut. 22:22). Adultery

---

[167]Contra R. Polzin, "'The Ancestress of Israel in Danger' in Danger," *Semeia* 3 (1975): 81–97.

was considered a "great sin" among many Semitic groups, as evidenced at Ugarit and in Egyptian marriage contracts (see 26:10; 39:9; also "clear conscience" in 20:5 below).

4. Lord. Abimelech uses a general term of deference, not a title for God (i.e., "LORD"). Abimelech knew the true God but not his salvation through Abraham's seed (see also Melchizedek, Gen. 14).

will you destroy an innocent nation? Abimelech's argument, like Abraham's, is based on the conviction that God does only what is right and good (see 4:7; 18:25). If God would spare the evil city of Sodom for ten righteous people, how much more an innocent nation? Abimelech's relational integrity with God is based on the king's moral rectitude with people.

nation. The king and his nation are inseparable. He is the breath in their nostrils (Lam. 4:20).

5. clear conscience. The Hebrew is literally "blameless of heart" (cf. 1 Kings 9:4; Job 1:1; Ps. 78:72). God judges those without the law by their consciences (see 3:8; Rom. 2:14–15; see also "blameless" in Gen. 6:9).

6. I know. The statement implies God's personal omniscience.

from sinning against me. See Ps. 51:4.

7. prophet. This is the first time this term is used in the Bible. Abraham is a man of God who, having received revelation, mediates God's word (Ex. 4:15; 7:1) and makes intercession (Gen. 12:7; 15:1; 18:18; cf. Num. 11:2; 14:13–19; 21:7; Deut. 9:20; 1 Sam. 7:8–9; 12:19, 23; 1 Kings 17:20; Job 42:8; Jer. 7:16; 37:3; 42:2; Amos 7:2, 5).[168]

pray. Moses prayed for Miriam after she defamed him (Num. 12:13) and Job interceded for his three friends who besmirched him (Job 42:8).

will live . . . will die. Life and death depend on obedience to God's word (cf. Deut. 30:15; Josh. 24:15).

Abimelech and Officials Become Afraid (20:8)

8. Early the next morning. This is another example of prompt obedience.

summoned all his officials. The entire royal council fears God. A good king produces a good nation (see 1 Kings 2; Prov. 25:4–5).

they were very much afraid. This is a primary response of pagans to God. It counters Abraham's worry that they did not fear God (see 20:11; cf. Jonah 1:10).

Abimelech Sues against Abraham (20:9–13)

9. Abimelech called Abraham. Armed with acquittal by God, Abimelech turns on Abraham. As before, Abraham must bear the reproach of a pagan king for failing to trust God.

---

[168]For more bibliography, see also Sarna, *Genesis,* 361, ch. 20 n. 6.

What have you done to us? Both Pharaoh and Abimelech ask, "What have you done?" Abimelech, however, demonstrates greater leadership. He speaks of "us" (meaning the nation), not "me" (2 Sam. 24; Ps. 72); appeals to a moral code, sin, and "things . . . that should not be done"; allows Abraham to explain himself (see 20:10); offers Abraham the best of his land; and protects Sarah's honor.

great guilt. See verse 3.

11. Abraham replied. In his attempt to mitigate his guilt, Abraham tacitly admits his sin and exonerates Abimelech. He failed to investigate the situation and to trust God.

I said to myself. Note the irony. Abimelech feared God more than Abraham did!

fear of God. This phrase should be distinguished from "fear of the LORD." The latter refers to respect for the special revelation of Scripture, while "fear of God" involves general revelation, moral standards known by humans through conscience and accepted by them out of fear of God's judgment.[169]

12. my sister. See 11:29; 12:11–12. The law against this kind of kinship marriage was not yet given (Lev. 18:9, 11; Deut. 27:22; Ezek. 22:11). Even after the giving of the law, its violation was considered a lesser wrong than some others (2 Sam. 13:13; Ezek. 22:11).

13. wander [$hit^c\hat{u}$]. If the root is t^ch, its plural form with God as subject is difficult to explain. Possibly the root is ^cwh, in which case the form is singular.

Everywhere we go. Abraham thought the kidnapping of foreign women was normal in the countries through which he must pass. He intended no insult in particular against Abimelech.

Abimelech Compensates Abraham and Sarah, and Abraham Prays for Abimelech (20:14–19)

14. Abimelech brought sheep . . . to Abraham. Abimelech gives gifts to Abraham (20:14–15) and to Sarah (20:16) to honor God and their special relationship with him, not to compensate for guilt (cf. 12:19–20). God not only delivers his elect out of dreadful peril but blesses them with unexpected and undeserved riches (see 12:16 and note).

15. live. The same word is used in 20:1 for his settling in the extreme south.

16. giving your brother. Social convention demands that the gift to Sarah be given through the male head of the family.

a thousand shekels. This is a fabulously large sum. A Babylonian laborer, usually paid a half shekel per month, would have had to work 167 years to earn such a sum.

---

[169]Human conscience commends God's special revelation to the Gentiles (see Deut. 4:6; Mic. 4:2; 2 Cor. 4:2).

cover the offense. Abimelech aims to restore in the eyes of others Sarah's honor, which he had tarnished, albeit innocently.

17. Abraham prayed. Abraham prays as God's prophet, responsible to be a blessing to the nations. In this act, Abraham would surely be reminded of God's power in his life and of the tremendous impact each of his deeds has on the nations around him in light of his call.

they could have children again. If God can answer Abraham's prayer for sterile pagan women, how much more for Abraham's wife?

18. closed up. Abraham and Sarah have convincing proof that the Lord gives conception (see 16:2; 21:1–2). Here also is dramatic irony: when Sarah is among them they become barren; when she leaves, wombs are opened but she remains barren.

THEOLOGICAL REFLECTIONS ON BOOK 6, ACT 2, SCENE 5 ————————————————

Grace to the Elect

Calvin declares, "In this history, the Holy Spirit presents to us a remarkable instance, both of the infirmity of man, and of the grace of God."[170] God's sovereign grace is clearly revealed in this chapter. On the brink of Isaac's conception (see 18:10–14; 21:1–2), Abraham places the program of redemption in jeopardy. God extends justice to Abimelech but mercy to Abraham and Sarah. Salvation depends on the faithful Lord, not on his unfaithful servants.

The Christian and Pluralism

Genesis begins with the formation of every person in the image of God. According to Paul, God has given everyone a general revelation of himself (Rom. 1:19–20). This basic recognition of God's ways can be broadly understood as "fear of God." As Whybray explains, there is a general "moral standard" to which all people adhere.[171] It is on this basis that God judges and interacts with humanity. And it is to this general understanding that God's covenant people, those who have responded to the "special revelation" of God's word, can appeal in their interactions with others. Of the Ten Commandments, no rationale is given for the four commandments dedicated to human relationships. These are understood to have broad appeal for all people.

Abraham provides a model for the Christian in the modern, pluralistic world. In that world, God holds each person accountable for a fundamental fear of God and essential consideration of human relationships. And at that level, God extends grace to the "pagan." Even to Pharaoh, who according to

---

[170]Calvin, *Genesis*, 521.

[171]R. N. Whybray, *Wisdom in Proverbs: The Concept of Wisdom in Proverbs 1–9* (SBT 24; London: SCM, 1965), 95.

Abraham might have committed murder, God sends warning of the mistaken choice. God also uses Pharaoh to reprove Abraham. To the God-fearing Abimelech, God speaks in a vision, and he confirms Abimelech's innocence. Mysteriously, God chooses the priest-king Melchizedek to anoint his special blessing upon Abraham. Finally, with circumspect justice, God destroys the people of Sodom and Gomorrah who arrogantly defy God and inflict others with their vile disregard of human dignity.

In this pluralistic world, Abraham walks with divine sensitivity, tailoring his relationships to people's level of relationship with God. The background of Melchizedek, the priest-king, is a mystery, but Abraham recognizes God's anointing, and he honors Melchizedek. For the evil Sodom and Gomorrah, which bring adversity to his nephew, Abraham pleads that God spare the cities for the sake of the righteous. Rightly Abraham must receive the rebuke of the pagan kings, but he must also intercede for Abimelech before God.

Intercession

Abimelech, a God-fearing Canaanite king, deals more righteously with Sarah than does Abraham. As a reward, God deals justly with the God-fearing pagan king by restraining him from adultery. Although God deals justly with him, Abimelech does not embrace by faith Abraham's election and forfeits the right to become part of salvation history. Abimelech does not recognize Abraham as the mediator of personal covenant blessing (see 17:5). Justice and salvation must be distinguished. Although Abraham is in the wrong, Abimelech must ask Abraham, God's elect instrument of salvation, to intercede for him. God's human covenant partner, who nearly brought death to Abimelech by his scheming (20:3), is still the means by which God gives life and blessing (20:17–18). Abraham intercedes as a prophet, not as one who has been wronged (unlike Num. 12 and Job 42). In his role as intercessor for the Gentiles, he prefigures Jesus Christ (Isa. 53:12; Rom. 8:34). We in the church are often sinful and failing, but still we are called to be the intercessors for those who do not receive Jesus Christ.

BOOK 6, ACT 2, SCENE 6: ISAAC'S BIRTH AND BLESSINGS IN LAND (21:1–21)

LITERARY ANALYSIS OF BOOK 6, ACT 2, SCENE 6 ————

Alternate Structure of 21:8–28:4

David Dorsey, citing his student David Carr, suggests that this scene representing the birth of Isaac opens up a new unit featuring Isaac and displaying the following chiastic structure:[172]

---

[172]Dorsey, *Literary Structure,* 58.

A Yahweh's choice of the younger son Isaac (21:8–19)
- family rift involving elder son Ishmael and younger son Isaac
- to protect favored younger son, matriarch proposes that elder son should leave0
- she appeals to husband
- blessing and promise of great progeny given to banished son

  B Marriage of nonchosen elder son Ishmael (an archer) to foreign woman (21:20–21)

    C Strife with King Abimelech of Gerar over Abraham's well (21:22–34)
- treaty at Beersheba with Abimelech, involving General Phicol
- unlike previous time at Gerar, matriarch is not taken by king
- naming of "Beersheba"

      D Risking everything for the covenant (22:1–19)
- Abraham's willingness to give up everything, even the life of his beloved son, for Yahweh's covenant

        E Nonchosen genealogy: family of Nahor (22:20–24)

          F Death of Sarah, Abraham's wife (23:1–20)
- her burial in the cave of Machpelah

            G CENTER: Yahweh selects Rebekah as chosen matriarch and Isaac's wife (24:1–67)

          F' Death of Abraham; Abraham's second wife (25:1–10)
- his death and burial in the cave of Machpelah

        E' Nonchosen genealogy: family of Ishmael (25:11–18)

      D' Scorning the covenant (25:19–34)[173]
- Esau's life is more important to him than the covenant; he shows contempt for his birthright

    C' Strife with King Abimelech of Gerar over Abraham's wells (26:1–33)
- treaty at Beersheba with Abimelech, involving general Phicol
- like Abraham's first time at Gerar, matriarch is taken by king
- naming of 'Beersheba'

  B' Marriage of nonchosen elder son Esau (an archer) to foreign women (26:34–35)

A' Yahweh's choice of the younger son (27:1–28:4)
- family rift involving elder son Esau and younger son Jacob
- to protect favored younger son, matriarch proposes that younger son should leave
- she appeals to husband
- blessing and prayer for great progeny given to banished son

---

[173]Unit D' exhibits no strong link to unit D.

This unit transcends Books 6 and 8 and features the successors to Abraham's holy patriarchy. A and A' begin and essentially end the life of Isaac as he passes on the patriarchal blessing to Jacob. Both Isaac and Jacob are divinely elected to their patriarchies by nonconventional means, not by smooth primogeniture rights. Isaac is a baby begotten by "dead" parents, and Jacob receives the family blessing from "blind" Isaac, who thinks he is blessing Jacob's older and profane brother.

B and B' show that the nonelect offspring marry foreign wives, unlike the elect Isaac and Jacob, who marry within the family. Their foreign marriages signal their lack of election and commitment to the covenant. C and C' show that Isaac inherits Abraham's blessings. D and D', though the weakest parallels in this chiastic pattern, contrast Abraham's radical commitment to the God of the covenant with Esau's lack of any commitment. At the same time, D' also signals Jacob's commitment to it. E and E' mark God's blessings on Abraham by multiplying even his nonchosen descendants. If they are blessed, how much more the elect! F and F' represent the first patriarch and matriarch stepping off the stage of sacred history. G features Rebekah's remarkable election as the matriarch to bridge the generations in this sacred history.

Structure and Plot of 21:1–21

After excruciating tension and delay, the promised birth arrives. But astonishingly, the birth story is reported in only a few short verses before the narrative dashes into more conflict (see also Theological Reflections of Scene 6 and Literary Analysis of Scene 7 below). Although one might anticipate the birth story as the act's climax, this narrative of Abraham's walk with God and faith in a seed will not crest until Abraham has faced the ultimate challenge to his faith, the sacrifice of his son.

The birth of Isaac does, however, bring resolution to the dilemma set out at the beginning of the account of Terah (11:27–32) and of Act 2 (see 16:1). Sarah, who until now has only observed the fruitfulness of others, is no longer barren.

The conflict of seed, however, is not just about waiting for the miraculous offspring but about faith's response to God's election of that seed. Abraham responds faithfully by naming his son "Isaac" (21:3; cf. 17:9) and by circumcising him (21:4; cf. 17:10), and Sarah responds with praise that breaks into laughter at God's goodness (21:6). However, Ishmael—a foil—reflects his mother's defiant spirit against Sarah (16:4–5) and mocks God's miraculous gift (21:9).

We have already noted the structural similarity of the framing scenes around Act 2 that involve the election of Sarah and her son and the rejection of Hagar and her son (see Act 2, Scene 1, 16:1–16). Scene 6 of Act 2 presents the Lord's gracious and mighty acts for Sarah and his provision and care for Hagar and Ishmael. This scene consists of two incidents, the birth of Isaac

(21:1–7) and the expulsion of Hagar and Ishmael from Abraham's household and inheritance (21:8–21). The episodes are held together chronologically by the smooth transition from the birth of Isaac to his weaning (21:8) and lexically by a pun on the name "Isaac" (see below). However, the two conflicting episodes cohere in their fulfillment of the divine word (21:1, 12): the birth of Isaac occurs as a fulfillment of "what [the LORD] had promised" (21:1), and the expulsion of Hagar and her son occurs as a result of God's word to Abraham that "through Isaac . . . your offspring will be reckoned" (21:12). Moreover, both episodes present the Lord's gracious and mighty acts for Sarah and his care and provision for Hagar and Ishmael.

Key Word and Naming

The key word, the root *ṣāḥaq*, occurs five times in the eight verses of the first incident (*yiṣḥāq* Isaac, 21:3, 4, 5; *ṣāḥaq*, "to laugh," 21:6 [2x]). In the second incident, the key word occurs in a pun (21:9). Instead of laughing with praise to God, Ishmael "mocked" (*mᵉṣaḥēq*) Isaac.

The narrator stylistically matches the Lord's exclusion of the mocker from salvation by not naming him. Instead, he speaks of the "son of Hagar" (lit., 21:9), "her son" (21:10), "his son" (21:11), "son of the handmaid" (21:13; cf. 11), and "the boy" (*naʿar*, 21:12, 17, 18, 19, 20; *yeled*, 21:14, 15, 16). Yet the text is ambiguous. The nonelect son is treasured. Everyone (i.e., the Lord, the angel, Hagar, Abraham) but Sarah agrees on the preciousness of Ishmael. Ishmael experiences God's promise (21:13, 18), provision (21:19), and presence (21:20).

Comparison

Abraham's natural and supernatural seed both experience God's testing and blessing. Hagar and Ishmael's rugged trek has striking parallels to the challenge Abraham and Isaac will have to face: (1) journey into the unknown at the command of the Lord; (2) provision for the journey; (3) child at the point of death; (4) intervention of God's messenger; (5) parent's sighting of the way out; and (6) promise of future blessing. Abraham must relinquish his natural seed in order to embrace God's supernatural promises. Yet even as God initiates an extraordinary future for the supernatural seed, he directs the destiny of the natural seed.

EXEGETICAL NOTES TO BOOK 6, ACT 2, SCENE 6 ———

Incident One: The Birth of Isaac (21:1–7)

The Lord Gives Birth and Keeps Covenant (21:1–2)

1. **was gracious** [*pqd*]. The Hebrew is literally "visited," connoting the direct intervention of God. The Hebrew here is also translated "come to your aid" in 50:24. God intervenes to shape destiny, sometimes for judgment, and often, as here, for salvation.

to Sarah. Sarah, not Abraham, is mentioned first, and it is she who speaks in this first episode. Sarah's role has significantly increased.

he had promised. This is matched by "as God commanded him" (21:4). God's promises are to be met with faith and obedience (see "Structure and Plot of 21:1–21" in Literary Analysis above).

2. Sarah became pregnant and bore a son. This is the resolution to the barrenness noted so long ago in 11:30.

in his old age. See 17:17, 24; 18:11–14.

Abraham Keeps Covenant (21:3–4)

3–4. Abraham gave the name . . . as God commanded him. In the naming of Isaac (see 17:19) and in circumcision (21:4; see 17:9–12), Abraham keeps covenant.

3. Isaac. The name means "he laughs," a pun with the laughter of disbelief and joy Abraham and Sarah have expressed.

4. eight days old. See 17:12.

Abraham's Age and Sarah's Laughter (21:5–7)

5. a hundred years. The ages of the postdiluvians have decreased substantially (cf. 11:10–26). To produce at one hundred years and at ninety years is miraculous (see 17:17).

6. Sarah said. Compare this statement with her earlier accusation of God (16:2). The narrator highlights Sarah, recording only her speech in this birth story (21:1–7).

God has brought me laughter. Sarah credits God with changing her laughter of incredulity (17:17–19; 18:12–15) into joy. All will now laugh in joy and amazement with Sarah.

7. children. The unexpected plural (cf. 21:2)[174] implies that she is looking beyond Isaac to his offspring who are destined to bless the earth.

Incident Two: The Expulsion of Hagar and Ishmael (21:8–21)

Setting of the Crisis (21:8–9)

8. The child grew. With this chronological notice, the second incident flows smoothly from the first.

weaned. This rite of passage from the dangerous stage of infancy to childhood usually occurred at about three years of age (1 Sam. 1:22–25; 2 Macc. 7:27). The Egyptian *Instruction of Any* (7.19), addressed to his disciple, speaks of "the mother's breast in your mouth for three years."[175]

---

[174]This is a countable plural. It cannot be explained by an appeal to plurals of collectives such as plural of result or plural of extension (see *IBHS*, §7.4.1; *pace* Sarna, *Genesis*, 146).

[175]M. Lichtheim, *Ancient Egyptian Literature. Volume 2: The Old and Middle Kingdoms* (Berkeley, Los Angeles, London: University of California Press 1975), 141.

9. Sarah saw. From her experience with Hagar (see Gen. 16), Sarah perceives the significance of Ishmael's disdain for Isaac and his threat to her son's inheritance.

son whom Hagar. Ishmael is never actually referred to by name in this scene, signifying his secondary position to Isaac and possibly his objectification by other characters. The references to Ishmael do differ in relation to the speaker. To Sarah, he is the "son whom Hagar . . . had borne" or "that slave woman's son" (21:9, 10). To Abraham he is "his son" or "the boy" (21:11,14). To God he is "the boy" (21:12, 17, 18, 20).

mocking [*mᵉsaḥēq*]. The Hebrew root means "to laugh" (see "Key word and Naming" in the Literary Analysis above), but the form here signifies "to laugh malevolently" (Gen. 19:14; Ex. 32:6; Judg. 16:25) rather than merely to play innocently.[176] Sarah perceives a real threat in the teenager's scoffing reaction to her joy and hope. The Lord's response to send the boy away validates this interpretation. The son of the slave woman persecutes the son of the free (see Gal. 4:29). His disdain for Isaac imitates his mother's for Sarah.

Conflict between Sarah and Abraham Regarding Expulsion of the Other Son (21:10–11)

10. Get rid of. Sarah's request is to disinherit Ishmael so he will never share in the inheritance (see 25:5–6).

11. distressed . . . because it concerned his son. Paternal love alone, not moral or legal concerns, explains Abraham's distress (see 16:6; 17:18). In the Lipit-Ishtar law code (ca. 1875 B.C.), a clause stipulates that if a slave bears children and the father then grants freedom to her and her children, "the children of the slave shall not divide the estate with the children of their (former) master."[177] Sarah's demand to expel Hagar and Ishmael from any share in the inheritance appears to be based on moral and legal grounds.

because it concerned his son. How much greater will be his distress about the sacrifice of Isaac?

Resolution: God Endorses Sarah (21:12–13)

12. God said. See 12:1; 15:1; 17:1.

maidservant. The same Hebrew word *ʾāmâ* is translated "slave woman" in 21:10 and differs from the one translated "maidservant" (*šipḥâ*) in 16:1. The former identifies Hagar as married to Abraham; the latter, as a possession and laborer for Sarah.

Listen to whatever Sarah tells you. Sarah's character has undergone a change. In her first conflict with Hagar, she lacked faith, blamed Abraham,

---

[176]Pace NRSV. HALOT (1019, no. 1 abs.) defines the root as "to joke (19:14) to make fun of (21:90)" or "to amuse oneself wildly (Ex 32:6)." This meaning, however, must be distinguished from its meaning with the preposition.

[177]ANET, 160, no. 25.

and mistreated her maidservant. Now her concerns are approved by God. God overcomes Abraham's hesitation on two grounds. Abraham's lineage will be reckoned through Isaac, and Ishmael's descendants will become a great nation in spite of his expulsion and wanderings in the desert.

your offspring will be reckoned. Everlasting blessing is pronounced only on those of promise (see 17:7, 19; Heb. 11:17–19; see also Theological Reflections below).

13. nation. Because of God's great love for Abraham, even his natural children, who will not directly participate in the redemptive kingdom, are blessed on earth (see 17:6). Since Abraham cannot provide for Ishmael, God will provide for him (21:18; cf. 16:10).

Abraham Obeys: Expulsion of Hagar and Ishmael (21:14)

14. Early the next morning. Once again, God's promise (21:12) is matched by Abraham's quick obedience (cf. 22:3).

skin of water. This would hold approximately 3 gallons or 24 pounds.

with the boy. The Hebrew literally reads, "He gave unto Hagar. He set upon her shoulders, and together with the boy [or, and the boy], and he sent her away." Previous translations, which left open the suggestion that Abraham put the lad, not the water, on Hagar's shoulders, have generated some confusion and been a favorite reading of source critics. Such a reading, however, is unnecessary and unwarranted.

boy. The Hebrew for *boy, na'ar,* simply means inexperienced and so can refer to any age. Even Solomon at forty years of age can say, "I am but a *na'ar.*" The word is somewhat misleading, for it does not conjure up the image of a sixteen-year-old (see next note). The NIV renders two different Hebrew terms "boy": *na'ar* (21:12, 17, 18, 19, 20) and *yeled* (21:14, 15, 16). Hamilton distinguishes them: With reference to God Ishmael is always called a *na'ar* ("boy," 21:12, 17, 18, 20). With reference to Hagar he is called a *yeled* ("child," 21:14, 15, 16). The use of *na'ar* in verse 19 is ambiguous, for God opened Hagar's eyes to give water to the *na'ar.* "From this passage one could conclude that *yeled* and *na'ar* are semantically distinct: *yeled* describes a biological relationship while *na'ar* suggests care and concern."[178]

Beersheba. See 21:31 and notes.

Ishmael Near Death (21:15 – 16)

15. put. Source critics think that this episode is a doublet of the same incident of Hagar's flight into the desert recorded in 16:14. They note that if these are two distinct incidents, according to the received chronology, Ishmael is at the time of the second flight about sixteen years of age (cf. 16:16; 21:5, 8). They wrongly interpret 21:14 to mean that Abraham set a young

---

[178]V. P. Hamilton, "*yld*," *NIDOTTE,* 2:457.

"boy" on Hagar's shoulders, a notion incommensurate with a sixteen-year-old youth (see notes 21:14). They further argue that she would not "put" a sixteen-year-old under a bush. The Hebrew form of the verb rendered "put" means more literally "to throw," as it is translated in 37:20, 22, 24. However, it can have the broader meaning "to expose, abandon" (Gen. 21:15; Jer. 38:6; Ezek. 16:5).[179] Cogan likewise renders it "abandon,"[180] a notion pertinent to a loving mother having to abandon her beloved teenager under the shade of a scrawny bush in the scorching desert.

God Intervenes (21:17–19)

17. angel of God. The term "God" reflects his role with the nonelect (see 2:4; 20:3).

from heaven. The angel speaks with divine authority (cf. 22:11, 15).

What is the matter, Hagar? See 16:8; 18:9.

God has heard. God's grace is not restricted to Isaac's line (see 16:11; cf. Ex. 2:23; 1 Sam. 7:8–9; Ps. 107:19).

the boy crying. Ishmael provoked their plight; his prayer now leads to their salvation.

19. opened her eyes. God affirms his promise with provision (see Gen. 22:13; 2 Kings 6:17).

Summary of Ishmael's Career (21:20–21)

20–21. God . . . wife for him. The persecutor's destiny is sealed; he will not inherit the divine promises of land and offspring that bless the earth.

archer. Ishmael survives by his weapons.

21. Desert of Paran. See 14:6 and note.

Egypt. See 16:1 and 24:3–4.

THEOLOGICAL REFLECTIONS ON BOOK 6, ACT 2, SCENE 6 ──────────────

Divine History

This brief domestic scene is played out on the larger stage of Abraham's international conflicts with Abimelech, first with reference to the seed (Scene 5, 20:18), then with reference to the land (Scene 7, 21:22–34). Against the backdrop of these political events, the birth narrative appears inauspicious, unless one understands the divine program. Both the birth of Isaac and that of Christ occur in the midst of immense political tensions. They seem like minor moments on the broad stage of history. The challenge is to discern the divine plan. Even today, events that appear insignificant to us may be part of God's great plans.

---

[179]F. Stolz, "šlk," TLOT, 3:1335.
[180]M. Cogan, "A Technical Term for Exposure," JNES 27 (1968): 133–35.

Covenant

The birth narrative underscores the covenant arrangement. God keeps his promise to give Abraham a son by Sarah (21:1−2; cf. 17:1−6, 15−16; 18:1−15), and Abraham obeys by naming him Isaac (21:3; cf. 17:16) and by circumcising him (21:4−5; cf. 17:9−14), while Sarah responds with praise (21:6−7).

The Supernatural Versus the Natural

The divine program does not depend on Ishmael's genetic connection nor on Isaac's righteousness but on divine choice (Rom. 9:6−8). God initiates covenant promises ("said," "spoken"); the promise bearer in faith believes and keeps covenant. The future lies in God's hands, which make the barren fruitful, not in human hands, which presume, plan, and seek to manufacture the future (cf. Gal. 4:4). In Gal. 4:21−31 Paul allegorizes this story, associating Judaism with Hagar and Ishmael, the way of human effort and so failure, and Christianity with Sarah and Isaac, the way of sovereign grace and promise embraced by faith and so success. Hagar and Sarah are types:

Hagar	Sarah
Mount Sinai	Mount Jerusalem
Necessity and coercion	Gift and freedom
Determination and planning	Gift and grace

God's promises will reach their fulfillment through supernatural offspring, not through natural schemes (see Rom. 9:7−8).

Conflict of Seeds

It is not the natural children who inherit the promise (Rom. 9:8); rather, they persecute the sons of promise (see Gen. 21:9; Gal. 4:29−30). They stand in opposition to Abraham's seed through Sarah (Gen. 17). The descendants of Ishmael, though the descendants of Abraham, in their hostility to the descendants of Israel belong to the seed of the Serpent.

Yet, the relationship of the Lord to Hagar and her son is ambiguous. Hagar showed disdain for Sarah, and now her son shows contempt for Isaac. The Lord rejects them for salvation history and grants them no inheritance in the land. Nevertheless, he hears their prayers and provides them with protection and progeny because of their relationship to Abraham. Ishmael has no name in this story. His future depends on his relationship with Abraham and Hagar.

BOOK 6, ACT 2, SCENE 7:
COVENANT WITH ABIMELECH (21:22–34)

LITERARY ANALYSIS OF BOOK 6, ACT 2, SCENE 7 ————

Plot and Structure

This scene occurs at the same time as the events of Scene 6 but focuses on different characters and tensions. This second conflict with Abimelech creates a bracket around the Isaac birth narrative. Whereas the first conflict, Scene 5 (20:1–18), concerned jeopardy of the seed, the second conflict, Scene 7 (21:22–34), concerns jeopardy of the land (i.e., well rights). In each scene God ensures Abraham and his offspring protection and provision. In this scene Abraham negotiates as more than an equal with Abimelech the Philistine king.

The scene consists of two covenant-making incidents. In the first, Abimelech sues for a nonaggression covenant in perpetuity with Abraham (21:22–24). In the second, Abraham sues for a covenant with Abimelech that the king acknowledges and guarantees Abraham's right to the well of Beersheba (21:25–34).

The two incidents are linked by Abraham's complaint about a well that Abimelech's servants have stolen from him. In light of the nonaggression pact the threatened king has sought, a confident Abraham now feels free to set matters right about his claim to the wells he has dug.

Inclusio

Three inclusios frame the scene: time references ("at that time," 21:22; "for a long time," 21:34); the approach and departure of Abimelech and Phicol (21:22, 32); and the acknowledgement of God (21:23, 33). Framing his account with these acknowledgements of God, the narrator leaves no doubt that Abraham's upward mobility and successful treaty are due to God's grace. Abimelech and the captain of his military forces open their request for a nonaggression pact in perpetuity with Abraham by acknowledging that "God is with you in everything you do" (21:23). Abraham responds to the well grant, implicitly from God, by setting the well apart as a worship site for the Lord, the eternal God.

Key Word

The two covenants are unified by the Hebrew root *šbᶜ*. This root, from which is derived both the verb "to swear" and the numeral "seven," occurs nine times in these thirteen verses. The verb "to swear" occurs three times, twice in the nonaggression pact incident (21:23, 24), and once in the well incident (21:31). The other derivative of the same root, "seven" (*šebaᶜ*) occurs three times in the second incident (21:28, 29, 30). The pun comes together in the place name "Beersheba" (21:31, 32, 33). Each of the names of the principal characters, Abraham and Abimelech, occurs exactly seven times.

EXEGETICAL NOTES TO BOOK 6, ACT 2, SCENE 7

Abimelech Sues for an Oath of Nonaggression (21:22–24)

22. At that time. This indicates that the events of Scene 7 occur at the same time as the events of Scene 6 (see Literary Analysis above).

Abimelech. Abraham's first encounter with Abimelech pertained to offspring and grazing rights (20:1–18); this one, to well rights. The Philistine king's visit gives further assurances that Isaac will receive the promised inheritance.

Phicol. This is an Anatolian name.

commander. The treaty at Beersheba is made between powerful forces.

23. Now swear to me. Abimelech sues for an oath of nonaggression. The supernatural blessing on Abraham, an alien shepherd, can be measured by a king and his commander coming to him for a nonaggression pact (see 14:23; 23:6).

before God. This formula signals oaths of consequence (see 21:31, 33).

my descendants. The covenant is to endure in perpetuity, indicating that Abimelech believes that Abraham will have an enduring posterity. Nevertheless, it is no more reliable than any other human document. The next generation will turn hostile to Isaac and out of envy stop up his wells (see 26:15–31).

not deal falsely . . . Show to me . . . same kindness. *Ḥesed* ("kindness") denotes a voluntary commitment by a stronger party to meet the needs of a weaker party. The term shows clearly that in Abimelech's mind the shepherd with his God is at least equal to him and his army commander.

Abraham Sues for Covenant Granting Him Beersheba (21:25–34)

25. complained [*ykḥ*]. The verb means "to determine what is right." The fact that the shepherd remonstrates the king about the wrongdoing of the king's servants and the king tries to excuse himself for their behavior reveals the respect that the king had for Abraham.

well of water. Water, so essential for survival and livestock, is a precious commodity.

26. But Abimelech said. He really may not know, or this comment may also be a negotiating tactic. It seems just as probable that a keen ruler would know about the activities of his servants. In fact, the tensions between his servants and Abraham might have prompted his request for a nonaggression pact.

27. So Abraham brought sheep and cattle. According to Wenham, the fact "that only Abraham gave gifts suggests he is the lesser party and principal beneficiary of the treaty."[181] In fact, however, Abraham, the greater in this partnership, is giving gifts to the lesser to guarantee no further infractions of Abraham's rights (see 21:23).

---

[181]Wenham, *Genesis 16–50*, 93.

30. Accept. By accepting the gift and swearing an oath before witnesses (see 21:31), Abimelech is obliged to acknowledge Abraham's right to the well.

31. Beersheba. The name means either "Well of oath" or "Well of seven," a pun on the key word. The name bears witness to the treaty between the two men and Abraham's right to the well. Beersheba marked the southern boundary of Israel during the monarchy.

swore. A verbal agreement of the covenant is not enough (21:23–24). It has to be ratified by an oath (21:31).

32. Philistines. See 10:14.

33. tamarisk tree. The planting of this small tree of the Negev probably serves as a landmark of God's grace, a pledge that Abraham will stay in the land, and perhaps as a symbol of God's shading presence (see note on 12:6).

called upon. See 12:8.

Eternal God. See 14:19. As on other occasions, Abraham refers to God by a name appropriate to his particular deeds. The well of Beersheba symbolizes life for Abraham's posterity.

34. stayed. The Hebrew here is translated elsewhere, "he stayed for a while." It denotes an alien, in this case a pilgrim. Though an alien, he is granted a settled place (see 20:15).

THEOLOGICAL REFLECTIONS ON
BOOK 6, ACT 2, SCENE 7 —————————————————

Blessing

"When a person's ways are pleasing to the Lord, he makes even his enemies sue for peace with him" (Prov. 16:7; author's translation).[182] The treaty with Abimelech, an intervening episode in the story about an heir, returns to the land. This report of a Philistine king and his commander suing for a nonaggression pact in perpetuity between Abraham and his descendants provides concrete evidence of God's blessing on Abraham and continued assurance that his seed will possess the land. Even though it is the Negev, Abraham has found a secure place to sojourn with a permanent well. This covenant is the small beginning of something much greater. The naming of the site in commemoration of that covenant, the planting of a commemorative tree, and the name of the Lord, "Eternal God," continues to strengthen the faith of pilgrims on their journey to the Promised Land.

---

[182]NJPS paraphrases, "When the Lord is pleased with a man's conduct, he may turn even his enemies into allies."

BOOK 6, ACT 2, SCENE 8: SACRIFICE OF ISAAC AND GOD'S OATH (22:1–19)

LITERARY ANALYSIS OF BOOK 6, ACT 2, SCENE 8 ————

Climax and Inclusio

The account of Terah's descendants (11:27–25:11), a narrative devoted to the growth of Abraham's faith within the context of God's call and promise to make him into a great nation, now reaches its climax. The tensions of Act 2 and of the entire narrative for Abraham's offspring and faith converge poignantly in this scene. The commitments of both the Lord and Abraham are now tested to their limits. With the perplexing command to Abraham to sacrifice his son, how will God fulfill his commitment to make Abraham into a great nation that blesses the earth? Confronted by such a costly sacrifice, how will Abraham remain obedient to his covenant commitment? This scene presents the radical nature of true faith: tremendous demands and incredible blessings. The crisis of Abraham's faith and the promises and provisions of God will be no greater than in this testing of Abraham (see Theological Reflections below).

God's demanding call and Abraham's radical obedience here match the opening scene of the account of Terah's descendants, bringing closure to the main body of this narrative. God's first call to Abraham was "go to [leḵ-leḵā] the land I will show you" (12:1). His last call is "go to [leḵ-leḵā] the region of Moriah . . . on one of the mountains I will tell you about" (22:2). The Hebrew phrase leḵ-leḵā occurs in the Old Testament only in these two passages, strongly suggesting that the narrator intends his audience to see the frame. The weighty demand on Abraham is evident in the threefold epithets of the command. Initially, Abraham was told to leave "your country, your people and your father's household"; now he is commanded to sacrifice "your son, your only son, Isaac, whom you love" (22:2). In each case God rewards Abraham's obedience with glorious promises: first, "all peoples on earth will be blessed through you" (12:3); then more specifically, "through your offspring all nations on earth will be blessed" (22:18; see also "Comparison" below).

Structure and Plot

Abraham's faith, not Isaac's submission, is the focal point of this scene. Hence the scene is framed by the twofold repetition of Abraham in 22:1 and 19. This story of Abraham's testing develops in three parts helpfully suggested by Ross: "presentation of the test [22:1–2], compliance with the instructions [22:3–10], and approval (or disapproval) of the compliance [22:11–19]."[183] The tension of the scene is heightened by the narrative's slow

---

[183]A. P. Ross, *Creation and Blessing: A Guide to the Study and Exposition of the Book of Genesis* (Grand Rapids: Baker, 1988), 392.

pace as the narrator attentively details each movement. Rather than simply stating that Abraham went (cf. 12:4), the narrator explains that Abraham "saddled his donkey," "took with him two of his servants," took "his son," "cut enough wood for the burnt offering," and "set out." The rest of the scene until the sacrifice progresses similarly, with the description of Abraham and Isaac's preparations for the sacrifice spanning five verses (22:6–10). At the scene's dramatic climax, Abraham grasps the knife to obediently sacrifice his son.

Key Word

The insistent repetition of the word "son" (*ben*, 10x) reiterates the severity of this test. Abraham has been asked to sacrifice his son, his "only son" (*yaḥîd*, 3x; 22:2, 12, 16).

Blanks

The narrator does not satisfy his audience's curiosity about the ages of Abraham and Isaac, the role of Sarah, or Isaac's reaction to his father's binding him to the altar of sacrifice. Since Sarah is entirely blanked here, it is best not to speculate on her role in this dramatic scene.[184] Isaac's reaction is essentially blanked as well; however, the narrator includes enough information to depict Isaac as having a habit of obedience, trust in his father, and trust in God's provision. A son strong enough to carry a load of wood sufficient for a sacrifice on his back is certainly able to resist an aged father if so minded. Instead, Isaac freely consents to Abraham's will. Deathe comments, "We scarcely know which to admire—the brave spirit of the patriarch or the meek resignation of the youth. The son exceeds in 'humble endurance.'"[185] Josephus, however, goes too far in his speculation on Isaac's reaction. Whyte summarizes Josephus's obviously apocryphal account: "Now, Isaac was of such a generous disposition that he at once answered that he was not worthy to be born at first, if he should now reject the determination of God and his father, and should not resign himself up readily to both their pleasures. So he went up immediately to the altar to be sacrificed."[186]

Comparison

This scene is the climax of the Abraham's radical obedience, but also the climax of God's guarantee of offspring to Abraham, the prime concern of Act 2. As a conclusion of Act 2, the scene shares parallels with scenes 1 and 6

---

[184]"Early exegesis has Abraham concealing from his wife the true purpose of his journey lest she hinder him from doing God's bidding" (Sarna, *Genesis*, 151). Søren Kierkegaard (*Fear and Trembling*, ed. and trans. by H. V. Hong and E. H. Hong [Princeton, N.J.: Princeton Univ. Press, 1983], 82–120) wrestles with whether it was ethically defensible for Abraham to conceal his undertaking from Sarah.

[185]Deathe, "Abraham," 145, cited by George Rawlinson, *Men of the Bible: Isaac and Jacob: Their Lives and Times* (New York: Revell, n.d.), 24.

[186]A. Whyte, *Bible Characters: Adam to Achan* (Edinburgh & London: Oliphants, 1900), 153.

(Gen. 16; 21). Abraham is required to surrender both his "natural" and "supernatural" seed, to which God accordingly responds with provisions and blessings for each of the sons.

The parallels with Act 2, Scene 1 include the following: a parent and child on a difficult journey (Hagar and Ishmael, 16:6; Abraham and Isaac, 22:4–8); intervention from the angel of the Lord (16:7; 22:11) with promise of numerous descendants, using the key word "I will [greatly] increase" (*harbâ ʾarbeh*, 16:10; 22:17); and the naming of the place of God's provision, using the key word *rāʾâ* "to see"/"to provide" ("Living One who sees me," 16:14; "The LORD Will Provide," 22:14).

Wenham also outlines significant similarities between the testing of Abraham and the journey of Hagar and Ishmael in Scene 6: God commands the protagonist to take a journey (Hagar and Ishmael, 21:12–14; Abraham and Isaac, 22:4–8); provision is made for the journey (21:14; 22:3); God commands Abraham to give up his son (Ishmael, 21:12–13; Isaac, 22:2); the son is on the verge of death (21:16; 22:10) when the angel of the Lord intervenes to save (21:17; 22:11); the angel uses the key word "fear" ("Do not be afraid," 21:17; "fear God," 22:12); the "eyes" of the protagonist are mentioned with reference to seeing the Lord's provision (21:19; 22:13[187]); "hear" appears as a key word (21:17; 22:18);[188] and the scene concludes with the promise of great descendants through the "lost" son (21:18; 22:17).[189] In order to attain God's provisions and blessings, Abraham has to surrender his sons to God in faith.

EXEGETICAL NOTES TO BOOK 6, ACT 2, SCENE 8 ———

Presentation of the Test (22:1 – 2)

1. Some . . . Abraham. Sarna explains, "This information is imparted to the reader, not divulged to Abraham, in order to remove any possible misunderstanding that God requires human sacrifice as such. Therefore, the purely probative nature of the divine request is emphasized. . . . Now the reader knows that the son will not be slaughtered."[190]

Some time later. See 15:1. At least a decade has passed since the last chronological notice that Isaac was weaned (see 21:8). He is now old enough to carry a load of firewood sufficient for the sacrifice of an animal.

God [Elohim]. Some debate surrounds the names for God in this story. In the first half of the story up to 22:10, God is referred to as Elohim, and in the last half as Yahweh. Based on this, source critics have argued that the story is composed of different sources with distinct theologies. Such a reading,

---

[187]"Looked up" renders the Hebrew "he lifted up his eyes."
[188]"Obey me" renders the Hebrew "heard me."
[189]Wenham, *Genesis 16–50*, 99–100.
[190]Sarna, *Genesis*, 151.

however, is unnecessary. As evidenced before (see 2:4; "Naming" in Literary Analysis of Book 6, Act 2, Scene 2; 20:3), the names for God are carefully chosen to emphasize particular aspects of God's relationship to his people. The name God (Elohim) focuses on God as Creator (see Gen. 1:1–2:3). By contrast, the term "the LORD" (*yhwh*) emphasizes God's covenantal relationship with Abraham and his descendants. This name suits God's oath to keep his covenant commitment to Abraham.

tested. The focal point of this story is not the danger to Isaac but the danger to Abraham in his relationship to God. The Hebrew word "tested" does not mean "to entice to do wrong." With a personal object it means "test another to see whether the other proves worthy" (1 Kings 10:1; 2 Chron. 9:1; Dan. 1:12, 14).[191] Youngblood summarizes, "Satan tempts us to destroy us (1 Peter 5:8; James 1:15; Rom. 6:23), but God tests us to strengthen us (Ex. 20:20; Deut. 8:2)."[192] Here the saint is torn between his faith in the divine promises and the command to nullify them, between his affection for God's gift and for God. Faith is living within the vision of trusting God and his promises.

He said. The narrator does not specify how God spoke to Abraham, that is, whether vision, appearance, or messenger (cf. 15:1; 18:1; 22:11). But Abraham knows he hears God's word (see 12:1).

Here I am. This formula is "a regularly used reply in ordinary speech, especially between persons related by intimacy or respect (father-son, king-subject)."[193] This emphatic particle *hinnēnî* is the only word Abraham utters to God in this scene (22:11). Although Abraham has not always been faithful, the repetition shows that in this climactic test of his faith he is attentive and receptive to God's word (cf. Isa. 6:8). Landy comments, "There is a background recognition of the special intimacy of Abraham and God into whose easy discourse the brutal command erupts. But primarily it also invokes Abraham as a speaking subject. The abstract distanced representation that encompasses the story (God—test—Abraham) is replaced by an Abraham who declares his presence and a voice that meets him."[194]

2. [Please] Take [*qaḥ-nāʾ*]. The so-called particle of entreaty ("please," *nāʾ*) preceding the command to "take" is rare in divine commands. Sarna takes this to mean either that God has something at stake in Abraham's response or that Abraham is free to decline it.[195] However, T. O. Lambdin has argued that the particle used with *hinnēh* (see *hinnēnî*, 22:1) "denotes that the command in question is a logical consequence."[196] The particle, then, conveys the con-

---

[191]G. Gerleman, "nsh," TLOT, 2:742.

[192]Youngblood, *Genesis*, 186.

[193]A. Jenks, *The Elohist and North Israelite Traditions* (SBLMS 22; Missoula, Mont.: Scholars, 1977), 25.

[194]F. Landy, "Narrative Techniques and Symbolic Transactions in the Akedah," in *Signs and Wonders: Biblical Texts in Literary Focus*, ed. J. Cheryl Exum (Atlanta: Scholars, 1989), 11.

[195]Sarna, *Genesis*, 151.

[196]T. O. Lambdin, *Introduction to Biblical Hebrew* (New York: Charles Scribner's Sons, 1971), 170; see also, *IBHS*, §34.7a.

sequential nature of Abraham's attentive and receptive response; in other words, "Since you are ready to obey me, take your son."

only son. Some argue on the basis of the Greek and other ancient versions that the term may indicate value and be better translated here "your favored son." The twelve uses of the adjective in the Old Testament, however, do not sustain that interpretation.[197] According to *HALOT*, the word signifies either "only" (referring to the only son, Gen. 22:2, 12, 16; Prov. 4:3; Jer. 6:26; Amos 8:10; Zech. 12:10; or the only daughter, Judg. 11:34) or "lonely, deserted" (Ps. 25:16; 68:6; the soul suffering and lamenting, Ps. 22:20; 35:17).[198] Since Ishmael has been expelled and Abraham's offspring will be reckoned in Isaac, the Lord designates Isaac as "the only son." Robert Alden comments, "The expression 'mourning as for an only son' (Jer. 6:26; Amos 8:10; Zech. 12:10 [cf. Judg. 11:34]) relates death and the end of the family line, therefore the death of the son signifies a terrible catastrophe."[199]

your son, your only son, Isaac, whom you love. The word *son* is repeated throughout the account (22:2, 3, 6, 7, 8, 9, 10, 12, 13, 16). The emphasis is inescapable. Abraham faces a monumental test.

go to. The Hebrew adds "by yourself." Abraham is called to "determinedly disassociate" himself from his familiar surrounding.[200] Just as Abraham had to leave all that he held dear to go to the land prescribed by the Lord (see 12:1), so he has to offer to the Lord what he holds most dear and worship where God chooses (see Deut. 12:5). Landy suggests, "The two primary commands, 'take,' and 'go,' suggest contrary movements, the one a retraction, of Isaac back into himself, the other a journey, from himself, the point where he says 'here am I' to an unknown place. The one is a tightening, a grasping, the other a perilous adventure that implies a certain loss of self. The story is a working out, to the point of exhaustion, of the dynamic of the two commands."[201] Faith is a lonely pilgrimage.

region of Moriah. Although there are some textual difficulties, this probably refers to Jerusalem (see 2 Chron. 3:1, followed by Josephus, the Targums, and the Talmud [*b. Ta`an.* 16a]). Sarna notes that none of the ancient versions transliterates Moriah but translate it according to its etymology, be it *r'h*, "to see" (cf. Aquila, "clearly seen"; Vulgate, "vision"), or *yr'*, "to fear" (cf. Targums, "to worship") or *yrh*, "to teach" (so some Jewish interpretations). He challenges the traditional identification on the basis that travel from Beersheba to Jerusalem would not have required three days or an accompanying supply of wood.[202] However, the distance from Beersheba (see 22:19) to Jerusalem is

---

[197]In fact, it never means "favored" or "unique" among many.

[198]*HALOT*, 406.

[199]R. Alden, "*yāḥid*," *NIDOTTE*, 2:435.

[200]T. Muraoka, speaking about the ethical dative use of the lamed ("On the So-called," 497); see also *IBHS*, §11.2.10d.

[201]Landy, "Narrative," 11.

[202]Sarna, *Genesis*, 391–92.

approximately 50 miles (80 km), which might well have required three days' travel, especially since a part of a day was counted as a whole day.[203] Sarna himself explains the need to split the wood beforehand: "since the exact destination is as yet unknown to him, he cannot be sure he will find fuel there."[204] T. C. Mitchell states, "There is no need to doubt ... that Abraham's sacrifice took place on the site of later Jerusalem, if not on the Temple hill."[205]

Sacrifice him. This is one of the most theologically difficult texts of the Old Testament. God's command did not contradict moral law because the firstborn always belongs to the Lord (Ex. 13:11–13); however, the command is extraordinary both morally and theologically. Kierkegaard wrestles with this text and finds God's command illogical and absurd (irrational).[206] An old man's only son is like a staff or cane to the old man. It is a sad thing when an old man's staff is left behind after his death but much sadder when the staff is taken away and the old man left. How illogical is God's request of Abraham to break his staff! How absurd to ask Abraham to negate the reality that had reversed his years of disappointed hope. How morally questionable to ask Abraham to violate a moral law that will latter become the sixth of his famous Ten Commandments, "You shall not take innocent life." Perhaps one can make a stab at justifying the command on the basis that the Lord owns Isaac's life. Nevertheless, the command teeters on the edge of morality. We are left with the inexplicable and exacting realization that faith demands radical obedience. Abraham is asked to behave in a way that it is illogical, absurd, and, to say the least, nonconventional from the human perspective. Within the biblical world view, however, such radical behavior proves the true nature of biblical faith. "Abraham had committed himself by covenant to be obedient to the Lord and had consecrated his son Isaac to the Lord by circumcision. The Lord put his servant's faith and loyalty to the supreme test, thereby instructing Abraham, Isaac and their descendants as to the kind of total consecration the Lord's covenant requires."[207]

the mountains. Wenham notes that "the mountains" (*hhrym*) is an anagram for Moriah (*hmryh*).[208]

I will tell you about. God's last command to Abraham echoes his first (12:1).

Abraham's Compliance with the Instructions (22:3–10)

3. Early the next morning. This is another example of Abraham's prompt obedience (see 20:8). The patriarchs live by the words of God (Deut. 8:3).

---

[203]For example, Jesus was in the tomb part of Friday, all day Saturday, and part of Sunday, yet this is reckoned as three days. Likewise, in John 20:26 (lit., "after eight days," NIV, "a week later"), two partial Sundays are implied and counted as eight days.
[204]Sarna, *Genesis*, 151.
[205]T. C. Mitchell, "Moriah," *NBD*, 794.
[206]Kierkegaard, *Fear and Trembling*.
[207]NIV study notes, 22:2 (p. 38).
[208]Wenham, *Genesis16–50*, 106.

Abraham got up. The bargainer falls silent: no debate (unlike with Ishmael [Gen. 17:18] or with Lot [18:22–33]), only movement, hurrying, saddling, taking, splitting, arising, going.

two of his servants [or slaves]. This is a sign of Abraham's eminence.

cut enough wood for the burnt offering. The narrator's skillful sequencing of verbs maintains the reader's tension and functions as indirect psychological characterization. With this act listed last, the reader is unable to forget the weight of the burden on Abraham as he begins the journey. That Abraham delays this emotionally laden act until the end also suggests his psychological dilemma.

4. third day. In the biblical world, three days was a typical period of preparation for something important (cf. 31:22; 42:18; Ex. 3:18; 15:22; 19:11, 15, 16; Num. 10:33; 19:12, 19; 31:19; 33:8; Esth. 5:1; Hosea 6:2; Jonah 3:3; Matt. 12:40; 1 Cor. 15:4; also Gilgamesh Epic 1.2.44; 1.3.48[209]). The extended interval of time shows that Abraham does not act rashly but proceeds with resolute faith. "It allows time for sober reflection; yet his resolve is not weakened."[210]

5. Stay here. Landy notes, "The servants are brought along to be left behind. This is their function, a very strange one in any narrative, characters who are introduced solely in order to take no part in it. It compounds our sense of Abraham's isolation."[211] Abraham must leave everything behind. His lonely journey up that mountain symbolizes the lonely, psychological journey of faith to the place of sacrifice.

boy. See 21:12.

we will come back. Although he does not know how God will work it out, his faith harmonizes God's promise that in Isaac his offspring will be reckoned (21:1–13) with God's command to sacrifice Isaac. According to Heb. 11:17–19, he expresses a type of "resurrection" faith, and according to Rom. 4:16–25 his faith is of the same quality and caliber as Christians who believe in Christ's resurrection from the dead.

6. wood . . . on his son. Isaac must be in his late teens to be able to carry sufficient wood for a sacrifice on his back up a mountain. This is a moment of tremendous tension—Isaac carries wood for his own destruction.

he himself carried the fire and the knife. This detail conveys the weight of Abraham's burden. He carries the weapons he must wield against his son. This word for "knife" (*maʾaᵏelet*) is used elsewhere only for the knife the priest uses to dissect his concubine (Judg. 19:29) and in parallel with sword (Prov. 30:14).

7. Isaac spoke up and said to his father. By the repetition of "father" and "son" the narrator relentlessly emphasizes the precious relationship.

---

[209] *ANET*, 74–75.
[210] Sarna, *Genesis*, 152.
[211] Landy, *Narrative*, 14.

8. provide the lamb. Abraham's faith in God's word enables him to see God's command in the light of the promises.

9. bound. See "Blanks" in Literary Analysis above. The term is found nowhere else in the Bible in the context of ritual sacrifice. The rabbis called this story the Aqedah, the Hebrew word for "binding."

9–10. laid him on the altar, on top of the wood . . . reached . . . took . . . to slay. The narrator develops this moment from the view of a slow-motion camera.

God's Approval of Abraham's Compliance (22:11–19)

11. angel of the LORD. See 16:7.

Abraham! Abraham! The repetition connotes the urgency (cf. Gen. 46:2; Ex. 3:4; 1 Sam. 3:10; Acts 9:4).

12. Now I know. The narrator does not wrestle with God's omniscience, which entails that he knew Abraham's faith commitment beforehand. Instead, he focuses upon the reality that God does not experience the quality of Abraham's faith until played out on the stage of history (cf. Deut. 8:2).

fear God. See 20:11. The "fear of God" entails an obedience to God's revelation of his moral will, whether through conscience or Scripture, out of recognition that he holds in his hands life for the obedient and death for the disobedient. Abraham is credited with obedience, which Roop describes as "an obedience which does not protect even what is most precious, but trusts God with the future."[212]

you have not withheld. Abraham's faith was not in words but in deeds (James 2:21–22).

13. looked up and there in a thicket. Providence is clearly at work.

a ram. Some MT manuscripts read, "a ram behind [him]."

instead of. This is the first explicit mention of substitutionary sacrifice of one life for another in the Bible, though it was implied in Noah's sacrifice (8:20–22).

14. The LORD Will Provide. A key word of the Abraham narrative rʾh, often meaning "to see," is here translated "provide."

to this day. The notice refers to a time after Moses (see "Composition and Authorship: Post-Mosaic Additions" in the introduction) and authenticates the story's historicity (see "Historicity and Literary Genre" in the introduction). After David takes Jerusalem, the "mountain of the LORD" refers to the Temple Mount in Jerusalem (see Ps. 24:3; Isa. 2:3; 30:29; Zech. 8:3).

16. I swear by myself. Having walked between the carcasses to confirm covenant and having assigned circumcision to affirm it, God now swears to his covenant promise. He does so "because God wanted to make the unchanging nature of his purpose very clear to the heirs of what was promised" (Heb. 6:17).

---

[212]Roop, *Genesis*, 148.

17. bless. See notes on 1:22 and 12:2.

descendants. See 13:16; 15:5.

18. offspring. See 12:3; 13:16; 15:5; 17:5–6, 15–16; 18:18.

all nations. See 12:2–3.

because you have obeyed me. This underscores the certainty of the covenant. Moberly says, "A promise which previously was grounded solely in the will and purpose of Yahweh is transformed so that it is now grounded both in the will of Yahweh and in the obedience of Abraham"[213] (see 17:9).

19. Then Abraham. Abraham alone is mentioned because the story is about the test of his faith, not about Isaac's submission. The name is repeated twice as in 22:1, forming an inclusio around the narrative.

THEOLOGICAL REFLECTIONS ON BOOK 6, ACT 2, SCENE 8

Faith in Action

Drawing from Erich Auerbach's reflections on biblical style, Fox comments that biblical style "favors one central preoccupation: a man's decision in relationship to God."[214] "The binding of Isaac" is the decisive moment in Abraham's relationship to God. In this scene the commitments of the Lord and of Abraham to one another are tested to their limits. The Lord committed himself to bless the earth through Abraham by making him into a great nation within the community of nations; Abraham committed himself to walk according to God's word. His commitment meant that he live radically in faith's imagination informed by God's promises to give him seed and land even though he and Sarah were no longer able to procreate. It also meant living radically in obedience to God's command. Abraham's lonely journey up the mountain symbolizes the lonely, psychological journey of faith to the place of obedience and sacrifice. As he did not fail to believe God's promises in spite of contrary visual evidence, he does not waver in his commitment to obey God. True faith expresses itself in action that accords with God's word, both his promises and his commands. When God calls, Abraham responds, "Here I am." Abraham is always ready to hear and obey (so also Moses, Ex. 3:4; Samuel, 1 Sam. 3:4; Isaiah, Isa. 6:8; and above all Jesus Christ, Heb. 10:7). He is a tremendous model of faithful response for the Christian.

Testing and Faith

God tests his saints often through adversity or hardship in order to prove the quality of their faith by their obedience in the actual time-space continuum we call "history" (see Ex. 20:20; Deut. 8:2; 2 Chron. 32:31; Matt. 4:1–11). In "the binding of Isaac," the saint is torn between his faith in the divine

---

[213]R. W. L. Moberly, "The Earliest Commentary on the Akedah," *VT* 38 (1988): 320.

[214]Fox, *Beginning,* 81.

promises and the command to nullify them, between his affection for God's gift and for God. For some reason God chose this history to validate reality. He does not test us to lead us into sin, but to test the quality of what we are. The proof of what we are is what we do (James 2:14–24). We are not to put God to the test (Ex. 17:2, 7; Deut. 6:16; Luke 4:12) but to respond humbly and obediently when God calls. This is Abraham's stance when he replies, "Here I am." Abraham's humility and obedient action are the models for Christian faith.

No one, however, has perfect faith. As we have seen, Abraham's faith falters on several occasions (cf. 12:10–20; 16:1–2; 20:1–13). Still, the Lord responds to Abraham's basic commitment of life to walk before God (17:1). One of the church's oldest confessions says: "If we are faithless, he will remain faithful, for he cannot disown himself" (2 Tim. 2:13). Instructively, however, when Abraham obeys, he blesses others and receives God's promises (12:1–3; 17:1–16; 22:15–18). When he disobeys, he is a burden around the neck of the nations. Faith requires vision and demands radical obedience to God's word.

Foreshadowing or Typology

In the Pentateuch, Abraham's journey to Mount Moriah and his sacrificial worship there foreshadow Israel's worship at Mount Sinai. After his three-day journey and his tremendous willingness to obediently sacrifice his son, Abraham is the first to offer without reservation a ram on Mount Moriah as an act of worship. Later, the Israelites want a three-day journey into the desert to worship God, presumably upon the mountain of God (Ex. 3:18; 4:27; 5:3). There the Lord appears to them, gives them the law, and promises a blessing to those who will keep the law. Every Israelite father redeems his firstborn son by an animal substitute (Ex. 13:12–13), just as the angel of the Lord spared the firstborn by the Passover substitute (Ex. 12:12–13).

Within the canon of Scripture, the story of Abraham's willingness to obediently sacrifice his son of promise typifies Christ's sacrifice. Abraham's declaration that "God himself will provide the lamb" (22:8) resonates with God's offer of the Lamb to save the world (Mark 10:45; John 1:29, 36; 2 Cor. 5:17–21; 1 Peter 1:18–19). God's provision of the ram on Mount Moriah typifies his sacrifice of Jesus Christ. Ultimately God provides the true Lamb without blemish that stands in humanity's place. This Lamb of God dies instead of the elect so that they might live (Gen. 22:13–14).

The obedience of Isaac and Abraham is a type of the Son of God, the true Suffering Servant. Like Isaac, Christ is a lamb led to the slaughter, yet he does not open his mouth. Just as Isaac carries his own wood for the altar up the steep mount, Christ carries his own wooden cross toward Golgotha (see John 19:17).[215] Just as Abraham sacrificially and obediently lays Isaac on the altar (Gen. 22:9), so Christ sacrificially and obediently submits to his

---

[215]See further Irenaeus and Tertullian in *ANF*, vols. 1, 3, 4.

father's will (Rom. 8:32; Phil. 2:6–8; 1 Peter 2:21–24). Abraham's devotion ("You have not withheld from me your son, your only son") is paralleled by God's love to us in Christ as reflected in John 3:16 and Rom. 8:32, which may allude to this verse. Symbolically, Abraham receives Isaac back from death, which typifies Christ's resurrection from the death of the cross (Heb. 11:19). In taking an oath to bless Abraham and all nations through him, God guarantees the promise to Abraham's offspring (Gen. 22:15–18). Abraham's obedience prefigures the active obedience of Christ, who secures the covenantal blessings for Abraham's innumerable offspring.

BOOK 6, ACT 3:
TRANSITION TO ISAAC (22:20 – 25:11)

LITERARY ANALYSIS OF BOOK 6, ACT 3 ————————

Structure and Plot

After the climactic conclusion of Act 2, everything now is preparation for the succession of the patriarchs. This final act of "The Account of Terah's Descendants" provides a transition from the patriarchy of Abraham to Isaac, although more so a transition to the patriarchy of Jacob (see Literary Analysis of Book 8).

This act concludes the concerns of Book 6, namely, the covenant promises to Abraham of seed and land. With respect to the land, the report of Sarah's death in Scene 2 (Gen. 23) prompts an extensive narrative of Abraham's negotiation to secure his first piece of real estate in the Promised Land, aside from his having secured rights to the well of Beersheba (see 21:22–34). With regard to the seed, Scene 3 (Gen. 24), an even more extensive narrative, depicts the negotiations of Abraham's servant to secure the matriarch for Isaac. This scene occupies the longest chapter in Genesis. It is framed by genealogies and death notices. While Scene 1 (22:20–24), the genealogy of Nahor, brother of Abraham, features the promised seed (pointing to the birth of Rebekah, the second "mother in Israel"), Scene 4 (25:1–6), the genealogy of Abraham through Keturah (the nonelect sons), features the granting of Abraham's inheritance exclusively to Isaac. While Scene 2 records Sarah's death and Abraham's negotiations to secure land, Scene 5 (25:7–11) is about Abraham's death and his burial on that land.

Scene 1: Genealogy of Nahor, including Rebekah (elect) (22:20–24)
Scene 2: Death of Sarah, Abraham securing real estate (23:1–20)
    Scene 3: Securing a bride for the promised seed (24:1–67)
Scene 4: Genealogy of Abraham through Keturah (nonelect) (25:1–6)
Scene 5: Death of Abraham (25:7–11)

The act prepares the narrative for a shift to Isaac's leadership. Genesis 23 and 24 relate Sarah's death and Isaac's marriage to Rebekah; 25:1–6, the dismissal of Abraham's other children, leaving Isaac sole heir; 25:7–11, Abraham's death.

Comparison

This wrapping up of loose ends in Act 3 at the conclusion of Abraham's life is not put together loosely. The narrator's crafting can be seen in the conclusion of each account of the major patriarchs (Abraham, Isaac, and Jacob), which all deal with the same issues in virtually the same sequence. Wenham sets out the comparison in a helpful chart:[216]

Death and burial of wife	23:1–20	35:18–20	48:7
Son's "marriage"[217]	24:1–67	35:21–22	49:3–4
List of descendants	25:1–6	35:23–26	49:5–28
Death and burial of patriarch	25:7–10	35:27–29	49:29–50:14
List of descendants	25:12–17	36:1–43	———
"This is the family history of…"	25:19	37:2	———

BOOK 6, ACT 3, SCENE 1:
REBEKAH'S FAMILY BACKGROUND (22:20–24)

LITERARY ANALYSIS OF BOOK 6, ACT 3, SCENE 1 ———

Inclusio

As Abraham's test of sacrifice (22:1–19) echoes Abraham's call to journey (12:1–8), this genealogy of Nahor (22:20–24) echoes the genealogy of Terah (11:27–31), forming an inclusio around the main narrative concerning Abraham (12:1–22:19).

A Genealogy of Terah (11:27–31)
    B Abraham's call to journey (12:1–8)
    B' Abraham's test of sacrifice (22:1–19)
A' Genealogy of Nahor son of Terah (22:20–24)

Form

Although the content of this unit is genealogy, it is given in the form of a narrative, as indicated by the narrative introduction: "Some time later Abraham was told."

Structure

After the narrative introduction (22:20), the genealogy of Nahor is presented as a segmented genealogy of twelve sons. Recall that a segmented genealogy aims to establish family relationships, whereas a linear genealogy aims to identify the final descendant as the legitimate ancestor of the first

---

[216] Wenham, *Genesis 16–50*, 156.
[217] Quotation marks are not in Wenham.

(see Book 1, "Excursus: Genesis Genealogies"). This genealogy is divided into two units: the first presenting the eight sons by Nahor's wife Milcah (22:20–23), and the second, the four by his concubine Reumah (22:24). The eight sons are clearly distinguished from the concubine's sons by the inclusio "Milcah . . . has borne sons to . . . your brother Nahor" (22:20, the voice of the reporter) and "Milcah bore these eight sons to Abraham's brother Nahor" (22:23b, the narrator's report). In this way the prominence of the first eight sons is featured. The narrator's explanatory gloss within this unit, "Bethuel became the father of Rebekah" (22:23a), suggests that he intends the genealogy to provide the background both for the marriage of Isaac to Rebekah (24:24) and for Jacob to Leah and Rachel (28:5).

Foreshadow

This genealogy completes the details of the descendants of Nahor and Milcah (11:29) and sets the stage for the introduction of Rebekah into the family line of the patriarchs (24:1–67; cf. 25:20). Sternberg comments, "Juxtaposed with God's blessing and placed in structural correspondence to Ishmael's marriage, the report virtually names the bride-to-be."[218]

Comparison

The twelve nonelect sons of Nahor, who probably become tribes, parallel the twelve elect sons/tribes of Abraham through his grandson Jacob. In each case there are eight by the principal wife/wives and four from the secondary wife/wives (22:20, 24; 29:31–30:24; 35:16–18). The number twelve also matches the twelve sons/tribes of Ishmael (see 17:20; 25:12–16).

EXEGETICAL NOTES TO BOOK 6, ACT 3, SCENE 1 ————

Narrative Frame (22:20a)

20. Some time later. For other temporal transitions, see 15:1; 22:1.

was told. This genealogy is reported in speech to Abraham. The report of his brother's children and daughter reminds Abraham of the unfinished task: securing the second generation of the promised family.

Nahor's Eight Sons by Milcah (22:20b – 23)

20b. Milcah is also a mother. The text assumes the audience's knowledge of 11:29.

Nahor. See 11:26.

21. Uz. See 10:23.

Buz. To judge from Jer. 25:23, his tribe settled in Northern Arabia. Cuneiform texts, however, mention Bazu/su located in East Arabia.[219]

---

[218]Sternberg, *Poetics*, 133.
[219]*HALOT*, 115.

Kemuel (the father of Aram). By adding "father of Aram," the narrator or a later scribe may have intended to distinguish this Kemuel from a leader in Ephraim (Num. 34:24) or from the father of a leader in Levi (1 Chron. 27:17). Kemuel's son Aram, grandson of Nahor, should also be distinguished from Aram son of Shem (Gen. 10:22–23; 1 Chron. 1:17) and Aram, descendant of Asher (1 Chron. 7:34).

22. Kesed. He is the eponymous hero of the Kasdim (Chaldeans) (see 11:31).

Hazo. *HALOT* identifies this as "[m]odern al-Ḥasa on the Arabian coast opposite Bahrain."[220]

Pildash, Jidlaph. These are unknown.

23. Bethuel. See Gen. 24:15, 47; 25:20; 28:5.

Rebekah. "The meaning of the personal name is uncertain, most probably *ribqa* is a dialect by-form of *biqra* corresponding to Arabic *baqarat* 'cow.'"[221] Rebekah is the only daughter mentioned in this genealogy, raising anticipations about Isaac's wife. She is related to both of Abraham's brothers. Her father Bethuel is son of Milcah, daughter of Haran and wife of Nahor (see 11:29). In the next generation, Leah and Rachel have a similar ancestry, for their father Laban is brother of Rebekah (see 29:10).

Nahor's Four Sons By His Concubine Reumah (22:24)

24. concubine. This Indo-European loan word refers to a second-class wife, acquired without payment of bride-money and possessing fewer legal rights (see 30:4; Judg. 19:1–4).

Tebah. His name means "slaughter" (i.e., "born at the time of slaughter").[222] The name may be related to the Ṭubiḫi (Egyptian Dbḫ) of the El-Amarna letters, an important city in southern Syria. Some conjecture it is the same as Betah in 2 Sam. 8:8 (MT) and Tibhath in 1 Chron. 18:8 (MT).

Gaham. This is also a personal name in the Arad inscriptions (seventh century B.C.).

Tahash. It may be related to the Egyptian place name Ta-ḫ-śi, in the Valley of Orontes south of Qadesh (cf. Taḫ-śi in the El-Amarna correspondence.)[223]

Maacah. This is the most southerly place name of the concubine's sons' names. Maacah designates a small Aramean state south of Hermon, near to Geshur (Josh. 13:13; 2 Sam. 10:6, 8; 1 Chron. 19:7). The Maacathites belonged to a small kingdom on the northern border of the half-tribe of Manasseh in Transjordan (see Deut. 3:14; Josh. 12:5). Their territory was deeded to the tribe of Manasseh, who was unable to drive them out (Josh. 13:11–13).

---

[220]Ibid., 301.
[221]Ibid., 1182.
[222]Ibid., 368.
[223]Ibid., 1721.

THEOLOGICAL REFLECTIONS ON
BOOK 6, ACT 3, SCENE I ────────────────

Historical Credibility

The known geographical attestations of these names tend to support the historicity of the genealogy. Ultimately, their authenticity depends on inspiration, not on human criteria.

Primogeniture

To judge from the sequence of names, which cites Uz as the firstborn, Bethuel father of Rebekah is the youngest of the eight prominent sons by Milcah. The narrator time and again makes the point that the family of God is based on election, not on the natural rights of the firstborn.

BOOK 6, ACT 3, SCENE 2: THE ACQUISITION OF THE CAVE OF MACHPELAH (23:1 – 20)

LITERARY ANALYSIS OF BOOK 6, ACT 3, SCENE 2 ────────

Structure and Plot[224]

The death of the honored matriarch Sarah (see notes on 23:1) occasions Abraham's first acquisition of property in the Promised Land. The fact that Abraham, "an alien and a stranger" in the land, has no place to bury his dead intensifies the crisis. The plot tension revolves around Abraham's careful negotiations to secure a firm contract guaranteeing him and his descendants a burial site. As a resident alien, he is not ordinarily entitled to purchase land. Initially the Hittites offer him a tomb to meet his immediate need to bury his dead, but not a permanent burial site. Assumedly, Abraham encounters the pervasive reluctance of landowners in the ancient Near East to part with their property. The negotiations become more complicated when Ephron offers to give him the cave along with its field to bury his dead. Had Abraham accepted this offer, his claim to the cave and field would not have been incontestable. The tension is resolved with Abraham's successful *purchase* of a cave and field. The negotiation dialogues are followed by the narrator's statements of acceptance agreement and payment formula (23:16), transfer of property, including property description (23:17), and witnesses. The dialogue contract form establishes Abraham's impeccable claim to the cave and field of Machpelah.

The narrator's introduction and conclusion to the scene (23:1, 20) and his summary of Sarah's death (23:2) and burial (23:19) frame the extended "dialogue contract,"[225] whereby Ephron's cave and field are deeded to Abraham

---

[224]Garrett (*Rethinking*, 150–56) classifies this as one of three negotiation tales in Genesis (Gen. 23; 24; 34). According to him, they have the common structure of crisis (23:1–2; 24:1–4; 34:1–2), circumstances (23:3–6, 10–11; 24:1–4; 34:1–2), decisive action (23:7–9, 12–13; 24:5–9; 34:3–12), result of action (23:14–16; 24:15–16; 34:18–29), and aftermath (23:17–20; 24:62–67; 34:30–31).

[225]This is a form attested in the Neo-Babylonian period. See G. M. Tucker, "The Legal Background of Genesis 23," *JBL* 85 (1966): 80–84.

as a permanent burial site for the patriarchs (23:3–18). The contract consists of three dialogues between Abraham and the Hittites of Ephron (23:3–6, 7–11, 12–16). Each dialogue becomes more specific in terms of participants and property (first: Hittites and a tomb; second: people of the land and Ephron's cave; third: Ephron and his cave and field).

Style

The narrator employs the legal terminology and detailed style one expects in a firm and binding contract. Each speech is introduced by at least an entire verse (23:3, 5, 7, 10, 12–13a, 14), and twice the narrator adds that the negotiations take place at the "gate of the city" (23:10, 18), the legal center of an ancient Near Eastern city.

The plot, editorial summaries, "dialogue contract form," and style show that the narrator's point of view does not focus on Sarah's death but on Abraham's firm and binding procurement of a sepulchre that will anchor Abraham's descendants in the Promised Land.

Key Words

The phrase "his/my/your dead," a metonymy for Sarah, occurs eight times (23:3, 4, 6 [2x], 8, 11, 13, 15). These phrases mostly occur climactically at the end of speeches. In the Hebrew Bible, the narrator introduces the main narrative with the verb "died" (23:2). The repetition keeps at the forefront the urgent reason for the negotiations. Abraham underscores the urgency by adding "before me" to "my dead" (23:4, 8 MT).

Correlatively, the root *qbr* occurs thirteen times, eight times as a verb "to bury" (23:4, 6 [2x], 8, 11, 13, 15, 19) and five times as a noun, either alone as "tomb" (23:6 [2x]) or in the phrase "[property] for a burial site" (*ʾaḥuzzat-qeḇer*, 23:4, 9, 20). The distinction between "[property] for a burial site" and "tomb" is the key to the negotiations. The Hittites are willing to give Abraham a tomb, but Abraham wants to purchase a permanent burial site for his descendants to anchor their identification with the Promised Land. The operative verb *ntn* "to give" occurs seven times; it is rendered "to sell" and "to pay" in the mouth of Abraham (23:4, 9, 13) and "to give" in the mouth Ephron (23:11[3x]). The narrator underscores the legality and irrevocable nature of the purchase in an aural, not a literary society, by the key words "to hear/listen" (23:6, 8, 11, 13, 15, 16), "ears" (23:10, 13, 16), and "eyes" (23:11, 18).

EXEGETICAL NOTES TO BOOK 6, ACT 3, SCENE 2 ───────

Introduction: Death of Sarah (23:1 – 2)

1. **lived.** The NIV fails to represent the inclusio surrounding the introduction. At the beginning and end of the verse the Hebrew mentions "the life of Sarah" to highlight this unique reference to her age and the greatness of this mother of Israel (cf. Isa. 51:2).

a hundred and twenty-seven years old. She is the only woman in the Bible whose life span is given, signifying her importance. She dies when Isaac is thirty-seven years old, three years before his marriage (see 17:17; 21:5; 25:20; cf. 24:67). Abraham outlives her by another thirty-eight years (25:7).

2. Kiriath Arba. See 13:18. The name means "City of Four." Perhaps the Hittites occupied one quarter in the amalgam of the City of Four.

Hebron. The narrator blanks the precise relationship and movement of the patriarchs with reference to Beersheba (21:34; 22:19), Hebron (23:2), and the Negev (24:62).

in the land of Canaan. This repetitive detail serves to link this story with God's earlier promise to give Abraham the land.

went. The Hebrew is literally "to enter, to come." The meaning of the verb is ambiguous here. Did Abraham "enter" her tent to mourn, since mourning rites were performed before the corpse (see 23:3)? Or did he "come" from Beersheba to Hebron to mourn? Or is it an idiom with another verb, meaning "to proceed" (cf. Deut. 32:44)?

to mourn . . . and to weep. The lack of detail regarding mourning (e.g., its duration and manner) stands in striking contrast to the amount of detail regarding the purchase of the land, showing the narrator's focus in this scene.

First Cycle of Negotiations with the Hittites: Abraham Requests a Permanent Sepulchre; Hittites Offer Him Their Best Tomb 23:3 – 6

3. rose. Abraham probably rose from sitting as a mourner on the ground (cf. Job 2:8; Isa. 3:26; Lam. 2:10). In the Hebrew text this initial verb *wayyāqom* functions as an inclusio around the dialogues. It occurs in the summary statement (23:17–18), translated "deeded."

Hittites. See 10:15; 15:19–21. These Hittites in the hill country of Southern Palestine have no obvious connection with the Hittite Empire, which fell to the Sea Peoples in approximately 1200 B.C. The Hittite Empire was restricted to the area north of the kingdom of Kadesh on the Orontes. Moreover, these Hittites do not reflect the customs and practices of that Hittite Empire. Furthermore, the Hittites of the patriarchal accounts have Semitic, not Hittite, names, and Abraham seems to converse with them without an interpreter.[226] Also, these Hittites have no connection to the Neo-Hittite states of Syria that had contact with Israel during the period of the monarchy (1 Kings 10:29; 11:1; 2 Chron. 1:17).

4. alien and a stranger. The hendiadys, meaning "resident alien," underscores that Abraham owns no land and ordinarily is not entitled to buy land. According to Gen. 34:20–22, it seems that sharing property depends on

---

[226]H. A. Hoffner, "The Hittites and Hurrians," in *Peoples of Old Testament Times*, ed. D. J. Wiseman (Oxford: Clarendon, 1973), 213–14.

intermarriage between ethnic groups. Marriage with the Hittites, whose moral practices were otherwise repulsive to the godly patriarchs, is unthinkable to Abraham (cf. 26:34–35; 27:46; see Theological Reflections).

Sell me. See "Key Words" in the Literary Analysis above. Establishing a place in the land of promise is an appropriate step of faith. God's full gift of the land lies beyond the lifetime of Abraham and Sarah.

property for a burial site. One could translate this, "possession for a burial site." This key word to the transactions denotes a sepulchre in perpetuity (Lev. 14:34; 25:25–28; Josh. 21:12). The word rendered "property" is also used in 17:8; 48:4 of Israel's eternal "possession" of Canaan.

6. mighty prince. The Hebrew (*neśîʾ ʾelōhîm*) literally means "a prince of God."[227] The Hittites recognize God's blessing and protection on this alien (see 21:23 and note). It is the landless one who bears all the promises and lives in hope.

among us. Their address becomes more personal: from "resident alien" to "great prince" and from "with you" (lit.) to "among us." Roop says, "Abraham has put himself at the bottom of the social ladder, and they put him at the top."[228]

Bury your dead in the choicest of our tombs. The change of terms from "property for a burial site" to "tomb" suggests that, while the Hittites are willing to grant this mighty prince the right to bury his dead on their land, they are reluctant to give him a permanent possession there.

Second Cycle of Negotiations with the People of the Land: Abraham Requests Ephron's Cave; Ephron Offers His Cave and Field (23:7–11)

7. rose and bowed down. This is an exceptional action for one who has just been addressed as "mighty prince." His bow signifies gratitude and dependence on their favor.

people of the land. Although in some later texts this expression may generally indicate the total population of a region, it is often used either as a technical term for the assembly of the men who are responsible for a region's political activity or for the upper class with the rights of citizenship. A. R. Hulst interprets its meaning here as the "fully enfranchised, landowning citizens."[229] Either interpretation finds support because the "people of the land" seem to be distinguished from the Hittites in general, who are addressed in the first round (23:3).

8. intercede [*pgʿ*]. The Hebrew means "to go and plead with someone" or "to press someone."

---

[227]This is possibly a superlative (*IBHS*, §14.5b).
[228]Roop, *Genesis*, 154.
[229]A. R. Hulst, "*ʿam*," *TLOT*, 2:902.

Ephron son of Zohar. The rare identification of a non-Israelite by his father's name (cf. 34:2) suggests that Zohar was an outstanding man among the Hittite citizens.

9. Machpelah. The name means "double-cave" or "split-cave." It is unclear whether its chambers were side by side or one above the other. Many of God's promises to Abraham for land and offspring, including the famous Abrahamic covenant (13:14–18:15), occurred at this site. Today this site is covered by the mosque of Ḥaram El-Khalil ("sacred precinct of the friend [of God]"), northeast of Hebron.

at the end of his field. This is probably either a legal detail or a bargaining point to show that Abraham's possession of the cave will not interfere with Ephron's activity. Ephron's addition of the field is more than Abraham requested or probably hoped for.

Ask him. Abraham may think he needs the support of the leading citizens in order to secure Ephron's favor, or he assumes negotiations of this sort must be conducted through the community.

full price. This is likely a legal term signifying full payment for an irrevocable sale. The term has been considered the equivalent of common Sumerian and Akkadian (and more rarely Ugaritic) legal terms, which indicated that a sale was for cash and final. These terms always accompanied clauses establishing the sale's irrevocability.[230]

10. Ephron . . . replied. Ephron does not wait for the leaders to act as mediators. His direct reply shows that he sells the cave and the field of his own free will, without social pressure, making Abraham's claim to the property even more incontestable.

in the hearing of all the Hittites. These details (see also 23:13, 16, 18) ensure that the transaction is proper and legal, with appropriate witnesses.

gate. Legal transactions usually took place in the gate of oriental cities (see Ruth 4:1–11).

11. I give. It is impossible to know for certain whether he really wants to give the cave and field as a gift out of respect for Abraham or whether he uses courteous language to show his willingness to sell the cave. The latter is more probable. The dialogues are infused with exaggerated politeness (e.g., "bowed," 23:7, 12; "mighty prince," 23:6; "my lord" ["sir" in the NIV], 23:6, 11, 15), of which this would be only another instance. A parallel in 2 Sam. 24:22–23a (= 1 Chron. 21:23) shows the seller also offering to give the buyer more than he requests. When David asks Araunah for the site of his threshing floor, Araunah adds to the offer the oxen for the burnt offering

---

[230]G. Tucker ("Legal Background," 79–80) calls this interpretation into question because the same expression occurs in 1 Chron. 21:22 (cf. 2 Sam. 24:24) and means simply "to give the full value." His argument, however, is not convincing. The other ancient Near Eastern texts do not exclude a price that is full value. More probably the term denotes the purchase paid in full value, which secures an irrevocable sale.

and the threshing sledges and oxen yokes for the wood! Probably, as Gene Tucker argues, "The object of the offer and of the excessive politeness as a whole is to put the other party on the defensive. . . . By offering more than was requested, he [the seller] would indirectly command a higher price."[231] In support of this interpretation, when Abraham counters Ephron's proposal, Ephron names a high price.

the field. Drawing from Middle Assyrian and Hittite laws prior to 1200 B.C., Lehman argues that Ephron adds the field in order to transfer to Abraham feudal obligations linked to the entire holdings.[232] The parallel in 2 Sam. 2:22–23a debunks this interpretation. Araunah is not trying to transfer feudal obligations to the king! Moreover, we already noted that these Hittites had no obvious connection with the Hittites of the Empire Period (ca. 1600–1200 B.C.).

Third Cycle of Negotiations, with Ephron and the Hittites As Witnesses: Abraham Offers to Buy the Field; Ephron Names His Price (23:12–16)

13. pay the price. Literally, "I will pay the silver." Abraham wants a final and irrevocable sale of property, as recognized by the Hittites.

field. Abraham speaks of the field, entailing his willingness to pay a higher price to purchase both the field and the sepulchre.

15. four hundred shekels. Since ancient land values and the extent of the property are unknown, it is impossible to evaluate with certainty the price according to market value. On the one hand, the price may accord with market value. Sarna notes, "Three texts from Ugarit . . . record real estate transactions involving a purchase price of 400 shekels of silver."[233] On the other hand, the price seems high when compared with David's purchase of the temple site for fifty shekels (2 Sam. 24:24).[234] Both Abraham and Jeremiah buy land as a sign that the land has a future.[235]

between me and you. The only real parties involved in the negotiations are Ephron and Abraham. It is a matter only between them (cf. Gen. 16:5; Judg. 11:10 ["our witness," lit., "witnesses between us"]; 2 Sam. 21:7). Sarna explains, "Only a payment that is manifestly accepted by the seller of his own volition ensures the unchallengeable nature of the transaction. That is why Ephron, not Abraham, must first state the price and why, once that is done, there is no further bargaining."[236]

---

[231]Ibid., 78.
[232]M. R. Lehmann, "Abraham's Purchase of Machpelah and Hittite Law," *BASOR* 129 (1953): 15–18.
[233]Sarna, *Genesis*, 160.
[234]Jeremiah's purchase of a field outside Jerusalem for seventeen shekels (Jer. 32:9) was probably as exorbitantly low due to the Babylonian besieging of Jerusalem as Abraham's was high due to the death of Sarah.
[235]Brueggemann, *Genesis*, 196.
[236]Sarna, *Genesis*, 157.

16. Abraham agreed [*šmᶜ*]. The Hebrew is literally, "Abraham heard." In the dialogue contract form, the term denotes agreement (see also "Key Words" in the Literary Analysis above). Abraham, wanting an unimpeachable sale and secure peace, buys the cave at beyond a fair price. Not to bargain is totally contrary to Near Eastern custom (see Prov. 20:14), but now no one can contest his right to the cave.

weighed out. They did not have coinage at that time.

according to the weight current among the merchants. The ancient Near Eastern contract clauses use similar language.[237]

Narrator Recounts the Deed of Sale (23:17 – 18)

17. all the trees. Trees were also considered appurtenances. Some ancient Near Eastern contract documents even record the number of trees.

deeded. In the Hebrew text, this word occurs first, a format precisely following the dialogue contract form. Literally, the phrase is "rose [and went over] to." That is, the deed "rose and went to Abraham." The detailed contractual form demonstrates that Abraham has an impeccable legal claim to the field in Machpelah. Goodwill, good faith, and sincerity exist between the three parties.

Narrative Frame (23:19 – 20)

19. buried his wife Sarah in the cave. On the framing aspect of these verses, see above on 23:1–2. Abraham aims to anchor his descendants in the sworn land (see 24:6–9; 25:9; 49:30; 50:13). Abraham bestows on Sarah the honor she rightly deserves by purchasing for her a proper tomb. His mourning goes far beyond conventional mourning rites: "As befits the mother of the nation, her grave was impressive, a worthy memorial to a great woman."[238]

20. field and the cave. This little piece of land gives promise of the whole land. It makes clear that the aliens and strangers are seeking a homeland (Heb. 11:13–14).

were deeded to Abraham . . . as a burial site. Abraham and Sarah, Isaac and Rebekah, Jacob and Leah will all express their faith by being buried here (Gen. 49:29–32, 50:4–14; Heb. 11:13–16).

THEOLOGICAL REFLECTIONS ON BOOK 6, ACT 3, SCENE 2 ————————————

Faith

God had promised that he would give Abraham the land, but when Abraham's wife dies, he has no land, not even a place to bury his dead. But Abraham uses what could be a crisis of faith as an opportunity to secure property. Even

---

[237]Ibid., 160.
[238]Wenham, *Genesis 16–50*, 130.

when he has to buy property that God has promised will be given to him, Abraham acts with faith and long-term vision. He could have simply buried his dead in a Hittite tomb, as the Hittites suggested (23:6). By firmly securing a piece of real estate in the land God promised him, Abraham demonstrates his unswerving commitment to the promise.

The Seeming Absence of God

Although the story appears quite secular, making no reference to God,[239] it is highly theological. The absence of God in style matches the seeming absence of God at death. Abraham did not even have a place to bury his dead (23:4, 13; cf. 19). In faith he purchases a cemetery plot as his first piece of property in the Promised Land. His faith exemplifies the faith of all believers, who buy their own graves without having obtained the promise (see Heb. 11:39–40), yet believing that the meek will inherit the earth (Matt. 5:5).

Aliens and Strangers

Abraham as an alien and a stranger in the land (Gen. 23:4) is a type of all saints, whose existence depends on God's gracious provisions (1 Chron. 29:15; Ps. 39:12; Heb. 11:13). The phrase "aliens and strangers" is often used by the people of God to denote their earthly pilgrimage toward the city of God. They have no abiding home on earth but like Abraham "live in tents" (Heb. 11:9), the most temporary dwelling, looking forward to their promised heavenly home, "the city with foundations, whose architect and builder is God" (Heb. 11:10).

Remembrance

Biblical faith is largely a matter of memory. Through memory each generation of believers commits itself to the faith of its ancestors. Abraham Joshua Heschel says, "Much of what the Bible demands can be comprised in one word: Remember."[240] To remember is not simply an empty mental act. Heschel argues, "'To remember' means literally to re-member the body, to bring the separated parts of the community of truth back together, to reunite the whole. The opposite of re-member is not forget, but dis-member."[241] Tangible symbols serve as memory's handmaidens. Abraham realizes that, for the succeeding generations to remember their identification with the founding patriarchs and matriarchs, they need a burial site by which they can memorialize their faith. In this Abraham is exceedingly insightful. Today Jews venerate Machpelah: "After the Western Wall in Jerusalem, it has remained throughout history the most sacred monument of the Jewish

---

[239]Except possibly for the expression "prince of God" in 23:6. Cf. Wenham, *Genesis 16–50*, 124.
[240]A. J. Heschel, *Man Is Not Alone* (New York: Farrar, Strauss & Giroux, 1951), 61.
[241]Ibid., 103.

people."[242] Christians, however, no longer look to this sepulchre but to the Lord's Supper in remembrance of their identification with Christ.

Burial Practices

The burial of Sarah is not ostentatious but respectful. The care with which Abraham buries her reveals great respect for life, the body, and death. Such respect is precisely Christian thinking. The body as a sacred gift of God is to be respected. The followers of Jesus show the same care and respect for his dead body and seek to give it honor by a proper burial (Mark 15:42–16:1).

BOOK 6, ACT 3, SCENE 3:
GIFT OF REBEKAH TO ISAAC (24:1–67)

LITERARY ANALYSIS OF BOOK 6, ACT 3, SCENE 3 ————————

Style

This scene, the longest single episode in Genesis, is a marvelous demonstration of the Hebrew talent for dialogue, repetition, and sparse—but vivid and informative—detail. "Its leisurely pace, attention to detail, and concentration on speeches as well as action belie the importance of what is being recounted."[243] This masterful, romantic tale is a theological reflection on divine providence (see Theological Reflections). On the story level, the scene presents the shift to Isaac's patriarchy and the miraculous adventure that leads to Isaac's marriage. On the theological level, the scene wrestles with the interplay of human responsibility (faith in action) and divine initiative (perfectly coordinated circumstances). Artistically, the detailed style functions to create a charming and engaging tale. Theologically, the attention to detail suggests God's providence is in the particulars.

Structure and Plot

The report of Nahor's family in Paddan Aram, especially of his granddaughter, Rebekah, in Scene 1, and the death of Sarah in Scene 2, form fitting background for Scene 3. This scene, recounting the providential gift of Rebekah as a wife for Isaac, features the Lord furthering the history of salvation through perfect timing and faithful people. Abraham's command to his servant, "go and take a wife" (24:4), is answered by Laban and Bethuel, "Here is Rebekah; take her and go" (24:51), and fulfilled with the statement, "So the servant took Rebekah and went" (24:61).

After an introductory statement of Abraham's age (24:1), showing the father's urgent need to secure a bride for his son, the scene develops geographically, chronologically, and logically through four settings. Abraham

---

[242]Sarna, *Genesis*, 159.
[243]Fox, *Beginning*, 87.

commissions his servant in his household (24:2–9); the servant providentially meets Rebekah at a well in Nahor in Aram Naharaim (24:10–27); in Bethuel's household, the family consents to the marriage (24:28–61); in the Negev, Rebekah and Isaac meet and as married couple enter into Sarah's tent (24:62–67).

Driving each scene of the Abraham narrative is the implicit question: How will God carry out his incredible promises? Abraham has been promised immeasurable seed that will bless the earth. What woman will the Lord find for Isaac to further this promise? How will he overcome the inevitable human stumbling blocks? This masterfully written scene has all the tension of a classic love story. The readers never doubt that somehow the hero and heroine will find each other, yet with each plot twist they hold their breath. Abraham makes the servant swear by "the Lord" that he will secure Isaac a bride from his own family and not from the Canaanites. The servant's first words—"What if the woman is unwilling?"—express the constant tension in biblical narrative. What kind of faith will each character embrace, and how will God overcome human folly? The servant's oath to Abraham commits him to a long and risky venture that Abraham says depends upon the "angel of the Lord" for success. At the well of Nahor the servant's success depends upon the Lord to identify the bride in answer to his prayer. In Bethuel's household, the servant must convince the family that his encounter with Rebekah was a providential answer to his prayer. Their acceptance seems secure until they fail to follow through on their commitment and leave the decision to Rebekah. In a moment of dramatic tension they ask Rebekah, "Will you go with this man?" She responds, "I will go," and the tension dissipates—a delightful confirmation of what we knew all along. The narrative confirms that this is a divinely designed marriage as the eyes of Isaac and Rebekah providentially encounter each other in their meeting.

Scenic Depiction

The narrator clearly intends this scene to mark the movement from Abraham's patriarchy to Isaac's. The prayerful and godly servant functions as the agent of transition. The scene opens with Abraham commissioning the servant to secure a bride (24:2–9) and concludes with the servant reporting directly to Isaac (24:66). This scene transferring patriarchal power is set in three homes: Abraham's household (24:1–9), Bethuel's household (24:28–60), and Isaac and Rebekah's new household (24:66–67). The shifts between these households occur fittingly at wells, which in Genesis typically mark marriage arrangements. The first well setting features Rebekah (24:10–27), the second, Isaac (24:62–65). Providential guidance is ever present. The household settings reveal human negotiations accomplished through faith; the well settings, providential timing in response to faith.

Characterization

In this scene four characters figure significantly in God's providential designs: the faithful Abraham, his prayerful servant, the virtuous Rebekah, and her not so virtuous kin. God's providence is worked out through his godly people, in spite of the ungodly.

Abraham continues in faithfulness: single-mindedly committing to the Promised Land, rejecting the corrupt Canaanites, and relying confidently in the Lord to lead his servant. He is unwilling to allow his son to return to the security of the old country even if the servant fails in his mission (24:5).

The anonymous servant is a model of sagacity and piety. By means of indirect characterization—actions and speech—the narrator develops a rich picture of the wise servant's gifts. His loyalty and prudence are exemplified by his stiff test of hospitality and health, his tactful request to Rebekah, his persuasive speech, and his refusal to be detained in his mission by an unscrupulous family. Abraham's astuteness in commissioning this servant is most apparent by the prayer and thankfulness that undergird each of the servant's actions. With the servant's lengthy speech to Rebekah's family—a retelling of the prior events—the narrator reveals much about the servant's character. In a comparison of the events (24:1–33) and his retelling (24:34–49), the servant's sagacity is revealed by the way he shapes his story to his audience, what he includes, and what he omits (see Exegetical Notes). Roth argues that the servant is the central character in this story, and his actions provide an instructive model to the listeners of a faithful and wise messenger: "The example story Gen. 24 demonstrates what typically happens when a trusted senior steward who belongs to a well-to-do, prestigious household fulfills his mission selflessly, patiently and prudently."[244]

The narrator describes Rebekah as "beautiful, a virgin." Her actions reveal her as a model of hospitality and faith: compassionate to people and animals (24:18–20), strong, energetic and industrious (24:19–20), and welcoming (24:25). She declares faith in Abraham's God by decisively leaving her immediate family to marry Isaac in a foreign land (24:58).

Laban and her other relatives function as foils. Rebekah's hospitality sharply contrasts with Laban, who rushes to the servant "as soon as he had seen the nose ring" (24:30). Her resolute faith contrasts with their indecisiveness and attempt to renege on their promise (24:50–58).

Key Words

"The LORD," who never speaks in this act, is nevertheless the chief actor. He is mentioned seventeen times in this scene, twice by Abraham (24: 3, 7),

---

[244]W. M. W. Roth, "The Wooing of Rebekah: A Tradition-Critical Study of Genesis 24," *CBQ* 34 (1972): 181. In his article (177–87), Roth notes links between the wise actions of the servant and instructive proverbs.

three times by the narrator (24:1, 26, 52), ten times by the servant (24:12, 27 [2x], 35, 40, 42, 44, 48 [2x], 56), and remarkably three times by Laban and Bethuel, who, although pagan, confess the LORD's blessing on Abraham (24:31, 50, 51).

As the journey of a loyal envoy, the narrative rests on the words "to go" (24:4, 10, 42, 56), "to bless" (24:1, 31, 35, 60), "to lead" (24:27, 48), "to make successful" (24:21, 40, 56; cf. 39:3, 23, of Joseph), and "loyalty" (24:12, 14, 27, 49), and "faithfully" (24:27, 48, 49).

The crucial verb hlk, "go" (24:4, 38, 51, 55, 56, 58 [2x]), "come/went back" (24:5, 8, 39, 61), "left" (24:10, 61), "set out" (24:10), "come/coming" (24:42, 65) also occurs seventeen times. Of these, seven occur with reference to Rebekah (24:5, 8, 39, 51, 55, 58 [2x]), as Sarna remarks, "a sure sign of its seminal importance."[245]

Comparison and Contrast

This scene contains many verbal allusions to the Lord's call of Abraham. Abraham's command to return to "my country," "my own relatives," "my father's household" (24:4; 7, cf. 24:40) and his emphatic instruction that Isaac not return there echo his initial departure in Act 1, Scene 1 (12:1–4). The narrator's assessment that God blessed Abraham (24:1), also put in the mouth his servant (24:35), signals the fulfillment of the promise of 12:2. Abraham's rejection of the depraved Canaanites (24:3) reflects God's rejection of them and his promise to give Abraham's posterity their land (15:16–20). Rebekah's firm resolve, "I will go [hlk]" (24:58), matches Abraham's venture to this land, "So Abram left [hlk]" (12:4). The subsequent blessing on Rebekah, "may you increase" and "and may your offspring possess the gates of their enemies" (24:60), parallels the one that the Lord pronounced upon the obedient Abraham (22:17).

Although the Lord elects both Abraham and Rebekah, his mode of revelation to them is strikingly different. To Abraham he speaks (12:7) in visions and auditions, to Rebekah he communicates through answered prayer and providential acts (24:27, 48, 50).

EXEGETICAL NOTES TO BOOK 6, ACT 3, SCENE 3 ————

Introduction (24:1)

1. old and well advanced in years. Old age is a sign of blessing on a great person (cf. Josh. 13:1, 23:1; 1 Kings 1:1) but also a difficulty because of the time pressure and limitations in settling family affairs before death.

blessed. See 1:22; 12:2–3; 15:15. God's promise to bless Abraham is now proclaimed as realized, even though some blessing remains in the future.

---

[245]Sarna, *Genesis*, 161.

Abraham and His Servant in Canaan (24:2–9)

2. chief. This unnamed servant is, in Roop's words, "the quiet hero of the story."[246] Abraham entrusts the crucial mission only to his most trusted manager. This servant, perhaps Eliezer (see 15:2–3), fully shares Abraham's faith (17:12–13).

Put your hand under my thigh. This is a euphemism for genitalia (Gen. 46:26; Ex. 1:5; Judg. 8:30[247]). When facing death, the patriarchs secure their last will by an oath at the source of life (see Gen. 47:29). The reason for this gesture is uncertain, but perhaps it is chosen because the oath involves the certainty of the posterity God promises.

3. the LORD, the God of heaven and the God of earth. See 14:22. The title is appropriate for beginning a perilous journey to a distant land.

not get a wife for my son from the daughters of the Canaanites. In the biblical world, parents usually arranged marriages. Abraham sets an example for his descendants to secure wives from the blessed Semites, not the cursed Canaanites (see 9:24–27; 15:16; 18:18–19; Deut. 7:1–4).

4. my own relatives. See 12:1. Abraham's family is characterized by family loyalty (see 11:27–32; 22:23; 31:50).

6. do not take my son back there. Abraham remained faithful to God's call to leave behind his homeland (see 12:1, 7; 23:19). Now he works to ensure that his descendants also do so.

7. who brought me out. Abraham orients his entire life, even at death, to God's promise (see 12:1–3, 7).

To your offspring I will give this land. The patriarch's last recorded words (24:6–8) express the essence of God's promise (see 12:7). Isaac's presence in the land symbolizes the fulfillment of God's promise.

his angel. See "angel of the LORD" in 16:7. The Abraham who engineered solutions with Hagar and the pharaohs has greatly matured. He has learned to trust God's supernatural provision of the promise (cf. Gen. 16).

8. If the woman is unwilling. He can count on God, but not on people. Abraham recognizes that the woman must also make a faith choice. If she refuses, she is unworthy.

you will be released. While Abraham acts on the basis of God's promises, he does not presume upon them, freeing the servant of his oath if the Lord does not prosper his mission. Abraham enters and leaves history on the basis of the divine promise.

9. swore an oath. Mention of the oath forms an inclusio around this dialogue (24:3, 9).

---

[246]Roop, *Genesis*, 155.
[247]In these verses, a literal translation for "descendants" is "those coming out of his body [yᵉrēkô]." The word "my thigh" in the Gen. 24:2 is yᵉrēkê.

The Faithful Servant and Rebekah at the
Well at Aram Naharaim (24:10–27)

10. Then the servant. The details about the journey are sparse in comparison with the details concerning the encounter and the answer to the servant's prayer. God's providence includes the ordinary and the extraordinary.

ten . . . camels. See 12:16. This was no doubt an impressive entourage. The details of the camels and the servants (see 24:32, 59) underscore Abraham's wealth and faith in the journey's success. The mention of camels also sets the stage for Rebekah's test at the well.

set out. See "Key Words" in Literary Analysis above.

Aram Naharaim. This is the area of Aram bounded by the Euphrates and the Habur rivers. The LXX took the dual form Naharaim as a reference to the two rivers (i.e., the area between the Tigris and the Euphrates) and so read the name Mesopotamia ("between the rivers").

town of Nahor. This is named in the Mari Tablets (eighteenth century B.C.) as the place Nahur, east of the Balikh River, in the vicinity of Haran.

11. the time. Timing is crucial in providence. The servant knew evening was the time women went to the well.[248]

12. he prayed. This is the first recorded instance of prayer for specific guidance in Scripture. The meeting with Rebekah is encircled by prayer (see 24:26–27). The servant's prayer is crucial to the story and the fulfillment of his mission.

Give me success. The Hebrew is literally to "make happen before me." The servant depends on God's providence. What appears to be chance from the human perspective is part of an orchestrated plan from the divine perspective (see Ruth 2:3).

kindness [ḥesed]. A key word in the servant's prayer (24:12, 14) and doxology (24:26–27), the Hebrew word ḥesed entails loyalty to a covenant relationship. The inferior partner depends on the kindness of the superior to meet desperate need. God's reliable kindness to his needy people is the basis of the covenant relationship (see Isa. 54:10).

14. I'll water your camels too. Hospitality is the determinant, over and above beauty and virginity (24:16). Since each camel could drink twenty-five gallons, the servant's sign is sagacious; it is a test of the woman's kindness, hospitality, industry, and willingness to help a stranger. Sternberg calls it "a shrewd character test." He states, "What touchstone could be more appropriate than the reception of a wayfarer to determine a woman's fitness to marry into the family of the paragon of hospitality? And it is a stiff test, too, since it would require far more than common civility to volunteer to water 'ten' thirsty camels."[249]

---

[248]The Samaritan woman went at high noon because she was an outcast (John 4:6–7).
[249]Sternberg, *Poetics*, 137.

By this I will know. A request for a sign is appropriate in connection with the servant's mission to advance a family meant to bless the earth (see Isa. 7:10–14). He is conscious of the angel's invisible presence (see Gen. 24:7).

15. Before he had finished praying. God's providential timing is key in this story and the other events of the patriarchs' lives (see the story of Joseph, Gen. 37–50; cf. Isa. 65:24).

Rebekah. See 22:23.

Bethuel son of Milcah. This note indicates Rebekah's social status. She was not the granddaughter of a concubine (see 22:20–24).

16. very beautiful. Beauty is valued in the Old Testament (cf. Prov. 6:25). Many stories about honored women note their sex appeal and/or beauty: Sarah (Gen. 12:11; cf. 20:2), Rachel (29:17), Tamar (38:13–19), Rahab (Josh. 2:1), Ruth (Ruth 3:1–9), and the queen consort (Ps. 45:11–15).

a virgin [*bᵉtûlâ*]. "Virgin" in this text does not mean chaste. It denotes an adolescent, nubile girl (i.e., a girl of marriageable age).[250]

no man had ever lain with her. This is a virtue, important to assure that her children unquestionably would be Isaac's.

went down . . . came up again. The comment underscores Rebekah's industry.

17. little water. The wise servant makes a request—simple, yet full of possibility. He is testing her character, while allowing space for God's providence.

19. until they have finished drinking. This generous offer from an obviously capable woman far exceeds the servant's request.

20. quickly . . . ran. Rebekah's actions "dramatize a single point: that the young woman's performance surpasses even the most optimistic expectations."[251]

21. Without saying a word. The perspicacious servant does not react hastily but carefully observes to ensure the Lord's leading. That his next act is to offer Rebekah gold suggests that he discerns admirable qualities in her as she serves.

22. took out a gold nose ring . . . gold bracelets. The servant does this to reward her, to win her goodwill, and to impress her family.

beka. This is one-fifth of an ounce (5.5 grams).

ten shekels. Four ounces (110 grams) of gold is a very handsome sum.

24. the daughter of Bethuel, the son that Milcah bore to Nahor. Bethuel is Isaac's cousin, a providence that exceeds Abraham's request for a kinsman.

25. plenty of straw and fodder. The narrator reports additional signs of hospitality, wealth, and Rebekah's extra care for this man.

---

[250]An Aramaic incantation text speaks of a *bᵉtûlâ*'s "travailing but not bearing." Esther 2:17–19 applies the term to new members of the harem both before and after they have spent the night with the king. In Joel 1:8 the *bᵉtûlâ* has a husband (see G. J. Wenham, "Betula," *VT* 22 (1972): 326–48.

[251]Sternberg, *Poetics*, 138.

26. worshiped the LORD. The meeting is framed by prayer and worship (see 24:12), a sign of the servant's faithfulness and God's favor.

27. Praise be to the LORD. God prospers his worshipers.

has led me [*nḥh*]. The connotation of the Hebrew is "to lead through difficulty." Elsewhere in the Pentateuch this word describes God's special angelic guidance of his people through the wilderness to the Promised Land (Ex. 13:17, 21; 15:13; 32:34; see also Theological Reflections below).

The Servant in Bethuel's Household (24:28–61)

28. mother's household. In that culture a girl's primary familial relation is with the mother (Ruth 1:8; Song 3:4; 8:2).

29. Laban. Laban took responsibility for the family either because the family government was fratriarchal, not patriarchal, or because Bethuel was incapacitated (see 24:50; cf. 20:16). Laban's name, which means "white" and is used elsewhere as a poetic metonym for the moon (*hallᵉḇānâ*, Isa. 24:23; 30:26; cf. Song 6:10), is perhaps another indication of his family's connection with the lunar cult.

30. As soon as he had seen the nose ring, and the bracelets. Whereas Rebekah innocently rushed to show hospitality to a stranger, Laban instead is gripped by greed. This picture of Laban racing after gold foreshadows his dealings with Jacob.

31. blessed by the LORD. His statement lacks sincerity, since he seems most concerned with material blessing.

33. I will not eat until. The servant puts his mission before his need and comfort. His prudent refusal to eat before stating his mission also allows him to control the situation and to avoid any sense of obligation to this host and hostess.

34. he said. Repetition of this sort is a standard feature of ancient Near Eastern epic literature. The servant varies the account to meet the exigencies of this situation (see notes that follow). His selective and creative retelling, meant to persuade Rebekah's family of God's providential leading, models the narrator's persuasive "retelling" of the biblical story.

36–38. he has become wealthy . . . to my own clan. These are also important details (see 25:5–6). The servant appeals to his listeners' venality by mentioning first his master's wealth (24:34–35) and Isaac's position as sole heir (24:36). By mentioning his master's request that Isaac marry within his own family and his refusal to allow marriage with the Canaanites, the servant assures them that Rebekah's children will be the sole heirs (24:37; cf. 29:26–27; 31:50).

36. in her old age. The servant is a skilled spokesman, carefully selecting the details that will motivate and encourage the family. Here his mention of Sarah's late age for childbirth assures them that Isaac is not too old. His later mention of the Canaanites explains why Isaac is unmarried.

everything he owns. This will be confirmed in the next scene (25:1–6, especially v. 6).

37. made me swear. It is a compliment to the family that Abraham is so seriously committed to arranging his son's marriage among his relatives. The servant tactfully omits reference to Abraham's departure from the family.

40–48. The LORD, before whom I have walked . . . the granddaughter of my master's brother. The repetition of the story is necessary to persuade the family to acknowledge the hand of the Lord. His detailed recounting of Abraham's faith, of his own prayers, and of his providential meeting with Rebekah challenges the listeners to recognize God's approval of this marriage.

45. Rebekah. The narrator blanks how he learned her name.

49. show kindness and faithfulness [*ḥesed weʾemet*] **. . . if not.** Finally he appeals to them for covenant loyalty to Abraham. If they fail to respond, he will look elsewhere for a bride.

50. Laban and Bethuel answered. The irregular sequence of mentioning the son before the father and the mention of only the brother and mother in 24:53 and 55 suggest that Bethuel is incapacitated.

This is from the LORD. They validate the hand of Providence.

one way or the other. The NIV offers a paraphrase of the Hebrew expression, "either good or bad" (cf. 31:24). They have no choice in the matter.

52. he bowed . . . before the LORD. This faithful servant never fails to credit and thank God.

53. brought out gold and silver. In addition to the personal gifts to Rebekah, he now gives the family a gift, probably the bride price. The bride price was payment for the loss of the bride's services and her potential offspring (see Gen. 34:13; Ex. 22:16).

55. Let the girl remain. This was customary (see Tobit 9:20).

ten days or so. The Hebrew is literally "days or ten." The amount of time is ambiguous. The Targums interpreted the phrase to mean "a year or ten minutes"; the LXX, as "a few days, say ten." It could mean a few days or a few years. Later, Jacob will unexpectedly remain twenty years (Gen. 31:38)!

56. The LORD has granted success to my journey. The servant gives an implicit warning that if they detain him they are acting against Providence.

58. Will you go. . . ? Since they had already consented to the marriage (24:51), the question is unethical. This story hints at Laban's unscrupulous conduct and greed, which will later trouble Jacob (see 29:23; 31:41). Had the servant and Rebekah stayed, they might have lost both the dowry and the marriage.

I will go. This is the most decisive remark in the narrative. Seemingly against her family's wishes, she complies with the Lord's direction, matching Abraham's faith to leave the family (see 12:1, 4).

59. their sister. The reference here is somewhat unclear. Does it mean relative?

her nurse. The Hebrew refers to her "wet nurse." To judge from Akkadian parallels, the wet nurse after suckling the child had the responsibility to rear the child and serve as guardian. This esteemed member of the family now accompanies Rebekah. Later this nurse, Deborah, will play a fateful role in Rebekah's story (see 35:8).

60. increase . . . possess the gates of their enemies. See 22:17. Once again, "the matriarch shares in the blessing."[252]

61. her maids. This marks Rebekah's social status.

got ready. Probably several days were required to prepare for the journey. The servant is away from southern Canaan for approximately three years (see 23:1; 25:20).

mounted their camels. It is now clear why ten camels were needed.

servant took Rebekah and left. The faithful servant has performed well his appointed task.

Isaac, Rebekah, and the Servant in the Negev (24:62–67)

62. Beer Lahai Roi. The name means, "The well of the Living One who sees me," named for Hagar's providential encounter with the Lord at that place (see 16:14). It is significant that Isaac is coming from a well, a symbolic meeting place for marriages (see "Scenic Depiction" in Literary Analysis above).

living in the Negev. The narrative reflects a shift of leadership and focus to Isaac. Abraham, who had initiated this journey, is not mentioned, nor is explanation given for Isaac's residence in the Negev. The servant will refer now to Isaac as his master (see 24:65, cf. 24:36, 39, 42, 44, 48).

63. to the field one evening. The Lord's providential hand in the situation and timing is again undeniable.

to meditate [śûaḥ]. The meaning of the unique Hebrew is uncertain. The ancient versions differ: LXX, "in order to gossip"; Vulgate, "in order to meditate"; Syriac, "so as to result"; Targums, "in order to pray." Modern translations vacillate accordingly. It may be paraphrased in 24:65 by "coming" (hlk) [in the field], suggesting the meaning "to walk, stroll, wander about." An Arabic cognate has the meaning to "travel, rove, roam." If this is the meaning, it would enhance the idea of providence.

as he looked up, he saw. This statement parallels Rebekah's first glimpse of him ("Rebekah also looked up and saw," 24:64), conveying the idea of simultaneity.

64. got down. A paraphrase of the Hebrew idiom, "the fall from" (see 2 Kings 5:21).[253] Rebekah dismounts to show respect to her intended husband (Josh. 15:18; 1 Sam. 25:23).

---

[252]Fox, *Beginning*, 95.
[253]M. Delcor, "Quelques cas de survivances du vocabulaire nomade en Hébreu biblique," *VT* 25 (1975): 313–14.

65. covered herself. Rebekah's veiling symbolizes to Isaac that she is the bride. Israelite women were not normally veiled (see 12:14; 38:14). It was customary, however, to veil the bride in the marriage ceremony.

66. told Isaac. Abraham lived another thirty-five years (see 21:5; 25:7, 9, 20), yet the narrative omits the servant's report to Abraham and focuses on Isaac. By this editorial choice, Isaac is presented as lord and successor of Abraham even as Rebekah is presented as mother and successor of Sarah.

67. the tent of his mother. Rebekah follows Sarah in salvation history.

loved her. God grants complete success to the journey.

comforted after his mother's death. Fox concludes, "As the story opened with Yitzhak's father in his last active moments, it closes with the memory of his mother. Yitzhak is on his own."[254]

THEOLOGICAL REFLECTIONS ON BOOK 6, ACT 3, SCENE 3

Guidance

The story reflects on how the divine promise to Abraham is fulfilled through his faith and commitment (24:12, 14, 27), through the divine presence in the angel of the Lord, through the prayer and prudence of the anonymous loyal servant, through the Lord's providence, and through Rebekah's willingness to leave her own land to join the promised family. In this way the Lord orchestrates the birth of the promised seed. The anonymous servant is the first person in Scripture who prays for direct guidance through providential signs. While the saint should pray without ceasing and with thanksgiving for every circumstance, the New Testament has no parallel of the apostles or the church asking for signs.[255]

Prayer

The servant's prayer is spontaneous, from the heart, directly to God without religious personnel to mediate it, a designated site, or ritual such as a sacrifice (24:12). These qualities may be appropriate in formal worship, but they are not necessary for the saint's direct relationship with God.

Providence

The details about the journey are sparse in comparison with the details concerning the encounter and the answer to the servant's prayer. God's providence includes the ordinary and the extraordinary (see "Structure and Plot" in Literary Analysis above). God provides for his covenant partners to effect his plan through providential acts (see 50:20; Ruth). To that end, the angel of

---

[254]Fox, *Beginning*, 108.
[255]See B. K. Waltke with J. MacGregor, *Knowing the Will of God* (Eugene, Ore.: Harvest House, 1998).

the Lord who goes before his people (24:7) is also spoken of in conjunction with giving Israel the land (see Ex. 23:20, 23; Num. 20:16; see also Gen. 16).

Faith

In faith, Abraham orients his entire life, even at death, on God's promise (see 12:1–3, 7). Because he believes God's promises of land and abundant offspring that will bless the earth, Abraham refuses to allow Isaac either to intermarry with Canaanites or to leave the Promised Land. Although Abraham *acts* on the basis of the promise, he does not *presume upon* it. The servant is free of his oath if the Lord does not prosper his mission. Abraham trusts God but also recognizes that Isaac's future wife must make her own faith choice. Abraham's faith is rewarded. A life committed to seeking God's kingdom will experience God's good hand (see Matt. 6:33).

Rebekah demonstrates her faith in Abraham's God by decisively leaving her family to go to a foreign land to marry Isaac. The Lord turns her family's treachery into a marvelous moment for her to assert her faith. Her faith is rewarded as she enters a family line destined to bless the earth.

Marriage

Isaac and Rebekah's marriage may be made in heaven, but this is no sure sign it will not fail. By the time their twins reach marriageable age, their own marriage has become dysfunctional. Each speaks and acts secretly against each other in their machinations to secure the divine blessing on the favored son. A good marriage not only requires a good beginning but also continued leadership, good character, and godliness.

BOOK 6, ACT 3, SCENE 4: ISAAC THE SOLE HEIR (25:1–6)

LITERARY ANALYSIS OF BOOK 6, ACT 3, SCENE 4 ————

Structure

Before concluding Abraham's story, the narrator presents final details concerning Abraham's children and the settling of Abraham's affairs. The scene was anticipated in 24:36. Abraham has given Isaac everything he owns. In addition to his supernatural offspring, Isaac, Abraham has many natural offspring. These children are significant as descendants of Abraham, hence their genealogical listing. However, they are not the inheritors of the promise, which was intended for Abraham's supernatural offspring, hence the importance of establishing inheritance rights (see Theological Reflections below). Scene 4 is divided into two parts: the first presents a segmented genealogy of Abraham's children by Keturah (25:1–4); the second, the distribution of the inheritance, naming Isaac as the sole beneficiary of the estate and promise (25:5–6). To his sons by concubines Abraham gives only gifts

(25:6). Isaac is the sole heir of the property even before Abraham's death and of the Promised Land in the future after his death.

The segmented genealogy is framed by the statement of Keturah as the progenitrix: "Keturah . . . bore him" (25:1–2) and "all these were descendants of Keturah" (25:4). This genealogy presents sixteen descendants: sons, grandsons and great-grandsons.

Here is a schema of this genealogy:

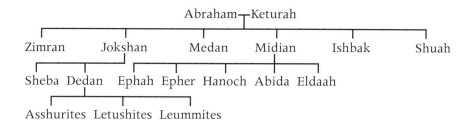

Keturah bore Abraham six sons (25:2). Through Jokshan, Abraham has two grandsons and three great-grandsons (25:3), for a total of five children of Jokshan. Through Midian, Abraham's fourth son through Keturah, he has five grandsons (25:4).

Comparison and Contrast

Although both Keturah (cf. 1 Chron. 1:32) and Hagar are concubines, the narrator gives the genealogy of Abraham's children through Hagar a separate book (25:12–18), suggesting the esteemed status of Sarah and God's grace to Abraham and Hagar. The differences between Hagar, an Egyptian slave concubine, and Keturah, a concubine, is Hagar's unique relationship to Sarah as a surrogate mother, Abraham's devotion to Ishmael, and God's promises to Hagar. Nevertheless, both genealogies form an inclusio around the final scene of Act 3, which records the death and burial of Abraham.

Anachrony

The text safeguards itself against the misinterpretation that this scene chronologically follows Scene 3. In the preceding scene, Abraham's servant asserts that Abraham has already given everything he owns to Isaac (24:36), a statement that assumes Abraham has other children. Also, Abraham already judged his body too old to beget children when he was one hundred years old (17:1, 17); it is biologically unlikely he fathered six sons when he was forty years older and "well advanced in years" (24:1). It is possible that God rejuvenated his body, but if he fathered them after 140 years of age, then they are even more supernatural than Isaac, which is theologically unlikely.

EXEGETICAL NOTES TO BOOK 6, ACT 3, SCENE 4 ―――――

Abraham's Descendants through Keturah (25:1–4)[256]

1. took. This is better translated "had taken" (see above Literary Analysis, "Anachrony"). No attempt is made to date this secondary offspring to Abraham, and most likely this event is anachronous. The placement of this genealogy at the end of the Abraham story functions to show that Isaac, the son of promise, is the elect patriarch and sole heir of the Promised Land.

another. This is presumably in addition to Sarah and before Hagar.

wife. Here she is named as a wife, but in 25:6b as a concubine (see Bilhah, 30:4). The difference may have affected the legal status of her sons. See "left everything he owned to Isaac" (25:5) below.

Keturah. This concubine's (25:6; 1 Chron. 1:32) name, which means "enveloped in fragrant smoke/incense," is probably explained by her sons' trade. Biblical and Akkadian sources name them as peoples or localities in Arabia involved with the production and trade of incense.

2. Zimran. The name is also a locality west of Mecca.[257]

Jokshan. He is to be distinguished from Joktan (Gen. 10:25–28). Although both are fathers of a Sheba, their names and paternity differ.

Medan. These desert dwellers are grouped together with the Ishmaelites and Midianites. The merchants shipping spices, balm, and myrrh from Gilead to Egypt are identified as Ishmaelites (37:25), Midianites (*miḏyānîm*, 37:28), and Medanites (*mᵉḏānîm*, 37:36). The name is otherwise unattested, unless it is a variant of a place named Badana, south of Tema.

Midian. A well-known Arabian tribe east of the Gulf of Aqabah and the Red Sea, from Moab to Sinai and Ephah (Num. 22:4, 7; Judg. 6–8), they traded in gold and incense (Isa. 60:6; cf. Gen. 37:25, 28). Moses' wife Zipporah was a Midianite, and her Midianite brother Hobab guided Israel through the steppe of Sinai (Num. 10:29–32).

Ishbak. This is a north Syrian tribe attested in cuneiform texts.[258]

Shuah. One should perhaps identify this with a place named in cuneiform texts that is situated in the region of the Middle Euphrates below the mouth of the Habur [River] (cf. Job 2:11).[259]

3. Sheba. This is a known region and people in the southern part of the Arabian Peninsula.[260] They are associated with incense and spice trade both in Akkadian and biblical texts (Isa. 60:6; Jer. 6:20; Ezek. 27:22).

Dedan. This is a well attested city—the modern oasis of el-ʿUlla some 68 miles (110 km) southwest of Taima—and people of Northwest Arabia, famous for their role in the caravan trade (Isa. 21:13; Ezek. 27:20). The city

---

[256]For indications of editing and the antiquity of this material, see Wenham, *Genesis 16–50*, 156–57.

[257]*HALOT*, 274.

[258]Ibid., 445.

[259]Ibid., 1439.

[260]Ibid., 1381.

lay on the well-known "incense route" from southern Arabia to Syria and the Mediterranean. Both Sheba and Dedan are also mentioned as sons of great-grandsons of Ham (Gen. 10:7). Hamilton explains, "One may explain the use of different patronymics for Sheba and Dedan as due either to the use of the same name by different persons and tribes in different parts of Arabia, or more likely, the convergence of Hamitic and Semitic lines in southern Arabia."[261]

Asshurites, Letushites and the Leummites. The exceptional gentilic forms (i.e., adjectival forms of proper names) may indicate that these are not proper names at all—so the Aramaic translation—but descriptions of the professions and or social status of the sons of Dedan. If so, the translation would be rendered, "they were peasants, smiths, and seminomads." However, gentilics also occur in the Table of Nations, and I will proceed with *HALOT* on the assumption that they are proper names.

Asshurites. This is an old Assyrian or Arabian tribe.[262] Although in the Hebrew Bible the name is the same as the infamous Assyrians (see 10:22), these Assyrians/Asshurites probably designate a tribe near Egypt known from South Arabian inscriptions. The same is true of the Asshurites in Num. 24:22, 24 and Ps. 83:8, whose circumstances do not fit Assyria.

Letushites. This is an unknown population in Arabia. If the name is read Loteshites, it denotes "manual craftsmen."[263]

Leummites. This is an Arabian tribe, but the word is understood by Montgomery to mean "hordes" and by Albright "tribal people."[264]

4. Ephah . . . Eldaah. The Midianites are probably made up of these five sons or tribes. Numbers 31:8 (Josh. 13:21) mentions five kings of Midian, presumably one from each of these tribes.

Ephah. Montgomery equates him with cuneiform Ḫaippa, whose habitat was the region of the Red Sea. In both cuneiform and biblical texts, the land of Ephah/Ḫaippa is associated with spices and incense (Isa. 60:6).[265]

Epher, Hanoch, Abida and Eldaah. These are otherwise unattested.

Keturah. Repetition of her name forms a frame around the genealogy (see 25:1 and Literary Analysis).

The Distribution of Property to Isaac (25:5 – 6)

5. left everything he owned to Isaac. See 24:36. Abraham dispossessed his descendants by Keturah as he had Ishmael by Hagar (see 21:10). Since the status of his sons by Keturah is uncertain, it is difficult to assess whether Abraham's actions conflicted with the Mosaic law and whether they comported

---

[261]V. P. Hamilton, *The Book of Genesis: Chapters 18–50* (NICOT; Grand Rapids: Eerdmans, 1995), 166.

[262]*HALOT*, 94, no. 4.

[263]Ibid., 528.

[264]Ibid., 513.

[265]*ANET*, 283b, 286a.

with ancient Near Eastern laws. In 25:1 Keturah is called a wife, but in 25:6, a concubine. If she were reckoned as a full wife, and assuming that Keturah bore these sons before Sarah bore Isaac, then according to the Mosaic law Abraham could not have deprived the actual firstborn, presumably Zimran, a share in the inheritance. However, since she is also called a concubine, this law may not have been applicable. In any case, Abraham lived before the Mosaic law, and, as in many other cases, the religious and social practices of the patriarchs differed from Israel's later laws (see "Historicity and Literary Genre" in the introduction). His actions may have comported with known ancient Near Eastern laws. According to the Code of Hammurabi, if a man does not own offspring from slaves as his sons, "after the father had gone to (his) fate, the children of the slave may not share in the goods of the paternal estate along with the children of the first wife."[266] Perhaps by making Isaac the sole heir and by sending the other sons away before his death, Abraham did not own them as legal sons.

6. while he was still living. Abraham himself secures Isaac's inheritance in the land.

gifts. This is their inheritance. "Sons of full wives could expect a definite share (Deut. 21:15–17; cf. Num. 27:1–11). Sons of concubines were completely dependent on their father's goodwill."[267] Since he is probably not legally required to give them gifts, his gifts are a gesture of goodwill. The result of this gesture, if not its purpose, probably wins their goodwill toward Isaac until the time of the conquest.

concubines. The plural refers to Keturah and probably Hagar. Although Hagar is described as a "maidservant" (16:2) and "slave woman" (21:10), she probably could be designated "a concubine." Similarly, Bilhah is called both a "maidservant" (30:3) and "concubine" (35:22).

the land of the east [$qedem$]. The unique phrase, "land of $qedem$," can be either a proper name for a specific territory, probably in the Syrian desert, that is known from Egyptian texts, or a general designation of the vast territory east of Israel extending from the Middle Euphrates to Arabia. The identification of Keturah's sons with place names in this vast territory favors the latter interpretation.

THEOLOGICAL REFLECTIONS ON
BOOK 6, ACT 3, SCENE 4 ————————————

Offspring

The text provides a striking tension between God's election of his mediatorial people through whom he will bless the earth and his generosity that embraces all people. The genealogies, prefaced (25:1–4) to Abraham's death

---

[266]Ibid., 173.
[267]Wenham, *Genesis 16–50*, 159.

(25:7–11) and appended after it (25:12–18), are of Abraham's natural sons. These genealogies show that the natural children, though they have a blood bond with the elect, do not inherit the promised blessings of property and especially of the Promised Land associated with the Abrahamic blessing. That inheritance is rightfully given exclusively to Sarah's son—Abraham's supernatural and, by divine reckoning, only son. On the other hand, the sons by the concubines are sent permanently away from the Promised Land.

Historicity

The attestations of many of these names in ancient, not modern, written sources inferentially help establish that other events in the Abrahamic narrative occurred in real history (see "Historicity and Literary Genre" in the introduction). Furthermore, the genealogy seems to be ancient. Though most of these tribes are located in Arabia, the name Arab is not used. That name does not occur in ancient sources until the ninth century B.C. Also, there is no suggestion that Midian, a half-brother of Isaac, would later become a bitter enemy of Israel. Thus Sarna concludes, "Given such a history of enmity between the two peoples, it is hardly likely that a narrator would have invented a record of kinship unless it rested on solid fact."[268]

Polygamy

Polygamy was practiced by godly men in the Old Testament. Indeed, the narrator presents David under blessing by contrasting his many sons of several wives with the impotence of the house of Saul (see 2 Sam. 3). He also presents David under divine wrath by having his wives taken from him (2 Sam. 12:8, 11). The practice, however, often led to strife among the wives and the siblings of the several wives (cf. Gen. 37:2; 2 Sam. 13), though the same can be said of the siblings by the same marriage (Gen. 4). The law did not forbid polygamy but regulated it. "If [a man] marries another woman, he must not deprive the first one of her food, clothing and marital rights" (Ex. 21:10). This law forbade a man from having a harem (cf. Deut. 17:17; 1 Kings 11:3) or from indulging his sensual pleasure without regard to the rights of his wife (contra Est. 1). Obviously, however, polygamy was not a violation of the command, "You shall not commit adultery" (i.e., taking another's person's spouse; Ex. 20:14; cf. Gen. 39:9). Nevertheless, polygamy was not the original intention. God gave Adam one wife, not several (Gen. 2:18–25), and the practice was introduced by depraved Lamech (4:19). Christ aimed to restore this original ideal in his church, for the law had only accommodated itself to the hardness of the human heart (Matt. 19:1–9). Therefore, an elder or deacon in the church was to be the husband of but one wife (1 Tim. 3:2, 12).

---

[268]Sarna, *Genesis*, 171.

BOOK 6, ACT 3, SCENE 5:
DEATH OF ABRAHAM (25:7–11)

LITERARY ANALYSIS OF BOOK 6, ACT 3, SCENE 5 ──────

Theme

The death and burial of Abraham forms a natural conclusion to Book 6, "The Account of Terah's Descendants." The obituary features Abraham's blessed state at the time of death (and in death) and God's continued presence with the next generation.

Structure

After an opening statement about Abraham's age at death, matching Scene 3 (cf. 25:7 and 23:1), the narrative records three chronological aspects of Abraham's passing: his state at death (25:8), his burial at Machpelah (25:9–10), and God's blessings on Isaac (25:11).

Anachrony

Isaac marries thirty-five years before the death of Abraham, and Abraham's grandsons are fifteen years old when he dies. This means that Scene 1 of Book 8 (Gen. 25:19–34) occurs before this scene.

EXEGETICAL NOTES TO BOOK 6, ACT 3, SCENE 5 ──────

Introductory Statement of Age At Death (25:7)

7. **a hundred and seventy-five years.** Abraham lives exactly one hundred years in the Promised Land (cf. 12:4). Isaac is now seventy-five years of age (see 21:5) and Abraham's grandsons fifteen (cf. 25:26).

Abraham's Blessed State at Death (25:8)

8. **Abraham breathed his last.** His death is developed by three verbs: expired, died, gathered to his people. The unnecessary addition of the first adds solemnity to the account (cf. 25:17; 35:19; 49:33).

died at a good old age. This is just as God had promised (see 15:15).

an old man and full of years. The addition "of years" is found in several manuscripts and the ancient versions. The majority of manuscripts read simply "full" (i.e., he had plenty). By the time of death he has enjoyed both abundant quantity and quality of life.

gathered to his people. Abraham's being gathered to his people occurs between his death and burial. It does not refer to his burial, because Abraham was not buried with his ancestors. The same is true of Aaron (Num. 20:26) and Moses (Deut. 32:50). Sarna argues, "It would seem, therefore, that the existence of this idiom [which is unique to the Pentateuch], as of the corresponding figure 'to lie down with one's fathers,' testifies to a belief that, despite his mortality and perishability, man possesses an immortal element that survives the loss of life. Death is looked upon as a transition to an after-life where one is united with one's ancestors."[269]

Abraham's Burial at Machpelah (25:9 – 10)

9. His sons Isaac and Ishmael. Jacob and Esau are also reunited at the burial of their common father. Here Isaac and Ishmael are listed in order of theological importance, not of age, as might be expected. Only the sons associated with Sarah share in this honor. They come together at death because of this common bond with their parents (see also 35:29). Ishmael is not a man without a story and future.

in the cave of Machpelah. See Gen. 23; 35:27–29; 49:29–32.

God's Blessings on Isaac (25:11)

11. God blessed his son Isaac. This functions as a transition to the account of Isaac, 25:19–35:29, and ends Abraham's story. God has the last word.

Beer Lahai Roi. The place where the angel of the Lord promised Hagar that she would have a son (see 16:14) is now occupied by Isaac. The allusion forms a transition to the account of the descendants of Ishmael and suggests that Isaac will displace him.

THEOLOGICAL REFLECTIONS ON BOOK 6, ACT 3, SCENE 5

Death

Ecclesiastes 12:1 describes old age as "the days of trouble" (*rāʿâ*, i.e., "evil," the opposite of "good"). However, the state of Abraham at his death shows that this truth can be qualified. He dies full of years, fully satisfied with life, and in a state that can still be called "good" (i.e., beneficial and desirable).

Immortality

See the note above on "gathered to his people."

Faith and Fulfillment of Promises

The book of Hebrews, in the list of the people of faith, normally gives one verse to each hero of faith. Abraham is given twelve verses as the example of faith par excellence. Moses is given six verses. The patriarchs die not having obtained the promises. Likewise, the saints under the new covenant, though fulfilling the promises, die not yet having consummated them. "None of [the Old Testament heroes of faith] received what had been promised. God had planned something better for us so that only together with us would they be made perfect" (Heb. 11:39–40). Together with them we are looking for a divine consummation, a new heaven and earth.

---

[269]Ibid., 174.

BOOK 7

THE ACCOUNT OF ISHMAEL'S DESCENDANTS (25:12 – 18)

THEME OF BOOK 7

This book, which features the descendants of Ishmael, follows up God's promises to Abraham and Hagar (16:10, 12). Because he is a descendant of Abraham and Sarah's maidservant, Ishmael is not a man without a future and a destiny.

OUTLINE OF BOOK 7

LITERARY ANALYSIS OF BOOK 7

Structure

After the stereotypical superscription (25:12), the book consists of three parts, which follow an A, B, A′ pattern: Ishmael's segmented genealogy presenting the twelve tribes (25:13–16), Ishmael's obituary notice (25:17), and the settlements and destiny of Ishmael's tribes (25:18). Ishmael's obituary is sandwiched between his offspring. The first part is clearly distinguished by the inclusio "these are/were . . . the sons of Ishmael" (25:13, 16). The third part begins, literally, "they settled," forcing the reader to jump over Ishmael's obituary to find the antecedent in the twelve tribal rulers. NIV eases the unusual syntax by offering, "His descendants settled." By this structure the narrator features the Ishmaelites rather than Ishmael without slighting him.

Comparison and Contrast

Ishmael's genealogy reveals both the blessings and curses promised in the calling of Abraham (see 12:2–3). As a son of Abraham, Ishmael experiences the physical blessing of progeny, but spiritually he stands apart from the Abrahamic line and the divine blessings that entails. Both Abraham and Ishmael are said to be gathered to their peoples after they die. The narrator records no burial site for Ishmael, but the separation of Abraham from Ishmael suggests that they were gathered to two different groups of people.

Although the narrator presents a segmented genealogy for Ishmael, like that of Keturah (25:2–4), this broad genealogy consists entirely of the twelve names of the first generation. Sarna's suggestion that this indicates "a very powerful primary confederation of tribes"[1] is validated by the additional notice, "and these are the names of the twelve tribal rulers" (25:16), a notice that is gapped in the genealogy by Keturah.

The twelve tribes of Ishmael correspond in number to the twelve tribes of Nahor (see 22:20–24), of Edom (36:10–14), and of Israel (35:23–26). If the rejected Ishmael and the twelve tribes that spring from him have a future and a destiny, how much more is that true of Isaac, through whom Abraham's lineage will be reckoned? In this sense, Ishmael is a foil to Isaac. Whereas God gives the Israelites land and makes them a light to the nations, he promises the Ishmaelites no land (though they settle from Havilah to the Egyptian border), and they live in hostility with all their brothers. Nevertheless, although the tribes of Nahor, of Keturah, and of Ishmael later fight against the tribes of Israel, Israel is chosen to become a blessing to them.

Repetition and Escalation

Book 7 repeats a segmented genealogy like that of Abraham's sons by Keturah (25:1–4, 13–16), ending with a notice of their settlement and their relationship with their brother(s) (25:5–6, 18) and also an obituary notice like that of Abraham (i.e., life span, expired, died, gathered to fathers [but not buried]; 25:7–8, 17). Each of these scenes ends with a statement about the relationship of the sons. Abraham sends the sons of Keturah away from Isaac, Isaac and Ishmael together bury Abraham, and the sons of Ishmael live in hostility against all their brothers.

EXEGETICAL NOTES TO BOOK 7 ——————————————

Superscription (25:12)

12. This is the account. See 2:4 and note.

Hagar the Egyptian. Where one might expect only the mention of the fathers in the genealogies of this patriarchal society, a number of wives,

---

[1]Sarna, *Genesis*, 175.

maidservants, and concubines are given due place in the genealogical records (see 22:24; 25:1). More surprisingly, however, the narrator devotes a whole book to the genealogy of a concubine. He does this because Hagar gave birth to Abraham's son as the surrogate mother of Sarah and to show that God has kept his promise to this maidservant (16:10, 12).

Ishmael's Segmented Genealogy (25:13 – 16)

13. in the order of their birth. See also 1 Chron. 1:29–31. For the function of a segmented genealogy in comparison to a linear genealogy, see "Excursus: Genesis Genealogies" and the Literary Analysis of Book 5.

Nebaioth. They are mentioned in various spellings in the accounts of the campaign of Ashurbanipal (ca. 668–633 B.C.) against the Arabs.[2] The tribe was located in the vicinity of Ha'il. They were wrongly assumed to be the ancestors of the Nabateans.

Kedar. Well attested in the Bible (Ps. 120:5; Song 1:5; Isa. 21:16–17; 42:11; 60:7; Jer. 2:10; 49:28; Ezek. 27:21) and in the royal Assyrian inscriptions (as *Qadr, Qadari, Qidri, Qidir*), they were a nomadic tribe of the Syrian-Arabian desert, more precisely in the region between Egypt and Dedan-Edom or alternatively in the Wadi aṣ-Sirhan.[3]

Adbeel. The Arab tribe *Idi-baʾilai*, subjugated by Tiglath Pileser III (see "Massa" below), is attested also in Old South Arabic inscriptions as *ʾbdʾl*.[4]

Mibsam. This is unattested, though the name is connected with the word for "spices." This person should be distinguished from the father of Mishma in the lineage of Simeon (1 Chron. 4:25).

14. Mishma. The Arab tribe *Isamme* in cuneiform sources, its location is unknown.[5]

Dumah. This is the same as cuneiform *Adummu, Adum(m)a/autu* and Nabatean *dwmt* and is identified with *Dumat el-Jandal* (Dumah of the Stones) in the oasis of el-Jof in northern Arabia.[6]

Massa. This is elsewhere attested in the Bible in 1 Chron. 1:30 (probably not Prov. 30:1; 31:1).[7] The Arab tribe *Masʾu* (gentilic *Masʾaia*) was subjugated by Tiglath-Pileser III (744–727 B.C.). Their abode was Tayma. Tiglath-Pileser III exacted from them "gold, silver, male and female camels and all kinds of spices."[8]

15. Hadad. An Aramaean tribe named *Ḥudadu* is attested, but not an Arabian tribe.[9]

---

[2]*ANET*, 298.
[3]*HALOT*, 1072.
[4]Ibid., 12.
[5]Ibid., 649.
[6]Ibid., 216.
[7]See B. K. Waltke, *The Book of Proverbs* (NICOT; Grand Rapids: Eerdmans, forthcoming).
[8]*ANET*, 283–84.
[9]*HALOT*, 291.

Tema. Like the Massa, they were subjugated by Tiglath Pileser III (see Massa above). Tema is also a place name for the famous oasis northeast of Dedan (see Job 6:19; Isa. 21:14; Jer. 25:23).

Jetur. The name is usually identified with Nabatean *Iatouros* in Hauran. The Jeturites are named together with the Naphishites, both as Hagrites, in 1 Chron. 5:19. The connection between Hagar and the Hagrites is uncertain.

Naphish. See preceding note.

Kedemah. This name is otherwise unattested.

16. names of . . . according to. Here it is clear that the names designate the eponymous ancestors who have given their names to both their tribes and places of settlement. This identification of personal names with place names tends to validate the identification of other biblical personal names with place names in ancient sources.

twelve . . . rulers. This is a fulfillment of 17:20.

tribal. The same Hebrew word is rendered "Leummites" in 25:3. The word is often parallel to *gôyim*, "nations," (cf. 25:23; Ps. 2:1; Isa. 34:1).

settlements. The word refers to permanent settlements without walls (i.e., without protection). The related Arabic *ḥazara* means "to make inaccessible, to confine cattle in fence."[10] The term points to the settlements of pastoral nomads.

Ishmael's Obituary (25:17)

17. lived a hundred and thirty-seven years. The report of the life span of a non-Israelite is exceptional, suggesting the importance of this descendant of Abraham (cf. 23:1). He outlives his father by forty-eight years (cf. 16:16; 25:7).

breathed his last . . . his people. The repetition of this formula with the death of Abraham (see 25:7–8) also suggests Ishmael's importance. The narrator does not slight him.

Settlements and Destiny of Ishmael's Tribes (25:18)

18. His descendants settled. The Hebrew literally says, "they settled" (see "Structure" in Literary Analysis above).

from Havilah to Shur. For Havilah, see 2:11 and 10:7; for Shur, see 16:7. The Ishmaelites are later displaced by the Amalekites (see 1 Sam. 15:7) and settle mostly in Arabia according to the personal and place names in the prophets and in the royal Assyrian inscriptions.

Asshur. See 25:3.

lived in hostility. This is a fulfillment of 16:12.

---

[10]Ibid., 345.

THEOLOGICAL REFLECTIONS ON BOOK 7

God's Incredible Faithfulness

God keeps his word to Abraham, as confirmed in the two accounts of Abraham's nonelect lines (Book 7, 25:12–18; 25:1–4; see "Theme" in Literary Analysis above). The account of Ishmael, however, also confirms the faithfulness of God's promise to the frightened and troubled maidservant Hagar.

Twelve Tribes and God's Sovereignty

Surely the mention of the twelve tribes of Arameans, of Ishmaelites, of Edomites, and of Israelites is not fortuitous. Christ even chooses twelve apostles, symbolic of the twelve tribes of Israel (Matt. 19:28; Luke 22:30; Rev. 21:12–14). The number twelve seems to represent God's ordering of creation and history, demonstrated by the fact that twelve is a basic unit for measuring time and organizing history (e.g. 24 hours [12 x 2] and 144 as the ideal number of the eschatological kingdom [12 x 12]). This suggests that all these tribes, one from Abraham's brother Nahor and three from his own loins, participate in God's common grace and elective purposes. The merciful God increases all of them and uniquely blesses Ishmael with longevity and a great nation (Gen. 17:20). Moreover, the Sovereign will later use these tribal confederacies to discipline his elect people. They also will be disciplined for their contentious spirit and fierce pride (cf. Isa. 21:13–17; Jer. 49:28–33). Ultimately, the gracious Sovereign will bring all under the sway of the kingdom of Jesus Christ (cf. Amos 9:11–12 with Acts 15:16–17; Isa. 42:11; 60:1–9).

Brothers, Spiritual and Political

Though of the same blood from Terah, these brothers are not gathered to the same people at death. Israel in the Promised Land stands apart. Isaac and Ishmael, though spiritually distinct from their inception, politically begin together in the burial of their father. The Primary History, however, traces a growing political hostility between Israel and these "brothers" that spring from Abraham (i.e., the various Arabian tribes through Keturah and Ishmael; cf. Judg. 8:24), from Abraham's brother Nahor (i.e., the Arameans; cf., e.g., 1 Kings 20; 2 Kings 5; 6:24–7:20), and from Haran (i.e., the Ammonites and Moabites from Lot; cf., e.g., Num. 20:14–21; 21:4; 22:1; Judg. 3:12–13; 11:1–18; 1 Sam. 14:47; 2 Sam. 8:2, 12–14; 1 Kings 11:14–22; 2 Kings 13:20). Instructively, although longevity and increase is a sign of blessing, apart from Gen. 17:20 the narrator mostly reserves the term *blessing* for Isaac and his seed (25:11; 26:3; 28:3), since the word also includes victory over one's enemies (see 22:17; 27:29).

THE ACCOUNT
OF ISAAC'S DESCENDANTS
(25:19 – 35:29)

THEMES OF BOOK 8

At the core of this account is God's promise of his protective presence (28:15; 31:42; 32:9, 12; 35:3) and blessing given to Abraham (24:7) and passed on to Isaac and Jacob (28:3–4; 31:1–5; 35:11–12). Overarching the entire story is God's sovereign good pleasure (Rom. 9:10–12) and blessing on Jacob. He opens Rebekah's barren womb, predicts the supremacy of Jacob over Esau, contravenes the primogeniture rights of human beings, and overrides Isaac's patriarchal authority, Laban's social position, and Esau's military might.

Election is worked out through a faithful covenant partner. The divine choice entails the gift of faith to Jacob, not Esau (Gen. 25:27–34). In contrast to Esau, Jacob shows covenant fidelity and vision by desiring the birthright and blessing and by remaining loyal to the promised seed and land. Covenant, however, rests on God's faithfulness. Though the chosen are often unfaithful, God always abides faithful to his elect.

At the same time, the moral laws of reciprocity are actualized: each reaps what he or she sows (cf. Isaac, Rebekah, Jacob). Isaac's sensuality will cost him his family and his full place of honor in the genealogical accounts. Esau's impatience, greed, and lack of covenant vision will cost him his birthright and blessing. Rebekah's deception will draw her into anonymity. Jacob's deception will bring him deception and alienation. Throughout this account is God's hand blessing and rebuking his chosen people.

Roop asserts,

The saga is not only about anger and division, but also about promise and hope. At the most dangerous moments God appears. God comes to the thief fleeing from the justified anger of his brother (Gen. 28). God protects the refugee trapped between the angry world of the present (Laban) and the murderous hatred generated in the past (Esau) (Gen. 31–33). God calls again to the family, even after they have returned evil for evil against their neighbors (Gen. 34–35). The promises which had called the family into being seem almost lost in the drama of this generation—almost but not quite. The promises are heard again at night by the dreaming Jacob (Gen. 28) and in the worship of the pilgrim family (Gen. 35). God's unfinished story provides unending hope for the faith community. God cannot be silenced by conflict and alienation nor chased away by exploitation, deceit and violence.[1]

Similarly, Paul writes, "We have this treasure in jars of clay to show that this all-surpassing power is from God and not from us" (2 Cor. 4:7).

OUTLINE OF BOOK 8

Act 1: Family conflicts in Canaan   25:19–28:9
    Scene 1: Births and genealogy, 25:19–26
    Scene 2: Esau sells his birthright to Jacob, 25:27–34
    Scene 3: Digression: Rebekah in foreign palace,
       pact with foreigners, 26:1–33
    Scene 4: Jacob steals Esau's blessing, 26:34–28:9
Act 2: Covenant blessings on Jacob
    and his exile in Paddan Aram   28:10–33:17
    Scene 1: Angels meet Jacob at Bethel, 28:10–22
    Scene 2: Jacob arrives at Laban's house, 29:1–14a
    Scene 3: Laban outwits Jacob: Leah for Rachel, 29:14b–30
    Scene 4: The birth of Jacob's children, 29:31–30:24
    Scene 5: Jacob outwits Laban, 30:25–43
    Scene 6: Jacob flees Laban, 31:1–55
    Scene 7: Angels meet Jacob at Mahanaim and Peniel, 32:1–32
    Scene 8: Esau's reconciliation with homeward-bound Jacob,
       33:1–17
Act 3: Transition to Jacob   33:18–35:29
    Scene 1: Digression: Dinah in foreign palace, pact
       with foreigners, 33:18–34:31
    Scene 2: Israel fulfills his vows at Bethel, 35:1–15
    Scene 3: Births and deaths, 35:16–29

---

[1]Roop, *Genesis*, 229.

LITERARY ANALYSIS OF BOOK 8 ————————————————

Gap

Instead of the account of Abraham's line (the narrative of Isaac), this book presents the account of Isaac's line (the narrative of Jacob). Isaac's account has been gapped, and his life must be pieced together from other accounts. Considering that even the nonelect such as Ishmael and Esau are given separate, even if brief, accounts (25:12–18; 36:1–43), Isaac's gap seems deliberate. Why would Isaac, who had such miraculous beginnings, be gapped? The first half of Isaac's life is full of God's providence and Isaac's faith: God's miraculous gift of birth (21:1–7), Isaac's superb theological education (cf. 18:17–19), Isaac's faith and obedience when facing death (22:1–19), God's providential gift of marriage (24:1–67), Isaac's reliance on God (25:20–21), and God's transmission of Abraham's blessing (26:1–24). However, in Book 8 the primary images of the aging Isaac are of a man whose mouth craves wild game and whose eyes cannot recognize God's leading (25:28; 26:34–27:46). In his old age, Isaac has become sedentary and stubborn, unwilling to lead the family through conflict and unwilling to submit to plans of God that differ from his own desires.[2] Isaac's gapping likely reflects his failure to remain faithful.

Innertextual Links

The account of Isaac's line and the account of Terah's line, as lengthy accounts of heroes of faith, share similarities. The accounts are driven by the characters' internal conflicts of faith and covenant commitment and external conflicts that arise as seeming barriers to the promises of seed and land. The timing of the accounts reveals God's providential guidance and presence.

The two accounts are distinct in their directions and prime concerns. Whereas the account of Terah's line proceeds in a vertical direction concerned with the transfer of promise from father to son, the account of Isaac's line proceeds in a horizontal direction concerned with overcoming conflict among family members. The account of Terah's line is concerned to establish the promise, and the account of Isaac's line is concerned to receive the blessings.

Structure

The "Account of Isaac's Line" is the narrative of Jacob in his progress of faith. The book's structure reflects this, placing Jacob's testing and transformation at the narrative's focal point.[3] Jacob's two encounters with angels

---

[2]See B. K. Waltke, "Reflections on Retirement from the Life of Isaac," *Crux* 32 (December 1996): 4–14.

[3]See also Brueggemann, *Genesis*, 211–13; Roop, *Genesis*, 166; esp. Fishbane, "Composition," 15–38; and Rendsburg, *Redaction*, 53–69.

of the Lord, preceding and following his sojourn in Paddan Aram, frame his time of testing and record his transformation of character.

A Births and genealogy: rivalry in the family, Jacob born (25:19–34)
    B Digression: Rebekah in foreign palace, pact with foreigners (26:1–33)
        C Jacob steals Esau's blessing (26:34–28:9)
            D Covenant blessings on Jacob and his exile (28:10–32:32)
                1 Encounter with angel at Bethel (28:10–22)
                    2 Arrival at Haran and conflict with Laban (29:1–30)
                        3 Rachel and Leah: Birth of tribal fathers (29:31–30:24)
                    2' Jacob's prosperity and flight from Laban (30:25–31:55)
                1' Encounter with angels at Mahanaim and Peniel (32:1–32)
        C' Esau's reconciliation with homeward-bound Jacob (33:1–17)
    B' Digression: Dinah in foreign palace, pact with foreigners (33:18–34:31)
A' Births and deaths (35:1–29)

The account opens with opposition and an oracle (A). Here is a foreshadowing of themes and tensions that will drive the account. The covenant family cannot avoid the barriers of barrenness and family strife exacerbated by self-determination and favoritism. The opening oracle also ensures God's continual directive presence disciplining and abundantly blessing the family. At the account's conclusion (A'), God's oracle and the fact of Jacob's abundant family living in the land declare that God has overcome barrenness and family conflict to bring about his good pleasure. With Isaac's death and Esau's separation from the covenant promises, Jacob is the confirmed successor of the promises to Abraham.

B and B' (Gen. 26; 34) have both plot and thematic functions. These interludes create and sustain tension. Both chapters have thematic similarities related to the wider account. Both involve endangering the sexual purity of women of the holy family, a wife and a daughter; both occur in the royal palace of the uncircumcised, a king and a king's son; and both tensions are resolved by a treaty. In addition, both relate to an inheritance of Abrahamic covenant blessing: Isaac's good fortunes give palpable proof that he has inherited Abraham's covenant; Jacob receives Abraham and Isaac's covenant at Bethel.

The brothers' conflict is the driving tension of the C and C' accounts. After deceiving his brother, Jacob must flee for his life. His return to the land entails reconciliation with the brother he has wronged. These sections also provide the narrator's evaluation of Esau. Jacob's theft of Esau's blessing is bracketed by Esau's marriage to Canaanites and Ishmaelites. From one human perspective, Esau, who functions as a foil to Jacob, is much more likeable than Jacob. From the divine viewpoint, however, he is rejected because he rejects his right to inherit the divinely given vision of his fathers.

With regard to D, Fishbane says, "Jacob came to Aram single, and left with Rachel; he found her barren, and left with her fertile; he came in flight from a brother whom he deceived and so he left."[4] At the center of the narrative and all of Book 8 is God's faithfulness to his covenant promises in the gift of the twelve tribes of Israel. Jacob's encounters with Laban also follow a chiastic pattern:

A Introduction: meeting of brothers in peace (29:1–14a)
  B Laban's deception regarding Rachel (29:14b–30)
    C God's blessing on Jacob's seed in spite of conflict (29:31–30:21)
      X Birth of Joseph: turning point to leave (30:22–24)
    C′ God's blessing on Jacob's property in spite of conflict (30:25–31:30)
  B′ Rachel's deception[5] regarding Laban's gods (31:31–42)
A′ Conclusion: parting of brothers in peace pact (31:43–55)

Framing this narrative with Laban are Jacob's encounters with God and the angels in which Jacob receives the covenant promises. The center of Book 8, the birth of the twelve tribes of Israel, becomes focused to a flash point in God's gift of a son to barren Rachel.

Conflict

As in the account of Terah's line, the plot of this account is driven by a series of conflicts, this time among family members: Isaac and Rebekah (25:19–27:46); Jacob and Esau (25:19–34; 27:1–46; 32:1–33:17); Jacob and Laban (29:1–31:55); fertile Leah and infertile Rachel (29:31–30:24); Jacob and Rachel (30:1–2); Jacob and his sons (34:30–31); and finally and decisively between Jacob and the angel of the Lord (32:22–32). The account is charged with energy and restlessness. Sleep is disturbed, and a riverbank at night is the scene of the climatic struggle.[6]

Jacob is in constant struggle particularly against culture and primogeniture rights. He contends with Esau, Rachel, and later Joseph (blessing Ephraim before Manasseh). Of primogeniture rights, Brueggemann says, "It is the linchpin of an entire social and legal system which defines rights and privileges and provides a way around internecine disputes. But that same practice which protects the order of society is also a way of destining some to advantage and others to disadvantage. That world of privilege and denial is here disrupted by the God of blessing who will sojourn with the 'low and despised' (cf. Luke 7:34). . . . The governing oracle and the narrative which flows from it are . . . an attempt to arrange the blessings in an alternative way."[7]

---

[4]Fishbane, "Composition," 31.
[5]Rachel even out-trumps Jacob. He is unaware (ibid.).
[6]Roop, Genesis, 167.
[7]Brueggemann, Genesis, 209.

Key Word

The key word of the cycle, "brother" (*'āḥ*), is often linked with strife and deceit and so marks the tensions of family and blessing driving this account.[8]

BOOK 8, ACT 1: FAMILY CONFLICTS IN CANAAN (25:19–28:9)

LITERARY ANALYSIS OF BOOK 8, ACT 1 ————————

Structure and Plot

Act 1 of Book 8 takes place in Canaan from the time of Isaac's marriage to the flight of the younger offspring of that marriage to Paddan Aram, the original home of the sojourning patriarchs. Scene 1 opens with answer-to-prayer twins struggling in the mother's womb and a prophecy that the older will serve the younger. In Scene 2 the conniving younger brother through hardfisted business practices inveigles the birthright away from the older brother. The contrasting natures of the twins—the younger, a cultured pastoralist with an immature faith; the older, a coarse hunter without faith—and parental favoritisms polarize the parents. The act climaxes in Scene 4 when mother and younger son thwart the father's spiritually reckless plan to bless the older. The scene ends with the younger twin fleeing the wrath of the older intent on murdering him.

Inclusio

The act's introductory reference to the sojourning family's original home in Paddan Aram paves the way for its conclusion with Jacob fleeing there. The prophecy that immediately follows the introduction, "two peoples from within you will be separated" (25:23), finds its fulfillment in the flight of Jacob from Esau. More importantly, the Lord's prophecy that the older will serve the younger (25:23) is matched in the climax of Scene 4 by the patriarchal blessing on the younger, "may nations serve you" (27:29). This frame shows that in spite of the family's machinations and mischief the divine purpose stands.

Intercalation

Scene 3 anachronistically interrupts the family conflict and presents Isaac as the recipient of the family's blessings, possessing fertility of flocks and fields and security in the midst of the hostile Philistines. The interrupting scene gives an insight into what the struggle for the birthright and blessing is all about and shows that the family turmoil is not the lack of blessing by the Lord, the divine partner, but the lack of blameless faith by Isaac's family, the human partners.

---

[8]See Fishbane, "Composition," 23.

Foreshadowing

The twins' struggle for supremacy in the womb foreshadows the conflicts in the scenes that follow. Moreover, the notice in 25:28 that Isaac loves the nonelect and coarse Esau because he has a taste for wild game, while Rebekah loves the elect, cultured Jacob, foreshadows the parental conflict in Scene 4. Tragically, Esau's preference for stew foreshadows his father's taste for game.

Repetition and Contrast

In both Scenes 1 and 4 Jacob deceives his twin brother, as Esau bitterly complains (27:36). Jacob steals the birthright by taking advantage of his brother's unreflective character and the blessing by taking advantage of his father's blindness. The repetition underscores the flawed faith of Jacob and the connection between the birthright and the blessing. Although Isaac and Esau believe blessing and birthright can be separated, the Lord disallows the severance (Heb. 12:16–17).

Scene 1 opens with a prayerful patriarch effectively interceding for his barren wife; Scene 4 represents the couple as prayerless and uncommunicative. In the end, however, they are again talking as they conspire to obtain an Aramean, not a Canaanite, wife for Jacob.

BOOK 8, ACT 1, SCENE 1: BIRTHS AND GENEALOGY (25:19 – 26)

LITERARY ANALYSIS OF BOOK 8, ACT 1, SCENE 1 ————

Structure and Plot

This scene is framed by the marking of Isaac's age (25:20, 26). The conflicts that form the plot set the stage for the entirety of Book 8. The first crisis is Rebekah's infertility; it is resolved when God answers Isaac's prayer for his wife, affirming that God gives the seed and establishes its destiny in response to faithful covenant partners. The second crisis grows out of the first: the struggle for supremacy by each twin in Rebekah's womb. This tension will not subside until the end of Book 8. The promised resolution is that "the older will serve the younger" (25:23).

Foreshadowing

The twins' struggle in the womb foreshadows the struggles between Jacob and Esau in the following scenes when Jacob secures the birthright (25:27–34), steals Esau's blessing (27:1–40), and prevails with Esau and secures his good will (32:1–33:16). Their struggle spills over into conflicts between Rebekah and Isaac (27:1–46), Jacob and his wives as well as his wives with each other (30:1–24), and Jacob and Laban (29:14b–31:55).

Naming

The names of the twins poke fun at both. The eldest answers to the name *Esau* (i.e., "Hairy," implying an animalish nature)[9] and later *Edom* (i.e., "Red," suggesting passion). The youngest answers to the name *Jacob* (i.e., "Heel," implying grasping) until his return to the land and his struggle with the angel. Afterwards, he will also answer to the name *Israel* (i.e., the one who struggles with God and humans and who prevails).

Time Markers and Characterization

The narrator carefully arranges the presentation of details to heighten the image of Isaac's faith. At the beginning of the scene, the narrator notes Isaac's age as forty. The following verse states simply, "Isaac prayed to the LORD. . . . The LORD answered his prayer" (25:21). Not until the end of the scene do we discover that this answer to prayer came twenty years later, when Isaac was sixty. This artful shaping of details displays Isaac's faith in two ways. As Wenham argues, "The [initial] absence of any reference to time enhances the impression of Isaac the powerful intercessor. Like those of his father Abraham, his prayers for barren women are answered by God."[10] The narrator's marking of time at the end of the scene with Isaac's age only heightens the picture of Isaac's faith. The man who prays persistently for twenty years is a man of strong faith.

EXEGETICAL NOTES TO BOOK 8, ACT I, SCENE I ———

Superscription to Book 8 (25:19a)

19. This is the account of Abraham's son Isaac. On the *tôlᵉḏôṯ* formula, see 2:4. This is better translated, "this is the account of the descendants of Isaac, son of Abraham." The account takes place while Isaac is the active patriarch; however, the story features Jacob: his gracious election to inherit the promises and his journeys of conflict and transformation in Canaan (25:19–27:40), in Paddan Aram away from the Promised Land (27:41–33:17), and back in Canaan with his family (33:18–35:29). After Isaac tries to thwart God's blessing on Jacob (27:1–40), he is not heard of again until his death (35:27–29).

Introduction to the Account: Family Genealogy (25:19b–20)

19b. Abraham became the father of. The sequence "*tôlᵉḏôṯ* of Isaac. Abraham became the father of. . ." is exceptional. The parallels in 6:9; 10:1; 11:10, 27 teach us to expect "*tôlᵉḏôṯ* of Abraham. Abraham became the father

---

[9]Ross, *Creation*, 440.
[10]Wenham, *Genesis 16–50*, 175.

of. . . ." Also, the account of Isaac's birth is exceptional; the *tôlᵉḏôṯ* pattern generally elsewhere does not include the birth of the eponymous head himself. These changes occur due to the gapping of the account of Abraham's line, which would be about Isaac (see "Literary Analysis of Book 8: Gap").

20. forty years. Abraham is now 140 years of age (see 21:5).

Bethuel. See 22:22.

Aramean. See Deut. 26:5. The stage is being set for Jacob's flight to Paddan Aram and his conflict with Laban (28:1–31:55).

Paddan Aram. This is another name for Aram Naharaim ("Aram of the Two Rivers," see 24:10). Paddan means either "field" (Hos. 12:12)[11] or "road" (so Akkadian).[12]

Barrenness (25:21)

21. prayed. The Hebrew word for prayer *ᶜtr* (not the same as *htpll* in 20:7, 17) is a general designation for prayer, which may also specifically mean "to intercede." Albertz summarizes, "Isaac entreats the LORD for the infertile wife . . . and Moses on Pharaoh's behalf for the aversion of the plagues (Ex. 8:4f., 24f., 26; [passim]). . . . *ᶜtr* here, then, describes the powerful, appeasing effect on God of a man of God. It always transpires in private."[13] Isaac follows his father's example (see 20:7). As Abraham's servant secured Isaac's wife by prayer, so also will Isaac obtain his offspring (see Theological Reflections below). Isaac and Rebekah do not resort to concubinage (cf. Abraham and Sarah; Jacob and Leah and Rachel).

his wife. He is the only patriarch who is monogamous.

barren. The right woman is again barren. The motif of barrenness highlighted the Lord's power to give Abraham numerous progeny over insuperable odds. Barrenness here is not an occasion for anxiety but for sovereign grace (cf. John 1:1–13; Gal. 1:15; James 1:18). This generation also has to learn the lessons of faith (cf. Gen. 12:10; 16:1) and to understand that theirs is not a natural but a supernatural seed (see 11:30; 17:15–16; 18:1–15; 21:1–7).

Problems of Pregnancy, Rebekah's Inquiry, and the Lord's Prophecy (25:22–23)

22. jostled. The children almost crush one another. Rebekah carries not only the next generation but the struggle and anxiety that accompanies it. The struggle for supremacy between Jacob and Esau in the womb and the Lord's sovereign choice forms a fitting introduction to this account, whose hallmark is rivalry. The conflict progresses from the womb, to the troubled delivery of the twins (25:26), to their differences in profession (25:27), and

---

[11]NIV's "country of Aram" glosses "field [*śāḏeh*] of Aram."

[12]*Pdn* means "yoke of oxen" or "a plow share"—hence, the stretch of land an ox plows in a day (i.e., a field). However, Akkadian *padānu* means "path, track, road."

[13]R. Albertz, "*ᶜtr*," *TLOT*, 2:962.

to the opposing preferences of the parents (25:28). This struggle also foreshadows Jacob's struggle with the angel of God (32:22–32).

Why is this happening to me? The Hebrew is difficult (literally, "Why this, I"). This anguished question spread across the pages of human history finds its answer in accepting that God's wisdom and sovereignty stands behind all things (Rom. 11:29–36).

she went to inquire of the LORD. She seeks a prophecy from the Lord, probably at a patriarchal altar (see 12:6–8).

23. The LORD said. God predicts the outcome at the beginning of each family history (12:1–3; 27:27–29, 39–40; 37:1–11). Wenham asserts, "This prefacing of each 'family history' with a word from God thus serves to highlight that every stage of the patriarchal history was guided by God. Despite the appalling mistakes of these fallible men, God's purposes were ultimately fulfilled."[14]

Two nations. See Num. 20:14; Deut. 23:7–8; Obad. 10; Mal. 1:2; Rom. 9:11–13.

the older. The Hebrew here for the eldest son has so far been found only in an Akkadian cognate from the middle of the second millennium. This points to the remarkable preservation of the received text.

will serve [ya‘ăḇōḏ; cf. ya‘ăqōḇ "Jacob"] **the younger** [ṣā‘îr; cf. śē‘ār "hairy"]. Jacob owes his supremacy to sovereign election, not natural rights (see 37:2; 38:29; 48:5, 19; Deut. 21:15–17). God's grace triumphs over human convention (see "Hope" in Theological Reflections below).

Birth of Twins: Neither Is Commendable (25:24–26)

24. twin boys. Their descriptions poke fun at both: a hairy monster and a heel-clutcher.

25. hairy. This symbolizes Esau's animalish nature. The Hebrew word also sounds like Seir, where Esau will live (see 32:3; 36:8).

Esau. The etymology of his name is uncertain. The connection between śē‘ār ("hairy," see 27:11) and ‘ēśāw (Esau) is not clear.[15]

26. Jacob [ya‘ăqōḇ]. Jacob's name signifies his character on a number of levels. The etymology of his name is probably from a shortened form of the phrase "May El Protect" or "El Protects/Rewards," a typical West Semitic name.[16] This aspect of his name recognizes God's divine election. Jacob, however, will tarnish this honorable name with his deceit and self-reliant efforts to achieve God's good pleasure (see 27:36; Hos. 12:3–4), so the name also puns with ‘āqaḇ, "to seize someone by the heel, go behind someone . . . to betray."[17]

---

[14]Wenham, *Genesis 16–50*, 169.
[15]*HALOT*, 893.
[16]Ibid., 422.
[17]Ibid., 872.

sixty years. The narrator notes a man's age in the important event of reproducing his seed (see Gen. 5:3–32; 11:12–26). Here it also shows that Isaac intercedes twenty years for his barren wife without losing hope (see "Time Markers" in Literary Analysis above). He knows that in his seed the promised seed will be reckoned, and he has learned from his parents' failure not to seek to fulfill God's promise through human effort. Rebekah's age is omitted because, unlike Sarah, she is not beyond the age of childbearing.

THEOLOGICAL REFLECTIONS ON BOOK 8, ACT 1, SCENE 1 —————————

Total Dependence

Christians, as part of the chosen family in Christ, must depend entirely on God, and not on human striving, for provisions and promise. In his reflections on Isaac's pleading with God for a child, Brueggemann states, "There are no natural guarantees for the future and no way to secure the inheritance of the family. It must trust only to the power of God. . . . Promise requires an end to grasping and certitude and an embrace of precariousness. It is only God who gives life. Any pretense that the future is secured by rights or claims of the family is a deception."[18]

God's Sovereignty

Through prophecy on the threshold of histories, God displays his sovereign control of Adam and Eve (3:15), of Noah's descendants (9:25–27), of Abraham's career (12:1–3), of Jacob and Esau (see also 27:27–29, 39–40), and of Joseph (37:1–11). God's orchestrating of the patriarchal history is also affirmation to us that God controls all history, even our own.

God's continual overturning of primogeniture rights in Genesis signifies God's sovereign control and gracious election, witnessed in the words of Christ to his disciples, "You did not choose me, but I chose you and appointed you" (John 15:16). On this basis Paul explains the election of the Gentiles over the Jews, who had all the natural advantages to appreciate Christ (Rom. 9–11). All praise accrues to God, who does "whatever pleases him" (Ps. 115:3).

Mercy

God's sovereignty also involves his mercy. His sovereignty to extend mercy to whom he will is most conspicuous in this scene, as Paul's inspired commentary reveals:

> Not only that, but Rebekah's children had one and the same father, our father Isaac. Yet, before the twins were born or had done anything good

———————————————

[18]Brueggemann, *Genesis*, 212, 214.

or bad—in order that God's purpose in election might stand: not by works but by him who calls—she was told, "The older will serve the younger." Just as it is written: "Jacob I loved, but Esau I hated."

What then shall we say? Is God unjust? Not at all! For he says to Moses,

"I will have mercy on whom I have mercy,
    and I will have compassion on whom I have compassion."

(Rom. 9:10–15)

Hope

God's election actually offers us hope. God's world offers more surprises than custom usually allows. Roop asserts, "Neither fairness, divine promise, nor pedagogical purpose adequately explains this inversion of the place of the firstborn—only the surprising openness that characterizes God's world."[19] Without God's sovereign grace and mercy, there would be no openness, only law and justice without hope. Brueggemann says, "The oracle is against all conventional wisdom. It makes a profound theological claim. It affirms that we do not live in a world where all possibilities are kept open and we may choose our posture as we please. It does not deny freedom. But it requires us to speak also about *destiny*. . . . This oracle speaks about an *inversion*. It affirms that we are *not fated* to the way the world is presently organized."[20]

Human Faithfulness

The children are supernatural—the offspring of faithful prayer based on God's promise. God works out his elective purposes through faithful, not perfect, covenant partners. Isaac waits patiently for the Lord for over twenty years to keep his word that in Isaac Abraham's seed will be reckoned (21:12). He has learned from his parents' experience with Hagar to avoid synergism. Rebekah, on her part, seeks meaning for her life through God's revealed word.

Test of Faith

God tests Isaac's faith the same as he had Abraham by restraining his wife's womb (25:21). So also, God leaves the Canaanites in the Promised Land to test the postconquest generation of Israelites and to teach them how to fight (Judg. 2:22–3:4). Each generation of the church must learn with Paul to fight the good fight of faith (2 Tim. 4:7).

Prophecy

The prophecy concerning the twins extends beyond their births. It is fulfilled throughout Israel's history (2 Sam. 8:13), even to the birth of Christ during the days of Herod, a descendant of Esau.

---

[19]Roop, *Genesis*, 172.
[20]Brueggemann, *Genesis*, 215.

BOOK 8, ACT 1, SCENE 2: ESAU SELLS HIS BIRTHRIGHT TO JACOB (25:27–34)

LITERARY ANALYSIS OF BOOK 8, ACT 1, SCENE 2 ────

Plot

As the previous scene has prepared us to expect, this scene is pervaded by family conflict. The tension between the boys is immediate in their opposite occupations and their polarized parents. The questions propelling the scene relate to how these tensions will play out. How will Jacob overturn primogeniture rights? And how will God's purposes be realized through such discord?

The tension is only heightened when, in a shocking maneuver, Jacob demands a trade of Esau's birthright for stew. The scene peaks when Esau swears to sell his birthright. With the staccato action of Esau—"he ate and drank, and then got up and left"—the scene abruptly ends.

Characterization

A central feature of this scene is the characterization of Jacob and Esau. This brief scene captures both the complexity of their characters and the primary spiritual characteristics of each man. The narrator's artful portrayal with direct (25:27) and indirect (25:29–34) characterization exposes Esau as a crass man driven by the immediate and Jacob as a devious, civilized man of foresight. The characterizations serve to demonstrate Esau's unworthiness without exaggerating Jacob's worthiness.

In his explicit characterization, the narrator sets in opposition Esau's skill in hunting with Jacob's civilized manner and Esau's habitat in the open field with Jacob's dwelling in tents as a pastoralist. While the law made provision for eating game, the biblical writers commend pastoralists and condemn predators (see Exegetical Notes).

Esau's actions—the narrator's indirect characterization—betray a profane person. He speaks coarsely and acts on immediate demands without reflection (see Exegetical Notes, 25:30–34). Lest the audience miss this evaluative viewpoint, the narrator explicitly interprets Esau's actions: he has only contempt for his family inheritance (25:34b). By this characterization, Esau functions as a foil to the nature of true Israel.

Jacob, in contrast, acts with foresight. The narrator dissipates his audience's spiritual revulsion against Jacob for his lack of compassion on his brother's misery by characterizing Jacob as a "civilized man" who values his heritage and future. He speaks with finesse and acts as one who reflects, who opts for future rewards over immediate sensual gratification. But this contrasting portrayal is not simplistic or moralistic. Speaking of Jacob's future orientation, Alter says, "This qualifies him as a suitable bearer of the birthright. . . . But this quality of wary calculation does not necessarily make Jacob more appealing as a character, and, indeed, may even raise some moral questions about him. The contrast in this scene between the impetuous, miserably famished Esau and the shrewdly businesslike Jacob may not be entirely to Jacob's advantage."[21] Jacob still requires God's transformation.

The boys also function to polarize the parents. Isaac loves Esau for his game; Rebekah loves Jacob presumably for his character and the Lord's election of him to rule.

Foreshadowing

With the minor detail of Isaac's love for wild game, the narrator has masterfully set the stage for the scene of imparting the blessing. Isaac's taste for wild game is the little fox that will spoil the vine in chapter 27.

EXEGETICAL NOTES TO BOOK 8, ACT I, SCENE 2 ————

Exposition: Conflict Between Isaac and Rebekah Regarding Twins (25:27–28)

27. The boys grew up. Since Abraham dies when the boys are fifteen (25:7), undoubtedly they knew the patriarch during their early years. One can imagine him holding them on his knee and pointing to the sky and land to explain the blessings of this family, yet these boys must make their own choices and face their own testing. Esau is profane, impulsive, and thoughtless about the future in the face of present need. Jacob has faith's far sight to value the inheritance but tarnishes it by his bartering to advantage himself at his brother's expense.

a skillful hunter, a man of the open country. This is generally an unfavorable description by biblical standards. While the law made provision for eating game, the biblical writers commend pastoralists and condemn predators. Nimrod, the founder of the cities that stood opposed to God, is identified as a mighty hunter (see 10:9). Later, Esau is described as one who lives by the sword (27:40). The biblical ideal for a leader is symbolized by that of a shepherd (Ps. 23; Ezek. 34; John 10:1–18; 1 Peter 5:3–4). True Israel, like his God, behaves like a shepherd, not a hunter.

quiet [tām]. This is better translated "civilized" or "fine." The basic idea of the Hebrew root (tmm) is "to be complete, finished, perfect."[22] The adjective tām, "perfect," is used of the beloved in Song of Solomon ("flawless," 5:2; "perfect," 6:9). To judge from Jacob's reprehensible method of inveigling the birthright from his famished brother, the adjective cannot refer to his moral behavior. In this unique occurrence of the adjective in narrative, it probably denotes Jacob as being "well-cultured," "civilized."[23] Koch suggests the gloss "fine man."[24] Jacob's "completeness" stands in opposition to Esau's particular skill of hunting.

[21]Alter, *Biblical Narrative*, 45.
[22]K. Koch, "tmm," *TLOT*, 3:1424–28.
[23]Westermann, *Genesis 12–36*, 415.
[24]Koch, "tmm," 3:1427.

staying among the tents. Jacob is a pastoralist (see 4:20).

28. Isaac, who had a taste for wild game. Adam fails in eating, Noah in drinking, and Isaac, a gourmand, in tasting. God's sovereign grace must now prevail over Isaac's efforts to thwart the divine intention (see 24:36; 25:5; 27:4).

Isaac loved . . . but Rebekah loved. Parental favoritism further rifts the family. Isaac's love is based on natural senses, Rebekah's on divine choice and enduring qualities (see 27:1–46). A marriage made in heaven (see 24:1–67) can end in dysfunction when a spouse gives priority to taste in the mouth over a voice in the heart (see 26:35).

Esau Sells Birthright for Stew (25:29 – 34)

29. famished. This is not hyperbole. Esau is in dire need of food and drink, and Jacob should not have taken advantage of him.

30. Quick, let me have. Esau is impulsive.

red stew [hā'ā₫ōm]. The Hebrew actually reads "red stuff, this red stuff!" His language is coarse.

Edom. The name is derived from the Hebrew verb 'ā₫ōm, "to be red."

31. First sell me. Jacob exploits his brother's misery. His lack of compassion and hospitality stand in stark contrast to that of his grandfather Abraham (18:1–8) and uncle Lot (19:1–8). His value is right, but his method is wrong. Later God will transform his ambition into virtue (see 32:28).

birthright [bᵉₖōrâ]. The word refers to the rights of the firstborn (cf. Ex. 4:22; Jer. 2:3). The firstborn holds a position of honor within the family. Israel as God's firstborn receives a position of honor and privilege among the nations (Ex. 4:22; Jer 31:9). The firstborn of the womb (Ex. 13:2; Deut. 15:19) and firstfruits of the soil (Deut. 18:4; Neh. 10:38–39) uniquely belong to the Lord. As Tsevat states, "It is not only the best that belongs to God, but also the first."[25] Offering the firstborn or firstfruits to the Lord acknowledges that life is the Lord's good gift. Consequently, the firstborn male has to be redeemed with a firstborn donkey (Ex. 13:11–13). The firstborn has privileged status (see Gen. 43:33; 49:3) and the right of succession (2 Chron. 21:3). For his birthright, he receives a double portion of the father's inheritance (Deut. 21:17). The father's inheritance is divided among the number of sons, and the firstborn always has right to two of these portions. So, for instance, if there are nine sons, the firstborn receives two portions and the other eight split seven portions. If there are only two sons, the firstborn inherits everything.[26] Accompanying the blessing of the birthright is also the responsibility to be the family protector, the leader of the family. This birthright is transferable; the youngest son can displace the eldest as in the cases of Joseph/Judah and Reuben, Ephraim/Manasseh, Moses/Aaron, David/his six older brothers, and Solomon/Adonijah. Since it concerns the

---

[25]M. Tsevat, "bᵉₖôr," TDOT, 2:126.
[26]See ibid.

future, its value is apprehended by faith. In Abraham's family, the one who possesses the birthright inherits the Abrahamic covenant. The writer of Hebrews treats these as a unity. Since Esau sells his inheritance rights he forfeits the blessing (Heb. 12:16–17). In sum, Jacob is inveigling the right to be heir of the family's fortune and define its destiny.

32. I am about to die. Esau lacks faith and lives for the moment. To his nearsighted vision, the birthright appears meaningless.

33. Swear to me. This makes the transaction irrevocable.

selling his birthright to Jacob. At the heart of Jacob and Esau's differences are clashing worldviews: deferred prosperity versus immediate satisfaction.

34. lentil. Some varieties of lentils are reddish-brown, but when cooked they often lose the red hue. Hence, some suggest that Jacob added something to the stew that made it unusually red, maybe even what is called a "blood soup."[27] Such theories, however, may be unnecessary, since, as Brenner's thorough study has demonstrated, the biblical term used for red actually has a semantic range much wider than our modern term *red*.[28]

ate and drank, and then got up and left. The staccato style of the verbs represents Esau's behavior to be as crude and nonreflective as his speech.

despised his birthright. Grisanti states, "one who despises (*bzh*) someone or something treats with irreverence, rejects, or devalues the person/thing held in contempt. Although *bzh* denotes an inner attitude, it clearly impacts relationships."[29] God hates the one who holds his promises in contempt (Mal. 1:3; Heb. 12:16–17).

THEOLOGICAL REFLECTIONS ON BOOK 8, ACT I, SCENE 2

Grace

Vos says, "[Jacob's] reprehensible features are rather strongly brought out. This is done in order to show that the divine grace is not the reward for, but the source of noble traits. Grace overcoming human sin and transforming human nature is the keynote of the revelation here."[30]

Covenant Seed and Faith

The narrator of Genesis aims to define the nature of the covenant seed. By contrasting Jacob, the elect seed, and Esau, the nonelect, he shows that the chosen people, in spite of glaring imperfections, are characterized by a commitment to be heirs of Abraham, the man of faith. The nonelect have no com-

---

[27]Daube, *Studies*, 191–96.
[28]A. Brenner, *Colour Terms in the Old Testament* (JSOTSup 21; Sheffield: JSOT Press, 1982), 60–62, 79–80.
[29]M. A. Grisanti, "*bwḥ*," *NIDOTTE*, 1:628.
[30]Vos, *Biblical Theology*, 93.

mitment to this hope in the promised seed and land. Jacob is distinguished from Esau by his faith in the promises and blessings of God. He wrongly schemes against his brother because he correctly believes that the birthright in the line of Abraham and Isaac holds tremendous blessing and promise. Despite all of his weaknesses, Jacob lives within the vision of faith.

BOOK 8, ACT 1, SCENE 3:
DIGRESSION: REBEKAH IN FOREIGN PALACE, PACT WITH FOREIGNERS (26:1–33)

LITERARY ANALYSIS OF BOOK 8, ACT 1, SCENE 3 ————

Structure and Plot[31]

As with similar scenes in Genesis, Isaac's encounters with the Philistines are characterized by conflict and blessing. The scene progresses from precarious existence to security and riches, moving from famine (26:1) to a well of plenty (26:33, "We've found water!"), from fear of violence by the men of Gerar (26:6–7) to a pact with them (26:28–31), and from conflict and confrontation to peace (26:31).

The scene consists of three encounters between Isaac and the Philistines (particularly Abimelech the king), marked by changes in setting: at Gerar (26:1–16), at the Wadi of Gerar (26:17–22) and at Beersheba (26:23–33).

The first and third encounters follow an alternating structure (A B C//A′ B′ C′):

Migration: Isaac goes to Gerar because of famine, 26:1
A Theophany (divine monologue) at Gerar: *yērā' 'ēlāyw yhwh*, 26:2–6
1 Blessing conditioned on staying in land, 26:2–5
2 Isaac stays in land, 26:6
  B Blessing (dialogue): protection of the matriarch, 26:7–11
    C Blessing (narrative): prosperity in crops and herds, 26:12–16
A′ Theophany (divine monologue) at Beersheba: *yērā' 'ēlāyw yhwh*, 26:23–25
1′ Blessing unconditioned, 26:23–24
2′ Isaac worships, 26:25
  B′ Blessing (dialogue): protection of the patriarch through pact, 26:26–31
    C′ Blessing (narrative): prosperity in the well at Beersheba, 26:32–33

The second encounter functions as a janus between these two encounters. It is linked to the first by the Philistines' stopping up the wells Isaac dug (26:15, 20–21) and to the second by drawing to a climactic conclusion with the digging of a well in peace (26:22 and 32–33). The second encounter, like the other two, consists of three parts:

---

[31]See also Act 1, Scene 2.

Isaac reopens his father's wells, 26:17–18
Philistines quarrel over two wells, 26:19–21
Isaac digs Rehoboth without a quarrel, 26:22

Comparison and Contrast

The details of this narrative further affirm the transfer of divine blessing to Isaac and his line. Striking repetitions from the narrative of Abraham punctuate this scene—famine, sister-wife motif, wealth and quarrels, separation, altars and calling on the name of "the LORD." The Lord appears to both Abraham and Isaac through theophany and in a divine monologue promises to bless them, featuring gifts of offspring and land. To both patriarchs, he promises to make them a great nation through whom nations will be blessed. God conditions the blessings on the patriarchs' obedience. When they obey, he repeats the blessing unconditionally. Isaac reopens his father's wells and gives them the same names, which the narrator highlights in the naming of Beersheba. With these repetitions the narrator asserts that Isaac has more than fully inherited the blessings of his father. Wenham comments, "Thus this account of Isaac's dealings with the Philistines portrays Isaac as very much walking in his father's footsteps. He receives similar promises, faces similar tests, fails similarly, but eventually triumphs in like fashion. Indeed, in certain respects he is given more in the promises and achieves more. He is promised 'all these lands' and by the end of the story he is securely settled in Beersheba and has a treaty with the Philistines in which they acknowledge his superiority."[32] Garrett outlines the striking parallels between the Abraham and Isaac stories that reinforce Isaac's legitimacy as the promised line of Abraham.

Abraham

A 12:1–3   Receives God's call and promise
B 12:10–20   Wife-sister deception episode
C 13:1–12   Quarrel with Lot's men; Abraham takes lesser land
D 15:1–21   Divine reassurance and a sacrifice
E 21:22–24   Treaty with Abimelech at Beersheba

Isaac

A′ 26:2–6   Receives same call and promise from God
B′ 26:7–11   Wife-sister deception episode
C′ 26:14–22   Quarrel with Abimelech's men and other local men; Isaac moves rather than fight
D′ 26:23–25   Divine reassurance and a sacrifice
E′ 26:26–33   Treaty with Abimelech at Beersheba[33]

---

[32]Wenham, *Genesis 16–50*, 196.
[33]Garrett, *Rethinking*, 136.

All this confirms that Isaac's God is the God of Abraham (26:24).

The narrative about endangering the ancestress, Rebekah, so closely parallels the narratives of Sarah's endangerment (see 12:10–20 and esp. 20:1–18) that source critics contend the three accounts are variations of the same historical event. However, the accounts differ enough that there is no excuse to think it is the same event told twice (see also Exegetical Notes below and "Structure" in the Literary Analysis of Book 6, Act 1, Scene 2).

Key Words

Two key expressions—"blessing" (26:3, 12, 24, 29) and "Abraham his father" or its equivalent (26:3, 5, 15, 18, 24)—point to the scene's theme. Isaac inherits his father's divine blessing.

Anachrony

Obviously this story is anachronous, for if Isaac and Rebecca had children, their marriage would have been apparent to the Philistines from the beginning. The narrator often arranges scenes by poetic and theological concerns rather than chronology.[34] This scene has been carefully placed between the deception stories of the birthright and blessing. God's obvious blessings to Isaac in this scene illustrate the protection and prosperity entailed in the inheritance of blessing. The twins' conflict is over this. In addition, the faith of this younger Isaac is to be contrasted with his factious family (Gen. 27). Here is a peace-loving man, mostly blessed without deception and conflict.[35] If Isaac could gain so much without deception, so could Rebekah and Jacob have attained the same without resorting to deceit or alienating Esau.

EXEGETICAL NOTES TO BOOK 8, ACT 1, SCENE 3 —————

Introduction: Famine Leading to Sojourn in Philistia (26:1)

1. famine. As was seen in the life of Abraham, there are famines in the ambiguities and hard reality of God's providence. In the light of later history, they can be interpreted as opportunities that God uses for his own purposes, such as perfecting his saints and spoiling his enemies.

besides the earlier famine of Abraham's time. In this scene God confirms his commitment to Isaac in a way so similar to Abraham that the narrator makes a point of distinguishing the events.

Abimelech. This is probably a favorite dynastic name (see 20:2).

king of the Philistines. This is the same people group with whom Abraham interacted (20:1–18), except the next generation, since at least forty

---

[34]For other examples, see Gen. 10–11 (Table of Nations and Tower of Babel) and Gen. 25 (children of Keturah).
[35]Even his deception about his wife proves unnecessary.

years have elapsed. Probably these people should be identified as the descendants of the Caphtorites of 10:14. They differ from the Philistines of Judges in locale and government style (see 10:14).

Gerar. Isaac may be stopping at this place of royal pasturage (see 20:1) on his way to Egypt (see 12:10).

Gerar (26:2–16)

Theophany at Gerar (26:2–6)

2. The LORD appeared to Isaac. Like his father, Isaac experiences a prophet's vision (see 12:7). The Lord's command and promise and Isaac's obedience are stylistically and substantively linked with those of Abraham's encounter with God (see 12:1–4).

live [*škn*]. Hebrew *škn* (related to the noun for "tent") denotes to dwell or rest in a more temporary fashion than *yšb*, "stay" (see 26:6).

3. Stay [*gûr*]. The Hebrew refers to living as a resident alien with a sense of subordination. Since Egypt is the traditional source of food, it takes faith to remain in Gerar.

and I will be. The conjunction "and" signifies purpose (= "in order that") or result (= "so that"). The conditional nature of the covenant is the same as in 12:2 and 17:2.

with you. The immediate promise to Abraham concerns the supernatural birth of a son; to Isaac, supernatural protection. Protection will also be a significant motif in Jacob's story (see 26:24; 28:15, 20; 31:3, 5, 42; 32:10).

bless you. See 1:22. Whereas Isaac mediates the divine blessing to Jacob (27:27–29), and Jacob to the twelve tribes (Gen. 49), the Lord directly blesses Abraham (12:2; 22:17) and Isaac.

give all these lands. See 13:15.

confirm the oath. See 15:18; 17:21; and especially 22:16–18. God's reiteration of his oath to Abraham assures Isaac of God's faithfulness.

4. stars in the sky. See 15:5.

offspring. See 12:2–3.

will be blessed. See 12:3; 18:18; 22:18; 28:14.

5. because. See 22:18. This is a reminder to Isaac that his participation in the blessing is conditioned on his obedience.

my requirements . . . my laws. The many synonyms for *law* connote Abraham's comprehensive obedience to God's rule over him. The narrator means either the teachings of piety and ethics known by the patriarchs prior to Moses or more probably the whole law of Moses. Genesis is part of the Pentateuch and should be interpreted within that context. In Deut. 11:1 the same list of terms refers to the whole law of Moses.[36] The text shows that the person of faith does not live by law but keeps the law (see Gen. 15:6; 22:1–19; Heb. 11:8–19).

---

[36]See Sailhamer, *Pentateuch*, 66–71.

6. So Isaac stayed. In faith, Abraham went out (12:4). In faith, Isaac now remains. Just as Abraham, Isaac meets the conditions of blessing.

Blessing: Protection of the Matriarch (26:7 – 11)

7. When the men of that place. The narrative about endangering the ancestress, Rebekah, closely parallels the narratives of Sarah's endangerment (12:10–20; and esp. 20:1–18). However, the accounts differ enough that there is no excuse to think that it is the same event told twice (see "Structure" in Literary Analysis of Book 6, Act 1, Scene 2).

sister. For this stratagem, see 12:13 and 20:13.

might kill me on account of Rebekah. Knowing the divine arrangement that led Rebekah to be his betrothed, Isaac still lacks faith in God's protection.

8. Abimelech. See 20:2.

looked down from a window. Whereas Abraham was spared by a special revelation to Abimelech (see 20:3), Isaac is spared by Providence.

caressing [*mᵉṣaḥēq*]. The Hebrew word is a variant form of the verb "to laugh" (*ṣāḥaq*). The same variant is translated "mocking" in 21:9. This play on Isaac's name may function to highlight the conflicts and triumphs of his life. Sarah "laughed" (*ṣāḥaq—tiṣḥāq*) in unbelief at the announcement of Isaac's birth (18:12–15) and then in joy at his birth (21:6). Ishmael "played in jest" when Isaac was weaned (21:9), and now Isaac "plays in joy" with his wife.

10. One of the men. In the case of Sarah, the king took her for himself (see 20:2). Here the king is not guilty and no compensatory gift is needed.

have brought guilt. The verb refers to the guilt or culpability that a person must bear for some offense. Abimelech fears God (see 20:9, 11).

upon us. Abimelech understands the solidarity of a group. One person's action affects the whole community. Achan's sin brings God's wrath upon all Israel (Josh. 7:1). Likewise, Pharaoh's and Abimelech's offenses against Sarah bring God's wrath upon their peoples (12:17; 20:7–9).

Blessing: Prosperity in Crops and Herds (26:12 – 16)

12. planted crops. Pastoral nomads in the ancient Near East occasionally engaged in small-scale agriculture.[37] The favorable agricultural conditions at Gerar probably encourage Isaac in this direction.

hundredfold, because the LORD blessed him. His obedience during the famine brings tremendous blessing. God's good hand is as evident upon the chosen successor of God's promises as upon the founder (see 21:22).

14. the Philistines envied him. Just as Abraham had experienced, material blessing leads to strife.

---

[37]V. Matthews, *Pastoral Nomadism in the Mari Kingdom, ca. 1830–1760 B.C.* (ASORDS 3; Cambridge, Mass.: American Schools of Oriental Research, 1978); idem, "Pastoralists and Patriarchs," *BA* 44 (1981): 215–18.

15. the Philistines stopped up. Now that Abraham is gone, the Philistines effectively negate their nonaggression pact (see 21:23). They may fear God, but they lack genuine faith.

16. Move away. See 13:17; cf. 20:15.

too powerful for us. See also 21:23. The nation of Israel experiences a similar relationship with the foreign power Egypt (see Ex. 1:9). This story of God's faithful protection of Isaac should have strengthened Israel's faith.

Wadi of Gerar: Digging Wells (26:17-22)

17. So Isaac moved away. None of the patriarchs rashly risk war for the Promised Land. Instead, they trust God to give their descendants the land at the right time (see 15:13-14).

18. that had been dug in the time of his father Abraham. The ancient versions (e.g., the LXX and the Vulgate) clarify "that the servants of his father Abraham had dug" (see 21:25, 30).

same names. Wells were given names to establish proprietary rights. By giving them the same names as his father had, Isaac aims to make his ownership incontestable. This underscores the injustice (see 21:23-33) but also commemorates God's provision and protection.

19. fresh water. The Hebrew is literally "living water" (i.e., a prized artesian well).

20. Esek. The Hebrew means "dispute." Disputes over water in such arid pastureland were common.

21. Sitnah. The word means "opposition." In the wilderness, Israel will also name its water sources after miserable events.

22. Rehoboth. The Hebrew means "space." Probably this is the location Reheibeh, about 19 miles (30 km) southwest of Beersheba. Several large and ancient wells have been found in this area.

Now the LORD has given us room. Space is part of God's blessing. God's protection of Isaac resembles his rewards to Abraham during the controversy with Lot (13:1-12).

Theophany at Beersheba (26:23-25)

23. Beersheba. This is the site of Abraham's original nonaggression pact with the Philistines (21:22-34). The commemorative tokens of God's blessing were still there, further confirming Isaac's inheritance of Abraham's blessing.

24. I am the God of your father. This title is confined to the patriarchal epoch but is not unique to the Bible. The special relationship that the father had with God will now be experienced by his son. The title is never used with reference to Terah, Abraham's father. Terah was an idolater (11:27).

I will bless you. Here the blessing includes protection (26:8-9, 11, 31), enjoyment of his wife (26:8, 11), yield of a hundredfold (26:12–13), herds and servants (26:14), water supply (26:17–22, 32), space (26:22), and triumph over his enemies (26:26–31).

my servant. See 18:3. The title "servant of the LORD" is a very high accolade, reserved for such as Moses (Deut. 34:5), Joshua (Josh. 24:29), Caleb (Num. 14:24), David (2 Sam. 7:8), and the anonymous Suffering Servant (Isa. 42:1; 49:3; 50:10; 52:13).

25. built an altar. Like his father, Isaac builds an altar in response to God's revelation (see 12:7–8; 21:33). Abraham's sanctuary at Beersheba becomes Isaac's (see 21:32–33).

Blessing: Protection of the Patriarch through Pact (26:26–31)

26. Ahuzzath his personal adviser. The Hebrew is literally "Ahuzzath his friend." The king's friend is one of the highest in the court. The addition of the king's chief adviser to the party adds even greater weight to the negotiations (cf. 21:22).

28. We saw clearly. Apparently, because of his successful wells, Isaac's transition from wealthy grazier to nomad miraculously does not result in the expected economic ruin. He went to the royal city because of its royal pasturelands. Sending the herdsmen into the desert would have inflicted economic ruin on Isaac if he had not providentially found wells.

28–29. the LORD was with you ... you are blessed.[38] Their statement validates the Lord's promise (26:3–4).

sworn agreement [ʾālâ]. This is literally a curse "as a legal aid for securing an oath (Gen. 24:41 ...), contract (Gen. 26:8 ...), or covenant (Deut. 29:19f.). ... In each case the term concerns a conditional curse that the speaker either accepts or places on another."[39] This oath finalizes the terms and secures the contract.

30–31. feast ... oath. Isaac, like his father, was equal to a king (see 21:22–32).

31. peace. "When a person's ways are pleasing to the LORD, he makes even his enemies sue for peace with him" (Prov. 16:7; personal translation).

Blessing: Prosperity in the Well at Beersheba (26:32–33)

32. well. The reference to the well links Beersheba with God's provisions related in 26:17–22.

33. Shibah [šbʿ]. The Hebrew can mean "oath" or "seven." Here it likely refers to the oath just sworn.

---

[38]The Queen of Sheba will make a similar statement to Solomon (see 1 Kings 10:9).
[39]C. A. Keller, "ʾāla," TLOT, 1:113.

name of the town has been Beersheba. In Gen. 21:25–31 the name of the town was associated by a pun on the root *šbᶜ*, a homophone meaning "seven" and "oath." Here it is associated with the "oath" Isaac and the Philistines pledge on the same day Isaac's servants dig the well. As before, Isaac has redug a well of Abraham and given it the same name.

THEOLOGICAL REFLECTIONS ON BOOK 8, ACT I, SCENE 3

The Blessings of the Abrahamic Covenant

This scene makes conscious links with God's promises to Abraham and Abraham's faith and obedience. God states clearly that Isaac's blessings are a result of Abraham keeping God's commands, decrees, and laws. Abraham is a type of Christ, who by his obedience fulfils the righteous requirements of the law and secures its blessings for his seed.

The Conditional and Unconditional Aspects of the Abrahamic Covenant

Just as God unconditionally obligated himself to bless Abraham after he had proved himself a faithful covenant partner, now he conditions his blessing on Isaac on the son's obedience (26:2–4). Isaac proves himself a faithful covenant partner by staying in the land during famine (26:6). God rewards him by granting him an unconditional covenant to bless him (26:24).

Faith

Faith manifests itself in many ways. Abraham displays his faith by obeying God's rule. The narrator describes Abraham's faith in the comprehensive terms of his keeping the entire law (26:5). Isaac manifests his faith by his willingness to accept "stones" (i.e., famine) in God's will rather than search for bread outside of God's will. His greater son manifests his faith in both ways (see Matt. 4:3–4).

Weakness

Neither patriarch is perfect. Isaac shares some of his father's weaknesses, but like his father he does not allow his failures permanently to damage his faith. The bearers of Christ's kingdom are sometimes strong and sometimes weak. The faithful celebrate God's grace and are not overcome with self-guilt or destroyed by self-contempt.

Historical Guilt

Isaac receives God's blessings, but, as the next chapter will reveal, blessing is not enough. Isaac will not remain obedient to God's plans, and the cost to his family will be great.

BOOK 8, ACT 1, SCENE 4:
JACOB STEALS ESAU'S BLESSING (26:34–28:9)

LITERARY ANALYSIS OF BOOK 8, ACT 1, SCENE 4 ————

Plot

The family conflict now becomes full-blown in pursuit of the patriarch's blessing. The future of the promises may be squandered by a family wrecked by jealousy, deception, and power struggles. The tension begins with Isaac's secretive plan to bless Esau (27:1–4) and mounts with Rebekah's deceptive scheme (27:5–17) and Jacob's ruse before Isaac (27:18–26). For a few palpable moments, Isaac suspects Jacob's identity, but then the scene climaxes as Isaac blesses Jacob with fertile land and political dominion meant for Esau (27:27–29). In a classic moment too late, Esau arrives and receives only an antiblessing (27:30–40). In the denouement, Rebekah plots the flight of Jacob to escape murder by Esau's hand (27:41–28:5).

Structure

The main narrative—Jacob's purloining of Esau's blessing (27:1–40) and his flight from Esau (27:41–28:5)—is structured almost entirely by dialogue between the conflicting parties. The family members are paired in seven dialogues: Isaac and Esau (27:1–4), Rebekah and Jacob (27:5–17), Isaac and Jacob under the guise of Esau (27:18–29), Isaac and Esau (27:30–40), Rebekah and Jacob (27:41–45), Rebekah and Isaac (27:46), and Isaac and Jacob (28:1–5). Jacob and Esau never meet, and Rebekah and Isaac only briefly. Typically in Hebrew narrative only two characters dialogue at one time. Here, however, the number of separate meetings and their manner imply intentional exclusion and reflect the deep division within the family.

The information about Esau's marriage to Hittite women and his parents' displeasure seems intrusive until it is recognized as a narrative frame (26:34–35 and 28:6–9) that supplies essential data for interpreting developments in the intervening narrative. The frame gives intelligibility to Rebekah's stratagem to seek the blessing for faithful Jacob and to prevent faithless Esau from receiving it. Moreover, it profiles the contrast between Abraham, who in faith provided for Isaac's future according to God's elective purposes (24:1–67), and Isaac, who tries to thwart the divine election (25:23). It shows that Isaac fails because he follows his mouth, not his heart. He seeks to bless Esau because he loves the tasty game Esau puts in his mouth and disregards the bitterness in his heart over Esau's willful marriages and lack of spiritual perspicacity. The little fox introduced in 25:28 now devours Isaac's promising vine.[40]

---

[40]See Waltke, "Reflections," 4–14.

Naming

The manner in which the narrator and the characters identify other characters also conveys the family rifts. At a significant point the narrator states, "Now Rebekah was listening as Isaac spoke to his son Esau. . . . Rebekah said to her son Jacob" (27:5–6; see also Exegetical Notes at 28:5, 14).

Irony and Characterization

The speech and actions of this scene's peculiar characters glaringly display their flaws: misguided and violent Esau, sensuous and weak Isaac, deceptive and manipulative Rebekah, and opportunistic and unprincipled Jacob (see Exegetical Notes).

Here, Isaac is a figure of irony. He tries to thwart God's plans as given in the prenatal oracle and predicted by Esau's sale of the birthright, but his own deception is thwarted by the deceit of Rebekah and Jacob. In an incredible moment of dramatic irony, he bestows the blessing on Jacob, believing he has given it to Esau. So great is his blessing to Jacob, he has no real blessing left for the son he favors.

The narrator purposefully gaps the account of Abraham's line. In this way, he censures Isaac, who in his old age becomes like his son Esau and gives priority to his physical appetite over his spiritual discernment. Isaac, the precious son of a great father, becomes the beguiled father of a scheming son. He victimizes himself by seeking to thwart the divine word and to give the blessing to Esau. Alexander Whyte, the most famous biographer of biblical characters, captures the poignant irony of Isaac's life, even if he states it too harshly:

> The patriarch Isaac presents but a pale appearance as he stands planted between two so stately and so impressive personages as his father Abraham on the one hand, and his son Jacob on the other hand. . . . And indeed, as we follow out the sad declension of Isaac's character to the end, it is forced upon us that it would have been well for Isaac, and for all connected with Isaac, that Abraham's uplifted hand had not been arrested by the angel of the Lord.[41]

Like his father, Esau lacks discernment. Epitomizing his folly and tragedy is his belated realization that his two Canaanite wives are an abomination to the family. Esau functions as a foil to Jacob. Along with Cain, he too belongs to the seed of the Serpent. As Cain impresses the casual audience for his religiosity, so the circumcised Esau impresses one for his humanness. He is a skillful hunter with the eyes of an eagle, arms of a bear, and feet of a gazelle. His father dotes on this man's man and loves his delectable stew. Later Esau will even be presented as a forgiving man. However, he lacks the one essen-

---

[41]A. Whyte, *Bible Characters: Adam to Achan* (Edinburgh and London: Oliphants, 1900), 151.

tial virtue to please God: faith. He inherits no God-inspired dream, no vision of the transcendent. He reacts to the immediate, without reflection on future. He despises his right to take part in Abraham's promised destiny.

Key Words

The repeated words "game" (8x) and "tasty food" (6x) exclaim Isaac's weakness. The Hebrew noun *berākâ* ["blessing"] occurs seven times and its verbal form twenty-one times.

Reciprocity

Although the blessing is bestowed according to God's good pleasure, the divine verdict on the family's actions is pronounced in the disastrous consequences. Esau resolves to murder Jacob (see also Gen. 4), and Jacob must flee the Promised Land and become an exile in Paddan Aram, where Laban deceives him again and again. Later Jacob mourns the loss of his youngest son due to deceit of his older sons. Rebekah loses both sons and dies without memorial (see 35:8). Isaac lives on without significance (see 35:28). The narrator blanks whether Isaac ever learned of his wife's role in the deception.

EXEGETICAL NOTES TO BOOK 8, ACT 1, SCENE 4 ──────

Frame: Esau Marries a Hittite to His Parents' Grief (26:34 – 35)

34. When Esau. The reports of Esau's marriages to Hittite women (see also 28:6–9) frame the narrative (see Literary Analysis above).

forty years. Abraham provided a wife for Isaac when Isaac was forty (see 25:20). After Jacob steals the blessing, Isaac and Rebekah make provision for Jacob's marriage to a wife from their own lineage, not from the Canaanites (28:5). In the case of Esau, is Isaac negligent or is Esau strong-willed and indifferent to his parents? In either case, Esau has broken with the accepted patriarchal practice by contracting his own marriages.

married. Profane Esau shows his disregard for Abraham's God-given vision to sanctify the earth through his offspring. Esau cannot be censured for his bigamy. Although bigamy was not the Creator's ideal for marriage, Old Testament saints often had more than one wife (e.g., 25:1). Moreover, he cannot be censored for exogamy (i.e., marrying outside the kin group), since other saints, such as Salmon who married the Canaanite prostitute Rahab and Boaz who married Ruth, abandoned endogamy.[42] However, as a son of Abraham, Esau is without excuse in marrying Hittites who are listed among the wicked Canaanites. He should have known that God condemned these people for their wickedness and would eventually give Abraham's offspring

───────────────────

[42]All the women from outside of Israel (i.e., Tamar, Rahab, Ruth, the wife of Uriah the Hittite) who participated in the lineage of Jesus Christ were loyal to the elect family (see Matt. 1:3–6).

their land (15:16–20). He must have known how solicitously his grandfather acted to prevent his father from marrying these women (24:3). By marrying these women without regard to his ancestor's initiative and benediction, Esau again signals his lack of commitment to the Abrahamic vision of Israel's destiny and so his unworthiness to receive the blessing.

Judith daughter of Beeri the Hittite, and also Basemath daughter of Elon the Hittite. The names differ from the genealogical data for Esau given in 36:1–2. Three suggestions have been made by those who seek to harmonize the text: lists have suffered in transmission; some names are nicknames; or Esau married more than three wives. There is, however, currently no satisfactory explanation for the variance (see "Sources of Ur-Genesis" in the introduction).

Hittite. They are reckoned among the Canaanites (10:15; 15:16–21; 23:3; 28:1).

35. grief to Isaac and Rebekah. They were literally "bitterness of spirit to Isaac and Rebekah." We may infer that the Hittites' lifestyle radically differed from the holy family's spiritual tastes and training (cf. 15:16, 20; 18:19; 24:3; 27:46). Isaac should have recognized Esau's spiritual unsuitability, yet he will cling to his physical senses and appetites when it is time to give the blessing.

Isaac and Esau: Isaac Instructs Esau to Prepare Blessing Meal (27:1–4)

1. When Isaac was old. He is one hundred years old (see 25:26; 26:34), beyond the age of procreation and already blind; however, he will live another eighty years.

eyes were so weak that he could no longer see. Blindness or near blindness commonly afflicts elderly people (cf. 48:10).[43] The notice explains Rebekah's scheme for Jacob to impersonate Esau. Moreover, it is probably symbolic. His physical blindness matches his spiritual blindness (see 25:23; 26:35; 27:3). Fox writes, "'To see' . . . was a term connected to prophetic powers. . . . So here, ironically, Yitzhak's blindness leads to both deception and to the proper transferal of the blessing."[44]

called for Esau. Why does he give the blessing privately to only one son? The blessing was a public affair (49:1, 28; 50:24–25; Deut. 33:1). In Gen. 27:36, Isaac's clandestine plan backfires: he has no blessing left for Esau.

Here I am. See note at 22:1.

2. don't know the day of my death. Although Isaac lives another eighty years, he does not appear well here. The narrator introduces Isaac as old and blind, and when Isaac's sons come to him, they ask him to sit up (27:19, 31). Esau assumes his father's death is imminent (27:41).

3. weapons [kēlîm]. The Hebrew means "vessels, gear." Esau's quiver and bow may be symbols of his masculinity. W. G. E. Watson cites a Ugaritic pas-

---

[43]Moses is a remarkable exception (Deut. 34:7).
[44]Fox, *Beginning,* 107.

sage suggesting that a youth underwent an initiation rite into manhood that involved hunting game.[45]

3–4. game . . . tasty food. The word *game* is repeated eight times and *tasty food,* six times. The narrator's repetition of these terms in conjunction with the phrase "tasty food I like" and its variants (27:4, 9, 14) suggests that the narrator's focus is on Isaac's sensuality, not the role the meal played in the blessing ritual.[46]

4. I like [ʾāhēḇ]. The Hebrew is better translated, "I love." The term is usually used for personal relationships, such as a man's love for a woman (24:67; 29:18, 20, 30, 32; 34:3). Even with impersonal objects the term has a passionate tone and is stronger than *ḥps* and *rṣh,* "to like, be pleased with."[47] Isaac may be understood as having left his former spirituality (see 25:21) to become like Esau, who sold his birthright for lentil stew (25:32–34).

so that I. The Hebrew is literally, "so that my life [nepeš]." God will mediate the blessing through the patriarch's passionate vitality (see 2:7).

blessing. See 1:28. The relationship of the blessing (bᵉrākâ) to the birthright (bᵉḵôr) is unclear. In Esau's mind they are separate, for he expects to receive the blessing even though he admits he lost the birthright (27:36). However, to the inspired writer of Hebrews, and so to God, they are inseparable. After noting that Esau sold his inheritance rights, he adds, "Afterward . . . when he wanted to inherit this blessing, he was rejected. He could bring about no change of mind, though he sought the blessing with tears" (Heb. 12:17). Both pertain to the firstborn's inheritance rights—the birthright, to property (see 25:31); the blessing, to divine potency, prosperity, and dominion (27:27–29). Together they make the inheritor the primary carrier of the family heritage (economic, social, and religious). Roop explains, "The elder son becomes the head of the family, the one who carries the family tradition: defining the family's understanding of itself, speaking for the family and carrying out the family's direction."[48] Theologically, for this family it also means bearing God's promises into the next generation. Although Esau at first despises the birthright and its implicit blessing, he changes his mind. But now it is too late. Esau wants the blessing but not the prerequisite lifestyle. God will not allow this blessing to take place.

Rebekah and Jacob: Rebekah Instructs Jacob to Deceive His Father (27:5 – 17)

5. Rebekah. She is the chief actor. Her spiritual values are sound (see 25:23, 29–34; 26:35; 27:46), but her method is deplorable. G. von Rad states, "To exploit a man's blindness was not only prohibited on grounds of humanity;

---

[45]W. G. E. Watson, "The Falcon Episode in the Aqhat Tale," *JNSL* 5 (1977): 75.
[46]See D. Pardee, "An Emendation in the Ugaritic Aqhat Text," *JNES* 36 (1977): 55 n. 25.
[47]Jenni, "*tṣh,*" *TLOT,* 1:49.
[48]Roop, *Genesis,* 183.

God himself watched over dealings with the blind and deaf (Lev. 19:14; Deut. 27:18)."[49]

was listening. The family is not working together but conspiring against one another because the patriarch offers no spiritual leadership. Unlike Abraham and Sarah, who listened to the spiritual counsel of one another regarding the inheritance (see 16:5–6; 21:8–14), Isaac and Rebekah are not communicating.

5–6. his son . . . her son. The narrator highlights the family rivalry and parental favoritism by designating Esau as Isaac's son and Jacob as Rebekah's (27:6). In speaking to Jacob, Rebekah identifies Isaac as "your father" (not "my husband"), Esau as "your brother" (not "my son" 27:6; but cf. 27:15), and Jacob as "my son" (27:8).

7. my blessing. The family blessing in patriarchal times was given at departures (see 24:60) or imminent death. It could not be altered. The blessing had sanction because the Lord, using the legal social customs of those times, mediated it through the faith of the patriarch (see Heb. 11:20). After the law was given, God's blessing was mediated to all his people through the priest (see Num. 6:22–27).

in the presence of the Lord. Rebekah adds this phrase to Isaac's statement in 27:4 in order to impress upon Jacob the significance of this critical moment in the family's history. They must act now to direct the family according to Abraham's vision and save it from Isaac's and Esau's faithlessness.

8. tell. The English is a weak gloss for Hebrew *ṣwh*, "to command." She commands, not suggests, her son obey her.

9. just the way he likes it. This is better translated "that he loves" (see 27:4).

11. hairy man . . . smooth skin. See 25:25, 27.

12. What if my father touches me? Jacob has no qualms about the morality of the plan, only about its feasibility. Hamilton comments, "He who is later capable of wrestling with God wrestles little with his mother or with his conscience."[50]

curse [*qᵉlālâ*, see 12:3]. Isaac fears being defamed socially and so bringing misfortune upon himself.

13. let the curse fall on me. See also Matt. 27:25. Rebekah stakes her life on her convictions. Knowing the oracle she has been given that the older will serve the younger, she can dismiss Jacob's fears. Although her faith pays off and no curse falls on her, she pays a price for her deception. Ominously she disappears from Book 8 after this scene. The narrator memorializes Deborah, her nurse, not Rebekah (35:8) and makes no notice of her death (cf. 23:1–2). At the end of Genesis, however, he notes that she was given an hon-

[49]von Rad, *Genesis*, 277.
[50]V. Hamilton, *Genesis 18–50*, 217.

orable burial with the other patriarchs and matriarchs in the cave of Machpelah (see 49:30).

14. his father. The narrator does not refer to Isaac as "her husband" (see "his son" 27:5).

15. clothes. Later, Jacob also will be deceived by clothes (see 37:31–33).

Isaac and Jacob: Isaac Blindly Blesses Jacob (27:18–29)

18. My father. Jacob's address contrasts starkly with Esau's fulsome introduction in 27:31, betraying Jacob's fear and hesitancy.

19. firstborn [*bkr*]. The Hebrew *beḵôr* ("firstborn") and *beḵôrâ* ("right of firstborn") play with the crucial noun of this chapter, *berāḵâ* ("blessing").[51]

you. This is literally "your *nepeš*" (see 27:4).

20. the LORD. Jacob compounds his lie with blasphemy (see Ex. 20:7).

your God. This is "[co]nsistent with Jacob's language elsewhere (31:5, 42; 32:9). Not until his safe return from Haran did he speak of the LORD as his own God (cf. 28:20–22; 33:18–20)."[52] The God of the patriarchs is not his God until he experiences the divine protection for himself (see 28:20–22; 33:18–20).

22. voice . . . hands. Hearing is regarded as a source of truth in the Bible (Deut. 4:12), but Isaac ignores this sense. He fails to achieve his purpose because he depends instead on his other senses—his groping hands, his sense of smell, his taste—rather than upon spiritual understanding (see Theological Reflections below; cf. 13:8–17).

23. blessed [*brk*]. This word can simply mean "to greet" or "to salute."[53] The two occurrences here (27:23, 27) suggest this is the blessing to admit Jacob into his presence, not the blessing of inheritance.[54]

25. so that I. See 27:4.

26. kiss. This physical contact may have been a part of the ritual; if not, it is a traitor's kiss (cf. Matt. 26:48–49).

27. Ah, the smell. What was perceived through the senses gives form to the blessing (see 27:27–28; cf. 3:14–15; Num. 24:5). The blessing pertains to fertility (Gen. 27:28) and dominion (27:29; see 1:22; 22:15–18; 48:15–19; Num. 24:3–9). Hamilton identifies three parts to the blessing: descriptions of Jacob (27:27), of what he will receive (27:28), and of his future relationships (27:29).[55]

28. heaven's dew. Dew from westerly and northwesterly Mediterranean winds plays an important role in the irrigation of crops in many parts of

---

[51]Fokkelman, *Genesis*, 106–7.
[52]NIV Study Bible, 46.
[53]J. Scharbert, "*brk*," TDOT, 2:291.
[54]It could also be interpreted as an ingressive: "he began to give him the blessing" (*IBHS*, §33.3.1a).
[55]Hamilton, *Genesis 18–50*, 221.

Palestine. Sarna notes, "To the present time, the end of the rainy season and the commencement of the rainless summer is marked in the Jewish liturgy by a prayer for dew."[56]

earth's richness. This is literally "oil of the earth," a metonymy for rain.[57]

grain and new wine. The image is of a banquet. A similar blessing will be given to the nation of Israel when it settles in the Promised Land (Deut. 7:13).

29. nations. Though expressed in personal terms, the blessing pertains to national destiny and dominion. The plural points to the comprehensiveness of Israel's dominion. The blessing of universal dominion ultimately falls on Christ and his church (Matt. 28:18–19).

Be lord over your brothers. This part of the blessing granting Jacob political ascendancy confirms the oracle on which Rebekah has banked her life (see 25:23).

brothers . . . sons of your mother. This stock parallel is better translated, "relatives . . . mother's children." The statement does not entail that Rebekah had other children beside the twins (see 27:40), but it would include all her descendants through Esau (see 36:1–43).

May those . . . be cursed. Jacob inherits Abraham's blessing and destiny (see 12:3; Num. 24:9).

Isaac and Esau: Isaac Gives Esau an Antiblessing (27:30–40)

30. finished blessing. Later Jacob prays for a blessing directly from God, perhaps to supplement or supersede this one gained by a ruse (32:26).

scarcely. Timing is a sign of Providence throughout the lives of the patriarch families (e.g., 24:15, 37:25).

32. Who are you? The tragic irony is unmistakable.

33. trembled violently. Brueggemann notes, "His whole beautiful dream for a peaceful and proper closure to his life has been irreversibly shattered."[58]

indeed he will be blessed! Although Isaac had the wrong son in view, still he exercised faith and accomplished what God had planned. The word mediating the divine blessing is as irrevocable as a vow made to God (see Theological Reflections below).

34. a loud and bitter cry. Esau has reaped the painful consequences of despising his birthright, but he has also suffered unfairly again from his brother's deception.

Bless me—me too. The halting phrasing captures the shock and agony of Esau. Esau knows the blessing on Jacob cannot be rescinded. He asks only for another blessing.

35. deceitfully. Such deceit will also greatly cost Jacob (see 29:15–30).

---

[56]Sarna, *Genesis*, 193.
[57]See M. A. Grisanti, "*šmn*" *NIDOTTE*, 4:174.
[58]Brueggemann, *Genesis*, 233.

took your blessing. God may use human sin to effect his purposes; compare Israel's choice of a king (1 Sam. 8; 12); Assyria's boast (Isa. 10); the death of Christ (1 Cor. 2:8).

36. rightly named Jacob. See 25:26. In Ugaritic ʿqb means "to deceive, impede."

He took my birthright. He refuses to accept his culpability even as Adam blamed the woman (3:12).

37. So what can I possibly do for you. Though Isaac knew God had elected Jacob, he had intended to give everything to Esau and nothing to Jacob. Ironically, now he has nothing but a antiblessing to offer the son he loves.

39–40. Your dwelling . . . brother. Esau inherits an antiblessing: he is denied both dominion over his brother and the earth's fertility (see 27:28–29; cf. Cain and Ishmael). The antiblessing is a parody on Jacob's blessing. In a clever pun, the Hebrew preposition twice glossed "away from" is the same preposition glossed twice as "of" in 27:28 (i.e., "of heaven's," "of earth's"). Also "dew" and "richness" are reversed, a rhetorical device to signal and/or intensify the reversed blessing.[59]

40. You will live. Esau is to have a hard life, but he is to live.

by the sword. Esau's descendants will subsist by hunting people, just as he has subsisted by hunting game.

brother. The Israelites will not fall prey to the predator.

throw his yoke. This is fulfilled in 2 Kings 8:20, 22. The fulfillment of the prophecy within Israel's history validates that Isaac's blessing on Jacob will also be fulfilled in Israel's ultimate destiny.

Rebekah and Jacob: Rebekah Advises Jacob to Flee (27:41–45)

41. The days of mourning for my father are near. See also 27:2, "don't know the day of my death." Perhaps it is ironic that Esau lacks any psychological insight, unlike his mother, who sees right through him (see 27:45).

will kill. The murder in Esau's heart (fratricide) identifies him as the seed of the Serpent as surely as it marked out Cain and Lamech (3:15; 4:8, 23; John 8:44).

44. for a while. She probably did not think Jacob's exile would last twenty years (31:41).

45. no longer angry. Rebekah is psychologically perceptive.

I'll send word for you. But Rebekah is not a prophetess. She never fulfills her wish.

lose both of you [škl]. The Hebrew means "bereaved." She probably has in mind that after Esau killed Jacob, he would be killed by an avenger of

[59]Cf. Grisanti, "šmn," 4:173.

blood or by judicial decree demanding his execution for taking an innocent life (cf. Gen. 4:14; 2 Sam. 7:14).[60] Ironically, she suffers even more than she anticipates, at least socially if not physically. Her relationship (if any) with Esau must have been irrevocably damaged, and she never sends for Jacob from his exile in Paddan Aram. Finally, she even loses a memorial in Scripture (Gen. 35:8). Though Rebekah parries Esau's violent resolve, nevertheless, she must taste the bitter consequences of her deception.

Rebekah and Isaac: Rebekah Maneuvers Isaac (27:46)

46. Rebekah said. As Sarah took initiative to provide for Isaac (see 21:10), Rebekah acts for Jacob. She provides for flight with a cover of legitimacy. Rebekah's counsel is to be read in the light of the reasons in both 27:41–45 and 28:2–5.

because of these Hittite women. See 26:34. *Hittite* here refers to any people not under the discipline of the covenant. The Aramean wives embrace the faith of their husbands, unlike the Canaanite wives, who seduce their husbands to join their lifestyles (see 24:4; 26:34–35; 31:50). The issue is one of purity versus syncretism (2 Cor. 6:14–18; cf. Gen. 34).

disgusted with living . . . my life will not be worth living. Rebekah's manipulative language to spare Jacob again displays the poverty of Isaac and Rebekah's relationship. As demonstrated by the previous deception, Isaac and Rebekah do not seem able to communicate honestly with one another on important spiritual matters. Her statement, however, must hit a sore spot in Isaac, for he knows as well as she that Esau has betrayed the Abrahamic covenant (see 26:34–35). Sarna notes, "Implicit in Rebekah's words seems to be a subtle rebuke to Isaac for his unmerited favoritism of Esau, a rebuke that is also calculated to allay any lingering uneasiness about his unwitting blessing of Jacob."[61]

Isaac and Jacob: Isaac Blesses Jacob and Sends Him to Paddan Aram (28:1–5)

1. blessed. The blessing in 27:27–29, given in the face of death, determined the patriarchal succession; this one, as the farewell for the journey (see 24:60; 27:7), links the blessing with Abraham. By this act Isaac publicly recognizes Jacob as the true heir of Abraham's blessing.

1–2. Do not marry . . . Take a wife. The negative and positive commands correspond to those of Abraham (see 24:2–4). Faith becomes endan-

---

[60]Hamilton, "šhl," NIDOTTE, 4:106. R. Youngblood (*The Book of Genesis: An Introductory Commentary* [Grand Rapids: Baker, 1992], 216) thinks she means that when Isaac dies Esau will kill Jacob, and she does not want to mourn the loss of two family members at the same time. But Isaac is not a near antecedent of "you."

[61]Sarna, *Genesis*, 195.

gered either by persecution or by accommodation (see Theological Reflections below).

2. Go. Contrast this with Rebekah's "flee" (27:43). Apparently Isaac knows nothing of Rebekah's other reason for Jacob's exile.

Paddan Aram. See 22:23; 25:20.

3. God Almighty. See 17:1. The blessing is a fresh expression of the covenant with Abraham in 17:1–8.

a community of peoples. See "father of nations" in 17:5. In 35:11 the expression means a community of nations coming from the patriarch, a fresh expression of 17:6. The blessing will be reversed against Israel under judgment, when she is attacked by a community of peoples (see Ezek. 23:24; 32:3) rather than being blessed and joined by them. The fulfillment is found in Christ and his church (see "First Motif: The Seed" in the introduction).

4. blessings given to Abraham. In contrast to the blessing Isaac gave upon his deathbed, he now explicitly mentions the numerous offspring and land specified in Abraham's blessing (see Gen. 17).

take possession. The Hebrew here entails "to dispossess," preparing the way for the concept of holy war against the Canaanites (see also 15:16).

live [māgûr]. The Hebrew noun is related to the verb meaning "to live as an alien" (gûr, see 12:10; 26:3).

5. Then Isaac sent Jacob. The chastened father now sends his son away.

Jacob and Esau. The narrator grants Jacob, though not the firstborn, pride of place (cf. 25:9).

Frame: Esau Marries an Ishmaelite (28:6 – 9)

8. Esau then realized. Esau is a figure of tragic irony, as Roop says, "a marginalized family member who deeply wanted to belong."[62] Despite his desires to belong and to please his father, he lacks that spiritual perspicacity that will connect him with his family. Unbelievably, only now does he recognize that marrying Canaanite wives is not appropriate in his family. Brueggemann describes Esau as the family member always beside the point.[63]

9. so he went to Ishmael. Psalm 83:6 mentions an alliance of Edomites and Ishmaelites against Israel. Again Esau is a figure of tragic irony. His journey parodies Jacob's. Ishmael is the rejected natural offspring of Abraham.

Mahalath. Her connection with Basemath daughter of Ishmael is uncertain (36:3).

Nebaioth. See 25:13.

in addition to the wives. See 31:50.

---

[62]Roop, *Genesis*, 187.
[63]See also Brueggemann, *Genesis*, 234–35.

THEOLOGICAL REFLECTIONS ON
BOOK 8, ACT I, SCENE 4 ————————————

Faith and Motives

Isaac's motives are suspect and his intentions certainly misdirected. But he speaks the blessing to Jacob, whom he believes to be Esau, with full faith in God's blessings and provisions. Most of us can recognize ourselves in Isaac. We often minister with impure motives and misdirected intentions, but we exercise faith and God still accomplishes his good work, often reproving us in the process.

Blessing

Blessing, the presence of God and his promises for abundance and dominion, is communicated through the spoken word. The transference of blessing must be spoken with faith, trusting in God's empowerment. With his benediction, Aaron, as God's priest, blesses the people to multiply as God's chosen and to subdue the land (Lev. 9:22). Later, Christ, at the ascension, extends his hands in blessing upon the church, enabling her to reproduce and fill the earth (Luke 24:50–51).

Grace

Fulfilling God's plans is a family of faith and failure: Isaac who depends on his fallible senses and lacks resoluteness, Rebekah who acts by domination and deception, and Jacob who deceives and blasphemously lies. This is a message of hope for the church, for the irruption of the kingdom of God ultimately depends on God's sovereign grace, not on human faithfulness. God's promise of hope overrides all of this failure, ultimately using these fallible people to accomplish his good work. Wenham asserts, "By setting this new step forward in the history of salvation in the context of such unprincipled behavior by every member of the family, each self-centeredly seeking his or her own interest, the narrator is not simply pointing out the fallibility of God's chosen, whose virtues often turn into vices, but reasserting the grace of God. It is his mercy that is the ultimate ground of salvation."[64]

Historical Guilt

Though the blessing is passed on according to God's good pleasure, the divine verdict on the family's selfish actions is pronounced in the disastrous consequences that follow. Esau resolves to murder Jacob (see also Gen. 4), and Jacob must flee the Promised Land and become an exile in Paddan Aram, where Laban deceives him again and again. Later, Jacob mourns the loss of his youngest son due to the deceit of his older sons. Rebekah loses contact

---

[64]Wenham, *Genesis 16–50*, 216.

with both sons and dies without memorial (see 35:8). Isaac lives on without significance (see 35:28). The people of Israel will also have to learn these lessons. When they reject God's kingship in favor of a king like the other nations, they gain both the blessings and the sufferings of their fallen kings. We can be encouraged that God will use us despite our failings, but we must also recognize that real consequences exist for our sin and arrogance.

Challenge to Primogeniture Rights

See the discussion of "Conflict" in the Literary Analysis of Book 8.

Persecution and Accommodation

Jacob flees from two threats in his flight to Paddan Aram: persecution and accommodation. The physical threat from his brother may have seemed most obviously harmful, but the threat of accommodating to the Canaanite lifestyle was just as grave a danger. Accommodation is as great a threat as persecution to the community of faith.

Prophecy

With divine blessing, this family can see the future but only with darkly tinted glasses. In terms of the family's ultimate destiny, they see the future but not its historical contingencies. Prophecy is like a seed or nut. It has within it the genetic code that determines its broad destiny, but historical factors give it a specific shape. Isaac in the blessings is a prophet, but he does not know the details.

BOOK 8, ACT 2: COVENANT BLESSINGS ON JACOB AND HIS EXILE IN PADDAN ARAM (28:10 – 33:17)

LITERARY ANALYSIS OF BOOK 8, ACT 2 ─────────────

Structure and Plot

Our narrator is fond of word plays (i.e., using the same word in various ways) and of "scene plays" (i.e., using scenes in more than one connection). His work is like a piece of embroidery with design intersecting design. On the large tapestry of this act, one discerns an alternating pattern:

A Angels of God meet Jacob at Bethel (Scene 1)
B Israel establishes equality with Aram (Scenes 2–6)
A' Angels of God meet Jacob at Mahanaim (Scene 7)
B" Israel establishes equality with Edom (Scenes 7 and 8)

This pattern features Israel becoming a distinct nation in the midst of developing nations. Although Israel is inferior in military might to Aram and Edom, God's election of and presence with Jacob establishes Israel as an equal among the nations.

One can also see a chiastic pattern.[65]

A Jacob flees Esau (27:42–28:9)
    B Angels of God meet Jacob at Bethel (28:10–22)
        C Jacob an exile in Paddan Aram (29:1–31:55)
    B′ Angels of God meet Jacob at Mahanaim (32:1–2)
A′ Jacob reconciled to Esau (32:3–33:17)

In the outer frame (A/A′) lies the tension with Esau; in its inner core (C), the tension with Laban. The tension with Laban subsides when Laban proposes a pact of peace. The tension with Esau subsides when Esau kisses Jacob.

The midpoint of this act (C) in fact marks the midpoint of Book 8 and the beginning of Jacob's transformation. It can also be analyzed by a chiastic pattern:[66]

a The empty-handed fugitive arrives (29:1–30)
    b The barren mother (29:31–30:21)
        x God remembers (30:22)
    b′ God adds the son, and Rachel rejoices (30:23–24)
a′ Jacob bargains as a man of power and authority (30:25–31:55)

At the center stands God's good favor on Rachel and Jacob. In fact, at the critical junctures in Jacob's life the Lord appears to him and gives him promises: on his flight from the land (28:10–22), on his return to confront Esau (32:1–2, 22–32), and in the face of the threat from Laban's sons (31:1–3) and from the Canaanites (35:1–15).

Characterization

Behind this foregrounded plot the narrator is developing his audience's understanding of what it means to be God's covenant people. His book is about God establishing his rule through his elect people (see "Theme of Genesis and Biblical Theology" in the introduction). On his part, the Lord elects his people even while they are in the womb (Book 8, Act 1, Scene 1). In Act 1 he providentially intervenes to give Jacob the blessing, leaving Esau with the antiblessing. At the beginning of Act 2 he promises to return Jacob safely to the land.

However, the elect are unfit to rule as they emerge from the womb. The obstacle to fulfilling God's covenant promises is his own people. What appear to be obstacles to its fulfillment, such as the barren wives and barren land and the hostility of other peoples, are in reality God's means of disciplining his people to mature their faith and make them capable of leadership through godliness. In this act, God disciplines Jacob through con-

---

[65]See also Literary Analysis of Book 8.
[66]See also Brueggemann, *Genesis*, 211–13; Roop, *Genesis*, 166; Fishbane, "Composition," 15–38; Rendsburg, *Redaction*, 53–69.

flicts with Laban and Esau. As Fox observes, "Yaakov's journey takes him not only to a foreign land, but to the portals of adulthood."[67] In this act the Lord transforms the ambitious Jacob who prevails through his physical strength and malevolent cunning into the ambitious Israel who prevails through prayer to God and humble shrewdness in his dealing with people.

BOOK 8, ACT 2, SCENE 1: ANGELS MEET JACOB AT BETHEL (28:10–22)

LITERARY ANALYSIS OF BOOK 8, ACT 2, SCENE 1 ————

Repetition

The second act, like the first, begins with a divine revelation predicting its plot.

Structure

In a sublime vision, God speaks to the fugitive Jacob. Even in his sinfulness and weakness, Jacob recognizes the incredible presence of the divine and has the spiritual sensitivity to respond with passion and humility. In a worshipful attitude, he chooses symbols to memorialize the event. The narrator's careful structuring of the event heightens the significance of Jacob's symbols.

God's revelation is paralleled by Jacob's response (see also "Key Words" below).[68]

I God's revelation (28:10–15)
A A certain place (28:10–11)
- stay the night
- stone under head
B Dream (28:12–13a)
- stairway "placed" (*nṣb*) to earth
- top (*rōʾš*) in heaven
- angels of God ascending and descending on stairway
- the Lord standing (*nṣb*) above it/beside it
C Oration (28:13b–15)
- I am "the Lord," God of fathers
- I am with you and will bring you back

I′ Jacob's response (28:16–22)
A′ To the place: awe (28:16–17)
- "Lord" in this place
- awesome place
- house of God, gate of heaven

---

[67]Fox, *Beginning*, 128.
[68]Many of these parallels are helpfully analyzed by Fokkelman, *Genesis*, 46–80.

B' To the dream: memorial pillar (28:18–19)
- stone under head set up as pillar[69] (*maṣṣēḇâ*, from *nṣb*)
- pours oil on top (*rō'š*) of stone
- names place Bethel ("house of God")

C' To the oration: vow (28:20–22)
- if (contextualization of audition) you will be my God
- stone will become temple
- I will bring tithes

Key Words

The key words of the vision (28:11–13) are repeated in Jacob's memorializing of it: "place," "took," "stone," "set," "top," "rest/stand/*maṣṣēḇâ*," "heavens," "earth," "God," "LORD."[70]

Scenic Depiction

The setting of God's encounter with Jacob matches Jacob's psychological condition. The security of the sun has been replaced by the dangers of the night. The comfort of his parents' tents has been replaced by a rock. Behind him lays Beersheba, where Esau waits to kill him; ahead of him is Haran, where Laban waits to exploit him. He is situated between a death camp and a hard-labor camp. After the God of the fathers appears to him with assurances of his presence, the sun rises upon a worshiping Jacob.

Blanks and Gaps

Of the lengthy journey Jacob must have endured to reach Haran, the narrator singles out only this one event, seemingly because this event gives new meaning to the journey and begins Jacob's character transformation.

Initially, the setting of this scene is identified only as "a certain place." Although this is later revealed to be the major Canaanite city Luz, here the narrator deliberately blanks any information about the place, including the fact that it is a city. The implication is that this place has meaning only when God reveals himself there (see also Exegetical Notes and Theological Reflections below).

EXEGETICAL NOTES TO BOOK 8, ACT 2, SCENE I ———

God's Revelation: A Certain Place (28:10–11)

10. Jacob left. This action of leaving his father and especially his mother marks the beginning of Jacob's pilgrimage as a patriarch in his own right.

left Beersheba and set out for Haran. He retraces the long, arduous route that Abraham traversed about 125 years earlier. His situation, however, is even more precarious than that of his grandfather. Back in Beersheba,

---

[69]The stone probably gives tangible evidence of the stairway linking heaven and earth (see ibid., 66).
[70]Ibid., 71.

Esau lies in wait like an angry lion. Ahead in Haran, Laban waits with his spider web to trap and suck the life from his victims.

11. reached [*pgᶜ*]. This is the same Hebrew word translated "met" in 32:1, linking the two accounts.

a certain place. See Literary Analysis above and Theological Reflections below.

he stopped. Since travel is impossible after sunset, he has to stop.

night. This is another image linking Jacob's two nocturnal encounters with God as he leaves and returns to the land (see 32:22, 31).

sun had set. Sunset and sunrise are common images of distress and deliverance (cf. 15:12, 17; 19:1; John 13:30). This sunset begins Jacob's dark journey to Paddan Aram, through which he must struggle with humans and God. The true "daybreak" for his soul will not come until the end of his twenty-year exile (32:26).[71]

one of the stones. What seems ordinary, a nameless place and a simple rock, will not remain ordinary. The rock anticipates the building of a sanctuary (see Theological Reflections below).

under his head.[72] The ambiguous expression may mean "at his head," presumably for protection (see 1 Sam. 26:7) or, more probably, "his headrest."[73] In Egypt, headrests were sometimes made of metal.[74]

God's Revelation: A Dream (28:12 – 13a)

12. He had a dream. The situation only superficially resembles the incubation ritual that some have suggested as lying behind it. In the ancient Near East, a devotee repaired to the sacred precincts of a temple in order to induce the deity to reveal his will in a dream (cf. 1 Kings 3:4–5). Here Jacob does not know he is at a temple site. God takes the initiative and surprises Jacob with the dream. God's revelation requires no scheming from Jacob. Brueggemann states, "The dream permits the entry of an alternative into his life. The dream is not a morbid review of a shameful past. It is rather the presentation of an alternative future with God."[75] In this unexpected event in a no-place, God, sovereignly and apart from Jacob's schemes, reveals himself to Jacob.

in which he saw. The Hebrew literally reads, "see [*hinnēh*], a stairway." The Hebrew presentative (i.e., "present-izing") *hinnēh* marks out the three images of this dream: a stairway touching heaven and earth, angels ascending and descending, and the Lord above as master (see also 29:2 and notes).[76]

71Ibid., 49.

72The noun "head" is plural, a *pluralia tantum* (i.e., the area of the head around the head while reclining; *IBHS*, §7.4.1c).

73*HALOT*, 631.

74See C. Aldred, *The Egyptians* (New York: Frederick A. Praeger, 1961), plate 8; P. Montent, *Eternal Egypt* (New York: New American Library of World Literature, 1964), plate 90.

75Brueggemann, *Genesis*, 243.

76*Hinnēh* often marks the perception of a character and indicates a shift in point of view (see Berlin, *Poetics*, 62–63).

stairway [*sullām*]. The precise meaning of this unique Hebrew word is uncertain.[77] To judge from the context, the Akkadian cognate *simmiltu*, and the LXX translation *klimax*, it signifies either a ladder[78] or a flight of steps,[79] such as on the slopes of a ziggurat (cf. Gen. 11:1–9).[80] A flight of steps would more readily accommodate angels ascending and descending than a ladder.[81] In Egyptian and Hittite sources, ladders and stairways enabled the dead and divine beings to ascend from the netherworld to heaven. In Mesopotamia, the stairway ramp on the ziggurat linked each stage of the tower with the next until its top reached "the heavens."

resting on the earth. The Hebrew is literally, "placed toward the earth." Whereas in Gen. 11:4 the vile rebels build a tower climbing toward heaven, here the stairway is represented as stretching from heaven down to earth. Houtman explains, "[T]he impression is made that the narrator wishes to express that the communication between heaven and earth is established by an initiative from on high, on [the] part of God. The contact between heaven and earth exists by the grace of God."[82]

angels of God. These angels are met uniquely in Book 8 in connection with Jacob's leaving and returning to the Promised Land (see 32:1). Angels are messengers from God sent to guard (see 3:24), communicate (18:2), and protect (19:1–22). In sum, they are "ministering spirits sent to serve those who will inherit salvation" (Heb. 1:14). The angels suggest that the Lord who makes his presence known at Bethel will also be present to Jacob through the angelic messengers.

ascending and descending. This motion is an image of commerce between the divine and human realms. Like Eden, this place forms an axis between heaven and earth. Brueggemann says, "Now it is asserted that earth is a place of possibility because it has not been and will not be cut off from the sustaining role of God."[83] This may also be an image of God's caretaking of the land and Jacob. Rashi posits that the angels ascending are responsible for Jacob's homeland and the angels descending are responsible for the land Jacob is going to.[84]

13. above it. The Hebrew may also be read "upon it" or "beside him/it." The almost identical expression is translated "standing nearby/beside" in 18:2 and 24:13. The meaning of the preposition (whether in reference to the stairway or to Jacob) was already disputed in rabbinic times.[85] The NIV trans-

---

[77]Cf. C. Houtman, "What Did Jacob See in his Dream at Bethel?" *VT* 27 (1977): 337–51.
[78]Cf. *ANEP*, plates 96, 306, 359.
[79]*HALOT*, 758.
[80]*ANEP*, plate 747.
[81]However, according to H. Hoffner Jr. ("Second Millennium Antecedents to the Hebrew ʾ*ÔB*," *JBL* 86 [1967]: 397 n. 30), the parallel is not without difficulties. Priests ascended to the top of the temple tower by the stairway, but deities never descended by it.
[82]Houtman, "What Did Jacob See," 351.
[83]Brueggemann, *Genesis*, 243.
[84]Wenham, *Genesis 16–50*, 222.
[85]Sarna, *Genesis*, 364 n. 6.

lation presents God as Master over heaven and earth. It also fits the image of a small shrine on the top of the ziggurat (see 11:4). The alternative reveals the sovereign God in intimate communion with Jacob (cf. Ruth 2:5–6). The alternative may be more favored by the verb "said," not "called" (cf. Gen. 22:11, 15), and by Jacob's interpretation that "the Lord is in this place."[86]

God's Revelation: An Oration (28:13b – 15)

13. and he said. Sarna notes, "The wording of the divine promises shows clear dependency on the promise made to Abraham in 13:14–17."[87]

I am the Lord. See 15:7; cf. 26:2. This text does not contradict Ex. 6:3, where God says that he was not known by his name Yahweh (see "Sources of Ur-Genesis" in the introduction).

the God of your father Abraham and the God of Isaac. The revelation to Jacob confirms Isaac's blessing (Gen. 28:3–4). The theophany recalls the promises that enabled an infertile woman (Sarah) to bear a child (Gen. 21), a landless refugee (Isaac) to grow strong and wealthy (Gen. 26), and even one connected with the promise-bearing ancestry (Lot) to be rescued from disaster (Gen. 19). Jacob, as the bearer of the blessing, is the inheritor of Abraham's covenant.

I will give. Salvation is a surprising gift of God not gained through human manipulation.

descendants. See 12:3, 7; 13:15; 28:14. This is the same promise given to Abraham. When Abraham received the promise, he was married but childless; Jacob has not yet even found a bride.

on which you are lying. The covenant blessing to give Abraham the land of Canaan is here adapted to the immediate situation.

14. like the dust of the earth. This escalates the promises given to Abraham of abundant land and seed (cf. Gen. 22:17).

will spread out. A fresh expansion of promises in 13:16, the Hebrew here denotes "to break out" with destructive force; it connotes holy war.

All peoples on earth will be blessed. The particular election of the chosen seed is always linked to its universal significance (see 12:3; 17:4–6; 18:18; 22:18).

15. I am with you. See Gen. 26:3; Ex. 3:12; Ps. 23; 46; Matt. 1:23; Heb. 13:5. This is the first of three personal promises made to Jacob. First, in addition to promises for the remote future, God graciously grants intimate assurances to Jacob to sustain his faith. Brueggemann asserts, "The introduction of this formula dare not be treated like a cliché. It is the amazing new disclosure of Jacob's God, one who is willing to cast his lot with this man, to stand with him in places of threat."[88] This promise undergirds all other promises.

---

[86]See Houtman, "What Did Jacob See," 349.
[87]Sarna, *Genesis*, 198.
[88]Brueggemann, *Genesis*, 245.

will watch over you. Second, God promises preservation and protection (Ps. 91:11–15).

will bring you back. Third, God promises homecoming. "His parents prompted his departure from Canaan; Yahweh will determine and direct his return to Canaan."[89]

I will not leave you.[90] Unlike the pagan deities of the ancient Near East, God is not limited to a particular land. These personal promises of God's constant and intimate presence will help Jacob to orientate his life appropriately.

until I have done. The Hebrew "until" does not entail a situation change after God has fulfilled his promises.

Jacob's Response to the Place: Awe (28:16–17)

16. Surely. Jacob embraces the promises of his dream. The world of his dream is more convincing than his world of fear and guilt (Rom. 8:38–39).

in this place. In the Hebrew, this is the same phrase as "this is . . ." in 32:2, providing an additional link between the scenes.

I was not aware. It is as if Jacob says, "I could kick myself for my ignorance."

17. He was afraid. Jacob's reaction differs from that of Abraham and Isaac when God revealed himself to them (12:1; 15:1; 17:1; 22:1; 26:1). Perhaps his fear is prompted by his realization that he has wronged his father and brother. Adam also feared God's presence after he had sinned (3:10). In God's presence, Jacob realizes that he is a sinful creature (see Isa. 6:5; Luke 5:8). As such, this is appropriate, worshipful fear in God's presence (see Ex. 3:6; 19:16; Judg. 6:23; 13:22; Ps. 2:11). This fear is also an appropriate contrast to his fleeing for his life. There are greater forces than his brother—personal and spiritual issues of faith and righteousness—that must be reckoned with.

house of God. The formerly unidentified and seemingly insignificant place has become the house of God.

gate of heaven. The Semites understood the name *Babylon* to have been derived from *bāb-ilī*, "gate of god" (11:9). The identification of Bethel as the "gate of heaven" may be intended as a counterpoint to Babylon.

Jacob's Response to the Dream:
Memorial Pillar (28:18–19)

18. a pillar [*maṣṣēbâ*]. *Maṣṣēbâ* denotes a single upright stone and forms a word play with "resting" (*muṣṣāb*, 28:12) and "stood" (*niṣṣāb*, 28:13). The pillar functions as a witness (see 31:45–59) and a monument to the stairway

---

[89]Hamilton, *Genesis 18–50*, 243.

[90]In ancient Near Eastern religions, the deities were local and understood to protect their people within their geographical borders.

from heaven and the Lord standing there. Fokkelman says, "Just as the ladder was a prefiguration of God's appearance, so Jacob now turns an erected stone into a postfiguration of the theophany."[91] In contrast to the Canaanite pillars that were thought to be repositories of deities' spirits and perhaps functioned to symbolize their fertility,[92] this one commemorates the Lord's theophany and promises. Appropriately, upon coming into the land, the nation of Israel is directed to smash the Canaanite pillars (Ex. 23:24; 34:13; Deut. 7:5; 12:3) and not to erect these abominations to the Lord (Deut. 16:22; see "Historicity and Literary Genre" in the introduction). However, as Martens explains, "The setting up of pillars as memorials to Yahweh (28:18; 35:14) of witness (Gen. 31:45; cf. Ex. 24:4 [Josh. 24:27]) [or to mark a tomb (Gen. 35:20)] is of another order and is appropriate."[93]

poured oil. This consecrates it (see Ex. 30:25–29).

on top [rōʾš]. The word play with the top (rōʾš) of the stairway (28:12) links the memorial with the vision. Fokkelman says, "Jacob commemorates the ladder's reaching to heaven, just as by setting up the *massebe* [sic!] he commemorated that this ladder was *muṣṣāb* on earth."[94]

19. He called that place. This is a verbal link with the same formula in 32:2.

Bethel. The name means "house [bêt] of God [ʾēl]." By introducing God's self-revelation with "I am the LORD [yhwh]," the narrator eliminates any possibility of associating Israel's God with the Canaanite high god, El.

Luz. Archaeology reveals this Canaanite city to have been very large, yet it was meaningless compared to God's revelation. Fokkelman asserts, "Before the theophany transformed the *māqôm* ["place"] into Bethel, it had already accomplished another thing. By the theophany, Canaanite Luz has been exposed, leached, purged to the zero-state of 'a place'. God does not want to appear to Jacob in a Canaanite town, but he wants to appear in a nothing which only his appearing will turn it into a something, but then no less than a House of God. Where the history of the covenant between Yhwh and his people begins, all preceding things grow pale. Canaan loses its face, Luz is deprived of its identity papers."[95]

Jacob's Response to the Oration: Vow (28:20–22)

20. made a vow. This is the longest vow in the Old Testament. In Brueggemann's words, "Vows are not contracts or limited agreements, but

---

[91]Fokkelman, *Genesis*, 66.
[92]They are usually found in cult complexes that included altars and the Asherah poles.
[93]E. Martens, "nṣb," *NIDOTTE*, 3:135. Sarna confuses the two notions of memorial pillars and witness pillars, contending that the stone pillar here functions as a witness to Jacob's vow (Sarna, *Genesis*, 201). However, this is a "fallacy of total transference" (i.e., the reading of data from one text where a word is used into another). Nothing in this text refers to the stone bearing witness to either the Lord's or Jacob's words.
[94]Fokkelman, *Genesis*, 67.
[95]Ibid., 69.

yieldings that reorient life."[96] Regarding Jacob's vow, Roop comments, "The vow reorients Jacob's journey. The journey had originated as flight to avoid assassination and a trip to find a wife suitable to his parents. Now, however, Jacob's journey becomes a pilgrimage with theological content. He goes to the same place for much the same purpose, but now he travels as a carrier of God's promises and with divine assurance of aid. In turn, accompanied by God's 'traveling mercies,' Jacob has committed himself to living with Yahweh as his God (v. 21). . . . The promise and the vow transform Jacob's journey as surely as an encounter with God changes a stony place into a sanctuary."[97]

If. Whereas in the covenants with Abraham and Isaac, the Lord made the fulfillment of his promises conditional upon the obedience of the patriarchs, Jacob makes his worship of the Lord at this site conditional upon the Lord's fulfillment of his promises. Since the Lord looked with favor upon vows in old Israel, Jacob should not be censured for making this vow (see Theological Reflections below).

21. then the LORD will be my God. He fulfills this part of his vow upon his safe return (33:2), but to his detriment lingers too long at Shechem before returning to Bethel (see Book 8, Act 3, Scene 1).

22. this stone . . . God's house. This is a concrete cultic form. "The stone will not only function as a monument and a symbol of the ladder and God's appearance, it will be the centre and seal of this holy ground—without stone there is no House of God."[98]

pillar. See 28:18.

give you a tenth. Jacob's promise of a tithe marks an important moment in his transformation—no longer grasper but giver. Fokkelman explains, "[T]he very thing that Jacob undertakes to do, to pay the tithe, is in itself defined and only possible through that which God does and gives. That is why he mentions himself only in the very last place, in the main clause."[99] The practice of giving tithes to temples (i.e., to priests and deities) or to the royal court (i.e., to kings) is well-attested in the ancient Near East.[100] Abraham gave his tithe to a priest-king (Gen. 14:20). To judge from the use of the Hebrew verb form (Piel) here and in its other two occurrences (Deut. 14:22; Neh. 10:37 [Heb. 38]) and in contrast to its other form (Qal), it may signify that Jacob intends to tithe his increase regularly, not give just a one-time votive offering.[101]

---

[96]Brueggemann, *Genesis*, 248.
[97]Roop, *Genesis*, 193.
[98]Fokkelman, *Genesis*, 79.
[99]Ibid., 80.
[100]Cf. R. E. Averbeck, "*maʿaśēr*," *NIDOTTE*, 2:1035–36.
[101]See *IBHS*, §24.4i.

THEOLOGICAL REFLECTIONS ON
BOOK 8, ACT 2, SCENE 1 —————————————

Covenant

The divine covenant partner commits himself to be present with, to preserve, and to protect his pilgrim-saint until he returns safely to the Promised Land (cf. Matt. 28:20). The pilgrim obligates himself to come to God's house to worship him with tithe in hand. These commitments commence the plot of Act 2. Jacob sets out to find a wife, but first God finds him.

Crisis and *Chronos*

The narrator singles out only this event in Jacob's journey, seemingly because this begins Jacob's character transformation. Life consists of *chronos* time (i.e., regularly scheduled time, cf. Gen. 1:14) and crisis time (life-changing and defining moments). On the one hand, the regularity of *chronos* time confirms character and prepares one for the decisive moments. On the other hand, crisis time transforms the shape of *chronos* time. God's encounters are moments of life-shaping decisions. Responding to crises in faith bears the wholesome fruit of virtue and eternal significance. Responding in unbelief bears the bitter fruit of vice and a meaningless existence.

God's Transforming Presence

Until God reveals his presence at Bethel, Jacob's place appears dark, stony, and hard. However, when his eyes are opened to see beyond his physical surroundings to the metaphysical, his hard place is transformed into an awe-inspiring sanctuary, the axis between heaven and earth. Later in Israel's history, this temple (i.e., "house of God") is replaced by a portable tent-shrine suitable for Israel's wanderings and then by a temple of stone and cedar appropriate to Israel's being firmly established in the land. These shadowy temples find their antitypical fulfillment in Christ (John 2:19–22) and his church (John 7:37–39; 1 Cor. 3:16–17; 6:19). The consummation comes in the heavenly Jerusalem of the new heaven and earth: "The Lord God Almighty and the Lamb are its temple" (Rev. 21:22).

The church often appears insignificant (1 Cor. 1:26–31) and our lives dark and hard until God opens our eyes to see God's presence transforming us into the axis between heaven and earth, the gateway to God (see "Mediation" below). The church receives this awe-inspiring revelation by hearing God's word and participating in his sacraments (cf. Luke 24:30–32). However, if the church thinks of itself as a significant worldly place, like Luz, it will not gain this insight (Phil. 3:7–11).

God's presence not only gives our identity eternal dignity and meaning but also transforms our secular journey from a touring expedition into a sacred pilgrimage (Heb. 11:13; 1 Peter 1:17; 2:11). After encountering God's presence, Jacob's life is reoriented through his vision and vow. Although he is still on the same journey, his spiritual sensitivity has been transformed. Simply becoming aware of God's presence transforms the meaning and sanctity of our chartered paths. Our life is not simply a solitary wandering but a journey to the holy city with the holy God (Heb. 12:22–24).

In sum, the story is filled with transformations due to God's presence: a man running away from home runs into God; a man afraid of his brother fears God; a certain place becomes nothing less than God's place; a rock becomes a temple; night turns to morning; Canaanite Luz becomes Bethel (i.e., "the house of God"). When the dream is fulfilled, Jacob ("Heel/Grasper") will become Israel ("one who prevails with God and humans").

Tribulation

God's presence does not entail a life of ease but a life of hardship through which the saint is perfected. Jacob describes his twenty years in exile, even while God was with him, as a time when he experienced extreme physical afflictions and was wronged endlessly by Laban (Gen. 31:38–42). If God rewarded our virtue immediately by alleviating suffering, we would confound morality with pleasure. We would use God for our selfish indulgences. Our ethics would be based on eudaemonism (doing good to get good), not on pleasing God by serving the community. By gapping reward from virtue, God allows the saint to develop spiritual graces such as faith, perseverance, character, and hope. Hence the saint glories in tribulations (Rom. 5:3; 1 Peter 2:20–23; 3:8–22).

Mediation

Bethel, the gate of God between the heavenly and earthly realms, typifies Jesus Christ (John 1:47–51), who is the only "mediator between God and men" (1 Tim. 2:5), who gives "access to the Father by one Spirit" (Eph. 2:18), and who sends his angels as ministering spirits "to serve those who will inherit salvation" (Heb. 1:14).

Worship

True religion consists of more than inner, spiritual feelings. It finds expression in corporate, public, tangible acts of worship. To the altar where the patriarchs publicly petitioned and praised God through their sacrifices, and to circumcision that publicly bore witness to the family's understanding of its destiny, this scene now adds the memorial pillars to God's unique presence with his people in his temple (his house) and the saintly practice of bringing a tenth of all of one's possessions as an acknowledgement of God's presence, preservation, and protection.

Monuments and Remembrance

See "Circumcision and Baptism" in Theological Reflections on Book 6, Act 2, Scene 2.

Vows[102]

The Old Testament looks with favor upon making well-considered, realistic vows. Isaiah prophesies of a golden age when the Egyptians "will worship with sacrifices and grain offerings; they will make vows to the LORD and keep them" (Isa. 19:21). The vow, which aims chiefly to secure the Lord's aid in crisis, is a vital part of Israel's worship. The Mosaic law provides for votive sacrifices (Lev. 7:16; Num. 30:1–15), and frequently the royal psalmists make or pay vows as part of their petitions and thanksgivings (vows) (e.g., Ps. 22:25; 50:14; 56:12–13; 66:13–15). These vows also signify a commitment to continue relationship with God even after being delivered from the adversity.[103] The Lord looks with favor on Hannah's vow to offer her son to God for life if he takes away her reproach of being barren (1 Sam. 1:10–20), and with her vow she indirectly delivers Israel from the Philistines. Although vows are not required, once made they have to be kept (Deut. 23:21–23 [Heb. 22–24a]; Prov. 20:25; Eccl. 5:4–5 [Heb. 3–4]). In the words of Cunliffe-Jones, the Old Testament requires "honesty of intention and execution."[104] The vow of the Nazirite to set himself or herself apart to God reflects another motive for making vows (Num. 6:1–21). These vows of dedication express separation *to* the Lord and *from* the corrupting influences of society. Paul takes this kind of vow in Corinth (Acts 18:18). However, since there are no precepts or practices of Christians making vows in connections with personal petitions (cf. Acts 21:23), the church should abstain from the practice.

Tithe

From ancient times people have recognized the appropriateness of giving God at least a tithe of their income. Malachi reckons giving God less than a tithe as robbing him (Mal. 3:6–12). While Jesus reckons tithing as a less important matter of the law than showing justice, mercy, and faithfulness, he nevertheless says, "You should have practiced the latter, without neglecting the former" (Matt. 23:23). After Christ sends the Holy Spirit, however, his apostles drop the principle of tithing for a higher spiritual standard. God's people first give themselves to God (Rom. 12:1–2; 2 Cor. 8:5). Then they return material blessings to those who bring spiritual blessing (1 Cor. 9:6–18; Gal. 6:6) and give gifts to needy saints (Rom. 15:25–28; 1 Cor. 16:1–3; 2 Cor. 8:1–15; Gal. 6:10; Eph. 4:28). The principle now is: "Whoever sows sparingly will also reap sparingly, and whoever sows generously will also reap generously" (2 Cor. 9:6; cf. Gal. 6:9). Christians are to do so eagerly, generously, and cheerfully, the amount depending on one's level of prosperity.

---

[102]Much of this discussion is drawn from R. Wakely, "*ndr*," *NIDOTTE*, 3:38–42.

[103]C. Westermann, cited by H. Kraus, *Psalms 1–59: A Commentary*, trans. H. C. Oswald (Minneapolis: Augsburg, 1988), 299.

[104]H. Cunliffe-Jones, *Deuteronomy: Introduction and Commentary* (London: SCM, 1951), 134.

The apostles never instruct nor motivate people to give on the basis of an obligation to tithe. Averbeck notes, "There are just too many golden opportunities for NT writers to use the OT tithe to persuade Christians, yet no one ever does."[105] Our practice should reflect the abundant generosity called for in the New Testament. But all too often, Christians tithe in order not to give too much and pastors teach tithing to assure that people give enough!

Typology

Jesus refers to the ascending and descending angels on the stairway as picture of himself as the true axis between heaven and earth (John 1:51). He is the only mediator between God and human beings (1 Tim. 2:5).

BOOK 8, ACT 2, SCENE 2:
JACOB ARRIVES AT LABAN'S HOUSE
(JACOB MEETS RACHEL AT THE WELL) (29:1–14A)

LITERARY ANALYSIS OF BOOK 8, ACT 2, SCENE 2————

Structure

The scene now shifts from Bethel (28:10–22) to a well close by Haran (29:1–2). Scenes 1 and 2 are marked off by verbs signifying this movement (28:10 and 29:1).

In Scene 2 three encounters of Jacob make up the three parts of the scene: with the shepherds (29:1–8), with Rachel (29:9–12), and with Laban (29:13–14a). Jacob has traveled to Haran to find a bride; like Abraham's servant, he providentially finds her at a well.

Comparison and Contrast

In what Alter calls a type scene, Jacob meets his future wife, Rachel, at a well. The similarity of this meeting at the well with the archetype well scene in 24:11–33[106] underscores the benevolence of divine providence but puts into relief the contrast between the prayerful servant and the prayerless patriarch.

This scene must be read in light of God's promise to be with Jacob (28:15). Upon his arrival in Paddan Aram, Jacob meets the right shepherds at an unusual but providentially arranged time, and "while he was still talking with them" (29:9), his bride-to-be happens to come along (cf. Ruth 2:3). However, though directed by Providence, his chance meetings—unlike

---

[105]Averbeck, "ma'ăśēr," NIDOTTE, 2:1054.

[106]Alter (Biblical Narrative, 51–57). The basic well type scene from 24:11–33 is as follows: (1) The hero (or his representative) goes to the distant land of his relatives; (2) he arrives at a well; (3) a girl, who is cousin of the groom to be, comes to draw water from the same well; (4) the hero or cousin draws water for the other; (5) the girl returns home and reports the meeting to a brother or father; (6) the hero is brought to the girl's house; (7) subsequently, a marriage takes place between the hero and the girl encountered at the well.

those of Abraham's steward (ch. 24) and of Ruth's chance meeting with Boaz—lead to extreme hardships. God's providence becomes a means of discipline to transform Jacob's character (cf. Prov. 3:12).

The journeys of Abraham's servant and Jacob begin much differently. As Sarna states, "What a glaring contrast between the well-laden camel train of the grandfather and the lonely, empty-handed Jacob who arrives on foot!"[107] Their well-meetings are also markedly different. The actions of Abraham's servant are characterized by prayer; Jacob's by his own efforts. Abraham's chief steward begins with prayer, petitioning God for his leading. He devises a test for the woman he meets in order to confirm God's leading. When Rebekah providentially arrives and exceeds the test, he responds with praise to God.

The narrator records no specific petition from Jacob to God for provision of a wife. Instead, Jacob seems to stumble into his good fortune unaware of God's presence. Rachel does arrive at the well providentially, but now it is Jacob working to impress Rachel rather than his studying her character. Then, when he is received by the family, there is no mention of his offering praise or thanksgiving to God.

Blank

The narrator does not explain why Isaac sent Jacob away empty-handed to make it on his own. Isaac pronounced a blessing on him but gave him no tangible wealth. As a result, Jacob has no bride price to give and will have to reduce himself to a hired hand to secure Rachel.

Symbol: The Stone

The storyteller will not allow us to get around the image (29:2, 3 [2x], 10). The stone at Jacob's head became a part of his encounter with God; this stone plays a role in his meeting of Rachel. The former rock speaks of God's presence, this one of Jacob's strength.

Characterization

This scene reveals more attributes of this complex Jacob—passion and incredible strength—that God will mold on Jacob's journey of transformation. In an impressive feat of physical strength, Jacob moves a well stone that ordinarily requires several men. Then this calculating, powerful man is moved by a beautiful woman and weeps as he embraces his relatives. This strength and passion will play important roles in his lengthy servitude to Laban and again in his transforming struggle with God.

Laban, on the other hand, is a flat character. Just as before (24:30), he is an avaricious, greedy individual who uses people.

---

[107]Sarna, *Genesis*, 201.

EXEGETICAL NOTES TO BOOK 8, ACT 2, SCENE 2 ─────

Jacob Meets Shepherds at the Well Rock (29:1 – 8)

1. Then Jacob continued on his journey. The Hebrew literally reads, "then Jacob lifted up his feet." The unique expression means "to put into action [his original journey]."[108]

the land of the eastern peoples. This is a general designation for the territory east of Palestine. Other texts specify the location as Paddan Aram (25:20; 28:7) and "the country of Aram" (Hos. 12:12 [Heb. 13]). The narrator could have been much more specific, but by this designation he suggests both that Jacob is unaware of his precise whereabouts and that he is in a place of danger (see "east" at 2:8).

2. There he saw. Literally, "he looked and behold [*hinnēh*]." The narrator brings his audience alongside of Jacob and freezes the scene (see note at 28:12).

well. Knowing Jacob has come to Paddan Aram in part to seek a wife (see 28:2), the reader is alerted by the well to compare this scene with the well scene of Abraham's prayerful servant (see Literary Analysis above).

The stone . . . was large [29:3, 8, 10]. Driver explains, "Cisterns—and sometimes also wells—are . . . covered in by a broad and thick flat stone with a round hole cut in the middle, which in its turn is often covered with a heavy stone, which it requires two or three men to roll away, and which is removed only at particular times."[109] The enormous rock features prominently in this scene (29:2, 3 [2x], 10) and speaks particularly of Jacob's strength (see Literary Analysis above).

3. When all . . . mouth of the well. The generous amount of detail signals future significance to the reader.

the shepherds would roll the stone away. The rock functions to keep the well clean and to safeguard against anyone accidentally falling into it, but more importantly its immensity restricts the use of the well to a select group of shepherds who together move it.

4. my brothers [*ʾāḥ*]. The Hebrew is a very broad term meaning "relative." It could be a general greeting, "my friends" (cf. 19:7), or a more personal greeting to ingratiate himself.

where are you from? Jacob clearly does not know that he has arrived at his destination.

5. grandson. The Hebrew also means "son" (cf. NASB 24:15, 29; cf. 11:24).

6. here comes his daughter. Rachel arrives providentially.

7. it is not time. This is a striking display of providence. At what appears to be the wrong time, Jacob meets the right people and the right girl.

take them back to pasture. Their presence is the proverbial fly in the ointment. The man in quest of a bride from his relatives at Haran wants to converse alone with the girl who has already caught his attention.

─────────────────────

[108]A. B. Ehrlich, *Randglossen zur Hebraeischen Bibel* (1901, repr.; Hildesheim: Olms, 1968), 52.
[109]S. R. Driver, *The Book of Genesis* (London: Methuen, 1916), 269.

8. We can't. Their excuse is unreasonable; they are shirkers, as Jacob has insinuated. These shepherds function as foil to Jacob's ambition, energy, and strength.

until all the flocks are gathered. Since three shepherds with their flocks have already gathered, they imply that it takes more than that many men to remove the large rock. Moreover, they are not about to break their lazy work habits (see 29:2–3).

Jacob Meets Rachel and Rolls Away the Stone (29:9 – 12)

9. shepherdess. She shepherds one of the flocks entitled to the well, but it could be a rough occupation for a woman (cf. Ex. 2:16–19).

10. When Jacob saw Rachel. Unfortunately, Jacob acts solely on the basis of physical attraction (29:17), not on the basis of prayer (see Literary Analysis above).

daughter of Laban, his mother's brother. The repeated identification (29:10, 12, 13, 14) establishes the fulfillment of Jacob's parents' wishes and his mission (24:43; 28:2).

rolled. He rolls away a stone that the shepherds could not move (see 29:8). In Jewish tradition, Jacob is a giant. The sequence of events in 29:10 suggests that his superhuman strength springs from his love for Rachel and his reunion with his relatives after the long journey.

stone. Fokkelman notes, "God is indeed with him, leads him to the circle of relatives and inside it he meets the woman who is to be his bride. Whenever Jacob acknowledges this and when he feels he is under God's special protection, he makes it clear with stones."[110] However, unlike his stone pillar that commemorates God's encounter with him at Bethel (28:16–19) and the stone heap that bears witness to his treaty with Laban in the sight of God (31:42–45), the stone in this scene is not connected to God either by Jacob or the narrator. The contrast suggests that Jacob is unaware of obvious Providence.

watered. This is a reversal of the previous well scene, where the shrewd servant arranged for Rebekah to water his flocks in order to test her hospitality and virtue (24:14, 19). Jacob waters Rachel's flocks and learns nothing of her character. On the other hand, his unexpected gesture probably helps bond her to him.

11. kissed. A kiss is a customary greeting among relatives (see 29:13; 31:28, 55).

weep aloud. Jacob does this probably out of emotional joy for having successfully completed his difficult journey. He finds himself unexpectedly at the right time in the right place. However, unlike Abraham's servant, he offers no praise, for he has made no petition. On the surface all seems well, but underneath lurks dark trouble.

---

[110]Fokkelman, *Genesis,* 125.

Jacob Meets Laban and Stays (29:13–14a)

13. he hurried to meet him. Earlier the gold jewelry of Abraham's servant attracted Laban's attention (see 24:30); now Jacob's strength impresses him with the kind of service Jacob might render. As Fokkelman says, "tricky Laban knows, even before he has seen Jacob, that a workman is on his way who is worth his weight in gold."[111]

14. You are my own flesh and blood. Laban implies that they must stay together (see 2:23).

THEOLOGICAL REFLECTIONS ON
BOOK 8, ACT 2, SCENE 2

Providence

This scene is chiefly about God's providence versus Jacob's prayerlessness (see "Comparison and Contrast" in Literary Analysis above). God's providence in crisis can be either completely serendipitous, as in the cases of the marriages of Isaac and Rebekah and of Boaz and Ruth, or disciplinary, as in the case of Jacob and Rachel. Under the Lord's good hand, Jacob meets the right shepherds at an unusual but providentially arranged time, and "while he was still talking with them," his bride-to-be happens to come along. However, Jacob's chance meetings lead to extreme hardships under the machinations of Laban. The different consequences in critical encounters stem in part from having conducted one's life according to wisdom, as in the case of the former couples, or folly, as in the case of Jacob.

Spiritual Sensitivity

Jacob's actions with Rachel at the well are a lesson about spiritual alertness. Unlike the wise and prayerful servant, Jacob learns nothing about this beautiful woman because he is more in tune with the physical and emotional than the spiritual. This offers an important lesson about being spiritually alert and not giving priority to the physical and the sensual.

Prayer

The presence of prayer and worship is a key point of comparison between the two well scenes. At each important moment the servant of Abraham prays for God's guidance and thanks God for his provision (24:12–14, 26–27). Of Jacob's encounter at the well, no prayers of praise or petition are recorded. The consequence of the lack of prayer seems apparent in the following scene, with the troubled and deceitful arrangements of Jacob's marriages. The narrative values prayer in the life of the community of faith.

---

[111]Ibid., 126.

BOOK 8, ACT 2, SCENE 3:
LABAN OUTWITS JACOB:
LEAH FOR RACHEL (29:14B – 30)

LITERARY ANALYSIS OF BOOK 8, ACT 2, SCENE 3 ──────

Structure

God's transformation of Jacob's character now begins in the ambiguity of the beauty of romantic love being frustrated by an insensitive father. Jacob's arduous labor for seven years is mitigated by his ardent love. Through the providence of discipline with grace, he will return to the land as Israel, not Jacob. Jacob is being humbled to become fit to rule his brother according to God's model of servant leadership.

This scene takes place a month after Jacob's arrival at Laban's home (29:14b). Whereas the first two scenes transpired in twenty-four hour periods (Scene 1: an evening and a morning; Scene 2: an afternoon and evening), this third scene transpires over fourteen years, divided into two seven-year periods. In the first seven, Jacob agrees to work for Laban for seven years in exchange for being betrothed to Rachel (29:14b–20); in the second, after being tricked into marrying Leah, he works yet another seven years for Rachel (29:21–30; see also Scene 4).

Key Words

The root ʿbd, "to work, serve," dominates this act, which represents Jacob's exile in Haran. In this scene alone it is used seven times (29:15, 18, 20, 25, 27 [twice], 30), always with reference to Jacob serving Laban to wed Laban's daughters. This key word both begins and ends the scene. Jacob has entered a dark night of slavery, a foreshadow of Israel in Egypt. Laban outwits Jacob and reduces family to an economic arrangement (cf. 25:23; 27:29, 37, 40).

Significantly, this key word is the same one used with reference to Esau serving Jacob (25:23; 27:29, 37, 40). Fokkelman explains, "Qualitatively, too, ["work, serve"] is the most important word. It is exactly the counter-weight to the core of 'rule' versus 'serve' in Gen. 25 and 27."[112]

Reciprocity

On the one hand, God is working out his moral law of reciprocity: one reaps what one sows (Gal. 6:7). As Jacob deceived his father with reference to sight, so now he will be deceived. Again Fokkelman explains, "In Gen. 27 two brothers were exchanged by a trick, before a blind man; in Gen. 29 two sisters are exchanged by a trick in the darkness of night and behind a veil, which eliminate Jacob's . . . sight."[113] On the other hand, in a way that defies

---

[112]Ibid., 130.
[113]Ibid., 129.

human logic, God is working out his sovereign purposes through the "wrong" wife. She will become the mother of Judah, David, and Jesus Christ (see Scene 4)!

Comparison

Again, Jacob struggles against primogeniture rights. In Act 1, he kicked against the social practice, beginning literally in his mother's womb, escalating in his inveigling of the birthright and climaxing in his purloin of the blessing. Now he is hurt badly by it; it will cost him seven years of hard labor.

Characterization

Jacob's character is being tested and refined in the crucible of living with his uncle Laban. Laban is cunning, deceptive, heartless, greedy, and ambitious. Jacob has already shown that he possesses many of these same weaknesses. However, he has also shown himself to have faith. In this scene he shows himself a man capable of romantic love, a good worker, and a man of integrity whom Laban can trust to fulfill his contract, even when wronged. No mention is made of God in this scene by either actor; the narrator allows him to stand in the shadow of providence. Jacob has yet to learn a life of petition and praise.

Blank

The narrator does not tell us what Rachel feels toward Jacob in his love-at-first-sight meeting. He also neglects to mention the emotions of both daughters as they are treated as objects for money by Laban. He allows them to vent their emotions against their father in 31:14–16.

EXEGETICAL NOTES TO BOOK 8, ACT 2, SCENE 3 ─────

First Seven Years of Service: Jacob Betrothed to Rachel (29:14b–20)

15. Just because you are. Literally, this reads, "Are you surely a relative of mine that you should work for me for nothing!"[114] A negative answer is expected. Since a family member would work for nothing, Laban is degrading the blood relationship between himself and Jacob (29:14a) into an economic arrangement. What Laban should have done as a loving relative is to help Jacob get a start on building his own home, as Jacob asks of Laban in 30:25–34 (esp. vv. 26, 30, 33). Instead, Laban keeps Jacob as nothing more than a laborer under contract, as Jacob bitterly complains in 31:38–42.

work. This is a crucial word of this act and of this particular scene (see Literary Analysis above).

---

[114]Cf. D. Daube and R. Yaron, "Jacob's Reception by Laban," *JSS* 1 (1956): 61–62. The question may be real (cf. 2 Sam. 9:1) or rhetorical demanding a negative answer (cf. 2 Sam. 23:19; Job 6:22).

for nothing. Laban's smooth talk reduces Jacob to a lowly laborer under contract.[115] Their relationship for the next twenty years is that of an oppressive lord over an indentured servant paying off a bride price, not of an uncle helping his blood relative.

Tell me. He would rather give any wage than give Jacob the dignity and help due a relative.

16. Leah . . . Rachel. Their names, meaning "cow" and "ewe," respectively, were appropriate in a shepherding family, but, sadly, Laban actually treats Leah and Rachel like shepherds' animals, commodities for bargaining and trading. Later, the women use business language to describe how they understood their father's treatment (31:15).

17. weak. Literally "soft," this description likely implies that Leah's eyes lack the fire and sparkle that orientals prize as beauty.

18. Jacob was in love with Rachel. Jacob is not interested in money. He came in quest of a bride, and the Lord graciously gave him the gift of romantic love for a particular woman, which is far better than money.

19. better that I give her to you. Laban's answer is shrewdly ambiguous. He does not explicitly agree to give Rachel to Jacob after seven years. The prayerless patriarch is not discerning enough either to see through his uncle's character or to detect the ambiguity of "her."

20. seemed like only a few days. The narrator uses a classic line, thus setting the reader up to experience Jacob's agony at Laban's deceptive switch.

Second Seven Years of Service: Jacob Wed to Leah and Rachel (29:21 – 30)

21. my wife. Though only betrothed, she is reckoned his wife (cf. Deut. 20:7; 22:23–25).

to lie with her. This is the celebrated goal of the mysterious, magnetic attraction of romantic love, sung of in the Song of Songs (cf. Prov. 30:18–19).

22. feast [*mišteh*]. The Hebrew word implies a drinking fest. Jacob probably was not in control of all his faculties on his wedding night. By befuddling Jacob with wine (cf. 19:32–35) and using the blindness of the bridal veil and the darkness of night, Laban pulls off his deception, just as his sister had deceived Isaac with hairy skin, the smell of clothing, and tasty stew.

23. evening. As Jacob took advantage of his father's blindness to deceive him, so Laban uses the cover of night to outwit Jacob (see "Reciprocity" in Literary Analysis above).

he took his daughter Leah. The customs of veiling the bride (see 24:65) and of marrying off the elder daughter first serve Laban's selfish intentions. He shamelessly uses an unloved daughter, and the rivalry he initiates denies

---

[115]Such economic arrangements are documented by ancient Near Eastern texts. See Sarna, *Genesis*, 204.

the possibility for love fully to blossom between Jacob and his other daughter (30:1–2; 31:15).

24. servant girl. The custom of a father presenting his daughter with a maidservant on her marriage is well attested in ancient Near Eastern sources. The information is anticipatory of the next scene; Zilpah is mother of Gad and Asher.

Zilpah. An Arabic cognate means "with a small nose."[116]

25. there was Leah! In dramatic irony, Jacob marries the wrong woman. In yet another dramatic irony, God will use the unloved daughter and wife to give birth to the Savior of the world.

deceived me [rāmâ]. This is the same word Esau uses to describe Jacob's deceit (see 27:35–36).

26. not our custom. According to Fokkelman, this is a "formula [that] always indicates a highly objectionable, action, morally speaking" (cf. Gen. 34:7; 2 Sam. 13:12).[117] Laban feigns outrage and takes a moral stance, as though Jacob did something wrong! An honest man would have made this custom clear in the original contract. His self-righteousness is hypocritical.

to give the younger . . . before the older. The vocabulary differs from 29:16. The narrator uses *haggᵉdōlâ* ("the older") and *haqqᵉṭannâ* ("the younger") in 29:16, but Laban in dramatic irony uses *habbᵉkîrâ* ("the firstborn") and *haṣṣᵉᶜîrâ* ("the younger"), the latter of which appears in 25:23.

27. bridal week. The week of feasting (see 29:22) toasts Laban's wit and the humiliation of Jacob and of Laban's daughters (cf. Judg. 14:12, 17).

then we will give. The arrangement entails that the family trusts Jacob to honor the contract.

28. Jacob did so. Jacob is powerless and still without the woman he loves, so he says nothing. Sarna notes, "The antiquity of the narrative is attested by the fact that Jacob's action is contrary to the prohibition of Leviticus 18:18 against a man marrying a sister of his wife during her lifetime. No attempt was made to rewrite tradition in conformity with the morality and law of a later age."[118]

29. Bilhah. An Arabic cognate means "carefree."[119] She becomes the mother of Dan and Naphtali.

30. loved Rachel more than Leah. Two marriage arrangements begin with a meeting at a well. The first, arranged by the prayerful and wise servant of Abraham, commences as a peaceful and providential love between Isaac and Rebekah. The second, arranged by fleeing and prayerless Jacob, commences in strife and rivalry among sisters (see 29:31–30:24). The preferential treatment of one family member over another in the first family is now repeated in the next generation. Jacob's family also becomes divided.

---

[116]*HALOT*, 272.
[117]Fokkelman, *Genesis*, 129.
[118]Sarna, *Genesis*, 205.
[119]*HALOT*, 132.

worked. A similar Hebrew expression was translated "serve" in 27:29 with regard to nations serving Jacob. The patriarch has reaped the deceit and pain he sowed (see Theological Reflections below and Gal. 6:7).

THEOLOGICAL REFLECTIONS ON
BOOK 8, ACT 2, SCENE 3 ————————————
Providence

Sin leads to death, neglect leads to loss, and selfishness leads to self-victimization, and one ends up alienated and alone. This is the law of moral reciprocity. As Galatians says, "Do not be deceived: God cannot be mocked. A man reaps what he sows. The one who sows to please his sinful nature, from that nature will reap destruction; the one who sows to please the Spirit, from the Spirit will reap eternal life" (6:7–8; see also "Reciprocity" in Literary Analysis above).

Typology

Jacob's experience in Paddan Aram is an exile of servitude, which foreshadows Israel's servitude in Egypt. Jacob comes out with great wealth despite Laban's intentions. The Lord looks down on Jacob, and so it will be for Israel from Egypt. All of this is a picture of the church being redeemed out of a world of sin and death by God's intervention.

BOOK 8, ACT 2, SCENE 4:
THE BIRTH OF JACOB'S CHILDREN (29:31–30:24)
LITERARY ANALYSIS OF BOOK 8, ACT 2, SCENE 4 ————
Structure and Plot

The scene continues in Haran, covering a period of at least seven years, according to the terms of the marriage contract (29:27, 30; 31:41). Whereas Jacob spent his first seven years of that contract unmarried, Jacob now has two wives, each with her own handmaid. Over the remaining seven years of his marriage contract, he begins to build his family.[120] The birth of eleven sons and one daughter over seven years entails that the births are not successive and that two or more of the four mothers were pregnant at the same time.

This fourth scene of Act 2 brings to a climax the building of Jacob's family (Scene 2: the meeting of the bride; Scene 3: the marriage contracts; Scene 4: the birth of Jacob's children).

On the one hand, the scene can be easily divided by the birth mothers—Leah (29:31–35), Bilhah (30:1–8), Zilpah (30:9–13), Leah (30:10–21), Rachel (30:22–24)—with each section following the same pattern: (a) occasion of

---

[120]These are the seven years described in Scene 3, 29:30.

the births, (b) conception and birth, (c) naming. However, the occasions for these mothers bearing children create three scene divisions that reflect the conflict driving the scene:

1. The Lord enables Leah alone (29:31–35)
2. Rachel and Leah struggle for children via Bilhah and Zilpah (30:1–13)
3. Leah and Rachel struggle via mandrakes and prayer (30:14–24).

In each section, four children are born, for a total of eleven sons and one daughter. The scene reaches a climax when God remembers Rachel and ends with hope for another (30:24); the twelfth son will be born after Jacob's exile.

Frame

This scene is framed by God's opening of the sisters' wombs: Leah's at the beginning (29:31) and Rachel's at the end (30:22). For all the maneuvering of the sisters, it is still God who opens the womb.

Key Words and Naming

Obvious key words because of the structure are "Lord" and/or "God," "conceive," "bear," and "named." The names are abbreviated forms of sentences. For example, Judah, "praise," expresses more fully "I will praise the Lord." As such, many contain a theophoric (i.e., a divine name) element. In naming their children, the wives reveal their own spiritual state, reflecting their struggle and their recognition of God's assistance to them in their unloved or childless states. Out of pride and self-exaltation, they use the names to hurl malicious shafts at one another. Armstrong says, "The atmosphere in the household was electric with tension and jealousy as the two sisters crowed triumphantly over each other as each successive son was born."[121]

Characterization

Until his name is changed to Israel, Jacob is ever trying to secure God's blessing through his own efforts. Tragically, in this important phase of his life, he continues prayerless. He is potent in physical strength, both to work hard and to sire a family, but spiritually he is impotent. He stumbles into a providential marriage with neither petition nor praise. He is duped by Laban into the marriage contract and is the toast of Laban's jest at his own marriage. As his wives struggle for God's blessing in children to validate their marriages, Jacob is reduced to a stud.

The narrator reflects Jacob's impoverished state in the minimal dialogue assigned to him. He is addressed once by Rachel, "Give me children," and

---

[121]Armstrong, *Beginning*, 86.

once by Leah, "I have hired you." Both statements reveal a dysfunctional home without a spiritual leader. In addition, Jacob speaks only once in response to Rachel: "Am I in the place of God, who has kept you from having children?"

Comparison and Contrast

The narrator intends at least three comparisons and contrasts. First, Jacob's angry retort, though theologically sound, contrasts sharply with Abraham's and Isaac's prayers for childless wives (20:17; 25:21). Second, in Scene 2 Jacob was hired by Laban; in this scene, by his wife (see Exegetical Notes, 30:26)!

Third, the struggle of the sisters to overcome each other, each in her own way, mirrors Jacob's struggle to overcome Esau. Fokkelman argues, "The meaning of the entire story 29:31–30:24 is . . . that the real issue of sisters' fret and fray is the same as that of the brothers Esau and Jacob's struggle: who will take the lead, who will be first and who will be he who must serve?"[122] Leah has the disadvantage of being unloved, but the Lord chooses the unloved to become a mother first. Rachel has priority in the home through her husband's love but is barren and threatened to be displaced. Rachel's disgrace is removed when she gives up access to her husband and turns exclusively to prayer. Jacob has the disadvantage of being second born, but the Lord chooses him to be first. He will finally prevail when the strength of his physique is replaced by strength in prayer (32:25–26). Both Rachel and Jacob are spoken of as struggling and winning (cf. 30:8).[123]

EXEGETICAL NOTES TO BOOK 8, ACT 2, SCENE 4 ⸻
The Lord Enables Leah Alone (29:31–35)

31. the LORD saw. See 1:4. This section reports the first four births. The merciful God graciously gives Leah, the unloved wife, the firstborn child and half of Jacob's sons. Her children include the priestly line of Levi and the messianic line of Judah. By giving birth to a daughter (30:21), she has more children than the other three woman combined and the perfect number of children, seven.

not loved. The Hebrew literally says "hated." Her husband's emotional rejection also entails her inferior social position within the household. According to the terms of the contract, he could not divorce her.

he opened. See Literary Analysis above.

barren. Just as with Sarah and Rebekah, the loved wife is barren. There is no easy, natural way to the future. The future will not be worked by human machinations, not even by a mandrake.

---

[122]Fokkelman, *Genesis*, 140.
[123]"[Rachel's] struggle with Leah is really a struggle for God's favour, and to this extent it can be compared to her husband's struggle" (ibid., 136).

32. It is because. That is, this is the meaning of the name.

Reuben. The Hebrew is literally, "See, a son." She creatively reinterprets the name as an acronym from "The LORD has seen [*rāʾâ*] my misery [*beʿonyî*]" and/or perhaps from "my husband will love me [*yeʾehābanî*]."

the LORD has seen my misery. Like Hagar, Leah, the subordinate woman, finds mercy in childbirth (see 16:11). The first and last of the children born in Paddan Aram are given by the Lord to compensate a disgraced wife: first Leah, then Rachel (see 30:22–23). Leah's response matches the inspired narrator's interpretation of the occasion. She recognizes that God's gift of mercy has merely passed through her hands. Leah names three of her first four children with reference to "the LORD" (29:32–33, 35). By giving these names, she confesses her faith in the God of Abraham, Isaac, and Jacob, not the gods of Laban, and validates the faith and reasoning of Rebekah and Isaac for sending Jacob into exile.

Surely my husband will love me now. She yearns to change her status from the rejected to the preferred wife (cf. 29:34). As Armstrong expresses, "Yet we see the depth of Leah's pain in the names she gives her children. When Reuben . . . was born, her triumph was mingled with bitterness and a forlorn hope. . . . Each time she conceived, she nurtured the same yearning, but always in vain."[124]

33. not loved. Again, this is literally "hated" (see 29:31), a striking contrast to her hope in 29:32.

Simeon [*šimʿôn*]. The name is from "The LORD has heard [*šāmaʿ*] that I am hated [*śenûʾâ*]." Sarna notes, "The names of Leah's first two sons replicate a pair of verbs ("to see," "to hear") that expresses God's providential concern and care for the unfortunate."[125]

34. Levi. This name is from "My husband will be attached to me [*yillāweh ʾîšî*]." In spite of having the Lord's favor and gifts, her hope is not realized (see 30:15–16). She must learn to find her emotional fulfillment in the Lord's grace alone. Levi's name will take on redemptive significance when the tribe of Levi becomes attached to the ark of the covenant (see Num. 18:2).

35. Judah. His name means "I will praise [*ʾôdeh*] the LORD." The unloved wife is able to transcend her distress. Jacob supplements the meaning with praise for Judah himself (49:8). This child of praise will heal the family and become a source of blessing and reconciliation.

she stopped having children. The narrator blanks the reason. Probably Jacob has stopped his conjugal duty (see 30:15; Ex. 21:10). If so, was it out of his love for Rachel? His absence, however, is brief, for Leah bears six children in seven years (see 30:20).

---

[124]Armstrong, *Beginning*, 85.
[125]Sarna, *Genesis*, 207.

Rachel and Leah Struggle via Bilhah and Zilpah (30:1 – 13)

1. When Rachel saw. This episode chronologically must overlap with the preceding. Rachel's jealousy and drive for social esteem and Jacob's refusal to intercede in prayer for his barren wife provides the occasion for the births of the four children through their handmaids.

became jealous. See also 26:14; 37:11. Rachel's jealousy of her sister is rooted in her social disgrace as a barren wife (see 30:23). She wants to gain respect and publicly to validate her marriage. Ironically, Rachel is jealous of a sister who has been pawned off to a husband who does not love her. Each woman wants what the other has, and neither treasures what she has been given for its own value.

Give me children. Reduced to a stud in the rivalry between Rachel and Leah, Jacob suffers the consequences of the favoritism Laban has imposed upon him (see also 30:16).

I'll die. This is hyperbole for her extreme grief (see 25:32; 27:46). Although loved by her husband, she does not consider life worth living without children (cf. 1 Sam. 1:7–12). Ironically, she dies in childbearing (Gen. 35:16–19).

2. Am I in the place of God? The rhetorical question is in fact a strongly negative assertion. This is a theological certitude but also an abdication of his role as godly leader (see Literary Analysis above).

3. Here is Bilhah. See 16:2; 29:29. In the narrative, the maidservants function as agents serving the plot. Their characters are not developed.

for me. The Hebrew is literally "upon my knees." This symbolic ritual is widely attested in the ancient Near East (cf. Gen. 48:12; 50:23; Job 3:12). Carried out by parents, grandparents, or even great-grandparents, it signifies the welcome and legitimation of a newborn child into the family.

4. as a wife. The terms *wife* and *concubine* are used more loosely in the patriarchal period. Three women in the patriarchal period are called both *wife* and *concubine:* Hagar (Gen. 16:3; 25:6 indirectly), Keturah (25:1; cf. 25:6; 1 Chron. 1:32), and Bilhah (Gen. 30:4; 35:22). Each of these concubines is an auxiliary wife to the patriarch, not a slave, but subordinate to the wife who is her mistress. After the patriarchal period, the term *wife* is never used as a synonym for concubine. Zilpah, though never called a concubine (cf. 30:9), has the same social position as Bilhah (cf. 37:2).

6. God . . . has listened to me. To judge from Isaac's example, the husband has a responsibility to intercede for births in the family. Without a husband willing to intercede for her, Rachel, like Hannah, prays for herself. Instead of using "LORD," God's personal name for his covenantal relationship with his people, she uses "God," denoting his transcendence in contrast to humanity's limitations.

Dan. The name comes from "God has vindicated me" (*dānannî*). Rachel does not consider the birth of her children merely as a God-given blessing but as the justice due her as a hopeless victim. She explains her vindication in the name of the next son; God has proved her right in her struggle with her fertile sister, who has been trying to win her husband's love away from her by exploiting her barren state (cf. 29:31, 33–34; 30:15).

8. great struggle. The Hebrew literally reads "struggles of God" and is better translated, "in the struggling with God [I have struggled with my sister]."

I have won. This is the same Hebrew word rendered "overcome" in 32:28. It literally states, "I have prevailed [*yākōltî*]," a key word in this cycle. Fokkelman argues, "Her struggle with Leah is really a struggle for God's favour, and to this extent it can be compared to her husband's struggle."[126]

Naphtali. This name comes from "with the struggling [*naptûlê*] for God, I have struggled [*niptaltî*]." Laban treats his daughters as pawns in an economic struggle, and now his daughters seem to view their children as pawns in a family conflict.

9. When Leah saw that she had stopped. The flashback to 29:35 indicates that the birth of the children of the contesting sisters through their maidservants (30:1–8 and 9–13) occurs contemporaneously, not successively.

wife. See 30:4.

11. Gad. His name comes from "What good fortune [*bāgād*]."[127] Does she attribute the birth to Fortune/Luck,[128] not God? She is not represented as in prayer or praise, unlike the case of her own children (29:31–35; 30:14–20).

13. How happy I am! Her happiness lies in her success over her sister. However, Leah does not receive what she truly desires, the love and recognition of Jacob.

Asher [*ʾāšēr*]. The name is from "Women will call me happy [*ʾiššᵉrûnî bānôt*]." Essentially, Leah is saying, "I am to be envied."

Leah and Rachel Struggle via the Mandrakes (30:14–24)

In this struggle, Leah, without the mandrakes, validates her children by her handmaid in connection with naming her last two sons as God's reward and gift (30:16–21). Rachel confesses that God, and implicitly not the mandrakes, gives children (30:22–24).

14. mandrake plants [*dûdāʾîm*]. The Hebrew term, "love fruits," sounds like the word for "lover" (*dôd*) or "love" (*dōdîm*). The mandrake was used as an aphrodisiac in the ancient world (Song 7:13). Aphrodite, the Greek goddess of love, beauty, and sex, was called "Lady of the Mandrake."[129] Mandrake, grown in fields and rough ground in Palestine and the Mediterranean

---

[126]Fokkelman, *Genesis*, 136.

[127]*HALOT*, 176.

[128]In extrabiblical references, *gad* was personified as the genius or fortune of an individual (i.e., a semidivine being). See J. Tigay, "Israelite Religion: The Onomastic and Epigraphic Evidence," in *Ancient Israelite Religion: Essays in Honor of Frank Moore Cross*, ed. P. D. Miller Jr., P. Hanson, and S. D. McBride (Philadelphia: Fortress, 1987), 163, 167, 185 n. 39.

[129]Sarna, *Genesis*, 209.

region, is reputed to have emetic, purgative, and narcotic qualities; its fruit exudes a heady, distinctive fragrance, and the peculiar shape of its large, fleshy, forked roots resemble the human torso.[130] The sale of the mandrakes (30:14–15) provides the occasion for this episode (see Literary Analysis above).

15. he can sleep with you. Youngblood suggests, "Apparently Rachel, as Jacob's favorite wife, had the questionable privilege of deciding which of Jacob's wives or concubines would sleep with him on any given night."[131] In their rivalry, the struggling sisters reach an agreement that meets the other's need. Fokkelman explains, "Both wives have a serious 'deficiency'— Leah in love and recognition, Rachel in children—which they plan to eliminate for each other by a creative compromise."[132]

for your son's mandrakes. Rachel is not free of her pagan background (cf. 31:19).

16. hired you. Literally, "I have surely hired you." The fourfold occurrence of this key word (*śkr*, "hire, wage, reward") in 30:16–18[133] links the marriage contract scene (29:15) with the birth scene. Just as Jacob's relationship with Laban is changed from "flesh and blood" to "wages," so now his marriage to Leah is reduced to a commercial contract. Laban's degradation of Jacob to a shepherd under contract outside his home now strikes him from within his own family! Fokkelman observes, "The family's life is rotten and broken by the dehumanizing atmosphere of service-wages."[134] Jacob seems helpless to challenge Leah's right. This is actually the fourth "commercial" exchange in the Jacob cycle (cf. exchange of birthright, exchange of blessing, exchange of wives, exchange of husband for sex-by-hire). In the first two Jacob is the victimizer; in the last two, the victim.

my son's mandrakes. However, Leah bore two more sons and a daughter without the aphrodisiac; Rachel went three more years with no children. With this dramatic irony, the narrator dismisses the folkloristic superstition about the fertility plant.

he slept with her. "Sleep" (*škb*), as a euphemism for sex, is never used for loving marital intercourse in this book, only for illicit or forced sex: Lot's daughters with Lot (19:32–35); the Philistines with Rebekah (26:10); Shechem with Dinah (34:2, 7); Reuben with Bilhah (35:22); Potiphar's wife with Joseph (39:7, 10, 12, 14).

18. rewarded [*śᵉkārî*]. The Hebrew is the same translated "hired" in 30:16, as if to say, "God has given me my hire." Leah's pun sums up Jacob's lamentable lack of leadership and God's grace.

---

[130]*Fauna and Flora of the Bible: Helps for Translators*, vol. 11 (London: United Bible Societies, 1972), 139; see also F. N. Hepper, *NBD*, 946.

[131]Youngblood, *Genesis*, 225.

[132]Fokkelman, *Genesis*, 137.

[133]"I have hired" in 30:16 renders a double use of the verb: *śākōr śᵉkartîkā* [= "I have surely hired"]. The root is used once in the name "Issachar."

[134]Fokkelman, *Genesis*, 137.

for giving my maidservant. Rachel regarded herself as victor through God in the struggle for preference through the maidservants. Now Leah, who had not referred to God in that struggle, associates those births with God, not with the sale of the mandrakes, and validates her own relationship with God. God's reason seems to be his mercy upon each of the struggling wives.

Issachar. Hebrew *yiśśākār*[135] (= "he rewards") is from "God has rewarded me [*śekārî*]."

20. presented me with a precious gift. Hebrew *zebādanî . . . zēbed* might be translated "endowed me with a good dowry." The word occurs only here in the Old Testament, but the name Zabad occurs for different individuals (e.g., 1 Chron. 2:36 and Ezra 10:33; cf. 2 Kings 12:2).

honor [zbl]. The word means "to raise [exalt], to acknowledge (a woman) as one's lawful wife."[136] She must hire her husband to achieve what she hopes will bring his honor of her.

six sons. This repeats her plea after the birth of her third son (29:34).

Zebulun. The word may be a creative combination of "God has presented me" (*zebādanî*) and "my husband will acknowledge me as a lawful wife" (lit., *yizbelēnî*).

21. Some time later. The birth did not take place during the seven years of the contract.

Dinah. See note at 29:31. She is the only named daughter of Jacob (see 46:7); however, no etymology is given for her name. Dinah will appear again in the horrific events of chapter 34.

22. God remembered. God remembers Rachel's prayer to remove her disgrace. The verb assumes that she is a daughter of the covenant.[137] This is the climax of 29:31–30:24 (see 8:1; Ex. 2:24) and occurs after Rachel gives up her husband. Both the narrator and Rachel attribute the birth of Joseph to God, not the aphrodisiac. As Fokkelman notes, "We have not heard of the *dūdāʾîm* again, so they are insignificant and cannot even be defined as the instrument which God uses to grant Rachel fertility."[138]

23. my disgrace [ḥerpâ]. This refers to reproach and shaming,[139] which denotes the shame one feels. At last the shame of 29:31 is overcome.

God has taken away [ʾāsap] my disgrace. She named him Joseph (*yôsēp*) and said, "May the LORD add [*yōsēp*] to me another son." The name foreshadows the birth of Benjamin (35:17). It may be a play on the words "taken away" and "may he add." If so, it may also be prophetic. He will be a son "taken away" and then "added."[140]

---

[135]Several variations of the name are found within the Masoretic tradition, giving rise to several meanings (*HALOT*, 443).

[136]Ibid., 263, citing Albright, *JPOS*, 16:18.

[137]See B. S. Childs, *Memory and Tradition in Israel* (London: SCM, 1962), 41.

[138]Fokkelman, *Genesis*, 139.

[139]In contrast to *bôš*, which refers to the shame one feels when one risks, fails, and loses position.

[140]Fox, *Beginning*, xvi.

THEOLOGICAL REFLECTIONS ON
BOOK 8, ACT 2, SCENE 4 ────────────

Reciprocity

Although both sisters recognize that Israel's God, "the LORD," gives them conception and though both validate their identity by recognizing God's favor upon them, their selfish struggles to gain supremacy in their husband's affections and in their social status through bearing children destroys the home. Their shameful competition heaps disgrace upon Jacob's head that feels like decay in his bones (Prov. 12:4), fills them with inner turmoil that rots their own bones, and sows the seed of the future destructive tribalism that will ruin the sons of Israel. Reuben bringing the mandrakes to champion the cause of his mother against her rival foreshadows the devastating tribal wars during the times of the judges and of the divided monarchy.

Jacob also suffers divine discipline. As Jacob exploitatively "exchanged" the birthright and blessing, Laban exchanges Jacob's wives, and Leah exchanges her marriage for a husband-for-hire.

Grace

God incorporates the most fallible and fallen people into his gracious plans. As Brueggemann puts it, "two competitive sisters, a husband caught between them, and an exploitive father-in-law are not the most likely data for narratives of faith."[141] The twelve tribes of Israel begin in oppression, social pain, and rivalry. In spite of Jacob's prayerlessness and Rachel and Leah's rivalry for supremacy in the household and society, God blesses the family with twelve sons. His grace is greater than our sins, and his purposes will not be thwarted by them.

Hope

Embedded in this agonizing story of people's emptiness and self-inflicted pain is God's gracious gift of hope. These people have half-lives, blocked by sorrow, hostility, and competition. Leah has children but not the love of her husband; Rachel, the love of her husband but no children. Roop offers, "To those caught in half a life, the Bible offers not reproach or platitudes but God's remembering. To those longing for love or stagnated by a sterile world, the faith offers not blame or jargon but one who has come that we might have a full life (John 10:10). . . . Some folks, maybe all, will find themselves living in a situation which blocks them from reaching the fullness of life. They know the anguish of Leah and the hostility of Rachel. Ministry, like the Bible, takes that agony utterly seriously even while offering a word of hope."[142]

───────────────

[141]Brueggemann, *Genesis,* 253.
[142]Roop, *Genesis,* 206.

Mercy

The sovereign God mercifully builds up Israel by championing the unloved and the needy (29:31; 30:22). Leah wants a true husband (29:34) but finds God's mercy in bearing six of the twelve tribes of Israel, including the priestly and messianic lines. Rachel needs the social esteem of bearing children (30:23), and eventually God "remembers" her. Amazingly, though sordid jealousy and superstition taints their faith, the merciful God grants them the twelve tribes of Israel. Once again, it is divine grace and mercy, not human merit, that establishes God's kingdom.

Barrenness

Rachel's anguish concerning barrenness is understandable, but from the biblical perspective, barrenness need not be an occasion for turmoil or fear, but rather an opportunity for sovereign grace. For instance, contrast Hannah's attitude to Rachel's. At first Hannah will not eat out of grief, but she pours her heart out to God and redirects her reasons for not eating to the Nazirite laws. And just as God does so many times in Scripture, he graciously grants her a child. Faith is bringing our fears and weaknesses to God and believing that somehow God will transform our pain into a moment of grace. Rachel transforms her barrenness when she gives up her husband and the mandrakes. Fokkelman explains, "Rachel gives up the only thing that shows her precedence, the access to Jacob, and after that God shows mercy."[143] Her barrenness was partly a symbol of her self-will and envy and her oppression of Leah. As soon as she gives up the high-handedness of Jacob's policy and is prepared to bend, God grants her children.

BOOK 8, ACT 2, SCENE 5:
JACOB OUTWITS LABAN (30:25–43)

LITERARY ANALYSIS OF BOOK 8, ACT 2, SCENE 5 ————

Comparison

This unusual scene with strange, seemingly pagan rituals must be read in tandem with Jacob's recounting of the events in the following scene (see Scene 6). The comparison provides insights into the often hidden hand of God.

Structure and Plot

In the theophany at Bethel, God promises to be with Jacob. His presence entails blessing in children and in property, not in the absence of conflict. In the preceding scenes, God has been building Jacob's house; in this scene, his property. Prudently, one should build up property before his family (Prov. 27:23–27), but Laban prevents his flesh and blood from acting pru-

---

[143]Fokkelman, *Genesis*, 140.

dently. During the first seven years of their marriage contract, Laban should have allowed Jacob to prepare for his household; instead, he left him empty-handed. Now Jacob builds up his property on his own.

This scene takes place in Haran over the last six years of Jacob's exile (31:41). It consists of two incidents: the contract for flocks (30:25–34) and the contest between the two schemers (30:35–43).

Characterization

Laban's character is flat; he is ever the selfish schemer and cheat. However, Jacob is ever developing. Whereas he was a passive victim of both Laban and his wives with reference to his marriages and children, now he is once again aggressive and shrewd. He speaks first, demanding that Laban honor his marriage contract (30:26), and proposes the terms of the flock contract (30:31–33). Jacob the manipulated becomes again Jacob the manipulator.

The next scene reveals that God in a dream gives Jacob the inspiration for how he should justly plunder his avaricious father-in-law, who has cheated him many times and in many ways over his twenty years in Haran (cf. 31:38–42). However, Jacob betrays his own unrighteousness by trying to cheat Laban through the vain rod trick. Unfortunately, whereas Jacob dealt righteously with regard to Laban's marriage contract, now in this folly he acts wickedly. In the Old Testament "righteousness" means "to serve the community under God," not self, and wickedness means "to serve self at the expense of others." With regard to the marriage contract, he fulfilled the remaining seven years, though he could have run away, and he did not divorce Leah, even though today a case could be made for annulment. With regard to his own flock contract, however, Jacob embraces the godless philosophy of "fight fire with fire" and "when in Rome, do as the Romans." But Jacob's success at outwitting the cheater comes not from his folly but God's grace (see note at 31:9).

Key Word

Key words linking the scenes in this act are "serve" and "hire, wages, reward" (see Literary Analysis in Book 8, Act 2, Scene 3; cf. also 29:15; 30:16, 28).

EXEGETICAL NOTES TO BOOK 8, ACT 2, SCENE 5 ————

The Contract for Flocks:
Occasion and Agreement (30:25 – 34)

25. After. Jacob has fulfilled his fourteen-year marriage contract (29:30; 31:41). Jacob was twenty years in Paddan Aram (31:38): fourteen years for hire for the wives and six years for the flocks.

Rachel gave birth. After the birth of Joseph, it seems Jacob feels free to leave Paddan Aram with his family, for Rachel is now bound to him by child. Evidently the women could make a choice to leave or not to leave with Jacob (30:26; cf. 31:1–16). Perhaps Laban would have tried to keep his disgraced, barren daughter from going with Jacob and Leah.

Send me on my way. If a slave owner was to send an indentured slave away with a liberal supply of flocks, grain, and wine, presumably to get a new start for his own household (cf. Deut. 15:12–14), how much more should Laban have sent away his own flesh and blood (Gen. 29:14) with a full supply (31:38–42). Instead, Laban seeks to continue to exploit Jacob, and when that does not work, Laban would have sent him away empty-handed (31:42). Jacob does not tell Laban what he later tells his wives, that he is acting in response to a dream that God has just given him whereby he will plunder Laban (31:10–13). He fully anticipates that Laban will not send him away without seeking to exploit him.

my own homeland. Jacob wants to make good his vow by which he reoriented his exile as a pilgrim (28:20–22). This blessed but flawed man has always had faith and been committed to the land and to the God of Abraham and Isaac (see 28:4, 13; 31:13).

26. Give me. Jacob's demand, "give me my wives and children, for whom I have served you," forms the transition between the earlier scenes to this one.

my wives. Jacob asks for his wives and children because, although *de jure* they belong to him (Ex. 21:3–6; cf. Lev. 25:35, 45–46), *de facto* Laban still regards them as his (Gen. 31:43). Jacob could have stolen away from Laban without his consent, but Laban and his sons would have overtaken Jacob with swords (31:22–25). Moreover, Jacob would have looked like a thief running away.

I have served you. The root ʿbd, "serve," is repeated three times in this one verse. Jacob characterizes his time with Laban as one of servitude. Under the terms of the contract, his status is not unlike that of an indentured slave.

27. But Laban said. Just as the Egyptians will try to keep Israel enslaved, Laban seeks to thwart Jacob's return to his homeland, where he has vowed to worship the Lord. But even as Israel will spoil the Egyptians, so now Jacob will spoil Laban (see Theological Reflections below).

If I have found favor. This is a formula of courtesy in negotiations.

learned by divination.[144] Greedy and foolish Laban can only learn through divination what must be most apparent from Jacob's labors and Laban's increasing wealth. Most of the extrabiblical texts from Mesopotamia pertain to divination; however, divination is forbidden in Israel (see Lev. 19:26; Deut. 18:10, 14) because it presumes that other spiritual forces control the world and therefore are not under God's control. In this case the Lord accedes to Laban's magic so that Laban himself has to confess the Lord's blessing on Jacob, even as the Philistine kings had to acknowledge God's blessing on Abraham (21:22) and Isaac (26:28–29).

---

[144]An Akkadian cognate means "I have become rich." See *HALOT*, 690; N. M. Waldman, "A Note on Genesis 30:27b," *JQR* 55 (1964): 164–65; J. J. Finkelstein, "An Old Babylonian Herding Contract and Genesis 31:38f.," *JAOS* 88 (1968): 34 n. 19.

Lᴏʀᴅ **has blessed me.** See 1:22; 28:14. Laban unwittingly confirms the Lord's promise to Abraham (see 12:3; 22:18). If even those who do not bless Abraham's offspring are blessed by their presence, how much more those who bless them? However, the Lord's "curse" is about to fall on Laban for failing to bless.

28. Name your wages. Laban is always focused on economics. His statement has haunting echoes of the first deal he offered Jacob. The reader should anticipate that he intends to deceive Jacob again.

30. increased greatly. The Hebrew is translated "spread out" (i.e., burst forth) in 28:14 (see also 30:43).

The Lᴏʀᴅ has blessed you wherever I have been. This is the first time Jacob bears witness to God's blessing on him. He probably comes to this awareness through the dream he has just had (31:10–13). Although the blessing has been to Laban rather than directly to Jacob, fortune is about to turn.

31. do this one thing. Jacob's proposal depends on God's dream (see 31:10–13). However, he tarnishes it with the faulty notion that vivid prenatal impressions affect the unborn. Despite Jacob's scheming, God's intention to bless Jacob is not thwarted.

tending. The Hebrew could be translated "guarding." The sheep are entrusted to the shepherd's care to protect them (cf. 1 Sam. 17:20, 28; Hos. 12:12 [Heb. 13]).

32. every speckled or spotted. Normally in the Near East goats are black or dark brown (cf. Song 4:1; 6:5) and sheep are white (cf. Ps. 147:16; Song 4:2; 6:6; Isa. 1:18; Dan. 7:9). His wages are to be the abnormally colored sheep and goats. Normally the hire of a shepherd is 20 percent of the flock, and rarely, if ever, would the speckled population be such a large percentage.[145]

sheep [*śeh*]. The Hebrew denotes "a small livestock beast, a sheep or a goat."[146]

every dark colored lamb. . . . This is better translated, "remove from them every speckled or spotted animal, that is,[147] every black lamb. . . ."

The Contest Between the Two Schemers (30:35–43)

35. That same day he removed. Laban is again cheating. As per the agreement, the unusually colored animals should have been Jacob's starting flock. Jacob begins with no abnormally colored flock, highlighting the supernatural blessing on him.

35–36. placed them . . . put a three-day journey. Laban's two precautionary measures validate further the supernatural blessing, allow Jacob to engage in selective breeding, and provide opportunity later for Jacob to steal away.

---

[145]Finkelstein, "An Old Babylonian Herding Contract," 33–35.
[146]*HALOT*, 1310.
[147]NIV omits the *waw explicativium* ("that is").

37. poplar, almond and plane trees. Sarna says that these three trees, which have toxic substances used medicinally in the ancient world, may have "had the effect of hastening the onset of the estrus cycle and so heightened [the animals'] readiness to copulate."[148] However, Jacob is thinking in terms of sympathetic magic, as Rachel had with the mandrakes. Neither superstition, but only God, produces the offspring, as they both confess (30:23–24; 31:5).

white [*lāḇān*]. Laban's name means "white," and so does "poplar" (*liḇneh*). Jacob is using "white magic." As Jacob took over Edom (i.e., red) by red stew, so he takes over Laban by white branches.

38. flocks. These are probably goats. The word *flocks* may be used here as a synecdoche of the genus (i.e., using a broader term for the more specific).[149]

39. And they bore. The scheme works because of God's sovereign grace, not because of pagan magic or the fallacious assumption of prenatal influence on inheritable characteristics (31:10–13).

40. This is a difficult verse to translate. NIV's "young of the flock" represents a Hebrew word rendered "lamb" in 30:32; NIV's "the rest" renders the Hebrew word translated "flock" in 30:32. A consistent translation would yield: "Jacob dealt separately with the lambs [or sheep]. He made [this] flock face. . ." (so NJPS, NRSV). Nevertheless, the identification of some of the streaked and dark-colored animals as belonging to Laban is confusing, since according to the terms of the contract, these animals belong to Jacob. It seems clear that Laban has changed the contract to give himself some of the streaked animals (see 31:7–8).

41. stronger. Jacob applies the breeding method of 30:37–39 selectively to the stronger animals. Sarna suggests vigorous animals are hybrids whose recessive coloring genes emerge when they are bred together.[150] Jacob can distinguish the stronger animals with the recessive gene by their copulating earlier than the weaker animals without that gene.

42. the weak animals went to Laban. Roop suggests, "The previous agreement left Jacob with two wives: one beautiful one and one with 'weak eyes.' He did not want the weak-eyed one. This agreement makes Jacob rich with large and beautiful flocks (v. 43), providing Laban with a few weak goats."[151]

43. grew. This is the climax of the scene. The Hebrew verb means "to break out," the same verb used in God's promise at Bethel (see 28:14), showing that the promise has been fulfilled.

exceedingly prosperous. Jacob barters the strong sheep and goats for servants, camels, and donkeys.

---

[148]Sarna, *Genesis*, 212.
[149]See E. Bullinger, *Figures of Speech* (1898, repr.; Grand Rapids: Baker, 1968), 614–23.
[150]Sarna, *Genesis*, 212.
[151]Roop, *Genesis*, 201.

THEOLOGICAL REFLECTIONS ON
BOOK 8, ACT 2, SCENE 5 ──────────────────

God's Sovereign Grace

Jacob and Rachel are two of a kind. Both tarnish their faith with superstitious practices: she uses mandrakes, and he uses "white magic." Nevertheless, in spite of their foolish maneuverings, the gracious God answers Rachel's prayer and gives her Joseph and rewards the wrongly used Jacob with large flocks. The Sovereign blesses Jacob's flocks at Laban's expense in spite of the inexcusable cunning of both men (see 25:19–35:29). Jacob appears to outwit Laban, balancing Laban's outwitting of Jacob, but he obtains his family (see 29:31–30:24) and wealth by God's sovereign grace. Even Laban has to concede God's blessing on Jacob. God has committed himself to this flawed man of faith. Wenham says, "Thus, both in itself and as part of the larger patriarchal story, this narrative makes points that were ever relevant in the life of the nation: that God is not frustrated by the cheat, that justice will finally be seen to be done, and that his promises to his people, here personified in Jacob, of land, protection, and blessing to the nations will, despite all opposition, eventually triumph."[152]

Ethics

The narrator does not commend Jacob's scheming. In the next scene Jacob credits God with his blessing (31:9), not his unethical and flawed scheming in this scene. God rewards Jacob and punishes Laban for Laban's oppression in this and the other scenes in this act. He rewards Jacob for his integrity with Laban, not for this isolated incident of cheating (see 31:4–9, 36–42).

Confession versus True Religion

Laban testifies to God's blessing on him through Jacob, but that confession does not translate into a conversion of his heart. He continues to cheat Jacob and implicitly to defy Jacob's God.

BOOK 8, ACT 2, SCENE 6:
JACOB FLEES LABAN (31:1–55)

LITERARY ANALYSIS OF BOOK 8, ACT 2, SCENE 6 ────────

Anachrony and Contrast

The Lord's dream to Jacob (31:10–13), inspiring him to draw up the flock contract described in Scene 5, chronologically precedes Scene 5. By this anachrony, the narrator presents two views of how God blesses Jacob and plunders Laban. In Scene 5 (30:25–43) the narrator presents the phenomenological interpretation of events. In Scene 6, he allows Jacob himself to

---

[152]Wenham, *Genesis 16–50*, 260.

testify to its theological interpretation. The contrast between the two perspectives is vividly illustrated in summary statements: "In this way [through selective breeding] the man grew exceedingly prosperous" (30:43), and "So God has taken away your father's livestock and has given them to me" (31:9; see also Theological Reflections).

In Scene 5 the narrator gaps that Laban has changed the terms of the contract ten times. By putting that information in Jacob's mouth, he again allows Jacob himself to testify to God's amazing protection and provision: "God has not allowed him to harm me" (31:7).

Structure

Jacob's flight progresses in six steps:

1. Jacob's reasons for flight (31:1–3)
2. Jacob's speech to his wives and their agreement to flee (31:4–16)
3. Jacob's flight and Laban's pursuit (31:17–24)
4. Jacob's apologia in his dispute with Laban (31:25–42)
5. Laban's nonaggression pact with Jacob (31:43–54)
6. The relatives' parting (31:55)

Plot

The tension between Jacob and Laban builds steadily throughout Act 2. It begins in Scenes 2 and 3 when Laban cheats Jacob in their marriage contract. Throughout the fourteen years of this contract Laban has the upper hand, experiencing Jacob's blessing while oppressing Jacob. The tension shifts in Jacob's favor with the flock contract. During the last six years the Lord blesses Jacob by plundering Laban. In this scene the tension crests and plateaus repeatedly. The tension mounts in the hostility of Laban and his sons against Jacob and levels off as the wives decide to disassociate themselves from their father in favor of their husband. The tension heightens in the physical flight and pursuit of Laban and levels off with the Lord's dream warning Laban not to harm Jacob. It escalates further in their legal disputation and becomes almost unbearable as Laban searches Jacob's tents one by one in search of the gods whose discovery would utterly destroy Jacob. It again levels off when, due to Rachel's deception, he finds nothing. The act peaks when the humiliated Laban proposes drawing up a nonaggression pact; once again the tension levels off with the description of the pact-making process. In the denouement the two groups part with a kiss and return to their lands. Although Jacob is greatly inferior in numbers, he walks away—not fleeing—every bit an equal with the Aramean.

Characterization

Jacob's twenty years of trial and the obvious presence of God to prosper him during the last years work a transformation in him. For the first time in this act, he emerges as a man of public faith, and he takes the leadership of his home. He acts promptly upon God's command to return to the Promised Land (31:3–4), bears witness first to his wives of God's presence and provisions and then finally to Laban's whole family, and willingly undertakes the dangerous and difficult journey in obedience to God. For the first time, his wives follow his lead.

In this scene Rachel and Leah define themselves as the wives of Jacob, not as the daughters of Laban. In that choice, they more fully define themselves as daughters of the Lord's covenant. Rachel is purged of her pagan background as she sits menstruating on Laban's gods (see Exegetical Notes; regarding Laban, see "Sin" in Theological Reflections).

Key Word

The key word "wages" (31:8) connects the scenes of this act (see Scene 5). The key word of this scene is *gnb*, "to steal" (31:19, 20, 26, 27, 30, 32, 39), and its synonym *gzl*, "to take away by force."[153] Laban accuses Jacob of stealing his heart (i.e., deceiving him, 31:26) and stealing his gods (31:30; cf. 30:33), yet he does not accuse Jacob of stealing his flock. His silence condemns him and confirms Jacob's interpretation.

EXEGETICAL NOTES TO BOOK 8, ACT 2, SCENE 6 ——————

Jacob's Reasons for Flight: The Hostility of Laban and His Family, Jacob's Fear, and the Lord's Promise of Presence (31:1 – 3)

1. Jacob heard. This verse is a janus between Scenes 5 and 6. The jealousy of Laban's sons over Jacob's amassing wealth forms an appropriate conclusion to Jacob's care of the flocks. Providentially hearing Laban's sons and observing Laban's face, Jacob is prompted to leave.

Jacob has taken. Their accusation could be construed as a partial truth. Jacob's scheming, denying the Lord his rightful praise, contrasts sharply with Abraham's dealings (see 14:23; 27:36). In their mouths, however, the accusation is a lie. Laban has cheated Jacob, and it is the Lord who plunders their father (31:4–9). The Lord and Jacob's wives agree with Jacob's interpretation of the situation, not with Laban's sons'.

2. Laban's attitude. The Hebrew literally reads, "his face was not with him," which contrasts sharply with God's promise to Jacob: "I will be with you." Laban's attitude is like the Philistines' envy of Isaac (26:14).

not what it had been. Alienation, first expressed physically in three-days' distance, is now psychologically complete. Laban will not passively accept disadvantage, and disaster is threatening Jacob.

---

[153]To steal refers to the furtive act of taking something from someone else. Jacob uses the synonym *gzl* (31:31), "to take by force," in his accusations against Laban. Laban, as the family head, could simply exercise his power and commit *gāzal*.

3. Then the LORD said. The Lord's command to Jacob to depart foreshadows the Exodus. When warned by a revelation of God, the people of faith will once again have to flee a place of servitude (see Theological Reflections below).

Go back to the land. Jacob and his family repeat the acts of faith of Abraham and of Rebekah (cf. 12:1–2).

of your fathers. What was an unknown land to Abraham (12:1) has now become the land of the fathers.

to your relatives. Contrast this with the Lord's command to Abraham to leave his relatives (12:1).

I will be with you. This phrase evokes the revelation at Bethel (28:15). As the Lord assured Jacob of his presence and protection and flight on the sojourn, so now the Lord confirms his protective presence upon the return.

Jacob's Speech to His Wives and Their Agreement to Flee (31:4–16)

4. So Jacob sent word. He acts promptly in obedience to God. With Laban's family ganging up against him, it is necessary that Jacob secure the allegiance of his own family before fleeing this house of bondage. He must convince them of the justice of their flight (31:6–7) and of God's overruling providence to be with them (31:8–9).

Rachel and Leah. The order, giving priority to the loved wife, suggests that Jacob is now in charge of his home. In the childbearing scene, he was a pawn being brokered by his competing wives. Here his full speech demonstrates that he has finally taken spiritual leadership. He testifies to God's provision and his willingness to undertake the difficult journey in obedience to God's command (see "Characterization" in Literary Analysis above).

to come out to the fields. The witness of God's blessing is in the fields. Moreover, here he can speak without fear of being overheard by the rest of the family or by servants and without fear of raising anyone's suspicion.

5. He said to them. This lengthy speech is an important moment in the character of Jacob. In contrast to his previously recorded speeches, here Jacob openly proclaims his faith and gives all credit to God for his blessing.

the God of my father has been with me. God has graciously supplied the blessings that Jacob needed as assurance for his faith (see Theological Reflections below). Jacob's speech begins, continues, and ends with God's victories over Laban: Laban is against him, but God is with him (31:5); Laban cheated him, but God did not allow harm (31:6–7); Laban changed wages, but God changed flocks (31:8–9).

6. your father. Jacob consistently refers to Laban as "your father." He probably contrasts the attractiveness of "my father" with the repugnance of "your father."[154]

---

[154]Hamilton, *Genesis 18–50*, 288.

with all my strength. This is an amazing service, considering his physical strength (see 29:10).

7. cheated me. The Hebrew literally reads, "made a fool of me" (see 29:23; 30:25). His spoiling of Laban is just (see 31:38–42).

ten. The symbolic number for completeness is a rhetorical way of saying "time and again." The figure implies "enough is enough!"

God has not allowed him. In spite of his machinations, Jacob recognizes that the Lord has blessed him.

to harm me. See also 31:24, 29.

8. The speckled ones. See 30:31–35.

9. So God has taken away. This corresponds to an Aramaic legal term for the transfer and conveyance of property.[155] "Jacob's explanation here represents his sobered reflections on the happenings of the last several years."[156] God curses those who curse Abraham's seed (see 12:3; 27:29). Has Jacob acted unethically in his selective breeding? Laban acts according to the law in giving him Leah, but in fact he deceives him. So also Jacob acts according to the agreement concerning the flocks, yet he deceives Laban. But Laban also changes the agreement any number of times and separates himself from Jacob to restrict Jacob's wages. The ethical issue is resolved by Providence: "for I have seen all that Laban has been doing to you" (31:12). The one who deceives Laban, the one who takes away Laban's livestock, is in fact God. Jacob has had many schemes, but God is the only effective factor.

10. a dream. Lest anyone seek to deconstruct Jacob's interpretation of his success by contrasting the narrator's reason for Jacob's prosperity in 30:37–43 with Jacob's defense by an appeal to divine inspiration, the narrator himself validates Jacob's apologia by recounting God's revelation to Jacob to be with him (31:3) and warning to Laban not to harm Jacob (31:24) and by recording the agreement of both wives with Jacob against their father.

11. angel of God. See 16:7. Behind the scene is God's providence. The vertical event, not the horizontal activity, is decisive.

12. Look up. The command to "lift up your eyes" and see is a symbol of providence (see 24:63).

male goats mating with the flock are streaked. Here is the real reason for Jacob's triumph over Laban, not his cunning (see 30:31 and note).

I have seen. The metonymy of cause[157] expresses God's compassion on the suffering (cf. Gen. 16:13; 29:31; 31:42; Ex. 3:7, 9; 4:31).

13. I am the God of Bethel ... go back to your native land. Jacob seems to have collapsed two dreams into one. In the first, the angel of the

---

[155]J. Greenfield, "Našû-nadānu and Its Congeners," in *Essays on the Ancient Near East in Memory of J. J. Finkelstein*, ed. M. de Jong Ellis (Hamden, Conn.: Archon, 1977), 87–91.

[156]Hamilton, *Genesis 18–50*, 288.

[157]Bullinger, *Figures*, 539–60.

Lord gives him the inspiration of the flock contract (31:11–12). In the second, this one, introduced by God's self-identifying formula "I am," Jacob is instructed to return at once. It may be his version of the dream told by the narrator in 31:3.

the God of Bethel. The Greek and Aramaic translations expand this to say "the God who appeared to you at Bethel," in order to convey the truth that the narrator does not limit God's presence to Bethel.

vow. God reminds Jacob of his vow.

leave . . . go back. This is the climax of God's speech. The command to leave is God's will, not Jacob's.

14. Rachel and Leah replied. Jacob's wives follow him both out of retaliation against their father (31:14–15) and in recognition of God's providence (31:16). Their grievances pertain to the past, present, and future. In the past, Laban sold them and used up what was paid for them; in the present, he counts them as foreigners; their future and that of their children depends on the wealth they now have and that rightly belongs to them but which they fear Laban will steal.

15. foreigners. As such, they are exploited in the same way as Jacob, rather than being treated as members of Laban's clan.

he sold us. They condemn their "bought marriages."

he has used up. The phrase, literally "to consume money," appears in similar contexts at Nuzi (ca. 1500 B.C.). Legally, the consummating sum given in marriage was to be transferred at least in part to the daughters. Some of Jacob's wages during the fourteen years he worked for them should also have belonged to them. Further, by cheating Jacob during the last six years, Laban has continued to cheat them.[158]

paid for us. Payment was made through Jacob's work, not with money.

16. took away. The Hebrew includes the idea of "plunder" (see Ex. 12:36).

belongs to us. God recognizes their claim in the place of Laban, who will never treat their claim justly (see 31:43).

whatever God has told you. They acknowledge God's blessing and are willing to risk a journey to the Promised Land.

Jacob's Flight and Laban's Pursuit (31:17–24)

17. Then Jacob. He continues to act decisively, losing no time.

on camels. In biblical narrative, no detail is extraneous. A camel saddle from these camels will play a crucial role in the flight from Laban (31:34).

18. all his livestock. Fleeing Laban is much slower than fleeing Esau. Nevertheless, he travels very fast (see 31:23).

with all the goods he had accumulated. See 15:14 and 46:6.

---

[158]See M. Burrows, "The Complaint of Laban's Daughters," *JAOS* 57 (1937): 259–76.

Paddan Aram. The Plain of Aram is well south of Haran (see 25:20).

19. to shear his sheep. This is an ideal time to flee. Sheep shearing was carried out in the spring. It entailed large numbers of men working at great distances from their homes for an extended period of time.[159] Consequently, Laban and his men are far away and very preoccupied, allowing Rachel to steal the gods and enabling Jacob to be gone for three days (31:22) before Laban becomes aware of it.

Rachel stole. This will lead to a climactic situation that almost ruins, but then saves, Jacob (31:33–35). Hamilton says, "The ancient reader would not miss the sarcasm in this story, for here is a new crime—'godnapping'!"[160]

her father's household gods [$t^e r\bar{a}p\hat{i}m$]. The meaning of the Hebrew term and the nature and function of these objects, elsewhere called "gods" (31:30, 32), is obscure. The term may be a parody, like other terms in the Bible for idols, such as $^{\jmath}el\hat{i}l\hat{i}m$, "worthless things," and $gill\hat{u}l\hat{i}m$, "dung pellets." If so, it could mean "impotent things" or "foul things." The LXX and Targums called them idols. We have no certain knowledge from archaeology of their size and shape, nor were they uniform in size. They could be small enough to be hidden beneath a camel cushion [or within a camel saddle] (31:34) or large enough to appear the size of David (1 Sam. 19:13, 16). They were probably images of gods or ancestors. Household gods provided protection and blessing,[161] and some scholars think there is a connection between heirship and access to the family's gods.[162] Rachel may have stolen them for this reason, or she may be acting out of spite. As Laban stole her from Jacob and stole her property (31:16), so she now steals his prized gods. She herself is probably not yet completely free of her polytheistic background and beliefs (see 30:14; 34; 35:2).

20. deceived. This is better translated "stole the heart." To "steal the heart" can mean "to deceive," but elsewhere it involves taking away a person's ability to discern and act appropriately (2 Sam. 15:6; 1 Kings 12:27).[163] The translations "deceived" and "outwitted" (NASB, NIV, RSV) lose the parallelism between Rachel's theft and Jacob's. Both steal from Laban: Rachel his means of divination, Jacob his ability to act rationally.

the Aramean. Contrast the narrator's designation of Laban here with his designation in 29:10 and Laban's self-identification in 29:14. The ethnic identity underscores the total alienation of Jacob and Laban; they represent two distinct groups of people. It presages the treaty between them.

---

[159]See R. Frankena, "Some Remarks on the Semitic Background of Chapters xxix-xxxi of the Book of Genesis," *OtSt* 17 (1972): 57.

[160]Hamilton, *Genesis 18–50*, 292.

[161]For a discussion on the significance of the gods, see M. Greenberg, "Another Look at Rachel's Theft of the Teraphim," *JBL* 81 (1962): 239–48.

[162]For a summary of opinions, see Hamilton, *Genesis 18–50*, 294–95 nn. 18–20.

[163]H. W. Wolff, *Hosea*, trans. G. Stansell, ed. P. D. Hanson (Philadelphia: Fortress, 1974), 83–84; Johnson, *Vitality*, 79.

21. fled with all he had. Ironically, he flees to the homeland that he first fled in search of safety (see 27:43).

Gilead. This fertile, high plateau in Transjordan lies between the Yarmuk that runs into the Jordan, just south of the Sea of Galilee, and the northern shore of the Dead Sea.

23. his relatives. See 29:5. This likely would be the whole clan. Laban has the military superiority (see 31:29), but Jacob, undergirded by the blessing and protection of God, will ultimately prevail.

pursued. This military language depicts an atmosphere of threatening war (see 31:26, 31).

seven days. Skinner says the distance from Haran to Gilead is "c. 350 miles as the crow flies,"[164] a seemingly impossible distance for Jacob to cover in seven days with his retinue. However, he has started from Paddan Aram, several days southwest of Haran, probably in its southern extremity (see 30:26; 31:18). Also, his progress cannot be measured by the normal shepherd's pace of about six miles per day; he is fleeing for his future. Still, "seven" may be a round number for about a week.

24. God came. God is fulfilling his promise to Jacob (28:15). He sovereignly protects Jacob as he has Abraham (see 12:17; 20:3) and Isaac (see 26:8).

in a dream. See 20:3. God revealed himself to Laban earlier in providence (see 24:50) and now through a dream. What Laban saw for himself with Abraham's servant, God must now threaten him to see.

Be careful not to say. Word and deed become almost synonymous.

either good or bad. See 24:50. He is not to take legal action that will harm Jacob (see 31:29).[165]

Jacob's Apologia in His Dispute with Laban (31:25–42)

25. pitched his tent. Hebrew *tqᶜ*, not *nth,* the normal word in Genesis for pitching a tent (12:8; 26:25; 33:19; 35:21). *Tāqaᶜ* denotes the pounding or thrusting of an object into something and often connotes hostility. Here and in Jer. 6:3 it denotes the sound of the hammer driving the tent pegs into the ground. With such language the narrator sets a suspenseful scene. What hostility might follow?

in the hill country of Gilead . . . there too. Actually, the Hebrew reads "in the mountain . . . in the hill country of Gilead." Probably two heights, such as Mizpah and Mount Gilead, are intended.

26. Then Laban said. Kutler thinks Laban is issuing a challenge for battle,[166] but Laban cannot carry it through because God has threatened him

---

[164]Skinner, *Genesis,* 397. Sarna (*Genesis,* 217) says, "approximately 400 miles."

[165]See W. M. Clark, "A Legal Background to the Yahwist's Use of 'Good and Evil' in Genesis 2–3," *JBL* 88 (1969): 269.

[166]L. W. Kutler, "Features of the Battle Challenge in Biblical Hebrew, Akkadian and Ugaritic," *UF* 19 (1987): 96, 99.

not to use his superior power to harm Jacob. He accuses Jacob of deception, treating his "daughters" as prisoners of war, depriving him of the courtesy due a father, and stealing his gods. Although his rhetoric may have impressed his kinfolk, his speech is a classic example of dramatic irony. He is unaware of what the audience already knows. He pictures his daughters on his side against Jacob, whereas in fact we know the aggrieved daughters have disassociated themselves from their father in favor of their husband. The silence of Rachel and Leah in this scene bears witness against him. However, he is so self-righteous that he fails to note their silent shout. As a result, he does not expect his daughters to deceive him and make an even greater fool of him.

What have you done? These are the same accusatory words Jacob spoke to Laban when Laban deceived him (29:25). Laban is reaping what he has sown.

deceived me [*gnb*]. This is a key word in this account, and the same expression is used in 31: 20. He accuses Jacob of stealing his daughters and his gods (31:30a), but not his flock. His silence on this condemns him.

my daughters. He is so deluded he does not even recognize Rachel and Leah as Jacob's wives, though Jacob has fully satisfied the terms of the marriage contract.

captives in war. If anything, Laban has held them captive.

27. run off secretly. Laban takes his stand against the secret flight on the basis of custom (see 29:26). His speech is pure hypocrisy, and Jacob and his family know it (contrast 31:30 with 31:42).

with joy and singing. These words would sound hollow to Jacob's family. They had already experienced Laban's version of a happy feast (29:22–27). His appeal to customs such as party festivities and a farewell kiss now mock him.

harps. Better understood as "lyres" or "zithers," they could be carried easily and had six to twelve strings.[167]

28. a foolish thing. Laban says this to disparage Jacob before his wives.

29. I have the power to harm. Laban probably would have made Jacob an indentured slave. However, as his next statement confirms, he only has as much power as God allows. He will not be allowed to harm Jacob (see 31:7, 24).

you. The Hebrew is plural, that is, "every one of you," which includes his grandchildren and daughters (31:28).

30. steal my gods. Were the idols found, Jacob would lose his moral authority and appear guilty. Through Rachel's deception he almost loses his freedom and his future, and she her life. As it turns out, however, it saves the day.

31. Jacob answered. Jacob tersely defends his flight and rebuts Laban's accusations about his daughters and Jacob's lack of courtesy by speaking what his audience knows to be true (31:31). However, his defense regarding

---

[167]See *ANEP*, plates 191–93, 199, 205–7.

the stolen gods, his invitation to Laban to search his tents, and his imprecation almost bring him to ruin (31:32, cf. 44:9). His past and future meaning
depend on this critical search.

take . . . by force [*gzl*]. "To rob by seizure" matches Laban's accusation
that Jacob took the daughters as captives of war.

32. he shall not live. See 44:9, where theft entailed slavery and/or a capital offense. Theft of temple property was a capital offense in the Code of
Hammurabi. Rachel will not be found out now, but she will die young in
childbirth (see 35:16–18).

did not know. Jacob and Rachel are again two of a kind. This time both
almost bring ruin on the family by their risk taking: she by her rash theft,
he by his rash vow (cf. his sons' rash vow in 44:6–12).

Rachel had stolen the gods. As Laban deceived his family, now in *lex
talionis* justice his daughter deceives him. She makes the already foolish
Laban look ludicrous.

33. into Jacob's . . . Leah's . . . of the two maidservants. Always the
skilled storyteller, the narrator builds suspense.

34. saddle. A relief from Tell Halif in northern Syria (ca. 900 B.C.) shows
a camel driver with a stick in his right hand, fully and securely seated on a
boxlike saddle. The box, about 18 inches long and 14 inches high, is bound
by straps to the camel and serves as both a riding saddle and a pack saddle.[168]

sitting on them. The contrast between Jacob's God and Laban's idols is
laughable (see Isa. 46:1–2). Rachel does not hold them in high regard. Sarna
states, "It implies an attitude of willful defilement and contemptuous rejection of the idea that Laban's cult objects had any religious worth."[169]

searched [31:34 and 37]. The Hebrew word here is translated "touched"
in 27:22. Trusting only their physical senses, neither Isaac nor Laban finds
the truth.

35. Rachel said. This is Rachel's final retaliation against her father who
has spoiled her marriage and taken her bride price. As in Genesis 27, the
younger child deceives the father.

I'm having my period. The gods were equivalent to a sanitary napkin.
The law later codified that women were ceremonially unclean at this time
(see Lev. 15:19–30, esp. v. 20).

searched but could not find. As Bal points out, "A woman would simply have checked, a man would not dream of trying."[170]

36. took . . . to task [*rîḇ*]. The Hebrew describes a quarrel or dispute
(see 13:7–8; 26:20–22). In Genesis it refers to quarrels between groups
regarding rights to pasturage (see 13:7–8), ownership of wells (26:20), and

---

[168]See *ANEP*, 59, plate 188.
[169]Sarna, *Genesis*, 219.
[170]M. Bal, "Tricky Thematics," *Semeia* 42 (1988): 151; see also N. Steinberg, "Israelite Tricksters,
Their Analogues and Cross-Cultural Study," *Semeia* 42 (1988): 7.

here possession of flocks (31:36). The "dispute is a 'war' in the prenational arena,"[171] but God prevents physical conflict between Laban and Jacob. In the legal realm *rîb* signifies hearing disputes before a court, using the entire legal process.[172] That may be part of the sense here, because Jacob asks the relatives to judge between him and Laban (31:37) and concludes that God has already handed down the verdict in his favor (31:42). He turns the table from being the accused to being the aggrieved party. Jacob's speech, which summarizes his twenty years with Laban, is comprehensive and almost poetic. Jacob proves his innocence from the present situation of being wrongly accused of stealing gods (31:36–38) and the past circumstances of wrongs (31:39–40), with an appeal to God's vindication of him in the past and in the present in Laban's dream (31:41–42). Moreover, the balance and parallelism create the effect of elevated rhetorical prose. In Wenham's words, "Here twenty years of angry frustration burst out in a diatribe of ferocious intensity."[173]

What is my crime? [*pšᶜ*]. The Hebrew normally implies rebellion, willful volitions by an inferior against a superior in the political realm. Although all-out war between the clans is not in view, Jacob's speech is necessary to assure that he leaves his reputation in Paddan Aram on sure moral footing. He will have no debts to pay, such as he has with Esau.

What sin [*ḥaṭṭaʾt*].[174] The etymology of the word, "to miss the mark," points to its use. The sphere of "error" is usually theological and rarely political (42:22; 43:9; 2 Kings 18:14), though in fact the sacral and secular realms cannot be strictly distinguished. Here Jacob—at least to judge from the specifics that follow—has in view standards of behavior concerning others that God and society uphold.[175]

37. what have you found. His first defense is innocence. He has stolen nothing.

let them judge [*ykḥ*; see 21:25; 31:42; cf. *rîb*, 31:36]. This is a legal term meaning to set matters right. The plaintiff calls upon the relatives to serve as judge and jury. The case of the household gods symbolizes the problem. He has been similarly wronged by Laban for twenty years.

38. Your sheep and goats. Just as Laban cannot justly accuse Jacob of the theft of his gods, he cannot fault Jacob in the care of his sheep.

not miscarried. This is due to Jacob's skillful and conscientious shepherding.

---

[171]G. Liedke, "*rîb*," *TLOT*, 3:1234.

[172]Ibid., 1235.

[173]Wenham, *Genesis 16–50*, 277.

[174]R. Youngblood, "A New Look at Three OT Roots for 'Sin,'" in *Biblical and Near Eastern Studies: Essays in Honor of William Sanford LaSor*, ed. G. A. Tuttle (Grand Rapids: Eerdmans, 1978), 201–5.

[175]Mabee thinks "crime" refers to "property crime" and "sin" to "legal offense" (Mabee, "Jacob," 203 n. 32).

39. I bore the loss. Jacob went far beyond the obligations later codified in the Code of Hammurabi (see also Ex. 22:10–11). A shepherd was not usually accountable for animals that were attacked.

demanded payment. Jacob is not taking credit for doing more than law demanded. He was liable for lost or stolen sheep.[176]

stolen. The key word in this dispute must stick in Jacob's throat. Laban is obsessed with property.

41. fourteen years for your two daughters. In consideration of his wives, he tactfully omits the marriage switch.

you changed my wages ten times. See 31:7. Jacob endured great hardship and instead of receiving reward was cheated time and again.

42. If the God of my father . . . had not been with me. See 28:15; Ps 124:1.

Fear of Isaac. This could also be translated, "the Awesome One of Isaac," that is, the One of Isaac who inspires dread (see 31:24, 53).[177] This is a unique epithet for God. The God who providentially provided for Isaac, as Laban knows, also providentially protects Jacob, as Laban is now learning.

sent me away empty-handed. See 30:25–27. Here was Laban's real culpability: neglecting to pay his workers (see Ex. 3:20–21; Deut. 15:13–14).

seen my hardship. This phrase is used in the Old Testament only two other times, both to describe Egyptian oppression (Ex. 3:7; Deut. 26:7).

rebuked [ykh; see "judge," 31:37]. God has taken up Jacob's case (see also 30:33).

Laban's Nonaggression Pact with Jacob (31:43–54)

After Laban's grandiose but empty claim to the property and thereby his refusal to assent to Jacob's complaint (31:43) and his proposal to make a treaty (31:44), the remainder of the episode pertains to the pact-making process (31:44–54).

43. All you see is mine. His empty rejection of Jacob's complaint pertains to the property and his daughters. Regarding the former, he continues to rewrite history, ignoring the contract he drew up and Jacob fulfilled. Regarding the latter, his daughters stand opposed (see 31:16). He is a pretender, like the king of Sodom, claiming goods to which he has no title (14:21). His pretense is as empty as Satan's boast that all the kingdoms of this world are his.

Yet what can I do today. Regarding his daughters, he claims to be powerless, blind to the reality that they have sided with Jacob by their flight and silence. The truth is that God has given everything to Jacob.

---

[176]Cf. "if he [a shepherd] has lost [the ox] or sheep which was committed to him, he shall make good ox for [ox], sheep for [sheep] to their owner" (Code of Hammurabi, ANET, 177, no. 263). See also, S. M. Paul, *Studies in the Book of the Covenant in the Light of Cuneiform and Biblical Law* (Leiden: Brill, 1970), 93; J. N. Postgate, "Some Old Babylonian Shepherds and Their Flocks," *JSS* 20 (1975): 1–21; Mabee, "Jacob," 192–207.

[177]See Sarna, *Genesis*, 366 n. 17.

daughters of mine. They feel like foreigners (31:15) and leave him as resolutely as his sister.

44. Come now. Laban is the initiator, proposing the treaty (31:44) and first naming the stones (31:47) and the place (31:49). As the Philistines sought a nonaggression pact with Abraham and Isaac, entailing Philistine inferiority, so now Laban acknowledges Jacob's right to independent status, a recognized family of equal standing with other tribes. By proposing the pact, he concedes that he has lost the lawsuit. Laban speaks to Jacob; Jacob only responds and talks to his kin. God has vindicated Jacob, so, having nothing to fear, Jacob has no need of a pact. By contrast, Laban, now the inferior, has been plundered and feels threatened by the Fear of Isaac (cf. 31:42, 53).

let's make a covenant. The Hebrew here is translated "make a treaty" in 21:27 and 26:28; it is like the nonaggression treaties between Abraham and Isaac with the Philistines, not like the covenant God made with Abraham (15:8–21). The treaty process occurs in pairs: two witnesses to the pact (the treaty itself, 31:44; stone monuments, 31:45–48); two stone monuments (a heap of stones and a pillar, 31:51–52); two names for the stone heaps (Aramaic and Canaanite [= Hebrew], 31:47); two meals (at the beginning, 31:46; at the end, 31:54); two treaty provisions (the protection of the daughters in a foreign land, 31:50; tribal boundaries, 31:53); and two gods to monitor the treaty (the God of Abraham and the god of Nahor, 31:53).[178] Sarna says that Laban "tacitly acknowledges Jacob as constituting a separate, independent social entity of equal status."[179]

witness. Instead of *ʿēd*, "witness," the original may have read *ʿād*, "treaty, contract."[180]

45. a pillar. This is a monument of a man released from servitude by God's presence. Jacob marks the end of both cycles of his life, in Canaan and now in Haran, with a *maṣṣēḇâ* commemorating God's presence and protection (see 28:18–19). He immortalizes his story to his wives and to Laban with this stone.

46. relatives. The term is probably used for the people in both camps.

47. Jegar Sahadutha. This means "Witness Heap."

Jacob called it. For naming of an altar, see Josh. 22:10–12, 34. By using the language of Canaan, rather than Aram, Jacob decisively identifies himself with the sworn land. Jacob and Laban are distinct peoples, each speaking his own language.[181]

Galeed. This also means "Witness Heap."

---

[178]Though not part of the pairing into two equal social entities, the true God also has two names, the God of Abraham and the Fear of Isaac (31:42).

[179]Sarna, *Genesis*, 221.

[180]*HALOT*, 787.

[181]D. I. Block, "The Role of Language in Ancient Israelite Perceptions of National Identity," *JBL* 103 (1984): 338 n. 74.

48. today. The chronological formula indicates the consummation and perpetual validity of the treaty.[182]

49. Mizpah. This means "watchtower." Laban names out of fear of God; Jacob names out of gratitude.

May the LORD keep watch. This is an imprecation that the Lord monitor the treaty, not a benediction. For each hearer the image of God's watch is different. Laban has learned by God's threat in a dream that the Lord keeps watch over him and Jacob. Jacob has learned the truth by God's blessing upon him.

50. If you mistreat my daughters. The irony escapes Laban. It is he who has mistreated them (cf. 31:14–16).

if you take any wives besides my daughters. Other wives would have been a threat to their share and their children's share of the family estate. A Nuzi contract reads, "If Wullu takes another wife, he shall forfeit the land and houses of Nashwi [his father-in-law]."[183]

51. this pillar I have set up. Laban is always claiming what he has not done or does not belong to him. According to deluded Laban, the relatives, including the women and children who heaped up the stones, belong to him.

52. a witness. It is assumed that the terms of the treaty will be passed on faithfully through generations by tradition (see Mic. 1:2).

will not go past. This is a boundary marker. By the time of Israel's settlement, the frontier population becomes mixed. Asriel was a descendant of Manasseh through his Aramean concubine (1 Chron. 7:14). During the divided monarchy, the Arameans and the Israelites fought over Gilead (1 Kings 22:3; 2 Kings 9:14). It is unlikely that a narrator composed this treaty later in Israel's history. He records an ancient pact.

53. the God of Abraham and the God of Nahor. This is better rendered, "the God of Abraham and the god of Nahor." The verb *judge* is plural, indicating that Laban has two deities in mind (see next note; see also Josh. 24:2).

the God of their father. In context, this should be translated "the gods of their father" (see Josh. 24:2). The Septuagint, however, omits this phrase altogether.

Fear of his father Isaac. Jacob, not equating the God of Abraham with the god of Nahor, swears by the "Awesome One of Isaac," whom he equates with the God of Abraham (see 31:42). Jacob now accepts him as his God.

54. sacrifice. Erecting a stone monument and offering a sacrifice that seals the treaty are two important aspects of the covenant-making process (cf. Ex. 24:5–8, 11).

---

[182]G. M. Tucker, "Witnesses and 'Dates' in Israelite Contracts," *CBQ* 28 (1966): 42–45; S. J. DeVries, *Yesterday, Today and Tomorrow: Time and History in the Old Testament* (Grand Rapids: Eerdmans, 1975), 156–57.

[183]Another marriage contract stipulates: "Zilikkushu shall not take another wife in addition to Naluya" (see references in R. Yaron, *Introduction to the Law of the Aramaic Papyri* [Oxford: Clarendon, 1961], 60 and n. 4; Van Seters, *Abraham*, 84).

54. invited his relatives to a meal. See 28:20. Jacob is now the leader and the host. The meal consists of the animals just sacrificed and constitutes part of the ritual.

spent the night there. The preceding night, the hostile camps had pitched their tents against each other. This night they celebrate a nonaggression pact.

The Relatives' Parting (31:55)

55. blessed. See 24:60; 28:1.

THEOLOGICAL REFLECTIONS ON BOOK 8, ACT 2, SCENE 6

Providence

The description of the expansion of Jacob's flock in 30:25–43 and the interpretation of those events in 31:4–13 are an instructive picture of the daily events in the lives of believers. The first telling of the events in chapter 30 is the view an audience might have. Without the interpretive retelling in chapter 31, one might assume that God was not actively involved, that Jacob was simply scheming. In chapter 31 Jacob's personal observations and interpretations offer a glimpse of God's continual presence and activity on behalf of his chosen. Now we become aware of God's hand. Rarely are we given the interpretation when we look at events. From an audience perspective, it may appear that God is not involved, but appearance rarely reveals all.

Behind the struggle between Jacob and Laban stands the Lord. The Lord's dream to Jacob, instructing him to flee Laban "at once" (31:3, 13), initiates the scene. God's dream to Laban not to harm Jacob leads to Laban's suit for a pact of nonaggression. Providence enables Rachel to carry off her climactic deception in which Laban's household gods are utterly debased. As the Lord enabled Abraham and Isaac to establish themselves as a distinct nation equal to the Philistines, he now enables Jacob to establish his equality with the Arameans. Whether leaving his home or returning to it, Jacob does not travel alone.

God graciously orchestrates each life differently, working with our strengths and weaknesses. Abraham's faith enabled him to envision the future and walk in God's path based only on God's voice and visions. For this faith God blessed Abraham greatly. Jacob needs the assurance of God's blessing to bolster his faith. God graciously extends that blessing to Jacob, strengthening his slowly developing faith.

God's providence even orchestrates negative human emotions and actions to achieve his own sovereign purposes. As the jealousy of Jacob's wives led to the birth of the tribes of Israel, so the jealousy of Laban and his sons leads to Jacob's return to the land of his fathers. The folly of Rachel in stealing the household gods enables Jacob to win his lawsuit.

Reciprocity

God's providence also entails justice. Laban exploited Jacob and his daughters for fourteen years and still experienced God's blessing because of his gifted nephew. In the end, however, God turns the tables. Jacob and his wives walk away with the riches they have earned and triumph majestically over Laban without lifting a sword. Laban's greed robs him, leaving him without wealth or daughters and their children (see Prov. 16:7).

Divine Guidance and Faith

In the scene's opening (31:1–3), we are given a cameo of God's program of guidance.[184] Jacob decides it is time to leave because of God's words to him to flee, his own discernment of the mischief intended by Laban's family, and his providential hearing of their hostile conversation (31:1–3). In addition, he has the consent of the community; his wives have their own grievances. Jacob responds at once, trusting God to protect him in his flight, knowing that Laban will pursue him with a greatly superior army.

Typology

The twelve tribes repeat Abraham's migrations to the sworn land from Paddan Aram (see 12:1–9; 35:23–26) and later from Egypt with great wealth (see 12:10–20). The tribes' exodus from the house of bondage also fore-shadows their Exodus from Egypt (see Deut. 26:5–8; Hos. 12:12–13). They go in response to God's call (Gen. 31:3) to worship in the land of Canaan (31:13, 17–18); they spoil their enemy of wealth and gods (31:17–21); they are pursued and overtaken by superior forces (31:22–23); and they are delivered by divine intervention (31:24). All this is an example of new Israel's pilgrimage to the heavenly land (see 1 Cor. 10:1–4).

Sin

Laban is a classic example of sin's irrationality (Prov. 16:2; Jer. 17:9). The deluded scoundrel, who has repeatedly cheated Jacob, unabashedly complains that Jacob has wronged him (Gen. 31:26–30)! He is blind to the significance of the dream that vindicates Jacob and condemns him. He is deaf to the silence of his daughters, which shouts out against his delusion. Although he does not even attempt to rebut Jacob's evidence of innocence, he continues to claim pretentiously his right to the property and offers no apology. Contrary to all evidence, he presents himself a loving father, full of beneficence, who would send his homesick nephew and family away with song. Though he has egregiously wronged his daughters, he makes Jacob swear not to wrong them! Laban is a man without excuse. On several occasions he testifies both to the providential protection and provision of

---

[184]Waltke with MacGregor, *Knowing*, 52–135.

Abraham's God on Abraham's family (24:50; 30:30) and to God's dream to him (31:29). He is without excuse for hardening his heart against God out of love for himself.

BOOK 8, ACT 2, SCENE 7:
ANGELS MEET JACOB AT MAHANAIM
AND PENIEL: PREPARATION OF JACOB
TO MEET ESAU (32:1–32)

LITERARY ANALYSIS OF BOOK 8, ACT 2, SCENE 7 ─────────

Structure and Plot

The runaway must now confront his past with his family and his future with God. Jacob's preparation to meet Esau is bracketed by two unexpected meetings with the divine. These meetings transform his meeting with Esau, and this vertical dimension of Jacob's life signals his personal transformation.

As noted in the Literary Analysis of Act 2, the structures of this act can be viewed from a number of angles. The chiastic pattern of Act 2 features the presence of God with Jacob as the fugitive leaves the Promised Land and returns to it (see Literary Analysis of Act 2). According to this design, Scenes 7 and 8 are actually episodes of one scene: "Jacob reconciled to Esau." Viewed as one scene, they follow an alternating structure.

> A Angels of God meet Jacob at "Two Camps" (32:1–2)
> B Jacob prepares to meet Esau in "Two Camps" (32:3–21)
> A′ Angel of God meets Jacob at Peniel (32:22–32)
> B′ Jacob meets Esau (33:1–17)

This pattern features Jacob's encounter with the angels of God at Mahanaim (Hebrew for "Two Camps") as part of his preparation to meet Esau in two camps. Moreover, his encounter with the angel of God[185] is part of his following encounter with Esau. Jacob himself equates his meeting Esau with his meeting God (33:10). Both encounters begin in hostility and end with Jacob prevailing in his brokenness.

I have chosen for this commentary to view all of chapter 32 as a distinct scene from 33:1–17. The subtitle "Preparation of Jacob to Meet Esau" is an intentional pun: Jacob prepares himself for meeting Esau, and God also prepares him. Viewed as a distinct scene, chapter 32 also follows an alternating structure (A B C//A′ B′ C′).

───────────────────────────────

[185]The term "God-man" is also fitting for the "man" in the context of this scene. Later, Hosea (12:4; cf. Heb. 5) identifies him as "the angel," but, of course, the angel of God is equated with God himself (see 16:7). I will use both "angel of God" and "God-man" for the divine being Jacob encounters (see also discussion in the footnote for "man" at 32:24).

Introduction/Setting: Angels of God meet Jacob at Mahanaim (32:1–2)
A Jacob sends messengers to Esau (32:3–6)
B Jacob divides family (32:7–8)
  C Jacob prays on basis of God's covenant promises (32:9–12)
A′ Jacob sends gifts to Esau (32:13–21)
B′ Jacob sends family across Jabbok (32:22–23)
  C′ Jacob prays as he wrestles the God-man (32:24–32)

The second parallels in this alternating pattern dramatically escalate the first (i.e., messengers/gifts; divides/sends; prays/wrestles).

A/A′ and B/B′ highlight Jacob's prudent actions to control an apprehensive situation. In A/A′ he sends messengers to gather information and then prudently tries to pacify his perceived adversary with a smothering of gifts. In B/B′, alarmed at learning that Esau is coming to meet him with a sizeable fighting force, he takes further precaution. First, he divides his family into two camps. Then he sends them across the Jabbok at night, presumably to prevent the surviving camp from returning to Laban and to ensure they fulfill their destiny in the land of his fathers. C/C′, however, reveal Jacob's dependence on God's blessing for success. First Jacob prays the longest prayer in Genesis, basing his future on God's covenant promises. Then God wrenches his hip so that he must depend on God alone. The man who prevails through decisive and prudent action in strength now prevails through prayer in weakness.

In additional support of this theme, the scene is framed by God intruding upon him first by the angels at Mahanaim and then by the angel of the Lord at Peniel.

Jacob has escaped one conflict, that with Laban, only to return to another conflict, his unresolved feud with Esau (27:45). The uncertainty of the potentially dangerous encounter with Esau drives the movement of this scene, creates a catalyst for Jacob's transformation, and grips the reader with tension.

The angels of God that met Jacob as he left the sworn land (28:10–22) meet him on his return. The narrator opens the vertical dimension of the story before the horizontal. Fox explains, "From this starting point everything is subsequently a matter of 'two camps' (v. 8) or two levels: the divine and the human. This is the key to understanding the meeting between Yaakov and his brother in its entirety: Yaakov will have to deal with God before he can resolve his problem with Esav."[186] Moreover, the heavenly messengers to Jacob serve as an exemplar of his messengers to Esau, and his conceptualization of his two camps of family and possessions.

The plot tension escalates from Jacob's unexpected and dangerous encounter with the angels as he approaches Edom's territory to the report that

---

[186]Fox, *Beginning*, 131.

Esau is coming with a full sized militia. The suspense only crescendos with
the division of the family into two camps, the dangerous fording of the Jabbok by night, and Jacob's match with the God-man. The wrestling scene
also encapsulates Jacob's internal struggle. Fox comments,

> The great wrestling scene at the Yabbok both symbolizes and resolves
> beforehand Yaakov's meeting with Esav, much as Shakespeare's pre-battle
> dream scenes (e.g., Julius Caesar, Richard III, Macbeth) will do with his
> characters. Struggle, the motif already introduced in the mother's womb
> (chapter 25), returns here, but that is not the only consideration. At issue
> is Yaakov's whole life and personality, which despite his recent material
> successes are still under the pall of Esav's curse (27:36).[187]

The scene peaks when Jacob's name is changed to Israel. In the denouement, the patriarch walks away from the struggle limping in the morning
light of a new day.

Naming and Key Words

Again Fox explains, "Central, then, is the change of name in v. 29, which
suggests both a victorious struggle and the emergence of a new power. This
is further supported by the Hebrew plays on sound: YᶜKV (Yaakov), YBK
(Yabbok), and Y'BK (wrestling)."[188]

The narrator also plays on the place name *maḥᵃnāyim* (= "Two Camps"),
the appellative *maḥᵃnēh* ("camp"), and *minḥâ* ("gift"). These are key terms
in Jacob's own preparation to meet Esau.

Another key word, "face" (*pānîm*), occurring six times (32:20 [3x], 21, 30
[2x] [Heb. 32:21, 22, 31],[189] is a focal point of Jacob's meetings. Fokkelman
explains, "That [Jacob] has been delivered comes home to him when seeing
God face to face. Jacob now understands that because he has seen God face
to face he will now also see his brother Esau properly, face to face, no longer
afraid, and that therefore he has been delivered."[190]

Comparison and Contrast

Jacob has three encounters with angels, and in each case he memorializes
the site: Bethel (28:19), Mahanaim (32:2), and Peniel (32:30).

The first encounter with the angels prepares him for meeting Laban, the
second encounter for meeting Esau. McKenzie suggests that Laban represents the people of Aram, and Esau represents the people of Edom. As such,
the events of Gen. 32:22–32 are primarily symbolic: "the point made by the

---

[187]Ibid., 135.
[188]Ibid.
[189]This does not include the preposition *lipnê*, which occurs four times (32:3, 16, 17, 20 [Heb. 32:4, 17, 18, 21]).
[190]Fokkelman, *Genesis*, 220.

writer is that the nation of Israel has prevailed, prevailed over all opponents, not just Edom and Aram."[191]

The encounter of the angels with Jacob at Mahanaim matches his encounter with them at Bethel. The plural, "angels of God," is restricted to 28:12 and 32:1. "This is the camp of God. So he named [*wayyiqrāʾ*] that place Mahanaim" (32:2 [Heb. 3]) echoes "this is . . . the house of God. He called [*wayyiqrāʾ*] that place Bethel" (28:17, 19). However, the scenes contrast. In the former, God encourages Jacob by assuring him of his presence and granting him the covenant promises; in this scene, the angels threaten his life, and Jacob embraces those promises.

Scenic Depiction[192]

As in his first encounter with the angels, the Jacob who meets God at night has a new orientation in the morning (28:10–22, esp. 16). So also in this parallel, his night of fear as Jacob (32:7) is transformed into his morning of hope as Israel (32:31). In this scene, however, his transformation is more gradual. He wrestles with "the man" at night (32:22); at daybreak (or "at dawn;" i.e., when the light of the sun just begins to show itself) his antagonist changes his name, and Jacob comprehends that the man is none other than God. Finally, as the sun rises above him (32:31), he walks away, better, limps away, a new man.

Characterization

See "Ambition, Perseverance, and Prayer" in Theological Reflections below.

EXEGETICAL NOTES TO BOOK 8, ACT 2, SCENE 7 ———

Angels Meet Jacob at Mahanaim (32:1–2)

1. **angels of God met him.** This is a sign to Jacob of God's protective presence and the fulfillment of God's promise, "I am with you" (28:15), even as he faces Esau. This is also a reminder to Jacob of his vow to worship if he returns in peace (28:21–22).

met (*pgʿ* [Heb. 32:2], not *qrʾ*, as in 32:6 [Heb. 32:7]). The text says the angels met Jacob, not vice versa. Moreover, the expression entails a threatening encounter.[193] Indeed, his following encounter with the angel of God

---

[191]S. McKenzie, "You Have Prevailed: The Function of Jacob's Encounter at Peniel in the Jacob Cycle," *ResQ* 23 (1980): 230.

[192]See also Exegetical Notes.

[193]Of the forty-six occurrences of the verb *pgʿ*, twenty-six are in the Qal stem with the preposition *bᵉ*, as in the construction in 32:2. The combination is used in the following situations: (1) one border "touched, reached" another (Josh. 16:7; 19:11 [2x], 22, 27, 34 [2x]; (2) a person "interceded, entreated" to God or to people (Ruth 1:16; Job 21:15; Jer. 7:16; 27:18); (3) someone "struck, killed" another (Num. 35:19; Judg. 15:12; 1 Sam. 22:17, 18; 2 Sam. 1:15; 1 Kings 2:25, 29, 32, 34, 46); and (4) someone meets another "to harm" him or her (Num. 35:21; Josh. 2:16; Ruth 2:22). The last two senses

also involves hostility, but both encounters are for his good. Jacob's close scrape with the army of God is meant to prompt him to advance cautiously and circumspectly in this dangerous region (cf. Mic. 6:8). As in Gen. 28:10–22, the angels play no role other than to impact Jacob's psyche in two ways. His safe passage past the angels assures him of God's protective presence (see 32:7) while also preparing him to be on his guard. This meeting sets the tone of "surprise, danger and attack."[194]

2. This is. The wording is a verbal link to Jacob's previous encounter with the angels (28:16–17).

camp [*maḥᵃnēh*]. This Hebrew word is also translated "group" in 32:7, 8, 10. He may be referring to the angels he had seen on the stairway at Bethel (28:12).

the camp of God [*maḥᵃnēh ᵓelōhîm*]. This is also translated "great army" (lit., "God's army," 1 Chron. 12:22). As Bethel was the gate of heaven (28:17), Mahanaim is God's camp on earth.

named that place. This is another verbal link to Jacob's previous encounter with the angels (28:19).

Mahanaim. Its location is uncertain. The name means either "two camps" or simply "camp,"[195] but the later references to two camps (32:7–8, 10) support the dual number. If dual, its significance is ambiguous. Does it refer to God's camp and Jacob's camp? Does it foreshadow the meeting of Jacob's camp with Esau's? Does it refer to the two angelic camps, here and at Bethel? Or do the two angelic camps prompt him to divide his household into two groups (32:8, 10), even as the dream of streaked, speckled, and spotted goats prompted him to draw up the terms of his flock contract (31:10–12). Perhaps the narrator, who loves puns, means to evoke one or more of these connotations. In any case, the narrator employs the number two throughout the scene: two camps, two families, two meetings—one with God and Esau—and two brothers. We observed a similar pairing in the nonaggression pact between Laban and Jacob.

Jacob Sends Messengers to Esau (32:3–6)

3. messengers. This is the same word translated "angels" in 32:1. Just as God has sent angels to Jacob, Jacob now sends messengers to Esau.

Seir. Esau during the twenty years of Jacob's exile has already dispossessed the Horites at Seir or is in the process of doing so (Deut. 2:12), suggesting his military might.

---

are attenuated. In Num. 35:21 the avenger of blood "meets" the murderer and kills him; in Josh. 2:16 the pursuers "find" the spies and will kill them; in Ruth 2:22 those who find Ruth in the wrong field will molest/abuse/harm her. Genesis 32:1 grammatically and contextually best suits the fourth sense. By contrast, the combination *pgᶜ ᵓet* means either "to strike" (Ex. 5:3) or "to meet unexpectedly in a context of danger" (Amos 5:19) or to "meet in a favorable context" (Ex. 5:20; 1 Sam. 10:5; Isa. 64:5 [Heb. 4]) or even "to meet and spare" (Isa. 47:3). But that ambiguous combination is not used here.

[194]Roop, *Genesis*, 209.

[195]See *IBHS*, §7.3d.

Seir, the country [śādeh] of Edom. Etymologically, śēʿîr (Heb. 32:4) means "hairy" (see 25:25 and note). In the archaic text of Judg. 5:4, "Seir" and "the land [śādeh] of Edom" parallel each other. Sarna comments, "The three Hebrew words seʿir, śadeh, and ʾedom are deliberately used to evoke memories of the hostile relations with Esau, the one covered with hair (seʿar), a man of the outdoors (śadeh), of ruddy complexion (ʾadmoni), who came in from the field (śadeh) and begged for the red stuff (ʾadom), and whose hairiness (saʿir) played a crucial role in the deception that precipitated Jacob's flight to Laban [see 25:25, 27, 29–30; 27:11]."[196]

4. my master Esau: "Your servant. . . ." Although this introductory greeting conforms to the customary epistolary style of the ancient Near East, nevertheless, through this courtesy Jacob begins to right the arrogance toward his brother that brought him in diametrical opposition to his promised destiny (27:29). Like Abraham with Lot, Jacob takes the first step toward giving up the rights of his election to the blessing (13:1–12), trusting God to fulfill the promise. His rivalry with Esau is about over.

Jacob says. The Hebrew literally says, "Thus says Jacob," a commissioning formula of prophetic literature. The messengers were to speak as though they were Jacob (see "angel of the LORD" at exegetical notes for 16:7).

I have been staying (gûr; see 12:10). He tactfully omits reference to the reason of his going to Laban. Hamilton says, "Jacob is able to telescope more than twenty years into six words."[197]

till now. This is the reason Esau has not heard from his twin brother.

5. I have. Herein lies an oblique hint of a gift, if necessary. He omits mention of the valuable camel (cf. 32:15) and understates his wealth.

that I may find favor in your eyes. The phrase is repeated in 33:8, 10, 15. This is a new Jacob (see 25:31). He throws himself on Esau's grace for acceptance.

6. coming to meet [hōlēk liqrāʾt]. The Hebrew expression is ambiguous; sometimes it denotes hostility (1 Kings 20:27; 2 Kings 23:29), but other times not (Gen. 24:65; Josh. 9:11; 2 Kings 8:8, 9; 9:18). Initially the audience is meant to feel the ambiguity, just as Jacob must feel the ambiguity. Jacob is terrified of Esau's tremendous numbers. But if Esau's intention is evil, why does he return the messengers unharmed in peace when he could have killed them and made a surprise attack? Subsequently, the audience sees the irony. Esau is coming to escort him (33:12).

four hundred men. This is a round number for a standard militia (1 Sam. 22:2; 25:13; 30:10; cf. Gen. 14:14).

Jacob Divides His Family (32:7–8)

7. great fear and distress. This very strong language is used for people in dire straits. Jacob has reason to fear (see 14:14; 27:40), yet he has survived

---

[196]Sarna, *Genesis*, 224.
[197]Hamilton, *Genesis 18–50*, 321.

Laban's stronger forces (see 31:29) and the camp of angels (32:1–2). His guilty conscience leads him to imagine the worst.

two groups. A retreat would violate his pact with Laban and incur Laban's wrath. So, in Sarna's words, "The most he can do is to minimize his losses."[198] As Jacob's thoughts indicate (32:8), he is hoping to save at least part of his family.

Jacob Prays on the Basis of God's Covenant Promises (32:9 – 12)

9. Jacob prayed. This is Jacob's first recorded prayer (32:9–12) and the only extended prayer in the book of Genesis.[199] Finally he is developing a right relationship with God and so can develop a right relationship with his brother. Structurally, the prayer stands in the center of the two embassies to Esau (32:3–8, 13–21), suggesting that Jacob trusts God to prosper his second gift to Esau. His prayer consists of invocation (32:9), confession (32:10), petition (32:11), confidence and motivation (32:12). The form resembles the so-called "penitential psalms."

God of my father Abraham . . . Isaac. Invocation. His address to God is the same as God's self-disclosure in 28:13. He means to hold God to the promise.

Go back. See 31:3; cf. 28:15. Obedience to God and his blessing are inseparable.

10. I am unworthy. Jacob's confession indicates that a spiritual transformation is taking place in Jacob: he submits to Esau and recognizes his unworthiness before God, casting his lot with the weak (cf. Judg. 6:15–18; 1 Sam. 16:11; Matt. 10:42; 18:6–14; 1 Cor. 1:18–25).

kindness [*ḥeseḏ*] and faithfulness [*ʾemet*]. *Ḥesed* relates to a superior who, out of kind character, meets the need of a covenant partner who cannot help himself or herself (see 21:23). *ʾemet* signifies that, although the superior has no obligation to meet the need, the superior can always be counted on. Sakenfeld writes, "Jacob attributes his prospering to God's loyalty and prays that he can count on Yahweh to follow through for him on this dangerous occasion. Loyalty manifest in family and flocks is meaningless if it is suddenly to be cut off. . . . While divine loyalty undergirds all that makes life meaningful, it comes to special expression when Jacob's well-being is threatened."[200]

your servant. Jacob is now a servant of the Lord ready to serve others (see 26:24). Biblical authors reserve the accolade "Servant of the LORD" for only the most choice servants: Moses, Joshua, Caleb, David, and Isaiah's anonymous Servant.

---

[198]Sarna, *Genesis*, 224.
[199]His vow in 28:20–22 is not formulated as a prayer.
[200]K. D. Sakenfeld, *Faithfulness in Action: Loyalty in Biblical Perspective* (OBT; Philadelphia: Fortress, 1985), 86.

this Jordan. Jacob regards the Jabbok River that flows into the Jordan as an extension of it. This may imply that he is back in the Promised Land.

11. Save me [nṣl]. This word marks the beginning of Jacob's petition. God's salvation and protection will come in an unexpected way (see the repetition of this Hebrew root, translated "spared," in 32:30).

12. But you have said. Jacob offers confidence and motivation for his petition. He bases his future on God's promise.

make your descendants like the sand. See 22:17; 28:14. He is concerned for the survival of his posterity, not just himself.

Jacob Sends Gifts to Esau (32:13–21)

13. spent the night . . . selected a gift. Note the chiastic inclusio in 32:13 and 21 (spent the night//gift) framing this episode.

gift [minḥâ]. Jacob sends his offended brother magnanimous gifts, in dramatic increments, and aims diplomatically to pacify his offended brother (Prov. 25:21–22). They are sent as free gifts (see 4:4–5; 43:11, 15, 25–26; 1 Kings 10:25), here to compensate a wrong, not as exacted tribute to a lord (2 Sam. 8:2, 6; 1 Kings 5:1; 2 Kings 17:4). Nevertheless, they are fitting tribute of wealth from a servant to his lord, to whom he owes his life. In 33:11 Jacob calls his gift "the blessing" ("present" [berākâ] in NIV). He is ready to restore the blessing and to recognize Esau as lord (see Prov. 25:21–22), trusting God to keep his covenant promises (see Gen. 13; 32:9–12).

14–15. two hundred female goats. . . . A total of 550 animals is a very large gift. In an attempt to appease Esau's anger, Jacob encircles Esau with gifts so he has no place, psychologically speaking, to move.

19. the third and all the others who followed. The repeating speech concerning Jacob's servitude to Esau emphasizes the genuineness of his statement.

20. pacify him [kippēr]. The Hebrew (32:21) is literally "cover his face." "Face" as the object of kippēr is unique in the Old Testament. Its Akkadian equivalent, "wipe the face" (kuppur panê), means "wipe (the anger from) the face."[201] Jacob's language resembles religious sacrifice (e.g., "I will pacify his face . . . perhaps he will receive me"). It is no less appropriate to pacify an offended brother than to appease an offended God.[202]

he will receive me. Literally "he will lift up my face," this may also connote "forgive me."

Jacob Sends Family across Jabbok (32:22–23)

22. That night. See "Scenic Depiction" in Literary Analysis above and 32:26. The evening is often an image of distress and a time for the awesome

---

[201]J. Milgrom, "Atonement in the OT," *IDBSup*, 81.
[202]The pericope of Prov. 16:1–15 joins together pacifying God (16:6, "atoned for") and pacifying the king (16:14, "appease").

revelations of God (see 28:11–22). This night will bring a true end to Jacob's dark nights since fleeing Esau.

eleven sons. Dinah is omitted because she plays no role in the founding of the nation, the concern of the narrator.

Jabbok. Today the Nahr ez-Zarqa ("Blue River"), the river flows through deeply cut canyons for about 50 miles westward from its source, moving from 1900 feet above sea level to 115 feet below sea level. It flows into the Jordan about 20 miles north of the Dead Sea. This natural, impressive boundary later constituted the limit of the territory Israel dispossessed under Moses (Num. 21:24; Deut. 2:37; 3:16; Josh. 12:2; Judg. 11:13, 22). In the patriarchal age, however, Esau has free access to march through it. The God-man will wrestle with Jacob at this boundary to prevent him from inappropriately entering this dangerous territory. Jacob the deceiver is not fit to enter it and prevail.

Jacob Prays As He Wrestles the God-Man (32:24–32)

24. left alone. The narrative emphasizes Jacob's aloneness. In the sequential detail of the story, Jacob's unprotected state functions as suspense. One whose life is in danger stands alone. In theological retrospect, Jacob's solitude serves an important spiritual purpose. Jacob must encounter God alone, without possessions or protection.

a man. The nondescript statement heightens the story's tension. Who has come to struggle with Jacob? Only later does the reader recognize the man as the invisible God.[203]

wrestled with him. The Lord unexpectedly initiates a match.[204]

---

[203]Hosea 12:4 identifies him as "the angel," but, of course, the angel of God is equated with God himself (see Gen. 16:7). Sarna follows a midrash that identifies the angel with "the celestial patron of Esau," the angelic protector of Edom, citing Deut. 4:19; 29:26; 32:8; Ps. 82; Isa. 24:21; Dan. 10:13, 20–21. Consistent with this interpretation the NJPS interprets *ʾelōhîm* in Gen. 32:28 and 30 as "divine being," not "God" (in contrast to LXX, Targum, Syriac, Vulgate, NKJV, NASB, NAB, REB, NIV, NRSV). However, even Sarna (cf. NJPS note) renders "Peniel" "face of God," claiming that the site already had this name. Moreover, the divine beings of the nations are in fact demons (Deut. 32:17; Ps. 106:37), that is, protective spirits opposed to God and his people. God's mediating of a blessing through a demon would be without parallel, and it is implausible to think that Edom's divine protector blesses Israel to conquer Edom. Recall too that a superior names an inferior. Does a demon give God's people their name? Only God controls life, land, prosperity, and destiny. See R. Hendel, *The Epic of the Patriarch* (Atlanta: Scholars, 1987), 105.

[204]God will come forcefully to others at night in order to prepare them spiritually for dangerous encounters. Exodus 4:24–26 records God's unusual attack against Moses, probably at night. This will prepare Moses for his dangerous meeting with Pharaoh. A number of people have cited the parallels between Jacob's encounter and other ancient Near Eastern accounts of such matches with divine beings. Such tales may have influenced the narrator's account, but they did not determine it. Wessner summarizes, "Quite possibly, the narrator of Genesis may have had such a parallel in mind, although he did not mimic it exactly. For example, Jacob was not completely victorious (he left with a limp), and although he received a blessing, the focus of the text seems to be on the changing of his name instead" (M. Wessner, "Face to Face: [*panim el panim*] in Old Testament Literature" [unpublished master's thesis, Regent College, 1998], 22).

could not overpower. Humbling himself, God has come to Jacob on some type of even terms. Jacob again displays his incredible strength (see 29:10).

25. touched. A mere touch of the divine conquers Jacob.

the socket of Jacob's hip. With severe mercy, God dislocates Jacob's hip (the acetabulum), the wrestler's pivot of strength (see 32:31). His natural strength shriveled, Jacob must prayerfully cling to God's grace.

26. Let me go. Jacob is physically broken but will not give up. Now it is a battle of words, and Jacob clings for a blessing. Jacob, who has already experienced the blessing of prosperity, now clings to experience the blessing of prevailing over his enemies.

for it is daybreak. One cannot see God and live.

I will not let you go unless you bless me. Jacob prevails with prayer, not with natural strength. This is the change of Jacob to Israel.

bless me. Jacob recognizes that the one who could wrench his hip is greater than he. Perhaps he already perceives the man to be a messenger of God. Jacob already had the divine blessing through his father to rule over his brothers. However, until now he has been unfit to experience his status.[205]

27. What is your name? The question forces Jacob to own up to his devious past and be purged from it by embracing his new name.

Jacob. This is an admission of guilt, as a name linked with deception (27:36).

28. will no longer be [$y\bar{e}^{\circ}\bar{a}m\bar{e}r\ ^{c}\hat{o}d$]. The Hebrew (32:29) literally reads, "it shall no more be said," indicating a spiritual metamorphosis.[206] In a sequel to this text, Gen. 35:10, it is literally said "Not as Jacob shall you be addressed" ($l\bar{o}^{\circ}$-$yiqq\bar{a}r\bar{e}^{\circ}\ \ldots\ ^{c}\hat{o}d$).[207]

Israel. This is an abbreviated form of $\acute{s}\bar{a}r\hat{t}\bar{a}\ ^{c}im$-$^{\circ}e l\bar{o}h\hat{i}m$ (see next note). The assailant has authority to impart a new life (see 17:5). Jacob's new name represents a reorientation from supplanter and deceiver into prevailer. Roop notes, "Re-naming marks a change of direction or context for the individual. It does not always mark a change in character or inner person."[208] The transformation pertains to the way in which Jacob prevails. Heretofore he prevailed over people by trickery. Now he prevails with God, and so with humans, by his words, not by the physical gifts conferred on him at birth or acquired through human effort. His ambition to prevail has not been changed but properly reoriented. Hosea matches "he struggled with the angel and overcame him" with "he wept and begged for his favor" (Hos. 12:4). This name, given to the victor, announces his true maturing spiritual character and destiny.

---

[205]S. Terrien (*The Elusive Presence: Toward a New Biblical Theology* [New York: Harper & Row, 1978], 88) explains Jacob's words less radically: "Because he needed a renewal of his being in order to face the ordeal of the next day."

[206]M. Weinfeld, "Jeremiah and the Spiritual Metamorphosis of Israel," *ZAW* 88 (1976): 18–19.

[207]See Hamilton, *Genesis 18–50*, 333.

[208]Roop, *Genesis*, 215.

struggled . . . and overcome.[209] By clinging to God, Israel overcomes in the face of insurmountable odds. God sanctifies Jacob's absolutely sincere and undivided commitment to the blessing.

God. The "man" (32:24–26) is now identified as God (cf. Josh. 5:13–15).

and with men. This includes in the womb, with Esau, with his father, and with Laban.

29. Please tell me your name. . . . Why do you ask my name? The scene is quite similar to Judg. 13:17–18. Manoah asks the angel of God, "What is your name. . . ?" and receives the reply, "Why do you ask my name? It is beyond understanding." In both cases, the answer on the part of the angel suggests that the inquirer has not yet fully grasped who he is. Hamilton comments, "In both instances the silence, the hesitancy, of the other being, begins to produce within Jacob/Manoah a realization of the supernatural status of that being. . . . [The angel's question] is another way of asking, 'Jacob, don't you realize who I am?'"[210] It is only after the disappearance of the deity that the protagonist fully realizes that he has encountered the deity.

blessed. Speiser, NJPS, Sarna, and Hamilton[211] prefer the translation "and bade him farewell/took leave of him" (cf. 28:1), because the angel had already blessed Jacob in changing his name.

30. Peniel. The Hebrew means "Face of God" and is an abbreviated form of "I have seen God face to face" [$᾽elōhîm pānîm ᾽el-pānîm$]. The location of the site is uncertain, but a good case has been made for modern Tulul edh-Dhahab, which stands on the bank of the Jabbok, four miles east of Succoth.

God. Jacob now definitively identifies the "man" (32:24–26) as none other than God, even though he received no definitive answer.

face to face. This unusual expression is used only of direct divine-human encounters, not necessarily of literal visual perception.[212]

yet my life was spared. God says explicitly to Moses: "No one may see me and live" (Ex. 33:20). Moses' face-to-face meeting is equated with "he sees the form of the LORD" (Num. 12:8). In the man Jacob sees a form of the Lord. The intensity of meeting his messenger is equivalent to meeting God face to face. The encounter is both terrifying and intimate.[213]

31. The sun rose. See "Scenic Depiction" in the Literary Analysis above. The scenic depiction portrays Jacob's spiritual landscape. The setting sun

---

[209]The term *struggle* means "to strive or contend" and is used elsewhere only in Hos. 12:3–4.

[210]Hamilton, *Genesis 18–50*, 336.

[211]Speiser, *Genesis*, 255; Sarna, *Genesis*, 228; Hamilton, *Genesis 18–50*, 327.

[212]According to M. Wessner's study, this expression is used of a "multi-faceted and unique encounter that the LORD Himself reserves for certain situations with specific criteria . . . 1) divine initiation, 2) complete solitude, 3) deep intimacy and 4) a display of the supernatural" (Wessner, "Face to Face," 103).

[213]See B. K. Waltke, "The Fear of the LORD: The Foundation for a Relationship with God," in *Alive to God: Studies in Spirituality Presented to James Houston*, ed. J. I. Packer and L. Wilkinson (Downers Grove, Ill.: InterVarsity, 1992), 17–33.

marked the beginning of this act depicting the fugitive's ignominious flight from the land of his fathers (28:10–11). It now rises upon him with hope and transformation after his years of oppressive darkness under the tyranny of Laban and his guilty conscience toward his brother. He is ready to enter the land that Israel will dispossess.

Peniel. The Hebrew is $p^e n\hat{u}^\hat{}\bar{e}l$,[214] a variant of Peniel.

limping. The limp is the posture of the saint, walking not in physical strength but in spiritual strength.

32. to this day. This dietary restriction, mentioned elsewhere only in later Jewish literature, served as a perpetual reminder that, when Jacob became weak in his struggle with God, Israel the victor emerged. The fateful encounter with God and the transformation of Israel is corroborated and memorialized both by the place name, Peniel (32:30–31), and by Israel's dietary ritual of not eating the sciatic nerve (32:32; see "Historicity and Literary Genre" in the introduction).

tendon [*gîd hannāšeh*]. This refers to the sciatic nerve, "the central nerve of the hip region."[215]

THEOLOGICAL REFLECTIONS ON BOOK 8, ACT 2, SCENE 7

God's Presence

Jacob's incredible encounter teaches us much about God's presence (see 28:15). First, it may be marked with ambiguity. Jacob wrestles with "a man"; only as the episode develops does he realize that he is wrestling with God (cf. Gen. 18–19; Josh. 5:13–15; Judg. 6; 13). Second, God's presence does not mean ease of conflict; in fact, it often brings unexpected difficulties. Both encounters with the angels of God seem hostile to Jacob's agenda. Third, there is a mystery about God's presence that defies human understanding. Jacob cannot see God nor know his name in order to control the situation. To be sure, God has revealed himself, but he is also *absconditus*. Fourth, God in humility makes himself available to humanity. Jacob is able to wrestle the man to a draw. Jacob's remarkable encounter reminds saints that they too may encounter God in ambiguity, even in apparent hostility, in mystery cloaked in darkness, and in such humility that he restrains himself from dominating their lives. When they stop wrestling with God and start clinging to him, they discover that he has been there for their good, to bless them.

The divine covenant partner promises his people that he will always be with them even as he was with Jacob during the foreboding night before Jacob's encounter with Esau. Each of the synoptic Gospel writers draws his work to a conclusion with a scene giving assurance that the resurrected

---

[214]See *IBHS*, §8.2b.
[215]See *HALOT*, 729.

Christ is present with his church. The scenes move geographically and chronologically from Galilee in the north of Israel (so Matthew), to Bethany in the south (so Luke), and finally to God's right hand (so Mark). On the mountain in Galilee, Christ promises "I am with you always, to the very end of the age" (Matt. 28:20). He ascends from the vicinity of Bethany with his hands—which had touched lepers and healed the blind, and which are now pierced—reaching out to bless the disciples (Luke 24:50). After Christ assumes his seat at God's right hand, the disciples preach everywhere and the Lord confirms his word by accompanying signs (Mark 16:19–20).

Ambition, Perseverance, and Prayer

The author of Genesis aims among other things to define the seed that establishes God's rule by prevailing in suffering over the seed of the Serpent. The seed of the woman is characterized by vision. Abraham "saw" beforehand the rule of God established through his offspring. He and all his true children share that God-given dream. Abraham functions in Scripture as the exemplar of the seed's faith. Isaac had the vision, but his late sensuality dimmed it.

Jacob, by his election already in his mother's womb, shares that inherited dream, wanting God's blessing. His virtue has been his faith, shown by his separation from Canaanite women and yet committed to that land. However, until now he has been ambitious to fulfill the vision and blessing by his own initiatives, sometimes unethically. In this scene, his ambition is harnessed into humble prayer. To be sure, prior to the encounter with the God-man he prays to God on the basis of God's promises, but he does not yet prevail because he has not been humbled. Only when he is "broken" does he prevail with God and humans. In the wrestling match, initiated by God, he loses his physical strength and prevails only through prayer. The God-man credits Jacob for his perseverance of faith. Jacob did not quit even when his strength was gone. When broken in God's severe mercy, he persevered in prayer. Quintillius said that ambition is a vice, but it can become the mother of virtue. It becomes virtue in Jacob when God breaks his hip, and he is left clinging to God to realize the blessing. If Abraham is a study in faith, Jacob is a study in spiritual strength through prayer. The man who was prayerless and caused so much trouble, sorrow, and anguish is now transformed as he commits himself to God in prayer.

Covenant

God's covenantal love and commitment to Jacob is amazing. In spite of all of Jacob's moral flaws, God could not deny himself his elect partner (2 Tim. 2:13). God is tied to his people with "ties of love" (Hos. 11:4). He delivered Jacob first from the Aramean; now he is about save him from the Edomite. No enemy, not even death, can separate the elect from that love (Rom. 8:38;

2 Thess. 3:2). Jacob exemplifies that among other virtues the human partner satisfies the covenantal relationship by accepting God's loving embrace. He confesses that he is unworthy of God's love and yet claims his promises.

Severe Mercy

The limp is the posture of the saint, walking not in physical strength but in spiritual strength. God's severe mercy allows Jacob a victory, but it is a crippling victory.[216] Paul expressed a similar truth in another oxymoron: "when I am weak, then I am strong" (2 Cor. 12:10).

Conscience

Conscience refers to the human ability to evaluate actions. A bad conscience may cause one to misinterpret another's good for evil. Jacob's condemning conscience for his treatment of his brother led him to misinterpret Esau's coming, and the guilty consciences of Joseph's brothers also led them to misinterpret his good intentions toward them (cf. 42:21–22, 27–28; 50:15–21). Bad behavior leads to bad feelings. The solution to a bad conscience is to give God glory by confessing sin and renouncing wrong behavior (Prov. 28:13).

Reconciliation

See the note on "pacify him" at 32:20. The covenant family is troubled by broken relationships, but God honors their efforts at reconciliation. Jacob models reconciliation as he works to appease the enemy he has created in his brother. One way of doing this is by "feeding" the offended party (Prov. 25:21–22; Rom. 12:20). Abigail spares her husband's life and David's honor by sending David a handsome gift (1 Sam. 25). Members of the covenant community are to seek opportunities for reconciliation, finding and meeting points of needs among their enemies.

BOOK 8, ACT 2, SCENE 8:
ESAU'S RECONCILIATION WITH
HOMEWARD-BOUND JACOB (33:1–17)

LITERARY ANALYSIS OF BOOK 8, ACT 2, SCENE 8 ———

Structure and Plot

The preceding scene ended with the breaking new day after Jacob's night encounter with the God-man (32:31). On this same day he encounters Esau. Act 2 peaks in this scene when Esau kisses Jacob. The scene brings resolution to Jacob's conflict with his brother and establishes Jacob's place as an equal with Esau (33:4). The rest of the scene belongs to its denouement.

---

[216]See Brueggemann, *Genesis*, 270.

This scene consists of two incidents: the reconciliation of the brothers (33:1–11) and their disengagement (33:12–17). In the first, Esau embraces his now humble brother (33:1–7) and accepts Jacob's gift as proof of his reconciliation (33:8–11). In the second, Esau offers to provide escort back for Jacob (33:12–15), but Jacob delicately separates himself (33:16–17). The scene ends with Jacob settled at Succoth.

The incident of Jacob's journey to Shechem (33:18–19) belongs with Act 3, Scene 1. The narrator explicitly connects Jacob's migration to Shechem with his departure from Paddan Aram, not from Succoth in Transjordan. Moreover, Jacob's arrival at Shechem sets the stage for the next scene in chapter 34.

Blanks and Gaps

Aside from implying that Esau migrated to the land of Seir (32:3) and prospered there (33:9), the narrator blanks the life of Esau for the twenty years of Jacob's exile in Paddan Aram. He also blanks Esau's radical emotional development from nursing a grudge to kill his brother (27:41) to welcoming his brother with a kiss (33:4). Does he allow Rebekah's evaluation of her son's character—that time itself will still his fury (27:44)—to suffice? Or was it Jacob's extremely generous gift and extravagant obeisance that pacified him? Or was it Esau's own good nature? It appears that Esau, unlike Laban, does not need a threatening warning from God. In all likelihood, all of the above factors transformed Esau's vile passions.

The narrator gaps, not blanks, Jacob's emotions upon seeing his brother approaching with the complement of a standard militia. The narrator recorded that, on the previous day when Jacob heard of Esau's approach, "In great fear and distress Jacob divided the people" (32:7). Now when Jacob sees them, the narrator says only, "So he divided the children.... He himself went on ahead ... as he approached his brother" (33:1, 3). By his silence, the narrator signifies that Jacob approaches without alarm.

The narrator also gaps evaluation of Jacob's statement to Esau that he will follow him to the land of Seir and his failure to carry through on his word. Whereas he says explicitly that in Jacob's flight from Laban "Jacob deceived[217] Laban the Aramean by not telling him he was running away" (31:20), he makes no similar evaluation in the peaceful parting of the brothers. He allows his audience to live with ambiguity regarding Jacob's motives for going the opposite direction from Seir. Does he have misgivings about the longevity of Esau's amiable mood?[218] Does he think going to Seir imprudent because that land cannot sustain both (cf. Gen. 13:1, 6)? Is he bent on completing his pilgrimage (33:20; 35:1–15)? Does he tactfully not mention the land of his fathers in order to entomb the past wrongs and not to resurrect

---

[217]Such deception is appropriate in war.
[218]See Sarna, *Genesis*, 230.

old grievances? Possibly all of these motivate Jacob to disengage. However, the narrator's omission of evaluation excludes the interpretation of deception.[219] Moreover, the narrator implies that Esau bears him no grudge, for he draws this book to conclusion with the brothers in peace together burying their father (35:29). Probably both men understand Jacob's final request, "let me find favor in the eyes of my lord," as a tactful request to disengage.

Comparison and Contrast

Jacob's encounters with God and with Esau provide another comparison between the two scenes. Jacob's meeting with God at Peniel was preparation for this uncertain encounter with Esau. These two scenes are related by seeing the face and by the sparing of Jacob's life (see 32:20, 30; 33:10), suggesting a comparison between Esau and God. The concentric arrangement of 33:9–11 reinforces this comparison.

A "I already have plenty"
  B "If I have found favor" ($h\bar{e}n$)
    C "Accept this *minḥâ* from me"
      D "For to see your face"
      D′ "Like seeing the face of God"
    C′ "Accept the *berākâ* that was brought to you"
  B′ "God has been gracious [*ḥnn*] to me"
A′ "I have all I need"

If Esau accepts his gift, then Jacob knows he has found acceptance, even as when God accepts the tribute of his people. Esau's kiss of reconciliation with his brother stands opposed to Jacob's kiss that alienated the brothers (27:26). Esau runs; Jacob limps.

Characterization

The actors in the preceding scene were God and/or his angels and Jacob. Now they are Jacob and Esau. A new Israel approaches Esau, not the old Jacob, who prepared for the encounter and whom God prepared. Whereas previously Jacob stayed behind (32:16, 18, 20) and apart (32:21) from his retinue, now he steps to the front. He confronts his warrior brother and his militia confidently but humbly. As he pacified his brother by overwhelming him with gifts, he now smothers him in obeisance. Moreover, whereas he brashly duped his brother out of the birthright and the blessing, now he gingerly avoids the sore wounds of the past. The malevolent schemer is replaced by the shrewd but nonmalevolent diplomat. However, one thing about Jacob has not changed; from first to last, he is a good shepherd.

---

[219]Hamilton disagrees; he thinks Jacob is not being "upright" but "uptight" (*Genesis 18–50*, 347). For a discussion of opinions, see his bibliography (347 n. 32).

On his part, Esau proves more than forgiving; he even offers to escort his brother back to his own land. Nevertheless, he does not reciprocate his brother's gift, showing that he accepts it as reparation for his brother's wrongs against him. Esau is presented as a forgiving man. However, he lacks the one essential virtue to please God, faith. He inherits no God-inspired dream, no vision of the transcendent. He despised his right to take part in Abraham's promised destiny (see Literary Analysis of Book 8, Act 1, Scene 4 for further characterization of Esau).

EXEGETICAL NOTES TO BOOK 8, ACT 2, SCENE 8 ———————

The Brothers Reconcile (33:1 – 11)

1. looked up and there. This phrase, literally "lifted up his eyes and saw," is a typical indicator of providence (see 22:13; 24:63–64; 31:10).

Esau. The encounters with God and with Esau occur on the heels of one another.

four hundred. See 32:6. The narrator has not yet relieved the suspense. Both scenes are linked by the mention that Esau is coming with four hundred men.

divided. See 32:8. Jacob divided his people and possessions the day before into two groups as a necessary precaution in case of flight. Here he divides the two groups among the four wives as preparation to meet Esau formally.[220]

2. Rachel and Joseph in the rear. He keeps his most loved from potential harm. The wives and their children approach Esau in ascending order of their social status. In the case of Rachel and Leah, that prioritization is based on Jacob's affections. The family is still plagued by favoritism.

3. He himself went on ahead. See also 32:18. The new Israel is a leader, not a coward.

bowed down. The term denotes touching nose and forehead to the ground in a prostrate position as a symbol of submission before a superior. Jacob, his face in the dust, is undoing his manipulative hold on the blessing he had taken from Esau through deception (see 27:29).

seven times. This is a well-attested practice of a vassal to his lord in ancient court protocol.[221] Vassals writing to Pharaoh say, "Beneath the feet [of the king, my lord] seven times, and seven times I fall."[222] Jacob greets Esau as a vassal greets a patron with the ceremony of a royal court: the solemnity of approaching as becomes rank (33:2–3, 6–7), the sevenfold obeisance

---

[220]Hamilton (*Genesis 18–50*, 339 n. 1) notes that the Hebrew distinguishes between "divide into" (32:7) and "divide among" (33:1) by *ḥṣh lᵉ* and *ḥṣh ᶜal*. See also *HALOT*, 343.

[221]See S. E. Lowenstamm, "Prostration from Afar in Ugaritic, Accadian, and Hebrew," *BASOR* 188 (1967): 41–43.

[222]*ANET*, 483, no. 147, lines 2–3; see also 483–85, no. 137, lines 1–4; no. 234, lines 5–10.

(33:3), the submissive address of a "servant" (33:5) to "lord" (33:8, 13), the presentation of gifts of homage (33:10–11).

as [ʿad]. This is better translated "until."

4. But Esau. Whereas Jacob greets Esau like a servant to a lord, Esau greets Jacob as a "brother" (33:9) after a long separation. Clearly, important events of Esau's life have been blanked (see Literary Analysis above).

ran . . . embraced[223] . . . threw . . . kissed . . . wept. These are normal ways of greeting loved relatives. The narrator represented Esau's despising of his birthright with five terse verbs (25:34); he now represents the reconciliation with another five verbs.[224]

kissed. The scribes put dots above this word in the Hebrew text to draw attention to some peculiar feature.[225] Possibly they thought the kiss was insincere, but the narrator gives no indication of insincerity.

wept.[226] The tears are a catharsis for years of negative emotions.

5. Esau . . . asked. Esau as the superior party opens the conversation.

children. Jacob mentions only the children. Does he silently sidestep the wives to avoid reference to the reason for his flight?

God. In his conversation with one outside the covenant, Jacob refers to God as ʾelōhîm, not yhwh.

graciously [ḥnn].[227] This is the Hebrew root rendered "favor" in 33:10, 15. Jacob hopes Esau will show him a similar grace and spare him. He tactfully avoids the provocative term "bless" and uses instead the word that entails forgiveness.

servant. In the international diplomacy of that day, this was unmistakable language for submitting oneself by treaty to be a subject (see 32:4; 33:14).

8. droves [maḥᵃneh]. Also meaning "camp" or "army" (see Exegetical Note at 32:2), this may be another pun on minḥa, "gift" (32:13, 18, 20 [Heb. 14, 19, 21]; 33:10). Jacob's "army" against Esau is his magnanimous gift.

To find favor. Whereas previously honesty was not one of Jacob's traits, now he is honest and forthright about his intentions.

9. brother. A striking contrast with Jacob's mode of address, "lord" (33:8), Esau embraces Jacob as "brother," but Jacob rejects this fraternal relationship in favor of the diplomatic relationship of a servant to his lord (cf. 33:8, 13, 14 [2x], 15).

---

[223]"Threw his arms around his neck" renders ḥbq, "embraced." Hamilton notes the word play between ḥbq and ʾbq, "to wrestle." "Both verbs imply physical contact, but for significantly different purposes" (Genesis 18–50, 343).

[224]Sarna (Genesis, 366 n. 2) compares this terse description with Gen. 29:11; 45:14–15; 46:29; Ex. 4:27.

[225]Waltke, "Textual Criticism of the Old Testament and Its Relation to Exegesis and Theology," NIDOTTE, 1:58.

[226]Some text critics gratuitously emend the text to the singular ("he wept"), against all ancient versions and Hebrew manuscripts.

[227]He employs paronomasia linking maḥᵃneh, "camp," with ḥānan, "grace."

I already have plenty. According to Isaac's blessing, he acquired it by war, not by farming or shepherding (27:39–40; see note on Seir at 32:3). Both sons, each in his own way, have been blessed.

Keep what you have. This is perhaps a double entendre for "keep the droves" and, more subtly, "keep the birthright and blessing."

10. No, please! Hamilton says, "Jacob is as insistent with Esau as he was with the man at Peniel. His 'I will not let you go unless you bless me' now becomes, in effect, 'I will not let you go unless you accept my gift.'"[228]

gift. See 32:13.

like seeing the face of God. As at Peniel, when Jacob saw God's face and his life was graciously spared (see 32:30), so also now he sees the dreaded face of Esau and is graciously received. Jacob treats Esau as one who stands in God's stead. He bows down, pleads for grace, identifies Esau's pacified face with the pacified face of God, and offers tribute when he finds favor. Sarna likens his offering of a gift to Esau to a pilgrimage to a shrine—one does not come empty-handed.

received me favorably [*rsh*]. This is another sacrificial term for acceptance in the cult. Since Esau accepts guilty Jacob, he is now to accept Jacob's tribute.

11. present [*birkātî*]. A deliberate and crucial change of term from "gift," the Hebrew is the same word for the "blessing" in 27:35–36, which Jacob had originally stolen. Though neither brother, with great sensitivity, mentions Jacob's purloining of the blessing, Jacob subtly makes reparation by offering a "blessing" to Esau in exchange for the "blessing" he had taken from him.

insisted . . . accepted. Although refusing a gift may be part of ancient Near Eastern courtesy and so not to be taken at face value (see 23:11–14), the narrator indicates the sincerity of Esau's refusal by editorializing, "because Jacob insisted" (33:14).

Esau accepted. By not offering a gift in exchange, Esau indicates that he accepts the gift as payment for the wrong done to him. Whereas conflict with Laban is resolved through a treaty of nonaggression, conflict with Esau is resolved through genuine expressions of repentance, extravagant gifts, and exaggerated humility. The reconciliation is sealed by accepting the reparation gift. His acceptance is witnessed by Esau's four hundred men and by Jacob's entire household. Similarly, Abraham's claim to Ephron's cave and field was sealed when Ephron accepted the payment before witnesses.

The Brothers Disengage (33:12 – 17)

The disengagement occurs in two parts: the brothers' exchange about Esau accompanying Jacob to the land of Seir (33:12–15) and Jacob's

---

[228]Hamilton, *Genesis 18–50*, 346.

departure to Succoth instead (33:16–17). One senses an underlying tension, at least on Jacob's part. Jacob is trying graciously to disengage himself from Esau without offending him. First he declines Esau's offer to escort him by contrasting the slower pace of pastoralists with that of hunters. Then, when Esau offers to leave some of his men with him, he politely declines, saying he will follow.

12. Let us be on our way. Esau thinks Jacob came to visit him (32:4–5, 18, 20; see also Literary Analysis).

13. knows. An army of four hundred hunters moves and lives differently than a shepherd with flocks and family. The lives of Esau and Jacob are incompatible.

die. Jacob is a good shepherd (see 31:38–42).

14. until I come to my lord in Seir. The narrator does not editorialize that Jacob deceived Esau (see Literary Analysis above).

15. Just let me find favor in the eyes of my lord. Esau probably knows that this is Jacob's polite way of declining his proposal (see 23:11). He could not refuse him directly without offending him and risking his anger.

16. Esau started on his way. Israel must live apart from both Edom and Laban (cf. 31:55–32:1). Except for the brief mention of burying his father in 35:29, the man who despised his birthright steps off the pages of salvation history. The "visionless" man has no part in the eternal kingdom of God.

17. Jacob, however. Jacob could not directly refuse without insulting Esau.

Succoth. The Hebrew means "shelters." According to the excavator Franken, Succoth is not modern Deir Allah, as had been supposed.[229] Jacob may have had to cross back over the Jabbok to reach this site on the north side of the Jabbok, midway between Peniel and the Jordan.

built a place for himself. The patriarch now settles back in the sworn land.

THEOLOGICAL REFLECTIONS ON
BOOK 8, ACT 2, SCENE 8 ————————————————————

Theology

The preceding scene (Scene 7) explicitly referred to God many times; this one rarely and only with reference to past blessings (33:10, 11). The connection between them, however, assures the audience that God is standing in the shadows of this scene. As God orchestrated the nonaggression pact with Laban to effect Jacob's reconciliation with Laban, he also orchestrates this reconciliation of the brothers through Jacob's skillful diplomacy. God directly intervened by a threatening dream to check Laban's unjustified

---

[229]H. J. Franken, "Excavations at Deir ʿAllā, Season 1964: Preliminary Report," *VT* 14 (1964): 417–22.

wrath against Jacob; he allows Jacob's enormous reparation gift and genuine expressions of humility and respect to reconcile the brothers.

Spiritual Life

By orchestrating reconciliation in these differing ways, God develops Jacob's faith in God through the former and his confident and truthful humility toward people through the latter.

Speech

The brash-speaking Jacob has become the wise-speaking Israel. He has learned to think before speaking to win a brother. He expresses his feelings with candor and yet with tact. The humbled wise man has learned the art of speaking the truth with grace.

Forgiveness

Jacob links Esau's forgiveness and sparing his life with God's sparing his life (33:10). Just as Esau accepts Jacob's tribute and receives him with forgiveness, God graciously receives the elect because of Christ's gift of himself for their sins.

Thankfulness

Jacob credits God for his children (33:5), for sparing his life (33:10), and for his property (33:11). Esau does not credit God for his plenty (33:9).

Submission

Only in giving up his rights does Jacob fully become the family leader. Israel's rule prefigures the rule of Christ (Phil. 2:9–11). So also God gives up his Son, who humbly gives up his rights to be equal with God, to reconcile the world to himself (see 2 Cor. 5:16–21; Phil. 2:6–8). Their model of servitude is an example to the church (Matt. 5:24; Phil. 2:5).

BOOK 8, ACT 3:
TRANSITION TO JACOB (33:18 – 35:29)

LITERARY ANALYSIS OF BOOK 8, ACT 3 ─────────

This final section of the account of Isaac's line (see the outline of Book 8), 33:18–35:29, like the closing section in the account of Terah's line (22:20–25:11), provides a transition of patriarchies (for the place of Act 3 in Book 8, see "Structure" in the Literary Analysis of Book 8). It is structured according to Jacob's itinerary back in the land moving toward Mamre, featuring, at varying sites, deaths that mark the passage of Isaac's generation and episodes that impact the account of Jacob's line, namely, the sins of Reuben, Simeon, and Levi.

BOOK 8, ACT 3, SCENE I:
DIGRESSION: DINAH IN FOREIGN PALACE, PACT WITH FOREIGNERS (33:18-34:31)

LITERARY ANALYSIS OF BOOK 8 ACT 3, SCENE I ————

Structure

The scene takes place back in Canaan on the outskirts of Shechem some time after Jacob's twenty years of exile in Paddan Aram. The scene is set by Jacob's arrival at Shechem, where he settles, buying land and building an altar "within sight of the city" (33:18–19). Following this settling are two violent acts that form the heart of the scene: the rape of Dinah and the revenge rape of the city. The acts of rape are framed by the chiastic arrangement of verbs, "Dinah went out [ysʾ] ... he took [lqḥ]" (34:1–2) and "they took [lqḥ] Dinah and left [ysʾ]" (34:26). The episode displays an alternating structure with the violation of Dinah by Shechem matched by the plunder of Shechem by Jacob's sons. Each of these "plunderings" is followed by varying reactions.

A Shechem son of Hamor rapes Jacob's daughter Dinah (34:1–4)
B Reactions to the rape (34:5–24)
    1. Reactions (or inaction) of Jacob and sons to defilement
    2. Reactions of Hamor and Shechem: proposed intermarriage
    3. Reactions of Jacob clan and Shechemites: a treacherous treaty
A′ Jacob's sons rape [city of] Shechem (34:25–29)
B′ Reactions to the plunder (34:30–31)
    1. Reaction of Jacob
    2. Reaction of sons

In the first half, the plot tension is between Jacob's family and the Shechemites; in the second, between Jacob and his sons.

Comparison and Contrast

Hamor talks rudely to his father, and Jacob's sons scold their father. Dinah acts imprudently. In both families, the fathers fail to give leadership. Nevertheless, Hamor and Shechem are united in their purpose to gratify Shechem's lust (see also "Characterization, Naming, and Identification" below). When Shechem goes to his father, he expects and receives responsive action. Their unity contrasts with the alienation of Jacob from his children. Jacob appears indifferent to the defilement of his daughter. He offers no response or appropriate action. Jacob's sons confront hostility with hostility; Jacob, with silence and noninvolvement. Once again, as in the birth of his sons (29:31–30:24), Jacob's household is dysfunctional because of his passivity. His sons are rash and unbridled, and he is passive. No one in this story escapes censure.

Blanks, Gaps, and Logic

The narrator blanks the date of this event, allowing the reader to infer from other chronological notices the ages of Jacob's children. The rape of Dinah could not have followed immediately upon the heels of Jacob's flight from Laban, because in that case Dinah would have been at best only seven years old (cf. 31:21; 31:41). The narrator does not say how long Jacob stays at Succoth (33:17), only that the children are "tender" when he arrives (33:13). He also blanks how much time elapses between the two portions of this scene (Jacob's settling and the rapes). However, Joseph, who must have been just a little older than Dinah (cf. 30:21), is seventeen some time after Jacob leaves Shechem (37:2), making Dinah at best about sixteen at that time. In all likelihood, the rape of Dinah takes place about a decade after Jacob leaves Paddan Aram; his sons are about sixteen to twenty-two, old enough to fight, and Dinah about fifteen, a nubile girl.[230]

The narrator's omission of God in the rape episode is an intentional gap, not an unintentional blank. Had Jacob pushed on to fulfill his vow at Bethel (28:20–22; 34:1) and to build his altar there, instead of buying land and building his altar at Shechem, this tragedy would not have happened. After the tragedy, God commands him to build his altar at Bethel, where God had appeared to him (35:1). It seems Jacob and his household have paid a high price for not fulfilling his vow at Bethel (see note on "Intermarry" at 34:9).

The narrator blanks Dinah's reactions (contra 2 Sam. 13:12). She is an object of passion to Shechem, a bargaining chip to Hamor, a source of moral outrage on her behalf by her brothers, and passive indifference by her father.

Because of his particular focus in this scene, the narrator also blanks that Jacob gives the field he purchases here with its valuable well to Joseph (John 4:5). In this homeland, Joseph will be buried (Josh. 24:32).

Characterization, Naming, and Identification

On this critical occasion of defining the family's relationship to the Canaanites, the family lacks good leadership. In pitching his tent within sight of the Canaanite city, Jacob fails to model for Dinah appropriate distancing from the Canaanites and exposes her to sexual defilement from the notoriously sensual Canaanites. At the beginning of this cultically defiling rape episode, Jacob by his silence is much too passive. At the end, when he finally opens his mouth, he betrays fear, not faith. He struggles neither with God nor humans. The narrator appropriately uses his old label, Jacob, not his new name, Israel. The narrator stresses Jacob's passivity by repeatedly noting the obvious family relationships that seem to have no impact on Jacob's actions (e.g., "Dinah, the daughter Leah had borne to Jacob," 34:1; "Dinah daughter of Jacob," 34:3; "his daughter Dinah," 34:5; "his sons," 34:5; "Jacob's sons,"

---

[230]Hamor refers to her as a "girl" (Heb. *yaldâ*, "female child").

34:7, 13, 25, cf. 27; "Jacob's daughter," 34:7, 19; "Dinah's father," 34:11). The disparity in name and action is made more apparent by the active relationship between the Canaanite ruler and his son. They too are repeatedly identified by the narrator by their familial relationship (e.g., "Shechem son of Hamor the Hivite," 34:2; "his father," 34:4, 13; "Shechem's father," 34:6; "My son," 34:8; "his son," 34:18, 20, 24, 26). But they often act in concert, and Hamor responds to Shechem's demands, even if inappropriate.

Jacob's sons, however, expose and counter Jacob's passivity with extreme violence. Simeon and Levi overreact, rashly killing off all the males and plundering their households. Their moral indignation turns to Lamech-like revenge. Even decades later on his deathbed, Jacob cannot forget the violence; he curses the anger of Simeon and Levi and denies the hotheads kingship (Gen. 49:5–7).[231]

EXEGETICAL NOTES TO BOOK 8, ACT 3, SCENE I ─────────

Jacob Settles in Shechem: Purchase of a Plot and Erection of an Altar (33:18–19)

18. from Paddan Aram. The narrator disassociates this scene from Act 2, Jacob's exile in Paddan Aram. Jacob has returned to the Promised Land (see 28:10–22).

safely. The word is ambiguous. It means either he arrived "safe and sound" back in the land (12:7) and/or he entered the city of Shechem peacefully (34:21). Both are true.

at the city of Shechem.[232] Here he walks in the footsteps of his grandfather Abraham, staking his future in the Promised Land. He sets up an altar where Abraham had (cf. 12:6–7), purchases land in faith (cf. Gen. 23), and, though not stated here, digs a well (John 4:5–6; it can still be seen today).

Shechem. This is Tell Balâṭah, about one mile east of modern Shechem (Nablus). Egyptian texts from the nineteenth, seventeenth, and fourteenth centuries B.C. mention this important city. It lay in the heart of the Promised Land in the strategic pass between Mount Gerizim to its south and Mount Ebal to its north.

in Canaan. The tautology alerts the reader to the wickedness of the area (see Gen. 19), foreshadowing the trouble to come.

within sight of the city. Compare Lot in 13:12. By choosing this location, Jacob puts Dinah in jeopardy (see Literary Analysis above).

19. pieces of silver [qᵉśîṭâ]. The weight and value of this Hebrew monetary term is not known.[233] If less than a shekel, it suggests a peaceful rela-

---

[231]Goldin, "The Youngest Son," 27–44.

[232]The Hebrew could be read as "at Salem the city of [prince] Shechem." Salem is a village about four miles east of biblical Shechem.

[233]It is used exclusively during patriarchal times (Josh. 24:32; Job 42:11).

tionship between Shechem and Israel. If more, it suggests Jacob had greater wealth than Abraham. The exact price is given to make the sale final and incontestable.

he bought.[234] In allowing Israel and his sons to buy land and settle among them, the Canaanites hope to intermarry with Jacob's clan and so absorb them as part of their people and culture (Gen. 34:21–23). Jacob may have bought the land as an additional and more northerly burial site in the land. It becomes a part of the inheritance of the sons of Joseph (48:22).

from the sons of Hamor, the father of Shechem. The note foreshadows the terrible scene with Dinah that is to follow.

where he pitched his tent. Although purchasing the land and erecting the altar were acts of faith, Jacob errs in settling into the land. He made a vow to worship in Bethel when he returned to the Promised Land, but it takes him at least ten years to fulfill this vow. The idle years near the Canaanite city reflect a general spiritual passivity on Jacob's part that has horrendous consequences (see Literary Analysis above).

20. There he set up an altar. Jacob symbolically builds his altar at Shechem, where Abraham built his first altar in the sworn land (see 12:6–8; 28:20–22; 31:5).

called. See 35:7; Ex. 17:15; Judg. 6:24; Ezek. 48:35.

El Elohe Israel. This literally means "God, the God of Israel." Jacob identifies his new self with the living God and claims the land in his name. This "flag" distinguishes Israel from the Canaanites whose language they speak (31:47).

Shechem Son of Hamor Rapes Jacob's Daughter Dinah (34:1–4)

1. Dinah. See 30:21. She is important to the narrative only for her role in this scene.

daughter Leah. See 30:2–3, 5, 7, 19. The notice clarifies the roles of Levi and Simeon, her full brothers (34:13, 25, 27, 31). The narrator does not intend to slight Jacob (cf. 34:5).

borne to Jacob. See also 30:3, 5, 7, 11, 19. The narrator's continual identification of the father-daughter relationship exposes the shame of Jacob's passivity in the events that follow (see also Literary Analysis above).

went out. This is an improper and imprudent act. Sarna comments, "Girls of a marriageable age would not normally leave a rural encampment to go unchaperoned into an alien city."[235] Rebekah and Rachel going to a well owned by the clan is quite different from going out unchaperoned among the Canaanites. Jacob has not modeled appropriate distancing from the Canaanites (see 33:18

---

[234]Stephen says Abraham bought this field (Acts 7:16). Is he confused, or does he telescope the two accounts of patriarchal purchases in the land of Canaan into one?

[235]Sarna, *Genesis*, 233.

and Literary Analysis above) and possibly has influenced Dinah's inappropriate friendliness with them. It is his responsibility to see that she is chaperoned.

to visit. Hamilton suggests that it was possibly "to be seen."[236]

women of the land. This is another critical comment on Dinah's behavior. The lifestyles of Canaanite women repulsed Abraham, Isaac, and Rebekah (see "Canaan" in 33:18).

2. Shechem son of Hamor. See 33:18. Besides qualifying Shechem's identity, the mention of Shechem's father serves the narrator's persuasive bent. The narrator repeatedly notes the blood relationship of these men who, after the rape, act in concert (34:4, 6, 8, 13, 18, 20, 24, 26). The contrast with Jacob and his children is stark (see Literary Analysis above).

Hamor. The men of Hamor during the period of the judges were also aristocrats (see Josh. 24:32; Judg. 9:8).

Hivite. See 9:25; 10:15, 17.[237]

the ruler[238] of that area. The term "area" rather than "city" may reflect the undeveloped nature of the city at the time of Jacob. According to the Bible's chronology, Jacob lived between 1800–1750 B.C. Urban occupation of the site began about 1900 B.C. By about 1750 the city was enclosed within a free-standing mudbrick wall 2.5 meters wide, set on a stone foundation, and the buildings within were substantial structures, also with mudbrick walls on stone foundations.[239] However, at the time of Jacob, the walls were probably just beginning to be built; hence the term "area."[240]

saw . . . took. The same sequence is used for the sexually unrestrained tyrants in Gen. 6:2.[241]

violated her. The Hebrew also includes the verb *škb,* "lay, slept with her," which refers to objectified and illicit sex (see note at 30:16). The NIV omits this verb, taking "slept with her and violated her" as a hendiadys. Doing so, however, diminishes the increasing brutality. Most scholars gloss his sexual abuse by "rape," but others by "seduced."[242] *HALOT* defines the term for Gen. 34:2; Judg. 19:24; 20:5; 2 Sam. 13:12, 14, 22, 32; Lam. 5:11 as "to do violence . . . to rape a woman."[243]

3. was drawn to . . . loved . . . spoke tenderly. The three verbs of tender affection counterbalance the three verbs of brutality. Nevertheless, though he makes commitment to her, he makes no apology or attempt to indemnify the family he has wronged.

---

[236]Hamilton, *Genesis 18–50,* 353.

[237]See R. North, "The Hivites," *Bib* 54 (1973): 43–62.

[238]Hebrew *nāśîʾ* (see 25:16).

[239]See L. E. Toombs, "Shechem (Place)," *ABD,* 5:1179. From Egyptian sources it can be inferred that the city-state of Shechem at that time extended its territory from Jerusalem and Gezer in the south to Megiddo in the north, a dominion of about 1000 square miles.

[240]The expression "out of the city gate" in 34:24 may be an idiom for every able-bodied man.

[241]See the sequence also in 3:6.

[242]For discussion, see R. Wakley, *"mōhar," NIDOTTE,* 2:860–61.

[243]*HALOT,* 853.

loved. The same natural emotion motivated Jacob (see 29:18). Shechem's aggressive feelings have turned to love. The narrator's presentation is truthful but not sympathetic to Shechem. As Sternberg notes, "[H]e first shocks us by the suddenness of the rape and only then proceeds to its aftereffects on the rapist."[244]

4. Get [*lqḥ*]. This is the same verb translated "took" in 34:2. The willful youth does not add the polite form of address "please" (*nāʾ*) to his father (cf. 34:8; so also Samson to his parents, Judg. 14:2).

girl [*yaldâ*]. The Hebrew refers to a female child. The narrator gives her dignity by calling her "young woman" (*naʿărâ*, 34:3), and so does Shechem when addressing her brothers (34:12), but his words to his father here probably more honestly reflect his poor attitude.

wife. Here he acts better. Unlike Amnon, he attempts to right the wrong. Deuteronomy 22:28–29 does not prescribe death for rape but marriage with a heavy monetary penalty and without possibility of divorce if the father consents (cf. Ex. 22:16–17; 2 Sam. 13:16). However, Shechem acts wrongly in holding Dinah captive in his house and negotiating while putting Israel under duress (see Gen. 34:26).

Reactions of Jacob and His Sons to Defilement (34:5–7)

5. defiled. The word tips the hand of the narrator's evaluation of the incident. This was an act not of mere guilt but of defilement (i.e., ritual uncleanness, an outcast state). Drawing from Ricoeur (*The Symbolism of Evil*), Brueggemann states, "an elemental notion of ritual uncleanness is more powerful, more compelling and (as here) more dangerous than a judgment of moral guilt."[245]

kept quiet. The gap of Jacob's emotions is remarkable. Elsewhere the narrator records his intense emotions (see 29:11, 18; 32:7; 33:4; esp. 37:34–35 at the assumed death of Joseph). The narrator also censures Jacob's passivity in the face of his daughter's defilement by contrasting his reaction to that of his sons: "They were filled with grief and fury, because Shechem had done a disgraceful thing [*nᵉbālâ*]." David was rightly furious when Amnon raped Tamar (2 Sam. 13:21) but wrongly did nothing (2 Sam. 13:20–21). Absalom, like Jacob's sons, was correct in his anger but sinful in his extreme hatred and violence (2 Sam. 13:22).

until they came home. Apparently Jacob does not view it important enough to send prompt word.

6. with Jacob. The ruler wants to speak to Jacob as father to father. Hamilton asks, "Will he become the rogue's father-in-law?"[246] Jacob's sons, however, quickly take charge and Hamor ends up negotiating with them.

[244]Sternberg, *Poetics of Biblical Narrative*, 447.
[245]Brueggemann, *Genesis*, 275–76.
[246]Hamilton, *Genesis 18–50*, 356.

7. as soon as they heard. The narrator blanks how they heard but does not credit Jacob with summoning them.

grief. The Hebrew here (*ʿsb* in the Hithpael) is found elsewhere only for God's reaction to human wickedness (see Gen. 6:6). These proper emotions are assigned to the brothers, not to Jacob.

because. The causal clause gives both the reason for the grief and fury and the narrator's evaluative viewpoint.

disgraceful thing [*nᵉbālâ*]. According to Phillips, this term of "extreme gravity [is] a general expression for serious disorderly and unruly action resulting in the break up of an existing relationship whether between tribes, within the family, in a business arrangement, in marriage or with God."[247] Those who commit a moral outrage of the vilest sort against the deepest realities and convictions of the community must be punished to protect the fabric of the community (Deut. 22:21; Josh. 7:15; Judg. 19:23–24; 20:6, 10; 2 Sam. 13:12; Jer. 29:23). As Sarna says, "For society's own self-protection, such atrocities can never be tolerated or left unpunished."[248]

in Israel. The narrator's anachronism, referring to the nation of Israel, puts Shechem's crime and the brothers' outrage into the perspective of true Israel (see 2 Sam. 13:12). Here is the narrator's point of view on the heinous crime (see "Post-Mosaic Additions: The Implied Author and Audience" in the introduction).

Reactions of Hamor and Shechem: Proposal for Intermarriage (34:8–12)

First Hamor, the ruler, speaks and proposes intermarriage between Jacob's household and the Canaanites (34:8–10). Then Shechem, the prince, asks for Dinah's hand in particular and offers to pay the bride price. Significantly, they offer no apology.

8. his heart set on your daughter. They speak as though the rape had never occurred and Dinah is not now captive in their city.

9. Intermarry. This is what Abraham and Isaac dreaded. Later the law forbids it (Deut. 7:3). To Israel it is perversion; to Hamor, an opportunity for cooperation. The narrator does not spell out precisely how Jacob's children should have secured spouses in the land of Canaan. After the hostilities between Jacob and the Arameans, the option of returning to Paddan Aram is essentially ruled out. Probably, since they had four different mothers, they could have married among themselves even as Esau married the daughters of Ishmael. Moreover, they could have honestly insisted upon the circumcision and religious purity of males who married their daughters, and their males could have married Canaanites such as Tamar and Rahab, who embraced their lifestyle and worldview.

[247]A. Phillips, "NEBALAH—A Term for Serious Disorderly and Unruly Conduct," *VT* 25 (1975): 241.
[248]Sarna, *Genesis*, 234.

your daughters. Jacob probably had other daughters besides Dinah. Also, the agreement anticipates the future children of Jacob's sons.

10. acquire property. This most valuable provision to meet the basic need of sojourners and to fulfill their destiny presents the greatest temptation to the holy family (cf. Luke 4:5–6).

12. price for the bride [*mōhar*]. This is a technical term for the payment made by a prospective husband for a bride. According to Wakely, the Hebrew denotes "a sum of money paid by the bridegroom to the bride's family at the time of betrothal and that, from this point onwards, the marriage, though not yet consummated, was legally in force."[249] The sum of money varied. In the case of a rape of an unbetrothed virgin, the law demanded payment of fifty shekels of silver and marriage without the possibility of divorce (Deut. 22:28–29).

gift. He probably added "gift" to the bridal price to make his bribe irresistible.

girl [*naᶜarā*]. This is better translated "young woman" (see note at 34:4).

Reactions of Jacob's Clan and Shechemites: A Treacherous Agreement (34:13 – 24)

The brothers deceitfully propose circumcision as the condition of intermarriage (34:13–17), and the ruler and his son deceitfully sell the treaty to their subjects on the basis that they will appropriate their property through intermarriage (34:18–24).

13. defiled. See 34:5. Israel sees the situation as one between the violated and the violator. The violator has damaged Dinah's participation in the covenant community. The brothers demand that Hamor and Shechem's people make themselves qualified to participate in the Hebrew community by agreeing to circumcise all their males.

Jacob's sons replied. Notably, Jacob does not respond. His reproach of his sons for their cruel treachery inferentially excludes him from their plan, and his request "Let me not enter their council" (49:6) explicitly excludes him and infers that Simeon and Levi alone hatch the plan.

deceitfully [*mirmâ*]. This word describing "betrayal, deceit, or treachery" in its nearly forty occurrences is always pejorative (e.g., Gen. 27:35; Jer. 5:27).[250] While deceit is expected by both parties in war, it is not acceptable in a peace treaty (cf. 2 Kings 9:23). The Hebrew *mirmâ* is not used for warfare situations. While the narrator approves of the brother's moral indignation, he does not approve of their tactics.

15. circumcising. See 17:9–14; Ex. 12:43–49. They sacrilegiously and reprehensibly empty the holy covenant sign of its religious significance,

249Wakely, "*mōhar*," NIDOTTE, 2:860.
250E. Carpenter and M. A. Grisanti, "*rmh*," NIDOTTE, 3:1123.

commitment by faith to Abraham's God, and abuse it to inflict vengeance. Sarna comments, "[T]he speech of the brothers is heavy with irony: The part of the body used by Shechem in his violent passion will itself become the source of his own punishment!"[251]

16. our daughters. This is spoken proleptically (see 34:9, 13).

17. take our sister and go. The brothers are remarkably undaunted by the fact that at the time Hamor and Shechem hold Dinah hostage (see 34:26).

18. seemed good. They are peaceful, there is plenty of room, and it is economically advantageous.

19. lost no time. Their role model immediately sets the example before addressing the townsmen.[252]

because he was delighted. The narrator emphasizes that he had what some call "true love" (34:3, 8). In the world's view, that is all that matters.

20. gate. In the ancient world, this was the place for council among the leaders (see 19:1; 23:18).

21. These men are friendly toward us. The ruler of Shechem and his "honored" heir apparent deceive the townspeople by not stating their ulterior motive (gratifying Shechem's passion) and by not specifying that allowing Jacob's household to settle in the land entails permitting them to acquire property as well. Instead, they substitute their common deceit to possess Israel with cultural genocide.

21. live[253] . . . trade. They omit "acquire property" (see 34:10).

22. circumcised. The word is emptied of theological significance. They have no intent to embrace Israel's worldview symbolized by circumcision. It is only a means of financial gain, reinforcing their own culture.

23. become ours. Like other political leaders in the world, they make their own lust appear to be in the interest of the community.

24. agreed. They are willing to accept the sign of the holy covenant as a means to advantage themselves without conversion. The whole city is avaricious, bent on disadvantaging Israel.

who went out of the city. This is an idiom meaning "every able-bodied man."[254]

every male. NIV omits the Hebrew "all who went out" after "every male." The repetition underscores that not one male is left to defend the city. The ruse of the sons is totally successful.

---

[251]Sarna, *Genesis*, 236.

[252]Or the narrator is noting Hamor's ardent feelings for Dinah by anticipating Hamor's circumcision (so Sarna, *Genesis*, 236).

[253]Hebrew *yšb*, also translated "settle" in 34:23.

[254]Speiser, *Genesis*, 263. Cf. a Phoenician inscription, "I conquered those who came out [in battle] [*hyṣ'm*] and their allies" (G. A. Cooke, *Text-Book of North-Semitic Inscriptions* [Oxford: Clarendon Press, 1903], 76–77).

Jacob's Sons Rape Shechem [the City]: Simeon and Levi Slaughter, the Other Sons Loot (34:25 – 29)

25. Three days later. The delay is because by then either all had been circumcised[255] and/or likely the pain was severest.[256]

were still in pain. The brothers responded with unmitigated violence and shameless barbarity.

Simeon and Levi. They were Dinah's full brothers.

killing every male. Though their desire to punish Shechem is just, they overreact and engage prematurely in a holy war without divine sanction (see 15:16 and note; Num. 31:3–24). By their unbridled, faithless, and rash revenge, Simeon and Levi lose leadership (see Gen. 49:6) and land in Israel (49:7; Matt. 26:52). Later, however, the zeal of the priest Phinehas (from the house of Levi), used properly, wins him a better inheritance (see Num. 25).

26. took . . . left. This reverses "went out . . . took" (34:1–2; see Literary Analysis above).

from Shechem's house. Now the reader realizes that Dinah has been held captive in Shechem's home all this time. Shechem and his father had never offered honest negotiations.

27. where their sister had been defiled. The narrator is at pains to explain that their motive was to avenge the defilement, not to enrich themselves.

28. They seized. This is an act of *lex talionis:* as the men of Shechem intended to appropriate the property of Jacob's household, his household appropriates their property.

The Reaction of Jacob (34:30)

30. Then Jacob said. Jacob reproves the sons for their imprudence; they scold him for his lack of moral indignation. Their contrasting reactions to the rape of the city match their contrasting reactions to the rape of Dinah. Jacob shows no moral outrage, and the sons justify their slaughter as just punishment.

trouble on me. Jacob's grievance is less than honorable. His rebuke springs from a faint heart. He is concerned about himself, not about Dinah's humiliation. As Hamilton states, "His concerns are tactical and strategic, rather than ethical."[257]

Canaanites. See 10:15. Jacob's fear of Esau's militia is replaced by his fear of Canaanites and Perizzites.[258]

Perizzites. See 13:7.

my household. These are ironic words from one who has abdicated his leadership in this scene.

---

[255]Sarna, *Genesis*, 237.
[256]F. C. Fensham, "Gen xxxiv and Mari," *JNSL* 4 (1975): 89.
[257]Hamilton, *Genesis 18–50*, 371.
[258]Ibid.

will be destroyed. The patriarchs had to survive in the land by faith, not war (see Gen. 26). Here Jacob displays fear, not obedient faith (see 35:1–5).

The Reaction of the Sons (34:31)

31. our sister. Dinah is not referred to as "your daughter," as the story began in 34:1. This is another symbol of the terrible family split.

Should . . . like a prostitute? The rhetorical question emphatically asserts the anticipated negative answer. The narrator gives them the last word.

THEOLOGICAL REFLECTIONS ON BOOK 8, ACT 3, SCENE I ——————————————

Vow and Worship

The logic of the story implies the importance of keeping one's vow. Jacob fails to keep his vow to build his altar at Bethel and then almost loses his household (see also Literary Analysis above). One cannot worship God as one pleases. Jacob builds an altar, but in the wrong place. Because he is not in the place where he is supposed to be, he brings a sword, not a blessing, upon the nations.

Moral Indignation

The narrator censures the rape by his terminology: "violated" (34:2), "defiled" (34:5), "grief" and "disgraceful thing in Israel" (34:7; see Exegetical Notes). For that reason, he gives the sons as his agents the last word to express his own point of view: "Should he have treated our sister like a prostitute?" Neither Shechem nor Hamor find anything offensive about the rape. Now that Shechem truly loves her, they overlook the offense and only want to negotiate a financial settlement for the marriage. Jacob here is sadly comparable to the Canaanites. He shows no moral indignation and wants only to settle the matter prudently. With the sons, however, the narrator affirms that it is a moral outrage in Israel that should be punished.

Leadership

The Canaanites have replaced Esau's militia in threatening Jacob's existence and God's covenant with him. In the last scene Jacob exemplified bold leadership based on prudence and faith; in this scene he exemplifies weak leadership based on prudence and fear.

This scene begins to answer the important question of who will rule the twelve tribes of Jacob. In the next scene Reuben, by his own immorality, like that of the Canaanites, disqualifies himself. Simeon and Levi, while rightly showing moral indignation against the cultic defilement of their sister, disqualify themselves by their rashness and unbridled revenge. Jacob acts as foil to them. He is prudent but lacks faith and moral indignation. In the last book, leadership will fall first upon the shoulders of Joseph, then finally upon Judah.

Typology

The slaughter and looting of the Shechemites foreshadow Israel's conquest of Canaan and their dispossessing the Canaanites from the land.

BOOK 8, ACT 3, SCENE 2: ISRAEL FULFILLS HIS VOW AT BETHEL (35:1 – 15)

LITERARY ANALYSIS OF BOOK 8, ACT 3, SCENE 2 —————

Structure

Jacob's movement to Bethel is part of his final itinerary in his return to Hebron (see Literary Analysis of Book 8, Act 3). The structure consists of two incidents in an alternating pattern: Jacob's return to Bethel and the renewal of the covenant at Bethel.

A God commands: ascend to Bethel, build an altar there (35:1)
B Jacob obeys: renews household, ascends to Bethel, builds an altar (35:2–7)
A' God appears to Jacob and renews Abrahamic covenant (35:9–13)
B' Jacob rededicates the stele and renews name of Bethel (35:14–15)

In A, God takes the initiative to call Jacob to renew covenant with him; in A', he proclaims Jacob's new name and escalates the covenant promises. Jacob's response escalates from the covenant renewal of his family (B) through radical symbolization and building an altar to his erection of a rock pillar as God's house (B').

These accounts, though both concerned with God's revelation to Jacob, are distinct happenings. They are divided by the death notice of Deborah (35:8). The first account is framed by historical reference: "God, who appeared to you when you were fleeing from your brother Esau" (35:1); "God revealed himself to him when he was fleeing from his brother" (35:7). The second account, the theophany at Bethel, is chronologically linked with his return from Paddan Aram (35:9).

Comparison and Contrast

This scene brings the Jacob cycle to its climactic, successful conclusion. As such, it coheres with many of the earlier scenes. (1) It fulfills Isaac's blessing on Jacob (28:3–4). (2) Most notably, the Lord's theophany to Jacob at Bethel (35:9–15) compares and contrasts with his original theophany at Bethel when Jacob was fleeing Esau. The narrator establishes the connection by framing the first account with the historical reference (35:1, 7)— "when you were/he was fleeing your brother Esau/his brother"—and by adding "again" to "God appeared to him" (35:9). In both theophanies, God, called by the rare term *ʾēl*, not the usual term *ʾelōhîm*, repeats provisions of the Abrahamic covenant: fertility, nationhood, blessing to nations, and possession of Canaan. After both theophanies, Jacob worships, first by setting up a pillar to commemorate the experience, then by rededicating it, both times in connection with naming the site. The theophanies are so similar that source critics think they are different recollections of the same event. However, Jacob is filled with fear after the first theophany, but not after the second. Moreover, the contexts differ. As Hamilton notes, "God's first appearance is to be read in the context of Jacob 'fleeing' (bāraḥ, v. 7). God's second appearance is to be read in the context of Jacob being blessed (bārak, v. 9)."[259] More important, the contents of the Abrahamic covenant differ somewhat (see below). Finally, whereas Jacob formerly named the site for its place where God appeared to him (i.e., "Bethel"), now he names the site for the God who appeared to him (i.e., "El-Bethel").

(3) The theophany of Genesis 35 completes the revelation of the Abrahamic covenant to Jacob. The first theophany coheres with God's covenant with Abraham in chapter 15; the second, with the expansion of that covenant in chapter 17. The similarities between the covenant to Abraham in chapter 17 and this covenant are striking. They have:

- the same opening: "Lord/God appeared" (17:1; 35:9)
- the same frame: God "appeared" and "went up" (17:1; 35:9; 17:22; 35:13)
- the same divine title: "God Almighty" (17:1; 35:11) [ʾēl šadday]
- names changed: Abram to Abraham (17:5), Jacob to Israel (35:10)
- similar phrases and promises: to be exceedingly fruitful, to consist of a community of peoples, kings to come from their own loins, and land to the descendants (17:6, 8; 35:11–12).[260]

(4) There are also striking comparisons and contrasts between this second theophany and Jacob's wrestling with the angel of God (32:22–32). In both, Jacob's name is changed to Israel and he is blessed. Here too the similarities are so striking that source critics assign the two scenes to two sources recounting the same event. However, now God encounters Jacob directly, not as an angel. Now Jacob's name is not merely changed to Israel, but from now on is to be proclaimed as Israel. The first change occurs outside the Promised Land; the second, within it. Significantly, the new proclamation of his name is made in connection with his becoming a community of nations. From the encounter with the God-man, he found boldness; now he exhibits boldness before the theophany. This theophany has come to a changed Jacob.

(5) The first two scenes of this act are both connected with "after Jacob came/returned from Paddan Aram" (33:18; 35:9). The refrain underscores a

---

[259]Ibid., 380.

[260]This comparison was arrived at independently from Gross's similar comparison (see W. Gross. "Jakob, der Mann des Segens: Zu Traditionsgeschichte und Theologie der priesterschriftlichen Jakob-süberlieferungen," Bib 49 [1968]: 321–44).

contrast in Jacob's obedience. By way of comparison, they share an alternating structure:

A Jacob settles at Shechem and builds an altar there (33:18–20)
B Rapes at Shechem (34:1–31).
A' Jacob settles at Bethel and builds an altar there (35:1–7)
B' God appears to Jacob and renews covenant; a community of nations (35:9–15).

In A, Jacob worships according to his own agenda; in A', according to God's. At Shechem (B), Jacob is neither blessed nor a blessing. His household inflicts death on the community. At Bethel (B'), Jacob is blessed, and nations become part of the worshiping community.

There are still more contrasts. The misplaced altar at Shechem (33:20) is replaced by the altar at Bethel (35:7). Jacob's fear of the Canaanites in the preceding scene (34:30) is replaced by the Lord placing holy war panic upon all the towns as a bold Jacob on pilgrimage marches through hostile territory (35:5). Both scenes emphasize Israel's uniqueness: in moral purity (Scene 1) and in religious purity (Scene 2). However, the removal of sexual defilement by violence (Scene 1) is replaced by removal of religious defilement through ceremonial ritual (Scene 2).

Blanks and Gaps

The mention of the death and burial of Deborah, Rebekah's nurse, is truly remarkable (35:8). The unique obituary immediately follows the notice "when he was fleeing from his brother [Esau]" (35:7), reminding the audience of Rebekah's last and seemingly unfulfilled words at the time of his flight, "I'll send word for you" (27:45). The audience expects Rebekah's obituary here, not her closest surrogate. The narrator records the death of each of the patriarchs and of their favorite wives, except Rebekah. Clearly, the narrator has intentionally gapped her death, leaving the audience to surmise that he omitted her obituary in order not to honor her after she had deceived her husband.

Scenic Depiction

See "Go up to Bethel" in 35:1.

EXEGETICAL NOTES TO BOOK 8, ACT 3, SCENE 2 ————

God Commands: Ascend to Bethel, Build an Altar There (35:1)

1. God said. The divine covenant partner takes the initiative to renew the covenant with his flawed human partner.

Go up to Bethel. Jacob had a vow to fulfill (see 28:20–22). Perhaps God's command is a double entendre. Bethel is geographically 1,000 feet above

Shechem, and that geographical ascent symbolizes Jacob's spiritual ascent to God.

settle there [*yšb*]. Jacob is not to settle at Shechem (cf. 34:10). His stay at Bethel replaces his "stay" (*yšb*) at Paddan Aram (see 27:43–44).

build an altar. This is the only time God directs a patriarch to build an altar (cf. 12:7–8; 13:18; 22:9; 26:5; 33:20).

to God. The Hebrew is *ʾēl*, not *ʾelōhîm*, just as in 28:20–22 (cf. 31:13).

who appeared to you when you were fleeing from your brother Esau. Jacob has come full circle. This is where Jacob should have headed instead of settling in Shechem (33:18).

Jacob Obeys: Renews Household, Ascends to Bethel, Builds an Altar (35:2–7)

2. Get rid. The expression signifies the people's rededication of themselves to the Lord (Josh. 24:14, 23; Judg. 10:16; 1 Sam. 7:3–4; 2 Chron. 33:15). Repentance entails renouncing whatever hinders or tarnishes worship of God. The covenant's primary requirement is exclusive allegiance to the Lord (see Ex. 20:3–5; Josh. 24:14; Judg. 10:16).

foreign gods. See Gen. 31:19; Josh. 24:23; Eph. 4:22–25; Col. 3:7–8; James 1:21; 1 Peter 2:1.

purify yourselves. The narrator seems to assume the purification rituals of the Mosaic law—bathing the body, washing clothes, and abstaining from sexual intercourse (Lev. 14:8–9; 22:6–7; Num. 8:7)—to effect passage from defilement of idols to purity before God (see Deut. 7:25–26; Jer. 2:23; 7:30).[261]

change your clothes. This symbolizes a new and purified way of life (cf. Gen. 41:14; Lev. 15:18; 16:23–24; 18:24–29; Num. 8:7, 21; 31:19, 24; 2 Sam. 12:20; Ezek. 44:19; Zech. 3:3–5; 2 Cor. 5:4; Eph. 6:13–17; 1 Peter 5:5; Rev. 3:4; 16:15). Hamilton connects the change of clothing with the change of names.[262]

3. let us go. It takes courage for the militant family to travel through hostile territory. They had been known as peaceful shepherds, but now they are known for their violent acts (see Gen. 34). They now face greater jeopardy.

to Bethel. Jacob finally makes the religious pilgrimage to pay his vows.

day of my distress. See 28:20.

4. they gave Jacob. He has recovered his spiritual leadership.

rings. These amulets (see 35:2) were perhaps part of the plunder from the Shechemites.

buried them [*ṭmn*]. The rare Hebrew term, rather than the usual *qbr* (see 35:8, 29), may signify that they were buried ignominiously (i.e., "dumped"). This is a unique procedure. Later leaders burned them (Ex. 32:30; Deut. 9:21;

---

[261]Sarna, *Genesis*, 367 n. 4.
[262]Hamilton, *Genesis 18–50*, 376.

1 Kings 15:13; 1 Chron. 14:12). The gods that had been sat upon are denigrated to their final burial.

oak at Shechem. This is the sacred tree associated with Abraham (see 12:6; Hos. 4:18).

5. terror of God. Contrast this with Jacob's fears in 34:30. The divinely induced panic of holy war (see Ex. 23:27; Josh. 2:9), validating Jacob's good confession of God's presence, is necessary because their reputation has changed from peaceful shepherds (34:21) to rapacious warriors (34:30). Had Jacob trusted in God in the first place, he would have had no need to fear.

7. built an altar. See 35:1. By their worship, the covenant family retains their separation from the Canaanites, their witness to them, and symbolically their claim to the land based on God's promises (see 12:7).

El Bethel. See also 28:18–22. Hamilton explains the change of names: "Jacob's memories of two experiences at Bethel (chaps. 28 and 35) will recall for a long time to come the God Jacob encountered there, rather than recall Bethel as a divine reside, a holy site. 'The God of the House of God' rather than simply 'The House of God.'"[263]

revealed himself. This is a prophetic experience. The verb is plural, suggesting the translation, "the divine beings were revealed,"[264] which matches his experience at Bethel (see 28:12–13).

Death of Deborah (32:8)

8. Rebekah's nurse. Scripture memorializes the death of the aged, faithful nurse of Rebekah (see 24:59), not the matriarch herself, probably because she deceived Isaac and because Jacob was not present when she died (see Literary Analysis above).

God Appears to Jacob and Renews Abrahamic Covenant (35:9–13)

9. Paddan Aram. See 25:20; see also 35:26 and "Comparison and Contrast" in the Literary Analysis above.

appeared. See 17:1 and "Comparison and Contrast" in the Literary Analysis above. The narrator does not report that God merely "said" (cf. 35:1).

again. See 28:10–22 and "Comparison and Contrast" in the Literary Analysis above.

blessed. See 12:2 and "Comparison and Contrast" in the Literary Analysis above.

10. called. "It will no longer be said" (32:28) is replaced by "it will no longer be called."

Jacob . . . Israel. The text assumes 32:28. His new status is emphasized before the covenant.

---

[263]Ibid., 380.
[264]Less likely, it could be a rare usage of the plural verb with God.

11. God Almighty. See 17:1 and "Comparison and Contrast" in the Literary Analysis above.

be fruitful. This is a hendiadys for "be very fruitful" and is a fresh expression of 17:2, 6 (see 1:22, 28; 9:1, 7; 17:20; 28:3; 47:27; 48:4; Ex. 1:7). The common-grace blessing on all humanity (1:28; 9:1, 7) is focused particularly on the covenant community (see 47:27; Ex. 1:7). The promise is normally given to childless couples, but Jacob already has twelve sons. The reference is to the nation and to the community of nations.[265]

a community of nations. This is a fresh expression of 17:4, "You will be the father of many nations."

kings will come from your body. Literally ". . . from your loins," the expression will not be repeated again until the Davidic Covenant (2 Sam. 7:12). The community of Israel will consist of many nations not from the body of the patriarchs, but the king(s) over this nation will come from the patriarchs.

Jacob Rededicates the Stele and Renews Name of Bethel (35:14–15)

14. stone pillar. Stones often mark the significant events in Jacob's life (see Literary Analysis of Book 8, Act 2, Scene 2). Perhaps by this ritual here Jacob restores the original sanctuary where he had vowed to return to the land (28:22). Sarna cites a parallel in which Sennacherib, king of Assyria and Babylonia (704–681 B.C.), rehabilitates a sanctuary: "When that palace shall have become old and ruined, may some future prince restore its ruins, look upon the stela with my name inscribed (thereon), anoint it with oil, pour out a libation upon it and return it to its place."[266]

THEOLOGICAL REFLECTIONS ON BOOK 8, ACT 3, SCENE 2

Covenant

The book of Genesis is largely about God establishing his kingdom through his covenant people (see "Theme of Genesis and Biblical Theology, Introduction: The Kingdom of God" in the introduction). In this scene God again takes the initiative (35:1–2) to effect his plan in which he inevitably must overcome many adversities, famine, barrenness, enemies, and the like. In actuality, there is only one real obstacle to its fulfillment: the depravity of his covenant people. Through the other adversities, he perfects his people. As Abraham failed in Egypt (12:10–20) and Isaac in Philistia, so Jacob fails at Shechem. These failures, however, became stepping stones in their faith. After the deba-

---

[265]Cf. Hamilton, *Genesis 18–50*, 381.
[266]Sarna, *Genesis*, 242, citing D. D. Luckenbill, *The Annals of Sennacherib* (Chicago: Univ. of Chicago Press, 1924), 130.

cle at Shechem, Jacob's household repents and renews covenant. In response, Jacob receives the full blessings of the Abrahamic covenant.

Worship

Jacob's tragedy at the wrong sanctuary of Shechem and the expanded covenant at the sanctuary of Bethel underscore the importance of worshiping God only according to his agenda. The church's form of worship is "God's face" in the world. The church must not deviate from his prescribed form lest they change his face. God will judge, not bless, a willful church.

Separation from the World

Jacob calls his family to purity. Thus Brueggemann asserts, "Israel must find a way to stay in the land with the Canaanites and yet practice faithfulness. The way chosen to do this without either destructiveness or accommodation is by way of *radical symbolization*. Israel engages in dramatic ritual activity as a mode of faithfulness" (cf. Josh. 24:23).[267] Philip Carrington has suggested that in the Christian tradition, this same disengagement is enacted in the sacrament of baptism (cf. Eph. 4:22–25; Col. 3:7–8; James 1:21; 1 Peter 2:1). To retain purity from the sensuality at Corinth, Paul took a Nazirite vow. To retain purity on an aircraft carrier, my brother prayed beside his bunk every night. The new community is formed by renunciation, renaming, reclothing, and, finally, receiving a promise.

Obedience and Promise

Wenham says, "Just as Abraham's three-day pilgrimage to sacrifice on Mount Moriah climaxed in the most categorical reaffirmation of the promises in his career, so, too, Jacob's sacred journey is crowned with the strongest statement of the promises that he ever heard, summing up and adding to what had been said to him on earlier occasions."[268]

BOOK 8, ACT 3, SCENE 3:
BIRTHS AND DEATHS (35:16–29)

LITERARY ANALYSIS OF BOOK 8, ACT 3, SCENE 3 ————

Structure

This scene provides the denouement to Act 3 as well as to Book 8 as a whole. It consists mostly of three incidents bound together by Jacob's itinerary: on the way to Ephrath (35:16–20), at Migdal Eder (35:21–22a), and at Hebron (35:27–29). By the end of this scene Jacob has lost his father, mother, and his dearest wife. The old generation is passing off the scene in preparation for the next, the topic of Book 10. The narrator anticipates this change

[267]Brueggemann, *Genesis*, 281.
[268]Wenham, *Genesis 16–50*, 325.

by inserting a genealogy of Jacob's sons according to their primogeniture rights (35:22b–26). This is fitting because the scene opens with the birth of Jacob's last born, Benjamin, and the second event is the misdeed of Jacob's firstborn, Reuben. The last event of the scene, the death and burial of Isaac, also concludes Book 8.

Subplot

Scene 3 is tightly linked with the preceding two scenes by continuing Jacob's itinerary back in the land after his exile in Paddan Aram. However, its four parts are best treated as a separate scene because they belong to the denouement of Act 3 after Book 8 peaks in Scene 2. Behind the foregrounded plot of Jacob's fortunes and misfortunes in connection with each site of his itinerary lies a subplot concerning Jacob's successor.[269] The genealogy inserted in this scene presents the twelve sons in the order of their primogeniture rights of succession. In Scene 1 Simeon and Levi, Leah's second and third sons, disqualify themselves by their cruel rashness. In this scene Reuben disqualifies himself by his high-handed debauchery. Accordingly, either Judah, son of Leah, or Joseph, the firstborn of Rachel, is next in line. According to the law (Deut. 21:15–17), the rights of primogeniture are based on chronology, not on the father's affection, which makes Judah, not Joseph, the rightful heir.

Comparison

The genealogy at the end of Book 8 coheres with the genealogy toward the end of Book 10. The genealogy of Jacob's sons in 35:22b–26 summarizes the births of Book 8 and forms a transition to the account of Esau's line and to the actors of the account of Jacob's line. The summarizing genealogy of Jacob's descendants in 46:8–25, after the climax of Book 10, forms a transition to the movement of that generation and the succeeding ones to Egypt.

The last event of this scene presents striking comparisons between the deaths of Abraham and Isaac: their ages at death (25:7; 35:28); the sequence of events (i.e., expired, died, gathered to their fathers, buried at good old age, 25:8; 35:29); their burials by two sons of principal wives (25:9; 35:29); the location at Mamre (25:9; 35:27).

Foreshadowing

By completing the list of Jacob's descendants with the birth of Benjamin, by disqualifying Reuben from leadership, and by cataloguing the sons according to primogeniture rights, this scene provides important information

---

[269]The same backgrounded macrostructure also informs Book 10. See R. E. Longacre, *Joseph: A Story of Divine Providence: A Texttheoretical and Textlinguistic Analysis of Genesis 37 and 39–48* (Winona Lake, Ind.: Eisenbrauns, 1989), 53–56.

for the interpretation of Book 10. In that book, God will perfect Judah for kingship. The presentation of Jacob's genealogy also signals an upcoming presentation of Esau's genealogy.

EXEGETICAL NOTES TO BOOK 8, ACT 3, SCENE 3 ———————

Journey to Ephrath: Death of Rachel and Birth of Benjamin (35:16 – 20)

16. to give birth. The birth of Benjamin completes the twelve tribes.

17. Don't be afraid. In death, Rachel had the comfort that God answered her prayer for another son (30:24).

18. Ben-Oni. The name probably means, "son of my sorrow/trouble," but other meanings, such as "son of my vigor/strength," are possible with the homonym *ʾônî*.[270]

his father named him. This is the only son Jacob named, suggesting his renewed leadership.

Benjamin. The Hebrew means, "son of the right hand." Does "right hand" symbolize the south in contrast to the north (cf. 1 Sam. 23:19, 24; Ps. 89:13; Ezek. 16:46)? Or does it symbolize power and protection (cf. Ex. 15:6, 12; Isa. 62:8)? Or does it symbolize good fortune as in Arabic (Gen. 48:12 – 14; Ps. 109:31; Isa. 63:12; Ezek. 21:22 [Heb. 27]; Hab. 2:16)?[271] The Mari texts, using the Akkadian equivalent of *binyāmîn*, support the first interpretation. The context, which would contrast Rachel's name (i.e., "misfortune") with Jacob's (i.e., "good fortune"), favors the last two interpretations.

19. Rachel died. See 30:1; 31:32 and notes.

Ephrath. This Ephrath is identified with Bethlehem (cf. Ruth 1:2; 4:11; 1 Sam. 17:12; Matt. 2:18). Rachel's tomb, however, is some distance from there, at "Zelza on the border of Benjamin" (1 Sam. 10:2; cf. Jer. 31:15). The location of Zelza is unknown. There was another Ephrathah "in the fields [region] of Jaar [i.e., Kiriath Jearim]" (Ps. 132:6; cf. 1 Sam. 6:21 – 7:1). Both Bethlehem and Kiriath Jearim became known as Ephrath[a] because the clan of Ephrath settles at both places (cf. 1 Chron. 2:50).

20. pillar. See 28:18.

At Migdal Eder: Reuben's Incest (35:21 – 22a)

21. Migdal Eder. The Hebrew means "watchtower of the flock." Micah 4:8 may identify the site with a section of Jerusalem because the expression is parallel to "a stronghold of the Daughter of Zion."

22. Israel was living. No mention is made of an altar at Migdal Eder, where Reuben sins.

---

[270]See "*ʾôn*," *HALOT*, 1:22.
[271]See *HALOT*, "*yāmîn*," 415.

Reuben. Reuben's terrible behavior here contributes to the poor characterization of him: "Turbulent as the waters, you will no longer excel" (Gen. 49:4).

slept with his father's concubine Bilhah. Bilhah is Rachel's maidservant. Reuben's shameful act is motivated more by politics than by lust. By defiling Bilhah, he makes certain that with Rachel's death her handmaid cannot supplant Leah as chief wife (cf. 2 Sam. 15:16; 16:22; 20:3).[272] The Mosaic law prohibits incest because it dishonors the father but exacts no penalty other than that God curses the criminal and holds him responsible (Lev. 18:8; 20:11; Deut. 22:30; 27:20). Moreover, according to known ancient Near Eastern cultural forms, by taking his father's concubine Reuben is attempting to seize Jacob's leadership (cf. 2 Sam. 3:7–8; 12:7–8; 16:21–22; 1 Kings 2:13–25). For his sin, Leah's first son, Reuben, is deprived of leadership (Gen. 49:3–4). Since Simeon and Levi have also been discounted from leadership, Judah, Leah's fourth son, will assume it.

Israel heard. The verb may connote impending action (cf. Num. 12:2), but Jacob remains silent until he gives Reuben an antiblessing in Gen. 49:3–4. The narrator gaps Jacob's emotions. Again he has not responded with moral outrage at another sexual offense (see "Characterization, Naming, and Identification" in the Literary Analysis of Book 8, Act 3, Scene 1).

Jacob's Genealogy (35:22b–26)

22b. twelve sons. With the completion of the twelve sons, they are listed in a summary catalogue (see Matt. 10:2–4; Rev. 21:12–14). They are presented based first on the social ranking of Jacob's wives and then on seniority.[273] Accordingly, the sons of Leah (35:23) and then of Rachel (35:24) are given before the sons of Bilhah (35:25) and Zilpah (35:26). Leah heads the list, and her maidservant ends it. Within that frame are the sons of Rachel and her handmaid. The same sequence is found in Ex. 1:1–4, with Joseph necessarily excepted in that context. Other sequences are given in Gen. 46:8–25 and 49:1–27, but Leah's sons always head the lists.[274]

24. Benjamin. See 35:16–18. Here Benjamin is listed as a son born in Paddan Aram (see 35:26), even though just six verses before is a description of Benjamin's birth on the way to Ephrath (see "Sources of Ur-Genesis" in the introduction). The list of sons may idealize all the sons as participating in an exodus from exile in Paddan Aram to the Promised Land (see note on 46:8). If so, the theological concern overrules the factual concern (see "Typology" in Theological Reflections on Book 8, Acts 2, Scene 6).

---

[272]He showed an analogous concern for his mother's leadership in the home in Leah's competition with Rachel in Gen. 30:14.

[273]That is, since the wives have a higher social ranking than the handmaids, their children are listed first. Within that constraint, the children are basically listed by birth order.

[274]See J. M. Sasson, "A Genealogical 'Convention' in Biblical Chronography?" *ZAW* 90 (1978): 179–84; Roth, *Numerical Sayings*, 12–13.

At Hebron: Death and Burial of Isaac
by Jacob and Esau (35:27 – 29)

27. came home to his father Isaac. His pilgrimage has come full circle. The account of Isaac ends with Jacob's reconciliation to him.

Hebron. See 28:10.

28. a hundred and eighty. Isaac's journey ends with a full length of years, but God passed him over after he tried to thwart God's purpose in the blessing (see Gen. 27). The *tôlᵉḏôt* of Abraham (i.e., the narrative of Isaac) has become lost in the *tôlᵉḏôt* of Isaac (i.e., the narrative of Jacob).

29. breathed his last . . . buried. See notes at 25:8.

Esau and Jacob. They are listed in order of birth. In 25:9, Isaac was listed first because Ishmael was from a maidservant.

buried. Like his mother and father, he was buried in the cave of Machpelah (49:29–32).

THEOLOGICAL REFLECTIONS ON
BOOK 8, ACT 3, SCENE 3 ——————————————

Covenant Grace and Judgment

God's glory consists in his grace (Ex. 34:6). In spite of Reuben's vile deed, the family remains intact, an earnest of the great nation to come. In Book 10, God will make the sons fit for covenant through famine. Nevertheless, he holds the guilty Reuben accountable (cf. Ex. 34:7). Though the firstborn with all the honor and privilege of that position, Reuben will not excel.

Covenant Faithfulness

The linking of birth and death in this scene shows vividly and acutely the transference of faith between the generations in the holy family. Death always happens in the context of life. Isaac, in spite of all his shortcomings, dies at a good old age and is gathered to Abraham's bosom, and Jacob completes his pilgrimage. Some saints soar with wings of eagles, others run, and some only walk; nevertheless, all complete the journey.

Prayer

Rachel's answered prayer for another son comforted her in death. A righteous person finds refuge in God even in death (Prov. 14:32).

THE ACCOUNT
OF ESAU'S DESCENDANTS
(36:1 – 37:1)

THEME OF BOOK 9

The two accounts of Esau's genealogy show the transition of Esau's descendants from tribal arrangement to designated kingship. This development of Esau in this microcosm reflects the later development of Israel (see Theological Reflections below).

OUTLINE OF BOOK 9

LITERARY ANALYSIS OF BOOK 9

Comparison and Contrast

The genealogies of Ishmael and Esau immediately follow the obituaries of their fathers (25:7–10; 35:29). As in the "accounts" of Abraham's sons, the rejected line of Ishmael (25:12–18) is presented before the elect line of Isaac (25:19–35:29), so now in the "accounts" of Isaac's sons, the rejected line of Esau (36:1–37:1) is presented before the elect line of Jacob (37:2–50:26). The accounts of the rejected descendants of the patriarchs are given because these sons are also under divine blessing (17:20; 27:38–40). This chapter is one of the longest in Genesis.

The contrast between the destinies of the nonelect seed out of the land and of the elect seed in it is underscored by the report: "So Esau . . . settled [*wayyēšeb*] in . . . Seir" (36:8) and "Jacob lived [*wayyēšeb*] in the land where his father had stayed, the land of Canaan" (37:1).

The twelve legitimate sons and grandsons (see note at 36:10–14) of Esau listed in 36:9–14 match the twelve sons of Nahor (22:20–24), of Ishmael (17:20; 25:13–16), and, of course, of Israel (35:22b–26). This consistent pattern, similar to the twelve months of the year, may intimate that these peoples existed as twelve tribe confederacies.[1]

Structure

The repeated superscription *ʾēleh tōlˤdōt ˤēsāw* ("this is the account of Esau's line" 36:1, 9) divides this chapter into two unequal halves. Both are genealogies, self-contained units with titles (36:1, 9) and colophons (36:8, 43b–37:1). The first account (36:1–8) presents a one-generation segmented genealogy of Esau's sons born in the land of Canaan. The second account (36:9–43) is framed by the inclusio "Esau the father of the Edomites." This account consists of two three-generation segmented genealogies of those born in Seir (36:9–19, 20–30) and one linear succession of kings for eight generations before an Israelite king reigns (36:31–43). These three lists are presented in an alternating pattern of a list of sons (or kings) followed by a list of chiefs (36:10–14//15–18, 20–28//29–30, 31–39//40–43).

The first account may be Mosaic from an early source (cf. Num. 20:14). However, the phrase "before any Israelite king reigned" (36:31) in the second account shows that it was added to the first account no earlier than the time David conquered Edom (2 Sam. 8:13–14) or Solomon confronted Hadad (cf. Gen. 36:39 with 1 Kings 11:14–22).[2]

EXEGETICAL NOTES TO BOOK 9 ———————————————————

Account 1, Genealogy 1: Esau's Genealogy in Canaan and His Separation from Canaan (36:1–8)

1. account. This is better translated, "This is the account of Esau's descendants" (see 2:4). The superscription functions as head to 36:1–8 (see Literary Analysis above). This first genealogy consists of two parts: Esau's marriages to Canaanite wives and the children born in Canaan prior to his

---

[1]Cf. M. Noth, *The History of Israel* (London: Adam & Charles Black, 1958), 85–97. However, his use of the term *amphictyony* (i.e., sacral league) is not appropriate. See R. K. Harrison, *Introduction to the Old Testament* (London: Tyndale, 1970), 332–34.

[2]Cf. M. Haran, "Observations on the Historical Background of Amos 1:2–2:6," *IEJ* 18 (1968): 207; M. Fishbane, "The Treaty Background of Amos 1:11 and Related Matters," *JBL* 89 (1970): 315.

migration to Mount Seir (36:2–5); and his migration to Seir (36:6–8). Both parts radically distinguish him from Jacob, who secures Aramean wives and eventually settles in the land of his fathers.

Esau . . . Edom. As Jacob's personal name is transformed to the national name Israel (see 35:10), so also Esau's personal name is transformed into the national name Edom (i.e., "Red" from "red stew," 25:30).

2. took his wives. See 26:34; 27:46 and notes.

from the women of Canaan. This is a derogatory expression (26:34–35; 27:46; 28:1, 6, 8; 33:18). "Canaan" designates the land inhabited by the Canaanites and along with them many other tribes (see 15:19–21), including the Hittites and Hivites mentioned in 36:2 (see 9:25; 10:15–19).

Adah . . . Oholibamah. The difference in sequence of names from the next genealogy (36:9–14) is due to lumping the despised Canaanite women together. As noted, these names do not match the names of Esau's wives listed in 26:34; 28:9:

Genesis 36:2–3

Adah	Oholibamah	Basemath
daughter of	daughter of Anah	daughter of Ishmael
Elon the Hittite	[granddaughter] of Zibeon the Hivite	sister of Nebaioth

Genesis 26:34; 28:9

Judith	Basemath	Mahalath
daughter of Beeri the Hittite	daughter of Elon the Hittite	daughter of Ishmael sister of Nebaioth

Adah. This is also the name of Lamech's first wife (4:19–20), perhaps linking Esau with the seed of the Serpent.

Oholibamah. This possibly means "tent [shrine] of a cultic high place."

granddaughter of Zibeon. The ancient versions read "son of Zibeon."[3]

Hivite. He is a Hurrian living in Palestine (see 10:17; 14:6; 36:20).[4]

4. Reuel. This means "friend of God" or "El is [my] friend."

5. Korah. The name means "bald head."

born to him in Canaan. See 35:26; Literary Analysis above; Theological Reflections below.

6. moved to a land. To some degree, Esau the nomadic hunter has already occupied Seir prior to Jacob's return to Mamre (32:3; 33:14, 16). Yet he does not vacate the land of his fathers (see 35:29) until Jacob's return. The

---

[3]Here and in 36:14 with the Samaritan Pentateuch, the LXX and the Syriac versions read "son of," not *bat*, "daughter of," as in the MT. This reading is probably due to a desire to harmonize these verses with 36:24 (cf. 36:20). The MT's more difficult reading of *bat* is interpreted in NIV by "granddaughter" without denying that Anah is the son of Zibeon.

[4]See R. North, "The Hivites," 56.

patriarchs of the holy people, who stake their future on God's promises, move toward the Promised Land (e.g., Abraham, 12:5; Isaac, 26:6; Jacob, 31:18), but the nonelect, who live by sight (i.e., focused on the social, political, and/or economic), not by faith, move away from it (e.g., Lot, 13:5–6, 11–12; Esau, 36:6).

7. the land . . . could not support them. This is due to God's blessings on both Esau and Jacob; paradoxically, Esau chooses to leave the land of blessing (cf. Gen. 13).

8. So Esau . . . settled in . . . Seir. With the migration of Esau from the Promised Land, the stage is now set for God to fulfill his promises to Israel.

Seir. Seir is the national territory of national Edom (see 25:25, 30; Deut. 2:5; Josh. 24:4).

Account 2 (36:9 – 43)[5]

Superscription (36:9)

9. Esau the father of the Edomites. Compare this with 36:8 "Esau (that is, Edom)." The superscription at 36:9 suggests an advance in status (i.e., from person to nation). However, the colophon to the first list of Esau's sons and chiefs (36:19) parallels that in 36:8.

Genealogy 2: The Sons and Chiefs of Esau to the Third Generation (36:10 – 14, 15 – 19)

10. These are the names. . . . Although most commentaries separate the lists of sons and chiefs, the text treats 36:10–19 as one unit. This is apparent from the colophon at 36:19 (see notes at 36:19).

Esau's sons. The following is a chart detailing Esau's twelve "grandsons":

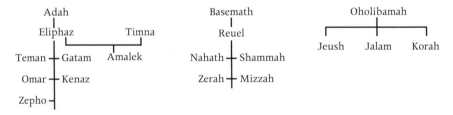

In all likelihood, the narrator has contrived this list in order to have twelve "grandsons" (see Literary Analysis above), counted as such by excluding Amalek the son of a concubine and by including the sons of Oholibamah. The sons of Oholibamah (wife of Esau) are placed on a line with the grandsons of Adah and Basemath by uniquely identifying her as a granddaughter, by placing her last, and by not listing her grandsons. Accordingly, the sequence of Esau's wives is given according to the descending number of

---

[5]See Literary Analysis above.

their respective offspring: five, four, three.[6] The list shows the transition of Esau from a family to a tribal arrangement.

11. Teman. Identified with Tawilan on the eastern outskirts of Petra, this important place name sometimes functions as a synecdoche for Edom (Jer. 49:7, 20; Ezek. 25:13; Amos 1:12; Obad. 9; Hab. 3:3).

Kenaz. See 15:19. The Kenizzites, although originally an Edomite clan, later identified themselves with the tribe of Judah.[7]

12. concubine . . . Amalek. As the offspring of a concubine, Amalek does not come under the umbrella of Edom's protected status with Israel (Deut. 23:8–9). The Amalekites are punished for their treacherous, unprovoked aggression against Israel during her Exodus journey from Egypt to the Promised Land (Ex. 17:8–16; cf. Judg. 3:13; 6:3–5, 33; 7:12; 10:12). Samuel commands Saul to annihilate the Amalekites in the area south of Telaim. When Saul spares Agag their king, Samuel himself slays him (1 Sam. 15). It remains for Mordecai, another descendant of Kish (1 Sam. 9:1; Esth. 2:5), to destroy Haman the Agagite (Esth. 3:1, 10; 8:3, 5; 9:23–25), presumably an Amalekite, as identified by Josephus.[8]

Amalek. The reference in Gen. 14:7 is an example of a later editorial description.

15. These were the chiefs. . . . The list is framed by the chiastic inclusio "chiefs of sons of Esau" (36:19) and "sons of Esau, their chiefs" (36:40). The following is a chart of the chiefs:

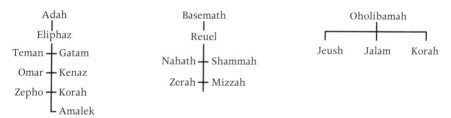

chiefs [ʾallûp]. These are "tribal chiefs."[9]

15–16. Kenaz . . . Gatam. The fifth son of Eliphaz is listed as his fourth chief, and his fourth son as his sixth chief (cf. 36:11).

16. Korah. Here Korah is listed as descendant of Eliphaz son of Adah, but in 36:14 as a son of Oholibamah. His inclusion boosts the number of Eliphaz's sons to seven (36:11–12). Probably, there are two descendants of Edom with this name.[10]

---

[6]Not all agree with this common analysis. See Hamilton, *Genesis 18–50*, 394; and Wilson, *Genealogy*, 171 n. 82.

[7]J. Milgrom, *Numbers* (JPS Torah Commentary; Philadelphia: Jewish Publication Society, 1990), excursus 31, 391–92.

[8]*Jewish Antiquities* 2.209.

[9]*HALOT*, 54.

[10]See Sasson, "A Genealogical 'Convention,'" 179.

19. These were the sons . . . and . . . chiefs. This colophon shows that the two lists of Esau's sons to the third generation (36:10–14) and of his chiefs (36:15–18) belong together (see also note at 36:10). By linking them, the narrator displays his interest both in the relationship of the Edomite clans and in their political organization and development.

Genealogy 3: The Sons and Chiefs of Esau, the Horites of Seir (36:20 – 30)

20–30. Lotan . . . chiefs. This segmented genealogy is bracketed by the inclusio listing seven identical Horite chiefs in Seir (36:20–21, 29–30). The genealogy presents the seven sons and one daughter of Seir the Horite (36:20–22) and extends to twenty sons of the third generation (36:21–28). The conclusion identifies the seven sons of the first generation as chiefs. Esau either destroys (see Deut. 2:22) or marries (see Gen. 36:20, 22, 25) these aboriginal inhabitants of Seir. The narrator again combines the segmented genealogy (36:20–28) with the political organization (36:29–30).

20. Horite. See 14:6.

22. Timna. She was Eliphaz's concubine (36:12).

24. Anah. See 36:2, 14.

hot springs [*yēmīm*]. This is the only anecdote in this genealogy. The meaning of *yēmīm* is uncertain. The Targum and Jewish tradition think it means "mules" (i.e., Anah was the first to crossbreed the horse and donkey). The Vulgate (and Syriac) has "hot springs," which may find support in Arabic *wamiha*, "to be hot." Others think it means "vipers," according to Arabic *yamm*, "spirits in the form of snakes."

28. Uz. See 10:23.

29–30. Lotan . . . Seir. See note at 36:20–30.

Genealogy 4: The Kings and Chiefs of Edom (36:31 – 43a)

31. These were the kings. This linear king list presents eight successive kings who reign in Edom before an Israelite reigns. The line of succession is related to their different capitals, suggesting an elective kingship, not a dynastic one. Perhaps they are chosen on the basis of their charisma, like the Hebrew judges who are contemporary with them.[11] It is the only known nondynastic king list among the national states of the ancient Near East,[12] raising the question whether Edom should be considered a nation at this time. This king list shows the transition from a tribal arrangement to designated kingship. One king, Hadad, is singled out for having defeated Midian in the country of Moab (36:35). This suggests the greatness of Israel under David, who will conquer Edom.

in Edom. This does not necessarily mean "over Edom."

---

[11]Cf. the use of "king" in Judg. 8:5, 12; 1 Sam. 14:47; 1 Kings 20:24.
[12]Its uniqueness suggests its historical credibility.

before any Israelite king reigned. It is unclear whether this means "reigned [in Israel]" (so the LXX) or "reigned [over Edom]." Actually, the two events are almost coterminous. Saul, Israel's first king, wages war against them (1 Sam. 14:47), and David subjugates them under his rule and puts garrisons throughout Edom (2 Sam. 8:13–14; 1 Kings 11:14–17).

32. Dinhabah. This is otherwise unidentified.

33. Bozrah. Modern Buseirah, approximately 20 miles (35 km) south-southeast of the Dead Sea and 35 miles (56 km) north of Petra, the name becomes a synecdoche for Edom as a whole (Isa. 34:6; 63:1; Jer. 49:13).

34. Temanites. See 36:11.

35. Hadad. This is the name of the Semitic storm god identified with Baal, the successor to El as the head of the Canaanite pantheon.

Midian. This refers to the five clans of Midian (see 25:1–6).

in the country of Moab. See Num. 22:1–7; 25:6–7.

Avith. This city is unidentified.

36. Masrekah. This is identified with Jebel el-Mushrak, about 22 miles (35 km) south-southwest of Maan.

37. Rehoboth on the river. Wadi el-Hesa is the natural border between Edom and Moab (see 10:11; 26:22).

38. Baal-Hanan. No capital is given.

39. Hadad. See 36:35. The Hadad who challenges Solomon may have been his grandson. If so, probably dynastic succession begins to prevail in Edom from the time Israel subjugates her.

Pau. This city is unidentified.

his wife's name. Hadad's wife's name, not his father's, is given, suggesting her distinguished ancestry.

40. These were the chiefs. These chiefs do not match the kings. Four,[13] however, are mentioned in the preceding two segmented genealogies. Perhaps these clan names, which are also names of their regions, represent administrative districts within the kingdom.

41. Elah. This is Elath on the Gulf of Aqabah, the southernmost boundary of Edom (Deut. 2:8).

Pinon. This is given as Punon in Num. 33:42–43. It is commonly identified with Feinan, a copper-mining area east of the Arabah, about 20 miles (35 km) south of the Dead Sea.

42. Mibzar. The word means "fortification." It may be the location Bozrah (cf. Ps. 108:10).

Colophon (36:43b – 37:1)

43. This was Esau. The death of Esau is not reported, perhaps because he has despised his birthright.

---

[13]Timna (36:40; cf. 36:12, 22), Oholibamah (36:41; cf. 36:2, 14, 18), Kenaz and Teman (36:42; cf. 36:11, 15).

37:1. Jacob lived. This unusual addition to the account of Esau's descendants contrasts with 36:8, "So Esau . . . settled in the hill country of Seir." It functions to show the geographical and spiritual divide between the brothers.

THEOLOGICAL REFLECTIONS ON BOOK 9 ————————

Covenant

God obligates himself to subjugate Edom to Israel (cf. 25:23; 27:29; 28:14; 35:11). These segmented genealogies of the twelve tribes of Esau and their conquest of the Horites at Mount Seir suggest the greatness of Edom. The inference is strengthened by the king list that precedes any king in Israel. The implication is that God raises up an even greater Israel able to rule Edom. More important, on the pages of sacred history, Israel's holy kingdom will rule over these representatives of human kingdoms (Num. 24:17; Obad. 21; Acts 15:17).

On its part, Israel commits itself to a life of faith in God and his promises. The first account of Esau's line (36:1–8), similar to the account of Ishmael (25:12–18), functions to show that Esau, like Ishmael, cuts himself off from the covenant line of blessing both by marrying Canaanite wives who were outside the family of Terah (36:2–3; cf. 24:3–4; 28:2; Deut. 7:3), and, like Lot, by leaving the Promised Land in search of greater prosperity (Gen. 36:7–8). To be sure, their possessions are too abundant for Jacob and Esau to remain together (36:7), but Esau could have migrated north to Shechem where there was room within the Promised Land (cf. 34:21). In contrast, Jacob visibly shows his faith by marrying from Terah's family, not the Canaanites, and by remaining committed to the land of the patriarchs.

Prophecy and Providence

The second account of Esau's line (36:9–40) demonstrates that God fulfills his promises. Edom does become a great nation, and, in spite of his greatness, the elder serves the younger (25:23; 27:39–40). If here God's word is true, it is reasonable to expect the great promises made to Abraham, Isaac, and Jacob to be fulfilled as well. If kings come from Esau's loins (36:31), how much more will Jesus Christ reign until his kingdom is coextensive with the creation (1 Cor. 15:24–28) and every tongue confesses him as Lord to the glory of God the Father (Phil. 2:11).

Typology

Jacob's children, who were exiles in Paddan Aram, by faith possess the land (Gen. 35:26), and Esau's children, who were born in it, walk away from it (36:6). Likewise, after Israel's exile in Babylon, the true seed return and possess the land. The church, the chosen today (1 Peter 2:9–10), is scattered abroad, but it will possess the Promised Land that never passes away (1 Peter 1:1–9).

Grace

In spite of Esau's unbelief, his descendants have a future. Under God they too have a story (cf. Deut. 23:7: "Do not abhor an Edomite, for he is your brother"). Today, in Christ, the remnant of Edom has been reconciled to his brother and has become a member of Christ's kingdom (Amos 9:4; Acts 15:16–18; Rev. 7:9).

THE ACCOUNT
OF JACOB'S DESCENDANTS
(37:2 – 50:26)

THEMES OF BOOK 10

The account of Jacob's line brings the book of Genesis to its climactic conclusion. The motifs of God's promises to Abraham to multiply his offspring, give them the land of Canaan, and bless the earth through them (Gen. 12:1–3) and God's covenant with Abraham and Sarah to bring forth kings through them (17:6, 16) escalate significantly in this account. It begins with twelve sons and concludes with seventy (a number of perfection and a microcosm of the nations; see Gen. 10) traveling to Egypt, where they become a nation. Even as they travel away, the land remains important to this covenant family. Jacob, though embalmed in Egypt, is buried in the Promised Land (50:4–14), and Joseph provides for the future exodus of his bones along with the covenant people to that land. In his benediction on his sons, Jacob prophesies that Judah will rule his brothers and the nations (see Gen. 10; 46:8–27). Joseph's rule over Egypt saves the world, authenticates the prophecy, and foreshadows that dominion.

Book 10 of Genesis primarily pertains to the transformation of Jacob's sons under Providence. More than a so-called "Joseph Story"—though it opens the curtain on Joseph as a teenager and closes it upon his death—this account concerns God's covenant dealings with the patriarchs and the establishment of his plans for the children of Israel. He keeps covenant by transforming all of Jacob's children, particularly Judah, to make them his worthy covenant partners. God uses Joseph to save the Israelites both physically, by giving them food, and spiritually, by separating them from the Canaanites and teaching them to love one another. Though the family's peace is shattered by their folly and rivalry, behind the scene God is working out their restoration (45:5–7), as foreshadowed by revelatory dreams and Israel's sojourn in Egypt (see 15:13; Ps. 105:23).

God's providence directs the covenant family's life. His providence is asserted in Joseph's double dream predicting his rule over the family. However, within this obvious theological frame, the story unfolds from a secular point of view (i.e., without angelic or other miraculous interventions). Instead, in retrospect everything happens at just the right time. Joseph providentially wastes time wandering around Shechem looking for his brothers when he happens to meet a man who had happened to overhear the brothers say where they would go. Without Joseph's delay, the Ishmaelite merchants would not have happened to come along at the right time. On the spur of the moment, it occurs to Judah to sell Joseph, so Joseph happens to end up in Egypt. The favoritism of a father, sibling rivalry culminating in selling the favorite into Egypt as a slave—"the crime of the century"[1]—and the cover-up all play a part in God's providence to save his elect! The narrative rejects humanism that believes in a God who "has no hands but ours to do the work." As Brueggemann asserts, "The narrative works its subtle way between a primitivism which believes too easily and a humanism which is embarrassed about faith."[2] Joseph summarizes the account's subtheme of God's providence in his famous insight: "You intended to harm me, but God intended it for good to accomplish what is now being done, the saving of many lives" (Gen. 50:20).

This account also addresses the question of who among the twelve sons will have the right of firstborn.[3] The obvious son to inherit this right is Reuben, the actual firstborn, but Reuben's foolish attempt to usurp Jacob's leadership by sleeping with his father's concubine backfires (cf. 2 Sam. 3:7–11; 16:21–22; 1 Kings 2:13–22), and he falls from Jacob's favor (Gen. 35:22; 49:3–4). Simeon and Levi, the next two sons in line, disqualify themselves by their rash overreaction to the rape of Dinah (Gen. 34; 49:5–7). The next in line is Judah, who emerges as the leader of the family and wins the right to rule his brothers (49:8–12; see "Characterization" below). The providential birth of Judah's twin sons, Zerah and Perez, confirms this choice. Zerah puts his hand out first and a red thread is tied around his wrist, but to everyone's surprise Perez comes out first. Likewise, Jacob had unnaturally assumed the position of first-

---

[1]Longacre, *Joseph*, 44.
[2]Brueggemann, *Genesis*, 294.
[3]This study is influenced by Goldin, "The Youngest Son," 27–44.

born over his twin brother Edom (i.e., "Red"). This preternatural similarity between the births of Judah's father and of his sons functions within the account as a sign that God once again chooses the younger son to rule over the older.

The narrative also develops the theme that God blesses those who bless Abraham and his seed, as seen in the divine blessings on Potiphar, who promotes Joseph (39:3), and on Pharaoh, who extends hospitality to Jacob's family (47:10–26).[4]

OUTLINE OF BOOK 10

---

[4]So B. A. McKenzie, "Jacob's Blessing on Pharaoh: An Interpretation of Gen 46:31–47:26," *WTJ* 45 (1983): 386–90.

LITERARY ANALYSIS OF BOOK 10 ————————————

Structure and Plot

The account of Jacob's line begins in Canaan and ends in Egypt, but with the hope of returning to the Promised Land. This account—between two lands—is driven by conflict with family and authorities of power, as illustrated below:

chs. 37–38   The family in conflict in Canaan
chs. 39–41   Joseph in conflict with imperial power in Egypt
chs. 42–44   The family in conflict in Canaan and Egypt
chs. 45–47   The family resolved in Egypt
chs. 48–50   The family blessed in Egypt, looking to Canaan

The account opens in Act 1 with the shattering of the covenant family's peace through internecine conflict (37:2–36) and with their intermarriage with the Canaanites (38:1–30). The rift between the sons and their father, begun in their births (29:31–30:24) and intensified in the rape of Dinah (34:1–31), now reaches it climax when the brothers sell Rachel's charismatic and hated son as a slave into Egypt. In Act 2 the setting shifts to Egypt, where Joseph must struggle with imperial power and triumph over it through his sterling character and charismatic ability to interpret dreams.

In Act 3 the setting shifts back and forth between the famine in Canaan and the food in Egypt. In this act Joseph, using his power of knowing and others' disadvantage of not knowing, struggles with his brothers and in cooperation with Providence refines them to love one another. The brothers' transformation begins when they confess their sin against Joseph (42:21–23, 28b) and culminates when Judah offers himself as a slave in Benjamin's stead for the sake of his father (44:33–34). The brothers' struggle ends when Joseph gives up his power of knowing, embraces them in tears, and relieves them of all guilt by his testimony that it was God, not they, who sent him into Egypt to save them (45:1–7). In the denouement to Act 3, Scene 4, the family migrates to Egypt, ending their struggle with the famine. At this point, as at the end of Book 8 (35:22b–26), the narrator presents a convenient genealogy of the seventy family members who migrate to Egypt.

Act 4, the denouement to the account and the transition to the Exodus, takes place in Egypt, where the family finds salvation and anticipates its future return to Canaan. The book draws to a close with the hope for the divine promises: (1) in Jacob's blessings upon his children, which look to their descendants as tribes settled in the land of promise with Judah ruling them and the world; (2) in Jacob's state funeral processing to Canaan; and (3) in Joseph's deathbed request for his bones to be carried to Canaan when the family is delivered from Egypt.

This plot is embroidered with the remarkable concentric pattern presented in the introduction to the commentary (see "The Alternating and Concentric patterns of the Ten *tôlᵉḏôṯ*" in the introduction). In addition to these seven concentric pairings, pivoting on the reconciliation of the brothers in Genesis 44–45, the story is characterized by many other pairings. Joseph has two escalating dreams (37:5–10), and he has escalating double trouble with his brothers (37:2–11, 12–36). Tamar's successful seduction of Judah is followed immediately with Potiphar's wife's unsuccessful seduction of Joseph (38:1–30; 39:1–23). Joseph interprets two sets of dreams: the two dreams of his prison mates (40:1–23) and the two dreams of Pharaoh (41:1–40). The brothers devise two plans to deal with him (37:21–27), and he devises two plans to deal with them (42:14–20). The brothers make two trips to Egypt (42:1–38; 43:1–34); Joseph's steward first tests the brothers and then Joseph himself tests Judah (44:1–13, 14–34); and the narrator twice tells of the family's migration there (46:1–27; 46:28–47:12). Jacob first blesses Joseph and his sons (48:1–22) and then all his own sons (49:1–28). The book closes pairing the deaths of two patriarchs, Jacob (49:33–50:13) and Joseph (50:22–26).[5] This striking symmetry and pairing in the account's style matches its theology; it subtly points to the unseen hand of Providence.

Characterization

Fox writes, "Initially the tale is one of family emotions, and it is in fact extreme emotions which give it a distinctive flavor. All the major characters are painfully expressive of their feelings, from the doting father to the spoiled son, from the malicious brothers to the lustful wife of Potifar, from the nostalgic adult Yosef to the grief-stricken old Yaakov. It is only through the subconscious medium of dreams, in three sets, that we are made to realize that a high plan is at work which will supersede the destructive forces of these emotions."[6]

Central in this story are the sons of Jacob, and of them Joseph and Judah. Reuben functions as a foil to both. After his incest with Bilhah (35:22), his leadership always seems ineffective (42:22, 37–38; 49:3–4; cf. 30:14–17). Perhaps he tries to win back his father's favor by his plan to rescue Joseph from his brothers' hands and "take him back to his father" (37:22); if so, this too backfires. Judah robs him of this opportunity to play the hero by getting his brothers to agree to his plan to sell Joseph into Egypt (37:26–27). Reuben is cowardly. Although he stands up to the murderous plan, he only hopes to rescue Joseph behind his brothers' backs. Instead, they sell him behind his back. After he learns his plan has failed, he cries out in hopeless desperation, "Where can I turn now?" He could have headed south and rescued Joseph from the merchants! Reuben's offer that Jacob kill his sons (Jacob's grandsons!) if he does not return Benjamin safely, which was also probably motivated by his desire to get back into his father's good graces, is "outrageous"[7] (42:37–38). By contrast, Judah offers himself.

---

[5]See J. Lichtig, *Storytelling in the Bible* (Jerusalem: Magnes, 1978), 142.
[6]Fox, *Beginning*, 152.
[7]Garrett, *Rethinking*, 174.

As the account begins, the heroes, Joseph and Judah, are immature and troubled. Joseph is a bratty talebearer. Judah is cold and spiritually insensitive. But in God's providential design, these men are refined through difficult trials.

Although Joseph begins immaturely, bragging and telling tales on his brothers, he is a noble character throughout most of the story (see also Literary Analysis of individual acts and scenes). Each scene in Egypt further depicts his virtues. He emerges as pious, loyal, discerning, and bold. Ultimately Pharaoh and his officials recognize the Spirit of God in him. His wisdom and discernment is most apparent as he tests and disciplines his brothers, retaining power of knowledge over them. He is also passionate, often weeping as he observes his siblings and then passionately embracing his brothers and his father when they are reunited.

Judah stands in glaring contrast to Joseph. While Joseph refuses immoral sex with Potiphar's wife and is forced to leave his identifying cloak behind in order to escape, Judah welcomes the invitation of a prostitute and willingly leaves his seal and staff as guarantee of a payment. Potiphar's wife accuses Joseph of making her a joke, but Judah actually becomes a joke. Yet Judah too is transformed by his suffering. His qualities of leadership, apparent throughout the story, are ultimately used to bring reconciliation to the family and to lead his father to safety in Egypt. In the end, Judah shows more sensitivity for his father than Joseph. His thoughtful and impassioned speech to Joseph allows Joseph to embrace his brothers and causes him finally to become concerned for his father's well-being (see also Literary Analysis of Act 1, Scene 2 and Act 3, Scene 3).

Dramatic Irony

This masterful tale is replete with dramatic irony. The reader often stands in a position of special knowledge, just as Joseph stands over his brothers (see also Literary Analysis of individual acts and scenes). From fermenting hatred to blood-soaked cloaks to a prostitute's veil to mistaken grief and mistaken identity, the narrator masterfully arranges the details so that the reader is often in the know but never fully aware of how the truth will emerge or how deliverance will be brought. This position of limited knowledge always draws the reader back to the omnipotence of the divine author who knows how he will bring about his good purposes.

BOOK 10, ACT 1:
INTRODUCTION TO THE DYSFUNCTIONAL FAMILY IN CANAAN (37:2 – 38:30)

LITERARY ANALYSIS OF BOOK 10, ACT 1 ——————

Janus

The reference in 37:1 to Jacob's living in the land of his fathers functions both to contrast Jacob's commitment to the Promised Land with Esau's migration to Mount Seir and to return to the main narrative of Genesis about the promised seed in the Promised Land.

Structure

The two scenes of this act take place in Canaan and occur at the same time (cf. 37:2; 38:1). Both show Jacob's family as dysfunctional. The first scene exhibits the brothers' rejection of Joseph and the second demonstrates Judah's rejection of his family.

Foreshadowing

The opening scene introduces Joseph as the central character in the rest of the account and sets the stage for God's providential deliverance of Joseph and of the nation through him. It also introduces Judah, who will emerge transformed by the end of Book 10, blessed to rule his brothers.

BOOK 10, ACT 1, SCENE 1:
JOSEPH REJECTED BY HIS BROTHERS AND SOLD INTO SLAVERY (37:2 – 36)

LITERARY ANALYSIS OF BOOK 10, ACT 1, SCENE 1 ———

Structure and Plot

The plot of this scene is driven by conflict. The scene establishes the devastating division of Jacob's household in two segments: Joseph hated by his brothers (37:2–11) and Joseph sold by his brothers (37:12–36). The first segment sets the stage for the horrendous crimes in the second by relating four brief events that capture the father's troubling favoritism toward Joseph and the terrible tension growing between Joseph and his brothers: Joseph tattles on his brothers (37:2); Jacob bestows a royal robe on Joseph (37:3–4); and Joseph declares his dual dreams (37:5–11). With the staccato presentation of these events, the tension mounts until its dramatic escalation in the second segment with the brothers' cry: "Here comes that dreamer! . . . Come now, let's kill him" (37:19–20). At the scene's peak the brothers trade Joseph to the Midianites for twenty shekels of silver. The denouement portrays a weak and wounded family: the impotent eldest son realizing his failed rescue plan, the hardened brothers deceitfully reporting Joseph's disappearance to Jacob, and Jacob grieving uncontrollably.

Key Words

The terrible irony of the conflict that drives this scene is thundered by the twenty-one uses of the word "brother"—fifteen times by the narrator (37:2, 4 [2x], 5, 8, 9, 10, 11, 12, 17, 19, 23, 26, 27, 30), three times by Jacob (37:10, 13, 14), once by Joseph (37:16) and twice by Judah (37:26, 27). The height of irony is Judah's words—"[let us] not lay our hands on him; after all, he is our brother (37:27)—for as Fox notes, "Shortly after Yosef, their '(own) flesh,' is sold into slavery and probable death."[8]

The key words that carry the story line of the mounting tension between the brothers in the first segment are "hate" (37:4, 5, 8) and "jealous" (37:11). This is an escalating hatred. The fourth generation of Abraham's seed enters the stage of sacred history outwardly united by flesh and blood and presumably by circumcision, but inwardly divided by faithless hatred, desiring to kill Joseph's God-given dream.

Characterization

No one escapes the narrator's censure. The vignettes chosen by the narrator portray each character's weaknesses. Jacob is a loving father to Joseph but utterly insensitive to his other sons (37:3–4). He seems completely unaware of the hatred he incites by his favoritism, as seen when, unsuspecting of mischief, he sends Joseph to the brothers who shortly before had slaughtered the Shechemites. Reuben is depicted as a failed leader. Although his plan to rescue Joseph from the pit shows him as a responsible older brother, he fails to accomplish his plan and stands feebly before the pit (37:29–30; see Exegetical Notes below). Judah is a coldly calculating leader: saving his brother from immediate death to profitably sell him into a living death (37:26–28). All the brothers, not just the concubines' sons, are driven by evil (37:2, 4, 8, 11, 20, 28, 31). Joseph is depicted as morally good but immature and bratty. His tattling, boasting, and robe parading inflames his brothers' hatred against him. As Sternberg states, "God's future agent and mouthpiece in Egypt could hardly make a worse impression on his first appearance: spoiled brat, talebearer, braggart."[9]

Foreshadowing

Joseph's destiny is sealed when he tells his dreams to his brothers. As in a Greek tragedy, the brothers make every effort to the kill the dreamer and his dreams. Joseph's arrival in Egypt at the end of the scene in retrospect is the first step in his exaltation.

---

[8]Fox, *Beginning*, 153.
[9]Sternberg, *Poetics*, 98.

Symbols

The story of Jacob features rocks; that of Joseph features robes (37:3, 23; 39:12; 41:14). These palpable objects symbolize something of the characters' social and/or spiritual situations.

Blanks and Gaps

In this scene the narrator blanks Joseph's emotions, perhaps to represent Joseph as a passive and helpless victim of his older brothers. In 42:21 he allows the brothers to express how Joseph felt and what he did.

EXEGETICAL NOTES TO BOOK 10, ACT 1, SCENE 1 ————

Superscription to Book 10 (37:2a)

2. This is the account of Jacob. This would be better translated, "This is the account of Jacob's line" (see 2:4). The account pertains to Jacob's sons, principally to Joseph and Judah (see Literary Analysis of Book 10).

Joseph Hated By His Brothers (37:2b – 11)

2b. Joseph. In the Hebrew text, the back-to-back conjunction of the names Jacob and Joseph—softened by the paragraph break in NIV—points to Joseph as the leading character of this account. He is the brother who will save the nation from extinction during the famine. The burials of Jacob and Joseph will close the book.

a young man . . . Zilpah. This is better translated, "Joseph at seventeen was tending the flock with his brothers. Now he was an assistant of the sons of Bilhah and the sons of Zilpah."

seventeen. Joseph lives with Jacob for the first seventeen years of his life, and Jacob lives with Joseph for the last seventeen of his life (47:28). Such symmetry reveals God's providence.

brothers. This is the key word of this scene (see Literary Analysis above).

sons of Bilhah and . . . Zilpah. This includes Dan, Naphtali, Gad, and Asher (30:4–13).

his father's wives. See 30:4 and note.

bad report. Although the narrator blanks the details, the word *report* (*dibbâ*) by itself denotes news slanted to damage the victim (see Prov. 10:18). Based on their previous behavior, it is likely the brothers were doing wrong, from which Joseph should rightly distance himself; however, Proverbs counsels that one should draw a veil over the transgressions of others (cf. Gen. 34:25; 35:22; 37:20; 38:1–26; Prov. 10:12; 11:12–13; 12:23). Such grace is a matter of life and death (e.g., Prov. 1:8–9). At the very least the young Joseph seems to be a pestering, tattletale little brother.

3. loved. Parental favoritism again provokes family discord, deception, and the disappearance of the preferred son, yet God's grace again uses the turmoil to achieve his good will (see 25:28). Nevertheless, the brothers' jealousy is wrong, and God will use Joseph to convert them.

more than any of his other sons. Jacob should have been aware of the damage his parents had inflicted upon the family by showing favoritism and working against each other.

because . . . his old age. Jacob did not love Joseph the most because he had loved Rachel more than Leah. Jacob is still kicking against primogeniture. Moreover, the birth of Joseph had signaled the changing fortune of Jacob's life (30:25).

richly ornamented robe. The word for "robe, tunic" is certain, but "richly ornamented" glosses the Hebrew *passîm,* which is of uncertain meaning because it occurs without further definition only in this chapter and in 2 Sam. 13:18–19. The "coat of many colors" is based on the LXX. "A long robe with sleeves" is based on Aquila's rendering and on the meaning of *pas* in postbiblical Hebrew and/or its connection with another Hebrew term meaning "extremity." Other proposals based on etymologies have not won a consensus. The richly ornamented robe is probably more than just a symbol of favoritism. The term is used elsewhere only for the garment of the princess Tamar (2 Sam. 13:18–19). Many commentators suggest it has something to do with royalty.[10] If so, it may foreshadow Joseph's royal rule in Egypt. By this regal apparel (see 2 Sam. 13:18) Jacob publicly designates Joseph as the ruler over the family. Jacob wants to pass on the rule to godly Joseph; in the end, he will pass it on to Judah.

4. could not speak a kind word to him. This could be translated, "could not so much as greet him." They behave like Cain, the seed of the Serpent (see Gen. 4).

5. dream. In the ancient Near East, dreams were a common means of divine communication and prediction; the brothers well understand its prophetic nature. This revelation at the beginning of the story shows God as the Director behind the entire account. This is the first dream in the Bible in which God does not speak (cf. 20:3; 28:12–15; 31:11, 24).[11] It forms a transition in the dominant means of God's revelation from theophany in Genesis 1–11, to dreams and visions in Genesis 12–35, and now to providence in Genesis 36–50. These three stages resemble the three parts of TaNaK (i.e., the OT). In the *Torah* ("Law"), God speaks to Moses in theophany; in the *Nebiim* ("Prophets"), he speaks in dreams and visions; and in the *Ketubim* ("Writings"), he works mostly through providence.

told it. Joseph is also responsible for his own downfall, bearing tales about his brothers (37:2) even before Jacob's preference for him is noted. He must gall them, insisting on telling his dreams to them and on repetitively sharing his second dream (37:9) even after they have begun to hate him "all

---

[10]For discussion, see Sarna, *Genesis,* 255.
[11]Hamilton, *Genesis 18–50,* 410.

the more." (37:8). Contrast his proud telling with Jacob's silent contemplation (37:11), yet by Joseph's telling the characters within the story one can learn of God's sovereignty.

they hated him all the more. This is not in the LXX.

7. binding sheaves. Pastoralists were also employed to gather the harvest.[12]

your sheaves gathered around mine. God has chosen Joseph as hero in this drama of redemption (see 20:3; 28:12; 42:6; 43:26, 28; 44:14).

bowed down. The prophecy is fulfilled in escalating stages: the brothers initially bowing once (42:6), then bowing twice to honor him (43:26, 28), and finally throwing themselves at his feet (50:18).

8. brothers said. As Sarna notes, "There is no record of an Israelite ever requiring the skill of an interpreter of dreams [contra 40:5–13; 41:1–33; Dan. 2, 4, 7]."[13]

rule. See Gen. 37:3; Deut. 33:16. Eventually, Joseph will receive the rights of the firstborn (see 1 Chron. 5:2), that is, the double portion of the inheritance, since Jacob adopts Joseph's two sons as his (see Gen. 48:5). The monarchy is coming into view even as it developed in Edom (see Gen. 36).

hated. Indirectly, they oppose the sovereign God who has given the revelation. They do not trust his program for them.

and what he had said. The Hebrew is literally, "and for his words" (i.e., not only for the information but also for the way he says it).

9. another dream. Dreams in this story come in pairs (see Gen. 40 and 41) to show that the matter is firmly decided by God and will come quickly (see 41:32). An isolated dream might be misinterpreted. Two dreams with the same meaning confirm the interpretation.

to his brothers. The LXX adds, "to his father and. . . ."

moon. This is probably a symbol of a mother (see. 37:10). Rachel had died when Joseph was about six or seven years old. Perhaps one of Jacob's other wives has become his surrogate mother.

10. When . . . brothers. This phrase is missing in the LXX.

rebuked. His dream threatens to reverse the social order of patriarchy.

your mother. See "moon" in 37:9.

will . . . I . . . actually come and bow down. Even Jacob has trouble overthrowing the priority of parents.

11. father kept the matter. Jacob may be mystified and confused, but he takes the dream seriously.

Joseph Sold by His Brothers (37:12 – 36)

12. his brothers had gone. The narrator blanks why Joseph is not with them.

---

[12]See Matthews, *Pastoral Nomadism.*
[13]Sarna, *Genesis*, 256.

Shechem. The rapes at Shechem occurred about two years earlier, when Joseph was about fifteen (see "Blanks, Gaps, and Logic" in Literary Analysis of Book 8, Act 3, Scene 1).

14. see if all is well with your brothers. Jacob has reason to worry about his sons at Shechem (see Gen. 34).

Valley of Hebron. Sarna notes, "One midrash sees in the extraordinary mention of this place a hint that the first stage in the fulfillment of the prophecy made to Abraham (15:13) is about to begin."[14]

Hebron . . . Shechem. Joseph traveled a distance of 50 miles (80 km).

15. a man. The anonymous man at Shechem provides the transition from the environment of a loving and doting father to that of hostile brothers simmering with rage. Joseph, alone and vulnerable, is safer with a Shechemite than with his brothers.

wandering around. Even wandering around in a field and a chance overhearing are part of God's providence. By this delay, Joseph's arrival times perfectly with the merchants' appearance (see 37:21–28; see Theological Reflections below).

16. I'm looking for my brothers. The narrator offers a moment of dramatic irony. This statement epitomizes Joseph's career. Read in retrospect, Joseph is the opposite of Cain (see 4:9) and has the qualities of leadership.

17. I heard. This is yet another providential act.

Dothan. Dothan was 13 miles (21 km) northwest of Shechem.

19. Here comes that dreamer! They identify him only by their resentment.

20. let's kill him. The same murderous word is used in 4:8. Brueggemann says, "the future is a deathly threat. But it can be resisted! They resolve to stop it."[15]

throw him . . . and say. After their hasty violence, the plan emerges gradually (cf. 37:31).

cisterns. Archaeologists have found a large number of cisterns all over Israel. They are large bottle-shaped pits hewn out of rock for retaining water. They range from 6 to 20 feet in depth. A dried-out cistern makes an excellent dungeon (cf. Gen. 40:15; Jer. 38:6).

21. Reuben. See "Characterization" in Literary Analysis of Book 10. As the eldest brother, he takes over the role of the father while the brothers are away (see 37:13–14). After his incest with Bilhah (35:22), his leadership always seems ineffective. Dumping Joseph's body in the pit leaves the problem unresolved.

he tried to rescue him. Better, "he came to his rescue."

Let's not take his life. This is better translated, "We must not take his life."

in the desert [midbār]. This is best translated, "in the pasture land."[16] In this area between villages, no one will hear Joseph's cries (see 42:21).

---

[14]Ibid., 258.

[15]Brueggemann, *Genesis*, 303.

[16]The Hebrew term *midbār* often means desert, but there are no deserts in the location cited; *midbār* can also designate pasture lands (*HALOT*, 547).

23. stripped. They dethroned the royal son (see 37:3) and exposed him to the chilly cistern.

24. empty . . . no water. This detail explains why Joseph does not drown. In addition, he has neither food nor drink and so could die of thirst.

25. they . . . meal. In callous indifference to their brother's cries in the bare dungeon (cf. 42:21), they enjoy a meal! Their next meal in Joseph's presence will be with Joseph at the head table (43:32–34).

Ishmaelites. Ishmaelites (see also 37:27–28; 39:1) and Midianites (37:28, 36) are alternate designations for the same group of traders (see 39:1; esp. Judg. 8:24). The descendants of Midian from Keturah and of Ishmael from Sarah may have intermarried (see 25:2, 17–18; 29:9).[17]

Gilead. See 31:21.

26. Judah. See "Characterization" in Literary Analysis of Book 10. Rather than Reuben, Judah emerges as the leader. His speech to his brothers at the climax of this scene stands in contrast to the ineffective speeches of Reuben before (37:21–22) and after (37:30).

kill our brother. Joseph could be killed either by violence or by leaving him in the cistern to die of exposure and/or starvation.

27. sell him. Kidnapping is a capital offense (see Ex. 21:16; Deut. 24:7). His cold and calculating plan only substitutes one evil for another.

our hands. Behind the scene is the hand of God (see 45:5; Ps. 105:17).

after all, he is our brother. The terrible irony seems lost on him (see Literary Analysis above).

28. Midianites. See "Ishmaelites" above.

pulled Joseph . . . sold him . . . took him. The Hebrew literally reads, "pulled Joseph . . . sold Joseph . . . took Joseph." "The bell solemnly tolls for Joseph," says Longacre.[18] The exceptional threefold repetition of his name "marks an extremely important and providential event in the family of Jacob and the history of the embryonic nation."[19]

twenty shekels. See "Historicity and Literary Genre" in the introduction.

Egypt. The sale of Asiatic slaves is well documented in Egyptian texts from about the time of Joseph. King Amen-em-het III (+ 1800 B.C.) provides for the disposal of four Asian slaves he received as a gift from his brother. A papyrus dated 1740 B.C. contains an inventory of thirty-seven Asiatic slaves out of ninety-five slaves.

30. Where can I turn. The feeble leader Reuben cannot come up with a plan. He should have turned first to his brothers to confront them and then pursued Joseph to rescue him (see 37:21). Now he must turn away from his father's face, to whom he owes an accounting.

---

[17]Hamilton thinks *Ishmaelite* here is not an ethnic term but "a catchall term for nomadic travelers." *Midianite* would be the ethnic term (*Genesis 18–50*, 423).

[18]Longacre, *Joseph*, 44.

[19]Ibid., 30.

31. robe . . . goat. Jacob's earlier deceptions have a terrible price. As Jacob deceived his father with goat skins and Esau's clothing (see 27:9, 16), he will now be deceived with goat's blood and his son's cloak.

32. whether it is your son's. The language continually betrays the divisions. They speak not of their brother but of Jacob's son.

33. ferocious animal. It is actually the work of the ferocity of anger and jealousy of Jacob's heartless sons.

34. sackcloth and mourned. His display of grief is much greater than Reuben's (see 37:30).

35. to comfort him. This is hypocrisy on the part of his sons.

to the grave. The Hebrew refers to Sheol; see Theological Reflections below.

36. Meanwhile. This verse sets the stage for Act 2.

sold. See Amos 1:6–7.

Potiphar. This is a shortened form of the Egyptian name "Potiphera" (41:45), meaning "he whom Ra (the sun-god) has given." The name, which cannot be dated before the thirteenth century B.C., may be a modernization of an earlier form.

THEOLOGICAL REFLECTIONS ON
BOOK 10, ACT 1, SCENE 1 —————————————————

Providence

God reveals his sovereignty through both dreams and providence (see "Themes of Book 10"). The message of dreams (predestination) is a "hard" word for God's sovereignty. Providence, as seen among other things in *lex talionis,* is a "soft" word.[20]

Dreams

Once again the revelation of God begins an account, this time predicting the rule of Joseph over his family (see 37:5, 8–9 in Exegetical Notes). The dreams given to Joseph will be fulfilled in Genesis 42–47. These certain revelations display the sovereignty of the Lord. God's sovereignty is also apparent in the dreams to the Egyptian prisoners and to Pharaoh. These sets of two dreams declare the Lord's predestination both in creation and in human affairs.

Election

It isn't just Jacob's favoritism or Joseph's manner that the brothers hate. It is the dream. Many today, like the brothers, are offended by the doctrine of God's election (see Rom. 9:10–24). God deals justly with all, but he has mercy on some (Matt. 20:1–16). The moral of his election is ambiguous; his

---

[20]Brueggemann, *Genesis,* 293.

choice of Joseph to rule promotes discord. The brothers have to learn to accept his election to kingship.

Lex Talionis

In God's sovereign justice, people reap consequences for their evil deeds. Jacob's crimes against Esau are matched by his sons' crimes against him. As he worked deception against Esau with a goat and a cloak, his sons' use a goat and cloak to deceive him. As Rebekah's desire to advantage Jacob and to disadvantage Esau led to Esau's desire to murder Jacob, so Jacob's desire to advantage Joseph leads to the brothers' desire to murder Joseph. God bestows great mercy upon Jacob, but he does not forego punishing Jacob's misdeeds.

Transformation

God makes the most surprising choices. Here he chooses a family divided by favoritism, immaturity, jealousy, and vengeance. Yet he will bring about his purposes through them and in the process will bring about their radical transformation and restoration. The road to kingship in Israel is much more tortuous than in Edom; the elect must be redeemed before they rule.

Grave

The Hebrew term for the grave is *šeʾōl*, which occurs sixty-six times in the Old Testament. Only eight of the occurrences are in prose. The prepositions frequently accompanying it indicate that it is a place below the earth, "the underworld." On the physical level it refers to the grave; on the metaphysical, to the realm of death as distinct from the realm of life. The emphasis is on the awfulness of death in comparison to life. Old Testament poets use rich and varied figures of speech in connection with the grave. It has a "mouth" (Ps. 141:7), which it "enlarges" (Isa. 5:14), and is "never satisfied" (Prov. 27:20; 30:16). It is so powerful that none escapes its grip (Ps. 89:48), and no one can redeem another from it (Hos. 13:14; cf. Ps. 49:7). It is likened to a prison with bars (Job 17:16). Here corruption is the father and the worm the mother and sister (Job 17:13–16). It is a land of no return (Job 7:9); an abode where socioeconomic distinctions cease. Rich and poor (Job 3:18–19), righteous and wicked (Job 3:17), wise and fools (Ps 49:10), and Israelite and foreigner lie together here. It is a land of silence (Ps. 94:17), darkness (13:3), weakness and oblivion (88:10–18). One errs to take such figurative descriptions of the grave as literal depictions of an intermediate state. Other texts teach the immortality of the saint (Job 19:26–27; Ps. 49:15; Prov. 10:2; 12:28; 14:32), a doctrine brought into full light through the resurrection of Jesus Christ from the dead (2 Tim. 1:10).

BOOK 10, ACT 1, SCENE 2: JUDAH SINS AGAINST TAMAR AND BEGETS TWINS (38:1–30)

LITERARY ANALYSIS OF BOOK 10, ACT 1, SCENE 2 ————

Structure and Plot

Where a weak and divided family ends Scene 1, the opening of Scene 2, with Judah's departure from the family to live among the Canaanites, only confirms the family's impoverished state. The plot of Scene 1 was driven by the tension of internecine strife that threatened to disintegrate the covenant family. In Scene 2 Judah exposes the family to even greater external threat by intermarrying with the Canaanites. This foolishness and his subsequent unrighteous acts create the plot tension for Scene 2. Who will rescue this family? As usual, hope and transformation is brought through an unconventional source—here, the Canaanite woman Tamar. The scene marks the beginning of Judah's transformation when he declares of Tamar, "She is righteous, not I" (lit., 38:26). The scene peaks when Tamar gives birth to twins, the sign of Judah's prominence over his brothers (see below, "Coherence with the Account of Jacob's Line").

This scene, set among the Canaanites of Adullam, can be divided into two segments, marked by the chronological notices "at that time" (38:1) and "after a long time" (38:12). The first segment pertains to Judah's foolish union with Canaanites, an unholy union that becomes more entangled when he secures Tamar as a bride for his wicked sons and then behaves dishonorably towards her. The second segment pertains to his unrighteous begetting of offspring by her. His Canaanite friend, Hirah the Adullamite, is involved in both follies.

The rapid presentation of multiple events in the first segment sets the stage for the crucial events of the second. The narrative time reflects this division: segment one covering a period of about twenty years, segment two covering a period of less than a year. Each concerns the birth of sons to Judah: Judah's three sons, Er, Onan, and Shelah, by the Canaanite daughter of Shua (38:1–11), and Judah's twins, Perez and Zerah, by his daughter-in-law Tamar (38:12–30).

During the same period of time that Judah is begetting children by his Canaanite wife, Joseph is begetting children by his Egyptian wife (41:50–52).

Coherence with the Account of Jacob's Line

The scene abruptly interrupts the main narrative that traces the sale of Joseph into Egypt (cf. 37:36 with 39:1). However, in the concentric pattern that unifies Book 10, this scene matches Jacob's blessing on Judah as ruler over his brothers (see "The Alternating and Concentric patterns of the Ten *tôlᵉḏôt*" in the introduction). In fact, Judah's prominence in Gen. 37:26–27 foreshadowed his rise to prominence in this scene. A key to this story is the remarkable similarity between the births of Perez and Zerah and of Jacob and Esau. Both births involve twins; in both the younger thrusts ahead of the elder and displaces him; and in both the one who is naturally expected to get the birthright, but loses it, is associated with red: red stew in the case of Esau and a red string in the case of Zerah. Judah Goldin argues convincingly that this striking similarity between the births of Judah's parents and of his sons shows that in the miraculous history of the covenant people a special divine election rests on Judah and his offspring.[21] Perez is like his grandfather Jacob, the one who strives and prevails.

As Robert Alter has demonstrated, this scene also coheres with the preceding and following scenes.[22] Scenes 1 and 2 have significant connections. Judah reaps a deception by his daughter-in-law matching his deception of his father (cf. 38:25–26 with 37:32–33). Once again a goat and clothes facilitate the deception (cf. 37:31; 38:14, 17, 20). In both scenes, as Fox notes, "a man is asked to 'recognize' objects [cf. 37:32–33; 38:25–26] and again a brother (this time a dead one) is betrayed."[23] Hamilton notes the fraternal rivalry in both scenes: "Onan feels about Er as Joseph's brothers felt about him."[24]

Scene 2 also bears meaningful connections to Scene 1 of Act 2. "Go down" links both Judah's descent and Joseph's (38:1; 39:1). There is delicious irony between these scenes. Promiscuous Judah grasps Tamar's seductive offer and expands his family; chaste Joseph resists Potiphar's wife's seductive demand and ends up in an undeserved dungeon. In both scenes the woman retains tokens of the man to produce condemning evidence. In the first three scenes of this account, personal possessions (cloak, cylinder seal and staff, and cloak) are used as factual evidence of a crime.

Providence also arranges an important alignment in the chronology of the fate of Jacob's two leading sons. A span of over twenty years expires between Joseph's rise to power and his encounter with his brothers during the famine. He is seventeen when he enters Egypt (37:2), and thirteen years later he rules Egypt with seven years of plenty (41:46–47). After the famine becomes severe, Judah again encounters Joseph (42:1–7), and after two years of famine the whole family arrives (45:6). Judah's story begins at the time he sells Joseph into Egypt. Assuming Judah begets his children immediately, Er is about eighteen when he dies. If Tamar waits a year for Shelah, the twins are born about twenty-one years after Judah's original marriage.[25] This

---

[21]Goldin, "Youngest Son," 27–44.

[22]Alter, *Narrative*, 3–12; see also U. Cassuto, "The Story of Tamar and Judah," in *Biblical and Oriental Studies*, vol. 1, trans. I. Abraham (Jerusalem: Magnes, 1973), 29–40.

[23]Fox, *Beginning*, 159. Hamilton (*Genesis 18–50*, 432) cites *Gen. Rabbah* 84:11–12: "The Holy One, Praised be He, said to Judah, 'You deceived your father with a kid. By your life Tamar will deceive you with a kid.' . . . The Holy One, Praised be He, said to Judah, 'You said to your father, *hakker-naʾ*. By your life Tamar will say to you, '*hakker-naʾ*.'"

[24]Hamilton, *Genesis 18–50*, 432.

[25]The narrator's mention of the sons of Perez among those who descended into Egypt with Jacob in 46:12 must reflect the same historical freedom he exercises when he lists Benjamin among the brothers born in Paddan Aram in 35:22b–26.

means that Judah's confession of wrong against Tamar occurs near the same time as the confession of all the brothers in their wrong against Joseph (cf. 38:26 with 42:21). Perhaps Judah's confession regarding Tamar prepares him for the other. This scene provides an essential piece in the characterization of Judah, whose greater Son will rule the universe.

Characterization

The narrator masterfully utilizes action, comparison, gapping, and dialogue (internal and spoken) to create a picture of the selfish and visionless Judah prior to his transformation (see also Theological Reflections). This characterization is encapsulated in Judah's own declaration "She [Tamar] is righteous, not I" (lit., 38:26). If Joseph steps onto the pages of sacred history as a bratty do-gooder, Judah enters as a slave trader who has turned his back on Abraham's God-given vision. He is callous toward his father and cynical about the covenant family. The narrator's report that he has entered intimate relationships with Canaanites speaks volumes (cf. 24:3; 27:46–28:8; 34:1). He marries a Canaanite woman, and his best friend is Hirah, a savoir faire Canaanite, not his brothers (38:1, 20–22). He also fails as a father. He raises two sons whom God declares wicked (38:7, 10), and there is no reason to think Shelah will differ from them. Judah's internal speech reveals him irreligious (38:11). He sees no connection between the sins and deaths of his sons; instead, he superstitiously blames Tamar. He is a profane fornicator who is quick to condemn another for the same crime. His immorality contrasts sharply with Joseph's behavior in Potiphar's house (37:26; 39:1–20). His lack of grief over the loss of his sons glaringly contrasts with Jacob's inconsolable grief over the loss of Joseph. The connections between Tamar's deception of Judah and Judah's deception of Jacob also reinforce the narrator's judgment. However, the events of this scene will spark Judah's transformation. His confession of failure (38:26) not only captures his flawed character but marks the beginning of his transformation (see Theological Reflections below and ch. 44).

Although the narrator describes little of Tamar's character development, she is the heroine of this scene. She rejects her Canaanite father's house and remains loyal to Judah. Presumably she could have married a Canaanite man or have become a cult prostitute in a Canaanite temple, but like Ruth, who will choose her flawed Israelite family over her Moabite roots, Tamar remains true to her Israelite family in spite of its glaring failures and becomes absorbed into it. Normally Canaanite women absorb Israelite men into their debased culture (Deut. 7:1, 3). In that light, her deception as a Canaanite prostitute to snare her widowed father-in-law into fathering covenant seed should be evaluated as a daring act of faith. Her "faithful deception" wins her a place in the messianic lineage along with the "faithful treachery" of Rahab. In her daring ruse she acts quickly, decisively, and shrewdly, qualities also commendable in a king.

Scenic Depiction

Judah's geographical descent from Hebron's heights (see 35:27) to Canaan's lowlands mirrors his spiritual condition (cf. Deut. 33:7). Judah dwells in the Promised Land, but instead of being a blessing in it, he conforms to the world and life view of those whom his ancestors despised and whom his progeny is destined to dispossess. In his compromised position he becomes a joke, like Lot in Sodom.

Blanks and Gaps

The narrator blanks Er's sin and Judah's relationship to his anonymous wife aside from sex. He also gaps Judah's remorse over the death of his sons, an absence that contrasts with Jacob's agonized mourning. As a result, Judah comes off as concerned only with sex and offspring.

EXEGETICAL NOTES TO BOOK 10, ACT 1, SCENE 2 ———

Judah's Descent to the Canaanites: Three Sons by the Daughter of Shua (38:1 – 11)

This segment can be divided in two: Judah's marriage to the daughter of the Canaanite Shua and Judah's fathering of three sons (38:1–5); and the arranged marriages of his three sons to Tamar (38:6–11).

1. At that time, Judah left his brothers. The narrator chronologically connects the sale of Joseph to Judah's intermarriage with the Canaanites. The events of this scene cover a span of approximately twenty-two years, twenty of which are summarized in the first eleven verses (see Literary Analysis above).

went down. See "Scenic Depiction" in Literary Analysis above. The expression "went down" also creates a link with the next scene (cf. 39:1).

Adullam. Tell esh-Sheikh Madhkur, about 3 miles (5 kilometers) southwest of Bethlehem (which is visible on the central ridge above it), was a royal Canaanite city at the time of Joshua (see Josh. 12:15) and may have already been so at the time of Judah.

2. met . . . married. The Hebrew literally says, "saw . . . took." "Took" by itself is the normal expression for "marry" (cf. Gen. 4:19; 11:29). The conjunction of the two verbs has overtones of lust (3:6; 6:2; 12:15; 34:2).

daughter of . . . Shua. She remains nameless in Scripture.

Canaanite. See 9:26; 12:1; 24:3; 28:1, 8; and Literary Analysis above. Hamilton comments, "One gets the distinct impression that ever since the Dinah incident (chap. 34) Jacob has less and less control over the behavior of his family."[26] Simeon will also marry a Canaanite (46:10) and Joseph an Egyptian (41:45). With regard to Judah and Simeon, the very thing that

---

[26]Hamilton, *Genesis 18–50*, 433.

Abraham and Isaac feared for their sons and that contributed to the rejection of Esau, intermarrying with the daughters of the land, Jacob's sons are doing. Possibly one reason God will lead the family into Egypt is to prevent their assimilation with the Canaanites.

lay with her. As Hamilton aptly states it, "Their relationship to each other is conveyed by six verbs: three for him (he meets her, marries her, and has intercourse with her, v. 2), and three for her (she conceives, bears a son, and names the child, v. 3). Judah and his wife relate sexually, but the text says nothing else about their relations."[27]

3. who was named. Several Hebrew manuscripts, one of the Targums, and the Samaritan Pentateuch read "she named."

Er. Wenham comments that the name of this son, ʿēr, spells "evil" (rʿ) backward (see 38:7).[28]

5. Kezib. This place elsewhere is called Aczib and Cozeba. It is located southwest of Adullam, though its precise modern location is controversial (see Mic. 1:14).[29] The town Kezib (Aczib) was later settled by a Shelatine clan (1 Chron. 4:21–22).

6. Tamar. This is probably a Canaanite name meaning "palm tree."

7. The LORD put him to death. Though not stated, his sin(s) must have been grave (cf. 6:5–8; 18:20–21). This is the first text to state explicitly that God put someone to death.[30]

8. Judah said. Having given her to Er, Judah was responsible for her.

duty to her as a brother-in-law. The law forbade marriage between a man and his brother's wife (Lev. 18:16; 20:21). However, if a brother died childless, then according to ancient Near Eastern and biblical laws (Deut. 25:5–6; Ruth 4:5, 10, 17), a brother of the deceased should marry her in order to raise up seed in the name of the brother and so give the deceased social immortality. The practice continued into the time of Jesus (Matt. 22:23–30; Mark 12:18–25; Luke 20:27–35).

offspring. This is a key term in this book.

9. offspring would not be his. With only one brother left, he would have inherited half of his father's estate. He does not wish to diminish the inheritance of his own offspring (see Ruth 4:6).[31]

whenever he lay with his brother's wife. He has intercourse with her but prevents conception. He abuses familial loyalty for his own sensuality.[32]

semen on the ground. His sensual and selfish act denies his brother the possibility of blessing the earth through progeny reckoned as his (cf. 17:6,

[27]Ibid.
[28]Wenham, *Genesis 16–50*, 366.
[29]Y. Aharoni reports an ambiguous reading of *lbyt ʾkzy[b]* on an ostracon ("Trial Excavation in the 'Solar Shrine' at Lachish," *IEJ* 18 [1968]: 168).
[30]Hamilton, *Genesis 18–50*, 434.
[31]See E. W. Davies, "Inheritance Rights and the Hebrew Levirate Marriage," *VT* 31 (1981): 257–58.
[32]For the distinction between coitus interruptus and masturbation, see E. Ullendorff, "The Bawdy Bible," *BSOAS* 42 (1979): 434.

20; 28:3; 35:11). As Simeon and Levi desecrated circumcision (see 34:15 and note), Onan desecrates a sacred duty. He abuses his brother and his wife (see 4:9; cf. Ruth 4:5).

10. wicked. See 38:7.

he put him to death. The Lord regards the abuse of levirate marriage a capital offense.

11. Live as a widow in your father's house. See Lev. 22:13; Ruth 1:8. Judah's response is also wicked. Judah, with his dignity and status, is expected to care for a defenseless widow. He violates his daughter-in-law by shirking his responsibilities, denying her right to well-being and status in the community, and shifting her problems onto others. Nevertheless, he still retains authority over her (see 38:24).

until my son Shelah. Judah's thoughts reveal this to be a lie. He has no intention of giving his youngest son to her.

For he thought. Judah, failing to perceive God's judgment on his folly and on his wicked sons, superstitiously regards Tamar as a wife who brings misfortune (see Literary Analysis above).

Judah's Deception by Tamar; His Twins by Tamar (38:12–30)

12. After a long time. The text literally reads, "After many days." Other chronological notices allow no more than a year (see Literary Analysis). The point is that enough time has elapsed for Tamar to know that Judah is acting deceptively.

died. Death plagues Judah. The notice explains, though not excuses, why he consorts with a prostitute (cf. 1 Cor. 7:2–6). It also defends Tamar's actions against the possible accusation of threatening Judah's home (cf. Matt. 19:9).

recovered from his grief. Contrast Judah with Tamar, who is still dressed as a widow from the much earlier deaths of her husbands (Gen. 38:14).

Timnah. This is either Tell el-Batashi (cf. Josh. 15:10; 19:43) in the territory of Dan or Khirbet Tibneh about 2 miles (3 kilometers) south-southwest of Beth-shemesh (cf. Josh. 15:57).

shearing his sheep. This was usually a time for partying and celebration (cf. 1 Sam. 25:11, 36; 2 Sam. 13:23, 28).

13. When Tamar was told. Though she plays on Judah's vice, Scripture commends her for her daring ruse to redress Judah's wrong and to build up the family (see Literary Analysis; 38:26; Ruth 4:12).

14. she took off. Her demand that her father-in-law father a child by her, since he refuses to give her his son, is probably consistent with accepted ethical practices at her time. Both Hittite (fourteenth–thirteenth century B.C.) and Middle Assyrian laws legislated that if a married man died and his brother also died, then "his father shall take her. . . . There shall be no punishment."[33] The Mosaic law did not go this far, but her actions are not inconsistent with the principle: "[the deceased brother's] widow must not marry outside the family" (Deut. 5:5).

widow's clothes. The mode is unknown. She probably intended to wear them until Shelah was given to her. Mourning clothes also play a role in the Joseph story (37:34).

covered herself with a veil. As the text explains, Tamar did this to hide her identity. According to a Middle Assyrian law (ca. 1200 B.C.), the daughters, wives, and concubines of free Assyrian males, as well as sacred prostitutes, must be veiled in public, but a whore must not veil herself. The penalty for the whore was severe: "they shall flog her fifty (times) with staves (and) pour pitch on her head."[34] If these laws were applicable in Canaan five hundred years earlier—a questionable assumption—Hirah calls her a shrine prostitute because her veil so identifies her. The narrator, however, makes no distinction. Whether dressed as a shrine prostitute or not, she is playing the part of a whore (see 38:15, 21; Hos. 4:14).

to disguise herself.[35] Deceptive clothing also plays a role in the Joseph story (cf. 37:31–33).

For she saw. The narrator's sympathy lies with Tamar. She meets trickery with trickery.

Shelah. He is not mentioned again, but his clan is in Num. 26:20; 1 Chron. 4:21.

as his wife. To her credit, she is loyal to her deceased husband, trying to raise up seed for him. She has not married another Canaanite.

15. prostitute [$z\bar{o}n\hat{a}$]. The Hebrew terms signifies a whore in contradistinction to a shrine prostitute ($q^e\underline{d}\bar{e}\check{s}\hat{a}$, 38:21; cf. Lev. 20:10; Deut. 22:22).

16. Not realizing. The narrator takes pains to explain that Judah is not consciously committing incest and adultery (cf. Lev. 18:15),[36] assuring the legitimacy of these births. Note that "he did not sleep with her again" (38:26).

Come now, let me sleep with you. In contrast to Tamar, Judah is a profane fornicator.

17. I'll send you. Judah obviously did not anticipate hiring a prostitute; he is acting on an impulse. This is "another example of the biblical motif of God using human frailty for His own purposes."[37]

a young goat. Compare Judg. 15:1; see also Literary Analysis above; 27:9–10, 16; 37:31.

give me something as a pledge. See Ex. 22:26; Deut. 24:6, 10–13; Prov. 6:1; Amos 2:7–8. Providence plays into the hands of her quick wit.

---

[33]*ANET*, 196, no. 193; cf. 182, no. 33.
[34]Ibid., 183, no. 40.
[35]On the basis of Semitic cognates and parallels in some Dead Sea Scrolls, some think it means "and she perfumed herself" (see *HALOT*, 836).
[36]See A. Phillips, "Another Example of Family Law," *VT* 30 (1980): 243.
[37]Sarna, *Genesis*, 268.

18. Your seal and its cord. The small, ornamented cylinder seal, made of stone or metal and worn on a cord around the neck, was the insignia of a prominent man. When it was rolled across soft clay, such as the legitimating clay seal on a document, the resulting impression identified the owner and/or sender of the object.[38]

staff. This symbol of authority had his mark of ownership etched on top of it. Scepter heads incised with names have been found throughout the ancient Near East.[39] Sarna notes, "Herodotus (I.195) reports that every Babylonian carried a seal and a stick with a carved ornamented top. Whether the same custom prevailed in Canaan in an earlier age is not known."[40]

20. sent the young goat. He has the honor to keep his obligation to a prostitute but not to his daughter-in-law!

by his friend. Is he now too ashamed to be found in a whore's company?

21. shrine prostitute [$q^e\underline{d}\bar{e}\check{s}\hat{a}$]. This is a different designation than Judah's (see 38:15). Judah's Canaanite friend elevates her social status from a common whore to a shrine prostitute. In any case, the notice shows the degradation of the Canaanite culture and the danger of intermarriage with them (see note at 38:15). The Lord detests such folk (Deut. 23:18).

23. we will become a laughingstock. Judah is like a reputable gentleman who unwittingly "loses" his credit card in a brothel. The prostitute running off with his valuable possessions makes him look like a fool for entrusting them to her. Only his reputation concerns him.

24. Judah was told. Judah leaps at the hearsay evidence to get rid of his bothersome daughter-in-law.

prostitution. This word can signify any immoral sexual act. Since she is betrothed to Shelah, it is wrong for her to have sex with anyone else.

Judah said. Though Tamar lives in her father's house, Judah still has legal authority over her. He is quick to condemn others for crimes he has also committed.

Bring her out. Presumably, Tamar is to be brought to the city gate (see Deut. 22:21, 24).

burned to death. In the Mosaic law, adultery is punishable by death (Lev. 20:10; Deut. 22:22). For some sex crimes, the law prescribes public stoning (Deut. 22:21, 24; Ezek. 16:40); for others, burning (Lev. 20:14; 21:9). On the basis of Josh. 7:15, 25, Sarna argues that they were first stoned and then burned.[41]

25. recognize. Again, the deceiver is deceived (cf. 37:33).

26. She is more righteous than I. This is better translated, "She is righteous, not I" (cf. 1 Sam. 24:17 [Heb. 18]).[42] Tamar is a heroine in Israel

---

[38]Cf. *ANEP*, 219–23, nos. 672–706.

[39]See ibid., 6, no. 14; 134, no. 383; 153, no. 445; 174, no. 513; 179, no. 530; 192, no. 576; 199, no 609.

[40]Sarna, *Genesis*, 269.

[41]Ibid., 270.

[42]A comparison of exclusion (*IBHS*, §14.4e).

because she risks her life for family fidelity. Judah is also being prepared for his restoration (see Gen. 44; 49:8–12). Confronted with his failure and deception, he owns up to his sin. As when the formerly self-righteous David is confronted with the sin of fathering an illegitimate child and owns up to it (2 Sam. 11:1–12:13), so also Judah's true character emerges with his confession. We may assume that, just as the Lord forgives the repentant David, he also forgives Judah (cf. Ps. 51).

did not sleep with her again. Judah is not guilty of incest.

27. When the time came. Unlike Rebekah, Tamar is not anticipating twins.

twin boys. The twins were perhaps a gift from God to Tamar to compensate her for the lack of children from her two husbands as well as a sign to Judah, who lost two sons due to their wickedness, that his sins are forgiven and a new day is dawning under God's favor.

28. scarlet thread. This is part of the sign of God's election (see "Coherence with the Account of Jacob's Line" in the Literary Analysis above).

29. she said. The midwife speaks; she displaces Judah in the narrative.

broken out [pereṣ]. Only his name is explained in this account. The Hebrew word here is translated "spread out" in 28:14. Once again the younger brother prevails in the struggle with the older (see 25:23; 37:2). The births match Tamar's own struggle for children. She has broken out from Judah's deceitful binding of her.

THEOLOGICAL REFLECTIONS ON
BOOK 10, ACT 1, SCENE 2 ————————————

Character Transformation

As Wenham states, "In its biographical sketches, character change is what Genesis is all about."[43] If Joseph enters the spotlight as an arrogant tattletale, Judah enters as a cold and selfish man who has cast aside Abraham's God-given vision for a covenant people (see Literary Analysis above). In these twenty-plus years, however, he is being transformed under the mighty hand of God. Fox summarizes,

> As the one who basically assumes responsibility, he will be made to undergo an inner development in the narrative, and again becomes the one to take discharge of the youngest son (Binyamin, chapters 43 and 44). The missing piece that begins to explain his nobility in this regard (chapter 44) is the present chapter. Yehuda here learns what it is to lose sons, and to want desperately to protect his youngest. Although his failure to marry off Tamar to the youngest son leads to public humiliation (twice, actually), his response shows that he immediately accepts blame . . . (v. 26). Such an interpretation is further confirmed by the restriction of the word "pledge" to

---

[43]Wenham, *Genesis 16–50*, 364.

her and 43:9. Yehuda has learned what it means to stake oneself for a principle. . . . In other words, Yehuda reaches full inner maturity just in time.[44]

Grace

It is utterly astounding that Judah in connection with the twelve sons of Jacob has his name written on the gates of heavenly Jerusalem (Rev. 21:12). He stands as a witness to God's amazing grace. He fails as a son of the covenant (i.e., intermarrying with Canaanites and behaving like them), as a father (i.e., his sons are wicked), and as a father-in-law (i.e., deceiving Tamar). Even the worst sort of sinners can enter heaven by God's redemptive grace.

Covenant

Once again the covenant family is confronted with barrenness, this time the result of the sterility of Judah's wicked sons. Again obedience and faithfulness overcome barrenness. The Canaanite woman models radical risk-taking faith for the covenant family.

Kingship/Messianism

In Book 10 both Joseph and Judah emerge as the leader among the brothers. Joseph occupies the central stage, Judah a secondary one. Nevertheless, in this opening act, the birth of his twins marks him out as the son to succeed his father as the leading patriarch, and by the end of Book 10 Judah wins the enduring crown. He becomes the spokesman for his brothers to their father (43:3–5), assumes a position of leadership on their behalf (44:14–34), is chosen by Jacob to spearhead the migration to Egypt (46:28), and is finally granted by the patriarch the blessing of kingship originally given to the first three patriarchs (49:8–12). His ascendancy to supreme ruler occurs in conjunction with the transformation of his very flawed character. His confessions of his wrongs against Tamar and Joseph (38:26; 42:21) begin his faith journey. His faith peaks when the once callous slave trader of his young stepbrother offers himself as a slave in the stead of his youngest step-brother (44:18–33). Judah, who once hated his brother and who was insensitive to his partisan father, in his maturation offers himself as the slave for his father's favored son because he cannot bear to "see the misery that would come upon my father" (44:34). The partisan father is not transformed; his wicked son becomes a saint.

Ten generations, the symbolic number of a complete and significant unity of time (see Gen. 5), separate David from Perez in Ruth 4:18–22 and 1 Chron. 2:5, 9–15. Sarna asserts that this "shows that the birth of Perez is taken to be a historic turning point."[45] In retrospect, then, this chapter is about the birth of royal seed in the continuity and discontinuity between the generations.

---

[44]Fox, *Beginning*, 158–59.
[45]Sarna, *Genesis*, 270.

God had promised Abraham and Jacob that they would have royal offspring from their own bodies. Of Jacob's twelve sons, Judah is singled out to carry on this royal lineage. Tamar, a wrong wife (i.e., Canaanite), saves the family by her loyalty to it. The four women in Matthew's genealogy of Jesus Christ (Tamar, Rahab, Ruth, Bathsheba) all come from outside of Israel and have a highly irregular and potentially scandalous marriage union.[46] But because of their faith, God deems them worthy to carry royal seed.

Separation

Judah's story illustrates the necessity of the covenant family separating from Canaan for now. As noted, persecution and accommodation threaten the existence of the people of God. The shattered family, who live in the land without an altar, begin to intermarry the cursed Canaanites and to lose their purpose to bless the earth (see 12:3; cf. 24:3; 26:34–35; 27:46; 34:2). God will meet this threat by sending Joseph ahead into segregated Egypt (see 43:32; 46:34). In Egypt, through famine and servitude the family can be preserved and prepared to be a great nation.

BOOK 10, ACT 2: JOSEPH'S RISE TO RULERSHIP OVER EGYPT (39:1–41:57)

LITERARY ANALYSIS BOOK 10, ACT 2 ——————————

Structure and Plot

Will the Lord be faithful to his promises to Joseph, this spoiled but charismatic and noble lad, utterly alone, sold as a slave in a foreign land? The narrator masterfully builds the tension of Act 2 around the hope for Joseph's future. Here the pattern of exaltation and humiliation set in Act 1 escalates until its climactic reversal with Joseph elevated to vizier of Egypt. After the janus in 39:1 linking Act 2 with Act 1 (37:2–36), the first two scenes, in Potiphar's house (39:1–20) and in prison (39:21–40:23), follow the same pattern of exaltation and humiliation, a pattern also reflected in the division of theological and phenomenological narration:

A Theological narration: exalted over Potiphar's house (39:2–6)
  B Phenomenological narration: incarcerated in prison (39:7–20)
A′ Theological narration: exalted over the prison warden's house (39:21–23)
  B′ Phenomenological narration: forgotten as a slave in prison (40:1–23).

The closing verse of each scene establishes the setting for the next. Scene 3 (41:1–57), however, breaks the pattern building throughout to the incredible exaltation of Joseph. This scene also does not contain a division between

---

[46]R. E. Brown, "Matthew's Genealogy of Jesus Christ: A Challenging Advent Homily," *Worship* 60 (1986): 483–90.

theological and phenomenological narration. Joseph himself and the Pharaoh, in their assertions of God's sovereignty (41:16, 25, 28, 32, 38–39), provide the theological narration that confirms the narrator's previous declarations of God's sovereign control. In this, explains Brueggemann, "The narrator offers an understanding of reality that is an alternative to every imperial presupposition of control."[47]

Characterization

Each scene adds a new dimension to Joseph's virtues. Scene 1 depicts his nobility: piety toward God, loyalty to those who trust him. To this Scene 2 adds his gift for interpreting dreams. Scene 3 adds his discernment and wisdom. He addresses the imperial power boldly, tactfully, and cogently, so much so that Pharaoh and his officials recognize the Spirit of God in him.

Key Words

A number of key words in this act—"Lord," "everything," "house," "in his hands," "eyes"—function to link the scenes, to build the tension between exaltation and humiliation, and to reinforce the truth of God's sovereignty (see Literary Analysis of individual scenes).

Patterning

The events of the biblical narrative often echo previous events. These echoes declare that God is sovereign over history. God instructed Noah to build an ark. Then he brought all creatures to Noah to redeem the covenant people and accomplish the salvation of creation in the midst of natural disaster. Now God leads Joseph to build storehouses, and all people are brought to Egypt. In the midst of the natural disaster of famine, God will redeem the covenant people and rescue the world.

Joseph's exaltation will complete the fulfillment of his childhood dreams. The three stages of his rise to leadership—Potiphar's assistant, prison governor's deputy, Pharaoh's vizier—will be matched by three acknowledgments of his power by his family: ten brothers bow (42:1–38), eleven brothers bow (43:1–45:28), the entire family bows (46:1–27).

BOOK 10, ACT 2, SCENE 1: JOSEPH IN POTIPHAR'S HOUSE (39:1–20)

LITERARY ANALYSIS OF BOOK 10, ACT 2, SCENE 1[48] ———

Janus

Genesis 39:1 recapitulates 37:36, moving from "sold" to "bought"—after the parenthetical chapter 38—and so forms a transition from Act 1 (37:36)

---

[47]Brueggemann, *Genesis*, 317.

[48]For extended analysis of the skillful use of repetitions in this scene, see Alter, *Biblical Narrative*, 107–13; Sternberg, *Poetics*, 423–27.

to Act 2 and sets the stage for Scene 1 of the latter. This semantic shift moves the scene from Canaan to Egypt and from Joseph's brothers and the Midianites to Joseph and Potiphar.

Structure and Plot

This scene is divided into two segments (see Literary Analysis of Act 2 above):

A Theological narration (39:2–6)
B Phenomenological narration (39:7–20)

The phrase "the Lord was with Joseph" forms an inclusio around the theological narration (39:2, 5; cf. 39:21, 23). The separation between theological narration and phenomenological narration is marked by "after a while" (39:7).

Joseph's rise to power follows a rugged path. In this scene he is exalted to the highest level in his master's home, only to be humiliated again. The narrator masterfully develops the tension of Joseph's circumstances. The theological narration sets the stage, detailing the five steps of Joseph's elevation through God's blessing: sold as a slave to an aristocrat; serving in the house, not in the field; winning the master's esteem; becoming the master's personal attendant; heading the entire household. This tremendous elevation is matched by an escalation of conflict in the phenomenological narration. The lust of Potiphar's wife to possess Joseph sparks a downward spiral of events: her initial solicitation, her violent proposition, her false accusations repeated twice, and finally Joseph's imprisonment. The threefold repetition of the tale of "he forced me to" (once by the narrator [39:10–12], and twice by the wife, first to her servants [39:13–15] and then to his master [39:16–18]) serves to characterize the wife and to build the scene's tension.

Key Words

Other than in this scene, the name "Lord" (*yhwh*) only appears three times in the rest of Book 10 (see 39:21, 23 [theological narration in Scene 2]; 49:18). The fivefold repetition of this name in the theological narration of Scene 1 (39:2, 3 [2x], 5 [2x]) signals the crucial role of God's providence in directing Joseph's life. Joseph's name occurs six times in 39:1–6. Although it may function to avoid ambiguity, more probably the narrator is sharply focusing the divine and human partners (cf. 26:3; 28:15; 31:3). The Hebrew *kōl* ("everything"), also repeated five times (39:3, 4, 5 [2x], 6), underscores God's unrestrained presence with Joseph and the extent of Joseph's exaltation. Other terms also highlight the extent of Joseph's success and the painful irony of his humiliation. In the theological narration, "in his hands" (Hebrew) marks his success (39:3, 4, 6, cf. 39:8; see also Scene 2 Literary

Analysis). The corresponding expression "in her hand" in the phenomeno-logical narration forms a painful contrast.[49] The word "eyes" similarly con-trasts the movement from exaltation to humiliation (39:4, 7) to exaltation in the opening of Scene 2 (39:21).

Historicity

It is often said this story is built on the Egyptian Story of the Two Broth-ers.[50] However, in detail Joseph's story has little in common with the Egypt-ian story. A hero spurning a wife's advances is found in many ancient tales.

EXEGETICAL NOTES TO BOOK 10, ACT 2, SCENE 1 ————

Janus (39:1)

1. had been taken down to Egypt. This signals a return to the main story line (see 37:36), but it also forms a link to Judah's descent to Canaan in 38:1 (see Literary Analysis of Act 1, Scene 3).

Potiphar. See 37:36.

captain of the guard. His full title is given to emphasize his importance and to signal the first step in Joseph's exaltation.

Ishmaelites. See 37:25.

Theological Narration: God's Blessing on Joseph and Potiphar (39:2 – 6)

2. The LORD was with Joseph. See 39:21–23; Acts 7:9. This is the theo-logical entrance to the story as it unfolds in Egypt, the frame of the next the-ological narration (39:3, 21, 23), and the link between Joseph and the patriarchs (see 28:15). God's beneficent presence is experienced even in slav-ery, out of the land of blessing (see 26:3, 24, 28; 28:15, 20; 31:3). "Though Joseph's situation changed drastically, God's relationship to him remained the same."[51] For this reason, Joseph "can rise again and again in situations that would surely have crushed others."[52]

prospered. Joseph has an insight into adversity and acts decisively.

lived in the house. In the theological narration, "house" is repeated five times, punctuating Joseph's elevation. Joseph's position as a house slave con-forms to documented Egyptian practices. An Egyptian papyrus (Brooklyn 35.14.46) from 1833–1742 B.C. details the names and occupations of nearly eighty slaves in an Egyptian household. In that list, Asian slaves were given superior status and skilled jobs over the Egyptian slaves, who were usually assigned strenuous field labor.[53]

---

[49]Alter, *Biblical Narrative*, 109–10.
[50]*ANET*, 23–25.
[51]NIV Study Bible, 65.
[52]Sarna, *Genesis*, 271.
[53]See ibid., 271.

3. saw that the Lord was with him. This entails that Potiphar knew Joseph's religious convictions. In Hamilton's words, "Joseph may be over Potiphar's household, but he is under Yahweh's blessing and guidance."[54]

4. in his eyes. See Literary Analysis above.

became his attendant. This is a work of personal service (cf. Ex. 24:13; Josh. 1:1; 1 Kings 19:21).

put him in charge. The Hebrew expression signifies to be installed as the official over an entire estate.

5. blessed. The Lord's power overflows through the Semitic Joseph to the Hamitic Egyptians just as the Lord promised Abraham (see 12:3).

in the house and in the field. This is a merism for every part of his property.[55]

6. except the food he ate. This figure of speech refers to Potiphar's private affairs.

well-built and handsome. This description, unique of a male in Scripture, protrudes forebodingly from the other details of Joseph's exaltation. It is included to explain the devious behavior of Potiphar's wife that follows.

Phenomenological Narration: Joseph and Potiphar's Wife (39:7 – 20)

7. his master's wife. The narrator does not honor her with a memorial name in Scripture. Her designation underscores Joseph's temptation not to displease such an aristocratic and powerful woman and/or to scheme through her to advance himself. Sarna also captures the dramatic irony: "She, the mistress of the house, is a slave to her lust for her husband's slave!"[56]

took notice of. Literally, she "lifted up her eyes." In the Code of Hammurabi, the expression means to look at with desire.[57]

Come to bed with me! (šiḵbâ ʿimmî). This is a mere two words in Hebrew, an expression never used of marriage (see note at 34:2). Her clipped proposition portrays brutish lust.

8. he refused. Joseph's lengthy speech contrasts with her brute proposition.

With me in charge. Joseph exemplifies a noble character. His refusal, though spontaneous, is well thought out from the world and life view of people of faith. His cogent reasons for refusing are abuse of trust and gratitude, the violation of her husband's marital rights, and sin against God. Joseph is disciplined. Sarna notes, "His moral excellence can be appreciated all the more if one remembers that he is a slave and that sexual promiscuity was a perennial feature of all slave societies."[58] He concedes nothing to imperial power.

---

[54]Hamilton, *Chapters 18–50*, 460.
[55]For merism, see Gen. 1:1.
[56]Sarna, *Genesis*, 273.
[57]*ANET*, 164, no. 25.
[58]Sarna, *Genesis*, 273.

9. sin against God. Joseph assumes that she can speak about God. All sin is against God (see 20:9; Ps. 51:4). God has set boundaries. Freedom is within law, and lovemaking within marriage.

10. though she spoke to Joseph . . . refused. She tries to wear him down, a tact twice successful against Samson (Judg. 14:17; 16:16–17).

11. to attend to his duties. This is a necessary detail to excuse Joseph for being in a foolish situation.

12. caught. The word describes an act of violence. Normally, a man rapes a woman by force with little dialogue and a woman violates a man with seductive speech (cf. Prov. 5; 7). Her masculine attack is unique in Scripture.

ran out. Literally, "he fled and went outside" (cf. 2 Tim. 2:22). Probably, he fled inside the empty house, and then once outside, he walked normally so as not to attract attention.

13. cloak. The NIV glosses the general Hebrew word for "garment" (same word in 38:14, 19), plausibly assuming that the synecdoche refers to "the loose-fitting outer garment of the well-to-do, which was removed on entering the house."[59] Once again, Joseph's cloak is a means of deception against him (see 37:33).

14. she called her household servants. She did so to fabricate witnesses. Now she speaks cleverly at length (cf. 39:7).

Hebrew. See 10:21; 14:13; 43:32. She appeals to xenophobia.

us. She shrewdly identifies herself with the slaves against him.

to make sport of us. As she was false to her husband with Joseph, she is now disloyal to him before the domestics (contrast 39:17).

I screamed. This necessary fabrication establishes that the sex was unwanted (see Deut. 22:22, 27). She knows none were close enough to hear. Ambiguous providence seems to be working against Joseph.

15. ran out of the house. The Hebrew is the same as 39:12, but her revisionist narrative adds to and reverses the real events.

17. slave. While to the slaves she speaks of Joseph generally as a man, to her husband she is careful to emphasize his slave status.[60]

you brought us came to me to make sport of me. Her summary version of her speech to the servants (39:14) is a masterfully ambiguous rebuke. As Alter notes, it could mean "the slave came to me—the one you brought us—to dally with me" or "the slave came to me, the one you brought us to dally with me."[61]

19. he burned with anger. Against whom? The statement is deliberately ambiguous, not asserting whether his anger is directed at Joseph or his wife. Is he also angry at losing Joseph's good services so that he has to take responsibility of his house again?

---

[59]Ibid., 274.
[60]See Sternberg, *Poetics*, 425–27.
[61]Alter, *Biblical Narrative*, 110.

20. put him in prison. Attempted rape was a capital offense. The milder punishment suggests that Potiphar does not altogether believe his wife. He probably knows her character.

king's prisoners were confined. This is further confirmation of Potiphar's good will. In any case, even in prison Providence again smiles on Joseph.

THEOLOGICAL REFLECTIONS ON BOOK 10, ACT 2, SCENE 1

Grace

The division between theological narration, framed by the phrase "the LORD was with Joseph" (see Literary Analysis above), and phenomenological narration clearly exposes the narrator's theological intention (see also "God's Presence" in Theological Reflections on Book 10, Act 2, Scene 2). Joseph arises from a succession of greater, unjust falls to higher advancements because of God's sovereign grace overriding his misadventures in the hands of people. After the theological expositions of Scenes 1 and 2, the name "LORD" (*yhwh*) will not be used again apart from 49:18. Things are theologically settled (39:1–6), but life must be lived at great risk, trusting in God's sovereign grace (39:7–20). Stephen, in his sweeping review of Israel's history and his apologia for his life, takes time to underscore that God was with Joseph (Acts 7:9). Even Joseph's master takes note of this truth (Gen. 39:3; cf. 26:28). Joseph exemplifies the blessed person portrayed in Psalm 1.

Sovereignty and Submission

The theological narration credits God with all of Joseph's advancements. He controls Joseph's future, and to be faithful Joseph must trust God even in the face of unjust treatment. He is learning to put aside cloaks, trusting the Lord to clothe him with dignity and honor (see 41:14, 42). This is a marked contrast to Joseph's father, who wasted many years relying on his own strength and wit. Joseph is a representative of true Israel.

Covenant Theology

The theological narration presents God's faithfulness to the covenant; the secular narration presents Joseph's faithfulness. Joseph's career is part of God's covenant faithfulness to his people to preserve and prosper them in peril. God orchestrates the most unlikely set of circumstances into an astonishing change of events that moves unerringly to redeem his elect (cf. Ps. 105:16–22). In the covenant, God is faithful and sovereign. As Brueggemann states, "The narrator offers an understanding of reality that is an alternative to every imperial presupposition of control."[62]

Joseph proves his faithfulness by remaining loyal and showing gratitude

---

[62]Brueggemann, *Genesis*, 317.

to his master. His refusal of Potiphar's wife's advances entails that he does not take advantage of his superior physique to dispossess his master but rather accepts his God-given social standing as a slave. Ultimately, he acts out of fear of sinning against God. Joseph participates in the eternal covenant: he has the law of God in his heart (see 41:38; Jer. 31:31–33; Ezek. 36:22–32).

Typology

The pattern of exaltation, humiliation, and exaltation experienced by Joseph will be worked out again in the Israelites' life in Egypt. Because of Joseph, they are first welcomed with honor. Then they face cruel bondage simply because of God's blessings, but finally God delivers them and raises them up as a great nation. Above all, the movement from exaltation to humiliation to exaltation foreshadows the career of the Son of God. Believers have an exemplar by which to interpret their experiences. They are assured that ultimately God controls history.

BOOK 10, ACT 2, SCENE 2: JOSEPH IN PRISON: INTERPRETER OF DREAMS (39:21–40:23)

LITERARY ANALYSIS OF BOOK 10, ACT 2, SCENE 2 ———

Janus

Genesis 39:20 functions as janus between the two scenes by repeating the catchword "prison." The last scene ended with Potiphar confining Joseph to the royal prison (39:20a), and the new scene opens with the Lord providing for Joseph in prison (39:20b–21).

Structure

This scene completes the alternating pattern of theological narration and phenomenological narration begun in Scene 1 (see Literary Analysis of Book 10, Act 2). Here the scene is divided as 39:21–23 (A') and 40:1–23 (B'). Once again, "the LORD was with Joseph" forms an inclusio around the theological narration, and the expression "Some time later" (40:1), similar to "after a while" in Scene 1, begins the phenomenological narration.

Comparison, Contrast, and Key Words

The theological narration of this scene follows the pattern of the theological narration of Scene 1. The two theological narrations are bracketed by the chiastic inclusio, "The LORD was with him and gave him success" (39:3, 23). Similarly, the Lord's favor leads to Joseph's favor with his master, which the narrator describes in the same terms, "favor in the eyes" (39:4, 21). The expression "in his hands" also signals his success (39:3 [not trans. in NIV], 22, 23). Again, Joseph's exaltation is attributed to God's providence. Here the threefold repetition of "give" (ntn ["put," 39:20; "granted," 39:21; "put," 39:22]) confirms God's, not Joseph's, providential control of the future.

Whereas the theological narration remains unchanged, the phenomenological narration differs. Again the narrator skillfully weaves the story to build anticipation. The previous scene began with Joseph as a slave; now he stands unjustly in an even lower position as prisoner. But where the tension of the previous phenomenological narration was built on events beyond Joseph's control and increasingly detrimental to his position, the tension of this narration is the hope of Joseph's elevation. The hope increasingly mounts with his providential assignment to the king's officials, his wise and divine interpretation of the dreams, and climactically their precise fulfillment. It is not until the scene's final pointed words, "he [the cupbearer] did not remember Joseph," that hope deflates. Not until the next scene will Joseph's humiliation actually change.

As in Act 1, Joseph's life is changed by dreams and a dungeon. However, whereas his dreams in the first scene brought him into a dungeon, this time the dreams begin his deliverance from a dungeon (Hebrew *bôr*, rendered "cistern" in 37:22 and "dungeon" in 40:15 and 41:14).

Characterization

The preceding scene revealed Joseph's noble character. Though severely tempted, he neither betrays Potiphar's trust in him nor abandons his trust in God. This scene implies the same faith but displays him as divinely and uniquely gifted. He depends on God for his gift to interpret dreams and possibly anticipates a fulfillment of his own when he asks the cupbearer to remember him. Joseph recognizes that he belongs to a higher authority than the Egyptian masters in whose houses he slaves. At the same time, Joseph's plea to the cupbearer to remember him makes him very human.

EXEGETICAL NOTES TO BOOK 10, ACT 2, SCENE 2 ———

Theological Narration:
God Places Joseph over the Prison (39:21–23)

21. the LORD was with him. God does not remove Joseph from suffering, but he remains with him in the midst of it. Only after substantial time does God provide the way out.

showed him kindness [*hesed*]. The Hebrew *hesed* means to act with love and loyalty to help a covenant partner in his need (see 32:10).

granted him favor. The Hebrew here is the same as in Exodus describing the Israelites with the Egyptians (see Ex. 3:21; 11:3; 12:36).

in the eyes of. This is a key word (see 39:4, 7; Literary Analysis of Book 10, Act 2, Scene 1). Hamilton says, "She [Potiphar's wife] saw a male figure to satisfy her sexual lust; he saw a reliable, model prisoner who could be trusted with responsibilities."[63]

---

[63]Hamilton, *Genesis 18–50*, 472.

prison warden. The warden is responsible to the captain of the guard (40:3).

23. the LORD was with Joseph. This is essentially a repetition of 39:6. This theological key to the story will not be repeated (see Book 10, Act 2, Scene 1, Literary Analysis and "Grace" in Theological Reflections).

Phenomenological Narration: Joseph Interprets His Inmates' Dreams (40:1 – 23)

1. Some time later. By this point Joseph has been in slavery and then prison for over ten years. The total period of slavery and imprisonment will be thirteen years (see 37:2; 41:46). The narrator does not specify how much time was spent in the house of Potiphar.

offended. The Hebrew is literally "sinned," a contrast to Joseph's imprisonment, which was unjustified.

2. chief cupbearer. Kings often feared being poisoned, so they would trust cupbearers with their lives. As a result, these officials were often wealthy and influential, as Egyptian texts testify (cf. Neh. 1:11). Kitchen explains, "These officials (often foreigners) became in many cases confidants and favorites of the king and wielded political influence."[64]

chief baker. Both of his royal inmates attended to Pharaoh's food: the cupbearer to the wine in his cup, the baker to the bread and cakes on his table. Both had close access to the Pharaoh, and both could play a sinister role in a conspiracy against him.

3. custody. They are awaiting Pharaoh's sentence.

house of the captain of the guard. The prison house under the warden is situated on the estate of the captain of the guard or is a portion of it.

captain of the guard. This is also Potiphar's position (39:1). He is over the "prison warden" (39:21). Joseph is responsible to the captain of the guard (see 41:12).

4. assigned them to Joseph. Joseph is functioning in the place of the prison warden (39:22).

he attended them. See also 39:4. He attends those who had attended the Pharaoh.

5. each dream had a meaning of its own. See 41:11. Otherwise, dreams came in pairs (see 37:5 – 11; 41:25) that confirmed the common fulfillment (41:32). Here the dreams come in pairs, but their meanings differ.

6. dejected. See Neh. 2:2. The anxious officials probably have discerned that their dreams reveal anticipated sentences.

7. So he asked. He shows a solicitous care of those for whom he is responsible.

in his master's house. This matches "the house of his Egyptian master" (39:2), first Potiphar and now Potiphar's peer, "captain of the guard" (cf. 39:1;

[64]K. A. Kitchen, "Cupbearer," *NBD*, 255.

40:3). Ironically, the slave in his Egyptian masters' houses exercises by his gifts and character an authority over Pharaoh's chief cupbearer and chief baker.

8. dreams. They are an important means of revelation (see 20:3; 31:1–55; 41:25). The three pairs of dreams—to Joseph (37:5–11), to the cupbearer and baker (40:1–23), and to Pharaoh (41:1–40)—show that God sovereignly controls destiny (see 41:28). Here is knowledge that lies outside of imperial power.

no one to interpret them. Dreams played an important role in ancient Egypt, and their interpretation was a specialized skill. As prisoners, the cupbearer and baker have no access to expert interpreters.

interpretations belong to God. They do not belong to learning and manipulation. God confers the gift on whom he pleases (see 41:16; Dan. 2:24–49; cf. 1 Cor. 12; Eph. 4:7–13). Joseph does not hesitate to express his faith.

God. The narrator uses "Lord," God's covenant name to Israel, in describing God's relationship to Joseph. When speaking to the Egyptians or of Providence, Joseph uses the universal title, "God." Though the Egyptians stand outside the covenant community, Joseph still assumes he can speak to them about the same God whom they both recognize.

Tell me. Joseph understands his prophetic role (see Theological Reflections below). He knows he belongs to a higher authority and power than Pharaoh (see 37:5–11).

10. three branches. The recurrence of the number three (see below) confirms the dream and the three days (see 40:12–13, 20).

budded . . . blossomed . . . ripened. Three actions match the three branches.

11. Pharaoh's cup. The cup is mentioned three times in this verse.

took . . . squeezed . . . put. As before, there are three actions.

into Pharaoh's cup and put the cup in his hand. The dream assumes he has been restored to his position, entailing the cupbearer's clean conscience and confidence.

his hand. The Hebrew is literally "Pharaoh's hand."

13. three days. Joseph probably knows Pharaoh will decide their fate on his birthday three days away (40:20).

lift up your head. The Hebrew idiom is subject to two interpretations, allowing a pun with 40:19. The Hebrew here is rendered "release" in 2 Kings 25:27 (= Jer. 52:31), also in a context of release from prison. The Akkadian equivalent means "to call someone into the presence of the king."

14. when all goes well. Joseph's faith remains strong.

remember. See 8:1.

15. Hebrews. See 10:21; 14:13; 43:32.

I have done nothing to deserve. The wrongly accused cupbearer should identify with Joseph. His insensitivity to Joseph's plight is inexcusable.

15. dungeon. The Hebrew here is translated "cistern" in 37:24. The hyperbolic identification of this place of house arrest as a "dungeon" establishes a link to Joseph's first imprisonment.

16. a favorable interpretation. The willingness of the cupbearer to share his dream suggests his innocence; he has nothing to hide. By contrast, the guilty baker will not share his until he hears a favorable interpretation for the cupbearer.

On my head. Egyptian art portrays a baker carrying a basket on his head. This is also a fitting image for the death the baker will suffer (see 40:17, 19).

three baskets of bread. This is better translated, "three baskets containing a batch of white flour."[65] The etymology of this unique word is disputed.

17. all kinds. Hieroglyphic texts list thirty-eight kinds of cake and fifty-seven varieties of bread.

birds were eating them. Though he had all kinds of delicacies on his head, he amazingly does nothing to protect them (contrast Abraham's action in 15:11). Sarna explains, "The baker has neither the strength nor the presence of mind to drive them away—an ominous detail."[66] Does his unclean conscience render him immobile? Does it symbolize his failure to protect the Pharaoh's table?

19. lift off your head. This is a play on words with the interpretation given to the chief cupbearer, "lift up your head."

hang you on a tree. This is better rendered, "impale you on a pole" or "hang you from a stake."[67] His corpse would be publicly exposed after execution and likely pecked by carrion birds.

birds will eat away your flesh. The severe punishment of an ignominious and defiling death, rather than a decent burial, probably entails that, unlike the cupbearer, he has committed a grave crime that demands public censure.

20. birthday. The word could mean "anniversary." Egyptian texts mention granting amnesties on these days.

lifted up the heads. See 40:13. This is another play on words. Here it refers to a ritual by which the king singles out a servant.

22. he hanged the chief baker. Better, "he impaled the chief baker."

23. did not remember. He does not act on his duty to help Joseph. Two years will elapse before the cupbearer remembers (see 41:1).

he forgot. This is not a mental lapse but a moral lapse. He self-centeredly does not bother to "re-member" himself with his former inmate. Sarna says, "The ingratitude of the Egyptian cupbearer prefigures the later national experience of the Israelites in Egypt (cf. Ex. 1:8)."[68]

---

[65]See *HALOT*, 353.
[66]Sarna, *Genesis*, 279.
[67]*ANEP*, plates 362, 368, 373.
[68]Sarna, *Genesis*, 280.

THEOLOGICAL REFLECTIONS ON BOOK 10, ACT 2, SCENE 2

God's Presence

The Lord's presence with Jacob entailed both his safe return home and his twenty years of hard labor under the harsh, wily, and unethical Laban (see also "Grace" in Theological Reflections on Book 10, Act 2, Scene 1). God's presence with Joseph entails both his exaltations in the houses of the captain of the guard and his unjust imprisonment and ungrateful rejection. Ultimately, the closing of prison doors is designed by the Lord to open palace doors (Acts 7:10), but only in his timing. But Joseph must remain loyal to God, not knowing the future of his own existence.

Dreams

Dreams were valued throughout the ancient Near East as a means for predicting the future (see 20:3). However, only God can dogmatically interpret dreams, which he does so through elect agents such as Joseph (see 41:6, 14, 18; Dan. 2:28). Joseph's ability to interpret dreams also gives him the prophetic ability to interpret Providence (Gen. 45:5–8; 50:20). He belongs to a higher power and authority than Pharaoh (40:8; 41:16, 25, 28, 32). This glimpse into another dimension of reality reveals God's rule, confirming God's control and supervision of all things. As God's spokesperson, the interpreter of dreams speaks the kerygmatic news of life and death. He speaks eschatologically, revealing God's coming resolution of human issues. He mediates God's revelation even as Israel mediates God's revelation to the nations (see 18:17 and note; 41:16, 28, 32; Rom. 3:1–2). God's greatest revelation, however, has come in his Son (Col. 1:15–23; Heb. 1:1–2), and the Spirit reveals the Son and all truth through the apostles (John 16:13–14). Jesus Christ continues to send gifted individuals to build his church (Matt. 16:18; 1 Cor. 12–14; Eph. 4).

BOOK 10, ACT 2, SCENE 3: JOSEPH IN PALACE: SECOND ONLY TO PHARAOH (41:1–57)

LITERARY ANALYSIS OF BOOK 10, ACT 2, SCENE 3

Structure and Plot

The first two scenes have been building to this climactic conclusion of the act. Joseph's previous exaltation was assurance of God's presence, but even his humiliation (i.e., being thrown into prison and being forgotten) laid the foundation for this true exaltation.

The setting of this scene is two years later in Pharaoh's palace. The narrative of Pharaoh's double dream with none to interpret it is a scenario familiar to the reader who knows the previous events. The development of the scene, which revolves around the dreams, is the increasing elevation of Joseph to the climactic declaration of Pharaoh, "You shall be in charge of my palace. . . . Only with respect to the throne will I be greater than you" (41:40).[69] The scene develops in four dream-related stages: Pharaoh's dreams and dilemma (41:1–8); Joseph's deliverance and Pharaoh's retelling (41:9–24); Joseph's interpretation, plan, and elevation (41:25–40); Joseph's rule according to the plan (41:41–57). In the last part, the scene's denouement, the Pharaoh in two monologues transfers powers to Joseph as his viceroy over Egypt in a public investiture ceremony (41:41–43), confers a new name on him, and elevates him to nobility by marriage (41:44–45). The extended narrative at the end of the chapter depicts Joseph's wise administration of the land (41:46–57).

Comparison

The scene has several analogues with earlier scenes: again Joseph is brought up from a dungeon; again his ability to interpret dreams plays a crucial role in his fate; again he finds himself in charge of a house, this time Pharaoh's!

Characterization

Previously Joseph showed himself unflinching before imperial power; now he addresses it wisely: piously, forthrightly, tactfully, and sensibly.

EXEGETICAL NOTES TO BOOK 10, ACT 2, SCENE 3 ———

Pharaoh's Dreams and Dilemma (41:1–8)

1–5. dream . . . second dream. Pharaoh's dreams of "cows," "reed beds," and "grain" "are all natural symbols of food."[70] The unity of the dream is suggested by repetition of the untranslated *hinnēh* (see below) and by the word pairs "seven," "coming up/growing up," and "gaunt/thin" (see notes).

1. When two full years had passed. Two full years of affliction (*chronos* time) contrasts with one quick deliverance (crisis time). Compare the fourteen years that will follow.

Pharaoh had. In the ancient Near East, royal dreams were believed to indicate a special bond between God and the king (see 40:8 and note; 1 Kings 3:4–15; Prov. 21:1). The dreams here penetrate Pharaoh's royal power and isolation.

He was standing. The Hebrew is literally, "Look! He was standing." The Hebrew text contains the presentative *hinnēh*, which draws the audience in

---

[69]Wenham notes interesting parallels around the dreams and their recitation: "Within the first two parts, there are close parallels in the general sequence, dream—failed interpretation—Joseph summoned: dream—successful interpretation—Joseph appointed, and very close verbal echoes, especially when Pharaoh recounts his dream in vv 17–24 (cf. vv 1–7)" (*Genesis 16–50*, 389).

[70]Sternberg, *Poetics*, 397.

as participants with Pharaoh's excited perception. The sixfold repetition (41:1, 2, 3, 5, 6, 7) of this word in the Hebrew texts also links the dreams.

Nile. This river was the source of Egypt's—and so Pharaoh's—power, fertility, and life (cf. Ex. 7:15–18).

2. out of the river there came up seven cows. To keep from heat and insects, cattle sometimes submerse themselves.

reeds. Hebrew *ʾāḥû* is an Egyptian loanword. Along with the other Egyptian terms, it contributes to the scene's historicity.

3. After them. The Hebrew literally says, "Look! Behind them. . ." (see notes on 41:1).

gaunt [*daqqōṯ*]. The same word appears in 41:4 and is rendered "thin" of the heads of grain (41:6, 7), further linking the two dreams.

5. Seven heads of grain. The Hebrew literally reads, "Look! Seven heads. . ." (see notes on 41:1).

were growing. The Hebrew is the same verb translated "came up" in 41:3.

single stalk. This is an exceptional phenomenon symbolizing abundance.

6. After them. The Hebrew is literally, "Look! After them. . ." (see notes on 41:1).

thin [*daqqōṯ*]. The word also appears in 41:7 (see "gaunt" above).

scorched by the east wind. Resembling the Palestinian sirocco, the Egyptian *khamsin* blows in from the Sahara desert (see Hos. 13:15) in late spring and early fall and often withers vegetation (see Isa. 40:7; Ezek. 17:10).

8. mind [*rûaḥ*]. The word also means "spirit." In contrast to Pharaoh's troubled spirit, Joseph has the spirit of God (Gen. 41:38).

troubled. See 40:6–7; Dan. 2:1–3. He is probably troubled because the Pharaoh attributes the bountiful harvests reaped during his reign to his good and magical relations to the grain god. One Pharaoh said, "I produced the grain, because I was beloved by the grain god. No one was hungry in my years."[71]

magicians. This is probably another Egyptian loanword referring to intelligent and very clever priests occupied with magic and soothsaying (see Ex. 7:11, 22; 8:7). But even they cannot do some things (Ex. 8:18–19; Dan. 2:10–11).

wise men of Egpyt. "Wise man" (*ḥāḵām*) signifies an individual with masterful understanding of a subject.[72] The mastery in view depends on the context. Here it refers to skilled activity in magic.[73] Accordingly, "magicians and wise men" is a hendiadys for the most skilled magicians of Egypt.

dreams. The text literally reads, "dream, but no one could interpret them."[74] To Pharaoh it is one dream; to his interpreters, two. The difference

---

[71]O. Keel, *The Symbolism of the Biblical World: Ancient Near Eastern Iconography and the Book of Psalms*, trans. T. J. Hallett (New York: Seabury, 1978), 286.

[72]G. Fohrer, "σωφία," *TDNT*, 7:483–88.

[73]See M. Saebe, "ḥkm," *TLOT*, 1:420.

[74]The Samaritan Pentateuch reads the expected plural.

helps explain why Pharaoh may be dissatisfied with the magicians' inter-pretations and satisfied with Joseph's.[75]

no one could interpret. See 40:8 and note. The Egyptian ways of know-ing fails (cf. Ex. 7–8; Dan. 2; 5). The first episode of scene 3 ends the same as the first episode of scene 2.

Joseph's Deliverance and Pharaoh's Retelling (41:9 – 24)

9. I am reminded. This is better translated, "I must make mention."

my shortcomings. The Hebrew *ḥēṭ*ʾ means "sin"; the same root was ren-dered "offended" in 40:1. As noted in 40:23, the cupbearer had turned his back on Joseph. The form is plural because by not telling Pharaoh about Joseph's talent he has wronged both Joseph and Pharaoh. However, in prov-idence, God arranges perfect timing despite people's wrong.

11. a meaning of its own. See 40:5 and note.

12. Hebrew. See 10:21; 14:13; 43:32.

13. exactly as he interpreted. His eyewitness testimony prepares Pharaoh and his officials to accept Joseph's interpretation as God's ordained word (see Ps. 105:19).

14. he was quickly brought. That is, they "rushed him." The verb plus the staccato style shows that the Pharaoh must not be kept waiting.

dungeon. See 40:15.

When he had shaved. He would have shaved his head and face. Egyp-tians were usually clean-shaven for hygienic reasons, while Asiatics usually wore beards.

changed his clothes. See 39:14 and note; 2 Kings 25:29. Here the change symbolizes his changing social status.

16. I cannot. See 40:8; Dan. 2:27–28, 30; 2 Cor. 3:5.

God. See note at 40:8. God gives dreams to Pharaoh as he did to Abim-elech. There is a bond between God and this pagan king, so Joseph and Pharaoh can speak of the same God. Joseph punctuates his interpretation of Pharaoh's dream with mention of God's favor and authority (41:16, 25, 28, 32). Joseph knows of himself that he is a prophet before he hears the dream.

will give Pharaoh the answer he desires. Literally, "God will answer the peace/well-being of Pharaoh," meaning that God will give an answer that brings Pharaoh peace and/or is about Pharaoh's well-being.[76]

19. I had never seen such ugly cows in all the land. This addition in detail is appropriate in the mouth of the eyewitness. The Pharaoh, regarded as a god, is impotent and afraid.

21. But even after . . . before. The entire verse is not in the original report of the dream. This additional detail explains Joseph's interpretation:

---

[75]See Sternberg, *Poetics*, 398–400.
[76]The genitive of the mediated object (= peace to Pharaoh); see *IBHS*, §9.5.2d.

"The abundance in the land will not be remembered, because the famine . . . will be so severe" (41:31).

22. In my dreams. The Hebrew literally says "in my dream." Pharaoh himself knows the dream is one.

Joseph's Interpretation, Plan, and Elevation (41:25–40)

25. one and the same. In both dreams, the fat is devoured by the lean.

God has revealed. Both the dream and its interpretation are from God (see 40:8). Joseph is an inspired interpreter, not a magician.

28. what he is about to do. God sovereignly rules the nations, controlling their economies and very life.

31. famine. He is helpless before the future of famine and barrenness.

33. And now. This is a logical consequence of the dream's interpretation, but Joseph takes a risk by offering unsolicited advice.

let Pharaoh. Joseph repeats "let Pharaoh" in 41:34 and adds "under the authority of Pharaoh" in 41:35. He carefully appeals to Pharaoh's authority and wisely does not promote himself. Implicitly, however, Joseph is risking himself on his interpretation.

look for a discerning and wise man. Pharaoh has just learned that he has none. Joseph may be tactfully saying, "Let Pharaoh not make the same mistake twice!"[77] Here *wisdom* (cf. 41:8) is qualified by "discerning" (i.e., to have an insight into the cause and effect nexus).

put him in charge. Joseph's plan is threefold: (1) appoint a vizier; (2) appoint local overseers; and (3) institutionalize a national rationing system.

36. may not be ruined [*krt*]. Literally, the Hebrew reads, "may not be cut off." The word connotes excommunication by extermination and may have cultic connotations (i.e., cut off by God; cf. 9:11; 17:14; Mic. 5:10–15 [Heb. 9–14]).

37. seemed good. The Hebrew is literally, "was good in the eyes of" (cf. 39:4, 21). Pharaoh wisely receives God's words and responds accordingly.

38. Can we find. The rhetorical question implies a strong negation: "We cannot find!"

spirit of God [*rûaḥ*; see 1:2]. The Hebrew also means "wind." Neither physical wind nor spiritual/psychic spirit can be seen, only the manifestations of exceptional energy and ability. That invisible, dynamic energy of God is manifest in the effected creation (Gen. 1:2; Job 33:4; Ps. 104:29). God's S/spirit is ubiquitous. He manifests his S/spirit uniquely in elect individuals, gifting them in an extraordinary way for the sacred task of establishing his kingdom through works such as leading the military (Judg. 6:34; 13:25; 14:6, 19; 15:14), building the tabernacle (Ex. 31:3; 35:31), prophesying (Num. 11:17, 25; Mic. 3:8), and leading with wisdom and discernment (Isa.

---

[77]Hamilton, *Genesis 18–50*, 499.

11:1–3). It is the extraordinary abilities of Joseph to interpret dreams and to plot an effective course of action that make Pharaoh aware of God's S/spirit in Joseph. Joseph confesses no intrinsic ability of his own.[78] He points to God's action in giving the dream (Gen. 41:16), and Pharaoh recognizes God's power at work in Joseph (cf. Dan. 5:14).

39. no one so discerning and wise as you. Pharaoh repeats Joseph's words (41:33). Joseph has just defeated Egypt's best wise men (cf. Luke 10:21–24).

40. You shall be in charge. Semitic rulers, known as the Hyksos pharaohs (1720–1550 B.C.), took over the existing Egyptian bureaucratic administration and later appointed naturalized Semites to high office. They scrupulously observed Egyptian conventions. The same is true of the Semitic nomad Yanhamu, who became Egyptian commissioner for Canaan and Syria in the days of Akhenaten (ca. 1353–1340 B.C.), and of Ben Ozen at the court of Merneptah (ca. 1224–1214 B.C.). Thus, Joseph's exaltation, though extraordinary, is not unique.

palace. The Hebrew means "house." Joseph is placed in full charge over a third house in Egypt (see 39:4, 22).

submit to your orders. The Hebrew literally reads, "kiss your mouth."

Joseph's Rule According to the Plan (41:41 – 57)

Joseph's installation as viceroy over Egypt consists of a public act of installation (41:41–43) and the family act of conferring a new name with the elevation to nobility by marriage (41:44–45).

41. So Pharaoh said to Joseph. Pharaoh speaks three times without Joseph answering: first of his intention to make Joseph ruler (41:39–40); second of his investiture of Joseph (41:41–43); third of his authority and approval. Joseph's silence reveals that Providence, not Joseph, arranges these honors.

put [*nātan;* see 39:20, 21 ("granted"), 22]. Joseph allows others to praise and exalt him, rather than praising himself (cf. Prov. 27:2).

in charge of the whole land. See Ps. 105:21–22. This reflects the Egyptian title "Chief of the Entire Land," an epithet applied to the vizier (i.e., the prime minister) and lesser officials. The narrative of the public installation of Joseph (41:41–43, see above) is framed by the expression "in charge of the whole land of Egypt," first in the mouth of Pharaoh and then by the narrator.

42. Pharaoh took. Pharaoh's investiture of Joseph consists of transferring the signet ring, dressing him in fine linen, putting a gold chain around his neck, and having him ride with pomp and ceremony in a chariot. These

---

[78]The Babylonian story of Ahiqar has similarities with the stories of Joseph and Daniel (see Dan. 2). However, the story of Ahiqar gives credit and praise to Ahiqar, "the wise scribe and man of good counsel," whereas Joseph and Daniel give credit and praise to God for dream interpretation and wisdom (see *ANET*, 427–28).

are all well-known symbols of investiture in Egypt. Lest the narrative sound like a fairy tale, compare this account of Ashurbanipal (ca. 668–633 B.C.), who follows Egyptian customs when investing Neco as Pharaoh: "I clad him in a garment with multicolored trimmings, placed a golden chain on him. . . , put golden rings on his hands; I wrote my name (phonetically) upon an iron dagger (to be worn in) the girdle. . . . I presented him with chariots, horses and mules as means of transportation (befitting) his position as ruler."[79]

signet ring. This reflects the Egyptian title "Royal Seal Bearer." This gives Joseph the authority to validate documents in the king's name.

robes. See 39:13 and note.

43. as his second-in-command. Joseph holds the position of vizier (i.e., prime minister), the highest executive office below the king.

men shouted before him. See 2 Sam. 15:1; 1 Kings 1:5; Esth. 6:9.

Make way [ʾaḇrēk]. The meaning of this unique Hebrew term is disputed. In Akkadian, *abarakku* denotes a chief steward. Egyptian *i.brk* means "homage," a meaning close to that chosen by medieval Jewish commentators who took the verb to derive from *bārak*, "to kneel." However Egyptian *ab-r.k* means "Attention! Make way!" Philologically, this is best.

45. gave Joseph the name. This renaming symbolizes Joseph's new identity, validates Joseph's Egyptian position, and signifies Pharaoh's greater authority (i.e., only he has the power to name Joseph). Joseph is no longer an Asiatic slave but an Egyptian vizier.

Zaphenath-Paneah. His unique name probably means in retroverted Egyptian, "God speaks and lives." Joseph's role in Egypt is like that of Daniel in Babylon. Both accept pagan names without accepting pagan religion.

Asenath. Her name means, "She belongs to (the goddess) Neith." She is not to be numbered among the cursed Canaanites (see notes on 38:2). Unless other marriages are blanked, Joseph is monogamous.

Potiphera. See note at 37:36.

priest of On. On (Heliopolis in Greek) is situated seven miles (11 km) northwest of Cairo. Sarna notes, "The high priest at On held the exalted title 'Greatest of Seers.' Joseph thus marries into the elite of Egyptian nobility."[80]

went throughout. This means either "(for inspection) to travel around" or "rose higher than all in the land."[81]

46. thirty years. See 37:2. Joseph's rise to power has occurred in only thirteen years.

traveled through Egypt. Joseph did so to familiarize himself with the land and to appoint local commissioners (see 41:34).

48. collected. Joseph holds the Egyptian office of "Overseer of the Granaries of Upper and Lower Egypt." This office collects tax payment on field

---

[79]*ANET*, 295.
[80]Sarna, *Genesis*, 288.
[81]*HALOT*, 426.

produce and stores the grain of bumper crops for distribution in years of famine.

50. Before the years of famine. The account of the birth of Joseph's sons (41:50–52) forms the pivot in the depiction of Joseph's administrative procedures during the seven years of plenty (41:47–49) and the seven years of famine (41:53–57). This arrangement resembles the same structure in Genesis 29–31. The account of the birth of his two sons is not accidental but pivotal.

51. Joseph named. The names of both sons praise God, first for his preservation and second for his blessing. The names celebrate Joseph's new life: the end of the old, the potential of the new. The one not "in the know" confirms the "in the know" narrator's viewpoint: "God was with him" (39:2–6, 21–23).

Manasseh. This name is derived from "forget" (*nāšâ*).

God has made me forget. He praises God for delivering him from the sorrows inflicted on him by his family in Canaan. Significantly, he gives his sons Hebrew, not Egyptian, names. He has not forgotten his father's household.

all my trouble and all my father's household. This is probably a hendiadys for "all my trouble associated with my father's household."[82] He was rejected by his brothers and embraced by foreigners. However, Joseph is strangely indifferent to his father; he makes no effort to contact him. Although some traditions censor Joseph,[83] the narrator never directly does so. Moreover, none reproaches Joseph when he finally sends for his father (45:9). It may be that Joseph lives in faith of the fulfillment of his dreams (37:5–11).

52. Ephraim. This is derived from "made me fruitful" (*hiprani*).

fruitful. The word refers to abundant posterity (see 17:6, 20; 28:3; 48:4; Ps. 105:23–24) and can be future ("will make me fruitful"). Ephraim is an earnest of God's greater blessings.[84]

in the land of my suffering. This is probably intentionally ambiguous. Does Joseph mean Egypt or Canaan? On the one hand, the birth of Ephraim in Egypt, where he has also suffered afflictions, favors the former. On the other hand, his identification of his sufferings with Canaan and his anticipated abundant posterity in the future favors the latter. Joseph forgot his afflictions in his father's household in Canaan but not the land promised to his fathers and his destiny in it (see 50:24–25).

57. all the countries came. This verse functions as a janus to the next act, when Joseph's brothers come to Egypt.

---

[82]So Sarna, *Genesis*, 289; followed by Hamilton, *Genesis 18–50*, 512.

[83]Hamilton (*Genesis 18–50*, 513) cites an arresting statement in *Midrash Tanḥuma, Vayyesheb* 8: "When Joseph found himself thus [promoted to supervisor of Potiphar's house] he began to eat and drink and curl his hair and said: 'Blessed is the Lord who has caused me to forget my father's house.' Said God to him: 'Your father is grieving for you in sackcloth and ashes and you are eating and drinking and curling your hair! Now our mistress will pair herself with you and will make your life miserable.'"

[84]It can be translated "will make me fruitful" (see *IBHS*, §30.5.1e). In his farewell blessing, Moses capitalizes on the name: "Such are the ten thousands of Ephraim; such are the thousands of Manasseh" (Deut. 33: 17).

famine was severe. The phenomenon and the motif of seven-year famines are well documented in Egyptian and other ancient Near Eastern texts (cf. 2 Sam. 24:13, but see 1 Chron. 21:12).[85] One Egyptian text speaks of a famine when "the entire Upper Egypt was dying because of hunger, with every man eating his (own) children."[86] However, it was unusual to have drought in both the Levant and the Sudan, the source of the Nile on which rainless Lower Egypt in the north depended.

all the world. The salvation of that world depends on one descendant of the patriarchs (see Theological Reflections).

THEOLOGICAL REFLECTIONS ON
BOOK 10, ACT 2, SCENE 3 ————————————————
God's Covenant Faithfulness

God's blessing is matched by Joseph's competence and unflinching loyalty. Roop observes, "Joseph appears in this story as one who lives the virtues celebrated in the ancient Near East, virtues that we too [and the biblical writers] hold dear: patience in the face of unjust suffering, steadfast loyalty in the face of threat to one's position and even life, and forthrightness before power."[87]

However, this is not so much a story about Joseph as about God's faithfulness to his promises through providential acts and charismatic gifting. After thirteen bitter years, God suddenly exalts faithful Joseph directly over all of Egypt and indirectly over the world by charismatically gifting him with the ability to interpret dreams (41:16), supernatural wisdom (41:33), statesmanship, and discernment (41:38). Joseph expresses the central theme of the account: God has decided the course of history, and he will do it (41:32). Everything is in twos to corroborate this truth (cf. 41:1, 5, 27, 30). Joseph gives glory to God by rejecting the royal flattery regarding the interpretation of dreams and by naming his boys in praise of God, who makes him forget his misery and later blesses him.

God's Sovereignty and Human Accountability

God's sovereignty lays the foundation for human activity. Referring to Joseph's interpretation and speech to Pharaoh, von Rad comments, "What is theologically noteworthy is the way in which the strong predestination content of the speech is combined with a strong summons to action. The fact that God has determined the matter, that God hastens to bring it to pass, is precisely the reason for responsible leaders to take measures!"[88]

---

[85]C. H. Gordon, *The Common Background of Greek and Hebrew Civilizations*, 2d ed. (New York: Norton, 1965), 171–78.

[86]J. Vandier, *La famine dans l'Égypte ancienne* (Cairo, 1936), 105, cited by Hamilton, *Genesis 18–50*, 497.

[87]Roop, *Genesis*, 262.

[88]von Rad, *Genesis*, 376.

Pattern: Tribulation to Glory Because of God's Presence

In the case of Jacob, this pattern was necessary to discipline Jacob and prepare him to become a true covenant partner in God's blessing. This is less obvious in the case of Joseph. His afflictions are unjust. But each person learns dependence on God. Roop states, "The pilgrimage of Joseph from slave to vice-regent parallels the journey of Israel as escapees from Egypt to the nation under Solomon, the life of David from shepherd's helper to king, and the story of Jesus from manger to the right hand of God.... The presence of God brings life in the place of death, honor instead of humiliation, and fertility over sterility.... The story depends not on the prowess of the people, but the presence of God, Immanuel (Matt. 1:20–23)."[89] This pattern of humility and exaltation is the pattern for all saints: "Humble yourselves, therefore, under God's mighty hand, that he may lift you up in due time" (1 Peter 5:6).

Typology

Joseph prefigures Moses at the founding of Israel and Daniel at the end of Israel's monarchy. All three, oppressed captives in a hostile land, come to power by pitting God's wisdom against the wise of this world and displaying the superiority of God's wisdom and his rule over the nations. They prefigure Jesus Christ, God's wisdom, who astonishingly is raised from the cross to rule the world (1 Cor. 1:18–2:16; Rev. 12:1–5). As all were commanded to bow before Joseph (Gen. 41:43), so "at the name of Jesus every knee should bow" (Phil. 2:10).

God's Universal and Mediatorial Kingdoms[90]

God's building of his mediatorial kingdom to bless the nations occurs in the wider context of his universal kingdom. He looks after the well-being of Pharaoh as well as of Jacob's household. The two aspects of God's kingdoms are interdependent. On the one hand, God's universal dominion provides the food for the preservation of the mediatorial kingdom. On the other hand, the mediatorial kingdom has the prophetic light that saves the nations. Today the church is indebted to the universal rule of God for many of its provisions, but the only way to God and eternal life is through the word of the church pointing to Christ.

In this universal kingdom God exercises ultimate control. As Pharaoh reserved the ultimate throne for himself, so does God. Neither Pharaoh nor his officials were in control; God and his servant were, as they will be centuries later in the time of Christ. Herod could not prevent the birth of Christ, and Pilate had only the power God granted him (John 19:11).

---

[89]Roop, *Genesis*, 260.
[90]See "Introduction: The Kingdom of God" in the introduction.

Accommodation

While in Egypt, Joseph, like Daniel and his friends, has to accommodate his appearance but not his principles to participate ("in the world, not of it"). Both Joseph and Daniel are willing to wear pagan clothing, bear pagan names, and in the case of Daniel and his friends receive pagan schooling. However, Daniel and his friends refuse to violate Israel's explicit dietary laws, and Joseph never violates the eternal law of God written on the heart. He takes an Egyptian wife (cf. Gen. 24; 26:34–35; Deut. 7:3–6), but he uses Hebrew names for his children and associates them with the praise of God and possibly with his destiny back in the land of his fathers.

Imperial Power

God's universal kingdom involves imperial power, and Joseph must know how to use it, without abusing it. Roop says: "Joseph must deal with the presence of imperial power as well as with the presence of God. . . . Joseph chooses to disobey the illegitimate request of the powerful. He pays a high price, though not as high as others have paid. . . . For Joseph, royal power is dangerous, but not evil. He lives sometimes as victim and sometimes as agent of that power. Nevertheless, for all its force, royal power does not control the future. The power of dreams exceeds the power of Pharaoh."[91]

On the one hand, as Brueggemann states, "Joseph is the model for those who are born to rule. . . . This narrative affirms that power is a good thing. It celebrates the capacity to make tough decisions, to face crisis boldly, and to practice prudence so that the empire can be fed. . . . This is public power for the public good."[92]

On the other hand, God will overthrow abusive imperial power. In the first three acts of Book 10 the reversal of roles dominates. The powerful brothers who enslaved Joseph will bow before him. So will Potiphar and his wife, who imprisoned him. Brueggemann also states, "The reversal of roles in which Israel dominates and Pharaoh is the suppliant is an anticipation of the reversal of the Exodus. The empire is destroyed (Exod. 14:30). The hopeless slaves dance the death of the empire (Exod. 15:1)"[93] (see Christ on the teaching that the first shall be last, Matt. 19:30; 20:16; Mark 9:35; 10:31).

Faith and Certainty

Pharaoh's faith in Joseph is founded on both the cupbearer's testimony of Joseph's ability and Pharaoh's spiritual discernment that God's S/spirit is in Joseph. Pharaoh is so convinced of the truthfulness of Joseph's words, which Joseph makes the word of God (see Gen. 41:25, 28, 32), that he turns over the

---

[91]Roop, *Genesis*, 261.
[92]Brueggemann, *Genesis*, 295–96.
[93]Ibid., 295.

entire empire to him. The survival of the empire—that it not be cut off by God—depends on acting by faith. Joseph's words could not be proved empirically beforehand. So likewise today faith comes from the testimony of the church and correlatively from hearing God's word, not from human proofs (cf. John 10:3–6; 2 Cor. 3:14–18; 1 Thess. 1:4–6; 2:13; Heb. 10:15). Calvin in his justly famous *Institutes* writes, "The testimony of the Spirit is more excellent than all reason. For as God alone is a fit witness of himself in his Word, so also the Word will not find acceptance in men's hearts before it is sealed by the inward testimony of the Spirit. The same Spirit, therefore, who has spoken through the mouths of the prophets must penetrate into our hearts to persuade us that they faithfully proclaimed what had been divinely commanded."[94]

BOOK 10, ACT 3: THE DYSFUNCTIONAL FAMILY RECONCILED (42:1 – 46:27)

LITERARY ANALYSIS OF BOOK 10, ACT 3

Setting and Frame

Temporally, the act takes place in the early years of the great famine (45:6). This famine drives the act, forcing the family to struggle to their reconciliation and finally to migrate to Egypt. The journeys to Egypt frame the act. The act opens with Jacob sending his sons down to Egypt to secure a supply of grain in order to survive what he thinks will be a short famine (42:1–2). The act ends with the whole family going down—lock, stock, and barrel—to secure pastureland during the protracted famine (45:8–13). Geographically, the act is set in Canaan with the family making journeys down to Egypt. By contrast, Act 4 covers a period of seventeen years (see 47:9, 28) and takes place in Egypt with the family looking forward to its return to Canaan. The narrator radically separates the acts by inserting the genealogy of the seventy (signifying total completeness) family members who go down to Egypt.

The act is also framed by the contrasting relationships of the family members. It opens with the guilt-ridden brothers "looking at each other," unable to talk and act in the face of the crisis, and with Jacob barking at them (42:1). It ends with the brothers tearfully embracing one another, free of blaming and guilt, and the whole family anticipating being reunited with Joseph in Egypt.

This double frame points to the act's themes: providence and family reconciliation. The macrostructure of the book concerns itself with providence. At the climax of the act, Joseph, who had not been in the know, catches up to the narrator and the book's audience. In retrospect, Joseph can see that the threads of his tortured pilgrimage—the hateful brothers' attempts to

---

[94]J. Calvin, *Institutes of the Christian Religion,* trans. F. L. Battles (The Library of Christian Classics 20; Philadelphia: Westminster Press, 1960), 1.7.4. (p. 79).

harm him, his being sold as a slave, his imprisonment—are all part of God's design to save the family. Three times he repeats "God sent me [to Egypt]" (45:5–8). We do not know when the man of faith reaches this conclusion. We do know, however, that his initial dream of his brothers bowing down to him suddenly floods his mind when, in the first scene, he sees ten of his brothers bowing before him (42:6, 9). The Lord himself authenticates Joseph's interpretation of the sacred family's tortured history at the end of the act. As Jacob sets out for Egypt, in a vision the Lord assures him: "I will make you into a great nation there. I will go down to Egypt with you, and I will surely bring you back again" (46:3–4). Joseph uses, not abuses, his power of knowledge over his brothers both to fulfill his manifest destiny and to test their love and loyalty to a brother in need. Joseph's providence in the microstructure of this act mirrors God's providence in the macrostructure of Book 10.

As Roop notes, "The interaction between 'knowing' and 'not knowing,' 'recognizing' and 'not recognizing,' flows throughout the saga."[95] The knowing Joseph and the unknowing brothers function as a microcosm of the knowing God and unknowing humanity.

Plot

After the exaltation of Joseph over Egypt in three scenes (Act 2), the story now returns to Jacob, who has been in Canaan for over twenty years (37:2; 41:46). The original prophecy to Joseph is about to be fulfilled quickly in the three journeys to Egypt: first by Joseph's ten hateful brothers (42:1–38), second by them and his younger full brother Benjamin (43:1–45:28), and third by all the brothers and his father, Jacob (46:1–27).

The plot tension pertains primarily to the theme of the alienated brothers struggling toward reconciliation and secondarily with the family's struggle to survive the famine. The two themes are inseparable. The family cannot find salvation in Egypt until the brothers are first reconciled with Joseph.

In Scene 1 (42:1–38), the first journey to Egypt, Joseph imprisons Simeon, promising his release upon their second journey with Benjamin in hand. However, by clandestinely placing money in their sacks, Joseph gives them the choice of either returning the money, guaranteeing Simeon's release, or of keeping it and jeopardizing his freedom.

In Scene 2, Joseph's steward returns Simeon to them as soon as, but only after, they return the money to him (43:23). At the end of that scene, Joseph tests the brothers by giving Benjamin preferential treatment, but without envy the joyous brothers drink freely together.

In Scene 3, Joseph puts the brothers to their final test of loyalty to a needy brother. This time he makes Benjamin alone appear guilty by clandestinely

---

[95]Roop, *Genesis*, 265.

placing his silver cup in his sack and counseling the other brothers to return home in peace. Judah, however, offers himself as a slave in his brother's place. Joseph is now free to discard his Egyptian mask; they prove they are brothers he can trust through thick and thin. He assures them of his good will. In Scene 4, the act's denouement, the whole family migrates toward Egypt to find salvation with Joseph.

Characterization

In connection with the spiritual transformation of the brothers, Joseph and Judah emerge as heroes (see "Characterization" in the Literary Analysis of Book 10). Joseph's strategy to retain his power of knowledge in order both to test and discipline the brothers is done so skillfully that even the narrator's audience is uncertain about his motives and is tempted to project its own reactions onto him. In Scene 3, he brilliantly regroups the brothers in the same way as in the first scene of this book. However, instead of the brothers ganging up against Rachel's son (Joseph), they rally round Rachel's son (Benjamin). Instead of being cold and indifferent to their father, as in Scene 1, they are now filled with compassion for him. In retrospect, it is clear that Joseph's harsh, accusing treatment of his brothers serves both to discipline them and to test them, not to vent his spleen. Through his severe mercy they confess their sin and renounce their hateful ways (42:21, 28; 44:16). At the end of the day, he does them only good, not harm. When he identifies himself to them as the brother they sold into slavery, he immediately reassures them of his goodwill. To the end, however, the brothers question if he can be totally free of anger against them (50:18); again he has to assure them in the same way as at the end of this act.

Besides being brilliant and good, Joseph is passionate. In each of the three scenes, with escalating outbursts, he cannot contain his weeping as he observes from behind his Egyptian mask both their change of character and lays eyes on his brother Benjamin (42:24; 43:30; 45:1–2).

Judah eclipses Reuben as the family leader. Reuben cowardly and foolishly offers the lives of his sons to guarantee Benjamin's safety; Judah offers his own life. His speech to Jacob in Scene 2 is so respectful, sober, and forthright that Jacob has no alternative but to accede to the force of his argument and send Benjamin with them. Judah's speech to Joseph in Scene 3 is so truthful, cogent, and straight from the heart that he enables Joseph to become authentic, to acknowledge his real self, by throwing off his Egyptian guise to weep and embrace his brother. Moreover, Joseph for the first time seeks his father's well-being.

Key Words

"Silver, money" (*kesep*) is mentioned twenty times (42:25–45:22). In the first scene of Act 1, the brothers put a total of twenty pieces of silver before a brother (37:28). Now they put their brother over a fortune in silver. As might be expected in an act about family reconciliation, other key words are "brother" (ca. 50x) and "father" (ca. 40x).

BOOK 10, ACT 3, SCENE 1: FIRST JOURNEY: JOSEPH DISCIPLINES HIS BROTHERS (42:1–38)
LITERARY ANALYSIS OF BOOK 10, ACT 3, SCENE 1 ———
Plot and Structure

After about twenty years—Joseph's rise to rulership at the end of thirteen years and seven years of plenty—the brothers meet again. At the end of Act 1, Scene 1, the family was divided and Jacob was mourning inconsolably for Joseph: "In mourning will I go down to the grave to my son" (37:35). This scene recounts the first stage of reconciliation between the family members (see Literary Analysis of Act 3 above).

The scene's plot tension is about the family's survival, both physical and spiritual. Through the famine God initiates the suffering that begins the process of reconciliation (see "Severe Mercies" in Theological Reflections below). Fox comments, "Worldwide famine creates the backdrop for the family drama that is about to unfold. God is the prime mover here. Joseph, the wise administrator, works with this providence to unite the brothers. Joseph is the powerful governor not only of all Egypt but of his family as well. He providentially leads the brothers to repentance and brotherly concern."[96] Longacre, expecting a negative answer, asks: "Would mere salvation from physical starvation . . . have been sufficient if the family of Jacob had been left at odds with each other?"[97]

The references to death that frame this scene—"so that we may live and not die" (42:2); "his brother is dead . . . you will bring my gray head down to the grave in sorrow" (42:38)—depict the desperate physical and spiritual condition of this divided family. This scene also begins and ends in Canaan with Jacob's preferential concern for Benjamin (42:3–4, 38). Jacob's favoritism toward Benjamin and the extension of the famine to Canaan so that the other ten brothers are sent to Egypt set the stage of this tense scene.

The scene consists of three segments: leaving Canaan—Jacob sends ten sons to Egypt (42:1–5); in Egypt—the brothers have two audiences with Joseph (42:6–26); returning to Canaan—the brothers face Jacob (42:27–38). The knowing brother escalates the tensions. In the first audience, he accuses the brothers of being spies, evidently to worm out of them their admission that they have another brother. In the second interview, he incarcerates Simeon until they return with Benjamin and prove their innocence. Here he

---

[96]Fox, *Beginning*, 173.
[97]Longacre, *Joseph*, 50.

adds his own confession, "I fear God" (42:18). Threatened with starvation and now imprisonment, the brothers begin the process of reconciliation by owning up to their crime against Joseph: "Surely we are being punished because of our brother" (42:21). Joseph escalates the tension still further by putting the money they paid for the grain back in their sacks. Here they come to an even fuller awareness of God's involvement in their lives. "What is this that God has done to us?" they ask in their first mention of God (42:28). To rescue Simeon, the returning "thieves" must now risk their own death or imprisonment (see 43:18).

Characterization

Joseph's motives in using harsh words against his brothers are ambiguous and probably complex. The narrator suggests two motives by repeating "he recognized his brothers" (42:7, 8). In 42:7 he links Joseph's harsh speech with his immediate recognition of them, suggesting that he is punishing them by giving them a taste of their own medicine. As they had threatened him with death and imprisonment, he now threatens them with the same. In any case, the brothers interpret their treatment as punishment. In 42:8–9 the narrator links Joseph's drilling inquisition with his recognition of them and with his recall of his dream about them, suggesting that his harsh words are part of his developing strategy based on his dream to discipline and test his brothers. Even as Pharaoh's dream of abundance and famine formed the basis of Joseph's strategy to save the world, so his dream that his entire family would bow to him probably inspires him to develop a strategy that will bring all of them as a reconciled family to Egypt. Longacre says: "[Joseph] cannot trust himself to them until he knows that they are trustworthy."[98] Garrett argues that the text clearly shows that he acts out of spite (45:1–15).[99] In the final analysis—whatever his motives—Joseph's interactions with his brothers under the good hand of God mark an important transformation in the brothers' characters from being untrustworthy to trustworthy and in their interrelationships from dysfunctional to functional.

Joseph's brothers (and even the audience) expect Joseph to hold a grudge against them (45:15) and to get even. Perhaps Joseph was so tempted and spoke harshly out of his hurt and bitterness with a desire to get revenge—a motive quite different from disciplining punishment, as parents know—but if so, he overcomes the temptation, for his biographer does not characterize him in this way. In the preceding act the narrator records Pharaoh's characterization of Joseph as wise and discerning; getting even is not wise. In this scene, the narrator connects his harsh accusation that the brothers are spies to his dream, not to their selling him as a slave (cf. 45:4). As the brothers own up to their crime against him, he does not gloat but weeps (42:24). Longacre

[98]Longacre, *Joseph*, 50.
[99]Garrett, *Rethinking*, 171.

notes, "Here the narrator graphically portrays the process of reconciliation at its mid-phase."[100] Joseph will subsequently weep three more times (43:30; 45:2, 14–15).[101] Joseph's tactics are harsh, but his emotions are tender. At the end Joseph interprets their situations as part of God's plan for good (see 45:8; 50:20). This characterization is consistent with Joseph's later reactions and comments. When Judah gives impeccable evidence of the brothers' complete transformation, with intense emotions of love Joseph gives up his power over them by revealing his identity (45:1–3). He weeps over his brothers and kisses them (45:14–15). Right to the end of the book, he refuses to hold a grudge against his brothers; he forgives them and speaks kindly to them (50:21). Neither the narrator nor the protagonists at any time suggest that Joseph is angry with them or motivated by revenge.

Framing the brothers' return to Canaan, Reuben appears weak and stupid. At its beginning, when the brothers express their remorse, he can rise no higher than "I told you so." At its peak, he commendably wants to take responsibility to return Benjamin unharmed, but his guarantee that he will kill his two sons is not thought out and cowardly. What good would killing two grandsons do for Jacob? And why offer his sons, not himself? Judah will offer himself, not his sons, as a slave.

The patriarch takes authority over his family and displays initiative to supply its physical needs, but he continues to destroy it spiritually by showing favoritism to the sons of Rachel. He still grieves over Joseph and acts overprotectively of Benjamin and indifferently to Simeon. God, using famine and Joseph, reconciles the family in spite of Jacob.

EXEGETICAL NOTES TO BOOK 10, ACT 3, SCENE 1 ———

Leaving Canaan: Jacob Sends Ten Sons to Egypt (42:1–5)

1. Jacob. The patriarch is responsible for the entire family (see 37:21 and note).

learned. The text literally says that he "saw."

grain in Egypt. See 12:10; 26:1–2.

just keep looking at each other. Jacob's expression may connote that they are still a dysfunctional family, not helping each other out of their common plight (see 12:12; 43:18; 46:3).

2. die. See 42:38; see Literary Analysis above.

3. ten. Whereas Abraham went down to Egypt as one man with his household, now ten men and their beasts of burden have to go, since each has his own family (see 43:8). Going as a convoy may also provide security. In any case, they take their first step toward acting together. However, for the dream to be fulfilled, Benjamin must ultimately join them.

---

[100]Longacre, *Joseph*, 51.
[101]Fox, *Beginning*, 173.

Joseph's brothers. By this designation the narrator foreshadows the impending meeting.

4. did not send Benjamin. See 42:38. Joseph's full brother has taken his place in his father's affections (see 37:3). The brothers' treatment of him and of their father will test whether they have had a spiritual change.

5. Israel's sons. This is better translated "the sons of Israel," to suggest their national identity, not their personal identity as Jacob's sons. The narrator identifies them by their national designation to number them among the ethnic groups inhabiting the land of Canaan that go to Egypt for grain. The brothers enter Egypt as an embryonic nation; they will leave it as a powerful nation.

famine. God will use a famine to restore his elect to one another and to himself.

In Egypt: First Audience with Joseph (42:6–17)

6. governor. One could also translate this "vizier."

bowed down. To preserve their lives, the killers of the dream unwittingly begin to fulfill the divine dream (see 37:5–7).

7. recognized. "Recognize" (37:32–33) was a key word in the brothers' deception of Jacob; now it is a crucial word behind Joseph's deception of them. The scene is an interplay of "knowing" and "not knowing," "recognizing" and "not recognizing" (see Literary Analysis above).

he pretended. Literally, "he made himself unrecognizable." There may be a word play between *hitnakkēl*, "they plotted" (37:18), and *hitnakkēr*, "he pretended." Joseph keeps the power of knowledge to himself. People who sell a brother as a slave are not trustworthy; it is better to retain this kind of power over them.

spoke harshly. This could be translated, "to speak harsh things," things set out in 42:9–17 (see Literary Analysis above).

8. Although Joseph recognized his brothers, they did not recognize[102] him. The Hebrew literally reads, "and he recognized," repeating 42:7 (see "Characterization" in Literary Analysis above).[103] They do not recognize him, since Joseph has grown from a lad of seventeen (37:2) to a thirty-year-old man (see 41:12, 46 and notes). Moreover, as a lad he had a beard, but as an Egyptian man he is clean shaven (41:14).

9. Then he remembered. Joseph had forgotten his afflictions in his father's household, but now he remembers the dream. Genesis 42:8, Joseph's recognition of the brothers, repeats 42:7. In 42:7 Joseph's recognition follows the brothers' bowing down. The repetition in 42:8 just prior to Joseph's recollection of the dream links "he remembered" with "they bowed down to him" (42:6). But there are only ten bowing down. Where is the eleventh of

---

[102]This is the same Hebrew word as "he pretended" but in a different verb stem.
[103]NIV adds "although" to make sense of the repetition.

the dream? When the narrative is read as a whole, it seems apparent he constructs a series of events, in accordance with the dream, and in so doing disciplines, punishes, and tests his brothers to transform their character and to heal the rift between them and him. Without God's providence the strategy would fail. Just as Joseph planned a strategy for saving Egypt based on Pharaoh's dream, now he plans a strategy to save the family both physically and spiritually based on his dreams.

You are spies! Syntactically 42:9 links Joseph's accusations with his remembering of the dream.[104] He now acts according to the first dream of all eleven bowing down to him by strategizing to get Benjamin to join them. In order to test their sincerity, but without losing his power of knowledge over them, he creates the fiction that they are spies to worm out of them the confession that they have a brother. Next he incarcerates one of them to force them to prove that they are not spies by bringing Benjamin back from Canaan with them. No wonder the Egyptians were impressed with his extraordinary wisdom.

His accusation would not seem farfetched to the brothers (see Ex. 1:9–10; cf. 2 Sam. 3:25; 10:3). Frontier guards at Egypt's Asian border routinely checked travelers to discover spies who might herald an imminent attack. Famished armies could be expected to seek out any weaknesses in the fortifications in order to plunder stockpiled grain.

unprotected. The word literally means "naked."

11. We are all the sons of one man. A family does not risk almost all of its sons in the dangerous venture of spying. This is dramatic irony, for the statement unwittingly includes Joseph.

honest. The covenant family must be more than honest; it must show loving loyalty toward one another. Nevertheless, Joseph will test this claim. Although dishonest about Joseph to their father, they begin to act honestly here.

12. No! The characteristic hammering of an accusation to unnerve defenseless spies is necessary for the ruse and to worm information out of them (see 43:7). He repeats his accusation of spying four times to break down their resistance (42:12, 14, 15, 20).[105] Joseph's own lying is a necessary part of counteracting spying and should not be faulted. Rahab is commended for lying in connection with espionage. Lying in war is as necessary as deception in chess and sports (cf. the "fake punt" in football and the "hidden ball" in baseball).[106]

13. they replied. Their rebuttal to the charge of espionage is so compelling that they repeat it. They think that adding details makes them more credible; in reality, they are giving Joseph the information he wants.

one is no more. They think Joseph is dead.

---

[104]See J. S. Ackerman, "Joseph, Judah, and Jacob," in *Literary Interpretations of Biblical Narratives*, vol. 2, ed. K. R. R. Gros Louis (Nashville: Abingdon, 1982), 87.

[105]C. Westermann, *Genesis 37–50: A Commentary*, trans. J. J. Scullion (Minneapolis: Augsburg, 1985), 108.

[106]See B. K. Waltke, "Joshua," in *New Bible Commentary: 21st Century Edition* (Downers Grove, Ill.: InterVarsity, 1994), 239.

14. It is just as I told you. The leaving behind of one son suggests that the father knows espionage is a dangerous venture and so keeps one son back to guarantee the family's future.

As surely as Pharaoh lives. Ancients swore by the life of the king (see 2 Sam. 15:21).

15. how you will be tested. They are assumed guilty until they prove their innocence.

unless your younger brother comes. See "Then he remembered" in 42:9.

16. will be kept in prison. This is the first threat.

if you are telling the truth. Although his accusation is a ruse, they have told a half-truth about Joseph.

17. all in custody. See 40:3. Given a taste of their own fate, they connect their fate with their sin against Joseph.

In Egypt: Second Audience with Joseph (42:18 – 26)

18. On the third day. They taste for three days what Joseph had tasted for thirteen years! He dares not detain them too long; their families back home are starving. It took a week for them to get to Egypt and will take another week to return.

Joseph said. Both he and his brothers replace their first plan for dealing with one another with a wiser and more gentle plan (see 37:20, 27).

you will live. See 42:2. Not only is the famine sent by God a threat, now Joseph also threatens them with death. Both threats contribute to their confronting their sin against Joseph and beginning a spiritual conversion (42:21–24).

fear God. By reversing his decision because he fears God, Joseph plants the thought that they also fear God. There is a common conscience to provide for the hungry and to protect the defenseless (see 20:11).

19. let one of your brothers stay. His change of mind to keep only one and send nine reveals that he is a person who fears God and demonstrates that revenge is not the motivating factor (42:21, 28).

20. that you may not die. Joseph knows that the amount of grain he has given them will not last the duration of the seven-year famine. They will have to return with Benjamin to survive.

they proceeded to do. They accepted their fate that they have to bring Benjamin. Realizing the offer is fair, they proceed to select the brother, leading to the ensuing conversation between them.

21. we are being punished. This is better translated, "we are guilty and being punished." The Hebrew ʾāšam refers both to guilt and to its punishment. The two are inseparable.

because of our brother. Though falsely accused of spying, they see human beings as the tools of God's higher justice, matching their punishment with their crime against Joseph. Without that faith, they could not have participated in God's redemptive kingdom (see 44:16). Genesis is full of implicit punishments for misdeeds (e.g., Jacob and deception, Jacob at Shechem), but this is the only time the narrator allows the characters to state their conviction that only God governs the universe by matching moral deed with palpable destiny.

distressed . . . distress. They realize that under God they are reaping what they have sown (Gal. 6:7).

we would not listen. A real conversion is taking place from their former hardness of heart to a new sense of guilt when they themselves are confronted with life and death.

22. Reuben. See "Characterization" in Literary Analysis above. In their deliberations about who should stay behind, Reuben may be arguing that he should be excused from consideration because he opposed harming Joseph in the first place. Until now Joseph has probably held his eldest brother responsible for casting him in the pit. Heretofore he did not realize that Reuben opposed this action and intended to rescue him out of it.

not to sin. See 37:22.

accounting for his blood. See 9:5–6.

24. weep. Until now Joseph has dealt harshly with his brothers. With their confession of guilt, implicitly giving God glory, reconciliation is possible. "Whoever confesses [i.e., gives God glory by acknowledging God's awareness and punishment of sin] and renounces [his sins] obtains mercy" (Prov. 28:13). When the brothers are honest to themselves, Joseph can be honest with his own emotions.

Simeon. Joseph intervenes and selects Simeon because he now realizes the responsibility for selling him into slavery fell upon the second-oldest brother. Also, he knows Simeon's reputation for being cruel (34:25; 49:5–7).

bound before their eyes. He does this to impress upon them the seriousness of his intentions and their situation. To see Simeon again, they must bring Benjamin.

25. silver back. Joseph's motives are not stated. Are they punitive (Gunkel), redemptive (von Rad), or befuddled (Westermann)? He may be punishing them, but to make them merely squirm is out of keeping with his otherwise known nobility of character (see Literary Analysis above). Not to think clearly through a situation is also inconsistent with a man put in charge of Egypt precisely because he administers brilliantly. Perhaps he wants to treat them generously, but he cannot do it openly and retain his power of knowledge (see 43:23). Sternberg, like von Rad, thinks it is redemptive; Joseph is forcing them to face their past.[107] They previously put more value on money than on life. In that connection, he is testing their loyalty

---

[107]Sternberg, *Poetics*, 293–94.

to Simeon. To return with Benjamin is easy enough, but not when they appear to be criminals (see 43:23).

Returning to Canaan: Facing Jacob (42:27 – 38)

27. One of them. According to the narrator, only one opens his sack and finds the money at the stopping place; the rest find the money upon their return home (42:35). According to the brothers' account, each of them finds the money in the mouth of the sack on the way (43:21). The brothers are not concerned with precision in their accounts (see 42:29–34). The narrator allows his account to stand against theirs, leaving his audience to resolve the apparent contradiction.

28. Their hearts sank. They appear to be thieves.

What is this that God has done to us? This is the first time the brothers mention God; their aroused consciences see God at work behind their crime and punishment (42:21–22).

29. all that had happened. "All" is a relative term; here it must be understood as relative to all they want their father to know. In addition to other important changes noted below, they say nothing about the three-day detention, the shackling and imprisonment of Simeon, their remorse and Reuben's protestations, or finding the money.

30. and treated us as. The Greek reads, "and had us put in custody as."

33. Leave one of your brothers. They leave the impression that he is an honored guest, not a prisoner. Their attitude toward their father is now sensitive, no longer callused. Joseph lacks this compassion.

34. you can trade in the land. Out of consideration for their father's feelings, they change Joseph's threat of life and death (42:18, 20) to a promise of economic opportunity. They deliberately omit the return of money in a sack.

35. emptying their sacks. Until now they had only opened the feed sack (see 42:27).

father saw. Up to this point, Jacob probably found their story credible. The money, however, makes them look guilty, especially since he probably knows that they are not always trustworthy. Does Jacob think they sold Simeon? The money in the sack widens the breach between Jacob and his sons but binds the sons more closely together.

frightened. Now they all look guilty of stealing.

36. Their father Jacob said. He begins and ends his speech with self-pity.

is no more. He either does not believe them or does not trust Egypt's lord. In any case, since he has no intention of anyone returning to Egypt to retrieve Simeon, Simeon from his point of view is as good as dead.

You have deprived me of my children. Jacob speaks more accurately than he realizes. Still, Jacob allows no time for the sons to explain themselves. The money in the sack suffices to prove to him that they are guilty. He too must learn to trust. The brothers are drawing closer to one another in this scene, but Jacob is not drawing closer to his sons.

Everything is against me! His self-pity is understandable but not excusable. What about Simeon! And what about the affliction he inflicts on his family by holding back Benjamin?

37. You may put both of my sons to death. His poorly thought-out proposal is unconvincing to Jacob. Would Reuben really put his half-brother before his own sons? Besides, how would killing the patriarch's grandsons console Jacob? Reuben's suggestion would only further jeopardize the existence of a family already perilously close to destruction.

38. with you. The form is plural.

he is the only one left. By considering Rachel's other child as his only son, he further alienates the sons of Leah and of the concubines.

grave. See 37:35 for Sheol.

THEOLOGICAL REFLECTIONS ON
BOOK 10, ACT 3, SCENE 1 ——————————————

Providence

See "Characterization" in the Literary Analysis above.

Severe Mercies

God uses the famine over which none has control to reduce mighty Egypt to save his people and exalt them. Joseph's harsh speech is another severe mercy that God uses to punish, test, and teach the shattered family. At the beginning of the scene, Joseph is counted by the family as dead, and he himself makes no effort to return to them; Jacob continues to grieve the loss of Joseph and perhaps suspects his sons; the brothers can only "look at each other" instead of acting together for their common good; and they suffer with a hidden guilty conscience. In sum, they are alienated from God and from one another.

God, through the famine, initiates the saving process by forcing the family to confront their past and each other. Joseph's harshness also helps to heal the fracture and to restore the family to God. Simeon's detention in Egypt reminds the ten brothers of how they treated Joseph, and for the first time they recognize the Moral Governor of the universe at work in their lives. Their consciences are awakened to confess their guilt (42:21–24) and to fear God (42:28). They take responsibility to retrieve Simeon from prison (42:19, 24) and to protect Benjamin from harm (42:37; see 43:1–45:28). Upon their return they show sensitivity to their father's emotions by retelling their adventures in a way that will assuage his fears. The confession of their guilt causes Joseph to weep. The faith, penitence, tender emotions, and loyalty that unite a family are now being fashioned. Through the famine Joseph comes to rule over Egypt and the sons of Israel become worthy to be called the people of God. Both God's famine and Joseph's harsh speech confront the brothers with life and death (42:2, 18, 20). Through these severe mercies the fractured family is being healed.

Knowledge and Power

With his knowledge, Joseph has a power over others, a power that provides a helpful analogy for God's providence directing people's lives. Where the family sees events in Egypt as affliction and trouble, Joseph is actually strategizing to bring about their good. However, the analogy to God's providence is limited by Joseph's humanity. He must be careful to use his power appropriately, and the success of his strategy is ultimately dependent on God's providence.

Roop says, "Joseph's power [over the brothers] rests as much in 'knowing' and 'recognizing' as in his imperial position in Egypt. The previous episode related that his position came from his 'knowing' and 'recognizing'. Jacob, the brothers, the cupbearer and baker, Pharaoh, remain relatively powerless because they do not know. Joseph, who does know, has the power to restore or destroy the family. He comes close to destroying it."[108] The "omniscient" Joseph acts in God's stead. He providentially brings events into their lives that to them are inexplicable, but they are intelligible to the one who knows (see 42:15; 43:25). "The brothers constantly confront the ominous world of 'not knowing.' Events seem to happen at random and the dark side of their imagination senses a threat to their lives."[109] The family confronts death, famine, execution for espionage, and inability to trade, but all these dark events mysteriously are in wise and good hands.

BOOK 10, ACT 3, SCENE 2: SECOND JOURNEY: JOSEPH ENTERTAINS HIS BROTHERS (43:1–34)

LITERARY ANALYSIS OF BOOK 10, ACT 3, SCENE 2 ————

Plot and Structure

This scene can be divided into two incidents marked by the two settings: in Canaan—family negotiations to return to Egypt (43:1–14); in Egypt—feasting with Joseph in his home (43:15–34). The scene's plot tension involves the developing reconciliation of the formerly estranged brothers. Jacob's favoritism and fears, the uncertainty of the brothers' behavior, and Joseph's disguised identity are seeming obstacles to reconciliation. In the two settings of this scene, food is the focal point for the movement toward reconciliation. In Canaan, the lack of food forces the family to confront a return to Egypt (43:1–14). The family's imminent starvation motivates Judah to speak wisely and boldly to his father and convinces Jacob to release Benjamin (see Exegetical Notes for further analysis). This episode begins and ends with Jacob's instructions to return to Egypt. In Egypt, the drama of reconciliation begins with Joseph's command to prepare a meal and ends

---

[108]Roop, *Genesis*, 265.
[109]Ibid., 267.

with the brothers feasting at that meal (43:15–34). The brothers are brought to Joseph's home for a dinner. Here at anxious moments they nervously try to return their silver, all eleven brothers bow before Joseph, and Joseph is moved by the sight of Benjamin (see Exegetical Notes for further analysis). At the peak of reconciliation in this scene the brothers freely feast with Benjamin, whom Joseph has lavished with favoritism.

Characterization

The narrator's use of dialogue and narrow focus upon certain details of the meal betray his intention to characterize the family members in their process of reconciliation. The double crisis of famine and Joseph's "harsh" stipulation that to buy food Benjamin must accompany them draws the family even closer together.

Jacob still foolishly dotes on Benjamin and is indifferent to Simeon, but unlike in Scene 1, this time he sends his sons to Egypt with gifts in hand and God's blessing on their heads. He finally resigns himself to his fate in God's hands.

Judah emerges as the new leader. While he accedes to the patriarch's direction, he speaks forcefully, sensibly, and soberly. The severe mercies of famine and Joseph's test coaxes the best out of him. Judah risks his own family fortune and life to save the rest of the family. Later he will offer himself as a slave for his brother for the sake of his father (44:33–34). His development in this scene should be held together with the depiction of his character in chapters 37 and 38 (see "Characterization" in Literary Analysis of Book 10 and in Literary Analysis of Book 10, Act 1, Scene 2).

Joseph now drops his hard front but retains his power of knowledge. He extends genuine hospitality to his family; beyond that, his authentic, tender emotions are bound up in his family, not in his Egyptian social superiority.

The brothers accede to the patriarch's direction and obey his instruction exactly, even when he maligns them. In connection with the "found" money, they prove their honesty; a divine benediction transforms their relationship with Joseph from fright to peace; they submit to legitimate authority by giving gifts and doing obeisance; and climactically, in spite of the fact that Joseph gives Benjamin preferential treatment, all twelve drank freely together. The steward sums it up: shalom has been restored (43:23)

EXEGETICAL NOTES TO BOOK 10, ACT 3, SCENE 2 ———

In Canaan: Family Negotiations to Return to Egypt (43:1–14)

1. **famine.** See 41:57.

2. **their father.** Jacob is still the head of the family. He takes the initiative and makes the ultimate decisions. He sends his sons to Egypt and at the end (45:26–28) agrees to settle there. Yet he is also a man of the past. Judah begins to lead the family.

buy us a little more food. See 42:1.

3. Judah. Judah is the oldest son in good standing with his father (cf. 34:30; 35:22). Jacob had earlier definitively refused Reuben's weak guarantee of Benjamin's safety (42:37), and Simeon is in Egyptian custody (42:24). From this point on Judah becomes the leader of his brothers (cf. 44:14–34; 46:28). His tribe will become preeminent among the sons of Israel (49:8–10; Matt. 1:2, 17; Luke 3:23, 33).

You will not see my face again. As in all the other retellings of this act, Judah is offering a free paraphrase of 42:18–20, omitting details and adding information possibly blanked by the narrator.

4. If you will send. Although presumably without Jacob's permission they could have grabbed Benjamin and run, they will not go without their father's direction. The sons, now grown men, accede to the patriarch's leadership. As Hamilton explains, "Joseph's word is final in Egypt; Jacob's word is final in Canaan."[110] The onus is totally on Jacob.

5. we will not go down. Judah accedes to his father's direction but also lays down a definitive condition to match his father's refusal.

6. Israel. This is his name as head of the clan.

7. questioned us closely about ourselves and our family. Again, this is not a precise correspondence to the narrator's account of their interview with Joseph (42:11–14). They are not doctoring the story to excuse themselves because in 44:19 Judah says the same thing to Joseph, who knows the facts and holds their fate. Probably the narrator has blanked material in chapter 42.

8. Judah said. Judah takes the leadership again and breaks the stalemate between the patriarch and his sons. He does not overstep the patriarch's authority, but, in Sarna's words, "his approach is forthright, firm, sober, and severely to the point."[111] Jacob must face the reality that there is no alternative.

boy [*na^{c}ar*]. The flexible term, meaning "lad," refers to a male from infancy (Ex. 2:6) to marriage (cf. Gen. 21:12, 17, 18; 34:19; 41:12). Since Benjamin was born before Joseph went down to Egypt, he was more than twenty-two years of age. Here the term describes Benjamin's social standing in the family as the youngest brother, not his absolute age (cf. 42:13, 15, 20; 43:29; 44:23, 26). Likewise, Joseph, who is about thirty-eight years old, addresses his younger brother as "my son" in 43:29.

we and you and our children. Jacob's intransigence threatens all three generations of the family. Judah mentions them "in ascending order of importance to himself."[112]

may live and not die. Judah repeats Jacob's words the first time he sent the brothers to Egypt (42:2). Here it is a double entendre, referring both to the famine and to Joseph's threat (42:18–20, 34).

---

[110]Hamilton, *Genesis 18–50*, 540.
[111]Sarna, *Genesis*, 298.
[112]Ibid.

9. I myself will guarantee his safety. The text literally says, "I will become surety for him." Proverbs 6:1–5 forbids one to assume responsibility for a debt contracted by a stranger, but Judah is assuming a responsibility to save the family. Should he default in returning Benjamin, Judah is willing to surrender his family's fortune to Jacob, who can then do with it as he wishes. This is the second time Judah saves a brother (see 37:27), for he implicitly saves imprisoned Simeon (see Literary Analysis).

you can hold me personally responsible. Reuben put his sons' lives on the line; Judah puts his own life on the line. This is the second time Judah outshines Reuben as leader (cf. 37:21–22 and 37:26–27; 42:37 and 43:8–10).

I will bear the blame before you all my life. The Hebrew literally reads, "I will have sinned. . . ." If he violates this agreement, Judah is willing to take whatever penalty Jacob wishes to inflict on him for the rest of his life, and the patriarch can and will treat his sons harshly (see 49:3–7).

10. if we had not delayed. Judah speaks directly and severely.

11. If it must be. As his later speech to Joseph will also display, Judah is a persuasive speaker. This is the turning point in their conversation. Jacob now concedes and prepares them for their encounter with Joseph by sending gifts, returning the money, and offering a prayer for them.

gift. The Hebrew is the same as in 4:4–5; 32:13 (see notes). It refers to giving a token of submission. When approaching a superior (political, 1 Sam. 16:20; military, 1 Sam. 17:18; or religious, 2 Kings 5:15), this is a way to demonstrate respect.

balm. See 37:25.

honey.[113] The honey Jacob sends is from the large quantity of wild honey found in hollows of rocks (Deut. 32:13), in trees (1 Sam. 14:25–26), and in animal carcasses (Judg. 14:8). Honey was the basic source of sweetening (Ex. 16:31; Prov. 24:13; 25:16), abundant and prized (Ps. 19:10; 119:103; Prov. 5:3; Song 4:11), thought to have medicinal properties (Prov. 16:24), a good gift (2 Sam. 17:29; 1 Kings 14:3; Jer. 41:8). An Egyptian would have prized it as a delightful sweet during a famine.

12. double. This covered the money found in the sacks plus the money needed for the new purchase of supplies (see 43:21–22).

must return the silver. Though found unexpectedly and its source unknown, it was not given to them by the Egyptians. The covenant family must act ethically and make restitution (see 42:11 and note).

Perhaps it was a mistake. In light of Judah's offer, Jacob has second thoughts about the guilt of his sons (see 42:36 and note).

14. God Almighty. This is God's title in connection with his covenant promises to make them into a great nation to bless the nations (see 17:1).

---

[113]Beekeeping was practiced in Egypt as early as the Old Kingdom. It was introduced into Mesopotamia in the eighth century and probably into Palestine in the Hellenistic period. Explicit mention is made of honey from bees in Judg. 14:8–9 (E. Firmage, "Zoology," *ABD*, 6:1150).

if I am bereaved, I am bereaved. Jacob resigns himself to fate, but not as stoic. He resigns himself to his destiny after praying for God's mercy on their journey (see Esth. 4:16).

In Egypt: Feasting with Joseph (43:15 – 34)

15. men took. They follow Jacob's instructions precisely.

16. saw Benjamin. This sighting pertains to Joseph's private conversation with his steward. In 43:29 "saw Benjamin" pertains to his public conversation with his brothers.

prepare dinner. This is the frame of the incident (see Literary Analysis above).

18. frightened. Since they are singled out from the other buyers, they interpret Joseph's "good" providence as evil.

wants to attack us and overpower us and seize us as slaves. They probably know that high Egyptian officials keep dungeons in their homes (see 40:3; 42:17). Again, this is an ironic image of their treatment of Joseph.

23. It's all right. The steward literally says, "Peace [šālôm] to you." Rites of greetings establish the social status and relationship. "Peace," repeated three times, is the key word in their new relationship (rendered "how is" in 43:27 [2x]).

Your God, the God of your father. This turning point in the relationship of the brothers toward Joseph, from fear (see 42:21–22, 28, 35; 43:18) to peace, is spoken by a foreigner who trusts in their God. He recognizes that Providence directs human acts (see 45:5).

has given you treasure. They are to keep the money even though they returned it.

I received. Literally, "has come to me," this legal formula confirms receipt of full payment.

Then he brought Simeon out. The narrator links the restoration of Simeon to the restoration of the money, not to the return with Benjamin. The unexpected connection validates the interpretation that Joseph placed the money in their sack to test their fidelity to a brother, though to be sure they were under extreme pressure to do so (see 42:25).

24. gave them water . . . provided fodder. These are acts of hospitality (see 18:2–5) and a transition to Joseph's arrival.

26. bowed down. The narrator reserves this detail until Simeon is with them; he blanks this gesture in 43:15. The first dream of all eleven brothers bowing down to him is now fulfilled.

27. how they were. The Hebrew literally says, "about peace" (see 43:23).

How is. Here the text literally reads, "Is there peace" (see 43:23). This is a question about his total well-being.

your . . . father. Joseph is not indifferent to his father. He is probably aware that he is playing on a stage larger than any individual life (45:5–7).

aged . . . you told me about. Obviously, information they gave about their father is blanked in chapter 42 (see 44:31).

Is he still living? See 45:3. This is a figure of speech in which the logical sequence is inverted.

28. bowed low to pay him honor. See 43:26. They literally "bowed down and made obeisance." Sarna suggests that this is "either as a sign of appreciation to Joseph for his solicitude in asking about their father's welfare or as a gesture of gratitude to God, a physical equivalent of the verbal 'Thank God.'"[114]

29. looked about and saw. This is an important providential sight (see 24:63–64).

his own mother's son. He has a special bond with his full brother.

God be gracious. This Aaronic benediction is not a common greeting.

my son. Though seemingly of unequal social status, this is an assurance that they are family.

30. a place to weep. Joseph can only retain his power of knowledge by withdrawing to weep three times (42:24; 43:30; 45:1–2, 14–15). Underneath the cloak of Egyptian appearance, his love for his family throbs.

private room. Examples can still be seen in burial chambers of important persons.

31. Serve the food. "Joseph hosts a meal for his brothers, who years before had callously sat down to eat while he languished in the pit."[115]

32. served him by himself. This is because of Joseph's exalted position.

could not eat. A fortiori, they cannot sleep with them. The taboo is probably based on the Egyptian notion of their ethnic and cultural superiority. They look upon shepherds and Israel's form of worship as detestable (see 46:34; Ex. 8:26).

detestable to Egyptians. Herein lies a clue to the rationale for the Egyptian sojourn. Whereas the Canaanites are willing to integrate and absorb the sons of Israel, the Egyptians hold them in contempt. Judah's intermarriage with the Canaanites in Genesis 38 shows the danger that syncretistic Canaanites present to the embryonic family. The Egyptian segregated culture guarantees that the embryonic nation can develop into a great nation within their borders. The Egyptian threat will take the form of tyranny.

33. had been seated. Literally, "they sat." The NIV gloss rightly interprets the seating arrangement as under Joseph's direction.

in the order of their ages. They see the hand of Joseph's ambiguous providence.

34. Benjamin's portion was five times as much. Joseph tests the brothers for jealousy. This preferential treatment is comparable to the preferential

---

[114]Sarna, *Genesis*, 301.
[115]Ibid., 302.

treatment Jacob gave Joseph. To be invited to a meal with a high official assumes a close relationship with him, but it is fraught with the potential for promotion or rejection. Proverbs 23:1–3 instructs the wise son not to be distracted by the official's food; the guest's character is either intentionally or unwittingly under surveillance by the higher official.

feasted and drank. These are the two parts of a dinner.

drank freely. Literally, "they drank and got drunk," but, as noted in Gen. 9:21, this does not necessarily have a negative connotation. As W. Brown argues, it means the celebrators "drank and became fully content.[116]

THEOLOGICAL REFLECTIONS ON BOOK 10, ACT 3, SCENE 2

God As Covenant Partner

The merciful (43:14), providing (43:23), and gracious (43:29) God of the fathers brings peace to the shattered family (43:23, 26–28) through his ambiguous providence. The brothers seem like pawns in a mysterious play of power between God (famine) and Jacob (refusing to allow Benjamin to go down to Egypt) and Joseph (insisting Benjamin come down). Joseph's privileged knowledge and his control over his brothers functions as a microcosm of God's omniscience and his ultimate control over all. The brothers get a brief insight into a knowing hand when they are seated in the order of their ages. Joseph himself will later discern the guiding hand of God over all, including the wrongs of his brothers against him.

Sons of Israel As Covenant Partners

Coming forth from this crucible, the formerly callous brothers emerge a bonded family, shining with integrity and love toward one another (see Literary Analysis above). At peace among themselves, they are ready to become a nation within proud Egypt, who holds them in contempt.

BOOK 10, ACT 3, SCENE 3: THE BROTHERS TESTED AND RECONCILED (44:1 – 45:15)

LITERARY ANALYSIS OF BOOK 10, ACT 3, SCENE 3

Structure and Plot

This scene exposes the anatomy of reconciliation: in the crucible of crisis the brothers respond with compassion and self-sacrifice. The crisis is sparked by Joseph's final test of the brothers' integrity. The scene develops through three incidents: the steward's test of the brother's integrity (44:1–13), Joseph's test of Judah's integrity (44:14–34), and Joseph's disclosure of his

---

[116]Brown, "Noah: Sot or Saint?," 36–60.

identity and assurances of peace (45:1–15). The tension quickly builds with Joseph's plot of putting his silver cup in Benjamin's sack, the steward's accusations of ingratitude and burglary, and the brothers' rash proposal if one is found guilty. At the center of the scene is Judah's impassioned plea, which forms the turning point not only of the act but of the entirety of Book 10. Judah's unusually long speech (44:18–34), a study in persuasion, represents a reversal of the brothers' transgressions. Brothers, angry and indifferent toward their father and so jealous of their brother they conspire to sell him into slavery, now beg for their father's well-being and offer themselves as slaves to save their father's now-favorite child. The scene peaks when Joseph lets go of his power over his brothers and with a loud outburst of emotions makes himself known to them (45:1–3). G. von Rad explains, "Judah's speech in every respect brings the climax to the suspense, both with regard to the brother's despair and to Joseph's inner emotion. . . . This seething of his emotion coincides precisely with the inner end of the test of the brothers, for Judah's words had shown that the brothers had changed. They obviously intend to treat Rachel's younger son, Benjamin, quite different from the way in which they had formerly treated the elder son."[117] In the denouement, Joseph relieves their terror by assuring them of God's good providence directing their lives (45:4–8). He sends a message to Israel to find refuge from the famine in Egypt (45:9–11) and embraces his brothers (45:12–14). The scene ends with the brothers talking to one another as brothers (45:15).

Key Words

In this scene about reconciling a family, "father" is used twenty times and "brother" sixteen times. Fourteen of the twenty uses of "father" occur in Judah's skillful speech.

Characterization

Judah is the hero (see "Characterization" in Literary Analysis of Book 10). He accepts that love is irrational, unpredictable, and elective. He now accepts the painful reality of favoritism without rancor. In spite of this election, he displays both paternal and fraternal love and loyalty. Alter says, "His entire speech is motivated by the deepest empathy for his father, by a real understanding of what it means for the old man's very life to be bound up with that of the lad. He can even bring himself to quote sympathetically (v. 27) Jacob's typically extravagant statement that his wife bore him two sons—as though Leah were not also his wife and the other ten were not also his sons."[118] The loss of his own two sons shortly before this scene (Gen. 38) probably contributes to Judah's becoming sensitive to his father's grief. His speech, a climactic moment in the book of Genesis, is respectful to his audi-

---

117von Rad, *Genesis*, 397.
118Alter, *Biblical Narrative*, 175.

ence, fully and carefully documented, and, above all, passionate and straight from the heart. As he persuaded his father in his first extended speech (cf. 43:3–10), he now reaches Joseph's heart and reconciles the brothers. He exhibits "in spades" Israel's ideals of kingship (see Theological Reflections).

Joseph gives up his power of knowledge, whereby he controlled his brothers, for the embrace of intimacy with them. For the first time he can be authentic; the once estranged brother can discard his facade and freely express his emotions within the family he loves. For the first time he shows real concern for the well-being of his father. For the first time he can interpret his narrative. Longacre says, "the central participant of the story has now caught up with its unfolding macrostructure. . . . Like the narrator and us, [he] can stand above the story and view it as a whole."[119] By this faith Joseph is able to reinterpret the barbarisms his brothers inflicted upon him as God's good design to save them through him.

The brothers collectively exhibit the virtues of reconciliation (see also Theological Reflections). They have become the kingdom of God, a family fit to rule the world.

EXEGETICAL NOTES TO BOOK 10, ACT 3, SCENE 3 ———

The Steward's Test of the Brothers (44:1 – 13)

1. Joseph gave these instructions. As God tested the reality of Abraham's faith (see 22:1), Joseph tests the genuineness of his once hateful brothers' conversion.

in the mouth of his sack. When the steward searches the brothers' sacks (44:12), they will all look guilty of theft. Nevertheless, the steward will clear all of them of any charges except Benjamin. If motivated by selfish interests, not the good of the family, the brothers are being given every reason to free themselves from slavery and abandon Benjamin.

2. put my cup. The Hebrew *gᵉbîaᶜ*, "goblet," glossed "bowl" in Jer. 35:5 (NIV), is a larger container for wine than *kôs*, "cup." They probably drank from it the night before; at least the brothers had access to it. Later Joseph's steward calls it a cup for divination (44:5). That here Joseph only refers to it as a silver goblet is telling. The claim of divination is part of the ruse (see 44:5 and Theological Reflections below).

youngest one's sack. The original crime pertained to the brothers' hatred of Joseph, Rachel's son and Jacob's favorite, and the brothers selling him into slavery. Joseph brilliantly recreates the same grouping. Will they remain loyal to Joseph's full brother even when he looks guilty of theft? Or will they abandon him in Egypt as they had innocent Joseph?

3. As morning dawned. Twenty years of unresolved conflict between the brothers will be reconciled on this critical day of testing.

---

[119]Longacre, *Joseph*, 51.

4. the city. This is in the region of Goshen but otherwise unidentified.
good with evil. See 50:20.

5. the cup. His expression assumes that they know their crime.

divination. The techniques of hydromancy (pouring water into oil), oelomancy (oil into water), and oenomancy (wine into another liquid)[120] were commonplace in the ancient Near East. Through the surface patterns formed by pouring one type of liquid upon another, the practitioner professed to determine the mind of the gods with reference to the future, to the source of trouble, or to the truth of guilt or innocence. Referring to the wine goblet as a divining cup contributes to the ruse. Joseph receives revelation from God alone (37:5–9; 41:16; see Theological Reflections below).

9. he will die; and the rest . . . slaves. The law does not prescribe the death penalty for offenses against property. Their alleged theft, however, also entails unforgivable ingratitude and sacrilege. Their rash oath (cf. 31:32) stems from the conviction of their innocence. They express their faith in one another in the strongest terms. Such faith is essential for a good family relationship.

10. let it be as you say. Brushing aside the rashness and rhetoric of their oath, the steward at the least concurs that the guilty should become a slave of the wronged party.

will become my slave. He would be the steward's slave immediately until turned over to Joseph. The steward's just modification of the brothers' offer (44:9) is necessary—the test pertains to their attitude toward making Benjamin a slave (see 44:17).

the rest of you will be free. They will be free from servitude.[121] When Benjamin is found to have the cup, they will be confronted with a choice that has significant similarities to their choice with Joseph. Benjamin, like Joseph, is innocent, but they are free to leave him in slavery in Egypt.

11. quickly lowered. This shows their innocence.

12. proceeded to search. The narrator blanks what happened to the silver in the mouth of each of the sacks (44:1) because it is overshadowed by the goblet in Benjamin's sack and because it is inconsequential to the reconciliation of the brothers.

the oldest . . . youngest. The narrator builds suspense in describing the progression of the steward's search (cf. 31:33). The steward knows the order of their ages from the dinner the night before (see 43:33).

13. they tore their clothes. Their actions confirm their character change. They now show affection for their father and brother (contra 37:34).

all . . . returned. They pass the test; they do not abandon their brother.

---

[120]In Mesopotamia, private citizens used lecanomancy (divination from observing liquids) because it was cheaper than extispicy (divination from animal entrails) (W. W. Hallo and W. K. Simpson, *The Ancient Near East: A History* [New York: Harcourt Brace Jovanovich, 1971], 158–63).

[121]D. R. Hillers. "*Běrît ʿām*: 'Emancipation of the People.'" *JBL* 97 (1978): 179.

Joseph's Test of Judah (44:14 – 34)

14. Judah. He is clearly the leader.

threw themselves [*npl*]. They did not "fall prostrate in obeisance" (*hištaḥᵃwâ*), as in 37:7, 9, 10; 43:26. They are now desperate, not deferring.

15. divination. See 44:5. His words are not to be taken at face value any more than his feigned anger. Ironically, this divination cup does not discern Benjamin's innocence.

16. Judah replied. In this first speech Judah makes three points: he protests the brother's innocence of the theft, confesses their dilemma as due to God's judgment for previous guilt, and finally offers all of the brothers as slaves. In that way he undoes the rash oath to kill the guilty and avoids having to face their father.

How can we prove our innocence? The circumstantial evidence against them is so overwhelming, it is pointless to defend themselves.

God has uncovered your servants' guilt. He cannot be referring to the goblet, for he has just asserted their innocence. He may be referring to guilt in general, but more probably to their crime against Joseph. If so, they confess their crime against Joseph twice in his presence (42:21).

my lord's slaves. Judah assumes family solidarity but wisely offers themselves up not to death but as slaves.

17. Far be it from me. His words have double meaning. It is not he who would make his brothers slaves.

Only the man. The situation is now reconstructed. Will they show compassion on their father and show loyalty to Joseph's brother (see 44:10)? His limitation to only the man is consistent with God's moral law—yet part of the test.

father in peace. It is impossible to return to their father in peace without Benjamin.

18. Judah went up to him. Judah must speak. In an impassioned address to save Benjamin, the longest speech in Genesis, Judah appeals to Joseph to show mercy to his father. He first rehearses the history of their two journeys to Egypt, focusing on their father's great reluctance to accede to Joseph's demand to send the son lest he suffer the pain of losing another son (44:18–29). He emphasizes that the loss of this son will kill the father (44:30–31). He culminates his appeal by asking Joseph to allow him to fulfill his pledge and become the slave in the boy's stead to spare his father misery (44:32–34).

though you are equal to Pharaoh. See 41:39–43. He is careful to honor his audience.

19. father. This is the key word (14x) of Judah's speech. Judah essentially begins and ends his speech by referring to his father (44:19, 34). Judah's speech is designed to convey to the ruler the impact of his actions on their father. It is even more powerful as it causes Joseph to realize the cost of his deeds to his own father.

20. His brother is dead. His account is unintentionally inaccurate, and Joseph knows it.

loves him. It is clear that Jacob has not changed. He still dotes upon his youngest son. But the brothers have changed. They have experienced a conversion of affections.

23. But you told your servants. Tactfully, he omits any reference to the accusations of spying and their imprisonment.

27. my wife bore me two sons. In effect, Judah willingly delegitimizes himself as a son.

28. I have not seen him since. This unnecessary addition by Jacob suggests that he suspects mischief as a possibility.

33. in place of the boy. This first instance of human substitution in Scripture reveals a different Judah than the one who sold his brother into slavery (37:26–27). Sternberg notes, "Simply, Judah so feels for his father that he begs to sacrifice himself for a brother more loved than himself."[122]

34. see the misery. A formerly callused Judah (see 37:34–35) is now compassionate. Sternberg explains, "That Judah should adduce the father's favoritism as the ground for self-sacrifice is such an irresistible proof of filial devotion that it breaks down Joseph's last defenses."[123] Judah's love excels (see 43:3). He is worthy of kingship.

Joseph's Disclosure of His Identity and Assurances of Peace (45:1–15)

1. Then Joseph. Judah's speech proves beyond doubt that the formerly hateful, selfish brothers are now motivated by love for one another and have integrity within themselves and with one another.

could no longer control himself. His emotional release is overwhelming. Roop states, "The imperial power broker who had controlled the course of events in this whole chapter, with only an occasional and very private lapse, suddenly lost control of himself. The man who had been able to keep separate his family and national world could do so no longer."[124]

before all his attendants. The Egyptian wisdom literature prized a "cool," controlled spirit. Now Egypt's wisest man gives expression to a higher wisdom of authentic passion.

Have everyone leave my presence! No outsider can share in this intensely intimate moment of reconciliation between the brothers. Heretofore he talked privately with his Egyptian steward (44:1–15); now he talks privately with his brothers. In doing this, Joseph affiliates himself with the struggling covenant family, not with the riches of Egypt (Heb. 11:22).

2. wept so loudly. This is the third time Joseph weeps. Each time he loses more control of his tender emotions toward his brothers (see 42:24; 43:30–

---

[122]Sternberg, *Poetics*, 308.
[123]Ibid.
[124]Roop, *Genesis*, 271.

31; 45:2). These emotional bursts give expression to his true identity with the elect family beneath his Egyptian veneer and release Joseph's pent-up emotions at the peak of Book 10.

the Egyptians. The LXX reads, "all the Egyptians."

Pharaoh's household heard. His authentic emotions are with his despised, shepherding brothers, not with the sophisticated, proud culture of the palace.

3. I am Joseph. See Acts 7:13.

Is my father still living? Joseph does not refer to "your father," as in his previous cordial interview (43:27). His question is now not cordial but genuinely concerned with the truth. Perhaps Judah's passionate concern for their father opened Joseph's eyes to see his own insensitivity while testing his brothers. He too had missed the intergenerational unity of the family.

not able to answer him. The family is moving close to true intimacy, but as long as they live in fear of the one they wronged and until they allow themselves to be embraced by forgiveness, they do not talk intimately to one another.

terrified. This is a term used of paralyzing fear as felt by those involved in war (Ex. 15:15; Judg. 20:41; 1 Sam. 28:21; Ps. 48:5). Their lives are clearly in the hands of the one they thought they killed.

4. Then Joseph said. This lengthy speech of Joseph's (45:4–13) without any response from his brothers may imitate the rush of speech when an emotional barrier has been broken.

the one you sold into Egypt. No rebuke is intended. He needs to prove his identity (cf. 45:12); only Joseph knows their secret. Moreover, with their secret out, they can be freed from suppressed guilt.

5. Do not be angry with yourselves. Joseph directs their gaze away from their sins to God's grace (see 50:19; Num. 21:8–9).

to save lives. Here Joseph's reference is general, likely including the lives of the Egyptians and others. In 45:7 he speaks more specifically ("your lives") of the covenant family.

God sent me. This statement, repeated three times, is the theological heart of the account of Jacob's line (see 50:19–21; Acts 7:9–10). God directs the maze of human guilt to achieve his good and set purposes (Acts 2:23; 4:28). Such faith establishes the redemptive kingdom of God.

6. two years. Joseph is thirty-nine years old at this time (see 41:46, 53).

plowing and reaping. This is a merism for crops (cf. Ex. 34:21).

7. remnant. The term denotes descendants who survive a great catastrophe. Here the incomplete metaphor signifies that the embryonic nation (see 46:8–27) "in narrowly escaping destruction is like a remnant which is the bearer of hopes for the future existence."[125]

great. The word here refers to something supernatural.[126]

---

[125]G. Hasel, *The Remnant: The History and Theology of the Remnant Idea from Genesis to Isaiah* (Berrien Springs, Mich.: Andrews Univ. Press, 1972), 154–55 n. 69.

[126]Speiser, *Genesis*, 338.

deliverance. Literally "survivors," this is another technical term along with "remnant" for the descendants of the patriarchs who survive the great catastrophes of their collective pilgrimage.

8. it was not you. Joseph alleviates the guilt and shame of his converted brothers by placing their crime against the broader picture of God's sovereignty. Since sin is part of his eternal counsel and foreknowledge—though human beings are still accountable—there is no basis for retaliation or bitterness. If they had not repented and renounced their sin, God at some time and in some way would have judged their guilt (see 44:16).

father. See 17:8.

ruler. His faith in the God-given dreams is validated (see 37:8).

9. Now hurry back. Joseph's counsel to migrate to Egypt provides the transition to Scene 4, which is itself a janus to Act 3.

God. He opens his speech to his father pointing to God. This is the key to all of their narratives.

God has made me lord of all Egypt. God made the impossible possible (see 45:26).

10. Goshen. The precise location remains problematic. Ward argues, "The basic requirement for Jacob and his family was pasturage for their herds (Gen. 46:32–34; 47:6, 11). The general region of the E Delta fits this admirably." Goshen was probably located in the specific region of modern Fâqûs, Saft el-Hinna and Tell ed-Dabʿa/Qantîr.[127]

11. five years of famine. Joseph tells them this to overcome resistance to a thoroughgoing and long-term migration from Canaan to Egypt.

12. my brother Benjamin. Joseph's words are so incredible that Jacob will need a credible witness. Benjamin is the only brother whose character is beyond reproach and whose testimony is completely credible.

I who am speaking. Joseph speaks to them face to face, in their own language, not through an interpreter (cf. 42:23).

15. kissed ... wept. See 43:30. These authentic gestures of emotion convince his brothers of his good will and finally free them from their stunned silence.

his brothers talked with him. This is the narrator's signal that the rift has been bridged (see 37:4); intimacy has been achieved. The narrator, however, blanks the conversation as inconsequential to the reconciliation. Intimacy is visceral, not cerebral.

THEOLOGICAL REFLECTIONS ON BOOK 10, ACT 3, SCENE 3 ──────────────

Providence and the Spiritual Life

G. von Rad comments, "Here in the scene of recognition the narrator indicates clearly for the first time what is of paramount importance to him in the

---

[127]W. Ward, "Goshen," *ABD*, 2:1076–77.

entire Joseph story: God's hand which directs all the confusion of human guilt ultimately [leads] toward a gracious goal."[128] Four times Joseph describes himself as God's agent (45:5, 7–8, 9; cf. 42:25; 43:23). Wenham says, "All the episodes in the Joseph story contribute to demonstrating how God's purposes are ultimately fulfilled through and in spite of human deeds, whether or not those deeds are morally right."[129] God in sovereign grace has guided Israel's history (42:2; 45:5–8; 50:20).

However, Joseph theologizes on the spiritual implications of that doctrine in a unique way. This truth enables him to reinterpret his narrative. From a worm's-eye view, his narrative reads like a nightmare, a cacophony of outrageous excesses unjustly inflicted upon him. A rational conclusion that it is all absurd from this perspective could have made him an existentialist, a cynic, or a nihilist. But he chooses the heavenly perspective that God is working through him to bring about what is good (Rom. 8:28 [NIV note]; cf. Prov. 16:1–4; 19:21; 20:24; 27:1). This enables him to forgive and encourage his brothers to do the same. Sin must be seen within the context of God's set and eternal purpose. The believer can count on God to bring to pass his good pleasure regardless of what people intend. Through Joseph's sufferings, the Lord saves Abraham's inspired dream. The holy seed survives the great famine, as Noah had survived the great Flood.

> Careless seems the Great Avenger; history's pages but record
> One death-grapple in the darkness 'twixt old systems and the Word;
> Truth forever on the scaffold, Wrong forever on the throne,—
> Yet that scaffold sways the future, and, behind the dim unknown,
> Standeth God within the shadow, keeping watch above his own.[130]

It is God's sovereignty that undergirds biblical love, joy, peace, and hope: "God sent me here to preserve life" (3x: 45:5, 7, 8). Wenham declares, "The God of Genesis is a God of mercy (43:14) and grace (43:29), who answered Jacob's forlorn prayer . . . (43:14) beyond his wildest dreams."[131] That interpretation of history produces the fruit of the Spirit: faith, love, joy, peace, and the like. Moreover, those who allow this truth to embrace them are able to forgive others and not to flagellate self.

Reconciliation

This scene exposes the anatomy of reconciliation. It is about loyalty to a family member in need, even when he or she looks guilty; giving glory to God by owning up to sin and its consequences; overlooking favoritism; offering up oneself to save another; demonstrating true love by concrete acts of

---

[128]Von Rad, *Genesis*, 398.
[129]Wenham, *Genesis 16–50*, 432.
[130]James Russell Lowell, "The Present Crisis," in *Masterpieces of Religious Verse*, ed. J. D. Morrison (New York: Harper & Brothers, 1948).
[131]Wenham, *Genesis 16–50*, 433.

sacrifice that create a context of trust; discarding control and the power of knowledge in favor of intimacy; embracing deep compassion, tender feelings, sensitivity, and forgiveness; and talking to one another. A dysfunctional family that allows these virtues to embrace it will become a light to the world.

Repentance

The brothers' sin against Joseph weighed upon them. Solomon declares mercy to whoever confesses and renounces sin (Prov. 28:13). "Confession" means to give God glory by acknowledging sin and God's right to punish it. The brothers, as represented by Judah, meet both conditions. They confess their corporate guilt in 44:16 (see also 42:21), giving God glory. Judah's plea for Benjamin shows how sincerely they renounce their former sin (44:33–34). Wenham asserts, "No more moving example of true contrition and repentance is to be found in Scripture, unless it be the parable of the prodigal son (Luke 15)."[132]

It is to Joseph's great credit that he recreates the therapeutic situation that enables his brothers to prove their conversion to him and themselves. Fox comments: "Some have questioned the morality of Yosef's actions, seeing that the aged Yaakov might well have died while the test was progressing, without ever finding out that Yosef had survived. But that is not the point of the story. What it is trying to teach (among other things) is a lesson about crime and repentance. Only by recreating something of the original situation—the brothers are again in control of the life and death of a son of Rachel—can Yosef be sure that they have changed. Once the brothers pass the test, life and covenant can then continue."[133]

Divination

The Hebrew *nḥš* (44:5) denotes the attempt to discover hidden knowledge through mechanical means. The law strictly forbade this form of divination (Lev. 19:26; Deut. 18:10) because it represented the pagan worldview that dark spiritual forces, not Israel's covenant-keeping God, ruled the world (cf. Gen. 30:27).[134] The unchanging, ethical God hates that worldview and its practices (2 Kings 17:17; 21:6; 2 Chron. 33:16). Joseph's description of his goblet to his brothers as a divining cup is as much a part of the ruse as putting the silver in their sacks and accusing them of burglary (see Gen. 44:2, 5 in Exegetical Notes above). In fact, the text is an insider's spoof on the pagan practice. Even with the retrieved goblet in his hand, Joseph cannot divine that Benjamin was innocent. As Judah confesses (44:16), God through history, not the goblet, uncovered their guilt.

---

[132]Ibid., 431.
[133]Fox, *Beginning*, 202.
[134]The Old Testament prescribed casting lots because it was understood that Israel's God, not sinister spiritual forces, directed the lot (Lev. 16:8; Num. 26:55; Josh. 14:2; Prov. 16:33; 18:18).

Kingship and Love

Jacob will crown Judah with kingship because he demonstrates that he has become fit to rule according to God's ideal of kingship that the king serves the people, not vice versa. Judah is transformed from one who sells his brother as a slave to one who is willing to be the slave for his brother. With that offer he exemplifies Israel's ideal kingship.

Intimacy

Once Joseph knows the changed heart of his brothers, he is free to be authentic. He allows his true identity to reemerge and becomes intimate with his brothers. The Hebrew word for intimacy is *sôd,* glossed in the NIV by "council," "confidence," "company," "confides," "fellowship," "intimate," and the like. It denotes fundamentally an inner circle of confidants. Within that circle of like-minded people, discussion, decision making, and plans take place. The Lord himself has a confidential relationship with the upright (Prov. 3:32) and those who fear him (Ps. 25:14). Outsiders are barred from that circle.

Remnant

God saves a remnant of humanity through the Flood and then multiplies the nations upon the earth. He also providentially spares through the great famine all the seed of the patriarchs. Although they are no more than a remnant of people, they will become a great nation. The doctrine of the remnant becomes a major theme in the prophets. Through the Exile God will preserve a remnant from whom the Messiah will come. The remnant with the Messiah will rule the earth (cf. Mic. 4–5). Today God preserves a remnant of ethnic Israel within the church, and Paul implies that the day will come when all of ethnic Israel will participate in the new covenant enacted through the blood of Jesus Christ (Rom. 11:1–27).

Typology

Both Joseph and Judah prefigure Jesus Christ. With regard to Joseph, the father's favorite son is sent to his brothers. They sell their guiltless brother for twenty pieces of silver, and he becomes their lord. The Joseph story also provides a remarkable parallel of Christ's death—God decides beforehand that through wicked hands he will nail Christ to the cross and so save the world (see Acts 2:23; 4:28).

Judah, on the other hand, is the first person in Scripture who willingly offers his own life for another. His self-sacrificing love for his brother for the sake of his father prefigures the vicarious atonement of Christ, who by his voluntary sufferings heals the breach between God and human beings. Joseph gets the double portion, but Judah gets eternal kingship.

BOOK 10, ACT 3, SCENE 4:
THE RECONCILED FAMILY MIGRATES
TO EGYPT (45:16–46:27)

LITERARY ANALYSIS OF BOOK 10, ACT 3, SCENE 4 ─────

Anachrony

The opening words of this scene, "When the news reached Pharaoh's palace" (lit., "the voice was heard at Pharaoh's household"), repeat the introduction to Joseph's disclosure, "and he . . . so loudly" (lit., "and he gave his voice . . . and Pharaoh's household heard," 45:2). By this technique the narrator indicates the speed of Pharaoh's response. The Pharaoh offers invitation without hesitation, confirming his wholehearted approval of Joseph and the welcome of his family. Of course, Pharaoh's invitation to Egypt chronologically follows Joseph's invitation. Although Sarna and Hamilton respectively say that Pharaoh "endorsed"/"ratified" Joseph's invitation,[135] the narrator never indicates that Joseph makes Pharaoh aware of his invitation. Pharaoh initiates the conversation and the invitation, at least as the story is narrated. No Egyptian was present when Joseph talked privately with his brothers, and were they there, they probably could not have understood the Hebrew language being spoken. Rather, Pharaoh independently extends hospitality to Joseph's starving family as his reasonable service to the man who saves Egypt.

Structure, Plot, and Escalation

As the denouement of Act 3, this scene brings together all the amazing details that resolve the family's struggles with one another and their struggle to survive the great famine. Act 3 began in Canaan with a broken Jacob at the head of a fractured family sending his sons to Egypt to buy grain so that, in his words, "we may live and not die" (42:2). In this final scene of the act, the now reconciled sons return to Canaan with the life-giving news that leads a renewed Jacob to declare, "I'm convinced! My son Joseph is still alive. I will go and see him before I die" (45:28). At the end of the scene the famished family resettles in the best of the land of Egypt, in what Pharaoh calls "the fat of the land" (45:18).

The narrative part of the scene (45:16–46:7) is unified in the Hebrew text by the narrative verbal form, sometimes rendered in the NIV by "so" (45:21, 25, 46:1) or "then" (45:24; 46:5) or in some other way (45:26, 27, 28; 46:6). It begins with Pharaoh commanding the brothers to bring their entire family to Egypt and to take some carts to transport their children and wives and father (45:19). It ends with brothers bringing their wives and children and father in Pharaoh's carts along with all their livestock and possessions.

─────────────────────────

[135]Sarna, *Genesis*, 310; Hamilton, *Genesis 18–50*, 583–84.

The narrative develops in three stages whose theological motifs deal respectively with generous hospitality, family reconciliation, and divine assurance. First, in Egypt, Pharaoh commands Joseph to extend to Jacob and the brothers every courtesy of hospitality as an inducement to come to Egypt (45:16–20), and Joseph adds to it his own largess (45:21–24). Second, in Canaan, the brothers announce to Jacob that Joseph is alive (45:25–26), and a convinced Jacob consents to migrate to Egypt to see him (45:27–28). Third, at Beersheba on the family's way to Egypt, the Lord reassures Jacob that he will fulfill his promises to the patriarchs to make them into a great nation by his presence with them in Egypt (46:1–4). After this, the entire family, lock, stock, and barrel, departs from Beersheba for Egypt (46:5–7).

The genealogy of children born in Canaan in 46:8–27 brings Act 3 in Canaan to closure and marks its division from Act 4 in Egypt. The expression "went to Egypt" frames the genealogy (46:8, 27) and links it to the narrative (46:6–7). This segmented genealogy (see "Excursus: Genesis Genealogies" at the end of Book 1) shows the relationships of the members of Jacob's family. Unlike the genealogy in 35:22b–26, the children of the concubines follow the corresponding wife (i.e., Leah, 46:8–15; Zilpah, 46:16–18; Rachel, 46:19–22; Bilhah, 46:24–25). Coincidentally, the arrangement parallels a decreasing number of offspring: thirty-three, sixteen, fourteen, seven. The wives produce twice the number of offspring as their concubines. The list concludes with a qualified total (46:26) and then a grand total (46:27). Benjamin has the most sons (ten); Dan, the least (one). With Judah and Asher, the lists extends Jacob's genealogy to the fourth generation. The catalogue of names includes the ten sons of Benjamin and the two sons of Perez, who are probably born in Egypt (see 46:21, 27; cf. 38:12). Similarly, the catalogue of those born in Paddan Aram (35:22b–26) included Benjamin, who was obviously born in Canaan (see 35:16–18, 22b–26). The narrator is more concerned with ideology than with historical precision, perhaps reckoning the sons in question as in the bodies of their fathers (cf. Heb. 7:10). He represents Israel as having the perfect number (see 46:27) and as a microcosm of the representative seventy nations to be blessed through Israel (see Gen. 10; Deut. 32:8). Biblical genealogies as a literary genre are patently somewhat artificial and idealistic and not written according to the dictates of legal historiography (cf. Gen. 10; 35:22b–26; Matt. 1:1–17).

Blanks

The episode in Egypt is all about hospitality—giving the best of one's land and property to a starving and needy family. The repetition of the invitation and gifts and the substantial detail about the provisions ensures that Pharaoh and his vizier anticipate and meet every physical and psychological need to encourage the family to migrate.

However, the episode in Canaan when the brothers arrive home is about family love, not property. The narrator puts in the brothers' mouths only,

"Joseph is still alive! In fact, he is ruler of all Egypt" (45:26). He puts in Jacob's mouth only, "I'm convinced! My son Joseph is still alive. I will go and see him before I die" (45:28). The narrator almost blanks the family's response to Pharaoh's and Joseph's extraordinary provisions and gifts. These serve only to convince Jacob that Joseph is alive. A father and brothers once driven by the pursuit of property and money now love the brother above all these things and use the provisions and the gifts to serve that relationship. The scene ends with Jacob willing to go to Egypt in order to see Joseph before he dies, not in order to enrich and enjoy himself.

Key Words

Key words in the first stage of the narrative are "do this" (twice) and "they did thus" (45:17, 19, 21) and "the best of the land of Egypt" (45:18, 20, 23); in the second stage, "Joseph" (45:26, 27 [2x], 28); and in the third, "Jacob"/"Israel" (8x).

Naming

Act 3 opens with "Jacob" speaking to his sons (42:1). By the close of Act 3, the narrator refers to the father's name as "Israel" to speak of his strength and leadership (45:28; 46:1) as he leads the embryonic nation to Egypt and as "Jacob" to speak of his weakness and dependence on God (46:2) and his sons (46:5–6).

Comparisons and Contrasts with Other Scenes

There are significant comparisons between the migrations of Abraham and Jacob. At the beginning of the patriarchal period, Abraham obeyed the divine revelation to go to the land of Canaan to become "a great nation" (12:2). Jacob obeys the divine command to leave the land to become a great nation of people in Egypt at its end (46:3). Just as the Abraham cycle, before its transition (Gen. 23–25), is encircled by God's promises given in theophany (12:1–3; 22:15–18), so also are Jacob's odysseys (28:13–16; 46:2–4). Famine drove Abraham to Egypt at the beginning of the patriarchal period (12:10); now it drives Jacob and the sons of Israel out of the land at its end. However, Abraham went to Egypt without God's direction and put the family in jeopardy. Jacob goes to Egypt according to God's revelation and preserves the family.

There are also striking links between this exodus of Jacob's family and the family's previous journeys. As an idealized genealogical list closed the period of Jacob's sojourn in Paddan Aram and his exodus from there to the Promised Land (see 35:10–26), so the idealized catalogue of sons, grown from twelve to seventy, closes the patriarchal period in Canaan and forms a transition to the Exodus from Egypt (see 46:8–27; Ex. 1:1–7).

The entire exodus to Egypt, beginning with chapter 45, follows an alternating structure. A/A': the inner circle of the family (45:1–15; 46:1–30); and

B/B': the settlement of the embryonic nation in Egypt (45:16–28; 46:31–47:12). In both cases, the incidents pertaining to the inner circle climax with Joseph throwing his arms over his relative(s) and weeping, first Benjamin and his brothers (45:14–15), then Jacob (46:29).

Finally, the genealogy in 46:8–27 functions like the genealogy in 35:22b–26. Both give evidence of the growth of the embryonic nation from Abraham, Isaac, and Jacob to twelve sons and now to seventy. In addition, both bring closure to a section: the former closed Book 8 and Jacob's exile in Paddan Aram; the latter closes the sojourns of the patriarchs in Canaan. The genealogy in 46:8–27 is repeated verbatim in abbreviated form in Ex. 1:1–5 to link the book of Exodus, which chronicles the history of the people of Israel as nation from Egypt to Sinai, with this account of the descent of the nation in embryonic form into Egypt.

Foreshadowing

With this scene, the patriarchal period in Canaan ends. The third stage of the scene pertains to the embryonic nation migrating to Goshen, where it will develop into a great nation as God promised. As such it foreshadows the opening scene in the book of Exodus. The title "God of your father" (46:3) in this last theophany to the patriarchs will feature prominently in the next theophany, 430 years later, to Moses (Ex. 3:6).

EXEGETICAL NOTES TO BOOK 10, ACT 3, SCENE 4 ————

In Egypt: Invitation, Gifts, and Provisions from Pharaoh and Joseph (45:16–24)

16. the news reached Pharaoh's palace. The text literally says, "the voice was heard in Pharaoh's palace," which links this verse back to 45:2 (see Literary Analysis above). Pharaoh has learned of the brothers' arrival, not of their conversation with Joseph. Joseph's attendants, barred from the brothers' conversation, hear only his loud weeping, not his words (see Literary Analysis above).

were pleased. Literally, "it was good in the eyes of. . . ." Pharaoh and his courtiers favor Joseph's family because they look upon Joseph with favor (contra Ex. 1:8). Pharaoh's offer of the best of the land in Egypt to Joseph's family is a proper response of gratitude to the man who saves Egypt and secures all the land of Egypt for Pharaoh (Gen. 47:20).

17. Pharaoh said to Joseph. He communicates his message to the brothers through Joseph because he needs an interpreter and they need an intermediary to have an audience with him.

animals. The reference is to donkeys (see 44:3, 13).

18. enjoy. The Hebrew word means "eat."

the fat of the land. This is the best land for agriculture (cf. Isa. 1:19) as can be inferred by Israel's later references to it (cf. Num. 20:5; Ps. 78:47). Pharaoh does not specify the pasturelands of Goshen, as Joseph had. In

46:31–32 Pharaoh seems unaware that Joseph's family are shepherds in need specifically of pastureland.

19. your children and your wives. He specifies the family members.

20. best of all Egypt. Its connection with "belongings" implies "the best [things] of Egypt" (i.e., houses, furnishings, etc.), not the best agricultural land, as in 45:18. The NIV renders a similar Hebrew expression in 45:23 "the best things of Egypt."

21. sons of Israel. This is the national term for Joseph and his brothers. The embryonic nation in unison acts to effect Pharaoh's good will.

as Pharaoh had commanded. The Hebrew literally reads, "according to the mouth of Pharaoh."

22. new clothing. Clothing is an important symbol in the Joseph story (cf. 37:3, 31–33; 38:14, 19; 39:12–18; 41:14, 42). Here it functions as a fitting token of Joseph's affection and esteem for his brothers (cf. 2 Kings 5:5, 22), for it stands in striking contrast to their stripping his robe off him (see 37:23). Sarna says, "Since an article of apparel had featured prominently in the tale of hostility between Joseph and his brothers, it is only fitting that their reconciliation should be marked by a gift of apparel."[136] The change also symbolizes their new situation (cf. 38:14; 41:14, 42): delivered from guilt, hostility, and famine, with the prospect of abundant provisions in the best of Egypt.

to Benjamin he gave three hundred shekels of silver and five sets of clothes. As sovereign, Joseph has the freedom to brush primogeniture rights aside and give a special status to the youngest. Moreover, he has no need to explain his action. The brothers have learned the lesson of sovereign grace and are now above petty jealousy. Even after Joseph gave Benjamin five times as much food (43:34), they were still willing to be enslaved for him (44:13).

silver. This is another key symbol in Book 10. Here the silver is given to bless a brother, not to sell him (contra 37:28).

23. ten donkeys . . . ten female donkeys. These are besides the brothers' donkeys.

24. Don't quarrel. See 42:22. The text literally says, "Don't get excited."[137] The brothers are not to make recriminations against one another regarding their crime, especially in explaining it to their father. If Joseph forgives them, how much more should they forgive one another (see Matt. 18:21–35).

In Canaan: Brothers' Announcement and Father's Response (45:25–28)

26. Joseph is still alive! The brothers are free of their guilt and can speak the truth. Their words concern their brother, not the possessions they have been given (see Literary Analysis above).

---

[136]Sarna, *Genesis*, 311.

[137]Wenham, following the rabbis, suggests that the term may refer to "fear" with reference to a highway robbery against their well-laden caravan (*Genesis 16–50*, 430).

he is ruler of all Egypt. They rejoice in, not envy, Joseph's exaltation.

27. when he saw the carts. Perhaps the grain, animals, and gifts could have been bought with the silver they had in hand or had stolen, but not the wagons.

28. Israel. This is his name of strength and leadership (see Literary Analysis above).

I'm convinced [*rab*]. The text literally says, "enough" (see Ps. 23:5).

I will go. The patriarch's consent to migrate is necessary before the brothers can begin to accept the commands of Pharaoh and Joseph to come to Egypt.

I will . . . see him. Jacob fought with Laban for possessions that were his due. Israel yearns for his son, not possessions (see 46:28, 30).

Migration from Canaan: God Meets Jacob (46:1–7)

1. Israel. See 45:28.

set out. The narrator assumes Hebron (see 35:27; 37:14), 20 miles (36 kilometers) northeast of Beersheba, as the starting place. Jacob journeys to see Joseph (cf. Luke 15:24), not to escape famine.

Beersheba. See 21:33; 26:23–25. This is the end of the Promised Land. Jacob's odysseys out of the Promised Land begin and end at Beersheba (28:10). God's revelation here resembles his revelation to Jacob at Bethel (28:10–22).

offered sacrifices [*zābaḥ*]. The Hebrew term occurs elsewhere in Genesis only in 31:54. This offering on the altar functions to establish communion between God and the worshiper and to establish the right spiritual milieu for the vision that follows.

God of his father Isaac. Beersheba was a liturgical site of Abraham (see 21:32–33) and Isaac (see 26:23–25), not Jacob (see 28:10–15; 35:6–15). By worshiping at the altar Isaac built, Jacob shows he worships the same God as his fathers. More specifically, he seeks divine assurance that God will be with the elect seed of the patriarchs outside of the Promised Land (cf. 26:2).

2. God spoke. This is the only report of theophany and promise in Book 10. Once again, upon Jacob's leaving of the Promised Land, God promises to be with Jacob and to bring him back (28:15). This last recorded speech of God to the patriarchs forms a preview of Israel's sacred history in the land of Egypt. The next recorded special revelation will be to Moses at the burning bush (Ex. 3:1–4:17), about 430 years later (Ex. 12:40).

in a vision at night. See 15:5, 12; 20:6; 26:24; 28:12; 31:24. The form is plural (possibly "visions"), but the versions read singular; the difference pertains to reading *mar'ōt* or *mar'at*. The patriarchs are prophets (see 15:1; 20:7). The night vision to Abraham and this one to Jacob pertain to Israel's sojourn in Egypt (15:13). No personal visions are directly addressed to any of Jacob's twelve sons. Joseph's dreams did not pertain to God's promises to the patriarchs to make them into a great nation in the land of Canaan, only to Joseph's rule over his brothers in his own lifetime. The promise to Jacob here returns to the themes of nationhood.

Jacob! Jacob! . . . Here I am. See 22:1, 11. God's address to the patriarch by his name of weakness suggests Jacob's psychological state.

3. I am God. The title "God" pertains to God's transcendence over time, space, and people.

the God of your father. Jacob worships the God of his father Isaac, and God responds as such. Weisman notes, "This is the only national promise in the patriarchal narratives which is not attributed to Yahweh or El Shaddai, but to the God, the God of your Father."[138] This also indicates an intentional link with Ex. 3:6. The communion between God and Jacob on this occasion is all about God's promises to the patriarchs—he repeats his assuring promises to Isaac (see 26:24) and Jacob (28:13–15; 32:9).

Do not be afraid. Peace is declared to each of the patriarchs (Abraham, 15:1, cf. 21:17; Isaac, 26:24; and now Jacob, cf. 35:17). The reassuring command implies disquiet in Jacob about the migration out of the Promised Land to Egypt, a land fraught with danger, and out of God's blessing (see 26:2).

I will make you into a great nation there. This is an elaboration of the promises to his fathers (see 12:2; 15:13–14; 17:6, 20; 18:18; 21:13–18). Egypt is the womb God uses to form his nation (see Ex. 1:7 for fulfillment).

4. I will go down to Egypt with you. God's presence does not eliminate pain, but it does assure provision and protection in the midst of it (see 28:15, 20; 31:3, 5, 42; 39:2–3, 21, 23). God will be Jacob's escort as he goes south to Egypt, just as he was his escort when he went north to Haran (see Theological Reflections below).

I will surely bring you back. The promise entails God's commitment to give the patriarchs the land of Canaan. The form is singular, referring both to Jacob, though in a coffin (49:29–32), and his sons in corporate solidarity with him. Jacob will remember this promise at death (47:29–31; cf. 12:1, 7; 13:15; 15:4), as will Joseph (see 50:24–25).

hand will close your eyes. The text literally says, "set his hand upon your eyes" (see 49:33–50:1). Sarna explains that this is "a reference to the custom that the eldest son or nearest relative would gently close the eyes of the deceased. Such has remained time-honored Jewish practice to the present day."[139] God's presence will be with him until death; he will die in peace, as Abraham had (see 15:13–16).

5. left [wayyāqom]. The Hebrew expresses quick and decisive action.

took their father Jacob and their children and their wives. Jacob, as this use of his name suggests, is weak and dependent on God's provision and

---

[138]Z. Weisman, "National Consciousness in the Patriarchal Promises," *JSOT* 31 (1985): 65.
[139]Sarna, *Genesis*, 313.

protection. The promises will not be realized through human strength but through divine grace. His sons now take charge in carrying out the migration.

in the carts. The narrator does not mention the details of the migration until after the theophany at Beersheba.

6. possessions. They do not presume upon Pharaoh's hospitality (cf. 45:20).

went to Egypt [bô']. This is a key word to link the narrative with the genealogy (see 46:8).

7. He took with him. Whereas 46:5–6 represent the sons of Israel taking Jacob, their families, and their chattel property to Egypt, this verse represents Jacob as the one taking his sons and their families. The former represents the practical reality; the latter, the ideal social ordering.

took [bô']. See 46:6, 8.

all his offspring. The migration is total and long-term. None is excluded from the divine blessing. The expression provides a janus to the genealogy that follows (see also 46:26).

Genealogy of the Israelites Who Went to Egypt (46:8–27)

8. These are the names.[140] See Literary Analysis above.

sons of Israel. This national term is often glossed "Israelites" (cf. Gen. 32:32; 47:27; Ex. 1:7). At this point the distinction between "sons of Israel" and "Israelites" is attenuated; they are a nation in miniature. As Sarna notes, "The promise of verse 3 is already being fulfilled in embryo."[141]

who went to Egypt. See "Structure" in Literary Analysis above.

10. Jemuel. So Ex. 6:15, but the name is given as Nemuel in Num. 26:12 and 1 Chron. 4:24.

Ohad. The name should be omitted. It is not in the Greek version or in Num. 26:12–13; 1 Chron. 4:24. Its deletion brings the number to thirty-three (see v. 15). The name likely came into the text through a scribal error involving Zohar, which in the Hebrew script resembles Ohad.

Zohar. So Ex. 6:15, but Zerah appears in Num. 26:13 and 1 Chron. 4:24. Both names mean "shining, brightness."

Shaul the son of a Canaanite woman. So Ex. 6:15. The opprobrium is not added in Num. 26:13 or 1 Chron. 4:24.

12. Er . . . Canaan. See 38:3–10; Num. 26:19.

The sons of Perez. The unique expression *wayyiheyû benê*, "the sons of Perez were," probably signals that they do not actually migrate to Egypt but are born there (see Gen. 38). Only two sons of Perez and not those of Zerah may have been included here for several reasons: (1) they replace the sons

[140]For a further detailed comparison of this genealogy with Num. 26:5–51 and 1 Chron. 2–8, see Hamilton, *Genesis 18–50*, 599.
[141]Sarna, *Genesis*, 314.

that died in Canaan, retaining the number of clans Judah sired as five; (2) they give Judah's genealogy seven sons, the divine number; (3) Perez's sons are the most important because David is their descendant.

13. Puah, Jashub. So the Samaritan Pentateuch, Syriac, and 1 Chron. 7:1, but the names are Puvvah, Iob in the MT.

15. Paddan Aram. See 25:20.

Dinah. She alone of the daughters is mentioned because she is featured in Genesis 34, and her inclusion contributes to the ideal and complete number.

thirty-three. This includes six sons, twenty-four grandsons (not counting Ohad but counting Er and Onan), two great grandsons, and one daughter.

16. Gad. The number seven is significant to him: seventh in the list of sons, numerical value of the letters of his name equaling seven, and seven descendants.[142]

Zephon. So the Samaritan Pentateuch, LXX, and Num. 26:15, but Ziphion in the MT.

Ezbon. This is Ozni in Num. 26:16.

17. Ishvah. So 1 Chron. 7:30, but the name is omitted in Num. 26:44.

Their sister was Serah. So also Num. 26:46 and 1 Chron. 7:30. Assuming Jacob's sons sire other daughters, the reason for her inclusion in the genealogy is unknown.

18. whom Laban had given. This is a reminder of Jacob's difficult exile in the past from which the ideal and complete family emerged. Jacob's family will emerge again from what will become a difficult exile in Egypt.

sixteen. The total includes two sons, eleven grandsons, two great-grandsons, one granddaughter. Zilpah's offspring are about half her mistress's total.

19. The sons of Jacob's wife Rachel. Rachel is given a superior status in the genealogy. She alone is designated his wife and given a title line.

20. Manasseh and Ephraim. See 41:50-52. The LXX adds five sons and grandsons of Manasseh and Ephraim named in Num. 26:29-36 (see Acts 7:14).

21. Benjamin. It is doubtful that Benjamin, now about thirty years of age, has had ten sons in Canaan (see above; cf. 35:26; Heb. 7:10). The genealogies of Benjamin in Num. 26:38-40, 1 Chron. 7:6-12; 8:1-40 differ somewhat from this one. The variants reflect different periods in Israel's history, different textual traditions, and different functions of the lists. For example, 1 Chronicles 7 functions as a military list, 1 Chronicles 8 expands lists to elevate Benjamin as equal to Judah, and Genesis 46 selects names to achieve the ideal and complete number of seventy.

Beker. He is not mentioned in Num. 26:38-40[143] or 1 Chron. 8:1.

Gera, Naaman. Both are grandsons according to the LXX of Gen. 46:1 and 1 Chron. 8:4, but only Naaman alone in Num. 26:40.

---

[142]Ibid., 315.
[143]But Beker is listed as a descendant of Ephraim in Num. 26:35.

Ehi. This is perhaps Ahiram in Num. 26:38. Aharah occupies this place in 1 Chron. 8:1.

Rosh. A grandson in the LXX, he is not mentioned in parallel lists.

Muppim. He is a grandson in the LXX. Shephupham is Benjamin's fourth son in the MT of Num. 26:39, and in 1 Chron. 8:5 Shephuphan is the eighth son of Bela.

Ard. In the LXX he is the son of Gera, but in Num. 26:40, one of Bela's sons; 1 Chron. 8:3 lists Addar as a son of Bela.

22. Rachel . . . fourteen. This includes two sons and twelve grandsons. Because God remembered Rachel (30:22), the once barren wife has a double portion of the divine number of offspring (see 1 Sam. 2:5).

23. son of Dan. The form is plural, "sons of Dan," probably a stereotypical phrase.

Hushim. In Num. 26:42, the name is Shuham. This is easily explained as an inversion of consonants.

24. Jahziel . . . Shillem. They are Jahziel and Shallum (most Hebrew manuscripts) in 1 Chron. 7:13.

25. seven. The total includes two sons and five grandsons. Rachel's handmaid also has the divine number of offspring but half of Rachel's (cf. Leah and Zilpah, 46:15, 18).

26. direct descendants. The Hebrew is literally, "from his own loins" (see 24:2).

sixty-six. The list includes twelve sons, fifty-two grandsons, four great-grandsons, and two daughters, for a total of seventy. However, Er and Onan, who died in Canaan (see 46:12), and Manasseh and Ephraim, who were born in Egypt (see 46:27), reduce the seventy children of Jacob to sixty-six.

27. seventy. The number is arrived at either by including the sons excluded in 46:26 or, more probably, by adding Jacob and Joseph (see Deut. 10:22).[144] The nation in miniature is represented as the ideal and complete number (see 5:5; 10:2; 46:8; Deut. 10:22) and as a microcosm of the nations (cf. 10:1–32; Deut. 32:8; see also Ex. 24:1, 9; Num. 11:16, 24–25; Judg. 1:7; 8:30; 9:2; 1 Sam. 6:19; 2 Kings 10:6; Luke 10:1, 17). Seventy is the multiple of two perfect numbers. In Acts 7:14, based on the LXX (Gen. 46:27; Ex. 1:5; Deut. 10:22), the sum is seventy-five (see above).

THEOLOGICAL REFLECTIONS ON BOOK 10, ACT 3, SCENE 4

Hospitality

Pharaoh and Joseph extend hospitality to Israel's family and as a result rescue the family from famine. Hospitality in the Bible is not entertaining.

---

[144]If the latter, then the expression "descendants of Jacob" is used loosely for Jacob and his descendants in Ex. 1:5.

It is, as Kerr summarizes, "'being food and drink for one another' (Wendy Wright, quotation from 'Weavings' calendar, 1992), about enlarging and extending ourselves just as we enlarge and extend our tables to fit another guest. Henri Nouwen states that 'the concept of hospitality is one of the richest concepts to deepen our insight in the relationship with our fellow human beings. [I]t may offer a new dimension to our understanding of the healing relationship and the formation of a recreating community.' Hospitality without the inner stretching of the heart becomes that inferior produce called entertainment."[145] Pharaoh shows hospitality as his reasonable service to the man who saves him. So also Christians show hospitality as their reasonable service to their Savior (cf. Matt. 25:31–45).

Sovereign Grace

As sovereign, Joseph has the right to honor Benjamin above his brothers. God also exercises his sovereign grace to honor whom he will. God's sovereign grace must not be confounded with his justice. God's justice demands that he reward obedience and punish disobedience. Beyond that, he shows mercy on whom he will, not because they deserve it (cf. Matt. 20:1–16; Rom. 9:1–29; 1 Cor. 12). Blessed indeed is the church and family that understands this doctrine.

In spite of a troubled life—the sharp conflicts among competing wives, harassment from Laban, dishonest and violent children in their youth—the man formerly exiled in Haran and his family now enter Egypt as an ideal and complete nation in miniature. Most of Jacob's grandsons, granddaughters, and great-grandsons go unmentioned in the narrative. Nevertheless, they too—even those from a Canaanite wife and an Egyptian wife—are known by name and numbered among God's people.

Typology

Both Abraham and Jacob figuratively receive their sons back from the dead. Both sons prefigure the death and resurrection of Christ, but Joseph even more so. Both are not only alive but rulers over all (cf. Acts 2:32–34; Phil. 2:6–11). Jacob's response on hearing the incredibly good news prefigures the response of the disciples when the women tell them that Christ is alive, having been raised from the dead. They too greet the news at first with stunned disbelief and finally with unspeakable joy when it is proved with many infallible proofs (cf. Luke 24:9–49; John 20:1–9, 24–29; Acts 1:3). Their faith, like Jacob's, revives them, reorients their lives, and makes them pilgrims venturing from land plagued by famine to the best land imaginable.

---

[145]P. E. Kerr, "Hospitality As the Christian Individual and Corporate Relational Reality That Reflects God's Character" (unpublished master's thesis, Regent College, 1994), 3, citing H. Nouwen, *Journal of Monastic Studies* 10 (Easter 1974): 7.

Hermeneutics

What God denies one saint he may permit for another. God commanded Isaac not to leave the land, but he promises his presence with Jacob out of the land. The interpreter must distinguish between God's universal commands to all saints and his personal commands to a particular saint. For example, Jesus tells the rich young ruler to sell all he has. Paul tells rich saints not to trust in their riches.

BOOK 10, ACT 4:
THE FAMILY BLESSED IN EGYPT
LOOKING FOR THE PROMISED LAND
(46:28 – 50:26)
LITERARY ANALYSIS OF BOOK 10, ACT 4 ————————

Plot

The plot tension of Act 4, the denouement to Book 10, pertains to the future of the fledgling Israelites exiled in Egypt by the great famine. Will they settle down and prosper in isolation? Will they retain their commitment to the Abrahamic covenant with its promise of Canaan? Who will lead them? These are the themes addressed in Book 10, Act 4.

The act opens in Scene 1 with the embryonic nation united under Jacob's patriarchy and Joseph's administration of Egypt. With the Pharaoh's initiative and full approval, it ends with Joseph settling the Israelites securely in Goshen, "the best of the land of Egypt." In Scene 2 the independence and prosperity of the Israelites during the last five years of the great famine stand in striking contrast with the plight of the Egyptians, who willingly accept enslavement by the Pharaoh in exchange for food. Nevertheless, the patriarch remains committed to Canaan; Joseph must swear to bury him there. The impending death of Jacob requires the settling of inheritance rights. In Scenes 3 and 4 Israel transfers the divine blessing in connection with his predictions of the family dwelling richly in Canaan. He contravenes primogeniture rights by adopting Joseph's two sons, Ephraim and Manasseh, thereby giving Joseph, not Reuben, the double portion and gives the younger Ephraim a greater blessing than his older brother Manasseh. Scene 4 climaxes when the dying patriarch blesses Judah as king over the twelve tribes of Israel and Joseph as "prince among his brothers" in the face of fierce opposition from without. The book and act come to their final resolution in the deaths of Jacob and Joseph in Scene 5 and Scene 6. Each scene transcends their deaths by describing and guaranteeing their pilgrimages even in death back to the Promised Land in the company of their unified family. In this way Jacob typifies Israel's Exodus out of Egypt and Joseph stakes his future on God's promises to the patriarchs, entailing their exodus.

Characterization

The two major players in this act are Jacob and Joseph. "Jacob," says Roop, "who fought his way into life, departs life just as dramatically. The life of Jacob, which has stretched over half the book of Genesis, has seen the family through moments of trust and betrayal, sterility and fertility, feast and famine, separation and reunion, all within the promise and providence of God."[146]

Scene 5 concludes Jacob's finest hour. On his deathbed (Scenes 3 and 4)—extending from 47:28 to 49:32—Jacob has assumed total and dynamic leadership of the family. Even Joseph bows down to him. Jacob gives the double blessing to the deserving firstborn son of the wife he loves, not to the detestable firstborn of Leah. With prophetic insight, he crosses his hands against even Joseph, the traditionalist. Without wavering, he looks forward to Israel's divine destiny in the land of promise. Renouncing even his love for Rachel, his last words instruct his sons to bury him with his unloved wife so he can rest in faith with his fathers.

He comes trepidly to Egypt not for its riches, comforts, and security but out of love for a son. While showing great respect and sensitivity to Pharaoh, he never bows his knee to the Egyptian, but instead, as the greater, he blesses the lesser. Isaac's old age shamed his youth, but Jacob's redeems his, just as Judah's heroic self-sacrifice redeemed his tragic beginnings.

All honor Jacob in his death. Joseph and his brothers mourn their father's death and faithfully carry out his instructions to bury him in the ancestral grave. The Egyptians mourn him for two and half months, as they would mourn their king. The skilled physicians embalm him for forty days, and the most senior dignitaries both from Pharaoh's own court and from the whole empire bear Jacob's body homeward from Egypt to Canaan in a grand and grave funeral cortège. With these details the narrator asserts Jacob's true redemption and exaltation.

Joseph remains loyal to God and his family to the end. In Scene 1 he saves the family from the great famine and, more than that, provides them with the best land where they can flourish and become a nation according to God's promise. His loyalty entails forgiveness, a forgiveness based upon his insight that God works even the evil machinations of the brothers against him to the good of his elect. At the end of the act, in the closing scene, they still do not comprehend his love and loyalty toward the family because of his piety. To protect themselves against the revenge they expect from him, they lie that his father commanded him to forgive them. Joseph weeps. Sternberg says, "No wonder Joseph bursts into tears. It is as though the whole ordeal has been in vain: if they have learned anything about him beyond externals—and the fear may well have haunted them all those years—the effect has evaporated. God-like to the last—and himself among the handful of gen-

---

[146]Roop, *Genesis*, 290.

uine learners — Joseph repeats his assurances in the hope of implanting the knowledge for good."[147]

Joseph voices all the feelings behind the tears: "He weeps because they believe a go-between necessary, because they are afraid of him, because they think him capable of such attitude, because he hears the father's voice. His youth, which had been poisoned by their hatred rises up before him, and it is they who in their self-humiliation remind him of it. These his last tears are really their tears."[148] The ruler of Egypt, second only to Pharaoh for over half a century, remains loyal to his ancestral fathers and their divine election to inherit Canaan and bless the earth. "By faith Joseph, when his end was near, spoke about the exodus of the Israelites from Egypt and gave instructions about his bones" (Heb. 11:22).

Comparisons and Contrasts with Other Scenes in Book 10

The introduction noted the counterpoint, concentric pattern to the plot development of Book 10 (See "The Alternating and Concentric Patterns of the Ten *tôlᵉdôt*" in the introduction). The narrative plot tension peaks in Act 3 when the brothers put Benjamin's well-being above their own and Joseph in response unmasks his identity as their brother with the greatest outburst of emotion, thereby relinquishing his power over them. In the concentric pattern of scenes and episodes, these two scenes form the pivot of the narrative. According to that analysis, the episodes of Act 4 show a remarkable chiastic matching with episodes of Acts 1 and 2. This pairing shows Providence transforming the family's misfortunes in the great famine into blessed fortunes after their pivotal reconciliation. Here, with the help of David Dorsey, is a fleshing out of those matched pairs.[149]

A Introduction: beginning of Joseph story (37:2 – 11)
- Joseph's dream that brothers will bow down
- brothers hate Joseph
- they cannot speak kindly to him
- Joseph's age
B Jacob mourns the "death" of Joseph (37:12 – 36)
- Jacob weeps at Hebron over "death" of Joseph
- Jacob refers to his own future death
- Joseph goes from Canaan to Egypt
C Interlude: Judah signified as leader (38:1 – 30)[150]
- Judah's first three sons bypassed
- Judah unnaturally begets two sons

[147]Sternberg, *Poetics*, 178.
[148]B. Jacob, *The First Book of the Bible*, ed., and trans. E. I. Jacob and N. Jacob (New York: Ktav, 1974), 341.
[149]Dorsey, *Literary*, 60.
[150]This analysis is based on Goldin, "The Youngest Son," 27 – 44.

- reversal of elder and younger sons of Judah as firstborn
- despite string tied to hand
- Judah signified as leader by birth of twins

D Joseph's enslavement in Egypt (39:1–23)
- he is sold, purchased, becomes a slave
- finds favor in the eyes of his master
- he is second only to his master
- in charge of Egyptian's bread

    E Joseph savior of Egypt through disfavor at Pharaoh's court (40:1–41:57)
- dishonoring and expulsion of Pharaoh's servants
- imprisonments
- life and death

    E' Joseph savior of family through favor at Pharaoh's court (46:28–47:12)
- honoring and welcome of Joseph's family in Pharaoh's court
- granted best of land of Egypt
- life and death

D' Joseph's enslavement of Egyptians (47:13–31)
- they are sold, purchased by him, and become his slaves
- seek to find favor in the eyes of their master
- in charge of Egyptians' bread

C' Interlude: Judah blessed as ruler (48:1–49:28)
- Jacob's first three sons bypassed
- Jacob unnaturally "begets" two sons
- reversal of elder and younger sons of Joseph
- despite Joseph's trying to uncross Jacob's hands
- Judah blessed as king by patriarch

B' Joseph mourns Jacob's death (49:33–50:14)
- Joseph weeps over death of Jacob
- Jacob buried at Hebron
- Joseph goes from Canaan back to Egypt

A' Conclusion: end of Joseph story (50:15–26)
- Joseph's brothers bow down before him
- fear that he will hate them
- he speaks kindly to them
- Joseph's final age and death

A/A': Book 10 opens by citing Joseph's age as seventeen (a combination of the two perfect numbers, seven and ten, 37:2) and closes by citing his death at a hundred and ten, the ideal age (50:26). Incidentally, he lives his first seventeen years under the care of Jacob, and Jacob lives his last seventeen under

Joseph's care (47:8, 28). The act's tension begins in the first episode. Joseph, his father's favorite, dreams his brothers will bow down to him (37:3–10), but they so hate the dreamer that they cannot speak a kind word to him (37:4). His God-given dreams find superlative fulfillment in the closing scene as his brothers throw themselves down before him as his slaves, begging his forgiveness, and he speaks kindly to them to reassure them of his goodwill (50:18–21).

B/B': The first scene of Book 10 closes with Jacob weeping over the "death" of his favorite son and expecting to mourn his loss until his death (37:35). Meanwhile, Joseph goes down from Canaan to Egypt as a slave (37:36). In the second scene from the end of Book 10 (Act 4, Scene 5), Joseph weeps over the corpse of his father, who is then carried from Egypt to Canaan as a king. Incidentally, Jacob is at Hebron when he mourns his loss of Joseph (37:14) and his embalmed body is buried in Hebron (50:13).

C/C': Act 1, Scene 2 (38:1–30), the third episode in the book, and Act 4, Scenes 3 and 4 (48:1–49:28) both interrupt the plot narrative that pertains to the movement of Israel from Canaan to Egypt. Instead, both pertain to family matters. Both point to Judah as the brother to succeed the patriarchs in leadership. In chapter 38 he is signified as leader through his twin sons (fourth in birth order), whose births resemble their grandfathers. In chapter 49 Judah, Jacob's fourth son, is explicitly blessed as king. In C/C' there is also an unnatural begetting. Judah unexpectedly begets Perez through Tamar's ruse, and Jacob adopts the first two sons of Joseph to give Joseph the double portion. In both, the primogeniture rights of succession are reversed in connection with hands. Although Zerah is marked as the first-born by a string tied to his hand, Perez supplants him. And although Joseph puts Manasseh as the eldest son under Jacob's right hand, the blind patriarch crosses his hands to give the greater blessing to Ephraim.

D/D': In the fourth episodes, Act 2, Scene 1 (39:1–20) stands in marked contrast to Act 4, Scene 2 (47:13–31). In the former an Egyptian official buys Joseph as a slave (39:1–3). Joseph finds such favor in his master's eyes that the official gives him charge over all he has except for the food he eats (39:4–6). In the chiastically parallel scene (Act 4, Scene 1, 47:13–31), all the Egyptians except the priests seek to find favor in Joseph's eyes (47:25) and sell all their possessions and even themselves as slaves for food.

E/E': The fifth episodes (39:21–41:57; 46:28–47:12) pertain to Joseph as a savior of Egypt and of his family, respectively. In the former, he becomes a savior (41:1–57) through Pharaoh's officials falling into disfavor in Pharaoh's court (39:21–40:23), but in the latter Israel finds salvation because, through the mediation of Joseph, the family finds favor at Pharaoh's court. Pharaoh imprisons his disgraced officials but gives Israel the best of his land. One official finds life, and another death, and Israel finds life in Egypt instead of death in Canaan.

BOOK 10, ACT 4, SCENE 1:
ISRAEL'S ARRIVAL IN EGYPT (46:28–47:12)

LITERARY ANALYSIS OF BOOK 10, ACT 4, SCENE 1 ————

Structure and Plot

The scene's tension pertains to whether the rudimentary and vulnerable nation will successfully resettle in peaceful isolation in Goshen (46:31–47:12; cf. 45:10). To develop into a great nation, they must be unified among themselves and have their physical and spiritual needs met. Goshen offers the shepherding clans the best pastureland with security and peace. This scene ends with the fledgling nation nested securely at the beginning of the exile in Egypt.

The scene opens with Jacob in the region of Goshen seeking directions and ends with Joseph settling the family in the best of the land, as Pharaoh directs. The resettlement takes place in three stages (46:28–30; 46:31—47:10; 47:11–12). Joseph warmly welcomes his father to the land. In the highly charged, emotional, and joyful meeting of Joseph and Jacob, Jacob pronounces his *nunc dimittis:* "Now I am ready to die, since I have seen for myself that you are still alive" (46:30).

The second and third stages concern the family's relationship to the Egyptians. Joseph articulates his plan to introduce the family to Pharaoh as shepherds so that Pharaoh will detest them and settle them in Goshen (46:31–34). Then, within Pharaoh's house, Joseph introduces five of his brothers, and Pharaoh directs the family to settle in Goshen (47:1–6). The scene peaks when the patriarch blesses Pharaoh (47:7–10). In the denouement, Joseph executes Pharaoh's directive and settles the Israelites in the land of Goshen, where all its needs are met (47:11–12).

Comparisons and Catchwords with Other Scenes

In Book 10, all the journeys to Egypt by the sons of Israel are prompted by Jacob's decision (42:1–2; 43:1–14; 45:28–46:7), climax with Joseph meeting his family (42:6–24; 43:26–45:15; 46:28–47:12), and tend to conclude with Jacob mentioning his death (42:38; 45:28; 46:30; cf. 47:29–31).

Act 4, Scene 1 is linked to Act 3, Scene 4 by catchwords: "die" with reference to Jacob (45:28; 46:30), "best of the land of Egypt" (45:18, 20, 23; 47:6, 11), now defined as Goshen (46:28; 47:4, 6) and "the district of Rameses" (47:11).

EXEGETICAL NOTES TO BOOK 10, ACT 4, SCENE 1 ————

Joseph Welcomes Jacob to Goshen (46:28–30)

28. sent Judah ahead. Judah is assuming the leadership (see 43:3; cf. Judg. 1:1–2; 20:18). Sarna says, "It is only fitting that Judah, who bore responsibility for separating Joseph from Jacob (34:26 [*sic:* 37:26]), should now be charged with arranging the reunion."[151] Jacob was separated from both Esau and Joseph for about twenty years, but here Judah forms a striking contrast to the messengers Jacob sent ahead to meet the dreaded Esau (32:3).

29. had his chariot made ready. He literally "hitched his chariot." This is not an exalted vizier waiting for his servants, but an anxious son racing to greet his father. Joseph, the second in command of Egypt, will not wait for his father to appear before him.

went to Goshen. The Hebrew literally says "went up," perhaps reflecting geographical movement (i.e., up from the Nile Valley to the Goshen plateau).

appeared before him [*rʾh*]. Except for here, this form of the verb with a personal subject (in contrast to an impersonal subject, cf. 1:9) is always used in Genesis of a theophany (cf. 12:7; 17:1; 18:1; 22:14; 26:3, 24; 35:6, 9; 48:3). The son Jacob believed to be dead for over twenty years now stands before him. Joseph, with his power, grandeur, and graciousness makes an overwhelming impression.

wept for a long time. See 43:30 and note.

30. Now I am ready to die. See Luke 2:29–30. The dreams and visions fulfilled, his attitude toward death revolutionized, Jacob pronounces his *nunc dimittis.* Hamilton says, "Jacob had a previous experience of seeing a face, the result of which he was never again the same. The face that time was God's. . . . He had seen God's face, yet he continued to live. Having seen Joseph's face, he needs to live no longer."[152] The man who feared his sons would bring him to Sheol in mourning now can die in peace. He will live peacefully another seventeen years.

Pharaoh Welcomes the Family and Jacob Blesses Pharaoh (46:31 – 47:10)

31. will go up. Egyptians refer to going south as "going up the Nile."[153]

speak to Pharaoh. The shrewd administrator will take every precaution to assure that Pharaoh gives the directive to the family to settle in Goshen.

32. shepherds. They are neither looking for jobs nor for food, just marginal land to pasture their flocks. He offers them the best pastureland. "[O]ne is struck by the precariousness of their situation in even this best of circumstances," notes Fox.[154]

they tend livestock. The livestock are defined here as flocks, not cattle. As Hamilton says, "They want to change residences, but not occupations."[155]

---

[151]Sarna, *Genesis,* 317.
[152]Hamilton, *Genesis 18–50,* 602.
[153]S. Shibayama, "Notes on *Yarad* and ʿ*Alah:* Hints on Translating," *JBR* 34 (1966): 358–62.
[154]Fox, *Beginning,* 189.
[155]Hamilton, *Genesis 18–50,* 603.

everything they own. It will be a long stay, and they need to be well-settled.

34. detestable. See 43:32. Even though shepherds are detestable to the Egyptians, he wants his family to be honest, not one of Jacob's virtues. He also wants to insulate his family so as to retain their unique identity until the patriarchal promises are realized.

1. with their flocks and herds. Joseph emphasizes that his family are shepherds to assure the Pharaoh that they entertain no social or political ambitions and to preserve them from an alien way of life and intermarriage with the Egyptians (see 34:9). The latter threat was more acute with the possession of property in Egypt (see 47:11).

Goshen. He plants the seed in Pharaoh's mind (see 45:10; 46:34; 47:4).

2. He chose five of his brothers. Literally, "from the extremity of his brothers [i.e., out of the totality],[156] he took five." The expression infers random choice. Five is perhaps a round number for several (see 43:34).

presented them. Hamilton explains, "Joseph delays in presenting his father to Pharaoh, possibly to avoid the embarrassment of having his esteemed father stand before Pharaoh to beg a favor, as did the brothers in v. 4."[157]

4. to live here awhile [*gûr*]. The Hebrew term is glossed "will be strangers" in 15:13 (see 12:10 and note; cf. Ex. 22:21; 23:9; Lev. 19:34; Deut. 10:19).

please let your servants. They cast themselves on Pharaoh's goodwill, not mentioning his promise (45:17–20).

5. said to Joseph. The Pharaoh's pronouncements and directives for the family are due to his favor for Joseph and/or Joseph's position as his vizier (cf. Ex. 1:7).

Your father and your brothers have come to you. This is official acknowledgment and legitimization of their presence.

6. in the best part of the land. See 45:18.

put them in charge. Egyptian inscriptions frequently mention superintendents—often foreigners—of the royal cattle. Within their own trade, Joseph's brothers can advance themselves in Pharaoh's royal administration and enjoy privileges and protection not normally accorded aliens.

livestock. Here the reference is to cattle, not sheep as in 46:32, 34.

7. his father Jacob . . . before Pharaoh. The patriarch bearing God's promise to become a great nation meets the lord of Egypt, juxtaposing vividly two modes of life. The Pharaoh is secure, royal, and condescending yet dependent on Jacob for blessing. Jacob, precarious and completely dependent on Pharaoh's goodwill, is the honorable benefactor of divine blessing. In Exodus, the sons of Israel will have the better part.

---

[156]*HALOT*, 1121, no. 2d.
[157]Hamilton, *Genesis 18–50*, 607.

blessed. This could be translated "greeted" (see 27:23). Such a greeting entails pronouncements of blessing. The sons do not bless Pharaoh at their meeting; only the patriarch does that.

8. How old are you? The question is perhaps prompted by a blessing of longevity from Jacob or possibly marks the honor of Jacob's long life and many children. Egyptians were preoccupied with death, and the pharaohs, who professed to be eternal, sought to immortalize their bodies. Jacob at 130—and he will live another seventeen years (47:28)—already exceeds the ideal Egyptian life span of 110 years (see 50:22).[158] His age must impress Pharaoh.

9. Jacob said. He does not exalt himself above Pharaoh, but he also does not refer to himself as Pharaoh's servant, as his sons did three times.

few and difficult. The emphasis is on *few*, about fifty less than Abraham and Isaac, who lived respectively to be 175 (Gen. 25:7) and 180 (35:28). With great humility and honesty, he confesses the humble state and difficulty of his years.

pilgrimage. This is the same root as the verb glossed "live . . . awhile" in 47:4. In radical symbolization, he announces his identity in awesome Egypt as a pilgrim. This pilgrim with a precarious, landless existence never doubts the promise of land. He is on a pilgrimage to the heavenly city (see Deut. 26:5; Heb. 11:9–10).

10. blessed. This could be translated "said farewell," again with pronouncements of blessing (cf. 24:60; 28:1; 47:7). Jacob apparently ends the interview. His blessings are strikingly fulfilled in 47:13–26.

Joseph Settles the Family in Goshen (47:11–12)

11. gave them property in the best part of the land. "Property" refers to an inalienable possession received from one with the authority to give it (cf. 17:8; 23:4, 9, 20). This is more than they ask for and remarkably differentiates the covenant family from the Egyptians (see 47:27).

district of Rameses. This is the region of Qantir or Tanis in the northeastern delta of the Nile.

12. provided . . . with food. This janus verse, which contrasts with the hunger in the next scene (see 47:13), highlights the miraculous provisions and protections bestowed on the family.

number. The Hebrew is literally "mouths."

THEOLOGICAL REFLECTIONS ON BOOK 10, ACT 4, SCENE 1

Family Love and Loyalty

It is family love and loyalty that open this scene. Jacob has journeyed to Egypt to see his son, whose loss he had been grieving for over twenty years.

---

[158]See *ANET*, 414.

Joseph forgets his exalted position and hitches his chariot to meet his father (46:29). The once separated father and son "run" to see each other in a meeting like the emotional embrace of the father and his prodigal son (Luke 15:24). Jacob exclaims, "Now I am ready to die." Joseph's only words are prolonged sobs. This is a family worthy to rule.

Hospitality

The hospitality initiated in the previous scene continues. Pharaoh carries out his promise by legitimizing the presence of the Israelites in Egypt and giving them "the best of the land of Egypt." In Hamilton's words, "[T]heir feet have hardly touched Egyptian soil, and already they are tantalized with the possibility of being placed in charge of royal cattle."[159] In response to Pharaoh's mercy, the patriarch Jacob blesses him, presumably with longevity and certainly with prosperity.

Suffering and Joy

The suffering of Jacob's family has been deep. Jacob characterizes his pilgrimage as "difficult." Joseph, who once "pleaded for his life" from a pit, has experienced great injustice. These saints greet relief from their sufferings, when wrongs have been righted, with deep emotion. Joseph, the imperial leader, is often overcome by tears (42:24; 43:30; 45:14; 50:1, 17). He openly clasps his family to him. As Hamilton says, "Tears of sorrow (ch. 37) are replaced by tears of joy (ch. 46)."[160] These saints are not stoic but are robust and authentic in expressing their emotions. It is a sign of their strength, not weakness.

Sovereignty and Human Accountability

At the beginning of the scene, God promises to make Jacob into a great nation in Egypt. At the end of the scene, he effects their settlement in the ideal location through the shrewd administration of Joseph.

BOOK 10, ACT 4, SCENE 2:
JOSEPH'S ADMINISTRATION OF
EGYPT DURING THE FAMINE (47:13−31)

LITERARY ANALYSIS OF BOOK 10, ACT 4, SCENE 2 ———

Plot and Structure

This scene consists of two incidents: Joseph enslaves the Egyptians to Pharaoh (47:13−26), and Joseph swears to bury Jacob in Canaan (47:27−31). They are held together by Joseph's administration over both events and his

---

159Hamilton, *Genesis 18–50*, 608.
160Ibid., 602.

loyalties to Pharaoh and to his father. Pharaoh, the Israelites, and Jacob depend on Joseph for their lands. The first incident picks up the plot from 41:54–57; it follows the course of the last five years of the famine. The second incident returns to the broader concerns of this book for the future blessing of Israel in the Promised Land.[161]

The plot tension of the first incident is precipitated by the continuing famine and involves the fate of the Egyptians. The plight of the people escalates. In exchange for threshed grain (47:14), food (47:17), and seed (47:23), respectively, they progressively give Pharaoh their money (47:14–15), livestock (47:16–17), land (47:20), and climactically their bodies and their liberty (47:21). The denouement also proceeds in three parts: Joseph gives the people seed at 20 percent interest (47:22–24); the people cheerfully accept their bondage (47:25); and the narrator explains that the royal tax of 20 percent continues until the time of writing (47:26). The plot tension of the second incident is precipitated by Jacob's approaching death. Though the episode begins during the five years of the famine, it shifts immediately to the climactic end of Jacob's seventeen years in Egypt. Jacob seeks assurances from Joseph that his son will bury him with his fathers. Joseph's pledge concludes the scene.

Janus

Israel's increase and acquisition of land stands in striking contrast to the Egyptians' loss of land and freedom. The notice about the contrasting fate of Israel forms the transition to Jacob's preparation for death.

Contrasts and Foreshadowing

The scene contrasts the fate of the Egyptians (47:13–26) with the Israelites in the famine (cf. 47:1–12, 27). Joseph makes the Egyptians slaves of the Pharaoh, while Israel acquires property and prospers. "Neither geography nor natural catastrophe can throttle God's commitment to his own,"[162] says Hamilton. Jacob pins his hope and destiny on the land promised to the fathers, not on Egypt's abundance.

Israel's increase in numbers foreshadows the continuing increase in the opening scene of Exodus, and Joseph's oath to bury Jacob in the land of the fathers foreshadows Israel's Exodus from Egypt. Note, however, the biting contrasts between these two scenes. In Ex. 1:8–11 the Pharaoh makes slaves of the Hebrews, and the Hebrews groan under the misery. In Gen. 47:21 a Hebrew makes slaves of the Egyptians, and the Egyptians praise Joseph for saving them. The double contrast implies the ingratitude and cruelty of the pharaoh of the Exodus. It also implies Joseph's wise administration.

---

[161]Longacre, *Joseph*, 29.
[162]Hamilton, *Genesis 18–50*, 623.

Characterization

To the end, Jacob remains committed to the faith of his fathers, expressed by his commitment of his body to the Promised Land. He is not bamboozled by prosperity in Egypt. Joseph continues to display his loyalty both to Pharaoh and to his father along with his wise and judicious administrative capabilities.

Intercalation

In contrast to the obituary notices of Abraham (25:7–10) and Isaac (35:28–29), the notice of the patriarch Jacob's life span of years (47:28) and his expiration and gathering to his people (49:33) is separated by much intervening material. Because of the unusual circumstance of being buried in alien soil, Jacob takes every precaution to assure that the holy family will return his body and themselves to the blessings of the Promised Land.

EXEGETICAL NOTES TO BOOK 10, ACT 4, SCENE 2 ———

Joseph Enslaves the Egyptians to Pharaoh (47:13–26)

13. Canaan. This is repeated three times in 47:13–15 to remind readers of Israel's fate if Joseph had not saved them.

14. grain [*šeber*]. This is threshed grain, corn, or cereal[163] used for food (see 43:2), not seed (*zeraʿ*), as in 47:23.

to Pharaoh's palace. Joseph takes nothing for himself.

17. he brought them through [*nāhal*]. The Hebrew means to escort through distress to safety.

18. the following year. The text literally says, "in the second year," but it is unclear to what it is second.

bodies [*gᵉwiyyâ*]. The term often means "corpse." It characterizes a person in weakness, oppression, or trouble.

19. Buy us. Joseph proposes the sale of livestock; the Egyptians propose the greater sacrifice of their bodies and their property.

Give us seed. In addition to food, they need seed for when the famine ends. It was not uncommon in the ancient Near East to give seed on interest.

21. servitude, from one end of Egypt to the other. The NIV is based on the Samaritan Pentateuch and the LXX (reading *hʿbyd . . . lʿbdym*). The MT, however, reads *hʿbyr . . . lʿrym* (= "and he moved the people into the cities"), a variant due to a very easy and common scribal error. If the MT is original, the Egyptians moved temporarily to the cities in a massive population transfer until planting seed could be distributed (see 47:23). However, the former better suits the context.

22. did not buy the land of the priests. Only the Egyptian priests and Israel, which will become a kingdom of priests, escape serfdom. Joseph is related to both: to Israel by blood, to the priests by marriage.

---

[163]*HALOT*, 1405–6.

23. I have bought you and your land . . . here is seed. He reduces them to tenant farmers on state land. Nevertheless, the narrator represents them grateful to keep 80 percent of the crop.

24. a fifth. Joseph took a 20 percent tax during the years of abundance to provide for the future. Now he takes a 20 percent royal tax for the privilege to farm the crown land and for the starting seed. By ancient Near Eastern standards, 20 percent interest is low; the average was 33 1/3 percent.

25. saved our lives. The Egyptians do not regard Joseph as a tyrant but as a savior (see 45:7; 47:15, 19).

we will be in bondage. They do not measure Joseph's actions according to the standards of Israel's practices. In Israel the Lord gave each family a portion of the Promised Land and forbade anyone, including the king, from taking it.

26. still in force today. See 1 Sam. 30:25. The coda assures the historicity of the narrative and contrasts the Egyptian state control of the land with Israel's ideal of private ownership of the land as a usufruct from God (e.g., 1 Sam. 8:13–16). Israel dreaded a monarchy that would insist on a royal double tithe.

Joseph Swears to Bury Jacob in Canaan (47:27–31)

27. Now. The independence and prosperity of the Israelites stands in striking contrast to the fate of the Egyptians.

the Israelites settled. In Hebrew the noun is singular, but the following verbs are plural, showing the corporate solidarity between the individual, Israel, and the nation descended from him.

fruitful and increased greatly. See Gen. 1:28. This is a fulfillment of the promise (cf. 46:3; 48:4) and a link with Ex. 1:7.

28. seventeen years. As Joseph spent the first seventeen years of his life in his father's care (37:2), Jacob spends the last seventeen of his life in Joseph's (see 47:9).

a hundred and forty-seven. Interestingly, the factorization of the life spans of the patriarchs follows a distinct pattern: Abraham 175 = 5 x 5 x 7; Isaac 180 = 6 x 6 x 5; Jacob 147 = 7 x 7 x 3. Sarna explains, "In this series, the squared number increases by one each time while the coefficient decreases by two. Furthermore, in each case the sum of the factors is 17. Through their factorial patterns, the patriarchal chronologies constitute a rhetorical device expressing the profound biblical conviction that Israel's formative age was not a concatenation of haphazard incidents but a series of events ordered according to God's grand design."[164]

29. Joseph. Jacob will elaborate upon this command to all his sons in 49:29–32, but Joseph is in charge and has the power to carry out Jacob's

[164]Sarna, *Genesis*, 324.

wishes. Moreover, he may be anticipating that he will reckon Joseph as his firstborn in the next scene.

If I have found favor in your eyes. This is normally spoken by a subordinate to a superior. It is used here because Joseph holds the power. The dying Jacob is dependent on Joseph's favor.

put your hand under my thigh. See 24:2 and note.

kindness and faithfulness [*ḥesed weʾemet,* see 32:10]. Covenant loyalty entails that the stronger party does what is right by the weaker; in this case, that the living bury the dead according to the covenant promises regarding the sworn land. Since kindness cannot be compelled, "faithfulness" is added to it in order to guarantee its reliability.

Do not bury me in Egypt. Jacob's reason is bound up in the Lord's promise to the fathers (see 48:21; cf. 50:24).

30. when I rest with my fathers. The notion is the same as being gathered to one's people (see 15:15; 25:8).

where they are buried. This is the cave of Machpelah (see 50:12–14). By faith Israel stakes his destiny in the sworn land, not in an embalmed body in the best land of Egypt (see 47:11; 50:2).

31. swore to him. See 50:1–14. Jacob demands an oath to make it official (cf. 25:29–33) and to make Joseph directly accountable to God. Also, Jacob needs assurance because he knows the difficulty of the assignment in light of Pharaoh's power. Pharaoh refers to the oath in granting permission (cf. 50:6).

worshiped. Jacob worshiped in thankful praise that his last wish will be fulfilled.

as he leaned on the top of his staff [*maṭṭeh,* so LXX and Heb. 11:21]. The MT says, "as he bowed down at the head of his bed" (*miṭṭâ*). This was a symbolic gesture of prostration. He is too feeble to bow to the ground (cf. 1 Kings 1:47).

THEOLOGICAL REFLECTIONS ON
BOOK 10, ACT 4, SCENE 2 ————————————————————

Blessing and Reciprocity

The prosperity of Pharaoh in this scene should be understood both as a divine reward for his kindness to Joseph and Israel and as the fulfillment of Jacob's blessings in the preceding scene. Pharaoh's acquiring of the Egyptian land (47:13–27) is bracketed by Israel receiving land in Goshen (47:1–12, 28). Because Pharaoh obeys the divine revelation (see 41:37–40) and honors Joseph (cf. 12:3), Joseph enriches Pharaoh and saves Egypt. Under Jacob's blessing on Pharaoh and Pharaoh's honoring of Israel, both prosper: Pharaoh gains control of all the property and people in Egypt, the Egyptians hail Joseph as a savior, and, remarkably, Israel prospers even more than the Egyptians. This mutual blessing and prosperity anticipates the contrasting situation 430 years later when another pharaoh curses Israel and is cursed himself.

Land

The biblical ideal of land differs radically from that of Egypt (see "Second Motif: The Land" in the introduction). The Egyptians accept that the land belongs to Pharaoh, to whom a 20 percent royal tax is due. God's inspired spokesman regards the Promised Land as God's land. As owner, he gives it freely as a usufruct to the tribes, clans, and families of Israel, allowing them to enrich themselves with the land, but only on the condition that they use their beneficiary responsibly; otherwise, the benefactor reserves the right to withdraw the gift.

BOOK 10, ACT 4, SCENE 3: JACOB'S BLESSING ON JOSEPH (48:1 – 22)

LITERARY ANALYSIS OF BOOK 10, ACT 4, SCENE 3 ————

Inclusio

Jacob's death instructions in 47:29–31 and 49:29–33 form a frame around Jacob's blessing of his sons. The first text announces his death instructions to Joseph; the second recounts it in detail to all his sons. This frame suggests the narrator intends Jacob's blessings on Joseph and on his own twelve sons set at his deathbed to be read together as Israel's transference of future blessings to the twelve tribes of Israel, based on the character and history of their founding fathers.[165] For ease of analysis we divide this unit into two scenes: Jacob on his deathbed first with Joseph and his two sons coming to Jacob for his blessing (48:1–22) and then with Jacob summoning all twelve sons so that he can foretell to them their future (49:1–28). Although here we analyze the scenes separately, they should be understood as one unit.

Janus

The notice of Jacob's approaching death at the end of the previous scene forms a transition to this scene. In both incidents, the protagonists are Jacob and Joseph, who depend on each other in connection with Jacob's death. In the first, Jacob depends on Joseph to bury him in the Promised Land. In the second, Joseph looks to Jacob to bless his descendants in the Promised Land. The incidents are so closely related that the writer of Hebrews links them together, citing the second before the first (Heb. 11:21).

Structure and Plot

The impending death of Jacob requires the settling of affairs (cf. 25:5–6). The inheritance of blessing is crucial for this covenant family. The scene

---

[165]The concentric pattern of events in Book 10, matching Gen. 38 with Gen. 48–49, supports this analysis.

is set with Jacob's deteriorating health and the arrival of Joseph with Manasseh and Ephraim (48:1–2). It proceeds with two formal ceremonies in which Jacob adopts Joseph's sons to elevate them to the status of founding fathers (48:3–12) and confers blessing on Joseph, who is represented by his sons (see note), declaring greater blessing for the younger Ephraim (48:13–20). The ceremonies progress in legal fashion, including distinct ritual gestures (see Exegetical Notes below). In the denouement, Jacob gives Joseph the portion of land he took from the Amorites at Shechem (48:21–22). The scene's underlying tension is generated by Jacob's continued fight against traditionalism and primogeniture rights. In the first ceremony Jacob replaces Reuben his firstborn by Leah with Joseph his firstborn of Rachel. In both ceremonies he overcomes Joseph's resistance to blessing the younger.

Anachrony

The narrator's subtle ordering of the events affirms the legality of the ceremonies and distinguishes the blessings. Jacob's introductory speech (48:3–7) to the adoption ceremony (48:8–12) was likely spoken to Joseph on an earlier occasion (see Exegetical Notes below) but is included by the narrator here to establish Jacob's authority to adopt and bless Joseph's sons. In the blessing ceremony, Jacob crosses his hands to bless the boys, but only after reporting the blessing on Joseph does the narrator record Joseph's objection to the placement of Jacob's hands (see Exegetical Notes below). This subtle shift in chronology assures a distinction between the blessing on Joseph and the greater blessing on Ephraim.

Blanks and Gaps

The author blanks the relationship of Jacob to Joseph and his family during Jacob's seventeen years in Egypt. More important, the deathbed blessings of Jacob to Joseph resemble God's blessings on Abraham, Isaac, and Jacob, with two notable differences. To all, God promises they will have numerous progeny in the Promised Land (Gen. 15; 17:2–8; 22:15–17; 26:4; 28:13–14; 35:11–12; 48:16) and, apart from Isaac, they will become a community of nations (17:6; 35:11; 48:19). However, God's blessings to Joseph are distinct. God does not appear to Joseph in a dream or theophany (cf. 17:1; 26:2–5; 28:12; 35:9–11) but mediates the blessing exclusively through the patriarch. Also, God does not promise that through the boys all nations will be blessed (cf. 22:18; 26:4; 28:14). The blessings pertain principally to protection and progeny (48:15–16, 20). The gapped blessings, however, may be derivative from their being called Israel (48:16).

The narrator also blanks that the number of tribes is retained at twelve, in spite of the adoption of Joseph's two sons making it thirteen, by eliminating Levi's territorial share (cf. Josh. 14:4).

EXEGETICAL NOTES TO BOOK 10, ACT 4, SCENE 3 ──────

The Setting (48:1 – 2)

1. Some time later. The Hebrew is literally, "after these things" (i.e., after the oath ceremony). Although the time of Jacob's death is relatively close, it is uncertain if the oath ceremony takes place in the closing year of Jacob's life.

was told. Joseph's position in the Egyptian court likely would keep him distant from family matters.

your father is ill. This is the first reference to the word *illness* in the Bible.

So he took. Joseph consecrates his sons of an Egyptian mother to the God of Israel and his covenant people. By bringing his sons to Jacob for this adoption ritual, he corrects any misunderstanding of their names to mean that he either forgot his family (so Manasseh) or that he hoped to be fruitful in the land of Egypt (so Ephraim; see 41:50–52).

his two sons. The sons are about twenty years of age (see 41:50; 47:28).

Manasseh and Ephraim. The order represents Joseph's viewpoint that by primogeniture rights the older will be greater than the younger. Jacob will reverse it (48:5, 13–14, 19).

2. rallied his strength. Jacob, whose spirit had died upon the news of Joseph's death (37:35), revived when he learned he was alive (45:27). Now, though ill, he renews his strength to impart the blessing, just as Isaac renewed his strength to bless his sons.

sat up [*yēšeḇ*]. Hamilton notes, "Jacob has deteriorated from 'dwelling' in Goshen (*yēšeḇ*, 47:27) to 'dwelling' in bed (*yēšeḇ*, 48:2)."[166]

Jacob Adopts Ephraim and Manasseh (48:3 – 12)

3. Jacob said. One could translate this, "Jacob had said" (cf. 12:1; 48:17).[167] The speech of Jacob in 48:3–7 probably took place earlier. Note the narrative flow from 48:2, "Israel rallied his strength...," to 48:8, "When Israel saw...." The speech of Jacob is inserted here because it establishes Jacob's authority to confer the blessing and to adopt Joseph's sons. Sarna notes, "The language and narration are noteworthy for their legal precision. The adopter is invariably called Israel (cf. 35:10); there is a declaration of intent comprising the careful, unambiguous designation of the persons involved and those excluded (vv. 5–6); the true identity of the boys present is established through interrogation of the father (vv. 8–9); certain physical acts reinforce the oracle declaration (vv. 10–12)."[168]

God Almighty. See 17:1 and note.

---

[166]Hamilton, *Genesis 18–50*, 628.
[167]*IBHS*, §33.2.3.
[168]Sarna, *Genesis*, 325.

appeared to me. Jacob's authority to legitimate Joseph's two sons as numbered among his twelve sons comes from the theophanies given especially to him. Joseph, having never experienced such theophanies, does not have this authority.

Luz. This is the ancient name of Bethel (see 28:10–22 and notes).

blessed. God's blessing on Jacob empowers him to bless the twelve tribes (48:5–49:28).

4. land . . . descendants. These are dominant themes of Genesis (see 12:7 and notes).

community of peoples. See 28:3 and note. The promise to Israel is narrowed down to Ephraim in 48:19–20. During the divided monarchy (930–722 B.C.) Ephraim's descendants, as the most powerful tribe, sometimes gave their name to all the peoples that made up the northern kingdom (e.g., Isa. 7:2, 5, 8–9; Hos. 9:13; 12:1, 8).

everlasting possession. This is a striking contrast to the Egyptians who lost their land and a subtle contrast to Israel's temporary holdings in Egypt (47:11, 27).

5. Now then. The logical particle shows that Jacob has recited God's past blessing on him to validate his present blessing on Joseph.

your two sons. He chooses Joseph's two sons out of his fifty-two grandsons (46:7–27).

reckoned as mine. The adoption ritual includes placing them upon his knees, symbolizing his giving them birth in place of Asenath daughter of Potiphera, priest of On. Intrafamily adoptions are attested in the Bible (cf. Ruth 4:16–17; Esth. 2:7) and in the ancient Near Eastern documents.[169] Mendelsohn cites an Akkadian legal document from Ugarit in which a grandfather adopts his grandson and makes him the heir.[170]

Ephraim and Manasseh. See 48:1 and note. He names Ephraim first because he intends to put Ephraim first in the blessing (48:19–20).

Reuben and Simeon. The first two sons of Leah are singled out because they are being bypassed to give the double portion to Joseph (cf. Gen. 35:23) through the adoption of his two sons. The Chronicler explains: "when he [Reuben] defiled his father's marriage bed, his rights as firstborn were given to the sons of Joseph son of Israel" (1 Chron. 5:1; cf. Gen. 49:3–4). Simeon and Levi may have been bypassed because of their crimes against Shechem (49:5–6). Besides, Joseph is Jacob's firstborn by Rachel, his favorite wife. Thus Rachel's firstborn supersedes Leah's firstborn, and

---

[169]A stipulation in the Code of Hammurabi (no. 170) illustrates verbal adoption: "[I]f the father during his lifetime has ever said 'My children!' to the children whom the slave bore him, thus having counted them with the children of the first wife, after the father has gone to (his) fate, the children of the first wife and the children of the slave shall share equally in the goods of the paternal estate with the first-born, the son of the first wife, receiving a preferential share" (*ANET*, 173).

[170]I. Mendelsohn, "A Ugaritic Parallel to the Adoption of Ephraim and Manasseh," *IEJ* 9 (1959): 180–83.

Joseph's two sons enjoy equal status with Reuben and Simeon among the twelve tribes of Israel.

6. will be yours. While Ephraim and Manasseh are now reckoned as sons of Jacob (see Num. 26:28–37; 1 Chron. 7:14–29), Joseph's other children are reckoned as his.

in the territory. Joseph's double portion in the land, implemented by Jacob's adoption of his two sons, is grasped by faith.

under the names. Though reckoned as Joseph's, they will perpetuate the names of Ephraim and Manasseh (see Gen. 38:8; Deut. 25:5–6). Joseph's territory could be divided into two tribes because Levi receives no share of the land (Josh. 14:4). The total number of tribal allotments remains twelve.

7. As I was returning. The Hebrew is literally, "Now as for me, when I was returning." Jacob is contrasting Joseph's prospect of having more children with his own lack of having more children by Rachel after her death. Having adopted Joseph's sons, they are also Rachel's sons, and as such they take the place posthumously of other children Rachel might have born to him.

Paddan. See 24:10 and note.

we were still on the way. See 35:24 and note.

I buried her there. Though Leah is buried in the family grave, Rachel is honored and memorialized in the double portion given her firstborn.

Ephrath. See 35:19 and note.

8. When Israel saw. This is probably chronologically linked to 48:1–2: "[Joseph] took . . . Israel rallied his strength and sat up on the bed" (see 48:3 and note).

he asked. Jacob certainly knows Joseph's sons; he has proposed adopting them by name! It seems unlikely that he has never met them during his seventeen years in Egypt. Possibly he cannot see clearly. More probably, the question to identify the beneficiaries is part of the legal ritual of adoption and/or blessing (cf. 27:18). Hamilton explains, "One thinks of the question at a baptism, 'What name is given to this child?' or the question at a wedding, 'Who giveth this woman to this man?'—neither of which is prompted by the ignorance of the clergyperson."[171]

Who are these? The Samaritan Pentateuch and the LXX add "with relationship to you."

9. God has given me. Joseph recognizes his children as God's gift. He gives the same answer as Jacob gave Esau to a similar question; he shares his father's faith (see 33:5; 41:50–52 and note).

bless them. One could translate this, "greet them with blessings" (see 47:7).

10. Israel's eyes were failing. See 27:1. The narrator's comment prepares the reader for Joseph's reaction when Jacob crosses his hands (48:14, 17–19).

---

[171]Hamilton, *Genesis 18–50*, 634.

The notice also may explain why Jacob does not comment on seeing them until they are brought close to him (48:11).

he could hardly see. Literally, "he could not see." The NIV adds "hardly" to harmonize with 48:8 and 11. Elderly people suffering from macula degeneration, a common malady, can be said both to see and not to see.

brought his sons close. Here they are brought close for the adoption; in 48:13, for the blessing.

kissed . . . embraced. He does this while the boys are on/between his knees (see 48:12). The two verbs occur together elsewhere in the Old Testament only in Gen. 29:13 and 33:4, where they are reversed. These gestures of genuine affection also have ritualistic significance, equivalent to saying "they are my children," as demanded by the Code of Hammurabi.[172] Such a ritual of kissing occurred in Isaac's blessing of Jacob.

11. God has allowed me to see your children. The adoption ceremony begins with Joseph crediting God for his sons and ends with Jacob praising God. God blesses both father and grandfather through these boys. To Joseph they are an incredible gift after years of affliction; to Jacob they are an incredible vision after he had lost all hope of ever seeing Joseph. Joseph's and Jacob's reflections of God's present blessings set the spiritual milieu for the blessings that follow.

12. Then Joseph removed them. The adoption ritual is over.

from Israel's knees. The Hebrew literally reads, "from with his knees." It is highly unlikely that a bedridden, dying old man had twenty-year-old boys on his knees. More probably they were "at/near Israel's knees." In any case, it is a legal gesture symbolizing their adoption (see 30:3 and note).

bowed down with his face to the ground. This is contra the dream (37:10). The one equal to the Pharaoh (see 44:18) humbles himself before the patriarch who mediates God's promises (cf. 24:52; 33:3; 42:6; 43:26). This concludes the adoption ritual.

Jacob Blesses Ephraim and Manasseh (48:13 – 20)

13. took both of them. The blessing ritual now begins (cf. 48:10).

toward Israel's right hand. Joseph "stage-manages"[173] the setting to give Manasseh the greater blessing by placing him under the right hand, the position of strength, honor, power, and glory (cf. Ex. 15:6; Ps. 89:13; Prov. 3:16; Eccl. 10:2; Matt. 25:33; Acts 2:33).

14. But Israel reached out. The gesture of blessing differs from the gestures of adoption (cf. 48:10).

crossing his arms. "Jacob may be losing his sight, but he is not losing his insight."[174] Sternberg reflects, "[T]he blind patriarch shows an insight into

---

[172]Hamilton (ibid., 635 n. 26) notes that both sequences occur in the Ugaritic texts.
[173]Sternberg, *Poetics*, 352.
[174]Hamilton, *Genesis 18–50*, 636.

the future denied to his clear-sighted (and occasionally clairvoyant) but for once earthbound son."[175]

15. Then. See 48:17–19 below and "Anachrony" in Literary Analysis above.

blessed. See 48:3. Jacob blesses as his father had blessed him (27:27–29). In the blessing to be given, Jacob's perspective shifts from God's miraculous blessings on him in Egypt in allowing him to see his favored son (see 45:28; 46:30) to the great blessing to come upon Joseph's sons when they return to the sworn land. By becoming part of the covenant family, Ephraim and Manasseh become heirs to all of its divine blessings of progeny and protection. The blessings are summarized by two epithets of God: Shepherd and Angel.

Joseph. He is represented in his two sons. In 49:22 Joseph will also be blessed with fertility but without distinguishing his two sons.

Abraham and Isaac. Jacob links his grandsons to his own father and grandfather.

before whom my fathers . . . walked. See 5:22; 17:1. God's covenant promises to Abraham and Isaac are certain because they walked before God. For their heirs to experience the promised blessings, they too must walk before him.

my shepherd. The first of two epithets is an intimate royal metaphor for God that signifies his provision, restoration, and protection (see Ps. 23:1; cf. Gen. 49:24). The aged shepherd acknowledges God's special shepherding of his life.

16. the Angel. The parallelism strongly suggests equating God with the angel. In other texts the distinction between God and his angel becomes attenuated (see 16:7). The incarnate God wrestled with Jacob and, having heard his cry to be blessed, blessed him and delivered him from Esau (see 32:25–26; cf. Hos. 12:4).

from all harm. This second epithet focuses on God's protection. Heretofore an angel has appeared in crises (Gen. 16:7–11; 21:17; 22:11–18; 31:11; 32:1–2, 24–30). Jacob has learned the reality of God's presence through experience (see 28:12; 31:11; 32:1–3, 22–32).

boys [*neʿārîm*]. This is better translated "young men." The word *naʿar* designates a youth of marriageable age (see 37:2; 41:12; 43:8; 44:22, 30–34).

May they be called by my name. That is, may they be reckoned among the twelve tribes of Israel and perpetuate the family line.

and the names of my fathers. That is, may they be reckoned as part of the family that is heir to the covenantal blessings God granted Abraham, Isaac, and Jacob.

may they increase [*dgh*]. The Hebrew verb occurs only here. It may be related to the word for "fish" (cf. Num. 11:22).

---

[175]Sternberg, *Poetics*, 353.

greatly. The combined number of males in Ephraim and Manasseh increases from 72,700 (Num. 1:32–35) in the second year after the Exodus to 85,200 forty years later (Num. 26:28–37). By contrast, the combined populations of Reuben and Simeon during the same period of time decreases from 105,800 to 65,930. The tribes of Joseph become the paradigm of spectacular increase (see. Gen. 48:20; cf. Deut. 33:17).

17. When Joseph saw. This could be translated, "When Joseph had seen." Although the grammatical form is ambiguous (the so-called *waw*-consecutive here and in 48:3 may signify a pluperfect situation),[176] the context suggests that Joseph voices his objection immediately after Jacob crosses his hands. The explanatory notice (48:17–20) is appended to the ritual so as not to interrupt the narrative but also to set apart the greater blessing on Ephraim.

he was displeased. Literally, "it was evil in his eyes." Joseph thought it wrong to disregard primogeniture rights. Like Abraham, he is reluctant to give another priority over the oldest son (cf. Gen. 17:18).

19. his father refused. The patriarch, empowered by God, is greater than the ruler of Egypt.

I know. This is an ironic touch. Blind Isaac blessed Jacob without knowing it. Jacob, though almost blind, knows and deliberately follows God's unconventional plan. If Isaac's unwitting blessing could not be reversed, how much more this conscious blessing?

his younger brother. God's ways in sovereign grace override human ways of social convention (see Isa. 55:8–9)—Abel versus Cain, Isaac versus Ishmael, Jacob versus Esau, Perez versus Zerah, Joseph versus Reuben, and Ephraim versus Manasseh. In Genesis, God often chooses the younger son, not the older, to carry the divine family's heritage (Deut. 33:17).

will be greater than he. See 25:25 and note. In the census taken in the second year after the Exodus, the male population of Ephraim is 20 percent more than that of Manasseh (see Num. 1:33, 35). In the second census a generation later, however, the male population of Manasseh exceeds that of Ephraim (Num. 26:34, 37) by 40 percent (cf. 1 Chron. 7:20–23). Eventually, however, Ephraim gains the numerical superiority (cf. Deut. 33:17).

a group of nations. The text literally reads, "the fullness of nations." The promise of 48:4 is narrowed down to Ephraim. As the most powerful of the northern tribes, he gives his name to all the tribes of that kingdom (cf. Isa. 7:5, 8–9; Jer. 31:9; Hos. 4:16–17; 5:3; 7:1).

20. your name. The form is singular, meaning "in the name of each of you." The blessing on the lads is now direct, not indirect as in 48:16.

Israel will pronounce. The Joseph tribes become the paradigm of God's fertility and blessing (cf. Ruth 4:11–12; contra Jer. 29:22–23).

So he put Ephraim ahead of Manasseh. If the reference is to the word order in the parallelism of 48:20b, the narrator removes ambiguity.

---

[176]*IBHS*, §33.2.3.

Jacob Gives Portion of Conquered Land to Joseph (48:21 – 22)

21. I am about to die, but God will be with you. Israel survives in spite of death.

you . . . your. The form is now plural to include Joseph and both his children (cf. 48:20).

as one who is over your brothers, I give the ridge of land. The Hebrew is ambiguous, literally reading, "I give to you Shechem/shoulder over your brother(s)." This may mean: (1) he gives Shechem, including its well, to Joseph, who is above his brother(s) (see Gen. 33:18–19; 37:12, 14; Josh. 24:32; John 4:5); (2) he gives Joseph a ridge—interpreting "shoulder" as a ridge of land; (3) he gives Joseph one more portion—interpreting "shoulder" to be a metonymy for portion—than his brother(s). The first is the best option because the other meanings of *šᵉkem* are unattested and unnecessary. Moreover, as the references cited show, the city is historically connected with Jacob and Joseph.

Amorites. See 15:16. This generic term refers to the pre-Israelite inhabitants of Canaan, including the Hivites (see 34:2).

my sword and my bow. Jacob denounced the raid of Simeon and Levi against the city (34:30; 49:5–7), making it odd that he would now take credit for it. He himself acquired land there through peaceful purchase (33:18–20; Josh. 24:32). However, in light of Jacob's comment here, it is unlikely that the narrator blanked some episode of his conquest of Shechem. Probably, in spite of Jacob's distaste for the overreaction of his cruel sons, he accepts the reality that in reprisal for Dinah's rape he conquered and took the city (see Theological Reflections below).

THEOLOGICAL REFLECTIONS ON BOOK 10, ACT 4, SCENE 3 ————————————

Theme and Foreshadow

The theme of Genesis, God blessing his elect people to become a great nation, entailing numerous progeny possessing the Promised Land, now becomes focused on Joseph and his sons, Ephraim and Manasseh. In this scene Jacob gives Joseph a double verbal blessing, after first adopting his sons and then blessing both of them, and a unique gift of land at Shechem. Moreover, he advances Ephraim in status over the firstborn Manasseh by giving him the greater blessing.

The scene lays the theological foundation within the Primary History for giving Ephraim and Manasseh equal status in the division of the land with their uncles and for the prophetic anointing of Israel's kings that leads to the emergence of the northern kingdom, of which Ephraim is the dominant tribe, to become a world power.

Sovereignty and Social Convention

All his life Jacob kicks against primogeniture rights with God's approval. He literally kicks against it in his mother's womb, and God gives him dominion over his twin brother. Now, on his dying bed, he twice opposes it with divine sanction. His preferential treatment of Joseph, giving him the double portion, and his preferential treatment of Ephraim, making his greater than Manasseh, reassert God's sovereignty to do as he pleases with his people.

Blessing

Through the patriarchal blessings the elect generations are linked in space and time and enabled to multiply and overcome their adversaries (see 1:2; 12:3). At first God directly blesses the patriarchs, Abraham, Isaac, and Jacob. In the case of Jacob, his father also mediates the blessing. Now Jacob mediates the blessing without the direct intervention of God to bestow it. Later, sacred personnel—the high priest (Num. 6:24–26) and king (1 Chron. 16:2)—mediate God's blessing on the generations of Israel, and the people's prayer for one another mediate blessing. The ascending Jesus Christ (prophet, priest, and king) and Son of God extends his pierced hands toward his representative church and blesses it (Luke 24:50–51). Today the Lord richly blesses all who call on him (Rom. 10:12).

Sovereignty and Sin

If the interpretation of 48:22 offered above is right, Jacob took Shechem through the cruelty of Simeon and Levi without acquitting them. Elsewhere God uses evil to achieve his aims without acquitting the guilty: for example, in his use of unbelieving Israel to establish the monarchy (1 Sam. 8–10); in his use of Assyria to punish Israel (cf. Isa. 10:5–11); in his use of wicked hands to shed the saving blood of Jesus Christ (Acts 2:23; 1 Cor. 2:6–10).

BOOK 10, ACT 4, SCENE 4: ISRAEL'S BLESSINGS FOR THE TWELVE TRIBES (49:1–28)

LITERARY ANALYSIS OF BOOK 10, ACT 4, SCENE 4 ————

Structure and Plot

This scene presents Jacob's deathbed blessings on the tribes of Israel. It is his third in a triad of blessings: on Pharaoh (47:7–10), on Ephraim and Manasseh (48:15–20), and now on his twelve sons.

This blessing, the first sustained poem in the Bible and one of the oldest of any length,[177] is the climax of Act 4.[178] The summarizing prose intro-

---

[177]See W. F. Albright, *Yahweh and the Gods of Canaan* (Garden City, N.Y.: Doubleday, 1968), 19–20. Because of its archaisms, it is difficult to translate, as can be seen in the Exegetical Notes.

[178]For other poetic blessings in Genesis, see 9:26–27; 14:19–20; 27:27–29, 39–40; 48:15–16, 20.

duction (49:1, Jacob's speech) and conclusion (49:28, narrator's summary) state its purpose: the identification of the twelve tribes of Israel and of their individual blessings prophesying their unique destinies within their common destiny as a nation. These summaries certify that the blessings are intended for the tribes that descend from the twelve sons, not just for the sons.

Paradoxically, what the narrator calls "blessings" (see 49:28) are often antiblessings, such as in the case of Reuben, Simeon, and Levi. However, in terms of the nation's destiny these antiblessings are a blessing. By demoting Reuben for his turbulence and uncontrolled sex drive, Jacob saves Israel from reckless leadership. Likewise, by cursing the cruelty of Simeon and Levi, he restricts their cruel rashness from dominating.

The narrator provides a frame to the patriarchal poetic blessings with a summarizing prose introduction (49:1) and a summarizing conclusion (49:28). After a summoning poetic introduction to hear the blessing (49:2), Jacob arranges his prophetic blessings according to the mothers, placing Leah's six children (49:3–15) and Rachel's two (49:22–27) in the outer frame and their handmaids' four children (49:16–21) in its inner core. The resulting chiastic pattern (Leah, Bilhah-Zilpah, Zilpah-Bilhah, Rachel) unifies the poem.[179] With the exception of Issachar and Zebulun, each group is presented in birth order of the sons.

The poem is also structured by a prayer. About midway through the blessings—what is known in poetics as a center line—Jacob interrupts the prophecies to address God (49:18). He petitions God for deliverance in this apostrophe because his prophecies explicitly and implicitly predict fierce hostilities against the tribes.

Peaking

Because of the structure of the poem, Judah and Joseph cannot be featured at climactic conclusions. Rather, the poem peaks on Judah and Joseph in other ways. First, ten of the twenty-five verses pertain to Judah (five verses [49:8–12]) and Joseph (five verses [49:22–26]). This 40 percent ratio corresponds to their importance in the preceding narrative and in the future narrative of the Primary History.[180] Second, Judah is promised kingship over the nation, and Joseph is named a "prince among his brothers." Third, the disqualification of the first three sons from leadership clearly moves toward the glorification of Judah's kingship. Fourth, Judah is praised with a term usually reserved for God, and God is uniquely celebrated as the blesser in connection with the creation blessings poured upon Joseph's head.

---

[179]Cf. Sarna, *Genesis*, 331.

[180]Another five verses of the blessing (49:3–7) concern brothers also mentioned by name in Book 10, i.e., Reuben and Simeon, whereas Zebulun, Isaachar, Dan, Gad, Asher, and Naphtali, who elsewhere appear just in lists, merit only eight verses among them.

Naming

The names *Jacob* and *Israel* occur five times each in chapter 49 (vv. 1, 2, 7, 16, 24, 28, 33), reflecting the weakness and strength of Jacob/Israel in his sons' future.

Paronomasia, Symbolization, and Catchwords

The prophecies of praise or blame are skillfully built on word plays with the names of the sons or comparisons to animals. The names and/or actions of the twelve sons portend the destiny of the tribes—*nomen est omen* (see Mic. 1:10–16). Some oracles are linked by catchwords, for instance, "brothers" of Simeon, Levi, and Judah (Gen. 49:5, 8; cf. 49:26), "lies down" of Judah and Issachar (49:9, 14; cf. 49:25), "heels" of Dan and Gad (49:17, 19), "doe" and "archers" of Naphtali and Joseph (49:21, 23).

Comparisons and Contrasts

The power of blessing and divine pronouncement has shaped the Genesis narrative. Jacob's life began and now ends with inspired prophecies. An oracle announced his destiny, and now he announces the future of his descendants. Unlike Isaac, who transferred the divine blessing behind closed doors, creating rivalry and conniving between parents and siblings, Jacob gives his blessing openly, summoning all his sons to gather round. The narrative of Genesis, which began with God's blessing of creation, now ends with Jacob conveying divine blessing on his children. Sarna says, "It is fitting that the Book of Genesis, which opened with the creative power of the divine word, closes with the notion of the effective power of the inspired predictive word of the patriarch."[181] The blessings of creation become focused on the chosen nation of Israel, particularly on Joseph (cf. 49:25–26).

Foreshadowing

The blessings upon Jacob's sons are meant for the tribes that stem from them. "In this chapter," says Longacre, "we have a glimpse of the embryonic nation—with the Judah and Joseph tribes destined to have preeminence in the south and north respectively."[182] These blessings will be expanded in the parallel "Blessings of Moses" (Deut. 33) given at his death on the threshold of Israel's conquest of the land.

EXEGETICAL NOTES TO BOOK 10, ACT 4, SCENE 4 ────

Introductions (49:1–2)

1. Then Jacob called. This is a striking contrast to Isaac's blessing given behind closed doors and to Jacob's deceptive scheme to gain blessing (Gen. 27).

---

[181]Sarna, *Genesis*, 331.
[182]Longacre, *Joseph*, 54.

his sons. All are still living.

Gather around . . . Assemble. The pairing of the synonymous parallel terms "gather" and "assemble" suggests that 49:1b functions as an introduction to the whole poem by Jacob.

tell you. He implicitly speaks as an inspired prophet. Jacob established his authority to mediate the blessing in the previous scene (48:3–7).

what will happen. The blessings are also prophecies. Jacob, like his ancestors, is a prophet.

in days to come [b^e'$ah^arît\ hayyāmîm$]. The same phrase is glossed "in the last days" in Isa. 2:2 and Mic. 4:1. This prophetic term refers to a future that brings the strivings of the present to a fitting outcome. There is a thickness to the expression, embracing both the near and distant future. Here it embraces the entire history of Israel from the conquest and distribution of the land to the consummate reign of Jesus Christ.

2. listen. See 37:6.

Leah's Sons (49:3 – 15)

3–7. Reuben . . . Simeon and Levi. The prophecies about Leah's first three sons pronounce punishment for crimes and do not employ animal imagery. Like Esau's blessing (27:39–40), they are antiblessings. The sins of the fathers are visited upon those children in corporate solidarity with them (see Ex. 20:5). As Wenham notes, "The [blessing] of Jacob, like Noah's (9:25), pronounces curses on sons guilty of unfilial conduct. Once again in Genesis the eldest son (cf. Cain, Ishmael, Esau, and Er) loses his privileged position because of his sin."[183]

3. Reuben. See 29:32; 35:23; 37:21, 29; 42:22, 37 and notes. This antiblessing first presents the eldest's inherited honor and power (49:3) and then takes it away for his high-handed sexual offense against his father (49:4).

you. The father censures his son in direct address.

firstborn. The unique position of firstborn normally should guarantee rights to a double portion and leadership. Deuteronomy 21:15–17 forbids a father from transferring the rights of the firstborn by his first wife to another son. The alteration of a man's inheritance in the ancient Near East was never subject to a father's arbitrary decision but was brought about in every instance by serious offenses against one's own family. De jure Reuben retains his status as firstborn in the genealogies (Gen. 49:3–4; Ex. 6:14; Num. 26:5; 1 Chron. 5:1), but de facto the double portion goes to Joseph (see Gen. 48). No prophet, judge, priest, or king comes from this tribe.

the first sign. This is better translated "the firstfruits" (cf. Ps. 78:51; 105:36). The agricultural metaphor signifies the choicest product. The parallelism equates "my might and the firstfruits of my vigor" with "excelling in honor, excelling in power."

---

[183]Wenham, *Genesis 16–50*, 471.

my strength. The reference is to sexual strength.

honor. One could translate this "exalted rank."

4. Turbulent. See Isa. 57:20. The Hebrew root means to be insolent, proud, undisciplined, reckless, uncontrollable, or unstable.[184] The parallel line explains the metaphor (i.e., Reuben's incest recorded in 35:22). Like Ham, Reuben's pride and passion cost him an eternal blessing (cf. Gen. 9:20–27).

no longer excel. This is a reversal of his preeminence of 49:3.

you went up onto. Most people in Jacob's world slept on a mat or sheet placed on the floor. Only the wealthy had a raised bed.

my couch and defiled it. The Hebrew is difficult, reading "you profaned; my couch he climbed."[185] Perhaps this is an aside to the other sons.

5. Simeon and Levi. See 29:33–34; 34:25; 35:23 and notes. Because they uniquely share the same criminal traits of violence, anger, and cruelty (49:5–6), they share the same condemnation and fate (49:7).

brothers. The word bears an additional sense of allies or confederates (cf. 1 Kings 9:13; 20:32; Prov. 18:9).

their. The switch from direct to indirect address provides an elegant variation of style.

swords [$m^e\underline{k}\bar{e}r\bar{o}\underline{t}$]. This is not the common word for "sword" used in 34:25. The NIV gloss of this unique word derives the noun from *krt*, "to cut," and may be related to the Greek *machaira*. Dahood thinks it means "circumcision knives." *HALOT*, deriving it from *mkr*, "to plan, counsel," glosses the noun "plan, recommendation."[186] The data is too meager to decide the meaning, and no scholarly consensus has been reached.

6. council. This is where one makes plans, such as for war.

men. The Hebrew is literally "a man," an individual representing the group.

anger . . . pleased. Whether angry or pleased, they destroy life.

hamstrung oxen. This is an image of senseless brutality. The incident of cutting the oxen's leg tendons is not recorded in Gen. 34:28. Actually, the Israelites seized the flocks of the Hivites because they were shepherds and destroyed their oxen because they were neither sedentary farmers nor cattlemen.

7. Cursed. This is the opposite of blessed (see Gen. 3:14 and note).

anger, so fierce. This is another reference to their massacre of all the men of Shechem in retaliation for the rape of Dinah.

scatter. This is better translated "divide" or "apportion." Simeon's descendants are eventually absorbed into the territory of Judah (Josh. 19:1, 9). Levi's descendants are apportioned forty-eight towns and pasturelands among the twelve tribes, including Ephraim and Manasseh (Num. 35:1–5; Josh. 14:4; 21:41).

---

[184]See *HALOT*, 923.
[185]For a discussion of proposed emendations, see Hamilton, *Genesis 18–50*, 645 n. 8.
[186]*HALOT*, 582.

disperse. This signifies a loss of power. The verb is also used to describe the dispersal of Israel among the nations (Deut. 4:27; 28:64; Jer. 9:16 [Heb. 15]; Ezek. 11:16; 12:15; 20:23; 22:15; 36:19).

8. Judah. See 29:35; 37:26–27; 38:1–30; 44:18–34; 46:28. The verse literally begins, "As for Judah." Jacob blesses Judah with the rewards of wisdom: kingship, dominion, eternity, prosperity. The blessedness of the ideal ruler was evidenced in his victories (49:10b), his wealth from the fertility of the land (49:11), and his beauty (49:12; see Ps. 45). Jacob overlooks completely Judah's sins of his youth, presumably because the repentant Judah later sacrificed himself for Jacob's well-being (see 44:18–34). In the wilderness Judah is by far the largest tribe (Num. 2:3–4; 10:14). In the frame of Judges, both in the settlement of the land after the conquest and in the civil war against Benjamin, God appoints Judah to lead the tribes (Judg. 1:1–19; 20:18). The book of Samuel celebrates David and Judah's hegemony over the other tribes. In the book of Kings the lamp of David remains lit.

Judah . . . praise . . . your hand. Note the word play between *yᵉhûdâ . . . yōdûkā . . . yādᵉkā*.

your brothers will praise you. Jacob addresses Judah directly in 49:8–9a and then shifts to third person, suggesting no significant difference between these forms in the two preceding oracles. His own brothers' accolades validate Judah's right to rule.

your hand will be on the neck. Seizing the fleeing enemy by the nape of the neck is a symbol of conquest (cf. 1 Sam. 18:7).

enemies. During the period of the judges and the monarchy, the enemies are Philistines in the west, Amalekites in the south, and Edomites in the east (cf. Deut. 33:7). Later the enemies are Assyrians and Babylonians from the north.

your father's sons. Jacob does not say "your mother's" (cf. 27:29), so he includes all the tribes here.

bow down to you. The brothers' words will be confirmed with their genuflecting gestures (see 37:10; 43:26).

9. lion's cub.[187] The lion, one of the largest and strongest carnivores, poses threat not only to animals but also to humankind (1 Kings 13:24; 20:36; 2 Kings 17:25; Mic. 5:8). "Its majestic appearance is heightened by its swift movements and fearlessness, and also by its mane. Thus it has become a proverbial symbol of majesty and strength."[188] This most powerful and daring beast of prey was a symbol of kingship in the ancient Near East (cf. Num. 24:9; Ezek. 19:1–7; Mic. 5:8).

return from [*ʿālîtā*]. The Hebrew means "to go up and away from" (cf. Jer. 4:7).[189]

---

[187]His lionesque image is denoted by three different words glossed in the NIV by "cub," "lion," "lioness." The difference between the last two Hebrew words is uncertain.
[188]*Fauna*, 50.
[189]*HALOT*, 829 no. 3e.

the prey. "The lion's lair is a hollow in the ground, hidden behind shrubbery. In Palestine they seem to prefer the sub-tropical vegetation of the Jordan valley. . . . The lion lies in wait for its prey, killing smaller animals by a blow of the paw, larger ones by a bite in the throat."[190]

he crouches. Here the lion does this in order to rest, not to pounce.

who dares to rouse him? Judah conquers his enemies and so inspires fear (see Num. 24:9; cf. 23:24; Deut. 33:20, 22; Nah. 2:11–12).

10. scepter. This is a symbol of eminence and kingship (see Num. 24:17).[191]

not depart. The prophecy is confirmed by the Davidic covenant (2 Sam. 7:16).

from between his feet. This probably has no sexual connotation. A Persian relief shows King Darius seated on his throne with a ruler's staff between his feet.[192]

until. Carl Brockelmann notes that in Hebrew "until" does not mean that the situation changes after the condition is fulfilled. "The sense of 'up to (a limit)' in a temporal sense easily shifts into one that places in the foreground the thought of the period thus demarcated."[193]

he comes to whom it belongs [*yābō' šîlōh*]. The meaning of the Hebrew is arguably the most debated in Genesis, as indicated by the three options listed in the NIV text and notes. One option, "until Shiloh comes," is unclear and unlikely. The interpretation that Shiloh, the cultic center in Israel during the time of the judges, denotes the defection of the ten tribes from Judah is incredible. Another option, "until he comes to whom tribute belongs," is based on emending *šîlōh* to *šay lōh* (= "tribute to him"). The actual gloss in the NIV text is based partially on Ezek. 21:27 [Heb. 32], where the almost verbatim expression is rendered in the NRSV by "until he comes whose right it is" (i.e., to wear the crown of 21:26). This is also the understanding of the ancient versions. All interpretations of this difficult phrase predict the rise of David and the establishment of the Israelite Empire and may imply the coming of one greater than David.

obedience of the nations is his. See 27:29 and note.

11. donkey. This was the ride of a chief in the period of the judges (Judg. 10:4; 12:14; cf. Zech. 9:9).

vine. The vine is a symbol of fertility, joy, peace, and prosperity. Here it is a hyperbole of tremendous prosperity. No one but an incredibly wealthy individual would tether a donkey to a choice vine, for the donkey would consume the valuable grapes.

wash his garments in wine. This is another image of incredible prosperity and/or power. If the former, the incomplete metaphor may signify

---

[190]*Fauna,* 50.

[191]For pictures of kings holding a scepter or mace, see *ANEP,* 154 nos. 442, 445, 447; 159 no. 461.

[192]Ibid., 159 no. 463.

[193]Cited by J. Barr, "Hebrew Especially at Job i.18 and Neh vii.3," *JSS* 27 (1982): 184–85.

that wine will be so plentiful and common that it can be used for scrub water.[194] The parallel, however, "blood of grapes," may connote his violent trampling of enemies (cf. Isa. 63:2–3). Perhaps a deliberate pun for both kinds of laundering is intended.[195] So Hamilton: "To his own this one will bring joy and fullness; to those who reject him he brings terror."[196]

12. darker. This is better translated "sparkling."[197]

13. Zebulun. Leah's sixth son is chronologically Jacob's tenth (see Gen. 30:20; cf. Josh. 19:10–16; Judg. 5:18). Curiously, he is listed both here and in Moses' blessing (Deut. 33:18) before his brother Isaachar, Leah's fifth son, giving him the preeminence. In both blessings, Zebulun is the more energetic and prosperous of the two. In fact, Isaachar is represented as lazy, submissive, and effete (see Gen. 49:14–15). This impression is reinforced by other texts. God gives Zebulun priority in drawing lots for the allotment of land (Josh. 19:16–17). The Song of Deborah celebrates both tribes but gives Zebulun priority (Judg. 5:14, 18). Isaachar is ignored in the prose account (cf. Judg. 4:4, 10). Zebulun, not Isaachar, is listed among those who join Gideon to battle the Midianites (Judg. 6:35). Of the western tribes, Zebulun contributes the largest military contingent to David's army; its soldiers are characterized as experienced and loyal (1 Chron. 12:33).

by [le]. The Hebrew preposition means "with reference to" or even "near."

the seashore. This prediction and its parallel, "they will feast on the abundance of the seas," in Deut. 33:19 is difficult to square with Zebulun's landlocked position of Asher and Manasseh in the west and Naphtali and Isaachar in the east (Josh. 19:10–16). Sharon Pace Jeansonne argues that the reference possibly "could refer to the tribe's Solomonic borders, which extended to the Mediterranean."[198] Or, "It is possible that Zebulun and Issachar shared some territory, since Deut 33:18–19 implies they had a mountain sanctuary in dual possession and because Moses' blessing to Issachar and Zebulun is given together."[199] If the latter, the "seashore" refers to the Sea of Galilee and "Sidon" refers to the Phoenician occupation of the Plain of Acco on Zebulun's western flank.

---

[194]See also Westermann, *Genesis 37–50*, 231: "The meaning is: 'There is so much wine there that one could....'"

[195]Cf. R. Alter, *The Art of Biblical Poetry* (Edinburgh: T. & T. Clark, 1990), 16.

[196]Hamilton, *Genesis 18–50*, 662.

[197]The Hebrew adjective *ḥaklîlî* has its only counterpart in the noun *ḥaklîlût* in Prov. 23:29. Lexicographers who equate the root *ḥkl* with a word meaning in Akkadian "to be dark" and in Arabic "to hide oneself" understand the Hebrew words to mean "dark" or "dull" either in appearance (i.e., bloodshot, red, etc.) or in vision (Del) from wine. *HALOT* (313, citing Bergsträsser, Bauer, and Leander) derive it from *kḥl*, "to paint." The metathesis of the first two consonants is well attested in Semitic languages. They suggest the meaning "sparkling" in both texts. This meaning best fits the contexts of both Gen. 49:12 and Prov. 23:29. However, since its sense is *bono partem* in Gen. 49:12 and *malo partem* in Prov. 23:29, "sparkling" and "flashing" are to be preferred, respectively. The LXX renders the adjective by *xaropoioi*, "causing joy," and the noun by *pelidnoi*, "livid."

[198]S. P. Jeansonne, "Zebulun," *ABD*, 6:1056.

[199]Ibid., 1057.

and become a haven for ships. The Hebrew is literally, "himself with reference to/near the shore of ships."

his border will extend toward Sidon. The text literally reads, "his flank by Sidon."

Sidon. This port city, about 25 miles (40 km) north of Tyre, by synecdoche, represents Phoenicia both in the Bible and in extrabiblical literature.[200]

14. Isaachar. See 30:14–18; 35:23. He is the fifth son of Leah and the ninth son of Jacob (see "Zebulun" above). The tribe is mostly slighted in the book of Judges. It is not mentioned in the inventory of the tribes in Judges 1 or in the prose accounts of the battle against Canaan and Midian (Judg. 4 and 6). This means that it played no significant role, and in fact an inglorious one, during this period. Whereas the flawed tribes do not exterminate the Canaanites, they at least subjugate them, but Isaachar presumably submits to the Canaanites for peace. Some biblical texts, however, speak well of Isaachar (Judg. 5:15; 1 Chron. 12:32).

rawboned. The distinction between the Hebrew *gerem,* used here, and *ʿeṣem,* the normal word for "bone," is unclear. Perhaps the former emphasizes hardness (see Prov. 17:22; 25:15).[201]

lying down. Though strong, Issachar stubbornly refuses to work, preferring comfort. He will be forced "to bend his shoulder to the burden."

saddlebags. The NIV reverses the translation and text note in Judg. 5:16. The word consistently denotes the two saddle-baskets of a pack mule.[202]

15. good . . . pleasant. Its territory lay in the fertile plateau of Lower Galilee, the best farming land in Israel.

forced labor. Jacob implicitly reproaches the tribe for allowing its material prosperity to make it submissive and effete to Canaanite overlords. Anson Rainey cites a cuneiform parallel in the Amarna correspondence that talks of corvée laborers in the same region settled by Isaachar.[203] This parallel has been viewed as evidence that Isaachar was resident in the land in the Amarna period and submitted to compulsory labor demanded by Canaanite overlords.

The Sons of Bilhah and Zilpah (49:16–17)

16. Dan. He is the first son of Bilhah and fifth son of Jacob (see 30:6; 35:25; cf. Josh. 19:40–48). Its priority as the first-mentioned of the concubines' sons is reinforced by its favored seventh position here and in 1 Chron. 2:1–2. In addition, Dan, along with Judah and Joseph, receives two separate blessings: to execute justice and, though relatively small, to strike back. In the wilderness censuses Dan is the second largest tribe (Num. 2:26; 26:43).

---

[200]Sarna, *Genesis,* 338.
[201]See NIV text note option, "strong."
[202]*HALOT,* 652.
[203]A. F. Rainey, "Compulsory Labour Gangs in Ancient Israel," *IEJ* 20 (1970): 191–202.

The imagery of a serpent on a road represents the tribe as small and in a vulnerable position, exactly its situation in the book of Judges. The book of Joshua does not define its borders.

will provide justice [*dān yādîn*]. Dan will execute judgment by pleading cases, not by condemning. This may be an allusion to Samson's exploits against the Philistines.

tribes of Israel. This is the first time the phrase is used.

17. Dan will be. This is better translated as a wish or prayer, "May Dan be."

a serpent. "Thirty-three different species have been found in Palestine and neighbouring countries, twenty of which are poisonous. . . . Other dangerous characteristics of the serpent . . . are its inconspicuous way of moving and the ease with which it hides itself."[204] Though small, Dan will be aggressive, dangerous, and strike unexpectedly to overthrow nations (see Judg. 18).[205] Samson, from this tribe, single-handedly wounds the Philistines (see Judg. 14–16).

Jacob's Prayer for Deliverance (49:18)

18. O LORD. Jacob inserts this petition to God because his prophecies explicitly and implicitly predict fierce hostilities against the tribes (see Literary Analysis above).

The Sons of Zilpah and Bilhah (49:19–21)

19. Gad. He is the first son of Zilpah and seventh son of Jacob (Gen. 30:10–11; 35:26; cf. 46:16). Four of the six Hebrew words in this oracle sound like *Gad,* using Hebrew roots meaning "fortune," "raid," and "troops": *gād gᵉdûd yᵉgûdennû wᵉhûʾ yāgud ʿāqēb.* The blessing predicts that Gad will lead a troubled life (49:19a) but will strike back at its enemies (49:19b; cf. Deut. 33:20–21).

will be attacked. Settled in the vulnerable Transjordan, Gad throughout its history endures attacks by Ammonites (Judg. 10–12; Jer. 49:1–6), Moabites,[206] Arameans (1 Kings 22:3; 2 Kings 10:32–33), and Assyrians (2 Kings 15:29). It obviously fights back after each defeat. Its people are celebrated as fighting warriors (Deut. 33:20; 1 Chron. 5:18; 12:8).

attack them at their heels. Not big enough to engage in full-scale warfare, it will resort to guerrilla raids.

19–20. their heels. Asher's. The MT reads *ʿāqēb: mēʾāšēr,* which translates "heel. From Asher." The NIV rightly follows other ancient versions by transposing the *mem* (m) to read *ʿqbm ʾšr.* This redivision brings 49:20 in

---

[204]*Fauna,* 72.

[205]In Deut. 33:22 Dan is likened to a lion's cub.

[206]On his victory stele (ca. 840/830 B.C.), King Mesha mentions that the Gadites had long dwelt in the land of Ataroth and that he conquered them.

line with the rest of the blessings, which start with a personal name without a prefix.

20. Asher. He is Jacob's eighth son, his second by Leah's maid Zilpah (see 30:13; 35:26). The name is attested as a Northwest Semitic personal name at Jacob's time.

food will be rich. This is a reference to its fertile land on the western slopes of the Galilean highland (see Deut. 33:24; Josh. 19:24–31).

21. Naphtali. He is the sixth son of Jacob and the second son of Bilhah (see 30:7–8; 35:25).

a doe. These were famous for beauty and fleetness. The image here is probably the Iranian fallow deer (*dama mesopotamica*), which reaches heights in excess of 2.5 feet (78.1cm) and weights about 64–121 pounds (29–55 kg). Only the male has antlers. It has a pale red or brown-gray coloring and speckled spots over the shoulder.[207]

set free. This could be translated "let loose." This is an allusion either to the freedom, agility, and frequent movements of the tribe or to its impetuosity. The references in Deut. 33:23 and Judg. 4:6, 10; 5:18b favor the former.

fawns. The form is a homonym with the common Hebrew word for "words."

Rachel's Sons (49:22–27)

22. Joseph. Joseph was the eleventh son of Jacob, the first by Rachel (Gen. 30:24; 35:24), and the favorite (Gen. 37:3; 45:28; 46:30). Because Jacob adopts Joseph's two sons, Ephraim and Manasseh, and gives them equal status with their uncles as inheritors of the Promised Land (48:1–20), Joseph here, and also in Numbers and Joshua, refers to the tribes of Ephraim and Manasseh. This is the longest and most complex prophecy. Joseph is compared to a fruitful vine (49:22), affirmed of his successful self-defense (49:23–24), and promised comprehensive blessing (49:25–26). In a chiastic pattern, the poem exclaims that his fertility (49:22) and his safety (49:23–24) are due to God, who protects him (49:24) and blesses him with the fertility of the soil and of the body (49:25). The comprehensive blessings of his father(s) (49:26) rest upon Joseph above his brothers. Jacob designates God as protector by the epithets "Mighty One of Jacob" and "Shepherd of Israel's sons" (lit., see below). He designates God as benefactor by the epithets "God" (as in transcendent Creator) and "Almighty [Shaddai]."

fruitful vine [*bēn pōrāt*]. This is a metaphor for fertility and a pun on "Ephraim." Barren Rachel produced the most fruitful tribe (see 30:2, 22; 41:52). The Hebrew has also been understood to mean "a wild colt."[208] This

---

[207]See A. Meinhold, *Die Sprüche* (ZBK; Zurich: Theologischer Verlag, 1991), 105.

[208]Hebrew *pōrāt* may be a Qal feminine participle of *prh*, "to be fruitful," used substantively (see *HALOT*, 963). If so, *bēn* is used metaphorically (cf. *ben-qešet*, "arrow" in Job 41:20 [Eng. 28]; *ben-šemen*, "oil," in Isa 5:1, "very fertile"; cf. Lam. 3:13). Support for the NIV text note, "a wild colt" instead of "fruitful vine," is found in Hos. 8:9, where Ephraim is compared to a wild donkey (*pere'*).

image would retain the animal imagery of the rest of the poem. If correct, the figure denotes the freedom and independence of the Joseph tribes.

branches climb over a wall. This is a metaphor for the expansion of their territory (see Josh. 17:14–18). The Hebrew may also be glossed "a wild donkey on a terraced hill" or "the foal of wild asses by a rocky rim." Either option has difficulties.[209] If the latter, it speaks of Joseph's vulnerability to the hunter (see 49:23).

23. With bitterness. This is better translated, "they embittered/provoked him[210] and shot [at him]" or, "they prevailed upon him militarily and shot."[211]

24. strong arms. The Hebrew is literally "the arms of his hands" (i.e., the strength of his arms that enables him to draw the bow).

stayed limber. They are supple, agile, and quick-moving.

the Mighty One [ʾăbîr]. This is a metaphor also used of heroic figures (Ps. 76:5 [Heb. 6]) and even of animals known for their strength (e.g., stallions, Judg. 5:22; bulls, Isa. 34:7).

because of the Shepherd. See 48:15–16. The MT text reads *miššam rōʿeh*, "from there the Shepherd." The Syriac (cf. Targum) reads *miššēm rōʿeh*, "by the name of the Shepherd." The former is unclear—maybe Jacob points heavenward as he speaks. The latter, which fits the parallel line well, is preferred.

the Rock of Israel [ʾeben yiśrāʾēl]. The NIV gloss may be misleading. The Hebrew reads "stone of Israel," which is never used of God, not "Rock of Israel" (*ṣûr yiśrāʾēl;* cf. 2 Sam. 23:3; Isa. 30:29). Hebrew *ʾeben* is used for field stones, marker stones, sling stones, and cult stones but not for "rock" or "mountain crag," as is *ṣûr*. If *ʾeben* means "stone," it is an appropriate image for the son of a man in whose life stones have been significant spiritual markers. More probably, this unique word means "son."[212] In that case, 49:24b would read:

> by the hand of the Mighty One of Jacob,
> by the name of the Shepherd of Israel's sons.

25. of your father's God. The title stresses the continuity of Israel's tribes with the God-blessed fathers. It is this continuity that makes the blessings meaningful.

the Almighty. The stereotypical phrase *ʾēl šadday* is here split apart (see 17:1 note).

---

[209]"Branches" is an unusual figurative meaning of *bānôt*, "daughters." "Climb" is an exceptional meaning of *ṣʿd*, "to march." On the other hand, "wild colt" for *pōrāt*, twice in 49:21a, would be a unique feminine poetic form of *pereʾ*, "male donkey." The second "wild colt" is based on an elliptical form of Arabic *ben bana ṣaʿdat*, "wild asses (see Speiser, *Genesis*, 368), and "terraced hill" or "rock rim" for Heb. *šûr*, "wall" (poetic) are pure guesses.

[210]See *HALOT*, 638.

[211]See Hamilton, *Genesis 18–50*, 679 n. 6.

[212]A. S. van der Woude ("*ṣûr*," *TLOT*, 2:1070) proposes that the *ʾaleph* is prosthetic.

blesses. Six times in the Joseph oracle alone the Hebrew root for "bless" is used. The blessings include fertility of land fed by beneficent water from heaven above and earth below (cf. 1:6–8) and fertility of body ("breast and womb"; cf. 1:22; Num. 6:24–26; Deut. 33:15; Hos. 12:8). The blessings given humanity at creation are concentrated on Joseph.

deep that lies. See 1:2 for "deep." The imagery, but not the theology, of the personified abyss crouching is probably borrowed from a pagan myth that represents the "deep" ($t^e h \hat{o} m$) as a sea monster.

breast and womb. Sarna explains, "The natural order (cf. Hos 9:14) is here reversed for reasons of sound-harmony (*shamayim*['heavens']-*shadayim* ['breast']; $t^e hom$ ['deep'] and *raham* ['womb'])."[213]

26. blessings of the ancient mountains. See Deut. 33:15–16.

of the ancient mountains, than. The NIV text note offers the option "Your father's blessings are greater than the blessings of my progenitors, as great as the bounty of the age-old hills." The Hebrew text can mean either. G. Rendsburg thinks that the pun is deliberate.[214] If so, "the blessings of my progenitors" parallels the preceding "the blessings of my fathers," and "the ancient mountains" parallels "the age-old hills."

bounty. The Hebrew is literally "the desirable [things]."

brow. The Hebrew literally means "pate."

prince [*nāzîr*]. The Hebrew designates something or someone—such as crops, Nazirites, or Joseph—who is consecrated to special acts.[215] It is never used of a king.

among his brothers. Note the descending hierarchical order from God (49:25) to fathers (49:26a) to the prince among his brothers (49:26b).

27. Benjamin. He is the twelfth and youngest son of Jacob and the second son of Rachel (Gen. 35:18, 24; cf. 42:4, 38; 44:1–34). The animal imagery of Benjamin as a predatory, ravenous wolf who shares his prey matches the tribe's high reputation for bravery and skill in war (cf. Judg. 3:15–30; 5:14; 20:14–21; 1 Sam. 9:1; 13:3; 1 Chron. 8:40; 12:2–27, 29; Esth. 2:5; Rom. 11:1). Deuteronomy 33:12 credits Benjamin's safety with God's protective, fatherly care of him.

ravenous wolf. The Hebrew is literally "a wolf who tears [prey]."

divides the plunder. Killing more than he could eat, he shares the prey.

Narrator's Conclusion (49:28)

28. tribes of Israel. They are not just the immediate sons.

he blessed them, giving each the blessing appropriate to him. The text literally says, "each according to his blessing he blessed them." Three times the narrator uses the word "bless" in the conclusion.

---

[213]Sarna, *Genesis*, 344.

[214]G. A. Rendsburg, "Janus Parallelism in Gen 49:26," *JBL* 99 (1980): 291–93.

[215]*HALOT*, 683.

THEOLOGICAL REFLECTIONS ON
BOOK 10, ACT 4, SCENE 4 ─────────────
Sovereignty and Covenant

These prophetic statements at the end of the patriarchal era exhibit God's sovereignty over the nations. He blesses the tribes but not independently from their character. The prophecies are based on praise or blame of the fathers.

Blessing

The family's future includes trouble as well as prosperity: "scattering, violence, violation, and turmoil follow the family as well as blessing and power."[216] These antiblessings, however, are in fact in the best interest of the nation, for they curb the baser elements of the tribes. Roop notes, "Through all this, the family remains the carrier of God's blessing into the future, as it was in the past (49:28)."[217]

Corporate Solidarity

Collectively, the descendants share the praise and blame together with their fathers. Their corporate solidarity is similar to the identification of the whole human race with the original sin of Adam and Eve.

Saving Grace

Jacob censures Levi for his past cruelty. Later, God will redeem that ferocity for good (cf. Deut. 33:8–11). In Ex. 32:25–29 the Levites rally around Moses and kill their idolatrous and fornicating brothers. In Num. 25:7–14 Phinehas, a Levite, kills a fornicating Simeonite. For these acts the tribe of Levi is set apart to the Lord and given the coveted priesthood. The Levites serve as fierce guards around the sanctuary and execute an encroacher on the temple's *terra sancta* (cf. Num. 1:51b). Sinners had to reckon with this tribe.

Messianism

In spite of the difficulties in the interpretation of *šîlōh* in 49:10, all interpreters agree that Jacob's blessing granting the tribe of Judah eternal kingship over the nations pertains to David and the Davidic covenant (see "Fourth Motif: The Ruler" in the introduction). One Qumran scroll (*Commentary on Genesis A* [= 4Q252; formerly called *Patriarchal Blessings*]) interprets it to mean "until the coming of the Messiah of Righteousness, the branch of David, for to him and to his seed has been given the covenant of the kingship over his people for everlasting generations."[218] An ancient

[216]Roop, *Genesis*, 289.
[217]Ibid.
[218]Hamilton, *Genesis 18–50*, 660.

Aramaic translation interprets *šîlōh* by "until the Messiah comes, whose is the kingdom, and him shall the nations obey." Sarna points out, "It has even been noted that the numerical value of the consonants *y-b-ʾ sh-y-l-h*, 'Shiloh will come' is equal to that of *mashiaḥ* 'messiah': 358."[219]

In sum, in the Old Testament the prophetic blessing on Judah is fulfilled in David and his house, and in the New Testament it is interpreted as being fulfilled and consummated in Jesus Christ (see Ezek. 21:27; Rev. 5:5). Jesus Christ—"Christ" is the Greek equivalent of Hebrew "Messiah"—may have signified his fulfillment by changing water into wine as his first miracle (cf. Gen. 49:11–12 and John 2:1–11). In the Apocalypse, John sees the prophecy consummated when "the Lion of the tribe of Judah" executes judgment upon all the nations (Rev 5:5).

BOOK 10, ACT 4, SCENE 5: JACOB'S DEATH AND BURIAL IN CANAAN (49:29–50:21)

LITERARY ANALYSIS OF BOOK 10, ACT 4, SCENE 5 ———————

Structure, Plot, and Resolutions

On the surface, this scene is about Jacob's death and burial, but on a deeper, ideological level it is about the unity of the holy family transcending the generations and the exaltation of the last patriarch as a king.

The affairs of Jacob's life are brought to resolution in this scene. The events concluding his life develop through three settings: Egypt to Canaan to Egypt.[220] Each act of Jacob in his final days has concerned his fundamental commitment to the holy family and to the land that his ancestors have embraced in faith. In the previous scenes he ensures the transference of the divine blessing, looking to the family dwelling richly in the land of promise. This scene opens in Egypt with Jacob's final words: a longing for the land of his ancestors (49:29–33). He makes his children swear an oath to bury him in Canaan, an oath the now fully obedient sons carry out toward the conclusion of the scene. The movement to Canaan in a grand funeral procession (50:1–14) symbolizes the holy family's commitment to Canaan even though they must remain yet in Egypt. The burial of Jacob develops in two parts. In the first the narrator interrupts the intrafamily's burial of Jacob with a remarkable picture of all Egyptians mourning Jacob's death and its leaders escorting the deceased to his home in the Promised Land. With this detailed insertion, the narrator creates a picture of the patriarch as an exalted king. This is a foreshadowing of Israel's future (see "Comparisons and Contrasts" below). The second part of Jacob's burial, however, rightly returns

---

[219]Sarna, *Genesis*, 337.

[220]The second incident is actually framed by the movement from Egypt (50:1–6) to Canaan (50:7–14) and back to Egypt.

to the obedience and grieving of his sons. Back in Egypt, Joseph's resolution with his brothers finally concludes the history that has troubled the family for years (50:15–21). The loss of an authoritative, restraining father might have threatened the cohesion of a family in which brothers had so wronged another. However, the offending brothers, on their part, acknowledge their sin and ask for forgiveness, offering themselves as slaves to Joseph, whom they regard as God's surrogate. Joseph, on his part, refuses to play God and assures them that retaliation has no place in a situation where God transformed their evil to bring about so much good. At the end of Jacob's life, his sons are united in faith in God's good sovereignty and in his promises for the holy land.

Characterization

"Jacob," says Roop, "who fought his way into life, departs life just as dramatically. The life of Jacob, which has stretched over half the book of Genesis, has seen the family through moments of trust and betrayal, sterility and fertility, feast and famine, separation and reunion, all within the promise and providence of God."[221]

This scene concludes Jacob's finest hour. On his deathbed—a scene extending from 47:28 to 49:32—Jacob has assumed total and dynamic leadership of the family. Even Joseph bows down to him. Jacob gives the double blessing to the deserving firstborn son of the wife he loves, not to the detestable firstborn of Leah. With prophetic insight, he crosses his hands against even Joseph the traditionalist. Without wavering, he looks forward to Israel's divine destiny in the land of promise. Renouncing even his love for Rachel, his last words instruct his sons to bury him with his unloved wife so he can rest in faith with his fathers.

At the beginning of the act he comes trepidly to Egypt, not for its riches, comforts, and security, but out of love for a son. While showing great respect and sensitivity to Pharaoh, he never bows his knee to the Egyptian but instead, as the greater, blesses the lesser. Isaac's old age shamed his youth, but Jacob's redeems his, just as Judah's heroic self-sacrifice redeems his tragic beginnings.

All honor Jacob in his death. Joseph and his brothers mourn their father's death and faithfully carry out his instructions to bury him in the ancestral grave. The Egyptians mourn him for two and half months as they would mourn their king. The skilled physicians embalm him for forty days, and the most senior dignitaries both from Pharaoh's own court and from the whole empire bear Jacob's body homeward from Egypt to Canaan in a grand and grave funeral cortege. With these details the narrator asserts Jacob's true redemption and exaltation.

---

[221]Roop, *Genesis*, 290.

Comparisons and Contrasts

This scene is written in the light of Israel's Exodus from Egypt under Moses four hundred years later. On the one hand, it foreshadows that Exodus. On the other hand, the escort of Jacob homeward to the Promised Land by all of Pharaoh's dignitaries together with his chariots and horsemen stands in striking contrast with the Mosaic Exodus (see Ex. 14:9; 15:4–5).

This grand funeral procession and this exaltation of Jacob as a king by the Egyptians foreshadows Israel's exodus from the world and gives a foretaste of the time when the nations hail a son of Jacob as King. Thus the narrator brings to conclusion his theme that God created humanity to rule the earth. The Creator's design will come to fruition when Israel lives in the Promised Land and a son of Judah rules the nations.

Key Words

In this scene of Jacob's death, the root *qbr* is a key word, repeated fourteen times (11x "to bury," 49:29, 31 [3x]; 50:5 [2x]; 50:6, 7, 13, 14 [2x]; and 3x "grave" 49:30; 50:5, 13). The other key term of this scene about the death of the leading patriarch and his longing for the land of his ancestors is "father," repeated fifteen times (49:29; 50:1, 2, 5 [2x], 6, 7, 8, 10, 14 [2x] 15, 16, 17, 22). In keeping with the intensity of this scene, another key word is *kābēd*, "heavy," rendered "very large" (50:9), "bitterly" (50:10), "solemn" (50:11).

EXEGETICAL NOTES TO BOOK 10, ACT 4, SCENE 5 ————

In Egypt at Jacob's Deathbed: Jacob's Burial Instructions (49:29–33)

29. these instructions. The two texts, 47:29–31 and 49:29–33, function as a transition between the scenes and form a frame around the blessing on the twelve tribes, including the adoption of Ephraim and Manasseh. The first announces his death; the second recounts it.

to be gathered to my people. See 49:33. Jacob's burial instructions and his death are framed by this phrase.

Bury. See "Key Words" in Literary Analysis above.

fathers. See "Key Words" in Literary Analysis above.

29–32. in the cave . . . bought from the Hittites. See 25:9 and note. The narrator has already slowed the narrative almost to a standstill on Jacob's deathbed for the blessings to the tribes. He frames these deathbed scenes with Jacob's instructions to bury him with his fathers, not in Egypt (cf. 47:28–31). Here the narrator stops his narrative altogether and allows Jacob to name the patriarchs and matriarchs, to locate the gravesite precisely, and to detail the business transaction entitling them to their final resting place. Jacob's recitation of history and the narrator's precision declare "This is the land!"

30. in Canaan. The narrator constantly reminds his audience that home is in Canaan, not outside of the Promised Land.

31. Abraham . . . Leah. He names his ancestors and family members individually.

Rebekah. The narrator had gapped her obituary earlier (see 35:8).

Leah. He refers to Sarah and Rebekah as their husbands' wives, but as Sternberg notes, "he cannot bring himself to refer to Leah as his wife"[222] (cf. 33:2; 46:19 notes). Nevertheless, "despite his lifelong passion for Rachel, buried on the way to Ephrath, [he] chooses to rest with his fathers at the side of Leah"[223] because he wants his body to rest in symbolic unity with the faith of his fathers.

33. drew. The same Hebrew root is rendered "gather around" in 49:1.

his feet up into the bed. Literally, he "gathered his feet" (see 48:2, where the setting of the last two scenes began). He had been sitting on the side of his bed while speaking to his sons. He is in control even in death.

bed [*miṭṭâ*]. This is a different word than in 49:4 (see note there).

The Procession to Canaan: Jacob Buried in the Cave of Machpelah (50:1 – 14)

1. Joseph. The narrator features Joseph, not his brothers, because this incident features Joseph and the Egyptians in relation to Jacob's burial, whereas the next incident (50:12–15) features the sons. Moreover, Joseph has the closest relationship with his father at the time of his death (see 46:4).

wept. Again, the wise ruler is also a man of deep compassion. This time he weeps not out of joy but out of grief.

kissed. This is an affectionate token of departure (see 31:28, 55; Ruth 1:9, 14).

2. embalm.[224] See also 50:26. Egyptians embalmed the honored dead to assist the afterlife journey. The Israelites did not embalm bodies, since they did not hold that conviction. Rather, they insisted that a corpse be handled properly because it was important especially for the living that the deceased rested peacefully in the grave until their resurrection (see Theological Reflections below). Joseph embalms his father to give him dignity and to prepare his corpse to make the extended journey to the Promised Land, the hope of Israel.

3. forty days . . . seventy days. Probably, but not necessarily, these days overlapped. Sarna explains, "Jewish exegetes have by and large understood that forty days were required for embalming, followed by another thirty days of mourning. The time of mourning would be in accordance with the period of public grief observed for Aaron (Num. 20:29) and Moses (Deut.

[222]Sternberg, *Poetics*, 353.
[223]Ibid.
[224]For bibliography on embalming, see Hamilton, *Genesis 18–50*, 692 n. 13.

34:8). Jewish law to the present time requires a thirty-day mourning period after burial . . . for close relatives, during which various restrictions are observed."[225]

the Egyptians mourned. Not surprisingly, the whole nation mourns the father of their Hebrew savior (see 47:25).

seventy days. They were the days of mourning for an Egyptian king. Diodorus describes a thirty-day preparation of the corpse with oil and spices and a period of public mourning for a king that lasted seventy-two days.[226]

4. to Pharaoh's court. Perhaps he cannot speak directly to Pharaoh because he is unclean by reason of mourning rites (cf. 41:14; Esth. 4:2).

5. swear an oath. See 47:31. Joseph tactfully omits the oath ceremony and prohibition against burial in Egypt.

I dug for myself. Joseph contextualizes Jacob's instructions in words Pharaoh understands.

6. Pharaoh said. Jacob is honored in death even by Pharaoh.

Go up. This is a rehearsal for the distant Exodus (see 50:24).

made you swear to do. He does not have to repeat "and return to me" to loyal Joseph.

7. All. . . . The narrator underscores the grand size of the funeral cortège. The Egyptian funeral retinue includes Joseph, the leading Egyptian officials, all the senior dignitaries from Pharaoh's court and the empire (50:7), and an army of chariots and charioteers. Accompanying them are all of Joseph's household and of Jacob's household (50:8), except the children and animals. The funeral procession occurs in two stages: the great cortège proceeds to Atad, and there they stop for seven days of mourning.

dignitaries. The Hebrew is literally "senior officials."

8. Joseph's household . . . father's household. Joseph continues to have a dual identity as ruler of Egypt and brother of the family (see 43:32 and note).

brothers. This is elaborated upon in 50:12–15.

Only their children and their flocks. They were left behind not only as a practical necessity but as an assurance to Pharaoh that Joseph intends to return.

children. This included their mothers.[227]

9. Chariots and horsemen. Compare Ex. 14:9, 17–18, 23, 26, 28.

very large [*kabēd*]. This is a key word of this episode, glossed also as "bitterly" (50:10) and "solemn" (50:11).

company [*maḥᵃneh*]. The same word is translated "army" in Ex. 14:20.

10. Atad. The sixth century A.D. Madeba mosaic map locates an Alon Atad (terebinth of Atad) near Beth Agla (Beth Hogla—modern Deir Hajlah)

---

[225]Sarna, *Genesis*, 347.

[226]*Histories* 1.72 and 1.91.

[227]D. Daube, *The Exodus Pattern in the Bible* (London: Faber & Faber, 1963), 47–48.

between Jericho and the Dead Sea. Is Jacob in his death showing his descendants the road to the Promised Land?

near. Literally "the other side of the Jordan," this expression means "Jordanside," and the context must decide which side is meant.[228]

loudly and bitterly. See "very large" in 50:9. The mourning is genuine, not just ceremony (cf. 37:35).

Joseph observed. See 50:1.

a seven-day period of mourning. This is in addition to the royal mourning in Egypt. Seven days, a full cycle of days, is the usual period of time to express great grief in Israel and in the ancient Near East (cf. 1 Sam. 31:13; Job 2:13; Ezek. 3:15). It is already attested in the Gilgamesh Epic. It may express the rite of passage, like seven days from birth to circumcision (Gen. 17:12), the rite of marriage (29:27), or the rite of consecration to priesthood (Lev. 8:33).[229]

11. Canaanites. This reference locates Atad in Canaan, not in Transjordan.

solemn ceremony. Literally a "very great" (see "very large" in 50:9) ceremony, this is not simply a ritual but a time of passionate grieving.

is called. The etiology brings the story to the date of the narrator and anchors it in history.

Abel Mizraim. The name involves a pun. Hebrew ʾēḇel means "mourning," and ʾāḇēl means "brook," but only as the first part of a Canaanite place name (e.g., 2 Sam. 20:14, 15; Judg. 11:33; 2 Chron. 16:4).[230] Hence the name means "brook of Egypt," a play with "mourning of Egypt."

12. Jacob's sons did as he had commanded them. The narrative returns to 49:29–32.

13. They carried him. They were accompanied by Joseph and the Egyptians (50:7–11).

14. Joseph . . . brothers . . . others. This is the appropriate sequence for recounting the family's burial as compared to the sequence Joseph-dignitaries-brothers for recounting the Egyptian mourning (50:7–8).

returned to Egypt. The iniquity of the Amorites was not yet full (see 15:13–16).

Settled in Egypt: Joseph Reassures His Troubled Brothers (50:15–21)

First the brothers start, under the pretense of their father's instruction, with a communication asking Joseph as God's surrogate to forgive them. When they learn of Joseph's tender emotional reaction, they follow up with a personal appearance offering themselves to him as slaves (50:15–18). Second, Joseph refuses to play God and reassures them that he has no grudge against them because God has used their evil to bring about good (50:19–21).

---

[228]See A. M. Harman, "ʿbr," *NIDOTTE*, 3:315; contra, G. H. Oller, "Atad," *ABD*, 1:508.
[229]J. Milgrom, *Leviticus 1–16* (AB; New York: Doubleday, 1991), 538.
[230]*HALOT*, 7.

15. saw that their father was dead. Realizing their vulnerability before their powerful brother without the restraining authority of their father before whom he bows, they act in fear of Joseph, not in faith. They are not yet rid of their guilt, in spite of Joseph's earlier assurances (45:1–15).

holds a grudge. Their fear is based on their uneasy consciences, not on Joseph's behavior. He has given them no reason to think that he is vindictive.

16. sent word. They do this to prepare the way for when they come to him (cf. 32:3–21; 33:1–11).

Your father. They know from experience that Joseph accedes to his father's authority in family matters. They hope he will respect Jacob's instructions to forgive them even as he acceded to the burial instructions.

left these instructions. This is probably a fabrication. The narrator connects their claim not to historical fact but to their fears (50:19).

17. sins and the wrongs. One could translate the pair as "transgressions"[231] and "sins." These are the strongest words for sin. Sin is ultimately against God, hence Joseph's response in 50:19.

they committed in treating you so badly. The Hebrew is literally, "[I say transgression and sin] because they treated you so badly." They already admitted their sin against him unwittingly in 42:21–22.

Now. Literally "so now," this provides the transition from Jacob's instructions to their request.

forgive. This is repeated twice. They regard Joseph as God's favored and standing in God's stead.

Joseph wept. He weeps for the second time in this scene: first for his father (50:1), then for his brothers. He probably weeps because, after seventeen years of kindness to them that reinforced his original forgiveness of them (45:7–8), they still misunderstand his goodness and think that he will at last take his revenge (see "Characterization" in Literary Analysis of Book 10, Act 4).

18. His brothers then came. They do so only after they have sent the messengers in 50:16–17 to prepare the way.

threw themselves down. This act draws a dramatic arc over the story beginning with Genesis 37.

We are. The text literally says, "So we are." The Hebrew *hinnēh* shows a logical connection between what they said through the messengers and what they now say.

slaves. The same word is translated "servants [of God]" in 50:17. They regard Joseph as God's surrogate. Becoming Joseph's slaves is equated with being "servants of God." Those who sold Joseph into slavery now again offer themselves to be his slaves. Again he refuses (see Gen. 44).

19. Don't be afraid. He has no need to forgive them but wants to reassure them.

---

[231]This is a strong word essentially signifying "revolt and rebellion" against God's rule.

Am I in the place of God? This is how they seem to regard him (cf. 50:17–18). The rhetorical question expects a negative answer (cf. 30:2). He is only God's instrument, not his surrogate.[232] Moreover, only God could use their evil to do good. Joseph directs their attention away from himself to the sovereign God who rules their history. He is aware of the limits of his authority.[233]

20. harm [*rāʿâ*]. The same word is rendered "badly" in 50:17. Joseph agrees with their confession.

God intended it for good. God transformed the brothers' evil intentions and actions to kill into his good intentions and actions to save life. Hence, there is no need for Joseph to hold a grudge. However, if they had not repented, they would still have been under divine wrath. Judas Iscariot also served God's purpose (1 Cor. 2:8), but it would have been better for him had he never been born (Matt. 26:24).

21. So then. See 50:17. The logic of God's providence to reckon their evil as for good leads to the logical conclusion that they need not fear, for Joseph will care for them. He is his brothers' keeper.

spoke kindly to them. He literally "spoke to their heart." The expression is used in difficult situations.

THEOLOGICAL REFLECTIONS ON
BOOK 10, ACT 4, SCENE 5 ———————————

Land and Covenant

After blessing his sons with a foretaste of Israel's future life in the Promised Land, Jacob, in his last words, looks back to his ancestors and expresses his longing to be buried with them in that land (cf. 46:4; 47:29–31; 48:21–22; see "Second Motif: The Land" in the introduction). His commitment to the Promised Land symbolizes his common faith with his ancestors in the covenant-keeping God. His family's stately procession to bury Jacob in the land also affirms their faith.

Providence

God's beneficent blessings come about through his sovereignty. The major theme of Book 10, God's providence, finds classic expression in 50:20. G. von Rad says, "The statement about the brothers' evil plans and God's good plans now opens up the inmost mystery of the Joseph story. It is in every respect, along with the similar passage in ch. 45:5–7, the climax to the whole. Even where no man could imagine it, God had all the strings in his hand."[234]

---

[232]Cf. E. I. Lowenthal, *Joseph Narrative in Genesis* (New York: Ktav, 1973), 156.
[233]Brueggemann, *Genesis*, 372.
[234]von Rad, *Genesis.*

Brueggemann adds, "[T]hey could not see that in the midst of their scheme was another plan about which none of them knew, a plan hidden but sure in its work."[235]

Accommodation and Contextualization

Joseph is willing to accommodate himself to Egyptian mourning rituals, including embalming, and to contextualize Jacob's burial request in words Pharaoh understands. He does so without compromising Israel's distinctive theology. The journey of Jacob's embalmed body takes him home to the grave of his ancestors in the Promised Land, not to the Egyptian understanding of the afterlife in the presence of their pagan gods.

Burial, Immortality, and Resurrection

The Israelites were certainly concerned with proper burial practices (2 Sam. 1:11–17; 3:31; Isa. 14:19; Jer. 8:1–3; 16:1–9; Ezek. 24:15–17).[236] Even sacred burial signified holy life with God. In biblical theology, life is essentially a relationship with God. According to Gen. 2:17 disruption of the proper relationship with the one who is the source of life is death. This life with God is an eternal, blessed state both before clinical death and after it. Spiritual death, by contrast, is associated with chaos and sterility.

The Old Testament focuses on laying hold and enjoying this blessed life with God before clinical death. After clinical death, the pleasures and opportunities of this life are no longer available in the grave (see "Grave" in Theological Reflections on Book 10, Act 1, Scene 1). Clinical death is a shadow along the trail. However, the continued presence with God that outlasts clinical death is both implied and asserted.

If God does not continue to be the God of his saints forever, the story of Cain and Abel, the first incident after the Fall, deconstructs the biblical teaching on justice. Without eternal life, the righteous Abel suffers martyrdom without deliverance from oppression. K. Farmer rightly says that "one either has to give up the idea of justice or one has to push its execution into some realm beyond the evidence of human experience."[237]

The exceptional translations of Enoch (Gen. 5:24) and of Elijah (2 Kings 2:1–15) point to the possibility of transfer into the heavenly realm to experience God's presence there. The salvific interventions by Elijah and Elisha that raise the dead (1 Kings 17:17–24; 2 Kings 4:31–37; 13:20–21) show that God, not the grave, has the last word (Deut. 32:39; 1 Sam. 2:6). If death had the last word for God's saints, then death would be god.

---

[235]Brueggemann, *Genesis*, 432.
[236]See Martin-Achard, "Resurrection (OT)," *ABD*, 5:683.
[237]K. A. Farmer, *Who Knows What Is Good: A Commentary on Proverbs and Ecclesiastes* (Grand Rapids: Eerdmans, 1991), 206.

Other texts explicitly teach the everlasting relationship of the pious with their God: they will know joy and eternal pleasures at God's right hand (Ps. 16:11); the grave cannot rob them of life in God's presence (Ps. 17:15; 73:24); they will dwell forever in his house (Ps. 23:6). Proverbs declares that righteousness delivers from death (Prov. 10:2) and that immortality is found on the path of righteousness (Prov. 12:28), and so even in death the righteous seek refuge in the Lord (Prov. 14:32).[238]

Although the doctrine of immortality and resurrection at the end of history is only brought into full light by the resurrection of Christ (cf. 2 Tim. 1:10), some Old Testament texts already anticipate that resurrection of the dead will liberate the bodies of the righteous from the grave (Job 19:25–27; Isa. 26:19; Dan. 12:1–3). No human being can redeem another from Sheol, the common fate of both the wise and fools (Ps. 49:7, 10), but "God will redeem my life from the Sheol," says the psalmist, "he will surely take me to himself" (Ps. 49:15).

The Anonymous Servant, identified as Jesus Christ in the New Testament (cf. Acts 8:30–35), pours his soul out as a guilt offering, yet he rises, ascends, and then is glorified (Isa. 53:12). After his atoning death, he prolongs his days and sees his seed (Isa. 53:10).

Robert Martin-Achard summarizes the hope implied in the Old Testament: "The dead lie sleeping in their tombs; at the moment of resurrection, they will rise up again (Heb. *qûm*: 2 Kings 13:21; Isa. 26:14, 19; Job 14:12). . . . The dead are sleeping now; they will be awakened (2 Kings 4:31; Isa. 26:19; Job 14:12; Dan. 12:2) and, finally, they will come back to life (1 Kings 17:22; 2 Kings 13:21; Isa. 26:14, 19; Ezek. 37:3, 5–6, 9–10, 14; Job 14:14)."[239]

BOOK 10, ACT 4, SCENE 6:
JOSEPH'S DEATH IN EGYPT AND
FUTURE BURIAL IN CANAAN (50:22–26)
LITERARY ANALYSIS OF BOOK 10, ACT 4, SCENE 6 ———
Structure and Repetition

The notice of Joseph's death brings the book of Genesis to conclusion. The heart of this brief scene, Joseph's final speech, recalls dominant themes of Genesis: faith in God's providence and provision and commitment to the Promised Land. Joseph repeats his father's demand that the children swear an oath to bury him ultimately in the Promised Land. Joseph's speech of faith is framed by the report of his age at death. The first report features his life of 110 years, seeing three generations; the second, his death. His ideal age signifies God's completed blessings on Joseph's life.

---

[238]See B. K. Waltke, "Theology of Proverbs," *NIDOTTE*, 4:1089–93.
[239]Martin-Achard, "Resurrection (OT)," *ABD*, 5:683.

Symbolism

The report of Joseph's age at death brings Genesis to a fitting conclusion. The years of the patriarchs are formed as a standard increasing integer multiplied by a standard decreasing square number:[240]

Abraham: $175 = 7 \times 5^2$
Isaac: $180 = 5 \times 6^2$
Jacob: $147 = 3 \times 7^2$
Joseph: $110 = 1 \times 5^2 + 6^2 + 7^2$

Hamilton explains, "Joseph is the successor in the pattern 7-5-3-1, and the sum of his predecessors $(5^2 + 6^2 + 7^2)$. In this way, Joseph is linked intimately with his family line.... [I]t appears that the narrator is suggesting that Joseph symbolically brings to a conclusion the patriarchal narratives."[241]

Blanks

The narrator blanks the obituary notices of the other sons of Israel as irrelevant to his purpose.

Janus

This scene predicting the Exodus provides a smooth transition from Genesis to Exodus. This concludes the formative period of Israel's history.

EXEGETICAL NOTES TO BOOK 10, ACT 4, SCENE 6 ———

Joseph's Years: A Notice of His Life's Conclusion (50:22-23)

22. stayed in Egypt. Although the family came down for relief in the famine, they remain throughout Joseph's lifetime and beyond that for another four hundred years.

a hundred and ten. This was regarded in ancient Egypt as the ideal life span and so a sign of God's blessing.[242] It is also the life span of Joshua (Josh. 24:29; Judg. 2:8).

23. third generation. Great-grandchildren are a sign of God's blessing in the Bible (see Ps. 128:6; Prov. 17:6; Isa. 53:10) and a valued prize in the ancient Near East.[243] Sarna notes, "A seventh-century B.C.E. Aramaic funerary inscription from Syria airs the notion that living to see 'children of the fourth generation' is the reward of righteousness."[244]

Makir. This is the most important clan of Manasseh, even identified with the whole tribe. The name, which means "one who is sold," is probably a word play with the life of Joseph.

---

[240]For bibliography, see Hamilton, *Genesis 18–50*, 709 nn. 10–12.
[241]Ibid., 709–10.
[242]Cf. J. Vergote, *Joseph en Égypte* (Louvain: Publications Universitaires, 1959), 200–1; *ANET*, 414.
[243]For bibliography and examples, see Hamilton, *Genesis 18–50*, 710 nn. 15–16.
[244]Sarna, *Genesis*, 350.

on Joseph's knees. See 30:3 and 48:12. As Jacob adopted Joseph's sons, Ephraim and Manasseh, Joseph now adopts Manasseh's son, Makir.

Joseph Last Words of Faith (50:24–25)

24. to his brothers. The word may mean "relatives." If it means "brothers" in the strict sense, then some or all of his older brothers outlive him.

I am about to die. The phrase is a link with the patriarchs (cf. 48:21).

come to your aid. The book ends with the expectation of God's visitation. The Hebrew here, which reads "to visit," connotes that God will change fortunes (21:1); it is translated "watched over" (Ex. 3:16) and "was concerned about" (Ex. 4:31) with reference to the Exodus.

take you up out of this land. This is a technical phrase for the Exodus from Egypt (see Gen. 15:13–14). Joseph speaks as a prophet, perhaps informed by God's promise to Abraham.

the land he promised. The theme of the patriarchs is on Joseph's lips at death. The land is a divine gift to the elect family.

Abraham, Isaac and Jacob. For the first time the three patriarchs are mentioned together; that era has passed, but not its hope. Throughout the Torah the cluster is used, as Sarna explains, "invariably in a context of the divine promises of national territory for the people of Israel."[245]

25. swear an oath. The oath is to bury him in the land (see 47:28–31).

carry my bones up. Moses fulfills the oath (see Ex. 13:19). Joseph is buried at Shechem in the land Jacob gifted to him (see 48:21–22; Josh. 24:32).

Joseph's Years: A Notice of His Death (50:26)

26. embalmed him . . . coffin in Egypt. He is outwardly Egyptian but inwardly Israelite (see 50:2).

THEOLOGICAL REFLECTIONS ON BOOK 10, ACT 4, SCENE 6 ──────────────

Covenant Blessings

The covenant themes of Genesis—blessing, seed, and land—continue through this final scene of the book. This closing scene of Genesis is about God's blessing on his chosen people through the generations. Joseph's genealogy to the third generation features God's faithfulness to give seed. Roop summarizes, "The blessing of God which enables one generation to follow upon another has undergirded the narrative from the orderly presentation of creation (Gen. 1) to this final genealogical note [50:23]. God's blessing has survived the raging flood of divine anger and the unexplained sterility of Sarah and Abraham. That quiet blessing, which makes it possible for the

---

[245]Ibid., 351.

human story to continue beyond a single chapter, will carry the family still further into the future."[246]

Also, that blessing is poured on the head of the covenant partner who in spite of great wrongs done against him remained loyal to God and Israel. He expresses his loyalties by prophesying that God will bring Israel back to the land promised to the patriarchs and by instructing his family to bury him in that land. "By faith Joseph, when his end was near, spoke about the exodus of the Israelites from Egypt and gave instructions about his bones" (Heb. 11:22). The similarity of the deaths of Jacob and Joseph, both having died in Egypt but being buried in the sworn land, unites Joseph's generation with the patriarchs. The covenant-keeping God showers blessings on those who keep the faith of the fathers.

This truth of covenant may also be seen in the word for "coffin," the same word for "ark" in Deut. 10:5. Ginzberg says, "Later Jewish tradition did not miss the parallel between Joseph being placed in an ʾārôn, and the two tables of the Decalogue also being placed in an ʾārôn (Deut. 10:5): All this time in the desert Israel carried two shrines with them—the one in the coffin containing the bones of the dead man Joseph, the other Ark containing the covenant of the Living God. The wayfarers who saw the receptacles wondered, and they would ask, 'How doth the ark of the dead come next to the ark of the Ever-living?' The answer was, 'The dead man enshrined in the one fulfilled the commandments enshrined in the other.'"[247] In truth, only Jesus Christ fully did that, and he did it for all the elect.

Faith of the Fathers

Although Joseph's bones were carried up to the land of the patriarchs, the writer of Hebrews explains that the people of God have not yet realized the complete fulfillment of the promises: "None of them received what had been promised. God had planned something better for us so that only together with us would they be made perfect" (Heb. 11:39–40).

God's Intervention

Throughout Israel's history, God intervenes to deliver his people. To each generation, he reveals his sovereignty and the hope of deliverance. God reveals to Abraham Israel's afflictions in Egypt, and to Joseph, the promise of rescue. A fuller visitation of God's aid comes in the birth of Jesus Christ (see Luke 1:68), and the New Testament ends with the expectation of his visitation from heaven when all believers will experience their final exodus from death and this world to meet their Lord (see Rev. 22:20).

---

[246]Roop, *Genesis*, 292.
[247]L. Ginzberg, *Legends of the Jews*, 7 vols. (Philadelphia: Jewish Publication Society, 1969), 2:183.

Bibliography

Ackerman, J. S. "Joseph, Judah, and Jacob." Pages 85–113 in *Literary Interpretations of Biblical Narratives*. Vol. 2. Edited by K. R. R. Gros Louis. Nashville: Abingdon, 1982.

Aharoni, Y. "Trial Excavation in the 'Solar Shrine' at Lachish." *IEJ* 18 (1968): 157–69.

Albright, W. F. *Archaeology and the Religion of Israel*. 4th ed. Baltimore: Johns Hopkins Univ. Press, 1956.

———. *Yahweh and the Gods of Canaan*. Garden City, N.Y.: Doubleday, 1968.

Aldred, C. *The Egyptians*. New York: Frederick A. Praeger, 1961.

Alexander, T. D. *From Paradise to the Promised Land: An Introduction to the Themes of the Pentateuch*. Grand Rapids: Baker, 1998.

Allis, O. T. *Prophecy and the Church*. 2d ed. Grand Rapids: Baker, 1978.

Alter, R. *The Art of Biblical Narrative*. New York: Basic, 1981.

———. *The Art of Biblical Poetry*. Edinburgh: T. & T. Clark, 1990.

Anderson, B. W. "From Analysis to Synthesis: The Interpretation of Genesis 1–11." *JBL* 97 (1978): 23–29.

Armstrong, K. *In the Beginning: A New Interpretation of Genesis*. New York: Ballantine, 1996.

Austin, S. A., and D. C. Boardman. *The Genesis Debate*. Edited by R. Youngblood. Grand Rapids: Baker, 1991.

Bal, M. "Tricky Thematics." *Semeia* 42 (1988): 133–55.

Balentine, S. E. "Prayers for Justice in the Old Testament: Theodicy and Theology." *CBQ* 51 (1989): 597–616.

Bar-Efrat, S. *Narrative Art in the Bible*. Bible and Literature Series, JSOTSup 70. Sheffield: Almond Press, 1989.

Barnouin, M. "Recherches Numèriques sur la gènèaloie de Gen. V." *RB* 77 (1970): 347–65.

Barr, J. "Hebrew Especially at Job i.18 and Neh vii.3." *JSS* 27 (1982): 177–88.

Barth, K. *The Work of Creation*. Vol. 3.1 of *Church Dogmatics*. Translated and edited by G. W. Bromiley and T. F. Torrance. Edinburgh: T. & T. Clark, 1960.

Berlin, A. *Poetics and Interpretation of Biblical Narrative*. Bible and Literature Series, JSOTSup 9. Sheffield: Almond Press, 1983.

Bierling, N. *Giving Goliath His Due: New Archaeological Light on the Philistines*. Grand Rapids: Baker, 1992.

Blanchard, W. M. "Changing Hermeneutical Perspectives on 'The Land.'" Ph.D. dissertation, Southern Baptist Theological Seminary. Ann Arbor, Mich.: University Microfilms International, 1986.

Blocher, H. *In the Beginning. The Opening Chapter of Genesis*. Downers Grove, Ill.: InterVarsity, 1984.

Block, D. I. "The Role of Language in Ancient Israelite Perceptions of National Identity." *JBL* 103 (1984): 321–40.

Bonchek, A. *Studying the Torah: A Guide to In-Depth Interpretation.* Northvale N.J./London: Jason Aronson, 1996.

Brandon, O. R. "Heart." Pages 498–99 in *Evangelical Dictionary.* Edited by W. Elwell. Grand Rapids: Baker, 1984.

Brenner, A. *Colour Terms in the Old Testament.* JSOTSup 21. Sheffield: JSOT Press, 1982.

_____. "Female Social Behaviour: Two Descriptive Patterns within the 'Birth of the Hero' Paradigm." *VT* 36 (1986): 257–73.

Brinkman, J. "The Akkadian Words of 'Ionia' and 'Ionian.'" *Daidalikon* (1989): 53–71.

Brooke, G. J. "Creation in the Biblical Tradition." *Zygon* 22 (1987): 227–48.

Brown, R. E. "Matthew's Genealogy of Jesus Christ: A Challenging Advent Homily." *Worship* 60 (1986): 483–90.

Brueggemann, W. *Genesis: A Bible Commentary for Teaching and Preaching.* IBC. Atlanta: John Knox, 1982.

Brown, W. "Noah: Sot or Saint? Genesis 9:20–27." Pages 36–60 in *The Way of Wisdom: Essays in Honor of Bruce K. Waltke.* Edited by J. I. Packer and S. K. Soderlund. Grand Rapids: Zondervan, 2000.

Brunner, E. "The Christian Understanding of Man." Pages 139–78 in *The Christian Understanding of Man.* Edited by T. E. Jessop. London: Allen & Unwin, 1938.

Buber, M. "Abraham the Seer." Pages 22–43 in *On the Bible.* Edited by N. N. Glanzer. New York: Schocken, 1982.

_____. "Leitwort Style in Pentateuch Narrative." Pages 114–28 in *Scripture and Translation.* Edited by M. Buber and F. Rosenzweig. Translated by L. Rosenwald and E. Fox. Bloomington and Indianapolis: Indiana Univ. Press, 1994.

Bullinger, E. *Figures of Speech.* 1898. Reprint, Grand Rapids: Baker, 1968.

Burrows, M. "The Complaint of Laban's Daughters." *JAOS* 57 (1937): 259–76.

Calvin, J. *Institutes of the Christian Religion.* Translated by F. L. Battles. The Library of Christian Classics 20. Philadelphia: Westminster Press, 1960.

_____. *A Commentary on Genesis.* Edited and translated by J. King. London: Banner of Truth, 1965.

Carson, D. A. *The Gagging of God: Christianity Confronts Pluralism.* Grand Rapids: Zondervan, 1996.

Cassuto, U. *A Commentary on the Book of Genesis. Part 1: From Adam to Noah.* Translated by I. Abrahams. Jerusalem: Magnes, 1961.

_____. *A Commentary on the Book of Genesis. Part 2: From Noah to Abraham.* Translated by I. Abrahams. Jerusalem: Magnes, 1964.

_____. "The Episode of the Sons of God and the Daughters of Man." Pages 17–28 in *Biblical and Oriental Studies.* Vol. 1. Translated by I. Abrahams. Jerusalem: Magnes, 1973.

_____. "The Prophet Hosea and the Books of the Pentateuch." Pages 79–100 in *Biblical and Oriental Studies.* Vol. 1. Translated by I. Abrahams. Jerusalem: Magnes, 1973.

_____. "The Story of Tamar and Judah." Pages 29–40 in *Biblical and Oriental Studies.* Vol. 1 Translated by I. Abrahams. Jerusalem: Magnes, 1973.

Childs, B. S. *Memory and Tradition in Israel.* London: SCM, 1962.

_____. "A Study of the Formula 'Until This Day.'" *JBL* 82 (1963): 279–92.

_____. "The Etiological Tale Re-examined." *VT* 24 (1974): 387–97.

Clark, W. M. "A Legal Background to the Yahwist's Use of 'Good and Evil' in Genesis 2–3." *JBL* 88 (1969): 266–78.

_____. "The Flood and the Structure of the Pre-patriarchal History." *ZAW* 83 (1971): 184–211.

Clines, D. J. A. "The Image of God in Man." *TynBul* 19 (1968): 53–103.

_____. "Noah's Flood: I: The Theology of the Flood Narrative." *Faith and Thought* 100 (1972–1973): 133–34.

_____. *The Theme of the Pentateuch*. JSOTSup 10. Sheffield: JSOT Press, 1978.

Coats, G. "Lot: A Foil in the Abraham Saga." Pages 113–32 in *Understanding the Word: Essays in Honour of Bernhard W. Anderson*. Edited by J. T. Butler et al. JSOTSup 37. Sheffield, JSOT Press, 1985.

Cogan, M. "A Technical Term for Exposure." *JNES* 27 (1968): 133–35.

Cooke, G. A. *Text-Book of North-Semitic Inscriptions*. Oxford: Clarendon, 1903.

Cross, F. M. *Canaanite Myth and Hebrew Epic: Essays in the History of the Religion of Israel*. Cambridge, Mass.: Harvard Univ. Press, 1976.

Cunliffe-Jones, H. *Deuteronomy: Introduction and Commentary*. London: SCM, 1951.

Daube, D. *Studies in Biblical Law*. Cambridge: Cambridge Univ. Press, 1947.

_____. *The Exodus Pattern in the Bible*. London: Faber & Faber, 1963.

Daube, D., and R. Yaron. "Jacob's Reception by Laban." *JSS* 1 (1956): 60–62.

Davies, E. W. "Inheritance Rights and the Hebrew Levirate Marriage." *VT* 31 (1981): 138–44, 257–68.

Delcor, M. "Quelques Cas de Survivances du Vocabulaire Nomade en Hébreu Biblique." *VT* 25 (1975): 307–22.

Delitzsch, F. *Biblical Commentary on the Psalms*. Vol. 1. London: Hodder & Stoughton, n.d.

_____. *A New Commentary on Genesis*. Vol. 2. Translated by S. Taylor. Edinburgh: T. & T. Clark, 1899.

Delitzsch, F., and C. F. Keil. *The Pentateuch*. Vol. 1. Translated by J. Martin. Grand Rapids: Eerdmans, n.d.

Denton, M. *Evolution: A Theory in Crisis*. Bethesda, Md.: Adler & Adler, 1986.

DeVries, S. J. *Yesterday, Today and Tomorrow: Time and History in the Old Testament*. Grand Rapids: Eerdmans, 1975.

Dorsey, D. A. *The Literary Structure of the Old Testament: A Commentary on Genesis-Malachi*. Grand Rapids: Baker, 1999.

Drake, Paul. "The Kingdom of God in the Old Testament." Pages 67–79 in *The Kingdom of God in 20th Century Interpretation*. Edited by W. Willis. Peabody, Mass.: Hendrickson, 1987.

Driver, S. R. *The Book of Exodus*. Cambridge Bible for Schools and Colleges. Cambridge: Cambridge Univ. Press, 1911.

_____. *The Book of Genesis*. London: Methuen, 1916.

Dumbrell, W. J. *Covenant and Creation*. Exeter: Paternoster, 1984.

Ehrlich, A. B. *Randglossen zur Hebraeischen Bibel*. 1901. Reprint, Hildesheim: Olms, 1968.

Eichrodt, W. *Theology of the Old Testament*. 2 vols. Translated by J. A. Baker. Philadelphia: Westminster, 1961.

Eliade, M. *A History of Religious Ideas*. Translated by W. R. Trask. Chicago: Univ. of Chicago Press, 1985.

Eslinger, C. "Knowing Yahweh: Exodus 6:3 in the Context of Genesis 1–Exodus 15." Pages 188–98 in *Literary Structure and Rhetorical Strategies in the Hebrew Bible.* Edited by L. de Regt, J. de Waard, and J. P. Fokkelman. Winona Lake, Ind.: Eisenbrauns, 1996.

Etz, D. V. "The Numbers of Genesis V 3–31: A Suggested Conversion and Its Implication." *VT* 43 (1993): 171–89.

Farmer, K. A. *Who Knows What Is Good: A Commentary on Proverbs and Ecclesiastes.* Grand Rapids: Eerdmans, 1991.

Fauna and Flora of the Bible: Helps for Translators. Vol. 11. London: United Bible Societies, 1972.

Fensham, F. C. "Salt As Curse in the Old Testament and the Ancient Near East." *BA* 25 (1962): 48–50.

_____. "Gen XXXIV and Mari." *JNSL* 4 (1975): 87–90.

Filby, F. A. *The Flood Reconsidered: A Review of the Evidences of Geology, Archaeology, Ancient Literature and the Bible.* London: Pickering, 1970.

Finkelstein, J. J. "An Old Babylonian Herding Contract and Genesis 31:38f." *JAOS* 88 (1968): 30–36.

Fishbane, M. "The Treaty Background of Amos 1:11 and Related Matters." *JBL* 89 (1970): 313–18.

_____ "Composition and Structure in the Jacob Cycle: Gen 25:19–35:22." *JJS* 26 (1975): 15–38.

_____. *Text and Texture.* New York: Schocken, 1979.

Fokkelman, J. P. *Narrative Art and Poetry in the Books of Samuel.* Vol. 2. Assen/Maastricht, The Netherlands: Van Gorcum, 1986.

_____. *Narrative Art in Genesis: Specimens of Stylistic and Structural Analysis.* 2d ed. Sheffield: JSOT Press, 1991.

Fox, E. *In the Beginning: A New English Rendition of the Book of Genesis.* New York: Schocken, 1983.

Franken, H. J. "Excavations at Deir ʿAllā, Season 1964: Preliminary Report." *VT* 14 (1964): 417–22.

Frankena, R. "Some Remarks on the Semitic Background of Chapters xxix–xxxi of the Book of Genesis." *OtSt* 17 (1972): 53–64.

Gage, W. *The Gospel of Genesis: Studies in Protology and Eschatology.* Winona Lake, Ind.: Carpenter, 1984.

Garrett, D. *Rethinking Genesis: Sources and Authorship of the First Book of the Pentateuch.* Grand Rapids: Baker, 1991.

Gaster, T. H. *Myth, Legend, and Custom in the Old Testament.* Vol. 2. New York: Harper & Row, 1969.

Gemser, B. "The Importance of the Motive Clause in Old Testament Law." VTSup 1 (1953): 50–66.

Gilkey, L. "Creationism: The Roots of the Conflict." Pages 56–67 in *Is God a Creationist? The Religious Case against Creation-Science.* Edited by R. Mushat Frye. New York: Scribner, 1983.

Ginzberg, L. *Legends of the Jews.* 7 vols. Philadelphia: Jewish Publication Society, 1969.

Gispen, W. H. *Genesis I: Kommentaar op het Oude Testament.* Kampen: J. H. Kok.

Goldin, J. "The Youngest Son or Where Does Genesis 38 Belong." *JBL* 96 (1977): 27–44.

Goldingay, J. "The Patriarchs in Scripture and History." Pages 11–42 in *Essays on the Patriarchal Narratives*. Edited by A. R. Millard and D. J. Wiseman. Winona Lake, Ind.: Eisenbrauns, 1983.

Gordon, C. H. "Biblical Customs and Nuzu Tablets." *BA* 3 (1940): 1–12.

_____. *The Common Background of Greek and Hebrew Civilizations*. 2d ed. New York: Norton, 1965.

_____. "Leviathan: Symbol of Evil." Pages 1–9 in *Biblical Motifs: Origins and Transformations*. Edited by A. Altmann. Cambridge: Harvard Univ. Press, 1966.

Gowan, D. E. *Genesis 1–11: From Eden to Babel*. ITC. Grand Rapids: Eerdmans, 1988.

Gray, J. *The Legacy of Canaan: The Ras Shamra Texts and Their Relevance to the Old Testament*. Leiden: Brill, 1965.

Greenberg, M. "Another Look at Rachel's Theft of the Teraphim." *JBL* 81 (1962): 239–48.

Greenfield, J. *Našû-nadānu* and Its Congeners." Pages 87–91 in *Essays on the Ancient Near East in Memory of J. J. Finkelstein*. Edited by M. de Jong Ellis. Hamden, Conn.: Archon, 1977.

Gross, W. "Jakob, der Mann des Segens. Zu Traditionsgeschichte und Theologie der priesterschriftlichen Jakobsüberlieferungen." *Bib* 49 (1968): 321–44.

Habel, N. "Yahweh, Maker of Heaven and Earth: A Study in Tradition Criticism." *JBL* 91 (1972): 321–37.

Hallo, W. W., and W. K. Simpson. *The Ancient Near East: A History*. New York: Harcourt Brace Jovanovich, 1971.

Hals, R. M. *Ezekiel*. FOTL. Grand Rapids: Eerdmans, 1989.

Hamerton-Kelly, R. *God the Father*. Philadelphia: Fortress, 1979.

Hamilton, V. P. *The Book of Genesis: Chapters 1–17*. NICOT. Grand Rapids: Eerdmans, 1990.

_____. *The Book of Genesis: Chapters 18–50*. NICOT. Grand Rapids: Eerdmans, 1995.

Haran, M. "Observations on the Historical Background of Amos 1:2–2:6." *IEJ* 18 (1968): 201–12.

Harrison, R. K. *Introduction to the Old Testament*. London: Tyndale, 1970.

_____. "Reinvestigating the Antediluvian Sumerian King List." *JETS* 36 (1993): 3–8.

Hart, I. "Genesis 1:1–2:3 As a Prologue to the Books of Genesis." *TynBul* 46 (1995): 315–36.

Hasel, G. "The Polemic Nature of the Genesis Cosmology." *EvQ* 46 (1974): 81–102.

_____. *The Remnant: The History and Theology of the Remnant Idea from Genesis to Isaiah*. Berrien Springs, Mich.: Andrews Univ., 1972.

_____. "The Significance of the Cosmology in Genesis 1 in Relation to Ancient Near Eastern Parallels." *AUSS* 10 (1972): 1–20.

Heidel, A. *The Gilgamesh Epic and Old Testament Parallels*. Chicago: Univ. of Chicago Press, 1949.

_____. *The Babylonian Genesis: The Story of the Creation*. 2d ed. Chicago: Univ. of Chicago Press, 1963.

Hendel, R. *The Epic of the Patriarch*. Atlanta: Scholars, 1987.

Henry, M. *A Commentary on the Holy Bible*. Vol. 1. London: Marshall Brother, n.d.

Heschel, A. J. *Man Is Not Alone*. New York: Farrar, Strauss & Giroux, 1951.

_____. *The Sabbath: Its Meaning for Modern Man*. New York: Farrar, Straus & Giroux, 1986.

Hess, R. S. "The Genealogies of Genesis 1–11 and Comparative Literature." *BSac* 70 (1989): 241–54.

Hexter, J. H. *Doing History*. London: Allen & Unwin, 1971.

Hiebert, T. *The Yahwist's Landscape: Nature and Religion in Early Israel*. New York: Oxford Univ. Press, 1996.

Hillers, D. R. "*Bᵉrît ᶜām*: 'Emancipation of the People.'" *JBL* 97 (1978): 175–82.

Hoekema, A. A. *Created in God's Image*. Grand Rapids: Eerdmans, 1986.

Hoffner H. A., Jr. "Second Millennium Antecedents to the Hebrew *ʾÔB̲*." *JBL* 86 (1967): 385–401.

————. "The Hittites and Hurrians." Pages 197–228 in *Peoples of Old Testament Times*. Edited by D. J. Wiseman. Oxford: Clarendon, 1973.

Houtman, C. "What Did Jacob See in His Dream at Bethel?" *VT* 27 (1977): 337–51.

Howard, D. *An Introduction to the Old Testament Historical Books*. Chicago: Moody, 1993.

Humert, P. *Études sur le Récit du Paradis et de la Chute dans la Genèse*. Neuchatel: Universite, 1940.

Ishida, T. *The Royal Dynasties in Ancient Israel*. New York and Berlin: Walter de Gruyter, 1977.

————. "The Structure and Historical Implications of the Lists of Pre-Israelite Nations." *Bib* 60 (1979): 461–90.

Jacob, B. *The First Book of the Bible*. Edited and translated by E. I. Jacob and N. Jacob. New York: Ktav, 1974.

Jenks, A. *The Elohist and North Israelite Traditions*. SBLMS 22. Missoula, Mont.: Scholars, 1977.

Jespen, A. "Amaʰ und Schiphchaʰ." *VT* 8 (1958): 293–97.

Johnson, A. R. *The Vitality of the Individual in the Thought of Ancient Israel*. Cardiff: Univ. of Wales, 1949.

Johnson, M. D. *The Purpose of the Biblical Genealogies*. Cambridge: Cambridge Univ. Press, 1969.

Johnson, P. *Darwin on Trial*. Washington, D.C.: Regnery Gateway, 1991.

Joüon, P. P. *Grammaire de l'Hébreu biblique*. Rome: Pontifical Biblical Institute, 1947.

Kaiser, W. C., Jr. "The Promised Land: A Biblical-Historical View." *BSac* 138 (1981): 302–12.

Keel, O. *The Symbolism of the Biblical World: Ancient Near Eastern Iconography and the Book of Psalms*. Translated by T. J. Hallett. New York: Seabury, 1978.

Kerr, P. E. "Hospitality As the Christian Individual and Corporate Relational Reality That Reflects God's Character." Unpublished master's thesis, Regent College, 1994.

Kierkegaard, S. *Fear and Trembling*. Edited and translated by H. V. Hong and E. H. Hong. Princeton, N.J.: Princeton Univ. Press, 1983.

Kikawada, I. M. "The Shape of Genesis 11:1–9." Pages 18–32 in *Rhetorical Criticism: Essays in Honor of James Muilenburg*. Edited by J. J. Jackson and M. Kessler. Pittsburgh: Pickwick, 1974.

Kikawada, I. M., and A. Quinn. *Before Abraham Was: The Unity of Genesis 1–11*. Nashville: Abingdon, 1985.

Kitchen, K. A. *Ancient Orient and Old Testament*. Chicago: InterVarsity, 1966.

————. "The Patriarchal Age: Myth or History?" *BAR* 21 (1995): 48–57, 88–95.

Klein, R. W. "Archaic Chronologies and the Textual History of the Old Testament." *HTR* 67 (1974): 255–63.

Kline, M. G. "Divine Kingship and Sons of God in Genesis 6:1–4." *WTJ* 24 (1962): 187–204.

_____. *Kingdom Prologue*. Hamilton, Mass.: Meredith Kline, 1993.

Kogut, S. "On the Meaning-Syntactical Status of *hinneh* in Biblical Hebrew." Pages 133–54 in *Studies in Bible*. Edited by S. Japhet. ScrHier 31. Jerusalem: Magnes, 1986.

Kraus, H. *Psalms 1–59: A Commentary*. Translated by H. C. Oswald. Minneapolis: Augsburg, 1988.

Kutler, L. W. "Features of the Battle Challenge in Biblical Hebrew, Akkadian and Ugaritic." *UF* 19 (1987): 95–99.

Lambdin, T. O. *Introduction to Biblical Hebrew*. New York: Charles Scribner's Sons, 1971.

Landy, F. "Narrative Techniques and Symbolic Transactions in the Akedah." Pages 1–40 in *Signs and Wonders: Biblical Texts in Literary Focus*. Edited by J. Cheryl Exum. Atlanta: Scholars, 1989.

Larsson, G. "The Chronology of the Pentateuch: A Comparison of the MT and LXX." *JBL* 102 (1983): 401–9.

Lehmann, M. R. "Abraham's Purchase of Machpelah and Hittite Law." *BASOR* 129 (1953): 15–18.

Leupold, H. C. *Exposition of Genesis*. Vol. 1. Grand Rapids: Baker, 1942.

Lichteim, M. *Ancient Egyptian Literature*. Volume 1: *The Old and Middle Kingdoms*. Berkeley, Los Angeles, London: Univ. of California Press, 1975.

Lichtig, J. *Storytelling in the Bible*. Jerusalem: Magnes, 1978.

Long, B. O. *The Problem of Etiological Narrative in the Old Testament*. BZAW 108. Berlin: Töpelmann, 1968.

Longacre, R. E. "The Discourse Structure of the Flood Narrative." *JAAR* 47 Sup (1976): 89–133.

_____. *Joseph: A Story of Divine Providence: A Texttheoretical and Textlinguistic Analysis of Genesis 37 and 39–48*. Winona Lake, Ind.: Eisenbrauns, 1989.

Lowell, James Russell. "The Present Crisis." In *Masterpieces of Religious Verse*. Edited by J. D. Morrison. New York: Harper & Brothers, 1948.

Lowenstamm, S. E. "Prostration from Afar in Ugaritic, Accadian, and Hebrew." *BASOR* 188 (1967): 41–43.

Lowenthal, E. I. *Joseph Narrative in Genesis*. New York: Ktav, 1973.

Luckenbill, D. D. *The Annals of Sennacherib*. Chicago: Univ. of Chicago Press, 1924.

Luther, M. *Lectures on Genesis 1–5*. Vol. 1 of *Luther's Works*. Edited by J. Pelikan. Saint Louis: Concordia, 1958.

_____. *Lectures on Genesis 6–14*. Vol. 2 of *Luther's Works*. Edited by J. Pelikan. Saint Louis: Concordia, 1958.

_____. *Large Catechism*. In *The Book of Concord*. Translated by T. Tappert. Philadelphia: Fortress, 1959.

Mabee, C. "Jacob and Laban: The Structure of Judicial Proceedings (Genesis xxxi 25–42)." *VT* 30 (1980): 192–207.

Malamat, A. "Aspects of the Foreign Policies of David and Solomon." *JNES* 22 (1963): 1–17.

Marcus, R. "The Tree of Life in Proverbs." *JBL* 62 (1943): 117–20.

Martin, G. *Reading Scripture As the Word of God: Practical Approaches and Attitude.* 2d ed. Ann Arbor, Mich.: Servant, 1982.

Mathews, K. A. *Genesis 1–11:26.* NAC. Broadman & Holman, 1996.

Matthews, V. *Pastoral Nomadism in the Mari Kingdom, ca. 1830–1760 B.C.* ASORDS 3. Cambridge, Mass.: American Schools of Oriental Research, 1978.

_____. "Pastoralists and Patriarchs." *BA* 44 (1981): 215–18.

Mazar, B. "The Historical Background of the Book of Genesis." *JNES* 28 (1969): 73–83.

McConville, J. G. *Law and Theology in Deuteronomy.* JSOTSup 33. Sheffield: JSOT Press, 1984.

McCreesh, T. P. *Biblical Sound and Sense: Poetic Patterns in Proverbs 10–29.* JSOTSup 128. Sheffield: Sheffield Academic Press, 1991.

McKenzie, B. A. "Jacob's Blessing on Pharaoh: An Interpretation of Gen 46:31–47:26." *WTJ* 45 (1983): 386–90.

McKenzie, J. L. *The Two-Edged Sword.* New York: Image, 1966.

McKenzie, S. "You have Prevailed: The Function of Jacob's Encounter at Peniel in the Jacob Cycle." *ResQ* 23 (1980): 225–31.

Meinhold, A. *Die Sprüche.* ZBK. Zurich: Theologischer Verlag, 1991.

Mendelsohn, I. "A Ugaritic Parallel to the Adoption of Ephraim and Manasseh." *IEJ* 9 (1959): 180–83.

Mendenhall, G. E. *Law and Covenant in the Ancient Near East.* Pittsburgh: Biblical Colloquium, 1955.

Milgrom, J. *Numbers.* JPS Torah Commentary. Philadelphia: Jewish Publication Society, 1990.

_____. *Leviticus 1–16.* AB. New York: Doubleday, 1991.

Millard, A. R., and D. J. Wiseman, eds. *Essays on the Patriarchal Narratives.* Winona Lake, Ind.: Eisenbrauns, 1980.

Miller, P. D., Jr. *Genesis 1–11: Studies in Structure and Theme.* Sheffield: Dept. of Biblical Studies, Univ. of Sheffield, 1978.

Moberly, R. W. L. "The Earliest Commentary on the Akedah." *VT* 38 (1988): 302–23.

_____. *The Old Testament of the Old Testament: Patriarchal Narratives and Mosaic Yahwism.* OBT. Minneapolis: Fortress, 1992.

Montent, P. *Eternal Egypt.* New York: New American Library of World Literature, 1964.

Morris, H. M., and J. C. Whitcomb. *The Genesis Flood: The Biblical Record and Its Scientific Implications.* Philadelphia: Presbyterian & Reformed, 1961.

Muraoka, T. "On the So-called *Dativus Ethicus* in Hebrew." *JTS* 29 (1978): 495–98.

Neugebauer, O. *The Exact Sciences in Antiquity.* 2d ed. New York: Harper, 1957.

North, R. "The Hivites." *Bib* 54 (1973): 43–62.

Noth, M. *The History of Israel.* London: Adam & Charles Black, 1958.

Olley, J. W. "'Righteous' and Wealthy? The Description of the *Saddiq* in Wisdom Literature." *The Australian and New Zealand Theological Review: Colloquium* 22 (May 1990): 38–45.

Packer, J. I. "Theism for our Time." Pages 1–23 in *God Who is Rich in Mercy: Essays Presented to Dr. D. B. Knos.* Edited by P. T. O'Brien and D. G. Peterson. Grand Rapids: Baker, 1986.

Pardee, D. "An Emendation in the Ugaritic Aqhat Text." *JNES* 36 (1977): 53–56.

Patrick, D. "Studying Biblical Law As Humanities." *Semeia* 45 (1989): 27–47.

Patten, D. *The Biblical Flood and the Ice Epoch*. Seattle, Wash.: Pacific Meridian, 1996.

Paul, S. M. *Studies in the Book of the Covenant in the Light of Cuneiform and Biblical Law*. Leiden: Brill, 1970.

Pfeiffer, R. H. *State Letters of Assyria*. New Haven, Conn.: American Oriental Society, 1935.

Phillips, A. "NEBALAH—A Term for Serious Disorderly and Unruly Conduct." *VT* 25 (1975): 237–41.

_____. "Another Example of Family Law." *VT* 30 (1980): 240–45.

Pitman, M. *Adam and Evolution: A Scientific Critique of Neo-Darwinism*. Grand Rapids: Baker, 1984.

Polzin, R. "'The Ancestress of Israel in Danger' in Danger." *Semeia* 3 (1975): 81–97.

Postgate, J. N. "Some Old Babylonian Shepherds and Their Flocks." *JSS* 20 (1975): 1–21.

Powell, M. A. *What Is Narrative Criticism?* Minneapolis: Fortress, 1990.

Pratt, R. L. Jr. *He Gave Us Stories*. Brentwood, Tenn.: Wolgemuth & Hyatt, 1990.

_____. "Historical Contingencies and Biblical Predictions." Pages 180–203 in *The Way of Wisdom: Essays in Honor of Bruce K. Waltke*. Edited by J. I. Packer and S. K. Soderlund. Grand Rapids: Zondervan, 2000.

Rad, G. von. *Genesis*. Translated by J. H. Marks. OTL. Philadelphia: Westminster, 1972.

_____. *Holy War in Ancient Israel*. Translated and edited by M. J. Dawn. Grand Rapids: Eerdmans, 1981.

_____. *Problem of the Hexateuch and Other Essays*. Translated by E. W. Trueman Dicken. London: SCM, 1984.

Rainey, A. F. "Compulsory Labour Gangs in Ancient Israel." *IEJ* 20 (1970): 191–202.

Rawlinson, George. *Men of the Bible: Isaac and Jacob. Their Lives and Times*. New York: Fleming H. Revell, n.d.

Rendsburg, G. A. "Janus Parallelism in Gen 49:26." *JBL* 99 (1980): 291–93.

_____. *The Redaction of Genesis*. Winona Lake, Ind.: Eisenbrauns, 1986.

Rendtorff, R. *The Problem of the Process of Transmission in the Pentateuch*. Translated by J. J. Scullion. JSOTSup 89. Sheffield: JSOT Press, 1990.

Ridderbos, N. H. "The Meaning of Genesis I." *Free University Quarterly* 4 (1955/57): 221–35.

Roberts, J. J. M. "In Defense of the Monarchy: The Contribution of Israelite Kingship to Biblical Theology." Pages 377–96 in *Ancient Israelite Religions: Essays in Honor of Frank Moore Cross*. Edited by P. D. Miller Jr., P. D. Hanson, and S. D. McBride. Philadelphia: Fortress, 1987.

Rodd, C. S. "Shall Not the Judge of All the Earth Do What Is Just?" *ExpTim* 83 (1971–1972): 137–39.

Rogerson, J. W. "Slippery Words: V. Myth." *ExpTim* 90 (1978): 10–14.

Roop, E. F. *Genesis*. Scottdale, Pa.; Kitchener, Ont.: Herald, 1987.

Ross, A. P. "Studies in the Book of Genesis, pt. 2: The Table of Nations in Genesis 10—Its Structure." *BSac* 137 (1980): 340–53.

_____. *Creation and Blessing: A Guide to the Study and Exposition of the Book of Genesis*. Grand Rapids: Baker, 1988.

Roth, W. M. W. *Numerical Sayings in the Old Testament: A Form-Critical Study*. VTSup 13 Leiden: Brill, 1965.

———. "The Wooing of Rebekah: A Tradition-Critical Study of Genesis 24." *CBQ* 34 (1972): 177–87.

Rowley, H. H. *The Growth of the Old Testament.* New York: Harper & Row, 1986.

Ruger, H. P. "On Some Versions of Genesis 3.15, Ancient and Modern." *BT* 27 (1976): 105–10.

Sailhamer, J. H. *The Pentateuch As Narrative: A Biblical-Theological Commentary.* Grand Rapids: Zondervan, 1992.

———. *Genesis Unbound.* Sisters, Ore.: Multnomah, 1996.

———. "A Wisdom Composition of the Pentateuch?" Pages 15–35 in *The Way of Wisdom: Essays in Honor of Bruce K. Waltke.* Edited by J. I. Packer and S. K. Soderlund. Grand Rapids: Zondervan, 2000.

Sakenfeld, K. D. *Faithfulness in Action: Loyalty in Biblical Perspective.* OBT. Philadelphia: Fortress, 1985.

Sarna, N. *Genesis.* JPS Torah Commentary 1. Philadelphia: Jewish Publication Society, 1989.

Sasson, J. M. "A Genealogical 'Convention' in Biblical Chronography?" *ZAW* 90 (1978): 171–85.

———. "The 'Tower of Babel' As a Clue to the Redactional Structuring of the Primeval History (Gen. 1–11:9)." Pages 211–19 in *The Bible World: Essays in Honor of Cyrus H. Gordon.* Edited by G. Rendsburg. New York: Ktav, 1980.

Schmidt, W. H. *Die Schöpfungsgeschichte der Priesterschrift.* WMANT 17. Neukirchen-Vluyn: Neukirchener Verlage, 1964.

Selman, M. J. "Comparative Customs and the Patriarchal Age." Pages 93–138 in *Essays on the Patriarchal Narratives.* Edited by A. R. Millard and D. J. Wiseman. Winona Lake, Ind.: Eisenbrauns, 1980.

———. "The Kingdom of God in the Old Testament." *TynBul* 40 (1989): 161–83.

Shibayama, S. "Notes on *Yarad* and ʿ*Alah:* Hints on Translating." *JBR* 34 (1966): 358–62.

Skinner, J. *A Critical and Exegetical Commentary on Genesis.* Revised ed. ICC. Edinburgh: T. & T. Clark, 1930.

Speiser, E. A. "Notes to Recently Published Nuzi Texts." *JAOS* 55 (1935): 423–43.

———. "*YDWN.* Gen 6:3." *JBL* 75 (1956): 126–29.

———. *Genesis.* AB. New York: Doubleday, 1964.

Steinberg, N. "Israelite Tricksters, Their Analogues and Cross-Cultural Study." *Semeia* 42 (1988): 1–13.

Sterchi, D. A. "Does Genesis 1 Provide a Chronological Sequence?" *JETS* 39 (1996): 529–36.

Sternberg, M. *The Poetics of Biblical Narrative: Ideological Literature and the Drama of Reading.* Bloomington: Indiana Univ. Press, 1987.

Strauss, L. "On the interpretation of Genesis." *L'Homme* 21 (January–March 1981): 11–13.

Strus, Adrzej. "La poétique sonore des récits de la Genèse." *Bib* 60 (1979): 1–22.

Terrien, S. *The Elusive Presence: Toward a New Biblical Theology.* New York: Harper & Row, 1978.

Thompson, T. L. *The Origin Tradition of Ancient Israel.* JSOTSup 55. Sheffield: JSOT Press, 1987.

Throntveit, M. "Are the Events in the Genesis Account Set Forth in Chronological Order? No." Pages 36–55 in *The Genesis Debate*. Edited by R. F. Youngblood. Nashville: Thomas Nelson, 1986.

Tigay. J. "Conflation As Redactional Technique." Pages 53–95 in *Empirical Models for Biblical Criticism*. Edited by J. Tigay. Philadelphia: Univ. of Pennsylvania Press, 1985.

_____. "The Evolution of the Pentateuchal Narratives in the Light of the Evolution of the *Gilgamesh Epic*." Pages 21–52 in *Empirical Models for Biblical Criticism*. Edited by J. Tigay. Philadelphia: Univ. of Pennsylvania Press, 1985.

_____. "The Stylistic Criterion of Source Criticism in the Light of Ancient Near Eastern and Post-biblical Literature." Pages 149–73 in *Empirical Models for Biblical Criticism*. Edited by J. Tigay. Philadelphia: Univ. of Pennsylvania Press, 1985.

_____. "Israelite Religion: The Onomastic and Epigraphic Evidence." Pages 157–94 in *Ancient Israelite Religion: Essays in Honor of Frank Moore Cross*. Edited by P. D. Miller Jr., P. Hanson, and S. Dean McBride. Philadelphia: Fortress, 1987.

Tsumura, D. T. *The Earth and the Waters in Genesis 1 and 2: A Linguistic Investigation*. JSOTSup 83. Sheffield: JSOT Press, 1989.

Tucker, G. M. "The Legal Background of Genesis 23." *JBL* 85 (1966): 77–84.

_____. "Witnesses and 'Dates' in Israelite Contracts." *CBQ* 28 (1966): 42–45.

_____. "Rain on a Land Where No One Lives: The Hebrew Bible on the Environment." *JBL* 116 (1997): 3–17.

Ullendorff, E. "The Bawdy Bible." *BSOAS* 42 (1979): 434.

VanGemeren, W. A. "The Sons of God in Genesis 6:1–4." *WTJ* 43 (1981): 320–48.

Van Seters, J. *Abraham in History and Tradition*. New Haven, Conn.: Yale Univ. Press, 1975.

_____. *Prologue to History: The Yahwist As Historian in Genesis*. Louisville: Westminster/John Knox, 1992.

_____. *The Life of Moses: The Yahwist As Historian in Exodus-Numbers*. Louisville: Westminster/John Knox, 1994.

Vawter, B. *On Genesis: A New Reading*. Garden City, N.Y.: Doubleday, 1977.

Vergote, J. *Joseph en Égypte*. Louvain: Publications Universitaires, 1959.

Vos, G. *Biblical Theology: Old and New Testaments*. Grand Rapids: Eerdmans, 1948.

Wakeman, M. K. *God's Battle with the Monster: A Study in Biblical Imagery*. Leiden: Brill, 1973.

Waldman, N. M. "A Note on Genesis 30:27b." *JQR* 55 (1964): 164–65.

Wallace, H. N. "The Toledot of Adam." Pages 17–33 in *Studies in the Pentateuch*. Edited by J. A Emerton. VTSup 41. New York: Brill, 1990.

Walsh, J. T. *1 Kings*. Collegeville, Minn.: Liturgical, 1996.

Waltke, B. K. "The Samaritan Pentateuch and the Text of the Old Testament." Pages 212–39 in *New Perspectives on the Old Testament*. Edited by J. B. Payne. Waco, Tex.: Word, 1970.

_____. "The Creation Account in Genesis 1:1–3." *BSac* 132 (1975): 25–36, 136–44, 216–28; 133 (1976): 28–41.

_____. "Relating Human Personhood to the Health Sciences: An Old Testament Perspective." *Crux* 25 (September 1989): 2–10.

_____. "The Literary Genre of Genesis 1." *Crux* 27 (December 1991): 2–10.

_____. "The Fear of the LORD: The Foundation for a Relationship with God." Pages 17–33 in *Alive to God: Studies in Spirituality Presented to James Houston*. Edited by J. I. Packer and L. Wilkinson. Downers Grove, Ill.: InterVarsity, 1992.

_____. "Joshua." Pages 233–60 in *New Bible Commentary: 21st Century Edition*. 4th edition. Consulting editors, D. A. Carson et al. Downers Grove, Ill.: InterVarsity, 1994.

_____. "The Role of Women in the Bible." *Crux* 31 (September 1995): 29–40.

_____. "Reflections on Retirement from the Life of Isaac." *Crux* 32 (December 1996): 4–14.

_____. "Textual Criticism of the Old Testament and Its Relation to Exegesis and Theology." Pages 51–67 of vol. 1 in *NIDOTTE*.

_____. "Circumcision." Pages 143–44 in *The Complete Book of Everyday Christianity*. Edited by R. Banks and R. P. Stevens. Downers Grove, Ill.: InterVarsity, 1997.

_____. *The Book of Proverbs*. NICOT. Grand Rapids: Eerdmans, forthcoming.

Waltke, B. K., and D. Diewert. "Wisdom Literature." Pages 295–328 in *The Face of Old Testament Studies: A Survey of Contemporary Approaches*. Edited by D. W. Baker and B. T. Arnold. Grand Rapids: Baker, 1999.

Waltke, B. K., with J. MacGregor. *Knowing the Will of God*. Eugene, Ore.: Harvest House, 1998.

Watson, W. G. E. "The Falcon Episode in the Aqhat Tale." *JNSL* 5 (1977): 75.

Weinfeld, M. "The Covenant of Grant in the Old Testament and in the Ancient Near East." *JAOS* 90 (1970): 184–203.

_____. "Jeremiah and the Spiritual Metamorphosis of Israel." *ZAW* 88 (1976): 17–56.

Weisman, Z. "National Consciousness in the Patriarchal Promises." *JSOT* 31 (1985): 55–73.

Wenham, G. J. "Betula." *VT* 22 (1972): 326–48.

_____. *Genesis 1-15*. WBC 1. Waco, Tex.: Word, 1987.

_____. *Genesis 16–50*. WBC 2. Dallas, Tex.: Word, 1994.

_____. "Pondering the Pentateuch: The Search for a New Paradigm." Pages 116–44 in *The Face of Old Testament Studies: A Survey of Contemporary Approaches*. Edited by D. W. Baker and B. T. Arnold. Grand Rapids: Baker, 1999.

M. Wessner. "Face to Face: [*pānîm ʾel pānîm*] in Old Testament Literature." Unpublished master's thesis, Regent College, 1998.

Westermann, C. *Genesis 1–11: A Commentary*. Translated by J. J. Scullion. Minneapolis: Augsburg, 1985.

_____. *Genesis 12–36: A Commentary*. Translated by J. J. Scullion. Minneapolis: Augsburg, 1985.

_____. *Genesis 37–50: A Commentary*. Translated by J. J. Scullion. Minneapolis: Augsburg, 1985.

Whybray, R. N. *Wisdom in Proverbs: The Concept of Wisdom in Proverbs 1–9*. SBT 24. London: SCM, 1965.

Whyte, A. *Bible Characters: Adam to Achan*. Edinburgh and London: Oliphants, 1900.

Widengren, G. *Literary and Psychological Aspects of the Hebrew Prophets*. Uppsala: Universitets Arsskirff, 1948.

Wilson, J. R. *Gospel Virtues: Practicing Faith, Hope and Love in Uncertain Times*. Downers Grove, Ill.: InterVarsity, 1998.

Wilson, R. R. *Genealogy and History in the Biblical World*. New Haven, Conn.: Yale Univ. Press, 1977.

Winnett, F. V. "Studies in Ancient North Arabian Genealogies." *JAOS* 107 (1987): 239–44.

Wiseman, D. J. "Abraham Reassessed." Pages 139–56 in *Essays on the Patriarchal Narratives*. Edited by A. R. Millard and D. J. Wiseman. Winona Lake, Ind.: Eisenbrauns, 1980.

Wolff, H. W. *Hosea*. Translated by G. Stansell. Edited by P. D. Hanson. Philadelphia: Fortress, 1974.

Woude, V. "Melchisedek als Himmlische Erlösergestalt in den Neugefundenen Eschatologischen Midraschim aus Qumran Höhle XI." *OtSt* 14 (1965): 354–73.

Wright, C. J. H. *An Eye for an Eye: The Place of the Old Testament Ethics Today*. Downers Grove, Ill.: InterVarsity, 1983.

_____. "A Christian Approach to OT Prophecy Concerning Israel." Pages 1–19 in *Jerusalem Past and Present in the Purpose of God*. Edited by P. W. L. Walker. Grand Rapids: Baker, 1994.

Yaron, R. *Introduction to the Law of the Aramaic Papyri*. Oxford: Clarendon, 1961.

Young, D. A. *Creation and the Flood: An Alternative to Creation and Theistic Evolution*. Grand Rapids: Baker, 1977.

Young, E. *Studies in Genesis 1*. Philadelphia: Presbyterian & Reformed, 1973.

Youngblood, R. "A New Look at Three Old Testament Roots for 'Sin.'" Pages 201–5 in *Biblical and Near Eastern Studies: Essays in Honor of William Sanford LaSor*. Edited by G. A. Tuttle. Grand Rapids: Eerdmans, 1978.

_____. *The Book of Genesis: An Introductory Commentary*. Grand Rapids: Baker, 1992.

church: Christ and his, 185, 206; his bride, 70; marriage in, 104; often appears insignificant, 395
circumcision, 396; and baptism, 264–65; as the condition, 465–66; set forth, 261; is the sign of, 198, 268
city, 163; of God, 182; hallmark of, 179–80; heart to, 183; of God, 175; of man, 175, 177, 182; refers to, 99
clean: means pure, 138; and unclean, 158
clothing, 95, 103, 148–49
Code of Hammurabi, 23, 253, 596, 598
commandment, followed by, 56, 61
concubine, 411
conscience, refers to the human ability, 450
corporate solidarity, 615
corrupt, 134–35
covenant, 51, 55, 297, 474, 488, 491, 522; with Abimelech, 298; with Abraham, 238–47; birth narrative and, 297, 627; blessings of, 372; blessings on Jacob, 385; confirmation of, 136, 146, 193; definition, 123; establishing God's kingdom through, 474; God's faithfulness to, 440, 479, 522; God's, 154; Jacob shows, 349; land and, 623; language of, 90; making, 244–45; Mosaic, 203; with Noah, 111, 124, 131; occurs for the first time, 123; renewal of, 469; sign, 145–46; sovereignty and, 615; the word, 257; theology of, 263; and faith, 364. (*See also* treaty between Jacob and Laban)
coverings, 95
crafty, 90
creation: account in Genesis, 17, 23, 67; of animals, 88–89; Babylonian account of, 23; to the fall of Israel, 44; literary genre of, 73–74; and myth, 74; order of this, 55; pattern of, 56–57; progress of, 57–58; and science, 74–75; seven progressive phases of, 128; by word, 60. *See also* creatures
creatures, apart from the other, 65
crime, 431
criticism: form, 26; literary, 26, 32
cultural mandate, 67, 100, 131
curse: of Cain, 98–99; of Canaan; 150, 164; the ground, 79, 142; promised in the calling, 344; of the serpent, 93

cursing: an allusion to the creation, 203; bless rather than, 206
Cush, 168
cypress wood, 135

Dan, 411, 610; Tell Dan, 232
Daniel, as righteous, 204
darkness, 60; existence of, 68
daughters of men, 116
David, covenant of, 52–53; fulfilled in, 616
Davidic covenant, 52
day, of creation, 56–64, 77
death, 341; definition, 87–88; enter the human race, 79; spiritual, 103; water symbolizes, 152
Dead Sea, 229
Deborah, 471, 473
Dedan, 336, 768
dependence, 359
depravity, 101
Deuteronomistic History, 44
devil, 90
diet, 158
Diklah, 174
Dinah, 414, 576; in foreign palace, 459; 458–60; Hamor's rape of, 461–67, 494
Dinhabah, 487
divination, 418, 560, 566
documentary hypothesis, 24–27
dominate, 94
doublets, 25
dove, 141
dreams: interpreter of, 523–32; of Jacob, 387–89, 421–22, 425; of Joseph, 495, 498, 504; mode of revelation, 285, 389, 500–501, 504, 526, 528
drunk, 148
Duma, 345
dust, symbolizes, 93, 95

earth sciences, evidences of, 77
earth: curse of, 79; end of, 151; is used, 59–60, 67
east, 178; represents, 85; symbol of, 222
eastern kings, victory over, 225–31
Eber, 173, 186
ecology, 155
economics, 223–24
Eden, meaning of, 85
Edomites, 47, 347; against Israel, 383, 488; Esau the father of, 484

Author Index